CHURCH LIFE IN ENGLAND
IN THE
THIRTEENTH CENTURY

CAMBRIDGE
UNIVERSITY PRESS

LONDON: BENTLEY HOUSE

NEW YORK TORONTO BOMBAY
CALCUTTA MADRAS: MACMILLAN

Plate I. Crucifixion with Saints: a painting *c.* 1250–1300 in Newport Church, Essex.

CHURCH LIFE IN ENGLAND IN THE THIRTEENTH CENTURY

BY

JOHN R. H. MOORMAN, B.D.
EMMANUEL COLLEGE, CAMBRIDGE

CAMBRIDGE
AT THE UNIVERSITY PRESS
1945

PRINTED IN GREAT BRITAIN

CONTENTS

PART TWO

LIST OF PLATES

MAP

PREFACE

There are two ways of writing history which may be compared to the film and the snapshot. The purpose of the former is to tell a story, to trace a sequence of cause and effect, to detect the movement and development of men's thoughts and actions. In the latter, or 'stationary' method, the historian sets out to paint a picture of life as it was at some particular moment in the past. Neither method can, of course, be wholly isolated from the other, for the narrator must, after all, present a series of pictures, while the painter cannot confine himself to so brief a period as to exclude movement altogether.

In adopting the 'stationary' method for this book I decided to limit myself to a single century. The older method of treating the four or five centuries from the Norman Conquest to the Reformation as a single whole seems to me to ignore too much the great changes which must inevitably take place in so long a period of time. On the other hand, to take a shorter period than a hundred years would have been to run the risk of drawing conclusions from inadequate evidence.

I have chosen the thirteenth century partly because it lies at the centre of what, for this country, may be regarded as the great medieval period, partly because of the wealth of information to be derived from contemporary documents such as bishops' registers and monastic chronicles and account rolls, partly because although there were many abuses there was also a strong spirit of reform, and partly because it was a century of great men and of a great experiment. During the eighteen years when Grosseteste was at Lincoln (1235–53) he numbered among his contemporaries S. Edmund of Canterbury and S. Richard of Chichester, Hugh Northwold, Alexander Stavensby, Walter Cantilupe, Ralph Maidstone, Walter Gray and Richard le Poore. Here then, in a single generation, were nine first-class men, all labouring for reform, supported by the energy and heroism of the early Franciscans and Dominicans. That the zeal of these men did not bring about greater reforms in Church life is disappointing; but at least they made great efforts, and one cannot fail to take courage from their example.

In writing this book I have received much help and advice from many friends. I would like to record my gratitude especially to Professor Powicke, who read the whole work in manuscript and gave me, from his vast store of knowledge, much helpful criticism. I should like also to mention the unfailing assistance and courtesy which I have received from the Librarian and Staff of the John Rylands Library in Manchester, where much of my work has been done.

But perhaps my greatest debt is to Miss Helen Dutton, who very kindly volunteered to type not only each chapter as it was written but also the very copious notes upon which the book has been based. As I was living in a vulnerable area during the air-raids of 1940–1 there was, for a time, a real danger that all my notes might, at any moment, be destroyed. Owing to Miss Dutton's kindness I was able to send a constant stream of duplicates to a safe place in the country where, fortunately, they remain untouched.

It remains only for me to thank the Syndics and Staff of the Cambridge University Press for the immense trouble which they have taken in seeing the book through the press.

JOHN R. H. MOORMAN

MANCHESTER
1944

NOTE. I regret that I have been unable to make use of the evidence given in Dr R. A. L. Smith's book, *Canterbury Cathedral Priory* (Cambridge, 1943), as it was published after my chapters were already in page-proof.

Jones, W. H. R. *Vetus Registrum Sarisberiense*, or, *Registrum S. Osmundi*, 2 vols. Rolls Series, 1883–4.

Knighton, Henry. *Chronicon*, ed. J. R. Lumby, 2 vols. Rolls Series, 1889–95.

Langland, William. *Piers the Plowman*, ed. W. W. Skeat, 2 vols. 1886.

Leach, A. F. *Memorials of Beverley Minster*, 2 vols. Surtees Society, 1898–1903.

—— *Visitations and Memorials of Southwell Minster*, Camden Society, New Series, vol. xlviii, 1891.

Luard, H. R. *Annales Monastici*, 5 vols. Rolls Series, 1864–9.

Lyndwood, W. *Provinciale, seu Constitutiones Angliae*, 1679.

Mansi, G. D. *Sacrorum Conciliorum Collectio*, 1758–98.

Map, Walter. *De Nugis Curialium*, tr. M. R. James, Cymmrodorion Record Society, ix, 1923.

—— *The Latin Poems commonly attributed to Walter Mapes*, ed. T. Wright, Camden Society, vol. xvi, 1841.

Oxenedes, J. de. *Chronica*, ed. H. Ellis, Rolls Series, 1859.

Paris, Matthew. *Chronica Majora*, ed. H. R. Luard, 7 vols. Rolls Series, 1872–83.

—— *Historia Anglorum*, ed. F. Madden, 3 vols. Rolls Series, 1866–9.

Raine, J. *Historical Letters from Northern Registers*, Rolls Series, 1873.

Record Commission. *Taxatio Ecclesiastica auctoritate P. Nicholai IV, c. 1291*, ed. 1802.

Reynolds, H. E. *Wells Cathedral, its Foundation, Constitutional History and Statutes*, c. 1880.

Richter, A. L. *Corpus Juris Canonici*, 2 vols. 1881.

Savage, H. E. *The Great Register of Lichfield Cathedral*, in *Collections for a History of Staffordshire*, 1924.

Simpson, W. J. S. *Documents illustrating the History of S. Paul's Cathedral*, Camden Society, New Series, vol. xxvi, 1880.

—— *Visitations of Churches belonging to S. Paul's Cathedral, 1249–52, 1297 and 1458*, Camden Society, New Series, vol. lv and *Camden Misc.* vol. ix, 1895.

Stenton, D. M. *Rolls of the Justices in Eyre for Lincolnshire, 1218–19, and Worcestershire, 1221*, Selden Society, liii, 1934.

—— *Rolls of the Justices in Eyre for Yorkshire, 1218–19*, Selden Society, lvi, 1937.

—— *Rolls of the Justices in Eyre for Gloucestershire, Warwickshire and Staffordshire, 1221–2*, Selden Society, lix, 1940.

Stevenson, J. *Chronicon de Lanercost*, Bannatyne Club, 1839.

Wendover, Roger of. *Flores Historiarum*, ed. H. R. Luard, 3 vols. Rolls Series, 1890.

—— *The Flowers of History*, ed. H. G. Hewlett, 3 vols. Rolls Series, 1886–9.

Wharton, H. *Anglia Sacra*, 2 vols. 1691.

Wilkins, D. *Concilia Magnae Britanniae*, 4 vols. 1737.

Woodruff, C. E. *Some Early Visitation Rolls at Canterbury* in *Archaeologia Cantiana*, xxxii and xxxiii, 1917–18.

Worcester, Florence of. *Chronicon ex Chronicis*, ed. B. Thorpe, English Historical Society, 2 vols. 1848–9.

Wright, T. *The Political Songs of England*, Camden Society, vol. vi, 1839.

BIBLIOGRAPHY

I. ORIGINAL SOURCES

(*a*) CHRONICLES, DOCUMENTS AND CONTEMPORARY LITERATURE

Bannister, A. T. *The Red Book of Hereford*, in *Camden Misc.* vol. xv, 1929.

Bliss, W. H. *Calendar of Papal Letters*, vol. i (1198–1304), 1893.

Bradshaw, H. and Wordsworth, C. *Statutes of Lincoln Cathedral*, 3 vols. 1892–7.

Cambrensis, Giraldus. *Opera*, ed. J. S. Brewer *et alii*, 8 vols. Rolls Series, 1861–91.

Capes, W. W. *Charters and Records of Hereford Cathedral*, 1908.

Capgrave, John. *Chronicle of England*, ed. F. G. Hingeston, Rolls Series, 1858.

Chadwyck Healey, C. E. H. *Somersetshire Pleas*, Somerset Record Society, 1897.

Chaucer, Geoffrey. *Works*, ed. W. W. Skeat, 7 vols. 1894–7.

Cotton, Bartholomew. *Historia Anglicana, 449–1298*, ed. H. R. Luard, Rolls Series, 1859.

Coulton, G. G. *A Visitation of the Archdeaconry of Totnes in 1342*, in *English Historical Review*, 1911.

Early English Text Society:

An Old English Miscellany, ed. R. Morris, 1872.

Handlyng Synne, by Robert Manning of Brunne, ed. F. J. Furnivall, 1901–3.

Instructions for Parish Priests, by John Myrc, ed. E. Peacock, 1868.

Lay Folks' Catechism, ed. T. F. Simmons, 1901.

Lay Folks' Mass Book, ed. T. F. Simmons, 1879.

Legends of the Holy Rood, ed. R. Morris, 1871.

Meditations on the Supper of Our Lord, etc., ed. J. M. Cowper, 1875.

Old English Homilies and Homiletic Treatises, ed. R. Morris, 1868–73.

Feltoe, C. L. and Minns, E. H. *Vetus Liber Archidiaconi Eliensis*, Cambridge Antiquarian Society, Octavo Publications, xlviii, 1917.

Fowler, J. T. *Memorials of the Church of Ripon*, 4 vols. Surtees Society, 1882–1908.

Gibbs, Marion. *Early Charters of S. Paul's*, Camden Society, Third Series, vol. lviii, 1939.

Gibson, Strickland. *Statuta Antiqua Vniversitatis Oxoniensis*, 1931.

Giuseppi, M. S. *The Wardrobe and Household Accounts of Bogo de Clare, 1284–6*, in *Archaeologia*, vol. lxx, 1920.

Gross, C. *Select Cases from the Coroners' Rolls, 1265–1413*, Selden Society, ix, 1896.

Hale, W. H. *Domesday of S. Paul's, 1222*, Camden Society, 1858.

Hudson, W. *Leet Jurisdiction in the City of Norwich*, Selden Society, v, 1892.

Jones, W. H. R. *Charters and Documents of Salisbury*, Rolls Series, 1891.

(*b*) BISHOPS' REGISTERS, WILLS, Etc.

Aquablanca, P. de. *Will of*, ed. C. E. Woodruff, in *Camden Misc.* vol. xiv, 1926.

Baldock, Ralph. *Registrum R. Baldock, G. Segrave, R. Newport, et S. Gravesend*, ed. R. C. Fowler, Canterbury and York Society, 1911.

Bronescombe, W. *Registers of W. Bronescombe and P. Quivil*, ed. F. C. Hingeston-Randolph, 1889.

Button, T. *Accounts of the Executors of Richard, Bishop of London and Thomas, Bishop of Exeter*, ed. W. H. Hale and H. T. Ellacombe, Camden Society, New Series, vol. x, 1874.

Cantilupe, Thomas. *Registrum*, ed. R. G. Griffiths, C. & Y. Soc. 1907.

Chichester, S. Richard of. *Vita*, in *Acta Sanctorum*, April, vol. i.

—— *Will of*, ed. W. H. Blaauw, in *Sussex Archaeological Collections*, vol. i, 1848.

Corbridge, T. *Register*, ed. W. Brown, Surtees Society, 2 vols. 1925–8.

Drokensford, John. *Calendar of the Register of*, ed. Bishop Hobhouse, 1887.

Gandavo, Simon de. *Registrum*, ed. C. T. Flower and M. C. B. Davies, C. & Y. Soc. 2 vols. 1914, 1934.

Geynsburgh, W. *Register*, ed. J. W. Willis Bund, Worcestershire Historical Society, 1907.

Giffard, Godfrey. *Register*, ed. J. W. Willis Bund, Worcestershire Historical Society, 1902.

—— *Will of*, in Appendix to Thomas, *Survey of Worcester*, 1736.

Giffard, Walter. *Registers of W. Giffard and H. Bowett*, ed. T. S. Holmes, Somerset Record Society, 1899.

—— *Register*, ed. W. Brown, Surtees Society, 1904.

Gravesend, R., of Lincoln. *Rotuli*, ed. F. N. Davies, C. W. Foster and A. Hamilton Thompson, C. & Y. Soc. 1925.

Gravesend, R., of London. *Accounts of Executors of Richard, Bishop of London and Thomas, Bishop of Exeter*, ed. W. H. Hale and H. T. Ellacombe, Camden Society, New Series, vol. x, 1874.

—— *Will of*, in *Philobiblon Society Miscellanies*, vol. ii, 1856.

Gray, Walter. *Register*, ed. J. Raine, Surtees Society, 1872.

Grosseteste, R. *Epistolae*, ed. H. R. Luard, Rolls Series, 1861.

—— *Rotuli*, ed. F. N. Davies, C. & Y. Soc. 1913.

—— *Fasciculum Rerum Expetendarum*, ed. E. Brown, vol. ii, 1690.

Halton, John. *Register*, ed. W. N. Thompson, 2 vols. C. & Y. Soc. 1913.

Hethe, Hamo of. *Registrum*, ed. C. & Y. Soc. 1914–16.

Neville, Ralph. *Letters to R. Neville*, ed. W. H. Blaauw, in *Sussex Archaeological Collections*, vol. iii, 1850.

Newark, Henry. *Register*, ed. W. Brown, Surtees Society, 1917.

Orleton, Adam de. *Registrum*, ed. A. T. Bannister, C. & Y. Soc. 1908.

Pecham, John. *Registrum Epistolarum*, ed. C. T. Martin, 3 vols. Rolls Series, 1882–5.

—— *Registrum*, ed. C. & Y. Soc. (unfinished), 1908.

Plantagenet, G. *Vita Galfridi*, in G. Cambrensis, *Opera*, vol. iv, Rolls Series, 1873.

Pontissara, John. *Registrum*, ed. C. Deedes, C. & Y. Soc. 1915–24.

Quivil, Peter. *Registers of W. Bronescombe and P. Quivil*, ed. F. C. Hingeston-Randolph, 1889.

Rich, S. Edmund. *Vita S. Edmundi*, in Martène et Durand, *Thesaurus Novus Anecdotorum*, vol. iii, 1717.

Roches, Peter des. *Pipe Roll of the Bishopric of Winchester, 1208–9*, ed. H. Hall, 1903.

Romeyn, John le. *Register*, ed. W. Brown, Surtees Society, 2 vols. 1913–17.

Sandale, John. *Registers of John de Sandale and Rigaud de Asserio*, ed. F. J. Baigent, 1897.

Stapeldon, W. *Register*, ed. F. C. Hingeston-Randolph, 1892.

Suffield, Walter. *Will of*, in Blomefield, *History of Norfolk*, vol. iii, 1806.

Swinfield, R. *Registrum*, ed. W. W. Capes, C. & Y. Soc. 1909.

—— *A Roll of the Household Expenses of R. de Swinfield during part of the years 1289–90*, ed. John Webb, 2 vols. Camden Society, vols. lix, lxii, 1854–5.

Welles, Hugh of. *Rotuli*, ed. W. P. W. Phillimore, 3 vols. C. & Y. Soc. 1907–9.

—— *Liber Antiquus*, ed. A. Gibbons, 1888.

—— *Will of*, in G. Cambrensis, *Opera*, vol. vii, Rolls Series, 1877.

Wickwayn, William. *Register*, ed. W. Brown, Surtees Society, 1907.

Winchelsey, R. *Registrum*, ed. C. & Y. Soc. In progress.

(Worcester.) *Register of the Diocese of Worcester during the Vacancy of the See*, or, *Registrum Sede Vacante, 1301–1435*, ed. J. W. Willis Bund, Worcestershire Historical Society, 1897.

(*c*) MONASTIC RULES, CHRONICLES, CHARTULARIES, Etc.

Butler, Dom C. *S. Benedicti Regula*, 1912.

Dugdale, W. *Monasticon Anglicanum*, ed. Caley, Ellis and Bandinel, vol. i for *Concordia Regularis*.

Lanfranc, Abp. *Decreta*, in Migne, *Patrologia Latina*, vol. cl.

Pantin, W. A. *Chapters of English Black Monks*, vol. i, Camden Society, 1931.

Canivez, J. M. *Statuta Capitulorum Generalium Ordinis Cisterciensis*, vols. i–iii, 1933.

Fowler, J. T. *Cistercian Statutes*, reprinted from the *Yorkshire Archaeological Journal*, 1890.

Clark, J. W. *The Rule of S. Augustine*, in *Observances at the Augustinian Priory of Barnwell*, 1897.

Salter, H. E. *Chapters of the Augustinian Canons*, 1922.

Duckett, G. F. *Charters and Records among the Archives of Cluni*, 2 vols. 1888.

—— *Visitations of English Cluniac Foundations*, 1890.

Gasquet, F. A. *Collectanea Anglo-Premonstratensia*, 3 vols. Camden Society, Third Series, vols. vi, x, xii, 1904–6.

Luard, H. R. *Annales Monastici*, Rolls Series, 1864–9:

Vol. i, Annals of Margam, Tewkesbury and Burton.

Vol. ii, Annals of Winchester and Waverley.

Vol. iii, Annals of Dunstable and Bermondsey.

Vol. iv, Annals of Osney and Worcester and of T. Wykes.

Vol. v, Index and Glossary.

Aberconway (Cist.)
Ellis, H. *Register and Chronicle of the Abbey of Aberconway*, in *Camden Misc.* vol. i, 1847.

Abingdon (Ben.)
Stevenson, J. *Chronicon Monasterii de Abingdon*, 2 vols. Rolls Series, 1858.

Albans, S. (Ben.)
Riley, H. T. *Gesta Abbatum Monasterii S. Albani*, vols. i and ii, Rolls Series, 1863.

Barnwell (Aug.)
Clark, J. W. *Observances at the Augustinian Priory of Barnwell*, 1897.
—— *Liber Memorandorum Ecclesiae de Bernewelle*, 1907.

Bath (Ben.)
Hunt, W. *Two Chartularies of the Priory of S. Peter at Bath*, Somerset Record Society, 1893.

Battle (Ben.)
Scargill-Bird, S. R. *Custumals of Battle Abbey*, Camden Society, New Series, vol. xli, 1887.

Bilsington (Aug.)
Neilson, N. *The Cartulary and Terrier of the Priory of Bilsington*, 1928.

Brinkburn (Aug.)
Page, W. *The Chartulary of Brinkburn Priory*, Surtees Society, 1893.

Bruton (Aug.)
Somerset Record Society, *Cartularies of Bruton and Montacute*, 1894.

Buckland (Aug.)
Weaver, F. W. *Cartulary of Buckland Priory*, 1909.

Burton-on-Trent (Ben.)
Wrottesley, G. *Abstract of Burton Chartulary*, in *Collections for a History of Staffordshire*, 1884.

Bury S. Edmunds (Ben.)
Arnold, T. *Memorials of S. Edmund's Abbey*, 3 vols. Rolls Series, 1890–6.
Jocelin of Brakelond, *Chronicle*, tr. L. C. Jane, 1922.

Canterbury, Christ Church (Ben.)
Sheppard, J. B. *Literae Cantuarienses*, 3 vols. Rolls Series, 1887–9.
Stubbs, W. *The Historical Works of Gervase of Canterbury*, 2 vols. Rolls Series, 1879–80.

Canterbury, S. Augustine's (Ben.)
Davis, A. H. *William Thorn's Chronicle of S. Augustine's, Canterbury*, 1934.
Hardwick, C. *Historia Monasterii S. Augustini Cantuariensis*, Rolls Series, 1858.
Thompson, E. M. *Customary of S. Augustine's, Canterbury, and S. Peter's, Westminster*, 2 vols. 1902–4.
Turner, G. J. and Salter, H. E. *The Register of S. Augustine's, Canterbury*, 2 vols. 1924.

Chester (Ben.)
Tait, J. *Chartulary of the Abbey of S. Werburgh, Chester*, 2 vols. Chetham Society, 1920–3.

Cockersand (Prem.)
Farrer, W. *The Chartulary of Cockersand Abbey*, 7 vols. Chetham Society, 1898–1909.

COLCHESTER (Ben.)

Moore, S. A. *Cartularium Monasterii de Colecestria*, 2 vols. Roxburghe Club, 1897.

CROWLAND (Ben.)

Riley, H. T. *Ingulph's Chronicle of the Abbey of Croyland*, 1854.

DIEULACRES (Cist.)

Wrottesley, G. *The Chartulary of Dieulacres Abbey*, in *Collections for a History of Staffordshire*, 1906.

DORE (Cist.)

Pertz, G. H. *Annales Dorenses*, in *Monumenta Germaniae Historica, Scriptores*, xvii, 1861.

DUNSTABLE (Aug.)

Fowler, G. H. *A Digest of the Charters preserved in the Cartulary of the Priory of Dunstable*, Bedfordshire Historical Record Society, 1926.

DURHAM (Ben.)

Blakiston, H. E. D. *Some Durham College Rolls*, in Oxford Historical Society, *Collectanea*, iii, 1896.

Botfield, B. *Catalogi Veteres Librorum Ecclesiae Cathedralis Dunelmensis*, Surtees Society, 1838.

Fowler, J. T. *Extracts from the Account Rolls of the Abbey of Durham*, 3 vols. Surtees Society, 1898.

Longstaffe and Booth. *Halmota Prioratus Dunelmensis, 1296–1384*, Surtees Society, 1889.

Raine, J. *Historiae Dunelmensis Scriptores Tres*, Surtees Society, 1839.

Richardson, R. K. *Gesta Dunelmensia A.D. MCCC*, in *Camden Misc.* vol. xiii, 1924.

ELY (Ben.)

Chapman, F. R. *Sacrist Rolls of Ely*, 2 vols. 1907.

Evans, S. J. A. *Ely Chapter Ordinances and Visitation Records*, in *Camden Misc.* vol. xvii, 1940.

EVESHAM (Ben.)

Macray, W. D. *Chronicon Abbatiae de Evesham*, Rolls Series, 1863.

EYNSHAM (Ben.)

Salter, H. E. *Cartulary of the Abbey of Eynsham*, 2 vols. 1907.

FINCHALE (Ben.)

Raine, J. *The Priory of Finchale*, Surtees Society, 1837.

FLAXLEY (Cist.)

Crawley-Boevey, A. W. *Cartulary of Flaxley Abbey*, 1887.

FOUNTAINS (Cist.)

Lancaster, W. *Chartulary of Fountains Abbey*, 2 vols. 1915.

Walbran, J. R. *Memorials of Fountains Abbey*, 2 vols. Surtees Society, 1863–78.

FRIDESWIDE'S, S. (Aug.)

Wigram, S. R. *Cartulary of the Monastery of S. Frideswide at Oxford*, 2 vols. 1895–6.

FURNESS (Cist.)

Beck, T. A. *Annales Furnesienses*, 1844.

Flower, C. T. *Coucher Book of Furness Abbey*, Chetham Society, 1935.

GLASTONBURY (Ben.)
Domerham, Adam de. *Historia de Rebus gestis Glastoniensibus*, ed. T. Hearne, 2 vols. 1727.
Elton, C. J. *Rentalia et Custumaria, 1235–61*, Somerset Record Society, 1891.
Glastonbury, John of. *Chronica*, ed. T. Hearne, 2 vols. 1726.
GLOUCESTER (Ben.)
Hart, W. H. *Historia et Cartularium Monasterii Gloucestriae*, 3 vols. Rolls Series, 1863–7.
Galbraith, V. H. *New Documents about Gloucester College*, in Salter, H. E., *Snappe's Formulary*, 1924.
GUISBOROUGH (Aug.)
Brown, W. *Cartularium Prioratus de Gyseburne*, 2 vols. Surtees Society, 1888–94.
HARROLD (Aug.)
Fowler, G. H. *Records of Harrold Priory*, Bedfordshire Historical Record Society, 1935.
HEALAUGH PARK (Aug.)
Purvis, J. S. *Chartulary of the Augustinian Priory of Healaugh Park*, Yorkshire Archaeological Society, 1936.
HEXHAM (Aug.)
Raine, J. *The Priory of Hexham*, 2 vols. Surtees Society, 1863–4.
HOLM CULTRAM (Cist.)
Grainger and Collingwood. *Register and Records of Holm Cultram*, 1929.
HYDE (Ben.)
Birch, W. de G. *Liber Vitae: Register of Newminster and Hyde Abbey*, 1892.
LEWES (Clun.)
Salzman, L. F. *The Chartulary of the Priory of Lewes*, 2 vols. Sussex Record Society, 1932–4.
LOUTH PARK (Cist.)
Lincolnshire Record Society. *The Chronicle of Louth Park Abbey*, 1891.
MALMESBURY (Ben.)
Brewer, J. *Registrum Malmesburiense*, 2 vols. Rolls Series, 1879–80.
MEAUX (Cist.)
Bond, E. A. *Chronica Monasterii de Melsa*, 3 vols. Rolls Series, 1866–8.
MERTON (Aug.)
Heales, A. *The Records of Merton Priory*, 1898.
MISSENDEN (Aug.)
Jenkins, J. G. *Cartulary of Missenden Abbey*, Pt. i, 1938.
MUCHELNEY (Ben.)
Bates, E. H. *Cartularies of Muchelney and Athelney*, Somerset Record Society, 1899.
NEWINGTON LONGEVILLE (Alien)
Salter, H. E. *Newington Longeville Charters*, Oxfordshire Record Society, 1921.
NEWMINSTER (Cist.)
Fowler, J. T. *Chartularium Abbathiae de Novo Monasterio*, Surtees Society, 1878.

NORWICH (Ben.)

Saunders, H. W. *Introduction to Rolls of Norwich Cathedral Priory*, 1930.

—— *First Register of Norwich Cathedral Priory*, 1939.

OLD WARDON (Cist.)

Fowler, G. H. *Cartulary of the Abbey of Old Wardon*, 1930.

OSNEY (Aug.)

Salter, H. E. *Cartulary of Oseney Abbey*, 6 vols. 1929–36.

PETERBOROUGH (Ben.)

Stapleton, T. *Chronicon Petroburgense*, Camden Society, vol. xlvii, 1849.

RAMSEY (Ben.)

Ault, W. O. *Court Rolls of the Abbey of Ramsey and the Honor of Clare*, 1928.

Hart, W. H. and Lyons, P. A. *Cartularium Monasterii de Rameseia*, 3 vols. Rolls Series, 1884–93.

Macray, W. D. *Chronicon Abbatiae Rameseiensis*, Rolls Series, 1886.

READING (Ben.)

Barfield, S. *Lord Fingall's Cartulary of Reading Abbey*, in *English Historical Review*, 1888.

RIEVAULX (Cist.)

Atkinson, J. C. *Chartulary of Rievaulx*, Surtees Society, 1889.

ROCHESTER (Ben.)

Thorpe, J. *Registrum Roffense*, 1769.

—— *Custumale Roffense*, 1788.

SALLAY (Cist.)

McNulty, J. *The Chartulary of the Cistercian Abbey of Sallay in Craven*, 2 vols. Yorks. Arch. Society, 1933–4.

SELBORNE (Aug.)

Macray, W. D. *Charters and Documents of Selborne and its Priory*, Hampshire Record Society, 1891.

STAFFORD (Aug.)

Parker, F. *Chartulary of S. Thomas, Stafford*, in *Collections for a History of Staffordshire*, 1887.

TRENTHAM (Aug.)

Parker, F. *Chartulary of Trentham*, in *Collections for a History of Staffordshire*, 1890.

VALE ROYAL (Cist.)

Brownhill, J. *The Ledger Book of Vale Royal Abbey*, 1914.

WETHERHAL (Ben.)

Prescott, J. E. *Register of the Priory of Wetherhal*, 1897.

WHALLEY (Cist.)

Hulton, W. A. *Coucher Book of Whalley Abbey*, 4 vols. Chetham Society, 1847–9.

WHITBY (Ben.)

Atkinson, C. J. *The Whitby Chartulary*, 2 vols. Surtees Society, 1878–9.

WINCHCOMBE (Ben.)

Royce, D. *Landboc, sive Registrum Monasterii de Winchelcumba*, 2 vols. 1892–1903.

WINCHESTER (Ben.)

Goodman, A. W. *Chartulary of Winchester*, 1927.

WORCESTER (Ben.)
Hale, W. H. *Registrum Prioratus Wigorniensis*, Camden Society, vol. xci, 1866.
Wilson, J. M. and Gordon, C. *Early Compotus Rolls of the Priory of Worcester*, 1908.
Wilson, J. M. *The Worcester Liber Albus*, 1920.
YORK, S. MARY'S (Ben.)
Craster and Thornton. *Chronicle of S. Mary's, York*, Surtees Society, 1934.

(*d*) THE FRIARS

Brewer and Howlett. *Monumenta Franciscana*, 2 vols. Rolls Series, 1858–82.
Denifle, H. *Die Constitutionen des Prediger-Ordens vom Jahr 1228*, in *Archiv für Litteratur und Kirchengeschichte*, vol. i, 1885.
Eccleston, T. de. *Tractatus de Adventu Fratrum Minorum in Angliam*, ed. A. G. Little in *Collection d'Études et de Documents sur l'Histoire Religieuse et Littéraire du Moyen Age*, vol. vii, 1909.
Reichert, B. M. *Acta Capitulorum Generalium Ordinis Praedicatorum*, vol. i, 1898.
Salter, E. Gurney, *The Coming of the Friars Minor to England and Germany*, 1926.
Trivet, N. *Annales*, ed. T. Hog, 1845.

II. SECONDARY AUTHORITIES

(*a*) GENERAL

Adams, Norma. *The Judicial Conflict over Tithes*, in *English Historical Review*, 1937.
Bale, John. *Illustrium Maioris Britanniae Scriptorum Summarium*, 1548.
—— *Index of British and other Writers*, ed. R. L. Poole with the help of M. Bateson, 1902.
Barraclough, G. *Papal Provisions*, 1935.
Barrett, William. *History of Bristol*, 1789.
Beck, Egerton. *Regulars and the Parochial System*, in *Dublin Review*, April 1923.
Bennett, H. S. *Life on the English Manor*, 1937.
Bishop, E. *Liturgica Historica*, 1918.
Blomefield, Francis. *History of Norfolk*, 11 vols. 1805–10.
Bridgett, T. E. *History of the Holy Eucharist in Great Britain*, 1908.
Brown, G. Baldwin. *The Arts in Early England*, vol. i, 1903.
Capes, W. W. *The English Church in the Fourteenth and Fifteenth Centuries*, 1900.
Chadwick, D. *Social Life in the Days of Piers Plowman*, 1922.
Chambers, E. K. *The Medieval Stage*, 2 vols. 1903.
Chambers, J. D. *Divine Worship in England in the Thirteenth and Fourteenth Centuries contrasted with the Nineteenth*, 1877.
Cheney, C. R. *English Synodalia of the Thirteenth Century*, 1940.
Cheney, M. *The Compromise of Avranches of 1172 and the Spread of Canon Law in England*, in *English Historical Review*, 1941.

Clark, J. W. *The Care of Books*, 1901.

Coulton, G. G. *Social Life in Britain from the Conquest to the Reformation*, 1918.

—— *Medieval Panorama*, 1940.

—— *Medieval Studies*, 1905–15.

—— *The Medieval Village*, 1925.

—— *Parish Life in Medieval England*, 1907.

Cox, J. C. *Notes on the Churches of Derbyshire*, 4 vols. 1875–9.

Cutts, E. L. *Parish Priests and their People in the Middle Ages in England*, 1898.

Dale, Edmund. *National Life and Character in the Mirror of Early English Literature*, 1907.

Dalton, J. N. *The Collegiate Church of Ottery S. Mary*, 1917.

Deanesly, Margaret. *The Lollard Bible*, 1920.

Dictionary of National Biography, 22 vols.

Gabel, Leona C. *Benefit of Clergy in England in the later Middle Ages*, Smith College Studies in History, October 1928–July 1929.

Gasquet, F. A. *Parish Life in Medieval England*, 1906.

Graham, Rose. *The Taxation of Pope Nicholas*, in *English Historical Review*, 1908; reprinted in *English Ecclesiastical Studies*, 1929.

Hargrove, William. *History and Description of York*, 3 vols. 1818.

Hartridge, R. A. R. *A History of Vicarages in the Middle Ages*, 1930.

Hobhouse, E. *Churchwardens' Accounts of Croscombe, Pilton, etc.*, Somerset Record Society, 1890.

Holdsworth, W. *A History of English Law*, 1903, etc.

Homans, G. C. *English Villagers of the Thirteenth Century*, 1941.

Hudson, W. *The Norwich Taxation and the Taxatio Nicholai*, in *Norfolk Archaeology*, vol. xvii, 1910.

James, M. R. *The Lists of Libraries prefixed to the Catalogue of John of Boston*, in *Collectanea Franciscana*, vol. ii, 1922.

Jones, W. Lewis. *Latin Chroniclers*, in *Cambridge History of English Literature*, vol. i, 1907.

Jusserand, J. J. *English Wayfaring Life in the Middle Ages*, 1889.

Kennett, White. *Parochial Antiquities attempted in the History of Ambrosden, Burcester, etc.*, 2 vols. 1818.

Ker, N. R. *Medieval Libraries of Great Britain*, 1941.

Leach, A. F. *The Schools of Medieval England*, 1915.

—— *Early Yorkshire Schools*, 2 vols. Yorkshire Archaeological Society, 1889 and 1903.

—— *Educational Charters and Documents*, 1911.

Le Neve, J. *Fasti Ecclesiae Anglicanae*, ed. T. D. Hardy, 3 vols. 1854.

Lightfoot, J. B. *England in the Latter Half of the Thirteenth Century*, in *Historical Essays*, 1895.

Little, A. G. *Theological Schools in Medieval England*, in *English Historical Review*, 1940.

Little, A. G. and Pelster, F. *Oxford Theology and Theologians, c. 1282–1302*, Oxford Historical Society, 1934.

Luard, H. R. *On the Relations between England and Rome during the earlier portion of the Reign of Henry III*, 1877.

Lunt, W. E. *The Valuation of Norwich*, 1926.

—— *Financial Relations of the Papacy with England to 1327*, 1939.

MacKenzie, H. *The Anti-foreign Movement in England, 1231–2*, in *Anniversary Essays in Medieval History by Students of C. H. Haskins*, 1929.
Maitland, F. W. *Roman Canon Law in the Church of England*, 1898.
Makower, Felix. *Constitutional History and Constitution of the Church of England*, 1895.
Manning, B. L. *The People's Faith in the Time of Wyclif*, 1919.
Maskell, W. *Monumenta Ritualia Ecclesiae Anglicanae*, 2nd edition, 3 vols. 1882.
Merryweather, F. S. *Bibliomania in the Middle Ages*, 1849.
Milner, John. *History and Survey of the Antiquities of Winchester*, 1839.
Newcourt, Richard. *Repertorium Ecclesiasticum Parochiale Londoniense*, 2 vols. 1708–10.
Owst, G. R. *Preaching in Medieval England*, 1926.
—— *Literature and Pulpit in Medieval England*, 1933.
Pendrill, C. *Old Parish Life in London*, 1937.
Phillimore, R. J. *Ecclesiastical Law of the Church of England*, 2nd edition, 2 vols. 1895.
Pollock, F. and Maitland, F. W. *A History of English Law before Edward I*, 2 vols. 1898.
Powys, A. R. *The English Parish Church*, 1930.
Rashdall, Hastings. *The Universities of Europe in the Middle Ages*, New Edition edited by F. M. Powicke and A. B. Emden, 3 vols. 1936.
Reichel, O. J. *The Treasury of God and the Birthright of the Poor*, in *Archaeologia*, vol. lx, 1906–7.
—— *Churches and Church Endowments in the Eleventh and Twelfth Centuries*, in *Transactions of the Devon Association for Science, Literature and Art*, 1907.
Richardson, H. G. *The Parish Clergy of the Thirteenth and Fourteenth Centuries*, in *Transactions of the Royal Historical Society*, 1912.
Rock, Daniel. *Hierurgia*, 2 vols. 1833.
—— *The Church of our Fathers*, ed. G. W. Hart and W. H. Frere, 4 vols. 1903–4.
Rogers, J. E. T. *History of Agriculture and Prices in England*, vols. i and ii, 1866.
—— *Six Centuries of Work and Wages*, 1891.
Russell, J. C. *A Dictionary of Writers of Thirteenth Century England*, Special Supplement No. 3 to the *Bulletin of the Institute of Historical Research*, 1936.
Savage, E. A. *Old English Libraries*, 1911.
Smalley, Beryl. *The Study of the Bible in the Middle Ages*, 1941.
Smith, A. L. *Church and State in the Middle Ages*, 1913.
Smyth, Charles H. *The Art of Preaching, 747–1939*, 1939.
Stephens, W. R. W. *The English Church from the Conquest to the Accession of Edward I*, 1901.
Stubbs, W. *Constitutional History of England*, 3 vols. 1874–8.
Swete, H. B. *Church Services and Service-books before the Reformation*, 1896.
Tanner, T. *Bibliotheca Britannico-Hibernica*, 1748.
Thompson, A. Hamilton. *Pluralism in the Medieval Church*, in *Associated Architectural Societies' Reports*, 1916–17.
—— *The Cathedral Churches of England*, 1925.

Turner, T. H. *Some Account of Domestic Architecture in England from the Conquest to the end of the Thirteenth Century*, 1851.
Tyrrell-Green, E. *Parish Church Architecture*, 1924.
Victoria County Histories.
Watson, E. W. *The Development of Ecclesiastical Organisation and its Financial Basis*, in *Cambridge Medieval History*, vol. vi, 1929.
Whitaker, T. D. *History and Antiquities of Craven*, 1805.
—— *History of the Parish of Whalley*, 1818.
Wordsworth, C. and Littlehales, H. *The Old Service Books of the English Church*, 1904.

(*b*) THE BISHOPS

Boussard, J. *Ralph Neville, Bishop of Chichester*, in *Revue Historique*, vol. clxxvi, 1935.
Churchill, I. J. *Canterbury Administration*, 2 vols. 1933.
Cole, R. E. G. *On the Canonisation of Robert Grosseteste*, in *Associated Architectural Societies' Reports*, 1915–16.
Creighton, M. *Bishop Grosseteste and his Times*, in *Historical Lectures and Addresses*, 1904.
Dixon, W. H. *Fasti Eboracenses*, ed. J. Raine, 1863.
Ghellinck, J. de. *Un Évêque bibliophile au XIVe siècle, Richard Aungerville de Bury*, in *Revue d'Histoire Ecclésiastique*, vols. xviii–xix.
Gibbs, M. and Lang, J. *Bishops and Reform, 1215–72*, 1934.
Hobhouse, E. *A Sketch of the Life of W. de Merton*, 1859.
Hook, W. F. *Lives of the Archbishops of Canterbury*, 12 vols. 1860–84.
Johnstone, Hilda. *Archbishop Pecham and the Council of Lambeth*, in *Essays presented to T. F. Tout*, 1925.
Knowles, Dom David. *Some Aspects of the Career of Archbishop Pecham*, in *English Historical Review*, 1942.
Morgan, Marjorie. *The Excommunication of Grosseteste in 1243*, in *English Historical Review*, 1942.
Oliver, G. *Lives of the Bishops of Exeter*, 1861.
Pegge, Samuel. *Life of Robert Grosseteste*, 1793.
—— *Memoirs of Roger de Weseham*, 1761.
Perry, G. G. *Life and Times of Bishop Grosseteste*, 1891.
Powicke, F. M. *Stephen Langton*, 1928.
—— *Stephen Langton*, in *Christian Life in the Middle Ages*, 1935.
Richardson, R. K. *The Bishopric of Durham under Anthony Bek, 1283–1311*, in *Archaeologia Aeliana*, Third Series, vol. ix, 1913.
Robinson, J. Armitage. *H. de Welles*, in *Somerset Historical Essays*, 1921.
—— *Bishop Jocelyn and the Interdict*, in *Somerset Historical Essays*, 1921.
Solloway, J. *Walter de Gray*, in *York Minster Historical Tracts*, 1927.
Stevenson, F. S. *Robert Grosseteste*, 1899.
Stubbs, W. *Registrum Sacrum Anglicanum*, 1858.
Sutcliffe, D. *The Financial Condition of the See of Canterbury, 1279–92*, in *Speculum*, x, 1935.
Thompson, A. Hamilton. *The Medieval Archbishops in their Diocese*, in *York Minster Historical Tracts*, 1927.
Thomson, S. H. *The Writings of R. Grosseteste*, 1940.

Ward, B. *S. Edmund, Archbishop of Canterbury, his Life by old English Writers*, 1903.

Waugh, W. T. *Archbishop Peckham and Pluralities*, in *English Historical Review*, 1913.

(*c*) THE REGULARS

Addy, S. O. *Historical Memorials of Beauchief Abbey*, 1878.

Aveling, J. H. *A History of Roche Abbey*, 1870.

Becker, G. *Catalogi Bibliothecarum Antiqui*, 1885.

Beeching, H. C. and James, M. R. *The Library of the Cathedral Church of Norwich*, in *Norfolk Archaeology*, vol. xix, 1917.

Bentham, James. *History of Ely*, 1771.

Berlière, Dom U. *Le Nombre des Moines*, in *Revue Bénédictine*, vols. xli and xlii, 1929–30.

Bishop, T. A. M. *Monastic Granges in Yorkshire*, in *English Historical Review*, 1936.

Brakspear, H. *Waverley Abbey*, 1905.

—— *The Cistercian Abbey of Stanley, Wiltshire*, in *Archaeologia*, vol. lx, 1906–7.

Burton, J. *Monasticon Eboracense*, 1758.

Butler, Dom C. *Benedictine Monachism*, 1924.

Cave-Brown, J. *The History of Boxley Parish*, 1892.

Chambers, E. *Eynsham under the Monks*, Oxfordshire Record Society, 1936.

Cheney, C. R. *Episcopal Visitation of Monasteries in the Thirteenth Century*, 1931.

Clapham, A. W. *Lesnes Abbey, Erith, Kent*, 1915.

Clay, R. M. *Medieval Hospitals of England*, 1909.

Coulton, G. G. *Five Centuries of Religion*, vols. i–iii, 1923–36.

—— *Scottish Abbeys and Social Life*, 1933.

—— *The Truth about the Monasteries*, in *Medieval Studies*, No. 6.

Cranage, D. H. S. *The Home of the Monk*, 1926.

Davidson, J. *A History of Newenham Abbey*, 1843.

Denholm-Young, N. *Edward of Windsor and Bermondsey Priory*, in *English Historical Review*, 1933.

Dugdale, W. *Monasticon Anglicanum*, ed. Caley, Ellis and Bandinel, 8 vols. 1817–30.

Fosbroke, T. D. *British Monachism*, 1843.

Fowler, J. K. *A History of Beaulieu Abbey*, 1911.

Frere, W. H. *The Early History of Canons Regular*, in *Fasciculus J. W. Clark dicatus*, 1909.

Gasquet, F. A. *English Monastic Life*, 1904.

Gibson, W. R. *A History of Dore*, 1927.

Gilbanks, G. E. *Records of a Cistercian Abbey: Holm Cultram*, 1899.

Gough, R. *A History of Crowland Abbey*, 1816.

Graham, Rose. *S. Gilbert of Sempringham and the Gilbertines*, 1901.

—— *The Finances of Malton Priory, 1244–57*, in *English Ecclesiastical Studies*, 1929.

—— *The Priory of La Charité-sur-Loire and the Monastery of Bermondsey*, in *English Ecclesiastical Studies*, 1929.

Gresley, J. M. *The Cistercian Abbey of Stoneleigh*, 1854.

Gunton, S. *History of the Church of Peterburgh*, 1686.
Hailstone, E. *History and Antiquities of Bottisham and the Priory of Anglesey*, Cambridge Antiquarian Society, 1873.
Haines, C. R. *Dover Priory*, 1930.
Harland, J. *Sawley Abbey*, 1853.
Heales, A. *A History of Tanridge Priory*, 1885.
Hearne, T. *History and Antiquities of Glastonbury*, 1722.
Hope, W. St J. *Fountains Abbey*, in *Yorkshire Archaeological Journal*, 1900.
Hope, W. St J. and Bilson, J. *Architectural Description of Kirkstall Abbey*, Thoresby Society, 1907.
James, M. R. *On the Abbey of S. Edmund at Bury*, Cambridge Antiquarian Society, 1895.
—— *Ancient Libraries of Canterbury and Dover*, 1903.
—— *Manuscripts from Essex Monastic Libraries*, in Essex Archaeological Society *Transactions*, 1937.
Jenkins, C. *The Monastic Chronicler and the Early School at S. Albans*, 1922.
Knowles, Dom David. *The Monastic Order in England, 943–1216*, 1940.
—— *The Religious Houses of Medieval England*, 1940.
Liddell, J. R. *Some Notes on the Library of Reading Abbey*, in *Bodleian Quarterly Record*, 1935.
Lobel, M. D. *The Borough of Bury S. Edmunds*, 1935.
—— *The Ecclesiastical Banleuca in England*, in *Oxford Essays in Medieval History presented to H. E. Salter*, 1934.
Mynors, R. A. B. *Durham Cathedral Manuscripts*, 1939.
Neilson, N. *Economic Conditions on the Manors of Ramsey*, 1898.
Oliver, G. *Monasticon Diocesis Exoniensis*, 1846.
Page, F. M. *Estates of Crowland Abbey*, 1934.
Pearce, E. H. *The Monks of Westminster*, 1916.
—— *Walter de Wenlok, Abbot of Westminster*, 1920.
Power, Eileen. *Medieval English Nunneries*, 1922.
—— *The Wool Trade in English Medieval History*, 1941.
Powicke, F. M. *Ailred of Rievaulx and his Biographer*, 1922.
Smith, R. A. L. *The Central Financial System of Christ Church, Canterbury, 1186–1512*, in *English Historical Review*, 1940.
—— *High Farming on the Canterbury Estates*, in *Canterbury Cathedral Chronicle*, May 1940.
—— *Feeding of the Canterbury Monks*, in *Canterbury Cathedral Chronicle*, August 1940.
—— *The Financial System of Rochester Cathedral Priory*, in *English Historical Review*, 1941.
—— *The 'Regimen Scaccarii' in English Monasteries*, in *Transactions of the Royal Historical Society*, 1942.
—— *Canterbury Cathedral Priory*, 1943.
Snape, R. H. *English Monastic Finances in the Later Middle Ages*, 1926.
Sparke, J. *Historiae Anglicanae Scriptores Varii*, 1723.
Speakman, E. *The Rule of S. Augustine*, in *Historical Essays by Members of Owens College, Manchester*, ed. T. F. Tout and J. Tait, 1902.
Stanley, A. P. *Memorials of Westminster Abbey*, 1868.
Swartwout, R. E. *The Monastic Craftsman*, 1932.
Sweet, A. H. *The Library of S. Radegund's Abbey*, in *English Historical Review*, 1938.

Tanner, T. *Notitia Monastica*, 1744.
Thompson, A. Hamilton. *English Monasteries*, 1923.
—— *The Premonstratensian Abbey of Welbeck*, 1938.
—— *The Priory of S. Mary, Bolton-in-Wharfedale*, Thoresby Society, 1928.
Thompson, E. M. *The Carthusian Order in England*, 1930.
—— *The Somerset Carthusians*, 1895.
Tindal, W. *History and Antiquities of Evesham*, 1794.
Trueman and Marston. *History of Ilkeston, together with Dale Abbey, etc.*, 1899.
Victoria County Histories.
Walcott, M. E. C. *The Abbey of S. Mary, Cleeve*, 1876.
Watkin, H. R. *The History of Totnes Priory and medieval town*, 3 vols. 1914–17.
West, J. R. *S. Benet of Holme*, Norfolk Record Society, vol. iii, 1932.
Wigram, S. R. *Chronicles of the Abbey of Elstow*, 1885.
Williams, L. F. R. *History of the Abbey of S. Alban*, 1917.
Williams, S. W. *The Cistercian Abbey of Strata Florida*, 1889.
Woodruff, C. E. and Danks, W. *Memorials of the Cathedral and Priory of Christ Church in Canterbury*, 1912.
Woodward, J. M. *History of Bordesley Abbey*, 1866.
Workman, H. B. *The Evolution of the Monastic Ideal*, 1913.
Zentralblatt für Bibliothekswesen, vol. ix.

(*d*) THE FRIARS

Barker, Ernest. *The Dominican Order and Convocation*, 1915.
Bennett, R. F. *The Early Dominicans*, 1937.
Bourdillon, A. F. C. *The Order of Minoresses in England*, 1926.
Bryce, W. Moir. *The Scottish Grey Friars*, 2 vols. n.d.
Cotton, Charles. *The Grey Friars of Canterbury*, 1924.
Coulton, G. G. *The Friars and the Deadweight of Tradition*, vol. ii of *Five Centuries of Religion*, 1927.
Cuthbert, Father. *Adam Marsh*, in *The Romanticism of S. Francis*, 1924.
Formoy, B. E. R. *The Dominican Order in England before the Reformation*, 1925.
Galbraith, G. R. *The Constitution of the Dominican Order*, 1925.
Gilbert, Father. *Blessed Agnellus of Pisa and the English Grey Friars*, 1937.
Goldthorp, L. M. *Franciscans and Dominicans in Yorkshire*, in *Yorkshire Archaeological Journal*, 1936.
Gratien, Père. *Histoire de la Fondation et de l'Évolution de l'Ordre des Frères Mineurs*, 1928.
Gwynn, A. *The English Austin Friars in the Time of Wyclif*, 1940.
Hutton, E. *The Franciscans in England*, 1926.
Jarrett, Bede. *The English Dominicans*, 1921.
Jessopp, A. *The Coming of the Friars*, 1888.
Kingsford, C. L. *The Grey Friars of London*, 1915.
Little, A. G. *The Educational Organisation of the Mendicant Friars in England*, in *Transactions of the Royal Historical Society*, 1894.
—— *The Grey Friars in Oxford*, 1891.
—— *Studies in English Franciscan History*, 1917.

Little, A. G. *The Franciscan School at Oxford in the Thirteenth Century*, in *Archivum Franciscanum Historicum*, 1926.

—— *The Friars and the Foundation of the Faculty of Theology in the University of Cambridge*, in *Mélanges Mandonnet*, tome ii, 1930.

—— *Franciscan History and Legend in English Medieval Art*, ed. A. G. Little, 1937.

—— *Brother William of England, Companion of S. Francis*, in *Collectanea Franciscana*, i, 1914.

—— *Records of the Franciscan Province of England*, in *Collectanea Franciscana*, i, 1914.

—— *Franciscans at Oxford*, in *Franciscan Essays*, 1912.

—— *The Mendicant Orders*, in *Cambridge Medieval History*, vol. vi, 1929.

—— *The First Hundred Years of the Franciscan School at Oxford*, in *S. Francis: Essays in Commemoration*, 1926.

—— *Franciscan Papers, Lists and Documents*, 1943.

Little and Easterling. *The Franciscans and Dominicans of Exeter*, 1927.

Mandonnet, P. *The Order of Preachers*, in *Catholic Encyclopaedia*.

Martin, A. R. *Franciscan Architecture in England*, 1937.

Parkinson, A. *Collectanea Anglo-Minoritica*, 1726.

Pfander, H. G. *The Popular Sermon of the Medieval Friar in England*, 1937.

Poland, E. B. *The Friars in Sussex*, 1928.

Sharp, D. E. *Franciscan Philosophy at Oxford in the Thirteenth Century*, 1930.

Wadding, L. *Annales Minorum*, 1731, etc.

Weare, G. E. *A Collectanea relating to the Bristol Friars Minors and their Convent*, 1893.

PART ONE

CHAPTER I

THE PARISHES OF ENGLAND

The thirteenth century 'is commonly regarded as the greatest of all in medieval history'. So wrote Dr M. R. James, adding that 'when we think of achievements such as Westminster, Amiens and Chartres, and of men such as S. Louis, S. Thomas Aquinas, S. Francis, Dante, Edward I, Roger Bacon, we must agree that the popular estimate is sound'.[1]

So far as this country is concerned the reigns of John, Henry III and Edward I saw changes of far-reaching importance and the growth and development of institutions which have profoundly affected our national history. It was not a century of unbroken peace. It began with the turbulent reign of King John and the disgrace of the Interdict; it included the Civil War in which Simon de Montfort perished, though his cause lived on; its peace was disturbed by constant attempts to subdue the Welsh and the Scots; and it ended with the first rumblings of what was afterwards known as the Hundred Years' War. Yet, in spite of these disturbances, the thirteenth century was one of solid achievement in the affairs of men. It witnessed the birth of a truly representative form of government, since it was during the reign of Henry III that the King's Council was enlarged by the calling up of two or more knights elected in each Shire Court to represent their fellows. It saw also the development of the legal system along the lines already laid down by Henry II, and the definition and codification of the law under the inspiration of Edward I. It watched the progress of learning through the foundation of our two ancient Universities, the one shortly before and the other just after the year 1200.

All these changes were destined to have a considerable influence on our history and on the history of other nations besides our own. It has therefore been the duty of historians to write of these things. But we must not be misled into supposing that

[1] M. R. James, *Wanderings and Homes of Manuscripts*, p. 39.

the people as a whole were aware of the constitutional and intellectual developments which were taking place. At the present day, government is largely influenced by public opinion which it is the duty of legislators to study and to respect. In the thirteenth century public opinion counted for very little. The peasant might grumble about the conditions of work imposed upon him, he might envy the comparative luxury of the rich; but he had no opportunity whatever of making his voice heard in the affairs of either Church or State.

The thirteenth century was certainly an age of achievement and of progress, and some at any rate of the liberties and privileges which later ages have enjoyed owe their origin to this era. But the purpose of the following chapters is not to tell the story of this achievement so much as to describe one aspect of the life of the country, namely, the religious life in the parishes and in the religious communities.

For us, living at a time when the Church has no power and little influence, it is almost impossible to realise what the authority of the medieval Church actually meant. To-day a man's duty to the secular power is regarded as inevitable and obligatory, while his duty to the Church is purely optional, a matter for his own conscience or his own taste. In the Middle Ages the allegiance demanded by the Church was just as great and just as indisputable as that required by the State. Every man was subject to the secular power, which had certain rights over his property and his labour; but he was equally in the power of the Church, which not only deprived him of a considerable proportion of his living, but also claimed to control his life and to give him his final passport either to unending joy or to unspeakable and eternal anguish.

The origin of the parochial system in this country has been the subject of some controversy in recent years. At one time it was believed that that organising genius, Theodore of Tarsus, mapped the whole country out into dioceses and parishes as long ago as the seventh century. This theory is no longer tenable, for it is known that the establishment of parishes was, in fact, far more casual and opportunist. After the flickerings of Christianity in England in the time of the Roman occupation the first real conversion of the country came from two centres—the Irish community at Iona and the Roman mission at Canterbury. Both were monastic. Both Columba and Augustine were monks, as were those who worked with them; and the first evangelistic missions were sent out from monastic centres. As time passed, however, the monasteries tended to withdraw more and more from the world and the initiative in evangelism passed from the monks to the bishops and to their households of secular priests.

For a time the country was organised on diocesan rather than on parochial lines; but, as more and more local churches were built, it was inevitable that, in the more remote districts, these should enjoy some measure of independence. These more independent churches, or 'minsters' as they came to be called, were served by communities or colleges of clergy similar to the bishop's *familia*, though on a smaller scale. Meanwhile local landlords had begun the practice of building, on their own estates, churches for the use of themselves, their tenants and their *nativi* or serfs. It is from these local churches that our parochial system really took its origin.[1]

So far as this country was concerned the local priest had in these early days a dual loyalty. He was responsible to his bishop, without whose sanction he could not function, but he was also responsible to his lord, without whose support he could not live at all. At his institution he would have to pay homage to his bishop, to whom he would be bound by an oath of canonical obedience; but at the same time he would be his lord's 'man', and therefore subject to his authority and jurisdiction.[2] We must not, however, think of the parish priest as a serf; he was a free man, exempt from the performance of servile labour[3] and endowed with a freehold from which he could not be dislodged. The sphere of his labours was more or less determined by the boundaries of his lord's estate, for originally the parish and the

[1] Hodgkin, *A History of the Anglo-Saxons*, ii, p. 425; Baldwin Brown, *The Arts in Early England*, i, p. 301; Watson, *Development of Ecclesiastical Organisation*, in *Camb. Med. Hist.* vi, p. 530; Hartridge, *Vicarages in the Middle Ages*, p. 2.

[2] See Dr Watson's essay in the *Cambridge Medieval History*, vi, pp. 531–2, where he says that the priest drew his income 'on terms that inevitably suggested a feudal relation'. Cf. Hodgkin, *A History of the Anglo-Saxons*, ii, p. 426, where he speaks of the English incumbent as 'a ceorl...like his fellow peasants'. Cf. also Hartridge, *Vicarages in the Middle Ages*, p. 3.

[3] This point was emphasised in Synodal Statutes, e.g. those of William of Blois (1229), where it is stated that the clergy must not perform 'opera servilia' (Wilkins, *Concilia*, i, p. 624).

manor were coterminous. But as estates changed hands or were broken up, the manorial boundaries shifted, so that in later years a parish often comprised land in several different manors, while a single manor might contain more than one church.

By the thirteenth century the parish boundaries were all firmly drawn; and, since they had been in existence for some five hundred years, they already had the sanction of antiquity. Moreover, not only were they firmly drawn, they were also rigidly observed, so that each parish was a self-contained community the members of which were forbidden to worship at any other church or to acknowledge the authority of any priest but their own.

Bishop Stubbs reckoned that during the Middle Ages the whole number of parishes in England was not much over eight thousand.[1] His figure is probably based on the *Taxatio Nicholai* drawn up in 1291. Mr Cutts, having counted up all the parishes in these returns, reaches the figure of 8085 parishes with 457 subordinate chapelries.[2] On the other hand Mr Powys thinks that he has evidence of a far larger number, amounting to a total of 12,280.[3] The true estimate almost certainly lies between these two figures. There are undoubtedly some eight thousand parishes mentioned in the *Taxatio*, but we know that this is not a complete survey of all the parishes in England. For example, in the Register of Bishop Pontissara there is a full list of the parishes in the diocese of Winchester at the end of the thirteenth century. Apart from the rural deanery of Winchester there are 345 churches mentioned, as compared with 300 in the *Taxatio*.[4] In this diocese, then, the returns of the *Taxatio* represent only 87 per cent of the whole. In the diocese of Hereford the returns of 1291 give 295 parishes, whereas a careful study of the episcopal registers reveals a total of 342. Once again the *Taxatio* represents almost exactly 87 per cent. Mr Hudson, who has made a special study of the diocese of Norwich, reckons that there were 1349 parishes in that vast diocese and not 1165 as in the *Taxatio*.[5] Again the *Taxatio* represents about 87 per cent. If, therefore, the *Taxatio* consistently gives this percentage, then

[1] Stubbs, *Constitutional History* (ed. 1874–8), iii, p. 367.
[2] Cutts, *Parish Priests and their People*, p. 385.
[3] A. R. Powys, *The English Parish Church*, pp. xv, 19.
[4] *Regist. J. Pontissara*, pp. 597–609.
[5] W. Hudson in *Norfolk Arch.* xvii, pp. 69–70.

the total number of parishes must have been somewhere in the region of 9500.

By far the majority of these were country parishes, covering a good many acres and often containing a number of villages or hamlets. The average population was about 300. It was, therefore, to a rural, agricultural community that the parochial system belonged; and it has never been quite at home in large towns, where boundaries are always arbitrary and loyalties loose. In the thirteenth century there were few towns, so few, in fact, that if we add together all the parishes in towns containing ten or more we get a total of some four or five hundred to set beside a total of nine thousand country parishes. London appears to have had about a hundred parishes,[1] Norwich a little over fifty,[2] Lincoln and York about forty,[3] Exeter, Winchester, Bristol, Stamford, Ipswich and Cambridge about twenty.[4] The average population of these town parishes was not more than 200.

The parish, then, was originally closely connected with the local lord, at whose instigation it had been brought into existence. Since he had endowed it and since he continued to be its chief supporter he considered that he had certain rights in it. In the first place he claimed the right to appoint the parish priest, a privilege which might be distinctly advantageous if he had a son or relative whom he wished to set up in life. In the case of the more wealthy livings the right of patronage was naturally much sought after, and advowsons have been freely bought and sold up to this day. On the other hand, the patron also claimed the right to give the income of the benefice away to some ecclesiastical body, so long as arrangements were made for the church to be served.[5] Since it was always possible to engage men to serve the churches at a salary of £3 or £4 a year, there was, except in the case of the poorest livings, a balance which might in fact go to the support of some member of the patron's family or be diverted to some other purpose. In either case there was a tendency, in the minds of patrons and their dependents, to regard a benefice much more as an estate than as a

[1] C. Pendrill, *Old Parish Life in London*, p. vi.

[2] W. Hudson in *Norfolk Arch.* xvii, p. 79.

[3] Baldwin Brown, *The Arts in Early England*, i, pp. 119, 289–90.

[4] For these, see *Taxatio Nicholai* (ed. Record Commission, 1802).

[5] See Hartridge, *Vicarages in the Middle Ages*, p. 3, and Coulton, *Five Centuries of Religion*, iii, pp. 156–7.

spiritual responsibility; and this is something which must be constantly borne in mind in any attempt to understand the parochial life of the Middle Ages.[1]

Much patronage, then, was in the hands of the laity, but the Church did its best to establish certain safeguards against indiscriminate presentations. One of these was the law against Simony. Although the Church tolerated, and even indulged in, the practice of bestowing large and important livings upon children of wealthy families who drew a large proportion of the income and did nothing in return, yet it looked with horror upon the purchase of livings, and passed a whole series of laws to stop it. Simony was regarded as a most serious offence,[2] and bishops sometimes made candidates for livings take the most solemn oaths not to hand over any money to their patrons.[3] Another safeguard against indiscriminate presentations was the bishop's power of institution and induction. No man, presented by a patron to a living, could enter upon his duties or draw his income until he had received the bishop's sanction.

Yet in spite of these safeguards there was certainly some disposal of livings which we can only regard as most improper. Bishop Drokensford of Bath and Wells himself collated a boy, who was not ordained at all, to a canonry at Wells in 1311 and received a sharp rebuke from his Archbishop for so doing. The boy, Ivo, was a member of the Berkeley family, who had probably put pressure on the Bishop to act as he did.[4] A layman was presented to the rectory of Cropthorne in Worcestershire and succeeded in turning out the existing incumbent, the learned Peter de Pyriton.[5] Children of ten years old and upwards were constantly presented and instituted to livings; and, though many

[1] See G. Barraclough, *Papal Provisions*, p. 54: 'The essentially material interests of the aristocratic classes...made it normal to regard the religious vocation from the standpoint not of *officium* but of *beneficium*.' Cf. p. 77: 'The whole endeavour of the canonists of the classical period was to minimise the differences between the benefice and secular property....They regarded it...as the object of private rights, not of public interests.'

[2] In a set of Constitutions issued about 1237 Simony is included among the sins for which only the Pope could grant absolution. It ranked as more deadly than homicide, sacrilege and incest: Wilkins, *Concilia*, i, p. 659.

[3] E.g. *Rot. H. de Welles*, i, pp. 94, 147.

[4] *Regist. J. Drokensford*, pp. xxiii, 41, 49.

[5] Wilson, *The Worcester Liber Albus*, pp. 49–52.

of them were in minor orders as acolytes, they were obviously incapable of serving the churches, since most of them were still at school.[1] Episcopal registers are, in fact, full of instances of men being appointed to benefices when they had no intention of living in the parish or of carrying out any pastoral duties.

Not only were benefices often given to men who were, by age, inclination and preparation, totally unsuited to the job, but they were also subject to the changes and chances which attended all estates. They might be stolen; for who was to prevent a member of some powerful family from intruding himself into a benefice and collecting his revenue by force of arms? The papal legates Otto and Ottobon both passed regulations designed to inhibit such as thrust themselves into livings and were prepared to use force of arms to prevent their being dislodged,[2] and we know how necessary such regulations were. Archbishop Wickwayn of York had to deal with a particularly flagrant case at Ferriby, where Richard de Vesci had intruded himself and from which he was only finally dislodged by the superior forces of the King.[3]

Another curious outcome of the relationship between the churches and the manors was that when an estate was divided up it was not uncommon for the benefice to be divided as well. Many livings were divided into medieties or portions; and, out of a great many, small sums were due to various people. In the institutions carried out by Robert Grosseteste in the archdeaconry of Lincoln there were no less than twenty-six parishes divided into halves, five into thirds, two into quarters and three into smaller portions.[4] In the Hereford diocese there were three portionists at Bouldon, Bromyard, Burford, Castle Holdgate and Pontesbury.[5] At Stottesdon the income was shared out between the Vicar, Shrewsbury Abbey, the Rector of Coreley, the Dean of Bridgnorth, the Abbot of Wigmore and the Precentor of Wenlock.

[1] E.g. Pecham, *Reg. Epist.* ii, pp. 555–6; *Regist. J. Pontissara*, p. 16; *Rot. H. de Welles*, i, pp. 11, 166; *Regist. J. Halton*, i, pp. 135–6; Wilson, *The Worcester Liber Albus*, pp. 42–3.

[2] Wilkins, *Concilia*, i, p. 651; ii, p. 6.

[3] *Regist. W. Wickwayn*, pp. 97–105, 262–5.

[4] *Rot. R. Grosseteste*, pp. 1–132.

[5] At Burford and Pontesbury the institution of three portionists survives to this day.

The unsatisfactory nature of dividing a church can readily be imagined. Where there were two or three portionists it would be extremely difficult to find any working agreement as to privileges and responsibilities; and it is therefore not surprising that Stephen Langton in 1222 and the legate Otto in 1238 tried to stop the practice of dividing benefices into portions, since it led only to neglect and to the appointment of unworthy men.[1] But neither an archbishop nor a papal legate was strong enough to challenge vested interests, and the practice went on for many years, the work in the parishes being done by some chaplain to whose stipend each of the portionists contributed a small amount.

In the early days all patronage had been in the hands of the local landlords except for those parishes known as 'peculiars' which owed their foundation to some bishop. But, by the thirteenth century, patronage was more or less equally divided between the laity and the clergy.[2] Among the former a few livings were in the gift of the Crown, but the majority were in the hands of local magnates who frequently presented members of their own families. Among clerical patrons the most powerful were the monasteries, but a few livings were in the gift of the Bishop or of some body such as the Dean and Chapter. The Bishop also collated from time to time by lapse, if the rightful patron failed to present someone within a specified time.

Behind the whole system of patronage in this country lay the papal claim to 'provide' men to benefices, an assumption of power and influence which was strongly resented by the growing nationalist spirit of the land. The system of providing Italians and papal favourites to English benefices received much impetus from John's submission to the Pope in 1213.[3] From this time onwards the papal registers are full of such appointments.

Most of the benefices which the Pope claimed were canonries and prebends at cathedral and collegiate churches. Into these

[1] Wilkins, *Concilia*, i, pp. 587, 652.

[2] E.g. in the diocese of Hereford 117 parishes were in the gift of the laity and 152 in the gift of the clergy. The patrons of the other parishes are not known.

[3] H. MacKenzie, *The Anti-foreign Movement in England, 1231–2*, in *Anniversary Essays in Medieval History by Students of C. H. Haskins*, pp. 183–4.

positions he put his relations and such men as he wished to reward for faithful service to his cause. In 1213 a nephew of the Pope was 'provided' to one of the wealthy prebends at York; in 1240 Peter Cinthii Guidonis, a papal chaplain and subdeacon, was to be found a prebend worth at least fifty marks a year; in 1263 John de Ebulo, a papal chaplain, was to have a prebend and dignity together with three churches in the dioceses of Durham, Lincoln and Worcester 'besides other benefices'; in 1292 Peter de Sabaudia, a kinsman of the Pope, was provided with a canonry at Lincoln 'notwithstanding that he is under age and already holds the treasurership of Llandaff and prebends and canonries at York, Salisbury and Hereford'; in 1298 Aymon, son of Amadeus, Count of Savoy, was to have a canonry at York although under age, not in holy orders, and already holding benefices to the value of 1000 marks; and in 1301 John, son of Octavian Brunforte, a member of the Pope's household, was to be provided with a canonry at Lichfield together with the archdeaconry of Stafford, although he was only twelve years old.[1]

Much more serious was the provision of foreigners to English livings. It was obviously absurd that an Italian should hold the little Yorkshire living of Kettlewell in Wharfedale,[2] or that a layman, Manuel of Genoa, a kinsman of Pope Honorius IV, should be Rector of Kettering,[3] or that the young son of the Marquis of Saluzzo should be Rector of Penistone.[4] It was even more improper that the Bishop of Worcester should be expected to provide a friend of the Pope with benefices to the value of 200 marks, or that these should continue to be his property after he became Bishop of Capua.[5]

It is not to be wondered at that such provisions caused resentment and dismay in the minds of patriotic Englishmen, or that this resentment finally led to acts of violence. The first sign of resistance appeared in the winter of 1231–2, when a number of Italian clergy were attacked and many barns containing the goods of foreigners were robbed or destroyed. For a time there was undoubtedly a good deal of armed hostility and some of

[1] Bliss, *Calendar of Papal Letters*, i, pp. 38, 188, 286, 388, 557, 578, 596. Many other examples could be quoted.

[2] *Regist. W. Gray*, p. 20.

[3] Bliss, *Cal. Papal Letters*, i, p. 265.

[4] *Ibid.* p. 569.

[5] *Ibid.* pp. 235, 278. Cf. M. Paris, *Chron. Maj.* iv, p. 526.

those who had benefited by papal provisions found it expedient to go into hiding until the tyranny was overpast. The agitation against the foreigners seems, indeed, to have been organised by a secret society, the leader, though perhaps not the organiser, of which was a man called Sir Robert de Twenge who held estates in Yorkshire and Westmorland and whose indignation was aroused by the fact that a living in his own gift had been twice seized and given to an Italian. The disturbance was quelled in the following year, but the country continued to feel resentment against the system of provisions until, in 1351, the Act of Provisors was passed with the object of bringing such appointments to an end.[1]

It is so natural for us to feel sympathy with those who agitated against the system whereby important and valuable benefices in this country were given to papal favourites and sycophants, many of whom never set foot on these shores, that we are in danger of exaggerating the evil and of failing to see the whole procedure in its right proportions. During the twelfth century the growing centralisation of church government had thrown more and more work on the curia at Rome and had therefore necessitated an ever-increasing number of officials. It was to pay these officials that the popes, in exercise of the *plenitudo potestatis*, came more and more to demand the proceeds of benefices all over Europe. It is important to realise that such demands were legal and not merely arbitrary and that the papacy could maintain that, though local churches might suffer, the Church as a whole benefited considerably from the greater efficiency which centralisation ensured.[2] Moreover the majority of benefices which the popes claimed were prebends and canonries at the secular cathedrals and collegiate churches.[3] These were undoubtedly more lucrative than most livings, but at the same time it could be argued that the normal holders of these positions did so little that was useful that no harm was done in transferring their emoluments to those who were engaged in valuable work

[1] H. MacKenzie, *The Anti-foreign Movement in England, 1231–2*, in *Anniversary Essays in Medieval History by Students of C. H. Haskins*, pp. 194–202; Stevenson, *Robert Grosseteste*, pp. 95–6; M. Paris, *Chron. Maj.* iii, pp. 208–11, 217–19; Roger of Wendover, *The Flowers of History*, ed. H. G. Hewlett, iii, pp. 16–19, 27–9.

[2] On this point see G. Barraclough, *Papal Provisions*, pp. 1–2, 90–110.

[3] E.g. in 1226 the Pope demanded two prebends from each cathedral: Stevenson, *Robert Grosseteste*, p. 94.

at Rome.[1] Much the same might be said of many of the parochial benefices which the popes annexed. Pluralism and consequent absenteeism were so common among the members of the more powerful English families that many parishes had to be content with the ministrations of a vicar or chaplain while they were obliged to pay their tithes and dues to a man whom they never saw. Under such circumstances it can have made very little difference to the inhabitants of such a parish whether their absentee rector were English or Italian or anything else.

The evil effect of provisions can therefore easily be exaggerated. That there was opposition to it in this country is true; but the source of such opposition was not so much solicitude for the spiritual welfare of the people as indignation at the thought of good English money going out of the country.[2] 'Where there used to be noble and generous clergy,' writes Matthew Paris, 'guardians and patrons of the churches, by their opulence bringing renown to the district, giving hospitality to wayfarers and feeding the hungry, now there are wretched men without manners, full of cunning, proctors and "farmers" of the Romans, seizing whatsoever in the country is precious and serviceable and sending it away to their lords living delicately out of the patrimony of the Crucified and despising what is not theirs.'[3] Whether there had ever been such a golden age of nobility and charity as is here depicted is exceedingly doubtful, nor should Matthew Paris' strictures on his own times be taken too seriously, coming, as they do, from one who saw the Church and the world only from within the cloister. But that they represent the opinion of a good many Englishmen, in whose hearts nationalist feelings were beginning to stir, is beyond doubt.[4]

[1] See below, pp. 19–21.

[2] M. Paris, *Chron. Maj.* vi, p. 111: 'in depauperatione ecclesiarum depauperatur regnum' (from *Gravamina Ecclesiae Gallicanae*). Cf. Barraclough, *Papal Provisions*, pp. 10–13.

[3] M. Paris, *Chron. Maj.* iii, pp. 389–90.

[4] See Barraclough, *Papal Provisions*, p. 15; H. MacKenzie, *The Anti-foreign Movement in England, 1231–2*, in *Anniversary Essays in Medieval History by Students of C. H. Haskins*, p. 202.

CHAPTER II

CHAPELS, CHANTRIES AND COLLEGIATE CHURCHES

The average English parish in the thirteenth century covered about four thousand acres, and often included, besides the main centre of population, a number of outlying farms and hamlets. To meet the needs of the people living far from the parish church it was most desirable that there should be chapels-of-ease in the more distant hamlets, especially in those parts of the country liable to be isolated by flooding, mist, or heavy falls of snow.[1]

According to the Winchester statutes chapels, with graveyards attached, were to be built in all villages which were more than two miles from their parish church;[2] but this was an ideal which could not possibly be attained. Some parishes, however, did have a considerable number of chapels. Sonning in Berkshire had eight,[3] Ashbourne in Derbyshire nine,[4] Bakewell perhaps as many as eleven,[5] and Clun in Shropshire twelve.[6]

The danger of a chapel developing an independent life of its own was one of which the medieval Church was fully conscious. When chapels were built, therefore, their privileges were always carefully stated and the rights of the mother church jealously guarded. Yet as time went by chapels became more and more self-sufficient, with their own graveyards and with rights of baptism and marriage, and it is impossible to see how this could have been avoided. If a conscientious priest found himself in charge of a chapel, it would be only natural that he should build up a church life there quite independent of the mother church, which might be several miles away. Many rectors were absentees, who were scarcely known to the people in the villages where they were supposed to live, and would be total strangers

[1] The Buttermere-Crummock valley in Cumberland was in the parish of S. Bees nearly twenty miles away. None could have hoped to go to church had not a chapel been built for them at Loweswater. Cf. *Regist. W. Gray*, p. xxxi; *Regist. W. Wickwayn*, p. 120.

[2] *Regist. J. Pontissara*, p. 210.

[3] W. H. R. Jones, *Reg. S. Osmundi*, i, pp. 277–82.

[4] Savage, *Great Register of Lichfield*, p. 218.

[5] Cox, *Churches of Derbyshire*, ii, pp. 7–8.

[6] Dugdale-Caley, *Monasticon*, v, p. 76.

to those living in scattered hamlets which they probably never visited at all. The danger of an outlying chapel regarding itself as a separate parish and becoming jealous of any interference from the mother church was the same as that which confronts 'mission churches' in our great cities to-day, but it was intensified by the isolation in which some small village communities lived, and by the fact that incumbents were often absent from their cures. It was in order to mitigate this growing independence that the people who normally attended such chapels were sometimes compelled to communicate at the mother church on certain great festivals,[1] while chaplains in charge were expected to take a vow of reverence and obedience to their rectors and to pay a small sum as a pledge of their subordination.[2] Occasionally a chapel separated from the mother church and became an independent parish, but this was not common.[3]

Many chapels were supported by endowments which in some instances were very generous. The chaplain of East Hoe (Hants), for example, was to receive all oblations at the chapel, together with the lesser tithes, and he was to be provided with a house, 50 sheep, 12 pigs and an annual gift of six cartloads of wood.[4] At Eastrington in Yorkshire the chapel was endowed with the tithes on corn which in almost all parishes belonged to the rector.[5] At the village of Osgodby in the parish of Kirby (Lincs) the parishioners were obliged to provide their chaplain with six loads of wheat and one of oats each year and to find him a house unless lodgings could be found in the village.[6] On the other hand the chaplain often received only a small proportion of the income of the chapelry. For example, the chapel of Chelmorton in the parish of Bakewell was worth 60 marks a year; but, of these, 40 went to the Prior of Lenton and the remaining 20 to the Dean and Chapter of Lichfield. The chaplain's stipend of

[1] For example, the parishioners of Faversham were obliged to attend the parish church on feast days and not the chapel at Ospringe: Turner and Salter, *Register of S. Augustine's, Canterbury*, ii, pp. 509–10.

[2] Cutts, *Parish Priests*, pp. 112–21.

[3] In 1282 the chapel of Patching separated from the church of Tarring and became a separate parish: *Regist. J. Pecham* (C. & Y. Soc.), p. 187. Archbishop Gray consolidated ten chapelries into five vicarages: Cutts, *Parish Priests*, p. 117.

[4] *Regist. J. Pontissara*, pp. 258–60.

[5] *Regist. W. Gray*, p. 7.

[6] Gibbons, *Liber Antiquus H. de Welles*, p. 42.

five marks a year was raised in the following way: the parishioners of Chelmorton paid half of it, the Chapter of Lichfield contributed one mark out of the 20 which they received, while the people of the neighbouring parish of Beeley were responsible for the remaining twenty shillings.[1] Where churches had been appropriated to religious houses the monks and nuns were often expected to endow the dependent chapels as well as the vicarage. Thus, the nuns of S. Mary and S. Michael at Stamford were obliged to provide a chaplain at Burghley besides a vicar at S. Martin's, Stamford, in which parish this chapel stood,[2] though the Abbot and Convent of S. Mary's at York obtained permission from the Pope in 1240 to provide for a chaplain at Kirkby Lonsdale in place of a vicar, who would have been more expensive.[3] In other instances the burden of providing the stipend of a chaplain rested on the lord of the manor upon whose land the chapel stood. At Edwalton in Nottinghamshire the lord of the manor was obliged to endow the chapel with two bovates of land, a meadow and a toft,[4] while at Lashbrook in the parish of Shiplake (Oxon) the local magnate was required to find everything necessary for the support of the chaplain.[5]

Most chapelries had their own local chaplain (who was often styled rector[6]), who lived in the village and carried on a more or less independent ministry. In some parishes, however, the outlying chapels were served from the mother church. At Ashbourne six of the chapels had their own resident chaplains, and three were dependent upon visits from the clergy of the parish church.[7] A few chapels, such as S. James', Pilton, were served by monks.[8]

In addition to public chapels in the villages there were, in some institutions, chapels which the public were allowed to attend on certain terms. At Bristol, for example, the canons of

[1] Savage, *Great Register of Lichfield*, p. 40.

[2] Gibbons, *Liber Antiquus H. de Welles*, p. 46.

[3] Bliss, *Cal. Papal Letters*, i, p. 190. The monks pleaded such poverty that persons wishing to join them had to buy their own habits.

[4] *Regist. W. Gray*, p. 18.

[5] Gibbons, *Liber Antiquus H. de Welles*, p. 9.

[6] E.g. Billingsley, *Regist. T. Cantilupe*, p. 302.

[7] Savage, *Great Register of Lichfield*, p. 218.

[8] Pilton was served by a monk of Malmesbury Abbey: Brewer, *Registrum Malmesburiense*, ii, p. 35.

S. Augustine built a chapel for the use of those who lived within the precincts of the monastery.[1] Hospitals generally had chapels to which the public were admitted, while to some of them full parochial rights were attached. This occurred at S. Paul's at Norwich, Armiston, S. Mary Magdalene at Durham, and the Leper-hospitals at Northampton, York and Lincoln.[2] In the hospital chapels which had no parochial status certain conditions had to be observed to ensure that there should be no trespassing on the rights of the incumbent. At S. Margaret's, Canterbury, for example, it was expressly stated that parishioners were not to enter the chapel of the Hospital of Poor Priests until after Mass had been said. The purpose of this regulation was to ensure that the people should hear Mass in the parish church in order that their oblations might accrue to the parish priest and not to the hospital.[3]

The custom of wealthy parishioners building and supporting private chapels in their own houses also became common during the thirteenth century. The earliest instance of this in the episcopal registers occurred in 1227 when the Archbishop of York gave permission for the Rector of Tuxford (Notts) to have a private chapel in his house since it was so far from the church.[4] In the following year Hugh of Welles tentatively gave permission to Ralph de Normanville to set up a private chapel in the manor-house of Newbold Grounds in the parish of Catesby (Northants). Since he allowed this only on condition that it was to be abolished on the death of Ralph's wife, it is clear that the Bishop regarded it as only a temporary arrangement.[5] In 1229 licence was given to Simon of Pelham Furneaux to build himself a chapel and to have his own chaplain. The chapel was to be 'wholly subject' (*plene subjecta*) to the parish church, and the family were to attend church on at least eleven days in the year unless the weather were too bad.[6] In 1231 Archbishop Gray gave licence to John de Romanby to have his own chapel,

[1] Barrett, *History of Bristol* (1789), p. 405.

[2] R. M. Clay, *Medieval Hospitals of England*, p. 203.

[3] Turner and Salter, *Register of S. Augustine's, Canterbury*, ii, pp. 557–9. The same conditions were made at the Hospital of S. John, Malmesbury: see Brewer, *Registrum Malmesburiense*, ii, p. 77.

[4] *Regist. W. Gray*, p. 16.

[5] *Rot. H. de Welles*, ii, p. 229.

[6] M. Gibbs, *Early Charters of S. Paul's*, pp. 148–50.

but he also was to attend the parish church on feast days. Strange to say, the vicar of the parish was expected to contribute half a mark each year to the stipend of the chaplain.[1]

In 1236 Grosseteste gave the first of a number of permits for the erection of private chapels. This was given to John Hansard of South Kelsey (Lincs), careful regulations being made to ensure that the parish church should not suffer. In the first place the rector and patron must give their consent; the chapel must have neither bell nor font; John Hansard and all his household must attend the parish church on Christmas Day, the Feast of the Purification, Easter, All Saints' Day, the Assumption of the Virgin Mary, the dedication festival and on 'all Sundays when there is a sermon', unless hindered by sickness or bad weather or through having distinguished guests in the house. All offerings taken in the chantry must be handed over to the parish church, and there shall be no marriages or churchings or 'such-like sacraments or sacramentals', no confessions or investitures. In exchange for the privilege of having his own chapel John Hansard was to give three and a half acres of land and a toft to the parish church.[2]

The majority of foundations of private chantries followed similar lines, care being always taken to ensure that there was no interference with the financial arrangements of the parish church. The constitutions of Ottobon in 1268 actually demand that all oblations received in private chapels must go to the parish church.[3] At Kellaways (Wilts) the chaplain might hear the confessions of the household and administer the sacrament, but he was strictly forbidden to baptise, bury, or give extreme unction.[4] In 1292 the parishioners of Hope All Saints in Kent complained that the lady of Crawthorne refused to come to church or make any contribution towards it, whereas she has her own chapel in which her chaplains baptise children, using a bucket since they have no font.[5] At Lymington it was ordained that at Ascensiontide the rector of the parish should join with the private chaplain, the latter to pay him *6d.* and *2d.* to his

[1] *Regist. W. Gray*, p. 45.

[2] *Rot. R. Grosseteste*, p. 12: cf. also pp. 25, 37, 173, 188, 208, 214, 258, 265.

[3] Wilkins, *Concilia*, ii, p. 9; cf. *Regist. W. Giffard*, pp. 266–8.

[4] *Regist. S. Gandavo*, ii, p. 786.

[5] Woodruff, *Some Early Visitation Rolls*, in *Arch. Cantiana*, xxxii, p. 151.

clerk together with 10*s.* for the poor of the parish.[1] At Gibbecrake in the parish of Purleigh (Essex) a chantry was founded by Reginald de Grey in memory of his wife. It was to be in the manor-house and was to be maintained by the Austin canons of Bicknacre, who were to provide a chaplain either secular or regular.[2]

Chantries in private houses became fairly common by the end of the thirteenth century. The custom of endowing chantries in churches and cathedrals was also growing but had not yet reached the proportions which made it so great an abuse in later years. Mr Leach says that the earliest chantry at Chichester was founded in 1180, that at Wells in 1198, at Ripon in 1234 and at Lincoln in 1235.[3] To these may be added S. Paul's Cathedral, where a chantry was set up before 1198.[4] In 1248 the Abbot and Convent of Wigmore endowed a chantry priest in the Cathedral Church of Hereford to pray for the soul of their benefactor, John Bacon, who had been one of the canons. The priest was to receive 5 marks a year, his only duties being to say Mass daily 'distinctly and in full'.[5] In 1277 the Austin canons of S. Thomas', Stafford, founded a chantry in Lichfield Cathedral in honour of Peter de Radnor, the late chancellor. Fifteen marks a year was the sum required, out of which seven marks went to the chantry priest, half a mark to his clerk, 12*s.* for the poor, 10*s.* for the Franciscans of Lichfield and a halfpenny a day to each of four vicars who were to assist at the Mass of Our Lady.[6]

Some chantries were founded in parish churches, many of them being well endowed. For example, Thomas Corbet founded a chantry for two priests in the chapel of S. Margaret in the parish of Westbury in 1272. The two chaplains were to have a house, 26 acres and a meadow, together with pasture for 16 oxen, 6 cows, 100 sheep, 2 horses and pannage for 50 pigs. When the priests grew old, Thomas Corbet was to see that they were adequately supported.[7] Even the monasteries had

[1] *Regist. J. Drokensford*, pp. 301–2.

[2] *Regist. R. Baldock, etc.* pp. 119–20.

[3] Leach, *Visitations of Southwell*, p. lxii.

[4] Gibbs, *Early Charters of S. Paul's*, p. 145.

[5] Capes, *Charters of Hereford*, pp. 82–4. In 1303 Wigmore got into trouble for not paying up (pp. 173–5).

[6] Savage, *Great Register of Lichfield*, p. 114.

[7] *Regist. R. Swinfield*, pp. 162–4.

chantries in them, served by secular priests. About 1240 Sir Peter Manley founded a chantry chapel at Meaux to be served by two priests and two clerks;[1] and about the same time Ralph de Willington and Olympias his wife built a chapel in the abbey of Gloucester and endowed two chaplains who were to do nothing but celebrate daily for the souls of the founders and their forebears. For these light duties they were to live in the monastery in a guest-house which Ralph had built for them, and were to be maintained by the monks on good and ample food provided from the monastic kitchens.[2]

Such was the chantry system in its early days; and it is easy enough to see that it was open to abuse. The duties tended to be very light and the remuneration at least equal to that of a hard-worked vicar in a parish. It is, therefore, no wonder that such jobs became much sought after by the indolent, or that many a man in Chaucer's day

> ran to Londone, unto Seynte Poules
> To seeken him a chaunterie for soules.

No study of the parochial system in England would be complete without some mention of the great churches which belonged more to communities than to the general public, but which yet had parochial responsibilities. Chief among these were the secular cathedrals of S. Paul's, Lincoln, Chichester, Hereford, Salisbury, York, Lichfield, Wells and Exeter. These vast structures were erected not to serve as places where huge crowds might assemble for worship (for every cathedral city was well supplied with parish churches), but rather to accommodate a small group of men who lived their lives under the shadow of the cathedral church in enjoyment of the wealth and splendour which were attached to it. The laity as a whole were no doubt allowed, and even sometimes encouraged, to attend the daily offices; but for the most part the members of the Chapter lived a life of superb detachment from the cares of pastoral work, while the proceeds of their prebends enabled them to employ subordinates to relieve them even of the burden of supporting the daily round of worship. In some of these cathedrals part of the nave was actually used as a parish church,

[1] Bond, *Chron. Melsa*, ii, pp. 60–1.

[2] Hart, *Hist. et Cart. Gloucest.* iii, pp. 279–81.

and in others there were nave altars set aside for parishioners, while at Salisbury one of the chantry priests acted as chaplain of the cathedral parish; but, as Professor Hamilton Thompson has pointed out, 'the neighbourhood of parish churches to our older cathedrals, either within the close itself or upon its verge, recalls the fact that the cathedral, if it was the Mother Church of the city and diocese, did not necessarily continue to provide parochial ministrations'.[1]

Similar to the secular cathedrals were the collegiate churches. Some of these were of ancient foundation, but many owed their origin to the work of benefactors in the thirteenth century. Ripon, Beverley, Southwell and S. George's, Windsor, are among the older foundations; Bishop Auckland, Lanchester, Chester-le-Street, Wingham, Glaseney and S. Edmund's, Salisbury, all came into being in the latter part of the thirteenth century. These foundations varied considerably in size. Merewell had but four priest canons, Wingham a provost and six canons; Glaseney a provost, sacrist and eleven prebendaries besides seven vicars and six choristers; Abergwilly had twenty-two prebendaries, four priests, four choristers and two clerks, while S. George's, Windsor, had a warden, twelve canons, thirteen priests, six choristers, four clerks and twenty-six poor knights. The average complement for a collegiate church was seven or eight prebendaries with about an equal number of vicars and a staff of singers and clerks.

The oldest collegiate churches were the 'minsters' of Anglo-Saxon times—communities of men living together to serve the church and the parishes connected with it. But as time went by and endowments increased it became more and more common for the canons to employ stipendiary priests to relieve them of their ministerial and liturgical duties. Each canon thus employed two vicars, a vicar-choral to deputise for him in the regular worship of the minster, and a parochial vicar to serve the parish which was appropriated to his prebend. Relieved thus of all responsibility, the canon or prebendary was able to live where he pleased in the enjoyment of an income for which little or nothing was demanded in return. Compared with the average benefice, prebends were well endowed. S. Martin's prebend at Beverley was valued at £80 a year, an equivalent

[1] A. H. Thompson, *Cathedral Churches of England*, p. 211; cf. pp. 103–4.

of several thousands in modern currency.[1] The prebends at Southwell worked out at an average of £20 apiece, at Ripon to £37. 10*s.* 0*d.*[2] At Wingham the canons received 1*s.* a day.[3] In addition to their regular income there were small payments to encourage the canons to attend services. At Hereford they received fourpence for each Mass which they attended,[4] at Southwell threepence for Mattins on ordinary days and sixpence on feast days.[5] At Beverley they received a bonus of 2*s.* for wine if they were present at church on certain festivals.[6]

The vicars, of course, were paid on a much lower scale. At Ripon they received £4 a year, but this was raised by the Archbishop in 1338 to £6, to the great indignation of the Chapter.[7] At Beverley each vicar celebrating at the high altar was to receive a penny or twopence a day;[8] at Southwell they received a regular stipend of 60*s.* a year.[9] In spite, however, of the fact that they were priests (whereas many prebendaries

[1] Leach, *Memorials of Beverley Minster*, i, pp. 215–17. The question of the comparative value of money in the thirteenth and twentieth centuries is a difficult one. Most writers adopt a rough-and-ready method of multiplying by twenty or twenty-five. Although some such method may be necessary for the general reader, it may also be very misleading. The average price of wheat in the second half of the thirteenth century was 5*s.* 4½*d.* per quarter, and of oats 2*s.* 3*d.* To-day the prices are 82*s.* 6*d.* and 77*s.* 1*d.* The former shows an increase of 15½ times, the latter of 34, an average for the two of 25. The average price of a cow at the same period was 7*s.*, whereas to-day it would fetch anything over fifty times as much. This, of course, would be partly due to the vast improvement of stock. Perhaps a better comparison is to be made in wages. In the thirteenth century a skilled workman—carpenter, mason, tiler, etc.—received about 3*d.* a day or 1*s.* 6*d.* a week, and a labourer half as much. Nowadays an artisan would expect at least fifty times this amount. The standard wage for a vicar was £3. 6*s.* 8*d.* (see below, p. 45). At the present day a curate receives about £250, which is seventy-five times as much. On the other hand, it was reckoned that a friar cost 4*d.* a day to feed (see below, p. 257), whereas nowadays it would take about ten times that amount to support him. Clearly, then, no general comparison can be made. (Note: for prices in the thirteenth century see J. E. T. Rogers, *History of Agriculture and Prices*, i, p. 245; ii, pp. 183–206, 274–86.)

[2] *Taxatio Nicholai*, pp. 302, 308.

[3] Dugdale-Caley, *Monasticon*, viii, pp. 1341–3.

[4] Capes, *Charters of Hereford*, pp. 168–9.

[5] Leach, *Visitations of Southwell*.

[6] Leach, *Memorials of Beverley*, i, pp. 336–7.

[7] Fowler, *Memorials of Ripon*, iv, pp. 10–18.

[8] Leach, *Memorials of Beverley*, i, p. 223; ii, p. 182.

[9] Leach, *Visitations of Southwell*, p. xlvi.

were only in minor orders), the vicars-choral were not much more than servants in a club of which the canons were the members.

The Chapter certainly had an uncommonly easy time. Although by their foundations they were intended to live together as a community, the time soon came when most of them had their own houses in the close, where they passed a comfortable existence, quarrelling with their neighbours[1] but free alike from the burdens of parochial responsibility and from the trouble of exercising a personal ministry. Rules as to residence and attendance at the services were made; but they were not always observed, and there were times when not a single member of the Chapter was in residence.[2] It was no wonder that prebends were eagerly sought after by those who regarded the Church as nothing more than a convenient milch cow to provide them with the cream of life.

The vicars, on the other hand, had a much harder time. It was they who did the work and kept the services going, though not always with the decorum which we nowadays associate with a great cathedral.[3] Nor did their private lives attain to any very high standard of dignity or rectitude. When colleges were visited by diocesan bishops there were sad tales of immorality and irresponsibility to be told. At his visitation of Beverley in 1314 Archbishop Greenfield found the chancellor diffamed with four women, John le Porter with five, another accused of keeping a wine shop and another of going on the corn exchange.[4] At Southwell in 1248 the vicars were found to be quarrelsome and incontinent, foul-mouthed and intemperate.[5] These may all have been exceptions, but the fact remains that the standard of manners and morals among the vicars and clerks was not generally very high. Confronted by the bad examples which

[1] The canons of Beverley enjoyed to the full the medieval passion for litigation. In 1306 they complain of some 'Satellites of Satan' and 'damnable sons of perdition', who have carried off some tithes to which they considered themselves entitled. In 1307 they excommunicated thirteen people who had not paid their dues, and in 1319 they quarrelled violently with the Abbot and Convent of Meaux, calling them 'devil's disciples' and excommunicating the whole lot (Leach, *Memorials of Beverley*, i, pp. 151–3, 187, 198, 370–1).

[2] Leach, *Visitations of Southwell*, p. xlvii.

[3] *Ibid.* p. 210.

[4] Leach, *Memorials of Beverley*, i, pp. 313–15.

[5] Leach, *Visitations of Southwell*, pp. 205–8, 210.

their employers set them, it is scarcely to be wondered at if this were so.

Most collegiate churches were also parish churches, and at Beverley the parishioners were expected to attend the altars in the nave.[1] The same was true of a certain number of monastic churches. In a good many Benedictine and Augustinian churches a nave altar was set aside for the use of the laity and a secular chaplain appointed to serve it. The arrangement, however, can never have been very satisfactory. The whole monastic system was closely bound up with the idea of claustration, of the monk's separation from the world; and it can therefore hardly have suited their ideal to have lay people wandering about their churches.[2] The attempt to make the same building serve both monks and laity was, therefore, not generally a success, as appeared in the prolonged quarrel at Leominster. Visiting this house in 1276, Thomas Cantilupe, Bishop of Hereford, found that the prior was in the habit of locking the church doors and so preventing the laity from entering their own church.[3] No doubt the action of the prior was designed to prevent not so much the laity from getting in, as his own monks from getting out. Cantilupe, however, insisted that the laity must have their rights and gave orders that the gates should be actually taken off their hinges. Seven years later Pecham, Archbishop of Canterbury, came to Leominster and was shocked to find what had been done. It was, to his mind, most improper that all kinds of 'nefarious people' should mingle with the monks, and he ordered the doors to be restored to their place, at the same time commanding the monks to build a separate chapel for the use of the laity.[4] Similar action appears to have been taken at Coventry, Evesham and Bury St Edmunds.[5]

As the medieval wayfarer, be he pilgrim or chapman, strolling player or strolling priest, pursued his way from parish to parish he would meet many different types of church and of clergy. There were the wealthy incumbents of rich livings, the 'club-

[1] Leach, *Memorials of Beverley*, i, pp. lxxvi–ix.

[2] A. H. Thompson, *English Monasteries*, pp. 53–5; Cranage, *The Home of the Monk*, p. 74.

[3] *Regist. T. Cantilupe*, pp. 46–9, 88–9.

[4] Pecham, *Reg. Epist.* ii, pp. 505–7.

[5] A. H. Thompson, *English Monasteries*, p. 55.

men' of the collegiate churches, the 'pore persouns' of those parishes which were but meanly endowed, the vicars fighting against poverty and exploitation, and the vast host of the unbeneficed, picking up a livelihood as best they might, struggling for existence and yearning for the security which many of them knew would never be theirs. Some of these certainly took their responsibilities very lightly, but the system was designed for one end only—to supply the spiritual needs of men; and there was not one square foot in England which was not a part of some man's parish or in which the writ of Christ's Church did not run.

CHAPTER III

RECTORS

We are so much accustomed nowadays to regard all parishes as being organised on the same system, with the parson, be he rector or vicar, residing in the parish and personally ministering to his flock, that it is easy to forget what great diversity there was among the parishes of England in the thirteenth century. Sir Francis Stevenson enumerated five different types: 'those in which dwelt resident rectors who received the whole of the proceeds and carried out the duties themselves'; 'those in which a rector, compelled for special reasons to be absent, made his own arrangements for the presence of a deputy for the time being'; 'those in which the rector put the living out to be farmed'; 'those in which the church was appropriated to a monastery, or to a chapter, or to some other religious foundation, and in which the services were performed by persons temporarily appointed for the purpose by those bodies'; and 'the appropriated churches in which vicarages had been established'.[1]

By the thirteenth century something like half the parishes were still rectories, but not all rectors approached their work from the same point of view. We shall understand the parochial system of the Middle Ages only if we constantly bear in mind the fact that, whereas some rectors regarded their livings as spiritual responsibilities, others were content to think of them as no more than financial assets. The distinction between the two was very largely one of class.

If we study the records of ordinations and institutions from the bishops' Registers of the time we shall discover that a great many of those who sought ordination and who eventually succeeded to livings were local men, sons of the smaller landowners and of the yeoman class.[2] Many of them were ordained on the title of their own property (*ad titulum patrimonii sui*), showing that they were men who had some private means, and were therefore in no danger of becoming a burden to the Church or to the community. Others were sons of craftsmen or tradesmen,

[1] Stevenson, *Robert Grosseteste*, p. 139.
[2] *Regist. G. Giffard*, p. cvii.

boys who had somehow managed to acquire enough learning to pass whatever tests the bishops demanded. The Ordination lists from the diocese of Canterbury between the years 1282 and 1300 provide us with a good many men whose surnames suggest that they belonged to this class. Among the names mentioned we find Barber, Carbonel (charcoal-burner), Chandler (candle-maker), Cordwainer, Cooper, Faber (smith), Grocer, Haymonger, Merchant, Mercer, Pistor (baker), Spicer, Taverner, Pastor (shepherd), Plumber and Flaoner (a maker of flat cakes or flans). Of the same class were the sons of men who held office in the big families, among whom we find Butler, Chamberlain, Cocus or Cu (Cook), Cofferer (treasurer), Falkener, Marshall, Forester, Gardiner and Archer. The cloth industry provides us with a Cissor, Textor, Tentour or stretcher, Fuller, Packer and Taylor.

Then there were those who belonged to the peasant class. A few of these rose to high rank in the Church either through intellectual brilliance or by showing great administrative ability as members of one of the religious orders. Robert de Insula, who became Bishop of Durham in 1274, was the son of poor crofters at Lindisfarne. He owed his preferment to his outstanding gifts as a Benedictine monk. Pecham advanced to the archbishopric of Canterbury after many years as a Franciscan friar; but he too sprang from humble origins. So also did Robert Grosseteste, whose elegant manners at table caused surprise to those who knew that he had come from a simple Suffolk home.[1] All these were men of exceptional ability, but this same class provided also a number of rectors of country parishes, men like the 'pore persoun' of the *Canterbury Tales* whose brother was a ploughman and carter of dung. Many of them made fine parish priests, for they understood their people and could speak to them in their own language.

Most of those who sprang from the yeoman class, or from craftsmen and tradesmen, or from the peasantry, were men who were willing to take their spiritual duties seriously by living in their parishes and ministering to their congregations. This is not to say that they were all good priests or even good men; but at least they made some show of spiritual activity in the parishes to which they were instituted.

[1] M. Deanesly, *The Lollard Bible*, p. 182.

It was far otherwise with many of those who belonged to the great land-owning families, the Clares, Nevilles, Foliots, Bohuns, Montforts, and others. However anxious bishops might be not to allow special privileges to men of high rank,[1] they would find it very difficult to resist the demands of those who belonged to the most powerful families in the land, in spite of the fact that, as our records show, to many of these men the taking of holy orders was more an opportunity for acquiring a secure and substantial income than the response to a call to pastoral ministration. Much of the patronage of the Church was in lay hands, and it was only natural that fathers should wish to see their sons well provided for. Moreover, it was generally a good financial investment to obtain a dispensation from Rome to hold several livings in plurality, since by this means the initial outlay could soon be repaid. Many of these men, having provided themselves with the necessary dispensation, relied upon the influence of their families to provide them with enough benefices to ensure a comfortable income. Since many of them took very little interest in the parishes from which they drew their money, they were enabled to live handsomely if not luxuriously, and to engage in such pursuits as interested them most, whether political, forensic or sporting.

Typical of this class was Bogo de Clare, a son of the Earl of Gloucester and Hertford. He obtained a dispensation from the Pope to allow him to hold benefices up to a total of 400 marks; but before he had finished he had far exceeded this limit. He began by being presented by his mother to the living of Adlingfleet in Yorkshire, though this led to a long and bitter dispute. By 1280 he had acquired livings in Northamptonshire, Cambridgeshire, Berkshire, Northumberland and Ireland, to which he shortly added fourteen others. This brought him to what was meant to be the limit of his acquisitions, but this did not deter him from proceeding further to much more lucrative emoluments. In 1282 he was instituted to the rectory of Settrington in Yorkshire, valued at 150 marks, and in 1285 he was appointed by the King to the office of Treasurer of York, valued at 600 marks. By the time of his death in 1291 he held two canonries, three dignities in cathedral and collegiate churches, and twenty-

[1] See T. de Cantilupe's letter to his official telling him to insist upon each man being properly ordained 'of whatever rank he might be' (quantaque prefulget dignitate): *Regist. T. Cantilupe*, p. 25.

four parishes or portions.[1] His total income from these benefices must have been something in the region of £2200, or about £150,000 in modern money.[2]

This enormous income enabled him to live a life of luxury and indulgence while he took only the smallest interest in the parishes from which he drew his money.[3] Some idea of his manner of living is to be derived from the extracts from his household accounts which have been preserved.[4] His *familia* included two knights, many squires, about thirteen servants (*garciones*) and two pages, besides a staff of clerks to look after his legal and financial affairs. He also kept a champion, Thomas de Bruges, whom he seems to have taken over from Bishop Thomas Cantilupe; and on one occasion employed no less than four champions at a cost of 17*s*. 9½*d*. Another regular member of the household was Adam the harper, and occasionally a troupe of professional actors was entertained.

His expenditure on food was immense, for he would have nothing but the best. He thought nothing of spending on preserved ginger as much as he would pay a chaplain to do his work for him in one of his parishes for a whole twelve months.[5] During the six months ending at Michaelmas 1285 his household expenses came to a total of £688, which included over £17 spent on sugar and spice. Wildly extravagant, he consistently lived beyond his income. In the six months from

1 A. H. Thompson, *Pluralism in the Medieval Church*, in *Associated Architectural Societies' Reports*, 1916–17, pp. 53 ff.

2 If a vicar in the thirteenth century was paid £3. 6*s*. 8*d*. this would be, at the most, one-seventieth of what he would expect to-day. On this basis an income of £2200 would be equal to £154,000. See above, p. 20, n. 1.

3 The writer of the *Lanercost Chronicle* says that he once visited the church of Simonburn in Northumberland, from which Bogo de Clare drew an income of 600 marks. It was Easter Sunday, but he found that in place of the retable above the high altar there was nothing but some dirty old sticks spattered with cow-dung. And yet, he says, Bogo could afford to send to the Queen of France, as a pleasantry, a tiny carriage made entirely of ivory and silver (*Chron. de Lanercost*, p. 158). Archbishop Pecham also complained of the way in which he neglected his parishes, in which he behaved 'as a robber rather than a rector': *Reg. Epist.* i, pp. 371–2. Cf. Roger of Wendover, *Flores Historiarum*, ed. H. R. Luard, iii, p. 93.

4 *The Wardrobe and Household Accounts of Bogo de Clare, 1284–6*, ed. M. S. Giuseppi, in *Archaeologia*, vol. lxx.

5 E.g. on p. 31 there is a record of 70*s*. for ginger while 66*s*. 8*d*. is the standard wage for a stipendiary chaplain.

Christmas 1285 to Whitsuntide 1286 his receipts were £564, but he cheerfully allowed his expenses during the same period to run up to a total of £939.

Thus he lived, luxuriously, recklessly and selfishly, with only the most trifling and conventional concern in the needs of those less fortunate. Mr Giuseppi points out how little he gave in alms and oblations, and how strongly this contrasts with what he was prepared to spend on his own personal interests and pleasures. 'It is sadly illuminating', he says, 'to find at the end of a long list of expenses on such a day as July 3rd, 1285, when the food and drink bill of a great banquet comes to as much as £8. *6s.* 0*d.* with additional payments of *6s.* 8*d.* to a wafer-maker...4*s.* to another, and 5*s.* to a harper, "on the same day in alms 1*d.*", the solitary item under this head.'[1]

A good many livings were held by men like Bogo de Clare, whose only interest in the parishes was as sources of the wealth which enabled them to live in luxury and indolence. As a result, the people in many a parish had never seen their rector, whom they knew only as a name and as the power behind the steward who came round to collect their tithes and their oblations.

Absenteeism was common in the thirteenth century and was due to many causes, of which perhaps the greatest was Pluralism.[2] Neither the decrees of the Councils nor the efforts of bishops were of much avail when they came up against the vested interests of the big families.[3] Perhaps another reason why the bishops' denunciations fell on deaf ears was that they themselves often had such bad records as pluralists. Thomas Cantilupe, for example, who was afterwards canonised, had been a flagrant offender. In the year before his elevation to the episcopate he was Archdeacon of Stafford, Canon of Lichfield, Precentor of York, Prebendary of S. Paul's and Hereford, and Rector of at least ten parishes: Wintringham, Deighton, Hampton Bishop, Ripple, Kempsey, Dodderhill, Snitterfield, Sherborne Decani,

[1] *Archaeologia*, lxx, pp. 17–18.

[2] See Professor Hamilton Thompson's article on *Pluralism in the Medieval Church* in *Associated Architectural Societies' Reports*, 1916–17, pp. 35 ff., and *Peckham and Pluralities* by W. T. Waugh, in *E.H.R.* 1913.

[3] Cf. *Regist. W. Wickwayn*, pp. 116–19, 259; Pecham, *Reg. Epist.* i, p. 91, ii, pp. 512–14, 531; Wilkins, *Concilia*, i, pp. 627–8; *Regist. W. Giffard*, pp. 266–8.

Bradwell and the family living of Aston Cantlow.[1] John le Romeyn, before becoming Archbishop of York in 1286, had been Chancellor and Precentor of Lincoln besides holding two prebends and at least three benefices.[2] Anthony Bek when nominated to the bishopric of Durham in 1283 was in possession of five livings besides being Archdeacon of Durham.[3] If the bishops themselves indulged in this evil, how can we wonder if they failed to restrict those who were only following where they had trod?

With the aid of a powerful kinsman, or with royal or papal favour, there was nothing to stop a man from collecting benefices to almost any number. John de Drokensford, one of the King's clerks, while only a deacon and under age, was Rector of Childwall, Hemingbrough, Kingsclere, Balsham, Barton and Dalston, besides holding canonries and prebends at York, Salisbury, Wells, Dublin, Kildare, S. Martin-le-Grand, Bishop Auckland and Darlington.[4] At the same time another royal clerk, John de Langton, who was only a subdeacon, was Treasurer of Wells, and rector of seven parishes, while holding canonries at eight other places. His income was over £1000 a year, representing many thousands in modern currency.[5] John Mansel, one of Henry III's most trusted advisers, was commonly supposed to hold three hundred benefices and to be the richest man in the world.[6] Gross exaggeration though this may be, there is no doubt that he was a particularly successful collector of ecclesiastical preferment. Bogo de Clare is described by Professor Hamilton Thompson as 'a man to whom the possession of livings was an occupation and a passion'.[7]

These were some of the most notorious cases; but there were a great many men who held two or more livings in plurality. Gregory IX, the friend of S. Francis, issued no less than seventy-eight dispensations to English clergy to hold several benefices at the same time,[8] and many were allowed to collect preferment up to a stated sum, such as 200 or 300 marks a year.[9]

[1] *Regist. T. Cantilupe*, p. xix. Cantlow = Cantilupe.

[2] *Regist. J. Romeyn*, ii, p. x; and cf. Bliss, *Cal. Papal Letters*, i, p. 484.

[3] Creighton's article in *D.N.B.*

[4] Bliss, *Cal. Papal Letters*, i, p. 577.

[5] *Ibid.* p. 583.

[6] A. H. Thompson, *Pluralism in the Medieval Church*, in *Associated Architectural Societies' Reports*, 1916–17, pp. 50–1.

[7] *Ibid.* p. 53.

[8] Bliss, *Cal. Papal Letters*, i, pp. 117–98.

[9] *Ibid.* i, pp. 132, 207, 261, 293, 312, 529, 575.

The evils of pluralism are obvious. A pluralist, even if he held only two benefices, was bound to have his interests divided; while the temptation to make his position an excuse for negligence was very great. No doubt there were some pluralists who were conscientious men, who visited their parishes regularly and maintained some contact with their parishioners; but there is no doubt, either, that many of them neglected their responsibilities in a shameful way, leaving it to mercenary priests to minister to the needs of their flocks. As so often, we find Grosseteste's penetrating eye seeing to the root of the evil. In 1236 he wrote to Hugh of Pateshull warning him not to fall into the temptation of seeking a dispensation to hold several livings in plurality. 'Enquire of your conscience', he says, 'whether you are seeking more benefices in order that love may abound among the sheep, or in order that you yourself may be enriched at their expense; whether it is in order that you may feed the sheep by word, by example and by prayer, or in order that you yourself may be fed from their milk.'[1]

But pluralism was not the only cause of non-residence. Many rectors failed to live on their cures for no other reason than that they preferred to live elsewhere. If a living were worth fifty marks a year, and a stipendiary chaplain could be found to do the work for an annual salary of three or four marks, the rector could enjoy a considerable income without the inconvenience of having to do any work. And many took advantage of this arrangement. As the bishops travelled around their dioceses they were constantly finding parishes totally neglected by their incumbents and left in the hands of ill-educated and sometimes quite inadequate stipendiaries. In 1289 Archbishop Romeyn, after one of his visitations, cited the rectors of fourteen parishes to answer for non-residence.[2] In the Register of Bishop Stapeldon of Exeter we read of one Nicholas Lovetot, Rector of Stokenham, who had deserted his parish and taken up his abode the Bishop knew not where. He had not been seen in his parish for over three years.[3] In the visitation of Godalming in 1220 the vicar was charged with the fact that he had never resided in the place.[4]

[1] R. Grosseteste, *Epistolae*, p. 99.

[2] *Regist. J. Romeyn*, i, p. 341.

[3] *Regist. W. Stapeldon*, p. 381. Nicholas Lovetot was a well-known pluralist whose misdemeanours occur in more than one Register.

[4] W. H. R. Jones, *Reg. S. Osmundi*, i, p. 296.

The worst case of all was in the diocese of York. Finding that the services in the church of Huggate had been shamefully neglected, Archbishop Corbridge instituted enquiries which revealed that no one knew whether there was a rector or not, for none had been seen in the parish for fifty years.[1]

Not all absenteeism was due either to plurality or to neglect, for many rectors were absent from their parishes either by permission or by compulsion. Exeats were readily granted to young men who wished to continue their education, for it must be remembered that benefices were often conferred by lay patrons on sons or kinsmen who were far too young to exercise a personal ministry. Boys of ten, twelve and fourteen were quite commonly instituted as incumbents of parishes from which they drew a substantial income while they themselves remained at their desks or took a course at the University. The episcopal registers of the thirteenth century are full of the names of those who had received a *licentia studendi* or who had sought and obtained permission to 'frequent the schools' for periods varying between one and seven years. Others obtained leave of absence to attend as clerks or chaplains upon noblemen,[2] or to go on crusade,[3] while licences were even granted to men who wished to visit their estates abroad,[4] or to take a holiday,[5] or merely to escape from bad weather.[6] Many also were away from their parishes by compulsion, for the ignorance of the younger clergy was so serious that many of the bishops ordered them to leave their parishes in order to go and learn something before undertaking a cure of souls.

In all cases of absenteeism efforts were made to see that the parish church was served either by a vicar or by a chaplain. P. de Rossignol, Rector of Droxford, obtained permission in

[1] *Regist. T. Corbridge*, i, pp. 188–9. A note on p. 189 tells us that the living had at one time been held by a non-resident Italian, Alberto Arcilis, a nephew of Innocent IV; cf. Bliss, *Cal. Papal Letters*, i, p. 496.

[2] See, for example, the list of dispensations for absence in *Regist. A. Orleton*, pp. 390–2.

[3] *Regist. W. Giffard*, pp. 278–86. This gives a list of about 300 who gave money for the Crusades, of whom 115 were priests. Of the priests, 39 were marked as *crucesignati*, but of course many of them never sailed.

[4] *Regist. W. Giffard*, p. 2.

[5] *Regist. S. Gandavo*, ii, p. 852 (*pro solatio*).

[6] *Ibid.* This was Master John de Chandoys, Rector of Castle Eaton (Wilts).

1235 and again in 1236 to put a vicar in his parish on the grounds that he himself was 'too busy to reside'.[1] In 1248 Guy de Rossilian was allowed to put vicars in all his benefices, while he himself was excused from the necessity of taking holy orders.[2] At Newchurch in Kent the rector had an income of 60 marks and installed a vicar with a stipend of 10 marks to do the work,[3] and in many parishes the rectory was definitely stated to be a sine-cure, the cure of souls being vested in the vicar.[4] In the archdeaconry of Buckingham there were both rectors and vicars in at least fifteen parishes.[5] Where there was no vicar the spiritual responsibilities were borne by a parish chaplain, paid by the incumbent, but with no rights and little security. It is not to be wondered that the men who took these positions were often little qualified for the tasks which they were expected to perform.

A popular method of avoiding the penalties of pluralism lay in the system of holding churches *in commendam*. Professor Hamilton Thompson has pointed out how this system, under which a man received the fruits of a living without being instituted to it, became a serious abuse despite the efforts of Councils to put an end to it.[6] The sharper the war that was waged against pluralism, the more the system of commendation grew. If pluralism was an offence, the holder of a plurality of livings could argue that he was not really incumbent of them since he held them only *in commendam*. As some men continued to hold their benefices on these terms more or less indefinitely there was nothing to choose between them and the most flagrant pluralists. In 1268 the legate Ottobon had declared that the system of commendations was to stop, and that any bishop who defied this decree was to be deprived of all right to collation and presentation,[7] and six years later the General Council at Lyons ordained that no man might hold more than one parish *in commendam*, nor for more than six months. Yet the system survived for some time, episcopal registers being full of

[1] Bliss, *Cal. Papal Letters*, i, pp. 148, 152. [2] *Ibid.* p. 242.

[3] Woodruff, *Some Early Visitation Rolls*, in *Arch. Cantiana*, xxxii, pp. 156–7.

[4] E.g. at Braintree and Chigwell: Newcourt, *Repertorium*, ii, pp. 87, 140.

[5] *Rot. H. de Welles*, ii, pp. 48–97.

[6] See his article on *Pluralism in the Medieval Church*, in *Associated Architectural Societies' Reports*, 1916–17, p. 47.

[7] Wilkins, *Concilia*, ii, p. 13.

instances of commendations granted by bishops and held, not for six months only, but for many years.

Another bad practice against which Church reformers were constantly fighting was that of 'farming' the revenues of a church. The major part of the income of a benefice was derived from tithe which, of course, had to be regularly collected. If the rector lived in his parish he could supervise this; but if (as so often) he lived elsewhere, the difficulty of collecting what was due to him became acute. In such circumstances the simplest thing was to invite some local man or neighbouring abbot to hand over a lump sum and to pay himself back with interest out of the fruits of the benefice.

Farming was viewed with much disfavour by the Church; and indeed rightly so, for it was a wholly commercial speculation which encouraged absenteeism and a niggardliness whereby the poor were often defrauded of what was their due.[1] We shall, therefore, not be surprised to find Grosseteste inveighing against it in a letter addressed to John le Romeyn, Sub-dean of York in 1235 and Rector of the parish of Chalgrave in Bedfordshire. After saying that he is willing to respect the rights of others in the disposal of benefices, he adds: 'Nevertheless, it ought to be quite clear to you that the putting out of a benefice to farm is not the same thing as a free disposal, but is rather degrading the free bride of Jesus Christ into a position of slavery.'[2] All the same, this 'degradation of the bride of Christ' continued for many years, and often with the connivance and co-operation of those who should have condemned it. In 1236 Grosseteste was overruled by the Pope, who commanded him to give permission to Hugh of Pateshull, one of the King's clerks, to farm his benefices; and we can picture the bishop's fury on having his own powers overridden by Rome.[3] Cantilupe allowed the Rector of Eastnor to farm his living for five years while he went on crusade;[4] the Rector of Opton was allowed by Bishop Giffard to farm his church for two years to the Abbot of Winchcombe;[5] the tithes of Rickling (Essex) were

[1] Wilkins, *Concilia*, i, pp. 502, 580, 588, 627–8, 651; ii, pp. 10, 58; R. Grosseteste, *Epistolae*, p. 158; Pecham, *Reg. Epist.* iii, pp. 948–50.

[2] R. Grosseteste, *Epistolae*, pp. 65–6.

[3] Bliss, *Cal. Papal Letters*, i, p. 154.

[4] *Regist. T. Cantilupe*, p. 6.

[5] *Regist. G. Giffard*, p. 69; cf. pp. 26, 28, 45–6, 94, 120, 146.

farmed to Reginald, the vicar, in 1236 for eighteen marks a year;[1] the tithes at Husborne Crawley (Beds) were farmed to the chaplain of the parish for twenty-three shillings a year,[2] while two parishes in the Hereford diocese, Diddlebury and Long Stanton, were farmed to a layman for an annual payment of £60.[3]

By one means or another a good many clergy managed to escape from any clerical duties by the simple expedient of keeping well away from their parishes. Another method was to remain all their lives in minor orders.

In the *Rotuli* of Hugh of Welles, Bishop of Lincoln from 1209 to 1235, we have records of many hundreds of men who were inducted into benefices in that diocese. The Registers are careful to give, where possible, the status of each man, whether priest, deacon, subdeacon or acolyte, though in many instances they use the words 'chaplain' (*capellanus*) or 'clerk' (*clericus*) without telling us precisely what these words imply. In the archdeaconry of Oxford, during these years, 104 rectors were instituted. Of these only 1 is definitely stated to be a priest, 5 were deacons and 1 an archdeacon, 45 were subdeacons, 5 were acolytes; 15 were described as clerks and 19 as chaplains; 1 was 'said to be a deacon', 1 was a physician, and 1 was the archdeacon's official. Of the remaining 10 no status or order is given. In the archdeaconry of Buckingham there were 96 rectors inducted. Of these not one is marked as priest, but there were 4 deacons, 34 subdeacons, 1 acolyte, 15 clerks and 29 chaplains. In the archdeaconry of Stow, out of 48 rectors none was described as priest, but, in addition to 1 deacon, there were 19 subdeacons, 3 acolytes, 9 clerks and 13 chaplains.

Before proceeding further it will be necessary to examine the words *clericus* and *capellanus* to see what they imply. The word *clericus* was used rather vaguely of men in minor orders.[4] Thus Gilbert son of Robert is described as *clericus* but is ordered to be ordained acolyte as soon as convenient;[5] several men (or

[1] Gibbs, *Early Charters of S. Paul's*, p. 231.
[2] G. H. Fowler, *Charters of Dunstable*, p. 99.
[3] *Regist. A. Orleton*, p. 239. For other instances see *Regist. R. Swinfield*, p. 85; *Regist. J. Pontissara*, p. 115.
[4] Cf. Rashdall, *Universities of Europe* (new ed.), iii, p. 394.
[5] *Rot. H. de Welles*, i, p. 32.

boys, to be more accurate) were designated *clerici* and were ordered to attend the schools before proceeding to holy orders. These lads had probably received the first tonsure and were known as 'holy-water carriers' or *aquaebajuli*.[1] Three vicars in the archdeaconry of Oxford are described as *clerici* and are instructed to be ordained subdeacon.[2] In one instance a rector who was marked *clericus* was apparently not ordained at all.[3] The Registers of other bishops bear similar witness, though in later years the word *clericus* became much less common.[4]

The word *capellanus* is generally used in episcopal Registers of a man who was working in a parish as an assistant to the incumbent, corresponding to what we call nowadays (quite inaccurately) a 'curate'. But in the appointment of rectors and vicars the word is commonly used in describing a man's orders, instead of one of the more precise terms—priest, deacon, etc. The fact that in the *Rotuli* of Hugh of Welles the scribe does occasionally use the word *presbyter* or priest[5] suggests that *capellani* were not in priest's orders; but the evidence on the whole is against this. For example, one rector who has been described as *capellanus* is ordered to reside in the parish to which he has been instituted and to minister 'in the office of a priest'.[6] Moreover in the later Registers the word *capellanus* becomes comparatively rare, being superseded by *sacerdos* or *presbyter*.[7] The probability is, therefore, that in the earlier Registers—those

[1] *Rot. H. de Welles*, i, p. 166; ii, pp. 48, 52, 53. The first tonsure could be given to a child of seven before receiving even minor orders: Gasquet, *Parish Life*, p. 77.

[2] *Rot. H. de Welles*, ii, pp. 5, 10, 12. Cf. *Regist. W. Giffard*, p. 22 (*clericus et acolitus*).

[3] *Rot. H. de Welles*, ii, p. 56.

[4] E.g. *Rot. R. Grosseteste*, p. 253 (a *clericus* who hopes to proceed to major orders); *Regist. W. Giffard*, p. 22 (*clericus et acolitus*).

[5] Vol. ii, p. 75; but it is only of very rare occurrence. In the *Rotuli* of Grosseteste it occurs on pp. 29, 54, 320, 360, 402, 414 and 415, but is still uncommon.

[6] 'In officio sacerdotali' (*Rot. H. de Welles*, ii, p.58). The medieval registrars were a little careless about the use of words. For example in the *Rotuli* of Hugh of Welles (ii, p. 55) we read of a certain deacon who is to serve in a parish 'in officio sacerdotali'. Cf. 'Sacerdotes in gradu diaconorum' (Dugdale-Caley, *Monasticon*, ii, p. 308).

[7] In the Register of W. Wickwayn (1279–85) out of the first 100 institutions 32 were priests and only 3 *capellani*; while in the Register of Richard Swinfield (1283–1317) out of 483 inductions 168 were priests and only 14 *capellani*, all of whom occur before 1291.

of Hugh of Welles, Walter Gray and Grosseteste—the word *capellanus* was used to indicate a man who had already served in some parish as assistant priest, as opposed to the boys and young men who were given benefices while still at school or only in minor orders.

If, therefore, we assume that all *capellani* were in priest's orders we find that, out of the 248 rectors instituted by Hugh of Welles in the three archdeaconries of Oxford, Buckingham and Stow, only 61, or less than one quarter were priests. In the register of Welles' successor, Grosseteste, we discover that out of 229 rectors appointed in the archdeaconry of Northampton only 45, or rather less than one in five, were priests. In the institutions of a later Bishop of Lincoln, Richard Gravesend (1258–79), only 16 per cent of the rectors were in priest's orders; in those of Archbishop Wickwayn of York about one-third, and in those of Bishop Swinfield of Hereford, nearly 40 per cent.[1] Some of these men no doubt proceeded to higher orders in due course, but others certainly did not. For example, Philip Lovel was ordained subdeacon in May 1285 and collated at the same time Rector of Wittersham in Kent: in the following Lent he received ordination as a priest, having apparently passed over the diaconate altogether.[2] On the other hand, William de Barewe was instituted Rector of Sutton-by-Shrewsbury as an acolyte in December 1315. He was away from his parish for the first eight years and seems to have made no attempt to proceed to any higher orders.[3] Henry Pancoke became Rector of the parish of Old Romney in 1289 when only a subdeacon, but was raised to the priesthood in the following year;[4] but Master Thomas of Esthall who was inducted into the living of Hothfield in 1284, having been ordained acolyte in the previous December, apparently never advanced even so far as the subdiaconate.[5] In the diocese of Carlisle, William de Brampton was appointed

[1] Of the 483 institutions and collations in Swinfield's Register 168 were priests, 36 deacons, 58 subdeacons, 68 acolytes, 4 clerks, 14 chaplains and 135 not stated. In Pecham's Ordination Lists, out of 183 rectors who came up for ordination 84 were deacons, 70 subdeacons, 24 acolytes and 5 below that.

[2] *Regist. J. Pecham* (C. & Y. Soc.), p. 47; and cf. Ordination Lists.

[3] *Regist. R. Swinfield*, pp. 543, 546; *Regist. A. Orleton*, p. 390; *Regist. T. Charlton*, p. 90.

[4] *Regist. J. Pecham* (C. & Y. Soc.), p. 86 and Ordination Lists.

[5] *Ibid.* pp. 131, 135 and Ordination Lists.

Rector of Asby while still a layman. The Bishop very rightly refused to institute him until he had been ordained subdeacon. This was done a few months later, but he does not seem to have advanced to any higher order.[1]

Rectors of parishes in the thirteenth century were, therefore, of two quite different types. There were the humbler men and those with a higher sense of responsibility who lived in their parishes and ministered day by day to their flocks. On the other hand there were those who regarded their parishes merely as a source of income. These men took no pains to qualify themselves for the ministry by receiving the necessary ordination, and most of them lived far from their cures. In a later chapter we shall see how efforts were made to control these two evils of absenteeism and lack of proper ordination.

[1] *Regist. J. Halton*, i, pp. 105–6.

CHAPTER IV

VICARS

It has been stated above[1] that local lords, having founded and endowed the parish churches on their estates, considered that they had the right to dispose of the income of the church in any way which they chose so long as the money was devoted to some ecclesiastical or charitable object, and so long as the parish church was served. In the religious revivals of the eleventh and twelfth centuries many laymen wished to give alms to monasteries[2] and a considerable amount of land passed then from lay to monastic ownership. But there came a time when people became chary of disposing of any more of their real property, and it was then that the idea of giving away the revenue of the Church came into being. There was nearly always a balance between the gross income of most parishes and the amount necessary to provide a parish chaplain. It was this balance that was so often conferred on the monasteries by the system of 'appropriations'.

Under this system a lay patron of a living, instead of appointing a man as rector, would hand over all his rights to a monastery which thereupon became rector, making itself responsible for collecting the income and seeing that the church was served. The net gain to the monasteries was often considerable, especially to those which acquired a number of such bequests. The rich living of Whalley, valued at over £200 a year, was appropriated to the new Cistercian Abbey there in 1296. Since the total outgoings were under £27 the monastery profited to the extent of £173 a year.[3] Skipsea Church in Yorkshire was appropriated to the Abbey of Meaux about the same time. The outgoings here were just under £14 out of an income of £23.[4] From fifteen parishes taken at random from the appropriations in the diocese of Lincoln the total income was £141, of which the monasteries had £89 to their

[1] See p. 5.
[2] Hartridge, *Vicarages in the Middle Ages*, p. 6.
[3] Hulton, *Coucher Book of Whalley Abbey*, i, pp. 205–6.
[4] Bond, *Chron. Melsa*, ii, pp. 235–6.

use, while the remaining £52 was set aside for the maintenance of the fifteen vicars.[1]

The system of appropriations does not seem to have arisen before the Norman Conquest, but in the twelfth century it became very common, and was continued throughout the following centuries.[2] The reasons given for the transfer of parish revenues were various. The most common was the poverty of the monasteries and the impossibility of providing hospitality for travellers and the poor. Richard Swinfield, for example, in sanctioning the appropriation of the comparatively rich living of Stottesdon to Shrewsbury Abbey in 1283, prefaces his injunctions with the following considerations:

> As part of the ceaseless care and great solicitude which attach to our office it behoves us to consider the well-being of the religious communities, lest among them divine worship should be neglected. Wherefore, considering the various setbacks and failing resources from which the monastery of S. Peter at Shrewsbury is suffering (whereby there is a slackening of divine worship and of hospitality and a danger of retrenchment and even complete cessation of alms-giving); in this evident necessity and dire need we are moved by affection and are anxious, so far as in us lies, to meet the aforementioned dangers. Wherefore we desire, ordain and decree that the Church of Stottesdon, with all its rights and appurtenances, which for the reasons already mentioned we appropriate to the abbot and convent of Shrewsbury, be given to them for ever for their own possession, saving a reasonable and adequate allowance for the vicar....[3]

Poverty was certainly the chief cause of appropriations, though the reasons for the poverty of the religious houses were not always given. Edgmond Church with its chapels was appropriated to Shrewsbury Abbey in 1254 because 'through various

[1] *Rot. H. de Welles*, i, pp. 181–7. It was customary for the appropriators to take about two-thirds of the living, leaving one-third for the maintenance of the clergy. Since the average living in England in the thirteenth century was worth about £11 the local clergy had to live on about £3. 10*s*. 0*d*. The standard rate for vicars was indeed fixed at 5 marks (£3. 6*s*. 8*d*.); see Council of Oxford, 1222, in Wilkins, *Concilia*, i, p. 587.

[2] Hartridge, *Vicarages*, pp. 23, 25; Coulton, *Five Centuries*, iii, p. 163. Stevenson exaggerates when he says that 'early in the twelfth century more than two thirds of the parish churches in England were already in the hands of the monasteries': *R. Grosseteste*, p. 138.

[3] *Regist. R. Swinfield*, p. 18.

unforeseen mischances' the monastery 'had become heavily burdened with debt for which there seems to be no remedy but to break up the House and surrender it to the creditors'.[1] Long Preston was appropriated to Bolton Priory in 1304, the reasons being heavy taxation, the poorness of the land, debts, poverty, lack of money for hospitality and dry rot in the canons' stalls.[2] Mattersey Church was appropriated to the Gilbertine Priory in the same place on the grounds that the canons had suffered great loss by fire,[3] and Birstal passed into the possession of the Augustinians of Nostell partly because Bamburgh Church, which they owned, had been destroyed by the Scots, and partly because of the expense to which they were put in providing hospitality for people going north to the Scottish wars.[4] Other appropriations were to increase the number of monks;[5] and some, such as Chipping Norton, were for the support of scholars at Oxford.[6]

For all the above appropriations there was some excuse. A monastery had met with misfortune, or an unusual strain was being put upon its resources, and it was perhaps justifiable that part of the income of some parish should be diverted in order to bolster up the financial position of the house and save it from total destruction. It was when parochial emoluments were annexed for no other purpose than to improve the domestic comforts of the monks that the system showed its worst side. Dr Coulton has drawn attention to the praise which Matthew Paris bestowed upon successive abbots of S. Albans who managed to secure the appropriation of various churches to improve the purely material pleasures of the monks—S. Stephen's to enable them to buy more food, Eglingham for the improvement of their beer, and Hexton to provide a feast on the abbot's anniversary.[7] Many similar appropriations could be found among the documents of the thirteenth century. Witcham Church, for example, was appropriated to the monks of Ely by the saintly Hugh of

[1] Savage, *Great Register of Lichfield*, p. 30.
[2] *Regist. T. Corbridge*, i, pp. 82–5.
[3] *Regist. W. Wickwayn*, pp. 70–2.
[4] *Regist. T. Corbridge*, i, pp. 68–70.
[5] E.g. Whalley: see Hulton, *Coucher Book of Whalley Abbey*, i, pp. 205–6.
[6] Dugdale-Caley, *Monasticon*, i, pp. 533–4.
[7] Coulton, *Five Centuries*, iii, p. 192, quoting M. Paris, *Gesta Abbatum Mon. S. Albani*, ii, pp. 252, 320–2.

Northwold for no other purpose than to buy them tunics,[1] Bretforton was appropriated to Evesham to improve their cheese, sauce and wine,[2] Gloucester Abbey received twenty marks a year from the church of Newport to provide the monks with French wine,[3] and S. Etheldreda's at Norwich was appropriated to the cellarer of Norwich to find table-cloths, napkins, glasses, spoons and pots.[4] Many parishes went for pittances (which meant extra food for the monks), and some to provide the brethren with pocket-money.[5]

The blame, however, must not be laid entirely upon the shoulders of the monks, for a certain number of churches were handed over to secular clergy for reasons no better than those which had led to monastic appropriations. Some of the bishops were offenders in this way. Lawrence of S. Martin, Bishop of Rochester 1251–74, was an active seeker for new ways of raising money. In 1252 he tried to seize a fifth of the revenue of all the benefices in his diocese for five years,[6] and shortly afterwards he appropriated to himself and to his own table the churches of Isleham, Dartford, and Frindsbury.[7] In 1283 Godfrey Giffard, Bishop of Worcester, appropriated the church of Cleeve to his own use, the excuse which he gave being the necessity of providing hospitality for those going to and from the Welsh campaigns.[8] In 1240 Hugh of Pateshull, whose rapacity had aroused the ire of Grosseteste some years before,[9] and who was now Bishop of Coventry and Lichfield, appropriated to himself the church of Wybunbury, near Nantwich, in order to provide himself with a convenient resting-place when journeying from Stafford to Chester, since the woods were filled with 'sons of perdition, who without fear of God molest travellers, so that the Bishop, who must pass that way in performance of his duty,

[1] Wharton, *Anglia Sacra*, i, p. 636.

[2] Macray, *Chron. Abb. de Evesham*, p. 275.

[3] Luard, *An. Mon.* iv, p. 422.

[4] Blomefield, *History of Norfolk*, iv, p. 75.

[5] Coulton, *Five Centuries*, iii, p. 194. A number of parishes were appropriated to foreign houses, such as Lydd in Kent to S. Maria de Gloria, Anagni, and Littlebourne to S. Maria di Monte Mirteto, both in 1247. Bliss, *Cal. Papal Letters*, i, p. 236; cf. p. 339.

[6] M. Paris, *Chron. Maj.* v, p. 273.

[7] *Regist. H. Hethe*, p. 51.

[8] *Regist. G. Giffard*, p. 222.

[9] See above, p. 33.

has no safe resting-place.'[1] Peter de Aquablanca, another prelate of remarkable financial astuteness, when Bishop of Hereford, appropriated to his own table the churches of Bosbury and Ledbury.[2] Upton Bishop was appropriated to the Dean and Chapter of Hereford about the year 1200 'for the increase of the canons' commons', and in 1272 they received the revenues of the churches of Holmer, Long Stanton and Pipe.[3] Boreham in Essex was appropriated to the Chancellor of S. Paul's, and Ardleigh in the same county to the Archdeacon of Colchester.[4]

By the end of the thirteenth century there is no doubt that at least half the parish churches of England had been thus appropriated, by far the majority having gone to the religious houses. The movement, however, had always had its critics. The early Cistercians, in the first flush of their ascetic zeal, 'considered it contrary to their profession to take the revenues of parishes, and attacked the Cluniacs and Benedictines for doing so';[5] but by 1284 they had earned for themselves a reputation so undesirable that Pecham could write to Edward I: 'though they be good men, if God please, still they are the hardest neighbours that prelates and parsons could have. For where they plant their foot, they destroy towns, take away tithes, and curtail by their privileges all the power of the prelacy.'[6] Yet the Cistercian conscience survived in some places, for, in the early years of the fourteenth century, the Abbot of Meaux was prevented for five years from appropriating the church of Eastrington by the opposition of his own Chapter.[7]

Many of the bishops were opposed to appropriations and would have liked to stop them, but their opposition was often overridden by commands from above. Swinfield, for example, did his best to prevent the monks of Worcester from seizing the revenues of the church of Lindridge, but he was finally

[1] Savage, *Great Register of Lichfield*, p. 257.

[2] See *Regist. T. Cantilupe*, p. 126. The date given there is wrong: it should be 1243; see *Regist. R. Swinfield*, p. 17. Other episcopal appropriations include Newland to the Bishop of Llandaff in 1286 (*Regist. R. Swinfield*, p. 113) and Dalston to the Bishop of Carlisle in 1301 (*Regist. J. Halton*, i, p. xxxi).

[3] Capes, *Charters of Hereford*, pp. 36–7, 127–8.

[4] Newcourt, *Repertorium*, ii, pp. 11, 71. At Ardleigh the monks of Colchester had the right to present a vicar: Gibbs, *Early Charters of S. Paul's*, p. 72.

[5] Hartridge, *Vicarages*, p. 16.

[6] Pecham, *Reg. Epist.* ii, p. 726 and cf. p. 769.

[7] Bond, *Chron. Melsa*, iii, p. 6.

overruled by the King.[1] Others who opposed the system were obliged to give way to mandates from Rome. Robert Grosseteste traced many of the evils of parochial life to the fact that so many churches had been appropriated;[2] while his successor, Oliver Sutton, in reluctantly allowing the nuns of Stamford to annex the income of Corby Church, wrote that 'appropriations of parochial churches, by converting the fruits and profits of them to the use of religious persons, were absolutely odious to the prelates of the Church...nor could be tolerable but in cases of manifest poverty or other great necessity'.[3] Even the laity were driven to complain that the monks had gone much further than was intended, for in 1259 a group of English patrons addressed a letter to Pope Alexander IV protesting that whereas they had originally handed over advowsons to the religious houses, thinking them to be better judges of men and better able to fill the posts, the monks had now 'by clandestine and indirect ways' obtained those churches to their own use.[4]

There is not much doubt in the minds of modern writers that the system of appropriations was thoroughly bad.[5] It was obviously unjust that money which was paid in tithes by hard-working peasants should go to the creature comforts of monks or other ecclesiastics who did nothing in return. The system led also to much spiritual neglect, for the monasteries tended to employ the cheapest hirelings who could be found, with results which were often tragic. Grosseteste thundered against a system which left the pastoral care of souls to men who were totally unfitted to be spiritual leaders.[6] Moreover, the modest stipends of vicars and chaplains left no margin whatever for poor-relief, with the result that much hardship was caused, many a family going with empty bellies while the monks were enjoying their pittances and anniversary feasts.

The system was immoral and therefore unjustifiable, but it would not be fair to the monasteries to leave it at that. As has

[1] *Regist. R. Swinfield*, pp. 160–1, 421–2, 433–8.

[2] Brown, *Fasc. Rerum Expetend.* ii, p. 253.

[3] Kennett, *Parochial Antiquities* (1818), ii, pp. 44–5.

[4] Luard, *An. Mon.* i, pp. 487–8.

[5] Even Cardinal Gasquet, who finds it so difficult to see the imperfections of the medieval Church, says: 'The practice of impropriation has been regarded by most writers as a manifest abuse, and there is no call to attempt to defend it' (*English Monastic Life*, p. 193).

[6] Brown, *Fasc. Rerum Expetend.* ii, p. 253.

already been said,[1] a benefice in the Middle Ages was often regarded much more as an estate than as a spiritual responsibility; and, from the point of view of the parishioners, there was little to choose between an absentee rector who took their tithes and spent the proceeds on living a life of idleness and luxury without ever setting foot in his parish, and a monastery who had appropriated the fruits of the living to its own use. Lay patronage was often abused by the appointment of children and others totally unfitted to exercise a cure of souls, but the system of appropriations had at least the advantage of giving the bishop an opportunity to ensure that the parish should be properly and continuously served by the ordination of a vicarage. Unjust and disastrous though it might be, the appropriation of a parish church to a religious house might not, in practice, lead to conditions any worse than they had been, while it might be the beginning of better times.

Where a church had been appropriated to a monastery it was customary for a vicarage to be ordained; but this was by no means always done. Many parishes, such as five which belonged to the Priory of Guisborough, had no vicars;[2] but the efforts of the bishops were consistently directed towards the establishment of a vicarage in each appropriated parish in order to ensure the provision of an adequate stipend and to give some feeling of security to the officiating clergy.

The history of the establishment of the vicarage system has been so well told by Dr Hartridge that it will not be necessary to do more now than give a bare outline. The system arose out of the custom of monasteries allowing churches which they had appropriated to be served by totally incompetent or unworthy people. The Lateran Council of 1215 had drawn attention to the fact that in some churches the parish priest was receiving only one-sixteenth of the revenue of the church 'whence it comes about that in those regions scarce any parish priest can be found who is even moderately well-educated'. The decree went on to declare that in future the priest must receive a decent wage and become a perpetual vicar. 'This canon', says Dr Hartridge, 'may be termed the Magna Carta of the parish priest.'[3] Vicarages had been mentioned in this country in a document of the year

[1] See above, p. 24.

[2] W. Brown, *Guisborough Chartulary*, ii, p. xvii.

[3] Hartridge, *Vicarages in the Middle Ages*, p. 21.

1173;[1] but the system really belongs to the following century. After 1200 the establishment of vicarages went ahead with great rapidity, Hugh of Welles creating nearly three hundred in the diocese of Lincoln during the twenty-six years of his episcopate from 1209 to 1235.[2]

The two foundation-stones of the vicarage system were security of tenure and a minimum wage. The annual chaplain was at the mercy of his employer, who was under no obligation to pay him any specified amount, and who could dismiss him at will. The vicar, on the other hand, had his freehold from which he could not be dislodged, and he had a wage which, if not princely, was at least secure. As early as 1222 we find the English prelates, at the Council of Oxford, declaring that, except in those parts of Wales where the churches were desperately poor, the minimum stipend for a perpetual vicar should be five marks a year.[3] Some vicarages were worth a great deal more than this. Gilling, Burniston and Kirkham in the deanery of Richmond (Yorks) were all valued at 40 marks in 1291,[4] S. Martin's, Beverley, was rated at 35 marks in 1269[5] and Stottesdon at 33 marks in 1286.[6] Many were worth £10 or more. But by far the majority were in the neighbourhood of £4 a year; though, even apart from the poor parishes of Wales, there were some in England which could not be raised above

[1] Wilkins, *Concilia*, i, p. 475.

[2] Gibbons, *Liber Antiquus H. de Welles*, passim. Dr Hartridge gives, in an Appendix to his book on Vicarages (pp. 209–12), an account of all the twelfth-century vicarages which he has discovered. To these should be added three in London and four in the diocese of Lincoln, all of about the year 1180.

The 'perpetual vicarages' in London were S. Pancras, S. Mary Magdalene in Milk Street and S. Edmund the King (where the Augustinian canons of Holy Trinity, Aldgate, became vicars). In 1183 the Bishop of Lincoln appropriated the four churches of Sandon and Ardeley in Hertfordshire, and Caddington and Kensworth in Bedfordshire, to the Dean and Chapter of S. Paul's, who were to appoint 'perpetual vicars' with 'adequate vicarages' on the death of the present incumbents. See M. Gibbs, *Early Charters of S. Paul's*, pp. 123, 170, 194, 229–30. Note that *Ardleigh*, in the last of these, should read *Ardeley*. Ardleigh is in Essex and was appropriated to the Archdeacon of Colchester.

[3] Wilkins, *Concilia*, i, p. 587. As the average wage for an artisan was 3*d*. a day or 78*s*. a year, a vicar was slightly worse off than this.

[4] *Taxatio Nicholai*, pp. 306–7.

[5] Leach, *Memorials of Beverley*, i, pp. 194–5.

[6] *Regist. R. Swinfield*, p. 123.

two, three or four marks a year.[1] Moreover, out of these miserably poor stipends the vicars were expected to bear heavy burdens, such as the provision of an assistant priest and clerk, the payment of repairs and renewals in the church, and the ever-pressing calls of hospitality and charity. Yet small though his stipend might be, the vicar had the great advantage over the casual priest in that his position and future were secure, and independence has always been prized above wealth.

In some parishes the vicar, instead of receiving a fixed salary, became an inmate of the local monastery. An arrangement such as this was known as a 'corrody'[2] and might be either for board or residence. The Vicar of Tywardreath in Cornwall, for example, was a resident in the local priory, where he was allotted a room, food for himself and his horse, and four marks a year for clothes and pocket-money.[3] Many corrodies applied only to food, the vicar sleeping in his own house at night. At Bourne the vicar had a house and garden but he took his meals each day at the abbey, as did also his page. He also received 20*s.* a year for clothes.[4] The Vicar of Missenden also normally had his meals at the abbey, but the regulation expressly stated that if he were out visiting at dinner time his food, and that of his clerk, was to be sent to his house.[5] The Vicar of Burwell was to have a corrody at the table of the Prior of Burwell together with two silver marks a year and 3*d.* on each of the great feasts.[6] The Vicar of Bishopthorpe, near York, was to have his Sunday dinner each week with the servants of the nuns of Clementhorpe to whom his church was appropriated. If he complains of the food he must wait until he is willing to receive it quietly.[7] The Vicar of Harrold in Bedfordshire fared better, for he was to be 'honourably fed' at the table of the Prioress of Elstow, who was also responsible for looking after his page and for providing him with a decent house where he could easily be seen by his parishioners.[8]

[1] Potsgrove in Bedfordshire was rated at 2 marks; Chicksands at 3 marks; Millbrook, Haynes and Cople at 4 marks. See *Rot. H. de Welles*, i, pp. 185–7.

[2] From *corredium*, meaning 'Provision for maintenance' (*O.E.D.* s.v.).

[3] *Regist. W. Bronescombe*, p. 188. Cf. the Rector of S. Andrew of Wich, who was to live with the Prior of Deerhurst for a year: *Regist. G. Giffard*, p. 48.

[4] *Rot. R. Grosseteste*, p. 29.

[5] Gibbons, *Lib. Antiquus H. de Welles*, p. 16.

[6] *Rot. R. Gravesend*, p. 28.

[7] *Regist. W. Giffard*, pp. 59–60.

[8] *Rot. H. de Welles*, i, p. 186.

Throughout the thirteenth century strenuous efforts were made by the bishops to safeguard the freedom of the vicars and to ensure that they received an adequate stipend. Since the vicarial portion was generally very much smaller than that of the average rectory the men who accepted these posts could not afford to pay others to do the work for them and were therefore bound to be resident. Moreover, as they had to work for their daily bread, it was more or less essential that they should be adequately ordained. Yet, even so, the reforming Councils of the Church thought it necessary to insist that vicars should be willing and able to do the work for which they were appointed. The Council of Oxford in 1222 passed a decree that vicarages should be given only to men who were willing to reside and to be ordained priest within a short time.[1] In the Constitutions of the legate Otto in 1237 it was declared that no one was to be instituted to a vicarage unless he were in priest's orders (or at least a deacon), and he must be resident.[2]

Yet we know that even these elementary rules were not always observed. Occasionally vicarages were acquired by foreigners who obtained dispensation not to reside, as, for example, in 1238 when Duraguerra di Piperno, perpetual vicar of Catterick, received a licence from Gregory IX to be non-resident since the parish was served by a chaplain and two clerks.[3] Again, Pecham had to write to the Bishop of Exeter about a man who held two posts, the Precentorship at the Collegiate Church of Crediton and the Vicarage of Bisham in Surrey, both of which demanded continuous residence (*continua residentia*),[4] while Hugh of Welles even went so far as to deprive the Vicar of Little Houghton for failure to reside.[5] In the records of institutions of vicars the duty of personal, uninterrupted residence is constantly stressed[6] in order that adequate provision may be made for the spiritual needs of the people.

If the bishops, then, made some effort to enforce the rule of residence upon vicars, they were equally anxious to ensure that men who were appointed to vicarages were adequately ordained.

[1] Wilkins, *Concilia*, i, p. 587. Lyndwood explains 'a short time' as meaning 'at the next ordination': *Provinciale* (1679), pp. 64–5.

[2] Wilkins, *Concilia*, i, p. 651.

[3] Bliss, *Cal. Papal Letters*, i, p. 174.

[4] Pecham, *Reg. Epist.* ii, pp. 583–4.

[5] *Rot. H. de Welles*, ii, pp. 270–1.

[6] E.g. *Rot. H. de Welles*, i, pp. 7, 9, 21, 39, 43, etc.; *Regist. W. Giffard*, p. 56; *Rot. R. Grosseteste*, p. 472.

The rule was that they must be at least in deacon's orders,[1] but it was not always observed. The diocese of Lincoln was well served in the thirteenth century by able and conscientious prelates, yet all of them instituted to vicarages men who were only in minor orders. For example Hugh of Welles, in the archdeaconries of Stow, Oxford and Buckingham, instituted 123 vicars of whom 6 were deacons, 5 subdeacons, 5 acolytes and 8 'clerks'; Grosseteste, in the archdeaconry of Northampton, instituted 71 vicars of whom 1 was a deacon and 3 had apparently no orders at all; and Richard Gravesend instituted 257 vicars of whom 41 were deacons, 6 subdeacons and 7 'clerks'.[2] The Canterbury Ordination Lists reveal the fact that Pecham ordained 7 vicars who were deacons, 3 who were subdeacons and 1 who was only an acolyte; while his successor, Winchelsey, ordained 16 who were deacons, 7 who were subdeacons and 4 who were only acolytes.[3] These figures make it clear that the Church's rule about the ordination of vicars was not always kept; but, compared with the rectors, the number of priests among those who were instituted to vicarages was relatively high. So far as rectors were concerned, the proportion of those who were in priest's orders was often no more than 20 or 25 per cent; among vicars the percentage of priests was generally about 80.[4]

The appropriation of churches to religious houses meant that the monks made themselves responsible for providing someone to serve those parishes. It might be thought that the easiest thing would be to allow some of their own members to do this; and it is sometimes rather loosely stated that many parishes were served by monks. The evidence, however, is against this. The monks lived under a system which was devised to separate

[1] Wilkins, *Concilia*, i, p. 651.

[2] See the *Rotuli* of H. de Welles, Grosseteste and Gravesend, *passim*. None of Welles' appointments was described as priest but the word 'chaplain' is very common. This almost certainly indicated a priest (see above, pp. 35–6). Among Grosseteste's men there is one definitely called 'presbyter' and 66 'capellani'. In Gravesend's lists there are 111 priests and 92 *capellani*.

[3] See Ordination Lists in the *Registers* of J. Pecham and R. Winchelsey (C. & Y. Soc.).

[4] Thus out of 548 vicars instituted in the dioceses of York, Canterbury and Lincoln, 441 were priests. This is based on the assumption which we have been making all along that the word *capellanus* indicates a man in priest's orders.

men from the world, and it would therefore be quite alien to the spirit of monasticism to take men out of the cloister and put them in vicarage houses where they would be cut off from the daily society of their fellow-monks and from the discipline of corporate life.[1] We should, therefore, be most suspicious of those who say that parishes were served by monks.[2] In later centuries the custom of monks serving parish churches became more common,[3] but in the thirteenth century it was practically unknown. The monks of Tewkesbury appear to have been serving the church of Fairford in 1231,[4] and in 1267 the Prior of Wetherhal, a dependency of the Abbey of S. Mary's, York, was admitted to the cure of souls of all the parishes appropriated to the Priory.[5] When the Cistercians moved from Stanlaw to Whalley in 1296 they were instructed to leave four monks in priest's orders to serve the old place.[6] Another Cistercian, William de Cameleyo, proctor-general of the Abbey of Aulnay in Normandy, was Rector of Mears Ashby in Northamptonshire in 1275.[7] But these are exceptions.

Canons of the Augustinian and Premonstratensian Orders were, however, quite commonly instituted to livings. Some, indeed, of the early Augustinian houses were founded with the

[1] In the Synodal Constitutions of 1237 it is expressly stated that it is *inhonestum* and even *canoni inimicum* for monks to serve parish churches: Wilkins, *Concilia*, i, p. 662.

[2] As Professor Hamilton Thompson says; 'Wherever we find it stated in print that an incumbent of a parish church or chantry was a monk we should hesitate to believe it without consulting the original record of his institution': *English Monasteries*, p. 28.

[3] Coulton, *Five Centuries of Religion*, iii, pp. 158–9, 388–9, 676–7.

[4] Luard, *An. Mon.* i, pp. 81–2. This should be remembered in connexion with Mr Egerton Beck's statement in the *Dublin Review* (April 1923, p. 237) that the only certain case known to him of Black Monks serving a parish church before the end of the fourteenth century is that of Cardigan Priory. Cf. also above, p. 14, n. 8.

[5] Craster and Thornton, *Chron. of S. Mary's, York*, p. 10. The same was granted to Giles Rousee, Prior of the Benedictine house at Stoke Courcy in Somerset early in the fourteenth century: *Regist. J. Drokensford*, p. 9.

[6] Bliss, *Cal. Papal Letters*, i, p. 499.

[7] *Rot. R. Gravesend*, p. 125. See also the letter from the Pope to the Prior and Convent of Rochester confirming an order made in 1245 to the effect that the church of Darenth should be served by chaplains not by monks (Bliss, *Cal. Papal Letters*, i, p. 325). This suggests that the church may at one time have been served by the monks themselves.

express purpose of serving a group of parish churches. This seems to have been the case at Barnwell, as Dr Frere has pointed out.[1] But in this instance the idea did not survive for very long, since the canons found it more convenient to delegate the parochial work to vicars and chaplains and to devote themselves to the life of the cloister and to the management of their estates. Nevertheless, all through the Middle Ages it was not uncommon to find canons regular in charge of parishes. For example, in 1216 the Prior and Chapter of Nostell obtained a licence from the Pope to enable them, on the deaths of the clergy serving their churches, to place two or three of their own number in the parishes, one of whom shall be presented to the bishop to receive the cure of souls.[2] Canons of Dunstable habitually served the parishes of Flitwick and Bradbourne;[3] there were canons of Hexham at Stamfordham and Warden;[4] and various Augustinians held livings at Bibury, Askham, Great Worldham and Hale.[5]

Yet in spite of many such appointments it was always considered unseemly for a regular to live alone in charge of a parish, and attempts were made to ensure that he should have a fellow-canon as his companion. Bishop Gravesend of Lincoln allowed a canon of Bridlington to be Vicar of Edenham only on condition that he had another canon always with him;[6] and Bishop Halton of Carlisle arranged for the appropriation of the churches of Shap and Bampton to the Prior and Convent of Shap, who were to serve the churches by two or three of their canons, one of whom would be vicar. He also insisted upon the maintenance of a secular priest in each parish to hear confessions.[7]

[1] *The Early History of Canons Regular*, in *Fasc. J. W. Clark dicatus*, p. 214, and cf. pp. 205–6.

[2] Bliss, *Cal. Papal Letters*, i, p. 42.

[3] Luard, *An. Mon.* iii, pp. 364, 391, and cf. *Rot. R. Gravesend*, pp. 191, 193, 195.

[4] Raine, *Hexham Priory*, i, p. cxxxvi and App. pp. xxxv–xl and xlix.

[5] *Regist. G. Giffard*, pp. 14, 177; *Regist. J. Halton*, i, p. 55; *Regist. J. Pontissara*, pp. 141–2 and Macray, *Charters of Selborne*, p. 78. Mr Egerton Beck reckons that in the twelfth and thirteenth centuries nineteen Augustinian houses served thirty or forty parish churches, while six Premonstratensian houses served ten or eleven more; see *Dublin Review* (1923), p. 248.

[6] *Rot. R. Gravesend*, p. 33.

[7] *Regist. J. Halton*, i, pp. 39–40.

The White Canons of the Order of S. Norbert of Prémontré, known as Premonstratensians, were more addicted to the practice of serving parish churches than were the Augustinians. The Abbey of Welbeck, for example, owned eleven churches, seven of which were served by canons, if not habitually at least occasionally.[1] The church of Kirkby Malham in Airedale was regularly served by canons from the house at West Dereham in Norfolk,[2] and Alfreton in Derbyshire was maintained by canons of Beauchief.[3]

Dr Hartridge has stated that 'one could probably find examples of male members of practically all religious orders and congregations serving churches',[4] but in some instances we should have to search the Registers of later centuries than the thirteenth. We have, however, already discovered Benedictines and Cistercians besides a number of Augustinians and Premonstratensians, while the Templars appear to have served the church of Guiting in 1223.[5] Finally, if the editor of Archbishop Pecham's Register in the publications of the Canterbury and York Society is right, there was actually a Dominican friar, Nicholas de la Dale, as Rector of Little Chart in 1284.[6] We know also that, in 1303, when a new rector was appointed to the parish of North Piddle, near Worcester, he could not be instituted since the previous rector had not resigned although he had entered the Dominican order.[7] There is no evidence of any Franciscan in charge of a parish during the thirteenth century.

1 A. H. Thompson, *The Premonstratensian Abbey of Welbeck*, pp. 35–53.

2 Whitaker, *History of Craven* (1805), p. 176; and cf. A. H. Thompson, *The Priory of S. Mary, Bolton* (Thoresby Society), p. 18.

3 Cox, *Churches of Derbyshire*, iv, p. 442.

4 Hartridge, *Vicarages in the Middle Ages*, p. 183.

5 Bliss, *Cal. Papal Letters*, i, p. 93.

6 *Regist. J. Pecham* (C. & Y. Soc.), p. 213. The entry reads, among the ordinations to the priesthood, 'Frater Nicholaus de la Dale, rector de Parva Chert, de ordine predicatorum'. The corresponding entry in Trice Martin's edition of Pecham's Register rather suggests that the Rector of Little Chart and Nicholas de la Dale were two separate persons (*Reg. Epist.* iii, p. 1035). He was D.D. of Cambridge and a regent master there: Little and Pelster, *Oxford Theology and Theologians, c. 1282–1302*, p. 185.

7 Worcester, *Regist. Sede Vacante*, p. 68.

CHAPTER V

ASSISTANT CLERGY

Working with the incumbents there were, in each parish, assistant clergy of different grades and varying remunerations. It is hard for us to realise how many there were of these men, or how they managed either to support themselves or to occupy their time. Dr Coulton estimates that the ratio of clergy to laity in the Middle Ages was about 2 per cent.[1] This would allow for a total of about sixty thousand ordained men in a population of three million.[2] Medieval arithmetic must always be treated with caution, but careful calculations, based on every available scrap of evidence, would suggest that there were, in fact, at least forty thousand secular clergy in this country as well as nearly seventeen thousand monks and friars.

How is this figure reached? First of all by the evidence of the Ordination Lists. Every year large numbers of men were ordained; but, as has been pointed out,[3] it is extremely difficult to give any satisfactory figures, partly owing to the fact that our records are so imperfect, and partly owing to the difficulty of knowing how far each candidate progressed. Many were, no doubt, ordained to each order, from what was called the 'first tonsure' right up to the priesthood. Many also never proceeded farther than the subdiaconate or diaconate. Careful calculations, based on the evidence which obtains, yield a total of some 1300 men joining the ranks of the clergy each year. For example, at Canterbury, between the years 1282 and 1292, John Pecham ordained 378 secular priests, 364 deacons, 343 subdeacons and 774 acolytes. This makes a total of 1859 ordinations, but of course a good many men came up for ordination more than once. If we trace the career of each man separately we find that the precise number of men whom Pecham ordained during this decade was 1113 from his own diocese, 431 from other dioceses, and 181 regulars. For the diocese of Canterbury alone this would mean just over 100 men each year, about half of

[1] *Priests and People before the Reformation*, pp. 13–14; cf. *From S. Francis to Dante*, pp. 292, 395.

[2] It is believed that the population of England in the thirteenth century was about three million: Coulton, *The Medieval Village*, p. 443.

[3] M. Deanesly, *The Lollard Bible*, p. 159.

whom apparently advanced no farther than the order of acolyte. Similar calculations for other dioceses of which records have been preserved show that Godfrey Giffard at Worcester ordained about 110 men each year; Thomas Cantilupe at Hereford about 56; Walter Giffard at York at least 50, and John Halton at Carlisle 10. This gives, for five dioceses, of varying sizes, a total of 325 men, an average of 65 for each diocese. If we now multiply by twenty-one, since that was the number of dioceses in England and Wales, we get a total annual ordination of no less than 1365 men. From this we can get some idea of the number of clergy in the country. If each man's ministry lasted, on an average, for thirty years, we arrive at a total of forty thousand ordained men at any given time.[1] Since there were about 9500 parishes in the country during the thirteenth century this would allow for something between four and five men in each parish.

This would be almost unbelievable were there not evidence of other kinds to support it. Though many of the thirteenth-century bishops held frequent visitations of their clergy, either personally or through their archdeacons or officials, not very many of their findings have been preserved. But the evidence of such records as we possess supports the contention that the parishes were, on the whole, very generously staffed. At the visitation of Sonning, conducted in 1220 by the Dean of Salisbury, the vicar presented no less than seven curates or chaplains to be examined. There was Simon, in priest's orders but very ignorant and apparently only temporary; Philip, who held the chapels of Wokingham and Sandhurst; Richard and Reginald; a chaplain of Sandhurst; Jordanus, chaplain of Ruscombe, and an old priest at Arborfield.[2] At Heytesbury the church was served by four canons, three of whom had vicars, and one also a subdeacon. There were also two chapels, one of which was in charge of a deacon. This gives a total staff, for this parish, of

[1] Miss Deanesly reckons an average ministry of 25 years, but we must remember that many ordination candidates were very young, mere boys in their teens. Some idea of the age of the clergy may be gathered from a list of thirty incumbents in the archdeaconry of Stow (Lincs) in the year 1278. Five were quite young men, two are of an unspecified age, while of the remaining twenty-three the average age is 58. All of these must have been in orders for well over 30 years. See *Rot. R. Gravesend*, pp. 351–3.

[2] W. H. R. Jones, *Reg. S. Osmundi*, i, pp. 304–6.

nine men.[1] At Snaith in Yorkshire Walter Giffard in 1275 found four chaplains and two clerks in addition to the rector, who appears to have been an absentee.[2] In the visitations of parishes in the diocese of Exeter recorded in the Register of Bishop Stapeldon, we find that at Colyton there were at least five men, at Dawlish four, and at Sidbury three or more.[3]

Further evidence is afforded by the episcopal Registers. For example, in 1236 Bishop Grosseteste insisted upon the vicar of S. Peter's-in-the-East at Oxford providing himself with two competent chaplains and the necessary ministers for two outlying chapels.[4] These 'ministers' would probably be a priest and a deacon or clerk. This would bring the total for the parish to seven men. At Barnburgh, near Doncaster, Archbishop Walter Gray made arrangements for the church to be served by two priests, two deacons and two subdeacons. They were to be paid by the canons of Southwell at the following rates: the priests £8 a year, the deacons £4 and the subdeacons £3. 6*s*. 8*d*.[5] At Sleaford in Lincolnshire, Bishop Gravesend arranged that the vicar should provide, presumably out of his own means, for a second priest, a deacon and other suitable *ministri* and *necessarii*;[6] while at Leighton Buzzard the vicar was to be assisted by three priests and two chaplains in order that the distant hamlets of Stanbridge, Egginton and Billington might not be deprived of spiritual comfort.[7]

Finally there is the evidence of the provincial and episcopal constitutions. This, in itself, would not count for very much, for such documents are bound to reflect the ideal to which their authors aspired rather than the standard actually attained; yet, added to the evidence already brought forward, they help to

[1] W. H. R. Jones, *Reg. S. Osmundi*, i, p. 292.

[2] *Regist. W. Giffard*, pp. 322–3.

[3] *Regist. W. Stapeldon*, pp. 111, 132–3, 368.

[4] *Rot. R. Grosseteste*, p. 451.

[5] *Regist. W. Gray*, p. 196.

[6] *Rot. R. Gravesend*, p. 72. In the *Liber Antiquus* of Hugh of Welles there are many cases where the staff consisted of a vicar, chaplains and clerks; e.g. pp. 7 and 24. Cf. *Rot. H. de Welles*, i, p. 195 (three chaplains at High Wycombe); p. 212 (two chaplains and two clerks at Burton-on-Stather); ii, p. 241 (two chaplains and necessary clerks at All Saints', Northampton).

[7] *Rot. R. Gravesend*, p. 211. Dr Hartridge, on p. 131 of his *Vicarages in the Middle Ages*, has collected some evidence on this subject from Gravesend's *Rotuli*. In the thirteen parishes which he mentions there is a total of something like sixty men, an average of nearly five to each parish.

strengthen the conclusion that in each parish of the country there were, on an average, about five ordained men. For example, section 18 of the Constitutions of the Council of Oxford in 1222 states that in large parishes there must be two or three priests in case of illness or infirmity.[1] These, with the necessary ministers and clerks, would bring the total staff of such parishes to seven or eight. Grosseteste expected to find, in each parish, besides the priest, a deacon and a subdeacon; while in even the poorest parishes the incumbent was to be assisted by a clerk.[2]

These figures will show that Jessopp was right when he wrote of England in the thirteenth century 'swarming with clerics'.[3] Every parish had, in addition to its rector or vicar, several of these men, each with an extra mouth to feed and an extra back to clothe when there was little enough to go round.

The most important of the assistant clergy were the chaplains in charge of outlying chapels, many of whom, as has already been said,[4] had their own endowments and lived in comparative independence. Next in importance to them were the 'annual chaplains', most of whom were obliged to live on very slender incomes. It is true that reforming bishops endeavoured to give them both security of tenure and a fixed stipend; but it is equally true that not all reforming bishops were successful in the improvements which they tried to make. According to the statutes of William of Blois at Winchester in 1229, annual chaplains were to receive three marks, or forty shillings, a year.[5] Even if we multiply by as much as seventy to raise it to modern standards of currency, it still seems very little. Yet when the Dean of Salisbury visited in the parish of Sonning in 1220 he found that the chapel at Arborfield was being served by a chaplain who received only twenty shillings a year.[6]

Below the annual chaplains came the parish priests and assistants, who had little security and were, as a rule, obliged

[1] Wilkins, *Concilia*, i, p. 588. [2] Grosseteste, *Epistolae*, p. 161.

[3] Jessopp, *The Coming of the Friars*, p. 83. [4] See above, pp. 13–14.

[5] Wilkins, *Concilia*, i, p. 625. In the statutes of Richard of Chichester in 1246 annual chaplains are to receive 5 marks a year, or £3. 6*s*. 8*d*.: *ibid*. p. 692. Peter Quivil of Exeter in 1287 demanded £3 a year for annual chaplains: *ibid*. ii, p. 147.

[6] W. H. R. Jones, *Reg. S. Osmundi*, i, p. 283. An unskilled labourer in the thirteenth century was paid 1½*d*. a day, which would amount to about 40*s*. a year. The chaplains were therefore paid at the same rate.

to offer themselves for hire to anyone who would employ them. Men were not supposed to be ordained without some title, that is, without a guarantee that they would have some means of subsistence; but in many cases the only guarantees which they could offer were very precarious, and some bishops were rash enough to ordain men with no title at all. As a result a good many men came on to the ecclesiastical labour exchange with little qualification and small hope of ever getting more than the barest subsistence. According to the statutes of Bishop Quivil of Exeter assistant priests were supposed to receive at least fifty shillings a year,[1] but many must have had to be content with less than this.

In his synodal statutes of 1238 Robert Grosseteste declared that 'in every church where funds permit there shall be a deacon and a subdeacon to minister therein as is fitting: in other churches there must be at least one adequate and suitable clerk who, properly attired, shall assist in the divine office'.[2] These were, presumably, the competent *ministri* and *necessarii* who are mentioned from time to time in the episcopal Registers.[3] The deacon was certainly regarded as an important member of the staff of a parish. In the course of a visitation of the parish of Churcham, Thomas Cantilupe discovered that the vicar was without the services of a deacon. He wrote therefore to the Dean of the Forest instructing him to see that this deficiency was put right with all possible haste.[4] But apart from the service which the deacon could render at Mass we know very little of how he assisted the priest. In the present Anglican service for the ordering of deacons it is stated that 'it appertaineth to the office of a deacon to assist the priest in divine service, to read the Scriptures and Homilies in the church, to instruct the youth in the Catechism, and to search for the sick, poor and impotent people of the parish that they may be relieved with the alms of the parishioners.' Similar tasks may well have been assigned to the medieval deacons, since these words in the Prayer Book are likely to have been based upon customs with which the

[1] Wilkins, *Concilia*, ii, p. 147.

[2] R. Grosseteste, *Epistolae*, p. 161. The same thing was decreed at Durham (Wilkins, *Concilia*, i, p. 707) and at Ely (Feltoe and Minns, *Vetus Liber Archidiaconi Eliensis*, p. 12).

[3] E.g. *Rot. R. Grosseteste*, p. 451; *Rot. R. Gravesend*, p. 131.

[4] *Regist. T. Cantilupe*, pp. 238–9.

Church had been familiar for some time. It is unlikely, however, that those who were employed in parishes as deacons and subdeacons were necessarily in those particular orders. The Ordination Lists which have been preserved make it clear that a great many men were ordained as acolytes who never advanced any farther.[1] These men must have been absorbed into the parishes in all kinds of capacities, thankful to get any job with a few shillings attached to it, while many incumbents would be satisfied to get men who were willing to come for a small salary without demanding to see their letters of orders or enquiring too closely into their qualifications.

The humblest but by no means the least important member of the staff in each parish was the clerk. The office of parish clerk is one which, having held an honourable place in the annals of the Church in England, has only latterly been allowed to disappear. In the thirteenth century the parish clerk held a position which, though of little substance, was of some security, for he was licensed by the bishop and held his office as a freehold.[2] In some parishes he was supported by the people, and, in addition to his regular stipend, might collect odd tips and fees, as did the 'joly Absolon', clerk of a parish in Oxford, who could

lete blood, and clippe and schave,
And make a chartre of lond and acquitaunce,

besides earning money by his skill as a dancer and actor and as a performer on the 'rubible'. Consequently he was able to dress as a dandy in fretted shoes, which reminded people of the windows in S. Paul's Cathedral, and to woo the carpenter's wife with gifts of 'pyment, mead, and spiced ale, and wafres piping hot'.[3] On the other hand many a parish clerk, less gifted than the 'joly Absolon', must have had a perpetual struggle against poverty and the terrors of old age and unemployment. Dr Hartridge has pointed out how vicars, living on miserably small stipends, were yet expected to support their own clerks,[4] and one can only wonder how any man managed to live on the

[1] Pecham ordained 794 acolytes and only 442 priests, and Winchelsey 779 acolytes and 480 priests; see their Registers published by the Canterbury and York Society.

[2] Cutts, *Parish Priests and their People*, p. 299.

[3] *Canterbury Tales, Miller's Tale*, ll. 126–200.

[4] Hartridge, *Vicarages in the Middle Ages*, p. 132.

few shillings a year which such an arrangement would allow. Matthew Paris' pathetic little story[1] of the parish clerk whose modest income of twenty shillings a year was reduced, by the rapacity of a papal collector, to eighteen, with the result that he had to sell his books in the cathedral close in order to keep body and soul together, is probably a fair commentary on the status of the parish clerk in most English parishes.

[1] M. Paris, *Chron. Maj.* v, p. 171.

CHAPTER VI

THE PARSONAGE AND ITS OCCUPANTS

The incumbent of a parish was generally provided with a house. This was often little more than a rough cottage of the type in which the peasants were housed. There were, however, in some of the richer parishes, better-built houses, much in the style of the manor-houses which existed up and down the country. Yet even these larger houses would seem very cramped according to our tastes. The manse at Hale, near Sleaford, consisted of a hall, two small rooms and a kitchen with a bakehouse and brewery.[1] The hall was the living room in which the vicar and his household spent most of their time, while the two chambers were bedrooms, one for the residents and one for visitors. At Kingerby in Lincolnshire the parsonage was big enough to be divided into two, the vicar having the use of the eastern part 'from the gable of the solar with the hall and other offices on that side', while the canons of Elsham, to whom the church was appropriated, were free of the rest.[2]

A few of these better-class houses have survived;[3] but, so greatly have our ideas of domestic comfort advanced, that even the best of them seem mean and cramped when measured by the standards to which we are accustomed. Yet, in their day, their traced windows, newel staircases and quoins of Caen stone[4] must have been looked upon with envy by those who were housed in the wooden shacks which were at that time by far the commonest form of parsonage house.

In various documents concerned with the establishment of vicarages the vicar is granted 'husbote', that is, the right to free wood for the building of his house.[5] In 1280 Bishop Thomas Cantilupe, finding that there was no manse at Churcham, wrote to the Dean of the Forest instructing him to order the Abbot and Convent of Gloucester to supply enough timber for the vicar to build himself a house, while the vicar is also told to

[1] Dugdale-Caley, *Monasticon*, i, pp. 635–6.

[2] *Rot. R. Gravesend*, p. 39. At Sutton-on-Trent the house was divided, the vicar having the southern portion from the kitchen wall southwards: *Regist. T. Corbridge*, i, pp. 230–1.

[3] See Cutts, *Parish Priests and their People*, pp. 151–3; and cf. Gasquet, *Parish Life*, pp. 88–9.

[4] Turner, *Domestic Architecture in England*, i, pp. 163–4.

[5] E.g. Dugdale-Caley, *Monasticon*, i, pp. 30 and 34; *Rot. H. de Welles*, ii, pp. 2–3.

proceed with the work without delay.[1] The building which emerged must have been little more than a rough cabin, the spaces between the timbers being filled in with clay, and the roof made of thatch or possibly of wooden shingles.[2]

But if the house itself was simple, the furniture was even simpler. We are accustomed nowadays to fill our houses with much furniture and stuff, but the medieval householder had to be content with only the minimum of domestic goods. A light is thrown upon this by an entry in the Register of Archbishop Corbridge of York. In the year 1303 the Vicar of Bradford was suspended from ministering in his church until he had done penance for certain misdeeds which had come to the knowledge of the Archbishop. During the time of his suspension he was to be paid at the rate of 2*d.* a day,[3] while his goods were sequestrated. An inventory of his property was then made which disclosed that his household goods consisted of the following: in the kitchen a brass pot (valued at 4*s.*) and a water pot (12*d.*), some plates (6*d.*), a tripod and andiron (6*d.*), and in the brewery one leaden vat (2*s.*) and a large tub with brewing apparatus (2*s.*).[4] It will be noticed here that there is no mention of any bedding or household furniture, possibly because these were reckoned as belonging to the house rather than to the incumbent himself.[5] On the other hand, the vicar probably managed with very little, for a similar inventory, made on the death of one Reginald Labbe, a smallholder who died in 1293 and whose standard of living must have been much like that of the smaller parish clergy, contains nothing more than a bolster and a rug, two sheets, a brass dish and a tripod.[6]

[1] *Regist. T. Cantilupe*, pp. 237–9.

[2] Cf. Turner, *Domestic Architecture in England*, i, pp. 70–2; Coulton, *Medieval Village*, pp. 99–100. Turner (p. 71) points out that in the Border countries there was a larger proportion of stone houses, built for protection against raids.

[3] I.e. just over 60*s*. a year, such being the amount allowed for a parish chaplain: Wilkins, *Concilia*, ii, p. 147. The vicarage of Bradford was reckoned at £13. 6*s*. 8*d*.: *Taxatio Nicholai*, p. 298.

[4] *Regist. T. Corbridge*, i, pp. 95–6.

[5] The contents of some vicarages were certainly not regarded as the private property of the vicars; cf. *Regist. J. Romeyn*, i, p. 326. According to the statutes of William of Blois in 1219, when a parson died his furniture was to go to his successor, viz. one table with two three-legged stools, a brass pot, a chest, a cask, a sheet of canvas and a cart: Wilkins, *Concilia*, i, p. 571.

[6] *Archaeological Journal*, iii (1846), pp. 65–6.

Simplicity was therefore the order of the day in these homes, which seem to have lacked so many of the things which later ages have come to regard as indispensable. But what would be the good of filling a house with possessions when it could be so easily broken into by rogues, or destroyed by fire or by storms? The stronger stone houses would, no doubt, have stood up pretty well to the weather; but the jerry-built, wooden shanties of the poor parsons often fell into a sad state of dilapidation. When the Dean and Chapter of Exeter visited a number of parishes in Devon in 1301 they found many of the parsonage houses in disrepair. Winkleigh vicarage was in a very bad way; at Harberton the house had entirely collapsed except for the priest's chamber, while at Shute the chaplain's house was in such a ruinous condition that the poor man had to sleep in the church.[1] A few years later, dilapidations on the clergy-house at South Warnborough in Hampshire were assessed at £23. 13*s*. 4*d*.[2] and at Denbury in Devon at £26. 13*s*. 4*d*.[3]

The cost of maintaining the buildings in good repair was very heavy, for in most parishes the parsonage house included a range of farm buildings in addition to the priests' living rooms. This was demanded by the fact that most country clergy were agriculturists on quite a considerable scale.[4] It was no unusual thing for a priest to keep cows, sheep and pigs, besides the horse which he would require for visiting the outlying parts of his parish. The Vicar of Chieveley in 1314 had as many as twelve cows, a hundred sheep and twelve pigs,[5] while a flock of fifty or sixty sheep with half a dozen milking cows was quite common.[6] Pigs were also very popular with the clergy.[7]

[1] *Regist. W. Stapeldon*, pp. 112, 170, 409.

[2] *Regist. J. Sandale*, p. 79.

[3] *Visitation of the Archdeaconry of Totnes in 1342*, in E.H.R. 1911, p. 114. In this archdeaconry a number of houses were in a poor way, but a good many were being maintained in a good state of repair, e.g. at Moreton Hampstead, Bigbury and Newton Ferrers (pp. 110, 117, 118).

[4] H. G. Richardson, *Parish Clergy of the Thirteenth and Fourteenth Centuries*, in *Trans. R. Hist. Soc.* 1912, pp. 108, 110.

[5] *Regist. S. Gandavo*, i, pp. 517–18.

[6] E.g. at East Witton (Yorks): *Regist. T. Corbridge*, i, pp. 294–6; East Hoe (Hants): *Regist. J. Pontissara*, pp. 258–60. At Lympsham (Somerset) the rector had 6 oxen, 6 cows, 6 bullocks, a mare, 50 ewes, a pig and 12 piglets, 4 hens and a cock: Somerset Record Society, *Rentalia of Glastonbury*, p. 51.

[7] The vicar of Wotton (Surrey) had 6: *Regist. J. Pontissara*, pp. 92–3; and the chaplain of Penshurst (Kent) had 8: *Regist. H. Hethe*, pp. 22–3.

Naturally such stock would need looking after, and we shall not therefore be surprised to learn that many parsonage houses were provided with stables, cowhouses and pigsties. Moreover, the storage of produce handed over as tithe made it necessary for the rector to have good barns and granaries, safe against marauding neighbours or dissatisfied tithe-payers.[1] The manse, therefore, presented the appearance, not of a detached villa with a pleasant garden of flowers all about it, but of a regular farm yard with all the customary sights, sounds and smells of such places. Here the parson lived and worked, dividing his time between the calls of his spiritual and his natural sheep; walking from the stable to the altar, and from there to look after his pigs and his cattle; sharing with his people in the task which occupied so much of their waking hours and of their thoughts, that of making the earth bring forth her increase.

The vicar did not live alone. However small and however dilapidated his house might be, it had to serve as lodgings for most of the parochial staff.[2] Even the single room belonging to the Vicar of Harberton might have to house three or four men at the least. It has been already pointed out that the average staff for an English parish in the thirteenth century consisted of four or five men,[3] a community of stipendiary priests, clerks, ministers and 'necessaries', who shared among themselves the work of the church. Since all of these were celibates, the natural and most sensible thing was for them to set up house together, though the conditions in which they must have lived would seem to us very crude and primitive.

The housework, such as it was, was done by a boy. The richer clergy employed a number of such attendants,[4] but even the humblest vicar was expected to have his page. In the ordination of vicarages we find many references to the vicar's boy, whose task it was to make his bed and look after his horse;[5] and, when vicars were granted corrodies at a local monastery,

[1] Cf. Dugdale-Caley, *Monasticon*, i, pp. 635–6; *Regist. W. Geynsburgh*, pp. 164–5.

[2] As Mr Richardson says, 'There is considerable likelihood that the vicar and his chaplains all lived under one roof': *Trans. R. Hist. Soc.* 1912, p. 92.

[3] See above, p. 53.

[4] Bogo de Clare kept fifteen; see above, p. 27.

[5] See, for example, *Rot. H. de Welles*, ii, p. 297.

provision for the boy was included.[1] The wages of this scullion were probably extremely small for he became proverbially one of the poorest in the village, so that Chaucer's mercenary Pardoner can declare:

> I wol have money, wolle, chese and whete,
> Al wer it yeven of the prestes page
> Or of the porest wydow in a village.[2]

But, in addition to these whom we have mentioned, there is no doubt that in a number of parsonage houses there was also to be found the priest's consort, be she wife or concubine. Although the teaching of the apostles seems to allow of clerical marriage, celibacy had, from the fourth century, been the rule of the Western Church. It had, however, never been very rigidly enforced until Gregory VII in 1074 adopted it as a part of his programme for Church reform. But while it was easy to say that clergy must be single men, it was very much more difficult to see that the regulation was enforced. In this country, clerical marriages had been quite common in the days before the Norman Conquest, and there is abundant evidence that attempts to abolish them were only very partially successful throughout the twelfth century.[3] Especially was this so in the North of England, where old habits died slowly.[4] Ailred of Rievaulx, for example, was son, grandson and great-grandson of priests, and several of the bishops of Durham and at least one archbishop of York had children.

It was clear, then, that so far as this country was concerned, the Hildebrandine reforms were not meeting with the success which was intended; and at the beginning of the thirteenth century another great reforming Pope, Innocent III, made a new effort to put an end to the irregularity of clerical marriages. His attempts seem to have caused some dismay, which is reflected in a number of poems written about the year 1216, in which the clergy are made to declare both their determination

[1] In the Middle Ages it was quite the usual thing for people to employ men to look after their personal needs. Even scholars at the Universities kept their pages; cf. *Regist. W. Giffard*, p. 103; Rashdall, *Medieval Universities* (new ed.), iii, p. 410 n.; Wright, *Poems attributed to Walter Mapes*, p. 251.

[2] *Canterbury Tales, Prologue to the Pardoner's Tale*, ll. 162–4 (Harleian version).

[3] Cutts, *Parish Priests*, pp. 261–70; Coulton, *Medieval Panorama*, pp. 171–4. For a fuller treatment of the subject see Lea, *History of Sacerdotal Celibacy*.

[4] Cutts, *Parish Priests*, p. 262 n.; *Regist. W. Gray*, pp. xxvii–xxix.

to keep their consorts, and also their inability to live without them.[1] Nevertheless, it is clear that throughout this century some progress was made. Although John Pecham had to take proceedings against a foreign bishop who had been officiating in the diocese of Canterbury and who was the father of five children,[2] no English prelate of the thirteenth century is known to have had wife or family. On the other hand, there is, in the Lanercost Chronicle, an agreeable tale which shows that papal decrees were perhaps not so successful in Scotland. A certain vicar, we are told, who kept a mistress, was informed that his bishop was coming to visit him to order him to put her away. The poor man was overcome with distress, but his good lady was more resourceful. She set out next day with a basket of pudding and chickens and eggs. By and by she met the bishop who asked of her where she was going. 'I am taking these gifts', she said, 'to the bishop's sweetheart who has lately been brought to bed.' The bishop said no more, but went on his way, called upon the vicar, but never a word did he say of the matter upon which he had come.[3]

So far as the parish clergy of England were concerned, there is no doubt that the rule of celibacy was not strictly observed. We can distinguish three types of union in which the clergy were partners. There were, first of all, those who were officially married, the *uxorati* as they were called. John de Boulton, Rector of West Rounton in Yorkshire, for example, having had his banns duly called, was openly married to Isabella, daughter of Thomas de Aslakeby, by Michael, parish priest of Goldsborough in 1276.[4] Similar stories appear from time to time in contemporary records,[5] though not enough to justify the wild

[1] Wright, *Poems attributed to Walter Mapes*, pp. 171–9.

[2] Wilkins, *Concilia*, ii, p. 40, and cf. Dugdale-Caley, *Monasticon*, viii, p. 1342.

[3] *The Chronicle of Lanercost, 1272–1346*, tr. H. Maxwell, pp. 2–3.

[4] *Regist. W. Giffard*, p. 289. The phrase is 'bannis editis, ut est moris, in facie ecclesiae matrimonialiter copulavit'.

[5] E.g. *Rot. H. de Welles*, i, p. 96; Pecham, *Reg. Epist.* i, pp. 170–1; Bliss, *Cal. Papal Letters*, i, p. 59; *Regist. W. Giffard*, p. 26; Bond, *Chron. Melsa*, i, p. 363; G. H. Fowler, *Charters of Dunstable*, p. 12. Cf. also the Wife of Bath who, following her fourth husband to the grave, was struck by the beauty of the clerk's legs, and

'at the monthis ende
This joly clerk, Jankyn, that was so heende,
Hath weddid me with gret solempnitee'.

Prologue to Wyf of Bath's Tale, ll. 596–8, 627–9.

statement of Giraldus Cambrensis that 'nearly all' the parish priests of England were married.[1] But that there were married priests admits of no doubt. The Church, moreover, was bound to take notice of such irregularities. Officially, clerks who married were liable to suspension, and vigorous efforts were made from time to time to enforce this,[2] though they met with much less success than their promoters might have desired, and the hunt for *uxorati* went on throughout the century.[3]

Besides those clergy who were formally married, there were those who lived with women, their wives in all but name.[4] The men who were guilty of this were known as *concubinarii* and their consorts as *focariae* or hearth-mates. If formal marriage was rare, concubinage was considerably more common, as contemporary records show. Alexander IV wrote to Archbishop Gray of 'the notorious cohabitation of clerks with their concubines', and Grosseteste tells his archdeacons that he has heard of many priests who keep their *focariae*.[5] There was certainly, then, in many a parsonage house a woman living with the incumbent on terms practically the equivalent of wedlock. Sometimes, as at Broadwas in Worcestershire, the priest attempted to introduce his mistress in the disguise of a dairymaid,[6] but in most instances the woman was recognised as the priest's 'lemmon or lotebye';[7] and, though the children of such unions were at a disadvantage legally, there is no reason to suppose that they were looked down upon by the community. Clerical moralists, like Robert Manning of Brunne, might cry shame upon those who were called 'priests' mares' and tell gruesome tales of fiends carrying off the corpse of a woman who had lived for many years with a priest and borne him four

[1] Giraldus was, of course, most familiar with conditions in Wales. It is worthy of note that in the Register of Godfrey Giffard, who was for thirty-four years Bishop of Worcester, there is only one recorded instance of a married priest: *Regist. G. Giffard*, p. 114.

[2] Bliss, *Cal. Papal Letters*, i, pp. 80, 84–6 and 90 for the dioceses of Durham, York, Lincoln and Worcester, 1221–3.

[3] Sometimes the authorities compelled the man to leave the church and support his wife: Bliss, *Cal. Papal Letters*, i, p. 29 and Bond, *Chron. Melsa*, i, p. 363.

[4] H. G. Richardson in *Trans. R. Hist. Soc.* 1912, p. 123.

[5] *Regist. W. Gray*, pp. 215–16; R. Grosseteste, *Epistolae*, p. 317.

[6] Worcester, *Regist. Sede Vacante*, pp. 170–2.

[7] *Piers Plowman*, C, iv, 188.

sons;[1] but on the other hand the daughter of the Rector of Trumpington in the *Reeve's Tale* was considered so well born and bred that

There durst no wight clepe hir but madame.[2]

If the laity grumbled about the priests' women and children it was generally on economic grounds, fearing that if a man had a wife and family to support he would inevitably try to get more money out of the people.[3]

In addition to those clergy who formed life-long attachments, there was also a certain amount of promiscuous intercourse between clergy and their female parishioners. Episcopal enquiries sometimes refer to those who have 'sinned with their spiritual daughters',[4] while Registers show that breaches of the vow of chastity were not uncommon. Giraldus thought that it was hopeless to expect the rule of celibacy to be observed; the temptations were too great.[5] Certainly women were, from time to time, brought into clerical households for immoral purposes, and clerks were sometimes up to no good when they visited the homes of their parishioners. Visits to 'spiritual daughters' sometimes resulted in a priest finding himself father of a family, and many problems, personal and financial, were thereby created.[6]

Such loose-living is without defence; but the man who took a woman to his bosom and was faithful to her was guilty of no sin worse than disobedience to ecclesiastical law. The married priest could claim that his behaviour, far from being a breach of divine law, was in fact in accordance with the teaching of S. Paul and with the practice of no less a person than S. Peter. He could, and did, point out that Zacharias, the father of John the Baptist, was a married priest;[7] and, though he probably had little idea of how celibacy came to be the rule of the Western Church, he might be aware of the fact that it was not enforced

[1] R. Manning, *Handlyng Synne* (1303), ed. Furnivall, E.E.T.S. pp. 253–6: 'And shame hyt ys euer aywhare, To be kalled a prestes mare.'

[2] *Canterbury Tales, Reeve's Tale*, l. 36.

[3] See Wright, *Political Songs*, p. 33.

[4] E.g. *Regist. W. Giffard*, pp. 266–8.

[5] A. L. Smith, *Church and State in the Middle Ages*, p. 19.

[6] See, for example, *Rot. H. de Welles*, i, p. 79; *Rot. R. Grosseteste*, p. 41; *Regist. W. Giffard*, p. 322; Pecham, *Reg. Epist.* iii, pp. 855–6; *Regist. H. Hethe*, pp. 198–200; Worcester, *Regist. Sede Vacante*, p. 143.

[7] Wright, *Poems attributed to Walter Mapes*, pp. 173, 178.

in England in Saxon times, and even by the thirteenth century might be regarded as something new.

At the same time, the Church had the right to demand that its discipline should be observed by those who accepted its authority and were its commissioned agents. There was no excuse for clerical unchastity, though the reason for it is not far to seek. The cause of it lay in the vast number of the clergy and in the fact that among so many of them their sense of responsibility was weak. Celibacy is a vocation. To make the vow applicable to a small number of men, such as members of a religious community, is reasonable enough; but to apply it to a class which numbered something like one in twelve of the adult male population is to create a tension which can scarcely be maintained.[1] Ordination was not confined to such as were moved by a strong sense of vocation, but was the normal thing for those who preferred professional work either to manual labour or to a military life. We know that many clergy took their duties very lightly, living far away from their cures, neglecting their education, and failing to acquire adequate ordination; and if their sense of responsibility in these things was so low, how shall we wonder if their self-control broke down altogether in the face of what must often have been powerful temptation?

[1] Nowadays the clergy and ministers in England of all denominations number some 50,000, or one in every thousand of the population. If celibacy were demanded of them all we should not be altogether surprised to hear of occasional lapses. But if there were, as in the Middle Ages, one ordained man in every fifty of the population, there would be a million clerics in the country and the chances of failure would be enormously increased.

CHAPTER VII

THE CHURCH AND ITS SERVICES

The scene of much of the parish priest's work was, of course, the church, which, in so many villages, stood majestically above the low huts of the people, a perpetual reminder to them of things spiritual and eternal. The twelfth century had seen the introduction of a new style of architecture, and gradually the small and solidly-built Norman and Saxon churches were being replaced by loftier and lighter buildings. It is true that the early years of the thirteenth century saw little church-building, for the times were unsettled and the Interdict crushed any such enterprise; but by the middle of the century the architects were busy again improving upon the Early English designs until they blossomed into that most beautiful of all styles, known as the Decorated or Geometrical.

That the thirteenth century was a time of active church-building is revealed by the constant references to the consecration of churches which appear in episcopal Registers and other official documents. Bishops and archdeacons were anxious to find out where new churches had been built, and the bishops themselves were kept busy on their visitation tours dedicating churches and altars.[1]

The fact of so much building is itself evidence of active Church life. Men do not part with their money for causes in which they have little interest—a fact which we shall do well to remember as we study the evidence of parish life during this century. Some of it is sad reading; but, if there were parishes where there was spiritual lethargy and gross neglect, there were undoubtedly others where Church life was virile and healthy, where the people were proud of their church, and loved and cared for it.[2]

Apart from any offices which the priest might choose to say,

[1] For example Bishop Bronescombe in 1259 visited a number of parishes in Cornwall and dedicated no less than twenty-one churches: *Regist. W. Bronescombe*, p. xii.

[2] Mr Powys has pointed out that any church which was totally neglected for forty or fifty years would fall into ruin. The fact that so many ancient churches are still standing is further evidence of the care which has always been bestowed upon them.

there were, on Sundays, three services which the laity were bidden to attend. Langland writes:

> Upon Sonedayes to cesse . godes seruyce to huyre
> Bothe matyns and messe . and, after mete, in churches
> To huyre here euesong . euery man ouhte.[1]

Unfortunately, however, men do not always do their duty in the matter of worship.[2] Of the three services the one which was best attended was the Mass, which was held fairly early in the morning. People were also encouraged to be present at Mattins which preceded it, but it is clear that some of them were content to arrive only for Mass, and, even then, were often late. The rich seem to have been the chief offenders, for Robert Manning tells us that many rich men, when they hear the church bell ring, prefer to stay in bed 'to lygge and swete and take the mery mornyng slepe', while 'of matyns ryche men take no kepe'.[3] As for Evensong, the evidence rather suggests that Sunday afternoons were more often given over to merry-making than to worship, so that the congregations at these services must have been rather thin.[4]

The Middle Ages would certainly have been surprised and shocked at the very small congregations which attend our churches nowadays, but the idea that in those days everyone went to church as a matter of course is not true. Archbishop Pecham in 1291 wrote to the Archdeacon of Canterbury complaining that Sunday was being so poorly observed and urging him to persuade more people to go to church,[5] and even fines for recusancy seem to have failed to induce some men to do their duty.[6] The reason for this neglect is not far to seek. Apart from the monks, who had a regular annual holiday for recreation,[7] no one in the thirteenth century had any chance of relaxa-

[1] *Piers Plowman*, C, x, 227–9.

[2] In 1201 Eustachius, Abbot of Flay, visited England and preached up and down the country on the duty of Sunday observance: Wilkins, *Concilia*, i, p. 510.

[3] R. Manning, *Handlyng Synne* (1303), ed. Furnivall, p. 143. He points out also that God's service is often neglected for playing at the ale-house: *ibid*. p. 152. Cf. *Vices and Virtues*, ed. Holthausen, E.E.T.S. p. 2.

[4] *Handlyng Synne*, pp. 36, 37, 38; *Regist. R. Baldock, etc*. pp. 73–4, 145–6.

[5] Pecham, *Reg. Epist*. iii, pp. 980–2.

[6] *Regist. H. Hethe*, p. 464; cf. B. L. Manning, *The People's Faith in the Time of Wyclif*, p. 5.

[7] Cf. below, pp. 342–3.

tion except such as was provided by the Church's year. Holy-days were the only holidays, the only break in the routine of hard manual labour, the only opportunity for recreation in any sense of the word. Not all men are natural worshippers; and if there were some then, as now, who made Sunday an occasion for sport or for merry-making, it was, after all, the only opportunity which they had.

But if the churchman of the thirteenth century would be surprised and shocked at the smallness of our congregations we ourselves should be equally startled at the apparent irreverence of theirs. Men and women gossiped and chattered during the most sacred parts of the liturgy; they lolled up against pillars and discussed where the best ale was to be had; young men and women stared and winked at one another and paid little attention to the priest and his whisperings.[1] In the *Lay Folks' Mass Book* there is constant warning against 'jangling' or chattering during the Mass, and in *A Lutel Soth Sermon* we are given a picture of lovers coming to church to talk of illicit affection, and to give each other the 'glad eye', while the beads which should encourage their devotions are left at home, locked up in the cupboard.[2]

The reason for this inattention and irreverence is twofold. In the first place the services were often performed with little dignity or reverence. Priests were accused of mumbling, clipping and whispering the words of the Mass in a way which must have destroyed any sense of corporate worship or of what is called nowadays 'the numinous'.[3] Moreover, it is quite untrue to suggest, as some writers have done,[4] that the average

[1] *Lay Folks' Mass Book*, pp. 4, 18, 170. Cf. *Handlyng Synne*, pp. 36, 292; Myrc, *Instructions for Parish Priests*, p. 9.

[2] *Old English Miscellany*, ed. R. Morris, E.E.T.S. pp. 189–91:

'Hwenne heo to chirche cumeþ
  to þon holy daye.
Euervych wile his leof i-seo
  þer yef he may.
Heo biholdeþ watekin
  Mid swiþe gled eye.'

[3] Wilkins, *Concilia*, i, pp. 505, 540, etc. Langland blames those whom he calls 'over-skippers': *Piers Plowman*, C, xiv, 123.

[4] See, for example, D. Rock, *Church of our Fathers*; T. E. Bridgett, *History of the Holy Eucharist*; F. A. Gasquet, *Parish Life*; J. D. Chambers, *Divine Worship in England*.

parish church in England was a treasure-house of costly vestments and ornaments which made the service rich in colour and beauty and which, by their very magnificence, would lift a man's thoughts up to heaven, and drive him to his knees in humble adoration. There were no doubt some cathedrals and larger parish churches where the services were conducted with much dignity and reverence, but in the average parish church the vestments and ornaments were often dingy and decayed, and, in many cases, missing altogether.[1]

The apathy of the celebrant and the poverty of the ceremonial were together one of the causes of irreverence. The other was the fact that the laity were encouraged to take so little part in the service. Every parish priest knows that one of the surest ways of developing a man's powers of worship is to allow him to take an active part in the service; but in the thirteenth century the laity could be little more than spectators. They communicated only rarely; they seldom heard a sermon; they sang no hymns. In Anglo-Saxon times some concession to the layman's desire to understand the service had been made by reading the Gospel in the speech of the people; but this practice died out soon after the Conquest.[2] For the few among the laity who could read, helps were provided in the form of Primers and Mass-Books, but these were of no use to the vast majority of illiterate worshippers. To them the Mass can have meant very little; and it is no wonder that tongues wagged and eyes wandered when the few prayers which they knew had been said. Had the priests been more willing to take the people into their confidence, to explain to them the nature and meaning of worship and to encourage them to take an active part in it, there would have been fewer complaints of 'jangling' and inattention.

There is nothing in the literature of the thirteenth century to suggest that the laity were ever encouraged to communicate frequently. The *Lay Folks' Mass Book* is concerned with 'messe herynge'[3] and gives no instruction to the communicant. Alexander Stavensby, Bishop of Coventry and Lichfield, encouraged the laity of his diocese to communicate three times a year,[4]

[1] See below, pp. 144–5.
[2] *Lay Folks' Mass Book*, pp. 210–11; cf. Manning, *People's Faith*, p. 7.
[3] *Lay Folks' Mass Book*, p. 2; cf. p. xxviii.
[4] Wilkins, *Concilia*, i, p. 640, and cf. G. Cambrensis, *Gemma Ecclesiastica*, i, cap. 9 in *Opera*, ii, p. 29.

but the usual thing seems to have been no more than one communion a year, on Easter Day.[1] At the communion of the people it was usual for the Sacrament to be administered in one kind only. From apostolic times down to the twelfth century there seems no doubt that the laity, as a matter of course, communicated in both kinds,[2] but from that time onwards the custom arose of withholding the chalice from the lay worshippers mainly with the intention of avoiding every possible risk of any particle of the Sacrament being lost or spilled. As devotion to the Host intensified, so fear of irreverence became greater, and the Church grew more and more anxious to communicate the laity in the species of bread only. The promulgation of the doctrine of transubstantiation by the Lateran Council of 1215[3] and the popular devotion to the Eucharist preached by the Franciscans served to emphasise the necessity of caution in the administration of the elements, with the result that the chalice came to be more and more generally withheld from the laity. At the same time the practice arose of giving to each communicant, after the reception of the wafer, a draught of unconsecrated wine and water from a chalice in order to prevent any crumbs remaining in the mouth. This custom, growing up at the time when the administration of the chalice was dying out, not unnaturally led to some confusion of thought in the minds of the worshippers, and Pecham in 1281 had to make it clear in his Statutes that this cleansing draught was by no means the same thing as participation in the consecrated element.[4]

During the thirteenth century, then, we may take it that

[1] In the *Lay Folks' Catechism* everyone is told to communicate 'anes in the yhere, that is at sai, at paskes' (E.E.T.S. p. 66); cf. *Handlyng Synne*, p. 321. In *Piers Plowman* (C, xxii, 390) once a month is recommended but this was not customary.

[2] 'The faithful always and everywhere, from the very beginning of the Church even to the twelfth century, communicated under the form of bread and wine': Cardinal Bona, *Rerum liturgic.* ii, p. 18. Cf. *Liturgy and Worship*, p. 611; Darwell Stone, *The Holy Communion*, pp. 312–14. In view of what is so generally acknowledged about the early Church it is a pity to find Dr Rock in his *Hierurgia* (i, pp. 277–89) trying to maintain that communion in one kind was the practice of the apostolic Church, and even quoting part (but only that part which suits his argument) of what S. Paul writes in *I Cor*. xi, 26–7 to support his theory.

[3] The word 'transubstantiation' is probably not older than the eleventh century; cf. D. Stone, *The Holy Communion*, p. 293.

[4] Wilkins, *Concilia*, ii, p. 52; cf. Lyndwood, *Provinciale*, p. 9.

infrequent communions and the administration of the bread or wafer only became, for the laity, the general rule.[1] But old customs die slowly, and there is evidence that communion in one kind was by no means universal in this country until some time later. The Statutes of the Council of Durham in 1220 refer quite naturally to the people receiving both the bread and the wine,[2] and the words are substantially reproduced in the Constitutions of the diocese of Exeter in 1287.[3] Even later than this there is a phrase in Robert Manning's *Handlyng Synne*, written in 1303, in which he tells the people not to feel doubtful of the Sacrament:

> . . .ȝyf on felë no sauour
> But ryghtely wyne and brede of flour.[4]

We may take it, then, that most of the laity attended Mass on Sunday morning, and that the more pious were present also at Mattins and Evensong.[5] As far as the weekdays are concerned there is little doubt that a daily Mass was considered the usual thing. Churches and chapels where this was not observed usually came in for censure, as, for example, at Blackmanstone, in Kent, where we learn that the custom of a daily Mass had been allowed to lapse.[6] Many days, moreover, were holy-days, and each Saturday was to some extent observed in England in honour of the Virgin, since she and she alone (according to tradition) had faith in the Resurrection throughout Easter Eve.[7] At the same time, it is unlikely that many of the laity attended these weekday celebrations.[8] The calls of labour and service

[1] S. Thomas Aquinas records that in his day (i.e. about 1270) many churches did not give the chalice to the laity: D. Stone, *The Holy Communion*, p. 214. The Council of Constance in 1415 made Communion in one kind for the laity the law of the Western Church: *ibid*. p. 215.

[2] Wilkins, *Concilia*, i, p. 578: 'Hoc accipiunt proculdubio sub panis specie quod pro nobis pependit in cruce. Hoc accipiunt in calice quod affusum est de Christi latere.'

[3] *Ibid*. ii, p. 133. [4] *Handlyng Synne*, p. 311.

[5] While Robert Manning says much about Mattins and Mass he does not mention any afternoon or evening service.

[6] Woodruff, *Some Early Visitation Rolls*, in *Arch. Cantiana*, xxxii, p. 155.

[7] *Handlyng Synne*, p. 34.

[8] Manning, *People's Faith*, p. 4. Myrc says:

> 'For a-pon þe werkeday
> Men be so bysy in vche way,
> So that for here ocupacyone
> Þey leue myche of here deuocyone.'
>
> *Instructions*, p. 28.

gave little opportunity for worship, even if the inclination were there. In addition to the daily Mass, priests were expected to say the canonical hours among themselves;[1] but Grosseteste complained that this was falling into neglect,[2] and there can be little doubt that among those clergy who took all their responsibilities so lightly many were unwilling to impose this discipline upon themselves.

As the village worshipper approached his church on a Sunday morning, what sort of thoughts were in his mind? Did he come to church just because he had done so all his life and his father and grandfather before him? Or had he some real conception of the meaning of worship, and, above all, of the Sacrifice of the Mass? These questions are hard to answer, for the laity were so little trained in the art of reasoned thinking, and had even less power of expressing their thoughts. But one or two things must have stood out clearly in his mind as he stood in the church and watched the priest vesting before the altar[3] and preparing to celebrate the divine mysteries.

One of these was the assurance of an ultimate destiny of either perpetual bliss or eternal torment. To one or other of these his soul would eventually be assigned, and the Church did what it could, in its instruction by ear and by eye, to keep this fact before him. On the walls of his church he would see the painting of the great 'doom', with its grim and highly imaginative scenes of the sufferings of the damned. To the scanty Biblical references to 'the fire that is not quenched' the Church had added every kind of detail to strike terror into the stoutest heart. *The Eleven Pains of Hell*, edited by Richard Morris in his *Old English Miscellany*,[4] is a good example of the sort of teaching which was given. Here is a description of Hell from one who claimed to have seen it in a vision.

[1] How far the laity attended the daily offices is hard to say: but it is interesting to note, in the Constitutions of the diocese of Norwich (1257), that priests were instructed to say the Creed and the Lord's Prayer every day, with their parishioners, at Prime and Compline, aloud and distinctly: Wilkins, *Concilia*, i, p. 732.

[2] Grosseteste, *Epistolae*, p. 317.

[3] It was a custom for priests in England to put on the vestments in public. That explains why so few English churches have vestries before the Perpendicular period. The vestments were kept in a chest under the altar. See *Lay Folks' Mass Book*, pp. 165–6.

[4] E.E.T.S. No. 49 (1872), pp. 147 ff.

There are burning trees upon which are hung the souls of those who would not go to church; there are vultures to gnaw people's vitals, venomous serpents to sting them, boiling lakes and frozen fens, heated ovens, vile dungeons—indeed every kind of torment which the macabre mind of man could devise.

The possibility of being condemned to such an existence was constantly in men's thoughts. The only things which could avail were the mercy of God, the prayers of the saints, and the worship of the Church. Of the mercy of God, as revealed in the Passion of Christ, the medieval man was fully aware. In the centre of his church hung the rood, the great crucifix with the attendant figures of the Virgin and S. John; and, as the rood overshadowed him in church, so the thought of the Passion of Christ overshadowed him in his life.[1] In the Cross lay his only hope of salvation, but to claim its virtue he must have recourse to the saints, and especially to the Virgin Mary.

Mr Bishop has described the spread of devotion to the Virgin which was 'so marked a feature of the English Church from the close of the tenth century to the Conquest'.[2] Throughout the succeeding centuries this devotion was developed and amplified. Once again, to the simple and moving stories of the Gospels the Church added a wealth of legendary matter which, while it enhanced the anguish of Christ's Mother, seriously diminished her dignity and courage. In Robert Manning's *Meditations on the Supper of our Lord*[3] we get a vivid account of the Passion of Christ and of the sufferings of our Lady, who first tries to rescue her Son from His tormentors, then ministers to Him in His agony, and finally swoons away crying 'Wuld god ȝe wulde byrye me with hym'.[4]

To her the layman was told to direct his prayers in that

[1] Manning, *People's Faith*, p. 25: 'The medieval Christian was a man of one event. The Passion of Christ was his daily meditation....Over the whole medieval world lay the broad shadow of the Cross.' See also *Legends of the Holy Rood* (ed. R. Morris, E.E.T.S. No. 46), which contains many strange and miraculous stories of the history of the tree from which the Cross was made, and of its discovery by S. Helen.

[2] E. Bishop, *Liturgica Historica*, p. 227.

[3] Edited by J. M. Cowper in E.E.T.S. No. 60.

[4] First she prays:

'He ys so buxum to do ȝoure wyl
Þat he nat chargeþ hym self to spyl,

delightful and almost wholly Scriptural form of address, the *Ave Maria*. This salutation came into general use in France at the beginning of the thirteenth century and rapidly became popular in this country,[1] for though the worshipper might understand little of the Mass he could easily kneel down and say a simple *Ave*, thereby adding his little contribution to the prayers of the saints.

Finally, his hope of eternal bliss lay in the worship of the Church, in which he was encouraged to meet his Lord face to face. The doctrine of the Real Presence was taught consistently throughout this century. When the priest held up the consecrated wafer the worshipper was taught to believe that he was looking upon 'Goddys flessh', 'Cristes own bodi...as hale as he toke it of that blessed maiden',[2] the very flesh and blood 'that iudas salde'.[3] This devotion to the Sacrament received considerable encouragement from the preaching of the friars,[4] and led to the establishment, in the latter part of the century, of one of the most popular of festivals, Corpus Christi.[5]

Helpeþ my sone fro cursed houndes,
Dere fadyr, bryngeþ hym out from here hondes' (p. 15).

Then we read:

'A! with what sorow hys modyr was fedde,
Whan she sagh hym so naked and alle bled!
Fyrþer more, þan gan she to seche,
And say þat þey had left hym no breche.
She ran þan þurgh hem and hastyly hyde,
And with here kercheves hys hepys she wryde' (p. 20).

For the final sorrows cf. pp. 25–31.

[1] See *Lay Folks' Mass Book*, pp. 6, 10, 26, etc. Canon Simmons is not quite accurate in saying that the first mention of it in England was in the Constitutions of Alexander Stavensby in 1237, for it is mentioned in the Durham Statutes of 1220: Wilkins, *Concilia*, i, p. 573 (cf. *ibid*. p. 646 and Rock, *Church of our Fathers*, iii, p. 260). Grosseteste in 1238 tells his clergy to teach children 'the Salutation of the Blessed Virgin': *Epistolae*, p. 156.

[2] *Handlyng Synne*, p. 310; *Lay Folks' Catechism*, p. 66.

[3] *Lay Folks' Mass Book*, p. 38.

[4] For S. Francis' views see *De Reverentia Corporis Domini* in *Opuscula S. Francisci*, p. 22.

[5] It first became popular in the diocese of Liège about 1246 and was taken up at Rome in 1264. It is mentioned in a letter from Stapeldon to the Benedictine nuns of Polslo (Dorset) in 1319: 'Item qe le serviez du corps et du sank notre seigneur Jhesu Crist soit fait oe grant solempnite entre vous chescun an le Judi prochein apres la Trinité et par les oytaves siwantes': Oliver, *Monasticon Dioc. Exoniensis*, p. 165.

Along such lines the thoughts of worshippers must have travelled; but it must not be supposed that any of them enjoyed any mental or spiritual independence. Though they might not always obey the dictates of 'halikirke', none of them would have questioned the Church's authority to command. Mostly illiterate, and with no opportunity of acquiring ideas except such as were given by the Church, the laity as a whole were willing to accept what they were told without question. 'Honour thy father and thy mother', they were taught, meant not only obedience to parents but also to their 'gastly fadirs', the clergy, and to their 'gastly modir', the Church.[1] The clergy, therefore, had a great and unrivalled opportunity in the realm of teaching and preaching. We must now see what they made of it.

In the thirteenth century a sermon was a rare event. The Council of Cloveshoo in 747 had encouraged the clergy to teach as well as to visit and baptise, while bishops were exhorted to travel about their dioceses and 'plainly teach those who rarely hear the word of God';[2] but it is clear that, whatever the practice of the Anglo-Saxon Church may have been, by the beginning of the thirteenth century the habit of preaching had been largely lost by the parish clergy of England. There were several reasons why this should be so. In the first place the typical sermon of the time was so abstruse as to be quite unsuited to a rustic congregation in a village church. Sermons belonged to the Schools, where they were composed more on the lines of a scholar's thesis than of a preacher's homily. Preaching is an art; but it was one in which the average parish priest was never instructed.

In the second place, effective preaching depends upon a knowledge of the Bible; but only a very few of the clergy possessed Bibles, and these were mostly the richer men who took little interest in their parishes. Chaucer's good parson was certainly a preacher of 'Christ's lore', but we must not be misled by this, since he belongs to a later period, after a considerable revival of preaching had taken place. If, then, the doctrinal sermon was too erudite for the masses, and the Gospel sermon beyond the wit of the preacher, it might seem that the laity would have little opportunity of receiving either instruction or exhortation.

[1] *Lay Folks' Catechism*, p. 44.

[2] Gee and Hardy, *Documents of English Church History*, pp. 18–20.

But things were not so bad; for the recognised medium both of teaching and of moral counsel was not the pulpit but the confessional. This had the advantage of being able to adapt itself to the needs of the individual, whereas the preacher can only throw out his advice and his condemnations in the hope that upon some head or other in his congregation the cap will fit.

In the earlier part of the thirteenth century no regular Sunday sermon was given in the parish churches.[1] Occasionally the priest would turn to give his people some simple explanation of the Creed, the Lord's Prayer or the Ten Commandments, or he would teach them about the Seven Deadly Sins or the sacraments.[2] In addition to these lessons, the preacher might have access to some book of homilies from which he might read to his people, for certain collections of sermons in English existed at this period,[3] though the number of churches which possessed such books was small.[4]

Preaching, therefore, in the first half of the thirteenth century was spasmodic and incidental. It was not considered a vital part of Sunday worship, though a certain amount of religious instruction was encouraged. In spite of such exhortation as was given by the Council of Oxford in 1222, that the clergy should not be 'dumb dogs, but with salutary bark drive away the affliction of spiritual wolves from the flock',[5] little preparation was made for preaching either in the training of the clergy or in the furnishing of the churches, for, as Dr Owst points out,[6] there are no examples of pulpits in England earlier than about 1340, while the absence of pews or chairs in the churches would have imposed a considerable strain upon the listeners' patience and endurance.

[1] When giving a man permission to have a private chapel in his house Grosseteste made it a condition that he should attend the parish church on certain festivals and 'when there is a sermon': *Rot. R. Grosseteste*, p. 12.

[2] Grosseteste, *Epist.* p. 156; Wilkins, *Concilia*, i, p. 573; ii, p. 144; Cutts, *Parish Priests*, p. 215.

[3] E.g. *Old English Homilies*, ed. R. Morris (E.E.T.S.); *Twelfth-Century Homilies* in MS. Bodley 343, ed. A. O. Balfour (E.E.T.S.).

[4] There was one at Heytesbury in 1220, at Kirkby in 1249, at S. Giles, Cambridge, in 1275, and at Heybridge and Kirkby in 1297; cf. *Reg. S. Osmundi*, i, p. 294: *Camden Misc.* ix, p. 31; *Vetus Liber Archidiaconi Elien.* p. 30; Camden Soc. N.S. lv, pp. 18, 25.

[5] Wilkins, *Concilia*, i, p. 586.

[6] G. R. Owst, *Preaching in Medieval England*, p. 161 n.

The revival of preaching in England during the latter part of the thirteenth century was largely due to the coming of the friars. From the very beginning, the mendicant orders had devoted much thought and time to preaching. S. Francis' sermons attracted large crowds upon whom they made a deep impression,[1] and the Order of Friars Minor no less than the sister Order of Preachers developed the technique of preaching to so high a pitch that the parochial clergy were bound to take notice of it and learn something from it. So much value did the friars set upon the sermon that S. Bernardino of Siena declared to the people: 'If of these two things you can only do one—either hear the Mass or hear the Sermon—you should let the Mass go rather than the sermon. . . . There is less peril for your soul in not hearing the Mass than in not hearing the sermon',[2] while the Dominican, Humbert of Romans, said: 'Christ only once heard Mass . . . but he laid great stress on prayer and preaching, especially on preaching.'[3]

Full of such ideals, and to some extent trained in the art of preaching, the Dominicans arrived in this country in 1221, followed by the Franciscan contingent three years later. Immediately they began their evangelistic tours which quickly made their mark. In contrast to the rather dreary and monotonous Sunday services which the parish churches offered, these preaching friars provided something which was almost an entertainment. Full of racy stories and the personal reminiscences of men who had travelled and seen something of the world, they offered an attraction which the English countryman found irresistible. Here was no monologue, but a display of pulpit fireworks, full of wit and repartee in which the congregation were encouraged to join. 'Stop that babbling' cries the preacher to a woman in the crowd. 'What about you?' she replies amid general laughter, 'you've been babbling for the last half-hour.'[4] The

[1] See the account by Thomas of Spalato in Golubovich, *Biblioteca Bio-bibliografica*, i, pp. 8–10, with translation in my *Sources for the Life of S. Francis*, p. 56.

[2] A. G. Ferrers-Howell, *S. Bernardino of Siena*, p. 219. Cf. the Wycliffite document in the *Lay Folks' Catechism*, where the worshipper is told to 'here godys lawse tawȝt in þy modyr tonge. For þat is bettyr to þe þan to here many massys' (E.E.T.S. No. 118, p. 41).

[3] C. H. Smyth, *The Art of Preaching*, p. 16.

[4] H. G. Pfander, *The Popular Sermon of the Medieval Friar in England*, p. 6.

preachers stopped at nothing. Stories and remarks which we should consider irreverent and profane, jokes and vulgarities, fantastic legends culled from folk-lore and bestiaries—all were made to contribute to this performance.[1] Sometimes the preachers added to the attraction of their sermons by delivering them in verse; often they were punctuated by applause and heckling.[2]

Such a contribution to Church life in England was bound to have its effect upon the old-established parish churches. Hitherto the parish priest had known no rival and had never had to face even the mildest competition. His parishioners were obliged to attend his church and no other, and he could snap his fingers at more gifted and attractive neighbours. But when the friars came, with the bishop's connivance, right into his parish, and even sometimes right into his church, their visit was bound to open men's eyes and must have stirred many a priest to reconsider the whole question of his relationship to his flock. As the years passed by we seem to detect a growing effort on the part of the Church to encourage the parish clergy to face their congregations and try to imitate what the friars were doing so supremely well. Grosseteste, who had worked with the Franciscans at Oxford, encouraged all his clergy to preach in English,[3] while he sent one young man off to the Schools to learn 'all the Sunday homilies' before he would institute him as Rector of Cossington.[4] Meanwhile we find Roger de Weseham at Coventry not only urging his clergy to preach in the vernacular but even going so far as to suggest topics for their sermons.[5] Pecham, the first Franciscan to become Archbishop of Canterbury, demanded that his clergy should preach at least four times

[1] See R. F. Bennett, *The Early Dominicans*, pp. 75–127; G. R. Owst, *Literature and Pulpit*, chap. i; C. H. Haskins in *American Hist. Review*, 1904; C. H. Smyth, *The Art of Preaching*, pp. 58–75. The use of *exempla* was already established before the advent of the friars; see Welter, *L'exemplum dans la littérature religieuse*, pp. 1–133.

[2] H. G. Pfander, *Popular Sermon*, pp. 8–9, 16. Cf. Owst, *Literature and Pulpit*, p. 227.

[3] Grosseteste, *Epistolae*, p. 155: 'doceant frequenter laicos in idiomate communi.'

[4] *Rot. R. Grosseteste*, pp. 402–3.

[5] Tanner, *Bibliotheca*, p. 758; Gibbs and Lang, *Bishops and Reform*, p. 42, and cf. *D.N.B.* Pontissara also encouraged his clergy to preach in English: *Regist. J. Pontissara*, p. 217.

Plate II. The Rectory, West Dean, Sussex.

Plate III. The Doom or Last Judgment: from Bagnot Church, Burgundy.

a year,[1] and appealed to their vanity by telling them that if they were not competent to do it they must call in the help of men specially set aside for this work.[2]

By the end of the century, then, preaching was becoming more common in the parish churches. The pyrotechnics of the friars had kindled a spark which burned ever more brightly in the following century. Already, at the beginning of it, we find evidence that the parish priests were more alive to their duties, for when the Dean and Chapter of Exeter visited a number of parishes in 1301 they received encouraging reports of the clergy, many of whom were regarded as good preachers whose efforts were gratefully acknowledged by their congregations.[3]

Apart from the preaching of sermons, the parish clergy were expected to do a certain amount of teaching. Grosseteste told his clergy that they were to teach the children the Creed, the Lord's Prayer and the *Ave*, and how to make the sign of the cross.[4] Richard le Poore in 1220 had instituted 'pupil teachers' by encouraging the clergy to call the children together and instruct one or two to become teachers of the others,[5] just as the little seven-year-old 'clergeoun' in the *Prioress' Tale* sought enlightenment from his fellow-scholars. Nor was it only the children who needed instruction. The *Lay Folks' Catechism* laments the ignorance of the people through the negligence of 'prelates, parsons, vikers and prestes',[6] and various reforming bishops urged their clergy to teach the elements of the faith to their parishioners.[7]

Besides the teaching of the faith, the clergy were exhorted to give practical advice, especially on questions concerned with the rearing of children. It is interesting and encouraging to find men like Grosseteste and S. Edmund ordering their clergy to warn mothers against overlaying their children,[8] Stavensby and

[1] Wilkins, *Concilia*, ii, p. 54.

[2] Pecham, *Reg. Epist.* iii, p. 949. The reference to men 'ad hoc specialiter deputati' must allude to the friars.

[3] *Regist. W. Stapeldon*, pp. 111, 130, 133, 194, 337, 368, 378.

[4] Grosseteste, *Epistolae*, p. 155.

[5] Wilkins, *Concilia*, i, p. 573.

[6] *Lay Folks' Catechism*, p. 4; cf. pp. 6 and 20.

[7] E.g. Grosseteste, *Epistolae*, p. 156; *Regist. J. Pontissara*, p. 217; Quivil in Wilkins, *Concilia*, ii, p. 144.

[8] Grosseteste, *Epistolae*, pp. 162 and 75; Wilkins, *Concilia*, i, pp. 635–40.

Walter Cantilupe worrying about the possibility of cradles being upset,[1] while the Durham Statutes of Richard le Poore required the clergy to announce every Sunday that children must not be left alone in a house where there is a fire, nor close to water.[2]

War, too, was waged against Superstition, an evil which so quickly rears its head if sound teaching is neglected. The medieval villager was full of superstition, some of which was clearly a relic of pre-Christian days. How otherwise should the Winchester Statutes consider it necessary to warn people against the dangers of worshipping stones or trees or wells?[3] Or why should Robert Manning refer to the custom of placing food at a baby's head, unless it were to propitiate some evil spirit which might draw near?[4] People were constantly warned against the dangers of trying to interpret strange dreams or the chattering of magpies.[5] The services and ornaments of the Church also lent themselves to superstitions, and bishops and moralists were obliged to order the destruction of basins used in private baptisms, to forbid people to use altar cloths as bed-spreads or to treasure bits of stone from ruined churches, and to stifle the belief that it was unlucky for a man to lie with his wife after one or other of them had received Extreme Unction and recovered.[6] False relics, the 'pigges bones' of the Pardoner, were a most fertile source of superstition.[7]

Thus, besides the teaching of the elements of the faith—'the Creed, the Lord's Prayer, the Ten Commandments and all other things which a Christian ought to know and believe to his soul's health'—the parish priest was expected 'to banish and drive away all erroneous and strange doctrines contrary to God's

[1] Wilkins, *Concilia*, i, pp. 640–6 and 668. [2] *Ibid.* i, p. 576.
[3] *Regist. J. Pontissara*, p. 217. [4] *Handlyng Synne*, p. 302.
[5] *Ibid.* p. 13:

> 'Beleue nouȝt yn þe pyys cheteryng,
> Hyt ys no trouþe but fals beleuyng.'

Cf. Manning, *People's Faith*, p. 96.

[6] Cf. Wilkins, *Concilia*, i, p. 624; *Handlyng Synne*, pp. 348–9.

[7] *Regist. J. Pontissara*, p. 217. The author of *Vices and Virtues* refers to people who are superstitious about the moon and think it better at new moon to move into a new house or lead a wife home. This, he says, is absurd; but he approves of a doctor watching the moon and of the carpenter who cuts his wood according to the moon (ed. Holthausen, E.E.T.S.), p. 26.

word' and to give practical advice about the problems of home life. One cannot help feeling that here was a great opportunity for the wise and sympathetic preacher, and one can only regret that so little was made of it, at least until the days when the parish clergy were goaded into activity by the rivalry of the friars.

The Occasional Offices are the point where the parish priest's pastoral and devotional work are brought most closely together. Concerned as many of them are with the great events of family life—birth, marriage, sickness and death—they provide an opportunity for the work and worship of the Church to impinge upon the intimacies of the home.

In the thirteenth century the parish priest was more closely associated with his people than the modern clergyman can ever hope to be. In a community of some sixty or seventy households, living closely together, and almost completely cut off from the sights and sounds of the outside world, the parson would find himself working side by side with his people in the open fields, would meet them from time to time at the common mill or at the village well, and would face, day by day with them, the dangers and disasters which so constantly threatened their security and their lives.

In such a community a birth was an event of considerable importance in which all could take a lively interest both in anticipation and in retrospect. Of equal importance to the child's birth was his re-birth through Baptism; for no one in the Middle Ages doubted the necessity of this sacrament. The babe who died unbaptised was indeed forlorn, for it had no hope of heaven's bliss. When Langland declared that

> A barne with-oute bapteme, may nouȝt so be saved,[1]

he was only expressing a view which everyone would have accepted without demur. So important, indeed, was the christening that holy water must be kept always at hand in the locked font so that the newborn child might be brought on the day of its birth to Baptism.[2]

[1] *Piers Plowman*, B, xi, 82.

[2] Gasquet, *Parish Life*, p. 189. The fonts were always supposed to be kept locked but the parochial visitations show that this rule was very frequently broken.

But if there were any danger of the child dying, then someone must cast water on it 'in the name of the Father, and of the Son, and of the Holy Ghost'. However simple the ceremony, this must be done, in order that the child's soul might be saved. If the baptiser knew not the Latin formula then he must say it in English or French, and if he only got part of the words right it would suffice, so long as his intentions were good.[1] To provide for such a contingency water was to be kept ready at every confinement.[2] If in the very moment of birth the child's life seemed to be in danger then the midwife must immediately christen it.

> And thaghe þe chylde bote half be bore
> Hed and necke and no more,
> Bydde hyre spare, neuer þe later
> To crysten hyt and caste on water.[3]

Indeed the spiritual life was considered of so much greater importance than the merely physical that the midwife is told to take a knife and, if necessary, risk the life of the mother if that be the only chance of sprinkling water on the half-born child.[4] Meanwhile the clergy were instructed to attack any of the foolish superstitions about Baptism, such as the current belief that it was unlucky for children to be baptised on Easter Eve or on the Eve of Whitsunday,[5] or that vessels and clothes used in Baptism had magical properties.[6] Strenuous efforts were also made to preserve as much dignity and cleanliness as was possible by ordering that all fonts should be made of stone and that the water in them should be changed once a week.[7]

Confirmation caused little trouble to the parish priest. It was administered (if at all) when children were very young, and therefore demanded no preparation. Clergy were sometimes warned of the approach of a bishop and told to see that any unconfirmed children were brought to him,[8] but this would involve little more than a visit to the parents, and possibly a

[1] Wilkins, *Concilia*, i, pp. 640–6; Lyndwood, *Provinciale*, p. 241; Myrc, *Instructions for Parish Priests*, p. 5. Lyndwood tried to confine baptism by the laity to such times as war, invasion or floods.

[2] Wilkins, *Concilia*, i, pp. 636, 639; cf. Myrc, *Instructions*, pp. 3–4.

[3] Myrc, *Instructions*, p. 4.

[4] Wilkins, *Concilia*, i, p. 576 and Myrc, *Instructions*, p. 4.

[5] Wilkins, *Concilia*, i, p. 650; ii, p. 2; *Regist. J. Pontissara*, pp. 207–8.

[6] Wilkins, *Concilia*, i, pp. 576, 636.

[7] *Ibid.* i, pp. 636, 656–7.

[8] *Regist. J. Romeyn*, i, p. 166.

short service in the church on the day of the bishop's arrival. Robert Manning describes Confirmation as a kind of charter whereby the bishop as overlord confirms what the priest has already done in baptism, but he expects those children who have been confirmed to have an added responsibility, as he calls them 'goddes champyons'.[1]

Marriages, on the other hand, were a source of endless problems and disputes. In the medieval Church many of the difficulties were due to the fact that Marriage, besides being a sacrament, was a legal contract which was often used for totally mundane purposes. As has been pointed out, the Church, in trying to codify and regularise the marriage laws, 'had to take account of Jewish tradition and ceremonial observances; of Roman law and the different types of marriage therein allowed; and of the tenacious Germanic customs varying in each tribal area....Outside and above all these was the Church's conception of marriage as a mystery, a symbol, a sacrament.'[2]

In the thirteenth century marriages among landed folk were generally arranged by the parents of the bride and bridegroom, often when their children were of very tender years and without any regard for the children's own wishes. Langland refers to this when he says:

For some, as I se now. soth for to telle,
For coueitise of catel . unkyndeliche ben wedded.[3]

Totally unsuitable unions were often arranged in this way, leading only to misery and perpetual discord.

It is an oncomely couple . bi Cryst, so me thinketh,
To ȝyven a ȝonge wenche . to an olde feble,
Or wedden any widwe . for welth of hir goodis,
That neuere shal barne bere . but if it be in armes!...
And though thei don hem to Donmowe . but if the deuel help
To folwen after the flicche . fecche thei it neuere....[4]

Young girls married to old men, boys to widows, children of four and five years of age espoused to grown-up men and women, simply in order to further the designs of ambitious

[1] *Handlyng Synne*, p. 307. For further information about Confirmations see below, pp. 195–6.
[2] A. L. Smith, *Church and State in the Middle Ages*, p. 61.
[3] *Piers Plowman*, B, ix, 154–5.
[4] *Ibid.* B, ix, 160–3, 168–9.

parents; all these aroused the indignation of sensible people.[1] Yet the initiative seems to have remained with the parents and guardians, or even with their agents,[2] the wishes of the young people themselves being regarded as of little importance.[3]

Once the marriage had been decided upon and the financial agreements concluded a ceremony took place known as the 'troth-plight' or, in later years, 'hand-fasting'. This appears to have taken the form of a solemn joining of hands, the giving and receiving of a ring, and the declaration of assent in words not unlike the formula in use at the present day. After this ceremony, if the ages of the parties permitted, the couple were bedded and the marriage was consummated.

So far the Church had played no part, and there was probably an interval between the troth-plight and the religious ceremony, an interval long enough for the bridegroom to know that his bride was capable of bearing children. Then and then only did the couple resort to church.[4] Here the ceremony was divided into two parts. The first took place at the church door, where, it will be remembered, the Wife of Bath, with all her faults, had most respectably married her five husbands. At the church door the priest enquired if there were any impediment to the intended marriage and the bridegroom stated the dower which he proposed to give his wife, at the same time making her an immediate gift of money together with a ring and a small sum to be distributed to the poor. Then came the declaration of assent, after which the priest led the bridal party into the church, where the nuptial Mass was celebrated. When the rite was concluded the couple were expected to provide a feast and could even be fined for not doing so.[5]

[1] *Handlyng Synne*, p. 60. Cf. Pollock and Maitland, *History of English Law*, ii, p. 392 and Coulton, *Medieval Panorama*, pp. 630–2.

[2] In B, xiv, 264–7 Piers Plowman says how much happier a woman is who can marry the man she loves instead of being 'maried thorw brokage'.

[3] G. C. Homans, *English Villagers of the Thirteenth Century*, pp. 160–2.

[4] I understand that in some country districts to-day it is quite usual for a young couple to postpone their marriage until the bride is known to be pregnant. Farmers whose families have lived for generations on the same farm are reluctant to run the risk of having no heir to succeed to the family acres.

[5] G. C. Homans, *English Villagers*, pp. 164–73. For the Church's struggle to make the religious aspect of marriage more important, see below, pp. 226–7.

The most intimate relationship between the priest and his people was in the sacrament of Penance. This was far more than a mere question of confession and absolution, for it was used as a thoroughgoing spiritual examination in faith and morals. The clergy were taught to probe into the most secret places of a man's life so that his confession might be full and nothing kept back from God. Some of the questions which he was told to put to the penitent were very searching. 'Have you ever borrowed things and not returned them?' 'Have you taught your children the Creed and the Lord's Prayer?' 'Hast þow wyþowte deuocyone I-herde any predycacyone?' 'If your children are "schrewes" have you tried to teach them good manners?' 'Have you ever ridden over growing corn?' 'Have you left the churchyard gate open so that beasts got in?' 'Hast þow ete wyth syche mayn, þat þow hast caste hyt vp a-gayn?'[1] This was indeed a searching cross-examination, from which no one could hope to emerge faultless. But not only was the penitent examined in morals; his faith and knowledge were also put to the test, especially upon the 'six points of belief' which, according to the *Lay Folks' Catechism*,

> Our fadir the Ercebisshop of his godenesse
> has ordayned and bidden that thai be shewed
> Openly on inglis o-monges the folk.[2]

This spiritual and intellectual examination must have taken so much time that it is not surprising that the laity were taught to confess only once a year in preparation for their Easter Communion.[3] Even so the burden on the parish priest must have been heavy, and it is no wonder that Pecham declared that if the clergy could not do all the work required of them in hearing confessions they were to summon good men to their aid.[4] Further, in order that there might be some continuity of advice and instruction the laity were taught to go to their own parish priest and to no one else,[5] a rule which was relaxed only in the case of wandering scholars, sailors, travellers and soldiers about to go into battle.[6]

[1] Myrc, *Instructions*, pp. 27–43.
[2] *Lay Folks' Catechism*, p. 22; cf. Myrc, *Instructions*, pp. 25–6.
[3] E.g. Wilkins, *Concilia*, i, p. 669; *Handlyng Synne*, p. 321.
[4] Pecham, *Reg. Epist.* iii, pp. 949–50.
[5] *Regist. J. Pontissara*, p. 209.
[6] Myrc, *Instructions*, p. 23.

Visitation of the Sick for the purposes of giving them their Communion and the administration of Extreme Unction where the patient was 'in periculo mortis' were strongly encouraged by the Church. Bishops commanded their clergy to be 'always alert and always prepared' to go when summoned,[1] and not to hesitate 'for reyne ne thonder'. Some bishops would not allow a parish priest to spend a single night away from his parish without leaving someone in charge in case of need.[2] The visit to the sick man, moreover, was to be carried out with dignity and reverence, the priest travelling along the country lanes or across the open fields clad in a surplice and preceded by his clerk carrying the cross and a lantern, and ringing the 'tintinabulum' which was regarded as one of the necessary ornaments of a church.[3]

'It is enough', said Bishop William of Blois in 1229, 'that the sick should receive the Body of the Lord once a week and unction once a year.'[4] The anointing of the sick, as practised in the Apostolic Church, was clearly intended to be a means of physical as well as spiritual health;[5] but it gradually came to be regarded more and more as a preparation for death. As such it was naturally associated, in the minds of the simple, with all kinds of superstition and terror. 'Many one', says Robert Manning,

> Many one þus hope and seye
> 'Anele hem[6] nat but þey shulde deye;
> For ȝyf he turne aȝen to lyfe
> He shulde lygge no more by hys wyfe'.

But this, he says, is nonsense. Everyone in sickness should seek the anointing with holy oil:

> Yn euery sykenes aske hyt al-weys;
> God almyȝty ys ryȝt curteys.[7]

Of Burials we know very little. Contemporary writers tell us little about them and there seem to have been no particular abuses demanding episcopal legislation or action. The Church

[1] 'Promptissimi sint et paratissimi, non solum diebus sed et noctibus' says Grosseteste (*Epistolae*, pp. 155–6).

[2] *Regist. J. Pontissara*, p. 209.

[3] Cf. Wilkins, *Concilia*, i, pp. 505, 579.

[4] *Ibid*. p. 623.

[5] *S. James*, v, 14–15.

[6] 'Anoint them.'

[7] *Handlyng Synne*, pp. 348–9.

honoured the dead, a funeral being not only one of the rare occasions upon which a priest was permitted to celebrate twice in one day, but also a solemn and dignified service. The dead were also remembered in the Sunday worship of the living. Largely under the influence of Franciscan preaching and practice, the Office of the Dead became more and more popular among the laity,[1] while each Mass was a commemoration of the dead, their names being read out to the congregation whose prayers were solicited.[2]

Thus from the cradle to the grave, and beyond it, the Church tried to keep in touch with the lives and souls of its members, to strengthen and sustain them, and to guide their feet so that they should not fall. Apart from what the Church offered, there was little to make life gracious or benign. Village life was often rough, and coarse, and brutal; but over it all lay the sweet influence of the Christian Church, which tried by ghostly counsel and by the recognised means of grace to set its members upon the 'strait and narrow way that leadeth unto life'.

[1] E. Bishop, *Liturgica Historica*, p. 233.

[2] Manning, *People's Faith*, p. 15.

CHAPTER VIII

THE EDUCATION OF THE CLERGY

Although the Church in this country has always tried to maintain a high standard of education among its clergy, the vast majority of those who served the parishes in the thirteenth century must have been only very partially instructed, while some were undoubtedly practically illiterate.

'The ignorance of priests', wrote Archbishop Pecham in 1281, 'casteth the people into the ditch of error',[1] for the clergy are like blind guides who will not seek for light where alone it may be found; and other scholars of the day were equally distressed and indignant at the very low standard of education among the clergy. Speaking of men who had risen to positions of eminence in the Church, Roger Bacon says: 'It makes no odds even if they do much studying, and read and argue and preach, and become even quite famous...for then they will only recite the words of others without knowing in the least what they mean, like parrots and magpies which utter human sounds without understanding what they are saying.' And he goes on to remark that just as choir-boys sing the Psalter which they have learnt by heart, so priests and country clergy (*sacerdotes rurales*) recite the divine offices, of which they understand little or nothing, like beasts.[2] Giraldus Cambrensis enjoyed himself enormously in collecting examples of clerical ignorance. He told with scorn of the parish priest who was unable to distinguish between Barnabas and Barabbas, and of another who bade his congregation honour the feast of S. Simon and S. Jude for the sake of the former only, since S. Jude was the man who betrayed Christ.[3] Another of his victims was a parish priest who asked the learned John of Cornwall who *Busillis* was. When John asked him in what Scripture this strange word was to be found, the man assured him that it occurred in the Missal and pointed out the words *in die* written at the foot of one column

[1] 'Ignorantia sacerdotum populum praecipitat in foveam erroris': Wilkins, *Concilia*, ii, p. 54.

[2] R. Bacon, *Compendium Studii*, cap. ii, in *Opera Ined.* p. 413.

[3] G. Cambrensis, *Opera*, ii, p. 341.

and *bus illis* at the top of the next.[1] When Robert Grosseteste delivered before the Pope at Lyons one of the most remarkable addresses which can ever have been made to the Vicar of Christ he referred to the ignorance of the clergy as one of the causes of decay and corruption in the Church.[2]

That, on the whole, the clergy of this country in the thirteenth century were only very partially educated allows of no contradiction. Episcopal Registers are full of examples of men who received benefices when almost totally illiterate, and strenuous efforts were made by the more conscientious diocesans to raise the standard of education. Grosseteste refused to institute a kinsman of John Blund, Chancellor of York, on the grounds that he was 'not sufficiently educated, not to say almost completely ignorant',[3] and, to prove his point, he enclosed, with his letter, the young man's examination papers. Another youth he turned down as being only 'in his Ovid',[4] while he complained that others had advanced no farther than their ABC.[5] Many of those who were inducted into livings he subsequently examined and re-examined year after year in order to ensure that some progress was made towards intellectual sufficiency.[6] The Viear of Cuddesdon was told that if he did not satisfy his examiners he would be deprived of his benefice, and a certain Reinotus, Rector of Alkerton, was found to be so ignorant, and so unfamiliar with the English language, that he was allowed to take only a small portion of the fruits of his living while another man was inducted as vicar.[7]

Grosseteste's predecessor, Hugh of Welles, had been equally severe. Many of his clergy he would only admit on condition that they continued their education,[8] and some he refused to

[1] Another man, having read that Herod killed all the children 'a bimatu et infra' supposed 'bimatu' to be the name of a district: G. Cambrensis, *Opera*, ii, p. 343. These examples are from the *Gemma Ecclesiastica* written in 1199.

[2] *Fasc. Rerum Expetendarum*, ii, p. 252.

[3] 'Insufficienter literatus, ne dicam fere omnino illiteratus': Grosseteste, *Epistolae*, p. 68.

[4] *Ibid*. p. 63.

[5] *Fasc. Rerum Expetendarum*, ii, p. 402; 'pueri abcdarii' is the phrase he uses.

[6] *Rot. R. Grosseteste*, pp. 36, 77, 151, 402.

[7] *Ibid*. pp. 463–4, 499–500.

[8] *Rot. H. de Welles*, i, pp. 7, 8, 13, 15, 16 (*bis*), 18, etc.; ii, pp. 8, 9, 32, 48, etc.

institute on account of their ignorance.[1] At Winchester the archdeacons were instructed to find out which of their clergy did not know the Ten Commandments, the Seven Sacraments and the Seven Deadly Sins together with the elements of the Christian Faith. The clergy were to be examined also to see whether they were capable of expounding these things in the vulgar tongue.[2] Walter de Kirkham had issued similar instructions for the diocese of Durham in 1255;[3] and in 1287 Peter Quivil of Exeter ordered his archdeacons to search out all who were woefully ignorant and suspend them from office. He also desired each incumbent or parish priest to provide himself with a written *summula*, or primer of the Christian Faith, which he was to learn by heart, under penalty of being fined six-and-eightpence.[4]

Some idea both of the education and of the character of the clergy is given by the record of a visitation of the parish of Sonning in Berkshire by William de Wanda, Dean of Salisbury in 1220. The parish contained a number of chapels, served by a miscellaneous collection of men, none of whom had much pretension to scholarship. Each in turn was examined by the dean, but only one of the seven was approved. The first was a man called Simon de Manston who was in charge of the chapel at Sindlesham, though he seldom ministered there. He said that he had been ordained subdeacon and deacon at Oxford by a certain Irish bishop called Albinus. He had received ordination as priest from Bishop Hugh of Lincoln in 1216. The dean examined him on the Gospel for the First Sunday in Advent, but he was found to be unable to understand what he was reading. So he was asked to construe the opening sentence of the Canon of the Mass: *Te, igitur, clementissime Pater, etc.*, but even this was too much for him. He could not say what case *Te* was, nor by what it was governed. 'And when he was told to look carefully and say what word could best govern *Te*, he replied "*Pater*, for the Father governeth all things".' He was then asked: Could he give any meaning to the word

[1] *Rot. H. de Welles*, i, p. 101.

[2] *Regist. J. Pontissara*, pp. 215–17. Simon of Ghent instituted a man as Rector of Winterborne Stickland (Dorset) on condition that he should provide himself with a chaplain to teach him the English language: *Regist. S. Gandavo*, ii, pp. 799–800.

[3] Wilkins, *Concilia*, i, p. 704. [4] *Ibid.* ii, p. 144.

clementissime? Could he say any of the antiphons? Did he know any part of the Divine Office, or of the psalms by heart? To each he answered 'No', protesting that the dean had no right to examine a man who was already ordained! Asked on what he had been examined when he was ordained priest he said that he could not remember. At this the dean dismissed him and wrote sadly against his name: '*Sufficienter illiteratus est*' ('He is ignorant enough').

The next man to be examined was a young chaplain at Hurst. He proved to be not only dismally ignorant but sullen and resentful, and observed a stubborn silence when questions were put to him. The same thing happened with some of the others, and it was at length discovered that they had made a conspiracy outside that they would not answer the questions put to them. So the dean was obliged to suspend some of them from office and to write them off as illiterate and insubordinate.[1]

There is no need, therefore, to search very long in order to find evidence of clerical ignorance in the thirteenth century; but it should be borne in mind that many of those who complained of it were scholars of international reputation, who were horrified to find men in positions of responsibility and leadership who were unable to construe the simplest Latin. To the uneducated, however, the clergy may have appeared in quite a different light. When the Dean and Chapter of Exeter visited a number of parishes in Devon in 1301, the laymen whom they interrogated gave almost universal testimony to the sufficiency of their clergy as preachers and teachers. It is true that the Vicar of Colyton did not satisfy them as a preacher, but the Vicar of Dawlish was regarded as an excellent teacher of spiritual things, as were also the Vicars of Sidbury S. Mary Church, and Staverton.[2] It was really a question of two quite different points of view: the scholar with his standard and the layman with his. Many of the clergy were drawn from the peasant or yeoman class and were men who had had little opportunity of education beyond what they could pick up from some sympathetic but probably ill-educated parish priest. They could stumble through the words of the Mass or of the Baptism Service, and they could

[1] W. H. R. Jones, *Reg. S. Osmundi*, i, pp. 304–6.

[2] *Regist. W. Stapeldon*, ed. Hingeston-Randolph, pp. 111, 133, 337, 368 and 378. Cf. Coulton, *Social Life in Britain from the Conquest to the Reformation*, pp. 260–3.

give some simple instruction in the elements of the Christian faith; but if deans and canons and other clever men came down and asked them to construe sentences or parse words they were immediately out of their depth. Then it was that they became sullen, and either made a conspiracy of passive resistance or were inevitably marked down as 'almost completely illiterate' (*fere omnino illiteratus*).

Giraldus Cambrensis might laugh, and Pecham and Grosseteste groan, at the illiteracy of the parish clergy, but it is only fair to remember that the facilities for receiving any sort of education were very meagre. Oxford and Cambridge were beginning to make their influence felt,[1] but they could affect only a small proportion of the many thousands of men who served the parishes. In the thirteenth century the number of incumbents who possessed University degrees was small, but it was growing. For example, in the diocese of Lincoln the proportion of 'masters' increased steadily as years went by. In the archdeaconry of Stow, Hugh of Welles (1209–35) instituted 86 men of whom 8 were *magistri*, a proportion of 9 per cent. In the same archdeaconry Grosseteste (1235–53) instituted 13 masters out of 85 men (about 16 per cent), and Gravesend (1258–79) raised the percentage to 21 (16 masters out of 76 appointments). In the archdeaconry of Oxford the proportion of masters was naturally rather higher. Welles instituted in this archdeaconry 18 graduates out of 149 men (12 per cent); Grosseteste 32 out of 191 (17 per cent) and Gravesend 42 out of 199 (21 per cent).[2]

Farther west, in the diocese of Hereford, things were not so good. Of 99 men ordained by Thomas Cantilupe at Leominster in 1277 only 2 had degrees, while at the following ordinations there were no graduates at all, though 275 men were ordained. On the other hand, when Cantilupe conducted an ordination at Tottenham on behalf of the Bishop of London in 1278 he had 7 masters out of 21 candidates.[3] In the diocese of Worcester the ordinations carried out by Godfrey Giffard appear to have included only 12 graduates out of over 5000 ordinands.[4] No

[1] The date usually given for the foundation of the University of Oxford is 1167, for Cambridge 1209 (Rashdall, *Medieval Universities* (new ed.), iii, pp. 15 and 277–8).

[2] Cf. *Rot. H. de Welles*, *Rot. R. Grosseteste* and *Rot. R. Gravesend*, *passim*.

[3] *Regist. T. Cantilupe*, pp. 299–312.

[4] *Regist. G. Giffard*, *passim*.

doubt some of these ordination candidates proceeded afterwards to the University, but it is unlikely that in these two dioceses the proportion of graduates was ever very high in the thirteenth century. The higher percentages in the diocese of Lincoln were due partly to the fact that the University of Oxford was situated within its borders, and partly to the succession of strenuous bishops who laboured to keep up a high standard among their clergy.

At the same time it is well to remember that though the possession of a University degree was assuredly a sign of some education, it did not guarantee any training in religious knowledge. The title of 'Master' was granted to those who had taken the standard 'arts' course.[1] This was divided into the *Trivium* (grammar, rhetoric and dialectic) and the *Quadrivium* (arithmetic, astronomy, music and geometry) and took seven years to complete. Students began by attending daily lectures by the regent masters, after two years of which they were obliged to join in the exercises or discussions with senior men. By the end of four years they were expected to be familiar with the standard text-books of Boethius, Priscian and Donatus besides some of the classical authors (mainly Cicero and Virgil) and a good deal of Aristotle. During the next three years they studied natural science and mathematics, and, besides taking part in daily disputations, delivered a number of lectures upon some book of Aristotle.[2] Most scholars came up to the University at about the age of fourteen,[3] and therefore 'incepted' about the time at which they reached manhood. Theology was a post-graduate course which was taken by only a few students and those principally men who intended to devote their lives to higher education. Thus, in spite of the close connection between the Church and the Universities, the average undergraduate received only a 'general education', which included no specifically religious or theological instruction beyond what he might pick up from attending University Sermons and the daily offices in church.[4]

[1] Rashdall, *Medieval Universities* (new ed.), i, p. 19. Note that the titles 'Master', 'Doctor' and 'Professor' were synonymous.

[2] For a full account of the Arts course see *Statuta Antiqua Vniversitatis Oxoniensis*, ed. Strickland Gibson (1931), pp. lxxxviii–cii.

[3] Rashdall, *Medieval Universities* (new ed.), iii, p. 352.

[4] *Ibid.* iii, pp. 450–1; M. Deanesly, *The Lollard Bible*, pp. 162–74.

Those among the clergy, then, who were graduates might be regarded as educated men; but they were not theologians. On the other hand, a number of incumbents were sent to the Universities for a few years not to read the usual 'arts' course but to study such subjects as would enable them to serve more efficiently in the parishes. Among the many licences which were granted to men who wished to leave their parishes for a time 'to frequent the schools' we find that some went to read theology,[1] some Canon Law,[2] while a few made the Bible the special object of their studies.[3]

The study of theology was by no means so common in the Middle Ages as is often supposed. Until well into the fourteenth century there were only three Universities in Europe which had theological faculties, Paris, Oxford and Cambridge.[4] The course of study for a theological degree was a formidable affair, lasting some sixteen or seventeen years and demanding lecturing as well as disputations and examinations.[5] The groundwork of theological study was the Bible, with which was closely associated the *Sentences* of Peter Lombard. 'It is the object of the "Sententiae"', says Dr Rashdall, 'to collect and harmonise the opinions of the Fathers upon every point of Christian theology, and to extract from their scattered and sometimes conflicting *dicta* a precise and explicit answer to every question which the dialectical activity of the age had suggested.'[6] In addition to the study of the Bible and the Sentences there was some effort made to use the *Historia Scholastica* of Peter Comestor as a textbook of theology, but this appears to have been abandoned about the middle of the thirteenth century.[7] The theological student, then, having first taken the arts course, and having subsequently studied arts and philosophy for a further seven

[1] E.g. *Regist. T. Cantilupe*, p. 29; *Regist. G. Giffard*, p. 54; Pecham, *Reg. Epist.* ii, p. 688.

[2] *Regist. T. Cantilupe*, p. 29; Pecham, *Reg. Epist.* ii, p. 688.

[3] Cf. 'in sacra pagina', *Regist. J. Pontissara*, p. 108; 'in sacra scriptura et canonibus', *Rot. H. de Welles*, i, p. 39.

[4] Rashdall, *Medieval Universities* (new ed.), ii, p. 167.

[5] For an admirable description of the Theological School at Oxford see Dr A. G. Little's article *The Franciscan School at Oxford in the Thirteenth Century*, in *Arch. Franc. Hist.* 1926, and reprinted the same year by the Quaracchi fathers; also Little and Pelster, *Oxford Theology and Theologians*.

[6] Rashdall, *Medieval Universities* (new ed.), i, p. 60.

[7] Little in *Arch. Franc. Hist.* (1926), p. 823, n. 3, quoting Roger Bacon in *Opera Ined.* p. 329.

years, underwent the ceremonies of 'opponency' and 'responsions' and was then allowed to lecture on the Bible and the Sentences until such time as he was qualified to take his 'vesperies' and 'inception'.[1]

This long and exacting course was meant only for such as intended to devote their lives to an academic career. Those who came from the parishes for a year or two to study theology can have done little more than attend a few of the more elementary lectures, without any intention of proceeding to a theological degree.

If a faculty of theology was comparatively rare in the thirteenth century, that of Canon Law was the most common of all, for every University in Europe possessed such a school.[2] The study of Canon Law was one of the gateways to preferment, for none could rise to high administrative office in the Church without some legal qualifications. In the thirteenth century the student of Canon Law devoted most of his time to a study of the *Decretum* of Gratian which had been published in 1143 and occupied, in the faculty of Canon Law, much the same position as the Bible and the Sentences occupied in the study of theology.[3] Canon Law, like theology, was a post-graduate course which demanded several years both of residence and of study; and, once more, we must assume that by far the majority of the beneficed clergy who left their parishes in order to read Canon Law in the schools did no more than attend a few of the more simple lectures.

Those who were sent from the parishes to read theology and what was called 'the sacred page' would devote most of their time to attendance at lectures on the Bible. The whole question of the medieval attitude to the Scriptures has been much misunderstood.[4] Those who seem to think that true religion in this country only began with the reforms of the sixteenth century lay great stress on the importance of what they call the 'open Bible'. The belief which they appear to hold is that, until the

[1] 'Vesperies' meant a disputation on some theological question or questions: 'inception' was the student's formal acceptance by the chancellor and proctors: Little, *Arch. Franc. Hist.* (1926), pp. 826–8.

[2] Rashdall, *Medieval Universities* (new ed.), i, p. 139.

[3] *Ibid.* i, pp. 130–4.

[4] Miss Margaret Deanesly's study, *The Lollard Bible* (1920), did much to rescue this subject from the fog of prejudice and misrepresentation. See also the latest contribution to the subject, Miss Beryl Smalley's *The Study of the Bible in the Middle Ages* (1941).

time when Henry VIII ordered that a copy of the Great Bible in English should be placed in every parish church, the Bible was regarded as the monopoly of the priesthood, who tried to prevent honest and God-fearing laymen from reading it. It is, of course, perfectly true that the Bible was not much read by the laity or by the inferior clergy of the Middle Ages, but the reason was not so much obscurantism on the part of the Church as the fact that so few of the laity could read, and that, even for those who could, a Bible was so costly that only the wealthiest of them could afford to buy one. The men who should be thanked for putting the Bible in the hands of the laity are not the reformers but the early printers, for it was only as a result of their discoveries that Bibles could be produced at a figure within the means of the public.

'The Vulgate was so valuable a book', says Miss Deanesly, 'that few individuals except bishops possessed it before 1300.'[1] With modern methods of printing and producing books we do not always realise what a very large book the Bible is, nor how costly would be its production were it not certain of an enormous sale. The Authorised Version (including the Apocrypha) contains just under a million words, which is about six times as much as the present volume. In manuscript it would occupy many hundreds of leaves even if inscribed in the smallest of hands.[2] The labour of writing out so big a work would be enormous, and it is therefore no wonder that Bibles fetched high prices. Archbishop Pecham refers in one of his letters to a Bible which his predecessor had had made at a cost of 113 marks, which would be the equivalent of many hundreds of pounds in modern currency.[3] Richard Gravesend, Bishop of London, had three Bibles—one a 'Little Bible' valued at £1, one at £4, and one in thirteen volumes at £10.[4] The average

[1] *The Lollard Bible*, p. 186.

[2] The Vulgate of course contains fewer words than an English version, and the medieval habit of contracting words, so that sometimes only a single letter was left, helped to reduce the labour of the scribes. But, even so, the copying of a whole Bible must have been a very laborious process.

[3] Pecham, *Reg. Epist.* ii, p. 542. Either this or another Bible which he possessed found its way into the library of S. Augustine's, Canterbury: M. R. James, *Ancient Libraries of Canterbury and Dover*, p. 198 (No. 33).

[4] *Philobiblon Society Miscellanies*, ii. The 'Little Bible' became very popular in the thirteenth century. Scribes vied with one another to see

price of even the cheapest Bibles, then, must have been something like £50 in modern money. If these prices obtained to-day, what proportion of the clergy or of the laity would be able or willing to pay them?[1]

Another criticism made about the medieval Church is that whereas the clergy read certain parts of the Bible with great frequency, there were large tracts with which they were quite unfamiliar. This, surely, would be no bad thing so long as the parts which they read were the right ones. Not every chapter of the Bible is of equal interest or significance, and there are whole books which, in point of fact, are very little read to this day, except by those whose Bible-reading is based on the plan that you begin at the beginning and having read straight through to the end, you turn back to the first chapter of Genesis and repeat the process. Any rational system of Bible-reading is bound to be selective: the important thing is that the selection should be well made. The selection with which the medieval priest was familiar was that which formed the framework of the liturgical books. The difference between this method of Bible study and that of modern times is that in the Middle Ages the Scriptures were regarded as a storehouse from which passages might be taken in order to enhance the worship of the Church, whereas in our own days Bible-reading is more commonly regarded as in itself a means of grace, a meeting-place of God and man.

into how small a compass the Bible could be packed, while a new kind of vellum was specially manufactured for the purpose, 'of astonishing thinness, often of the texture of modern India-paper'; see E. G. Millar, *English Illuminated MSS., tenth to thirteenth century*, pp. 51–2.

[1] This, of course, would apply to all books, and makes it unlikely that any of the clergy would possess many of their own. I know of only one contemporary book-list of the library of a parish priest. This belonged to Geoffrey de Lawath, Rector of the church of S. Magnus in London, a list of whose books is contained at the end of a *Liber Decretorum* now in the library of Pembroke College, Cambridge. There are forty-nine books altogether, mostly on theology, grammar or dialectic, though there are also three medical treatises. See M. R. James, *Catalogue of MSS. in Pembroke College Library*, p. 158. In the *Rolls for Justices in Eyre for Lincolnshire, 1218–19, and Worcestershire, 1221* (Selden Society, liii, 1934), p. 574, there is an account of how the men who farmed the toll at Wychbold took and detained for six weeks two carts which were carrying the books of Richard, rural dean of Worcester, so that he suffered loss to the value of 100*s*. I am indebted to Professor Powicke for this reference.

The almost prohibitive price of Bibles in the thirteenth century, combined with this difference of attitude towards the purpose of Bible-reading, certainly caused much less sustained study of the Scriptures than has been common in later centuries. At the same time it would be entirely false to suppose that the Bible was in any sense ignored, or that people as a whole were ignorant of its contents. Miss Deanesly has examined very closely the question of Bible-reading by clergy and laity before the days of Wycliff.[1] It is unnecessary, therefore, to go over the ground again, but there are certain points not mentioned in her chapters which contribute something towards the solution of the problem.

That the leading scholars were familiar with the actual text of the Vulgate is a fact well known to historians.[2] It is perhaps not always sufficiently realised how profound that knowledge was. For example, in the 131 letters from Bishop Grosseteste which have been preserved there are actually 565 Biblical quotations, an average of over four texts to each epistle. Moreover these quotations are drawn from practically every book in the Bible, showing that the writer must have had as close a familiarity with the Scriptures as the most devout of bibliolaters in recent years. Grosseteste was, of course, a very brilliant man, from whom we should expect striking evidence. But if we turn to a much lesser man, Godfrey Giffard, Bishop of Worcester, we find that his knowledge of the Bible was by no means confined to the great passages with which Christians have always been familiar, for in the course of his visitations he preached on texts drawn from sixteen books of the Old Testament and eleven of the New.

In the Constitutions of Walter Cantilupe, Bishop of Worcester, issued in 1240, there is a paragraph devoted to Bible-reading. The Bishop draws up a lectionary, most carefully devised to correspond with the ideas suggested by the Church's year. Thus, Septuagesima signifies the Captivity of Babylon and our own captivity in the world from which we hope to escape to the heavenly Jerusalem. At this season we should therefore read of the cause of our captivity—the story of the fall of Adam and the exile of Abraham. From Passion Sunday to Easter the

[1] *The Lollard Bible*, pp. 156–224.

[2] Gasquet, *English Biblical Criticism in the Thirteenth Century*, in *Dublin Review*, 1898, pp. 1–21.

Book of Jeremiah is recommended, since in his lamentations he foreshadows the sufferings of Christ. For three weeks after Easter the Apocalypse is chosen because of its references to the Lamb that had been slain. From then until Ascension Day the reader should turn to the Epistles, since they preach Christ and His Passion; and from the Ascension to Whitsuntide the Acts of the Apostles are to be read. Between Whitsunday and August 1st readings are suggested from the Books of Kings, since the battles of Saul against the Philistines and David against Goliath signify our struggles against vice and demons after our admission into the Church. In August the Book of Wisdom shall be read because August is the middle of the year and in the middle period of our life we ought to seek Wisdom above all things. In September we think of patience in sufferings, since towards the close of our lives we often need such patience. Job, Tobit, Esdras, Esther and Judith are the books recommended for this period. The month of October is apparently associated with the joy of the Resurrection, and the reader is directed to Maccabees, since in these stories the Jews praised God for the resurrection of their national life. From November 1st to Advent Ezekiel and Daniel are especially recommended because of the accounts of their visions of the future, and in Advent Isaiah is to be studied because of his references to the coming of Christ. Presumably the lessons from Christmas to Septuagesima were to be taken from the Gospels, though this is not actually stated.[1] Anyone who followed this lectionary conscientiously would become familiar with a very large part of the Bible; but how many of the clergy possessed the necessary text or the ability to read and understand it is a matter upon which these Constitutions throw no light.

There is reason, then, to suppose that knowledge of the Bible was in fact more widespread, even in the thirteenth century, than is commonly supposed. That even the laity were accustomed to read their Bibles in the days of Chaucer is suggested by the description in the *Canterbury Tales* of the 'doctour of phisik', of whom it is written that though he read his medical text-books with diligence 'his studie was but litel on the Bible'.[2] This could only have been said if Bible-reading were regarded as the normal practice of the educated laity. Moreover the Church did its best, by preaching and by art, to acquaint even its most humble

[1] Wilkins, *Concilia*, i, p. 677.

[2] *Canterbury Tales*, *Prologue*, l. 328.

members with the more picturesque of the Bible stories.[1] Their ideas were no doubt often muddled, and much of their knowledge of the Bible was confused with apocryphal and legendary stories,[2] but it is questionable whether the average peasant or artisan of the thirteenth century was actually any less familiar with the Bible narratives than his descendant of the present day.[3]

The difference between those clergy who were graduates and those who were not was not a difference in theological or biblical knowledge but in the level of general education and culture which they had reached. The graduate should, after seven years of study, have been able to read and write Latin with some fluency; the non-graduate would have had to scrape together such education as he could. If the records of illiteracy and ignorance which we possess are typical of the clergy as a whole, then the standards demanded by bishops of their ordinands must have been very low. Perhaps this was inevitable, for the facilities for even primary education were not very great, especially for boys living in small villages and hamlets at some distance from the centres of population.

The renaissance of learning in the twelfth century and the rise of the universities had led to a good deal of educational activity in this country. Most towns of any size could boast of a school of sorts, and the schoolmaster was coming to be

[1] Professor Tristram has shown us that the walls of most of the parish churches in England were covered from floor to ceiling with pictures of Biblical and other scenes.

[2] The same is true to-day. If anyone were to ask what animals were present in the stable where Christ was born, nine people out of ten would reply 'ox and ass', though there is nothing in the Bible to say so. They would also be quite sure that three kings came to worship, though again there is nothing in the canonical Gospels to say that the magi were kings, or that there were three of them. Adam's 'apple' and Moses 'in the bulrushes' (which ought to be flags) are also examples of the mixture of legend with the word of the Bible itself.

[3] This statement will, no doubt, be challenged. It rests upon two suppositions; one that knowledge of the Bible stories was more general in the thirteenth century than is sometimes imagined; the other that knowledge of the Bible is extremely limited at the present day. Only an historian can test the first, and only someone who has worked for some time as a parish priest can test the second. The experience of those who have worked in parishes in recent years is that a great many people have only the very slightest acquaintance with the Bible, while a generation is growing up containing a certain number who are ignorant of even the most familiar passages.

recognised as an officer of some standing. The most important schools were the grammar schools attached to the cathedral and collegiate churches, some of which could trace their existence back through many years. Mr Leach has assured us that 'there can be no doubt that all the cathedral and collegiate churches kept schools, and that the schoolmaster was one of the most important of their officers and school-teaching one of the most important of their functions'.[1] These grammar schools were under the jurisdiction of the chancellor, who is sometimes known by the alternative title of schoolmaster. The purpose of these schools was to give boys enough education to qualify for ordination or to enable them to take the entrance examinations demanded by the Universities.[2] Little or no attempt was made to give any 'general education', since the only knowledge necessary for either of these tests was a certain degree of familiarity with Latin. The priest was expected to be able to read his Bible and service books and to write reasonably good prose, and the student at the University was obliged to understand Latin in order to follow the discourses of his lecturers.[3]

Besides these grammar schools attached to secular churches there were a good many owned by the monastic houses and supported by them. It now seems clear that the monks themselves did not, as a rule, teach in these schools (which were generally outside the precincts of the monastery), but employed secular clerks as schoolmasters.[4] Many of these schools had originally belonged to secular bodies but were handed over to the regulars at a time when the religious houses were gradually getting more and more control over various public services.[5] Certainly a good many schools in England, as at Canterbury, Bury S. Edmunds, S. Albans, Reading and Dunstable, were organised in this way. At Bicester the schools belonging to the priory were lodged in a tenement in School Street which was hired

[1] Leach, *Schools of Medieval England*, p. 115; and cf. *Early Yorkshire Schools*, i, p. xxi.

[2] Rashdall, *Medieval Universities* (new ed.), iii, pp. 341–2, 351–2.

[3] Cf. *Education in the Fourteenth and Fifteenth Centuries* by G. R. Potter in *Camb. Med. Hist.* viii, p. 692.

[4] Butler, *Benedictine Monachism*, p. 325; Coulton, *Five Centuries*, i, pp. 200 n. and 252, and cf. his *Medieval Studies*, No. x.

[5] Leach, *Schools of Medieval England*, p. 120. It is unfortunate that Mr Leach's admirable work of research into the history of English schools is marred by prejudice against the regulars.

from Osney Abbey,[1] and at Dover in 1284 a school was being supported by the monks, who were obliged to keep a master.[2] These schools must not be confused with the novices' schools, which catered for lads destined for the cloister, for they clearly opened their doors to all. John Pecham in a letter to the Abbot of Cluny in 1285 suggests that he was educated at Lewes either by the monks of that place or in a school supported by them,[3] while about the same time Archbishop Wickwayn wrote to the Augustinian canons of Guisborough about their school, forbidding them to make distinctions between rich scholars and poor.[4] Other monasteries were expected to support boys at the local grammar schools, for in 1180 Simon of Farlington presented a manor to the Priory of Durham for the maintenance of three scholars at Durham School,[5] while the Prior of the dependent cell of Finchale was expected to feed and clothe a boy and send him to the same school for six or even ten years.[6] It appears, then, that though the monks may have taken little part in popular educational movements during the thirteenth century they were not entirely inactive.

In addition to the schools attached to the cathedrals there were in many places smaller parish schools. In the year 1200 the Council of Westminster passed the following decree: 'that priests shall keep schools in the towns and teach the little boys free of charge. Priests ought to hold schools in their houses, and if any devout person wishes to entrust his little ones to them for instruction they should receive them willingly and teach them kindly. They ought not to expect anything from the relatives of the boys except what they are willing to give.'[7] Twenty-

[1] Kennett, *Parochial Antiquities* (1818), i, p. 301.

[2] C. R. Haines, *Dover Priory*, pp. 350–1.

[3] Pecham, *Reg. Epist.* iii, p. 902. Such has been the usual interpretation of Pecham's reference to Lewes. Dom David Knowles has, however, pointed out that Pecham does not definitely say that he was educated at Lewes, which Knowles considers 'unlikely': *E.H.R.* 1942, p. 3 n.

[4] Brown, *Guisborough Chartulary*, ii, pp. 360–2.

[5] Leach, *Medieval Schools*, p. 135. [6] Raine, *Priory of Finchale*, p. 29.

[7] Wilkins, *Concilia*, i, p. 508; Leach, *Educational Charters*, pp. 138 ff. This decree only repeats what had always been aimed at since the eighth century: Coulton, *Medieval Panorama*, p. 386. A decretal of Gregory IX orders each priest to provide himself with a clerk who shall teach the boys in the parish: *Decret. Greg. IX*, lib. III, tit. i, c. 3. How far this was ever carried out is very uncertain: Rashdall, *Medieval Universities* (new ed.), iii, p. 350.

three years later the Bishop of Salisbury gave his support to such schools by endowing schoolmasters with benefices in order that the boys might be educated free of charge.[1] How far these injunctions were observed it is hard to say, but there are occasional references to parochial schools in the documents which have been preserved, which show that they were playing a definite part in the life of the community under the protection and with the support of the bishops. In 1276 Archbishop Walter Giffard was paying two shillings a week to three schoolmasters at Beverley, and a few years later we find Archbishop Romeyn issuing a decree to prevent anyone holding a school at Kinoulton except the parish clergy.[2]

Since the 'novices' schools' in the monasteries were designed only for 'oblates', that is, boys destined to be professed as monks, the only other type of school for those preparing for ordination was the song or choir school attached to the cathedrals and larger parish churches.[3] Just as the organisation of the grammar schools was under the supervision of the chancellor, so that of the choir schools was the responsibility of the precentor.[4] Although these schools were primarily concerned with providing choristers they were obliged also to give some general education, and some at any rate of the parish clergy may have received the rudiments of knowledge in this way.[5]

Such were the educational facilities which were offered for boys who aspired to the ministry. With schools established in all the larger towns and even in some of the villages, it might seem that there was little excuse for the low standards of education which prevailed among the clergy. Yet the opportunities for lads to take advantage of these facilities were not so great as they might appear at first sight. If a boy lived in a town of any considerable size, or where there was a large

[1] Constitutions of Richard le Poore in Wilkins, *Concilia*, i, p. 600.

[2] *Regist. W. Giffard*, p. 272; *Regist. J. Romeyn*, i, p. 285.

[3] The schools in the monasteries had largely disappeared by the thirteenth century owing to the dying out of the practice of putting quite young children in the cloister. See below, pp. 261–2.

[4] Leach, *Medieval Schools*, pp. 158, 214 ff. See also Sydney Nicholson, *Quires and Places where they sing*, pp. 24–7.

[5] 'Small and often ephemeral institutions that have left few records of importance, the song schools none the less accounted for most of the education that many humble folk in the Middle Ages ever received' (G. R. Potter in *Camb. Med. Hist.* viii, p. 689).

church or a cathedral, he would be able to go to the schools, if necessary free of charge. But if he lived in the country—and the names of the clergy show that most of them came from tiny villages—opportunities for going to school must have been small. Younger sons of the manorial family might be sent to the local grammar school, or they might receive some instruction through living as pages in the household of some nobleman or bishop, but the struggle for existence in which most of the village community were engaged occupied every member of the poorer families from earliest years. Nowadays a village boy who shows signs of awakening intelligence is taken by 'bus to a central school where he will, if necessary, be given free meals in addition to free education, so anxious are we to encourage those who have talents to use them. But in the thirteenth century any village which was more than a mile or two from a town was almost completely isolated, and no child from such a place could hope to reach any school, apart from the difficulty of any pair of hands, however small, being spared from the labour of the fields and the home.

We must assume, therefore, that many of those who came up to the bishops for ordination, and who subsequently found their way into the parishes, were men who had had no opportunity of being educated beyond what they could pick up from some sympathetic priest. The clergy of England have always been associated with the instruction of children, and many parish priests would be willing to help a boy who felt that he had a call to the ministry and lacked only the necessary qualifications of learning to enable him to achieve his ambition. Such a system would not make for a high standard of education among the clergy, for many of those who sought to give the instruction may have been themselves but poor scholars; but at least it would help to fill the gaps in the educational system of the day. And when all is said and done, although it is right and proper that the clergy should be educated men, the scholar does not always make the best parish priest, nor is intellect to be identified with intelligence. Giraldus Cambrensis tells of one parish priest who was unable to distinguish between the Latin for 50 and for 500 in the parable of the two debtors.[1] When his examiner remarked that, if the sums were identical, there was

[1] *S. Luke*, vii, 41.

no point in the story, the man replied that in one case the coins were Angevin and in the other sterling.[1] If this story is true, it shows that what some men lacked in knowledge they made up in wit and intelligence.[2]

Nowadays it is too readily assumed that once a man has reached the standard of education necessary for entry into the trade or profession of his choice there is no need for him to advance any further. In the thirteenth century efforts were made to provide what we should call 'refresher courses' for those who had already been ordained and instituted but who realised that they had still much to learn. Reference has already been made to the comparatively large number of men who were given leave of absence from their parishes to attend the schools and universities for varying periods to study either the customary arts course, or to read theology or Canon Law. Opportunities were also afforded for those who were unable to proceed to the schools by the establishment of lectureships at the cathedrals.

The Lateran Council of 1179 passed a decree that every cathedral church should provide a master with a benefice that he might teach the clerks of the church and other poor persons free of charge.[3] Thirty-six years later the Fourth Lateran Council repeated this, extending the order beyond the cathedrals to all other churches of sufficient means. The master was to be elected by the Prelate or Chapter and the income of a prebend was to be assigned to him. In every metropolitan church a theologian besides a grammarian was to be elected, and the theologian was to lecture to priests and others on the Scriptures.[4] That the chancellor was primarily a teacher is clear from the fact that up to about the year 1200 the titles 'chancellor' and 'schoolmaster' are interchangeable,[5] while there is evidence that each of the secular cathedrals in England maintained a school of theology presided over by the chancellor

[1] G. Cambrensis, *Opera*, ii, p. 343.

[2] The same might be said of the priest at Sonning who, on being asked what governed 'Te', replied 'Pater, quia omnia regit': W. H. R. Jones, *Reg. S. Osmundi*, i, pp. 304–6.

[3] Mansi, *Concilia*, xxii, col. 227; Leach, *Educational Charters*, pp. 122–3.

[4] Mansi, *Concilia*, xxii, cols. 986, 999; Leach, *Educational Charters*, pp. 142–3; Little, *Studies in English Franciscan History*, pp. 158–9.

[5] Leach, *Early Yorkshire Schools*, i, p. xx; *Schools of Medieval England*, p. 107.

himself.[1] But it is doubtful how far these schools actually functioned. Giraldus Cambrensis tells of William de Monte lecturing at Lincoln about 1200, and in 1293 John le Romeyn writes to his official telling him not to molest, on grounds of non-residence, those who were attending the theological lectures given by the Chancellor of York;[2] but Dr Little points out that 'most of the references to chancellors in this connection after the middle of the thirteenth century are usually concerned with dispensations from or neglect of their duties as teachers'.[3] Whether the practice fell into desuetude through the indolence of the chancellors or through the reluctance of the clergy to take advantage of this means of improving their education there is no saying. Had the courses been wisely planned to meet the requirements of the clergy some good might have come out of them, but it is unlikely that many of the country clergy would have had either the opportunity or the inclination to travel to the cathedral city for such a purpose.

The thirteenth century also produced a new type of school for those who wished to pursue their studies a little further, namely the 'friary school'. Roger Bacon's boast that these schools sprang up 'in every city, castle and borough'[4] is probably an exaggeration born of pride in this new venture sponsored by the order to which he himself belonged. Nevertheless, these schools became an important part of the educational system of the country, for though they were primarily intended for the friars themselves there is good reason to suppose that they were also frequented by some of the secular clergy who were glad of this opportunity of acquiring some education without the necessity of attending a University course.[5]

[1] Leach, *Schools of Medieval England*, pp. 158 ff., where the dates of the foundations are given; cf. A. G. Little, *Theological Schools in Medieval England*, in *E.H.R.* 1940, pp. 624–30.

[2] *Regist. J. Romeyn*, i, p. 36; Raine, *Historians of York*, iii, p. 220.

[3] Little, *Studies in English Franciscan History*, p. 160, n. 4. Cf. article on Simon of Ghent in *D.N.B.* and see Gibbs and Lang, *Bishops and Reform*, pp. 154–6. Cf. also *Regist. S. Gandavo*, i, pp. 41–2.

[4] R. Bacon, *Opera Ined.* p. 398.

[5] Dr Little points out that 'evidence of individual seculars attending courses in the friaries (except at the universities) is almost non-existent'; but he adds that 'indications are not wanting that in the thirteenth century the clergy did frequent the new schools of theology': *Studies in English Franciscan History*, pp. 169–70.

All the evidence which we possess goes to show that education in England in the thirteenth century was spasmodic and local. In or near towns where a good school was established a fairly high standard of knowledge might be attained; in more isolated districts the ordinand must consider himself fortunate if he could scrape together the barest rudiments from some sympathetic but perhaps ill-educated priest. Again, if, after his ordination, he found himself near a cathedral town where the chancellor took his duties seriously, or near to one of the new friary schools, he might have opportunities for continuing his education; but if he were placed in some remote parish, far from the fountains of knowledge, he would have little chance of making use of such facilities as existed.

CHAPTER IX

CLERICAL INCOMES

(*a*) FROM THE LAND

'The labourer' (so the Apostles were told) 'is worthy of his hire.' Whether or not this remark was meant to be the foundation of an elaborate system whereby the Church collected money for the maintenance of its ministry, may well be doubted; but it was certainly taken as such by medieval apologists, by whom this text was cherished and often quoted. S. Paul had always insisted on working at his trade as a tent-maker in order that he might support himself, and not become a liability to those to whom he preached; but with the growth and organisation of a professional priesthood some method of providing the clergy with a livelihood became essential.

There are various methods whereby this money may be raised. The one which seems at first sight most natural is that the clergy should take their place along with other professional men, and support themselves either by fees or from the freewill offerings of the laity. Yet both of these are open to grave objections. A man's right to enjoy the ministrations of the Church should never be dependent upon his ability to pay an adequate fee, nor should any temptation be put before the clergy to seek out the richer patrons to the neglect of the poor. The services of the Church and of its ministers must be open to all, regardless of class or substance, and any plan which threatens this principle should be sternly opposed. On the other hand, to make the clergy dependent, for the necessities of life, upon the charity of their congregations is also fraught with great danger. It is not to be desired that a spiritual guide will always behave just as his flock wishes, nor is it tolerable that if a difference of opinion show itself the laity should be able to starve the clergy into surrender by cutting off supplies. Though in all ages there have been men in the Church big enough to face penury and hardship rather than give up some principle which appears to them inviolable, yet there have also always been a good many men weak enough not only to choose submission rather than persecution, but also to conduct their ministry with that complaisance which invariably shrinks from any action likely to provoke criticism.

If, then, the priest is to be spared the dilemma of trying to serve two masters, the Church which commissions him and the laity who support him, either there must be some common fund administered in the name of the Church by its own authorities, or each individual priest must be endowed in such a way that he can proceed with his duties uninfluenced by the fear or favour of those to whom he ministers. Such a system of endowments can only be secured where the Church has either sufficient resources to support its clergy or sufficient power to claim some portion of the national income for its maintenance.

The medieval Church was both wealthy and powerful, and, if it had not been for the scandals of pluralism and appropriations, it would have been able to give its clergy a reasonable income. It presented each incumbent with two things—a benefice, or living, and a cure of souls. The first of these meant that the rector of a parish entered into the possession not only of a certain quantity of land but also of the right of collecting, for his own use, what was equivalent to an income-tax of two shillings in the pound from every one of his parishioners, rich and poor alike. The second meant that he received the spiritual jurisdiction over a certain number of people from whom he, and he alone, was entitled to collect what he could in the way of voluntary offerings or fees. The possession of these two means of support was a source of much strength. If he irritated his flock he was in no danger of being forced into the ignominious position of having to submit to economic pressure: if on the other hand his parishioners were dilatory or reluctant over the paying of their tithes he, as their parish priest, could exclude them from the privileges of Church membership.

There is no doubt that, whatever may have been the procedure of individual clergy, the medieval Church, as a whole, was determined to get as much as it could. Financial matters figure prominently in synodal statutes and episcopal Registers, and the clergy were encouraged, and even commanded, to take their pound of flesh. The parson who hesitated to take the full measure, or who was willing to forgo any of his rights, was liable to be severely reprimanded by those who believed that the Church had a duty to exact all that was its due. Hubert Walter, Archbishop of Canterbury, in the Council of York held in 1195, issued instructions to the clergy to collect their tithes in full 'without any reduction'; and the statutes, referring to the custom whereby some incumbents gave banquets at the tithe-paying seasons, tell the laity that they must pay their tithes in full, banquet or no banquet.[1] To modern minds this sounds rather severe; but we must remember that the relationship between the Church and the laity was very different in the Middle Ages from what it is to-day. Nowadays a man belongs to the Church of his own free will, and, if he supports it, he does so because he desires its welfare. In the thirteenth century the Church was just one of the great powers to which a man had to submit whether he wished it or not. And just as many an otherwise good and respectable citizen of to-day will shamelessly cheat the government out of customs money by smuggling contraband articles into the country after a holiday abroad, so the medieval layman would have had little scruple in under-paying his Church dues if he thought he could do so with impunity. Whenever a man is pitting his wits against an institution with vast powers over him, he becomes more than ever determined to look after his own interests, for he knows that no one else will do it for him. Unfortunately this battle of wits tends to make each side drive as hard a bargain as possible. So in all our study of medieval Church finance we shall do well to remember that if the Church had shown less stringency and more consideration it would have become the prey of those who would have had no hesitation in cheating it of its rights.

The medieval parson, then, drew his income from his benefice and from his cure of souls. As holder of a benefice he owned a certain area of land, commonly known as glebe, and had the right to collect tithes from the whole parish; while as holder of a cure of souls he was entitled to the voluntary offerings of the people.

Ancient law declared that no church could be consecrated without some land being set aside for the use of the rector.[2] In early days property meant land and land only. Few people possessed much in the way of personal property, and capital was of little use so long as usury was forbidden and there was no police force. So 'real' estate meant land; and the parson, by the possession of his glebe, counted as a man of property.

[1] *Regist. J. Pontissara*, p. 213.

[2] Kennett, *Parochial Antiquities* (1818), i, p. 314.

The glebe varied enormously in different parishes. By old custom the parson was entitled to twice as much as the villein,[1] but it is clear that often enough the glebe was very extensive. At Evenly in Northamptonshire it is said to have been thirty virgates, which must certainly have meant some hundreds of acres,[2] while at Ringstead in the same county it amounted to 220 acres,[3] at Queen Camel in Somerset to 145 acres (of which 9½ were meadow land),[4] and at Colston Bassett (Notts) to 126 acres besides 'a toft and a croft'.[5] In theory, at any rate, the land was held as a freehold for which no labour could be demanded by the lord of the manor, though in ancient times the parson was expected to provide male animals for the use of the village.[6] But it is clear that this theory of the glebe land being free of service was not always observed, for at Longbridge Deverill (Wilts) we find Parson Walter who holds 80 acres rent-free 'but must be ready with his plough when the lord requires him'.[7] It is possible, however, that these acres were not part of the glebe, for a good many country clergy, in addition to the land belonging to the Church, owned or rented land on their own account. Thus we find the Rector of Sturminster Newton (Dorset) paying twelvepence a year to the Abbot of Glastonbury for a croft called Colfrot,[8] while the Rent Roll of Malmesbury Abbey includes among its tenants William, priest of Ramsbury, William le Gaunt, *capellanus*, Walter le Chapelaine, and the Vicar of Westport.[9]

The clergy were, therefore, closely connected with the soil. They might own merely a few strips or selions, or they might

[1] Watson, *Development of Ecclesiastical Organisation*, in *Camb. Med. Hist.* vi, p. 531.

[2] *Rot. H. de Welles*, i, p. 203. It is impossible to state what this exactly meant, as the virgate varied so much in different parts of the country. According to the *Oxford English Dictionary* a virgate 'averaged thirty acres', but it was sometimes considerably less.

[3] Hart and Lyons, *Cartularium Monasterii de Rameseia*, i, p. 405.

[4] Adam de Domerham, *Historia de rebus gestis Glastoniensibus* (ed. Hearne), i, pp. 203–6.

[5] *Regist. W. Gray*, p. 22.

[6] Watson, in *Camb. Med. Hist.* vi, p. 531.

[7] Glastonbury, *Rentalia et Custumaria, 1235–61*, Somerset Rec. Soc. v, pp. 133–4.

[8] *Ibid.* p. 93.

[9] Brewer, *Registrum Malmesburiense*, i, pp. 123, 133, 132 and 124. Cf. Richardson, *Parish Clergy of the Thirteenth and Fourteenth Centuries*, in *Trans. R. Hist. Soc.* 1912, p. 110.

be holders of hundreds of acres. Whatever the extent of their holdings their connection with the land was of the highest value for their work. As freeholders they could hold up their heads in any society, while as husbandmen they would share with the poorest in the joys and the disappointments which close contact with nature brings. The country clergyman of more recent times, whose salary arrives punctually by cheque from London, is in a far less satisfactory position than the man whose livelihood, like that of his neighbours, depends upon his success in fighting the common enemies of mildew, murrain and drought.

In addition to his glebe the parson was provided with a house,[1] often including a whole range of farm buildings, yards, paddocks, gardens and orchards.[2] But like all freemen in his village he had also certain rights to which he was entitled. Perhaps the most important of these was the right of allowing his stock to graze on the common pastures. The Vicar of East Brent (Somerset), in addition to holding 49 acres of arable land and 9 acres of meadow, had also the right of grazing six oxen, five cows, five bullocks and a mare;[3] and the Vicar of Wotton (Surrey) was granted pasturage for sixty sheep, a ram, six cows and six pigs.[4] Another manorial privilege which many of the clergy enjoyed was that of collecting fallen timber, known as 'husbote, haybote and fyrbote' for repairing their houses, building their fences, and burning on their hearths.[5] At Westbury in Wiltshire the vicar was entitled to collect one 'Yule log' each Christmas from the park belonging to the Bishop of Bath and Wells;[6] and at Eaton (Notts) the vicar had the right of cutting peat.[7]

Important and valuable though the glebe or demesne land might be, it was worth much less than the income which the parson drew from tithe. The rich living of Whalley in Lancashire, which at the end of the thirteenth century was appropriated to the new Cistercian abbey lately moved there from Stanlaw in Cheshire, was valued at over £200 a year, of which about £50

[1] The parsonage house was normally rent-free, but at S. Giles', Oxford, the vicar was expected to pay *6d.* a year for his house. Gibbons, *Liber Antiquus H. de Welles*, p. 2.

[2] See above, p. 61.

[3] Dugdale-Caley, *Monasticon*, i, pp. 325–6.

[4] *Regist. J. Pontissara*, pp. 92–3.

[5] Dugdale-Caley, *Monasticon*, i, p. 34; *Rot. H. de Welles*, ii, pp. 2–3.

[6] Bates, *Cartularies of Bruton and Montacute*, p. 33.

[7] *Regist. J. Romeyn*, i, p. 293.

was provided by the glebe, perhaps £10 or £20 by oblations, and the remainder by tithes.[1] Again at Queen Camel, where a vicarage was ordained in 1317, the glebe land was worth just over £5 and the tithes more than £18,[2] and at Sturminster Newton the house and glebe were valued at nearly £4 and the tithes at about £10.[3]

The origin and sanction of the tithe-system is to be found in the Book of Genesis. In the picturesque story of Jacob's Ladder the patriarch, in gratitude for the assurance of divine protection, makes a vow to God in the words: 'of all that thou shalt give me I will surely give the tenth unto thee'.[4] From this resolution sprang a system of taxation which became an essential part of the religious and economic life of the Hebrews, which was later adopted by the Christian Church, and which has only finally been abolished in this country within the last few years. If, instead of dreaming of angels, the patriarch had dreamt of the trouble and litigation to which he was giving birth, he might have hesitated before making his vow.

Although the earliest Christians were Jews, who must have been familiar with the tithe-system, this form of raising money does not appear to have been contemplated in the early centuries of the Church's history. Although they deal with most matters of ecclesiastical law and practice, the great Councils of the fourth and fifth centuries make no mention of tithes. The Church had other means of supporting its ministers; yet in the minds of many ecclesiastical lawyers and financiers there must have lain a hope that one day the Christian Church would revive a system which must have proved very lucrative to the Jewish hierarchy. That hope was in due course fulfilled; and the tithe-system, once established in Christendom, soon became the most important and the most fruitful source of wealth to the Church.

At first it was only a voluntary offering, made by devout souls who wished to support the Church and to fulfil the divine law. But with a body as powerful and influential as the early medieval Church it was an easy matter to turn a generous impulse into

[1] Hulton, *Coucher Book of Whalley Abbey*, i, pp. 205–6.

[2] Domerham, *Hist. de rebus Glaston.* i, pp. 203–6. The demesne here consisted of 5 acres of rich arable land valued at 2*s.* 8*d.* an acre, 9½ acres of good meadow at 2*s.* 6*d.* an acre, and 131½ acres of indifferent arable land at only 6*d.* an acre.

[3] Dugdale-Caley, *Monasticon*, i, p. 34; and cf. *Taxatio Nicholai*, p. 178.

[4] *Genesis*, xxviii, 22.

a pious duty, and a pious duty into a universal obligation. So far as this country is concerned tithes are mentioned in the seventh-century *Penitentiale* of Theodore of Tarsus, though they did not become a legal imposition upon all landowners until the following century.[1] In the laws of Edmund (A.D. 944) and in those of Edgar (A.D. 958) tithes are accepted as a regular and ineluctable tax upon all land.[2]

'Will a man rob God?' asks the prophet Malachi. 'But wherein have we robbed thee?' protests an indignant people. 'In tithes and offerings,' replies the Almighty. Larceny against God is, no doubt, a serious offence, and the medieval lawyers and moralists were determined that it should not be allowed to go unchallenged in their own day. If tithes were due to God, tithes should be paid 'to the uttermost farthing'. So throughout the century with which we are concerned we find the Church making an energetic and sustained effort to ensure that there was no leakage in this system of collecting its income tax. Bishop after bishop refers to it in his decrees, emphasising the importance of stringent enforcement, while lawyers were busy solving the infinite problems to which it gave rise.

The greatest source of tithe was the produce of nature, whether of the soil or of beasts. These tithes were commonly divided into two classes—the greater or 'garb'[3] tithes on corn of every variety, and the lesser tithes which were levied on every kind of natural production, and on the labours of men. In nearly all the assessments of clerical incomes which we know, garb tithes form the major part. They varied, of course, according to the size of the parish and the nature of the land, whether good arable land, meadow, forest, moor, fen or waste. They also depended upon the amount of land in the parish under monastic control, since by the thirteenth century the monks as a whole had made good their claim to hold all their land exempt from tithe.[4]

[1] Stubbs, *Constitutional History*, i, p. 227, n. 3.

[2] *Ibid.* i, p. 228; Reichel, *The Treasury of God* in *Archaeologia*, lx, pp. 398–9.

[3] The word 'garb' means a wheat-sheaf, and is still in use in heraldry as such.

[4] Cf. e.g. Walbran, *Memorials of Fountains Abbey*, i, p. xliv; ii, p. 66; Luard, *An. Mon.* ii, pp. 400–1; iii, p. 65; Duckett, *Visitations of English Cluniacs*, p. 25. The monasteries did, however, sometimes pay a small sum in lieu of tithe 'pro bono pacis': Bond, *Chron. Melsa*, i, p. 312; ii, p. 12, and cf. i, p. 380; ii, p. 152.

Chief among the lesser tithes was the tithe on hay.[1] This was especially important to those clergy who kept beasts, and more particularly in the North where cattle have to be kept indoors for more than half the year. Church law was most insistent that a tithe should be paid on all grass cut for hay. If the season were such that a farmer got his hay in early and was able to reap a second crop later in the year, the Church took its tithe just as strictly as on the first mowing.[2] Moreover if a man went out with a sickle and gathered in a little hay from the grass verges by the roadside, he was to pay his tithe on that as he would on his best meadow.[3]

Next in importance to the garb and hay tithes came those on all other crops, whether wild or cultivated. Flax was grown extensively in some parts of the country and yielded a tithe at Ilminster which was valued in 1268 at 60*s*. a year with a further 8*d*. on hemp.[4] Orchards could also be a profitable source of income,[5] and even the tofts and gardens, the land 'dug by foot' as it is frequently termed, in which a man might grow a few leeks and onions, a little parsley or mint to savour his changeless diet, or a few lettuces or cabbages, were rigidly taxed.[6] And as the produce of the field or garden had to yield its tenth to the Church, so also did nature in the wild, the moment her gifts were turned to man's use. If a man felled a tree, a tenth of the wood must be given to the priest; or if a cloth manufacturer went out into the fields to pick a few teasels for fulling, tithe must be paid on these.[7] But not only did the Church expect to receive a tenth of the labours of man in producing food out of the earth, it demanded also its share of what either man or beast chose to pick up. If a man drove his pigs into the woods to find acorns, or if he sent his children to gather a little dead

[1] This was occasionally included with the greater tithes, but strictly belongs to the lesser. See Hartridge, *Vicarages in the Middle Ages*, p. 38.

[2] *Statuta Sinodalia* in *Regist. J. Pontissara*, p. 230.

[3] Lyndwood, *Provinciale* (1679), p. 192. The expression for the roadside is 'in chiminis'.

[4] Bates, *Cart. of Muchelney and Athelney*, p. 54; cf. Macray, *Charters and Documents of Selborne*, p. 65.

[5] E.g. *Regist. W. Gray*, p. 219.

[6] Lyndwood, *Provinciale*, p. 192, where leeks, onions, hyssop, cabbages, parsley, turnips, lettuces, sage and garlic are all stated to be tithable.

[7] *Rot. H. de Welles*, i, pp. 251, 253 and 195. The tithe on fullers' teasel was at High Wycombe (Bucks) and is called 'decimae cardorum qui ad officium fullonum pertinent'.

wood for kindling, the tithe must be duly rendered if he would keep on the right side of the law both human and divine.[1]

In addition to the produce of the soil, both cultivated and wild, the issue of animals and their natural products were taxed. The young of every kind of animal—cow, sheep, goat, pig, horse, geese, fowls, even swans, doves and bees—had to provide the rector with his tithe. So also could he claim his share of all that these creatures produced, such as wool, milk (and all that is made from it), honey, bees-wax and even the down of geese. With meticulous care and thoroughness the lawyers of the Church searched out every possible source of man's income and clamped down on it the burden of the tithe.

Every problem that might arise was anticipated and provided for. For example: a number of sheep might change hands during the course of the year. Who, then, was responsible for paying tithe? The Church had its answer ready. 'Since by driving flocks to different pastures', say the Statutes of Winchester, 'contentions sometimes arise between rectors concerning tithes, we, in order to make peace, decide that to the churches of those parishes in which the sheep are fed and folded from their shearing-time until Easter, even if afterwards they are removed and shorn elsewhere, the tithe of wool shall be paid.'[2] Again, what was to be done in the event of sheep being fed by day in one parish and folded by night in another? or what if they were kept for the summer in one parish and wintered elsewhere? In order to avoid the possibility of such an arrangement leading to neglect or defalcation, arrangements were made whereby the tithes were to be divided among the clergy concerned.[3] Or again, what of those cases where there were only a few beasts to be taxed? This problem must often have arisen in connection with animals like horses of which only a few were kept, as also on the farms of little men who had only very limited stock. How could a tenth be taken of six lambs or a single foal? To this question Archbishop Winchelsey, in the Statutes of Merton in 1305, gave a careful answer. If a man

[1] For tithe on pannage see *Regist. J. Pontissara*, pp. 230–2; and, for tithe on kindling, Lyndwood, *Provinciale*, p. 190.

[2] *Regist. J. Pontissara*, p. 231. According to the Council of Merton the statutory period was from shearing-time to Martinmas (11 November): Wilkins, *Concilia*, ii, p. 279; cf. Lyndwood, *Provinciale*, p. 194.

[3] Wilkins, *Concilia*, ii, p. 279.

has six or less lambs, then his tithe shall be commuted to a money payment of threepence. If he has seven lambs, he shall present one to the rector who shall pay three-halfpence for it. The basis of this reckoning was that a lamb was considered to be worth fivepence. A tenth of the value of six lambs would be threepence, of seven lambs threepence-halfpenny. Thus by selling the seventh lamb to the rector for three-halfpence the farmer was giving just one tenth of the value of his seven lambs.[1]

Finally, tithe was levied on artisans and tradesmen of all kinds who earned their living not from the soil but from the labours of their hands. They too were expected to pay a tenth of their profits with no allowance being made for expenses. At Tadcaster the Church claimed a tithe on the incomes of all merchants, bakers, carpenters, quarrymen, masons, limeburners, carters and brewers, besides hired servants and those who were employed in casual labour.[2] At Silkstone, near Barnsley, iron-miners are specifically mentioned,[3] and at Brading, in the Isle of Wight, those who made their living from the sea.[4] No matter what a man's occupation was, no matter how he made his living nor how slender it was, the Church's net was made with so fine a mesh that not even the smallest could escape.[5]

In theory, at any rate, the income from tithe was not the exclusive property of the parish priest. An ancient custom, which seems to have died out in England by the thirteenth

[1] Wilkins, *Concilia*, ii, pp. 278–9; Lyndwood, *Provinciale*, p. 193.

[2] *Regist. J. Romeyn*, i, pp. 106–7. Cf. N. Adams, *The Judicial Conflict over Tithes*, in *E.H.R.* 1937, p. 18.

[3] *Regist. W. Wickwayn*, pp. 292–4.

[4] *Regist. J. Pontissara*, p. 173: 'decimae batellorum et retium.'

[5] It is not often that we get definite figures of what the various lesser tithes were worth, but there are a few statements which have been preserved. Thus at Sturminster Newton the figures were as follows: wool, 6*s.* 8*d.*; lambs, 12*s.* 6*d.*; calves, 9*s.* 4*d.*; hens and pigs, 1*s.* 8*d.*; eggs, 10*d.*; geese, 4*s.*; hay, 43*s.*; milk and cheese, 1*s.* 8*d.*; flax, 16*s.*; merchants, 4*s.* 6*d.*; gardens and dovecotes, 3*s.*; mills, 20*s.* (Dugdale-Caley, *Monasticon*, i, p. 34). At Ilminster the figures were: wool, 16*s.*; lambs, 14*s.*; calves and foals, 2*s.*; cows, 4*s.*; pigs, 3*s.* 6*d.*; cheese, 10*s.*; apples, 25*s.*; geese, 18*d.*; honey, 18*d.*; flax, 60*s.*; hemp, 8*d.*; pigeons, 8*d.*; small gardens, 13*s.*; and mills, 13*s.* 4*d.* (Bates, *Cartularies of Muchelney and Athelney*, p. 54). At Churcham (Glos) the tithe on hay is reckoned at 22*s.* and those on wool, calves, lambs, foals, geese, ducks, hens, milk, cheese and eggs, 18*s.* (Hart, *Hist. et Cart. Monasterii Gloucestriae*, i, pp. 249–50).

century, divided it into four parts. One of these was to go to the bishop, one for the relief of the poor of the parish, one for the fabric of the church, and one for the stipend of the rector. But it is clear that from early times the rectors, whether parish priests or religious houses, secured for their own use very much more than one-quarter of the revenue from tithe.

In the first place the custom of reserving a fourth part for the bishop seems to have disappeared at quite an early date.[1] How it came to be abandoned is not known, but at any rate by the thirteenth century the bishops had come to look for financial support almost entirely to the manors which they owned. The amount which they collected from the parishes was comparatively small.

At the same time, by Canon Law as well as by ancient custom, every bishop was entitled to collect certain small sums from each parish in his diocese. The most common of these was the payment known as 'synodals' which arose out of a bishop's right to demand a sum of two shillings from every person cited to attend his Synod.[2] In England the parishes were assessed according to some scale, the details of which cannot now be determined. At Hinckley in Leicestershire the mother church and a chapel paid *3s. 6d.* each per annum,[3] the parishes in the archdeaconry of Ely paid *2s. 4d.* each in two instalments,[4] and the churches belonging to S. Paul's Cathedral mostly paid only 12*d.*[5] Other small contributions to which the bishop was entitled were the see-due or *cathedraticum*, which also amounted to a few shillings,[6] and a payment known as 'quadragesimals' or *Laetare Jerusalem* to be made by the parish clergy on the fourth Sunday in Lent towards the cost of the chrism which they fetched from the bishop for the font on Easter Eve.[7]

[1] Coulton, *Five Centuries*, iii, p. 151; Hartridge, *Vicarages*, p. 2.
[2] Hale, *Domesday of S. Paul's* (Camden Society), p. cxiii.
[3] *Rot. H. de Welles*, i, p. 248.
[4] Feltoe and Minns, *Vetus Liber Archidiaconi Eliensis*, p. 304.
[5] Hale, *Domesday of S. Paul's*, pp. 147 ff.; cf. *Rot. H. de Welles*, i, p. 255.
[6] Hartridge identifies the *cathedraticum* with synodals: *Vicarages*, cf. index. But they must have been two separate taxes since the Vicar of Sturminster Newton paid 22½*d.* synodals and a further 18*d.* for *cathedraticum*: Dugdale-Caley, *Monasticon*, i, p. 34. The *cathedraticum* was sometimes known as *senagium* (Hart, *Hist. et Cart. Gloucestriae*, ii, p. 224; Bond, *Chron. Melsa*, ii, pp. 235–6).
[7] Salter, *Eynsham Cartulary*, i, pp. 344–6.

In addition to the small sums paid as synodals and the like, a certain amount went from each parish annually in the form of 'procurations' payable to the bishop or the archdeacon. Ecclesiastical discipline provided for a regular visitation of the parishes by diocesan officials who could demand hospitality from the rector for the time of their visit. We know from such a record as that of Bishop Swinfield that they did not always exercise this prerogative in the course of their tours. No doubt many parsonage houses would be quite unable to provide the sort of hospitality which a bishop would expect. But if the bishop demanded lodging he could not be refused.

The entertainment of a dignitary in the course of a visitation tour was no light matter. Bishops and others were accustomed to take their households with them on these occasions, and many a country parson must have groaned at the thought of having to provide hospitality for a party of some thirty or forty men and their horses. It was in order to protect the clergy against exploitation of this nature that the Council of London in 1200, following the lead of the Lateran Council of 1179, put some limits on the number of retainers which these visitors might bring with them. An archbishop was to confine his equipage to no more than fifty men, a bishop was to be content with thirty, an archdeacon with seven and a rural dean with two. It was further enacted that they were not to bring with them packs of sporting dogs or birds.[1] In 1222 the Council of Oxford repeated this injunction, and declared that though the rector of a parish might invite guests to meet his visitor, the visitor himself might not invite anyone to add to the burden which his presence was already imposing upon the incumbent. All of this was very natural and just, as was also the decree that archdeacons who came to hold their Chapters must choose churches in or near the towns, so that those who attended could get their food in the shops and inns and not expect to be fed by the rector of the parish.[2]

But even with these regulations the burden of entertaining the bishop or archdeacon must have been considerable and far beyond the capacity of many parsonage houses. Nor were the regulations always observed, as the following protest from the

[1] Wilkins, *Concilia*, i, p. 505.

[2] *Ibid.* i, pp. 588, 653; and ii, pp. 9, 150–1. Cf. *Regist. J. Pontissara*, pp. 215–16.

clergy of the Deanery of Holderness in 1281 will show. They write as follows:

To the venerable, etc. . . . his loyal sons the rectors, vicars and parish priests of the deanery of Holderness, greeting etc.

If the beginnings of the early Church are called to mind it will be remembered that its members were one in faith, one in spirit, one in baptism, and that having pooled their resources (*in unum etiam facultatibus contributis*) they all promised to supply the wants of the poor and to regard the needs of all as their own. Moreover the robe of Christ is one and seamless, and the bride of Christ has never been divorced nor borne the reproach of being a stranger and a harlot. As the Bridegroom Himself bears witness in the Song of Songs 'My dove, my undefiled, is but one' (*Cant.* vi, 9). And although there are many churches, yet are they compactly joined together in one body so that if one member suffer all the members suffer with it, or if one church be desolate or oppressed all the others must needs share in her grief. For God Himself once spake of the Church: 'I will make thee an eternal excellency, a joy of many generations. Thou shalt also suck the milk of the Gentiles and shalt suck the breast of kings' (*Isaiah*, lx, 15–16). But to-day the Church is not only without nourishment but is even abandoned and rejected, weighed down with new burdens and unwonted oppressions, and there is scarcely anyone to bring her solace in all her troubles.

For when long since, beyond the memory of living men, the archdeacon's official with the rural dean and his clerk, or sometimes with only one of them, used to visit us and our churches to hold their chapters, they came with three or four mounted retainers (*evectionibus*) at the most; but nowadays the official brings his companion and the rural dean his clerk, with your sequestrator in addition, and an apparitor—recently inflicted upon us by your official—and thus they descend upon us with a retinue of eight or nine for holding their chapter. In this way not only the rectors and vicars but also the parish priests are unduly burdened at a time when their livings have been greatly reduced by various disturbances in the realm in these latter days, while at the same time the number of poor people (to whom the goods of the Church belong) is daily increasing. Thus are the clergy grieved by reason of this oppression as were the Children of Israel under Pharaoh.

Wherefore we approach your Grace in whose sympathy and help we have the deepest trust in Christ, beseeching you, father, of your paternal affection to restore us to that condition which previously we enjoyed.

Farewell.

(Since our own seals are not known to you we have had the authentic seal of the deanery of Holderness attached to this letter.)[1]

[1] *Regist. W. Wickwayn*, pp. 248–9.

Instead of providing hospitality, most parishes made an annual payment either to the bishop or to the archdeacon, or to each, for 'procurations'. The amount varied considerably. For example in the Archdeaconry of Ely the poorer parishes paid 12*d.* a year and the others 18*d.*;[1] on the other hand at Childs Wickham the vicar paid 6*s.* 8*d.* a year to the archdeacon, and the Abbot of Bordesley, to whom the parish had been appropriated, had to pay £2. 13*s.* 4*d.* to the bishop.[2] Parishes belonging to the Augustinian priory of S. Frideswide at Oxford paid 6*s.* 8*d.* as procurations, but both Whalley and Whetstone (Leics) had to pay 40*s.*[3] Wymondham and Skipsea each paid one mark (13*s.* 4*d.*), but the Abbey of Meaux, who held Skipsea Church, had to pay a further 20*s.* to the Chapter of York.[4]

A certain amount of the money collected in tithe, therefore, went out of the parish or had to be allocated to the entertainment of the bishop or some other dignitary. A third portion was intended for the relief of the poor, and a fourth for the upkeep of the church; but there is considerable doubt as to how far these obligations were carried out.[5] What remained was the property of the rector, though not all of it would go into his pocket for his own use, since he was responsible for the payment of his assistants.

In parishes which had been appropriated the heaviest expense would be the stipend of the vicar, though in the richer parishes this might represent only a small proportion of the total income. In addition, money would have to be found for various chaplains (especially in those parishes which had a number of outlying, unendowed chapels), besides deacons and ministers, clerks and cleaners, sextons and manual workers in and around the church. For the stipends and wages of such men there were no parochial or central funds such as we have nowadays. Each individual incumbent was therefore solely responsible for the provision of a staff adequate to the needs of the parish.[6]

[1] Feltoe and Minns, *Vetus Liber Archidiaconi Eliensis*, p. 304.

[2] Wilson, *Worcester Liber Albus*, pp. 79–83.

[3] Wigram, *Cart. of S. Frideswide's*, ii, p. 40; Hulton, *Coucher Book of Whalley Abbey*, i, pp. 205–6; *Rot. H. de Welles*, i, p. 239.

[4] Dugdale-Caley, *Monasticon*, iii, p. 324; Bond, *Chron. Melsa*, ii, p. 233.

[5] See below, pp. 138–45.

[6] In appropriated parishes the burden of supporting assistant clergy was often borne by the vicar. See Hartridge, *Vicarages*, pp. 130–7.

Yet even with all these outgoings, there is no doubt that many tithe-owners, whether the rectors themselves or the religious houses, found this source of income a lucrative one. A 10 per cent tax on income would yield a very considerable sum in any large agricultural parish. But it must not be supposed that the clergy found the collecting of their tithes an easy task, or that the burden was one which the tithe-payer bore willingly or cheerfully. Indeed the whole question of tithe was one which led to constant friction and litigation which is only now being finally settled. In those parishes where the rector resided and ministered personally to his people the natural reluctance of the tithe-payer might be mollified by the respect and affection which he bore towards his parish priest; but in those parishes which had fallen into the hands of courtiers and civil servants who made no attempt to fulfil their responsibilities, and in those which had become the property of the religious houses, the laity naturally resented the payment of so much money for which they had so little in return. That each layman in a parish, according to his means, should make a regular contribution towards the maintenance of his parish priest is a reasonable thing; but that he should be expected to surrender one-tenth of his income in order to satisfy the creature comforts of some monastic house was regarded as intolerable; and it needed all the weight of the Church's legal system to ensure that payment was made regularly and in full.[1]

But not only was there a legal system which could be brought to bear against the reluctant or deceitful tithe-payer, the Church also claimed to decide man's ultimate destiny and to give him his passport either to a future of joy unspeakable or to one of endless and pitiless torment. One would like to think that the power to inflict such punishment on a man would be used only for some heinous offence, some defiance of the basic laws of God and man, some sin against the Holy Ghost. But it was not so. For many misdemeanours which we should not regard as serious the Church was not afraid to use the weapon of excommunication; and, of these misdemeanours, failure to pay tithe was one.

[1] Church Councils had constantly to condemn the practice of tithe-payers deducting expenses, or paying hired servants their wages, before reckoning their tithable income; cf. Wilkins, *Concilia*, i, pp. 507, 578, and Lyndwood, *Provinciale*, pp. 190–2.

It is true that the delinquent was to be warned;[1] but, after due admonition had been given, the priest was ordered to curse—and that with all the grim ritual of tolling the bell and dashing the candle to the ground. The sinner was to be accursed by Father, Son and Holy Spirit and all the host of heaven, 'sleeping and waking, going, sitting, standing, lying above ground and underground, speaking, riding, eating, drinking, in wood, in water, in field and in town'. He was to be excluded from every kind of service in the Church and condemned to share in the pains of hell 'with Judas that betrayed our Lord Jesus Christ' and he is to be 'put out of the book of life'.[2] After reading this fearsome doom we shall not wonder that Chaucer wrote of the good parson:

> Ful loth were him to curse for his tythes.

[1] According to the Constitutions of Archbishop Gray he could be warned three times but no more: *Regist. W. Gray*, p. 220.

[2] For the full form of the curse see John Myrc's *Instructions for Parish Priests*, pp. 66–7.

CHAPTER X

CLERICAL INCOMES

(b) THE OFFERINGS OF THE PEOPLE

As holder of a benefice a rector had two sources of income, the glebe land with which the rectory was endowed and the right to collect tithes: as administrator of a cure of souls he had also the opportunity of collecting certain offerings and fees from his people.[1]

In the Synodal Statutes of the diocese of Winchester[2] it is stated that 'all parishioners who have passed their eighteenth year, provided that they have any movable property of their own or are employed outside their parents' houses at fixed wages, must pay their due and accustomed oblations at the four festivals, namely: Christmas, Easter, the Festival[3] and the Dedication of the Church'. On these and other feast days the members of the congregation were expected to make some contribution to the Church or, more accurately, to the rector.[4] No doubt these offerings would vary a good deal in different parishes, but they must often have amounted to a considerable sum. At Sturminster Newton the oblations on the three chief festivals were reckoned at *34s. 4d.*[5] At Bygrave (Herts) the offerings amounted to *7s.* at Christmas, *6s. 8d.* at Easter, *1s.* on All Saints' Day, *3d.* at Candlemas, and, on S. Margaret's Day (the Dedication Festival), *16s.*[6] At Upton (Bucks) the offerings at Christmas, Easter and the chief festivals amounted to *30s.*;[7] at Churcham (Glos) to *27s.* with a further *20s.* for

[1] The word used for these oblations was 'altarage'. Although this word was often used in the Middle Ages to mean all that an incumbent received apart from the greater tithes, yet strictly speaking it should have been applied only to the offerings of the people, whether those were made voluntarily or by compulsion. Hartridge, *Vicarages*, pp. 36–7.

[2] *Regist. J. Pontissara*, p. 214; cf. p. 231.

[3] Pontissara's Register gives *die Festivitatis*. Wilkins, who prints the statutes in vol. ii of his *Concilia*, pp. 293–301, gives *festivitate sancti loci*, whatever that may mean.

[4] These offerings were compulsory, and defaulters could be reported to the bishop: *Regist. J. Drokensford*, p. 91.

[5] Dugdale-Caley, *Monasticon*, i, p. 34.

[6] *Rot. H. de Welles*, iii, p. 40.

[7] Heales, *Records of Merton Priory*, p. 67.

the rest of the year;[1] at S. John's, Peterborough, to 48*s.* 8*d.* with a further 13*s.* 4*d.* from the daughter church of S. Botolph;[2] at Ilminster to 60*s.*;[3] and at Norton Hibbert to 37*s.* 8*d.*[4] At Tadcaster, however, the various offerings in the chapel of Catterton amounted to only 12*d.*[5]

In the parishes which had been appropriated it was usual for the rector to allow some share of these offerings to go to the vicar. Occasionally, as at Shipton-under-Wychwood and Bygrave, the vicar received the total offertory, but the more usual arrangement was for him to receive a small honorarium of threepence at Christmas, twopence at Easter and a penny on other feast days.[6] In some parishes a different arrangement was made, as at the two Hertford churches of S. Mary's and S. John's, where the vicar received no specified sum at Easter but was allowed to take all that was offered at the first Mass—a shrewd bargain, since the worshippers at this early service would probably be the poorer parishioners.[7] At Cassington the vicar was allowed to take all the oblations except on the two feasts of S. Peter when he took only half, and at High Wycombe half the offerings on some of the festivals, but nothing on the others.[8]

In addition to the bigger offertories on the greater festivals the faithful were encouraged to make some contribution each time they came to Mass, though this was not enforced.[9] Bishop Walter Cantilupe of Worcester included in his statutes a decree that the poor must not be compelled to contribute to the Church every time they communicate,[10] but others were clearly expected to do so. The collections on these occasions cannot have been very great, for the vicars of the parishes belonging to Osney Abbey were told that they might have one penny from the oblations at Mass 'if so much as that is offered'.[11] On the other

[1] Hart, *Hist. et Cart. Gloucestriae*, i, p. 249.

[2] *Rot. H. de Welles*, ii, p. 127.

[3] Bates, *Cart. of Muchelney and Athelney*, p. 54.

[4] Heales, *Records of Merton Priory*, p. 68.

[5] *Regist. J. Romeyn*, i, pp. 106–7.

[6] E.g. Bicester (Gibbons, *Liber Antiquus*, p. 7), Deeping S. James (*Ibid.* pp. 41–2), Bardney (Dugdale-Caley, *Monasticon*, i, p. 634), Humberstone (*Rot. R. Grosseteste*, p. 49), Canons Ashby (Gibbons, *Liber Antiquus*, p. 35).

[7] *Rot. H. de Welles*, i, p. 138.

[8] Gibbons, *Liber Antiquus*, pp. 3 and 7.

[9] In the *Lay Folks' Mass Book*, ed. T. F. Simmons, p. 22, the worshipper is told that he may make an offering or not just as he likes. Cf. p. 230.

[10] Wilkins, *Concilia*, i, p. 671.

[11] Gibbons, *Liber Antiquus*, pp. 1–2.

hand at Bingham (Notts) the vicar received three-halfpence from the collections every Sunday,[1] and at S. Botolph's, Peterborough, his 'Sunday pennies' (*denarii dominicis diebus*) amounted to 13*s.* 4*d.* by the year's end.[2]

Similar to the 'Mass-pennies' were the offerings made at anniversaries and trentals. An 'anniversary' was a Mass said *pro defuncto* on the day of the man's death each year; a 'trental' was a series of thirty Masses said either on thirty consecutive days or on thirty specified days during the year.[3] On such occasions it was customary for an offering to be made.[4]

Besides the offerings at the Sunday services there was a certain amount to be gleaned from the occasional offices. In the ordinations of vicarages the vicar is often allowed some portion of the money collected for banns or weddings (*sponsalia*), for the churching of women, and for funerals.[5] All these are common enough, but it is rare to find any fees or offerings for baptisms. One of the few examples of this from the thirteenth century is at Blyth (Notts), where the vicar was allowed to take any money offered 'at the baptising of children'.[6]

On the other hand penitents who came to make their confession were encouraged to make some contribution before leaving the church. Such offerings, especially in the busy times, when people came to prepare for their Easter communions, could be a profitable source of revenue, for at S. John's, Peterborough, the 'Confession pennies' (*denarii confessionum*) were reckoned at twenty-two shillings a year.[7] Again, the visiting of the sick was regarded as an occasion when some thank-offering to the Church might reasonably be expected.[8]

[1] *Regist. J. Romeyn*, ii, p. 326.

[2] *Rot. H. de Welles*, ii, p. 127.

[3] Rock, *Church of our Fathers*, ii, pp. 260–1.

[4] E.g. Gibbons, *Liber Antiquus*, pp. 13, 29, 64–5; *Regist. J. Pontissara*, p. 151. Church law made it perfectly plain that though free-will offerings might be made, no fees could be charged for sacraments: Wilkins, *Concilia*, i, pp. 506, 581, 635–40, 650, etc.

[5] Gibbons, *Liber Antiquus*, pp. 7, 35, 41–2; *Regist. J. Pontissara*, p. 151; *Rot. R. Grosseteste*, pp. 29, 49, 90; *Regist. J. Romeyn*, i, p. 106.

[6] *Regist. W. Wickwayn*, p. 77. It was illegal for a priest to charge fees for the sacraments, but it was sometimes done, as at Bristol where the clergy were charging 2*d.* for each child that they baptised: *Regist. W. Geynsburgh*, p. 7.

[7] *Rot. H. de Welles*, ii, p. 127.

[8] E.g. Gibbons, *Liber Antiquus*, p. 65 (Spalding).

In addition to these money-offerings the clergy were accustomed to receive also a certain number of oblations in kind. The most important of these was the bread offered at the altar.[1] This was the *eulogia* or 'pain bénit', some of which was used in the service, while the remainder became the property of the priest. Its use in the service was as follows: 'As soon as Mass had been ended a loaf of bread was blessed, and then, with a knife very likely set apart for the purpose, cut into small slices for distribution among the people, who went up and received it from the priest, whose hand they kissed. This holy loaf, or *eulogia*, was meant to be an emblem of that brotherly love and union which ought always to bind Christians together.'[2] The faithful were encouraged to make an offering of a loaf each Sunday for this purpose, and the priest was allowed to have, for his own use, what remained after the service.[3]

Similar to the offering of bread was the gift of wax or candles, some of which would be used in the church and some in the priest's house.[4] Moreover the clergy were accustomed also to receive from their parishioners offerings of eggs at Easter,[5] cheese at Whitsuntide, and fowls at Christmas.[6]

Adding together the various oblations on the festivals of the Church, Mass and confession pennies, fees for the occasional offices and various offerings in kind, the parish priest was able to make an appreciable addition to what he received from his own land and from the lands of others. We have not much evidence of what these amounted to, for oblations and lesser tithes were often lumped together under the word 'altarage', but we do know that at Norton Hibbert the offerings of the

[1] See Gibbons, *Liber Antiquus*, pp. 6, 17, 29, etc.; *Regist. J. Romeyn*, i, pp. 106, 326; Dugdale-Caley, *Monasticon*, i, p. 34, where it was reckoned at 7*s.* 7*d.* Note that there is a rubric in the Book of Common Prayer stating that 'if any of the bread and wine remain unconsecrated, the Curate shall have it to his own use'.

[2] Rock, *Church of our Fathers*, i, pp. 110–11; see also H. E. Salter, *The Churchwardens' Accounts of S. Michael's Church, Oxford*, pp. viii–x.

[3] Wilkins, *Concilia*, i, p. 714. The Vicar of Keynsham received offerings of corn for making holy bread: Hunt, *Two Chartularies of Bath*, p. 121.

[4] E.g. Gibbons, *Liber Antiquus*, p. 31; *Regist. J. Romeyn*, i, p. 326; *Rot. H. de Welles*, i, p. 195; Dugdale-Caley, *Monasticon*, i, p. 34 (where the wax is valued at 7*s.* 4*d.* a year).

[5] Gibbons, *Liber Antiquus*, p. 7; *Rot. H. de Welles*, iii, p. 40; Hale, *Reg. Prioratus Wigorn.* p. 32b.

[6] Gibbons, *Liber Antiquus*, p. 65; *Rot. H. de Welles*, i, p. 108.

people amounted in 1212 to £5. 4*s*. 0*d*.,[1] at Ilminster in 1268 to £4. 3*s*. 4*d*.,[2] and at Newland (Glos) in 1304 to £4. 6*s*. 8*d*.[3] In the town parishes where, of course, there was much less tithe, the clergy lived almost entirely on the offerings of the people. At S. Stephen's, Norwich, for example, in 1303 the oblations were valued at £11. 15*s*. 0*d*., while tithe brought in only 5*s*.[4]

But if we are to make a complete list of the various sources of income we shall have to include, besides glebe, tithes and altarage, the various perquisites which a parish priest was entitled to claim. The chief among these was the 'mortuary' or 'second legacy'. If the Scriptural sanction underlying the theory of tithes was the law of Moses, and if the authority for the various alms and oblations was the saying of S. Paul that 'they who wait at the altar are partakers with the altar', the only passage of Holy Writ which might be claimed in support of the mortuary gift is the text 'Where the body is, there will the eagles be gathered together'.

The theory whereby the Church sought to justify the annexation of part of a man's property when he died was that he might have—and indeed almost certainly had—neglected at some time in his life to pay tithes in full. Since strict payment of tithe was necessary to salvation it would be unwise to run any risks, and a gift to the Church 'in lieu of any unpaid tithes' would help to put a man on the safe side. Thus when a man died, his widow and children had not only to part with their best animal to the lord of the manor, but they had also to surrender their second-best animal to the Church; for though theory demanded that the payment of the mortuary should be voluntary, the ecclesiastical eagles saw to it that it became compulsory.[5] Nor was this death

[1] Heales, *Records of Merton Priory*, p. 68. The total was made up as follows: S. John the Baptist's Day, 13*s*. 4*d*.; confessions, Easter and Whitsun offerings, 13*s*. 4*d*.; Christmas Day, 8*s*.; Candlemas, 3*s*.; offerings of wool, 26*s*. 8*d*., flax, 6*s*. 8*d*., cheese, 6*s*. 8*d*., calves and poultry, 3*s*.; churchings and banns, 10*s*.; bequests and trentals, 13*s*. 4*d*.

[2] Bates, *Cart. of Muchelney and Athelney*, p. 54. At Basingstoke the oblations were divided into three parts, one for the Prior and Convent of Selborne, one for the vicar, and one for the repair of the churches: A. W. Goodman, *Chartulary of Winchester*, p. 174.

[3] *Regist. R. Swinfield*, pp. 411–12.

[4] Blomefield, *History of Norfolk*, iv, p. 146.

[5] *Regist. J. Grandisson*, ii, p. 1177; Coulton, *Five Centuries*, iii, p. 292; *Medieval Village*, p. 448; *Medieval Studies*, No. VIII; H. S. Bennett, *Life on the English Manor*, pp. 144–5; Hartridge, *Vicarages*, pp. 227–9.

duty confined to the wealthier parishioners, for by the express command of Archbishop Langton's Provincial Constitutions the 'mortuary' was to be collected from any man who left three or more animals.[1]

Another perquisite which might be made lucrative was in connection with the making of wills. In the thirteenth century a man had far less freedom in the disposal of his property than he has to-day. In all testamentary matters there were definite rules, the testator being obliged to provide for his wife and family. At the same time there was generally a certain sum to be devoted to charity or to the work of the Church. Every will was a religious instrument made in the name of the Trinity, and from the twelfth century onwards it became customary to have witnesses who normally acted as executors.[2] Since literacy was largely confined to the clergy it was inevitable that most of these witnesses would be clerks, and the Church took advantage of this to turn what was really no more than a practical convenience into a universal obligation by declaring that no one was to make a will except in the presence of a priest.[3] The priest would naturally expect some return for the trouble to which he was put, and there is little doubt that in the making and witnessing of wills the clergy managed to get some remuneration, for the Vicar of S. John the Baptist's at Peterborough reckoned to receive ten shillings a year from this source.[4]

Yet another perquisite which occasionally proved fruitful was the sale or letting of seats in church. In the nineteenth century many clergy were largely supported by pew-rents which had a ready sale and brought in large sums of money. This could never happen in the Middle Ages since there were practically no pews to let. In some churches, however, there was some system of

[1] Wilkins, *Concilia*, i, pp. 530–1. At Sturminster Newton the mortuaries amounted to ten shillings a year: Dugdale-Caley, *Monasticon*, i, p. 34. Some rectors were accused of taking not only the mortuary gift to which they were entitled but a ninth, sixth or even a third of the dead man's property: Bliss, *Cal. Papal Letters*, i, pp. 252–3.

[2] Pollock and Maitland, *History of English Law*, ii, pp. 330–46.

[3] Statutes of Durham (1220) in Wilkins, *Concilia*, i, p. 583, and Constitutions of S. Edmund, *ibid.* p. 639. Cf. Coulton, *Medieval Studies*, No. VIII, p. 9: 'Apart from the very small minority who were rich enough to make written wills, every man was obliged to dispose of his property on his deathbed by word of mouth in the presence of his parish priest.'

[4] *Rot. H. de Welles*, ii, p. 127.

hiring seats, for Bishop Peter Quivil of Exeter included in his statutes a clause designed to prevent the confusion and bad blood which was sometimes caused through seats in church being sold to two or three different persons.[1]

Finally, the parish priest was entitled to a fairly large number of taxes in addition to all his other sources of revenue. Perhaps the most important of these was the 'churchset', a church rent on corn payable each year at Martinmas.[2] It is hard to say how much it amounted to, though we know that at Sturminster Newton it was valued at 21*s.* 2*d.*[3] In some cases it was commuted to a payment in hens.[4] Similar to the churchset were the various taxes known as 'ploughpenny', 'wax-set' and so forth, which probably never amounted to very much but were a small but perceptible addition to the Church's income.[5]

With all these sources of income—glebe, tithe, oblations and perquisites—we should expect to find the beneficed clergy well provided for. Many of them certainly were; and a few who had the luck or skill to collect a number of livings were undoubtedly very wealthy men. Others, however, were obliged to live on very small incomes, made less by the various outgoings for which they were responsible. It is hard for us nowadays to state with any degree of accuracy the exact value of any living in the thirteenth century. This is partly due to the fact that the revenue varied so much from year to year according to the seasons and the state of the harvest, and partly to the difficulty of reckoning in terms of cash an income which was largely drawn in kind. Nevertheless it was necessary from time to time, for purposes of taxation, to make an official estimate of clerical incomes. The earliest assessments of which we have any record were made in 1217 and 1229; but we know very little of these.[6] The first valuation of which we have any considerable knowledge was made in 1254–5 for the purpose of levying a tax of one-tenth of all ecclesiastical revenues in order

[1] Wilkins, *Concilia*, ii, p. 140.

[2] Anglo-Norman scribes had some difficulty in spelling this word, which appears as *cherset*, *cyrceatta*, *cuhrseth*, *curescet*, etc.

[3] Dugdale-Caley, *Monasticon*, i, p. 34.

[4] Stevenson, *Chron. Monast. de Abingdon*, ii, pp. 301, 304–6, 309, 330. Cf. Luard, *An. Mon.* v, p. 416.

[5] Cf. *Regist. W. Wickwayn*, p. 291; Gibbons, *Liber Antiquus*, p. 31; *Rot. H. de Welles*, iii, p. 40 (Bygrave, where the plough-tax amounted to 9*d.* a year).

[6] W. E. Lunt, *Valuation of Norwich*, pp. 17–20.

to meet the expenses of a crusade in which Henry III undertook to engage.[1] This assessment goes by the name of the 'Norwich valuation', since it was prepared by Walter Suffield, Bishop of Norwich, assisted by the Bishop of Chichester and the Abbot of Westminster. The assessment was carried out in each deanery by the rural dean and three or four incumbents selected from the Chapter.[2] The assessors, though competent and conscientious, clearly had no heart for the job, and in the following year they were superseded by Boniface, Archbishop of Canterbury, and Rostand, a papal nuncio, both of whom were more sympathetic with the King and the Pope than their predecessors had been.[3] The revised assessment, made by the archdeacons and rural deans, caused some consternation among the clergy, who complained bitterly of the burden which this levy would impose upon them;[4] consequently the revision was dropped and the former Norwich valuation readopted.[5]

There is no doubt that the Norwich valuation was a generous one, being considerably below the estimates of clerical incomes which were subsequently made. Mr Lunt has collected a great deal of information about this valuation and has produced some striking statistics. For example, for thirty-three churches in the dioceses of Durham, Ely, Hereford, Lincoln, Norwich and Salisbury the Norwich estimate gives a total revenue of £609. 13*s*. 4*d*., whereas we know from other sources that the incomes of these churches amounted to over £1150. Or again, for seventy-four vicarages in the diocese of Lincoln the Norwich figures give a total of 699 marks while the registers of Hugh of Welles and other documents show that they were actually rated at a total of 1007 marks.[6]

The comparative leniency of the Norwich valuation was not allowed to go long unchallenged. In 1266 a new tax was imposed, and a new assessment was ordered by Ottobon, the papal legate, which was to be 'according to the true value and not according to the ancient estimation'.[7] The new valuation,

[1] W. E. Lunt, *Financial Relations of the Papacy with England*, p. 255.

[2] W. E. Lunt, *Valuation of Norwich*, pp. 52, 65; and cf. Luard, *An. Mon.* i, p. 325; M. Paris, *Chron. Maj.* v, p. 451.

[3] W. E. Lunt, *Valuation of Norwich*, p. 84.

[4] See the protests sent in by the clergy of the archdeaconry of Lincoln and the diocese of Coventry and Lichfield in Luard, *An. Mon.* i, pp. 360–3.

[5] W. E. Lunt, *Valuation of Norwich*, p. 87.

[6] *Ibid.* pp. 568–72.

[7] W. E. Lunt, *Financial Relations*, p. 293.

which appears to have shown an increase over the Norwich figures of 33⅓ per cent, was again bitterly opposed by the clergy; but the added burden of this levy was light compared with a later estimate of 1276 which more than doubled the demands of the Norwich assessors.[1]

The valuation of 1276 arose out of a decree of the Council of Lyons, two years previously, that money should be raised for a crusade. In England the tax was to be one-tenth of all clerical incomes for a period of six years. The Pope appointed one of his chaplains, Raymond de Nogeriis, and a Dominican friar, John of Darlington, to make the new valuation. Again both the figures and the method were denounced as utterly unreasonable, and John of Pontissara, at that time Archdeacon of Exeter, and two others made representations to the Pope complaining that never before had assessors stooped so low as to take money from leper-houses, hospitals, the poorer monasteries, benefices worth less than six marks a year, and even from the salaries of vicars, priests, clerks and parish chaplains. They also complained that no allowance had been made for expenses in the cultivation of land or in the collecting of tithes. The religious houses joined in the general protest and showed such reluctance to pay their quota that John of Darlington had to coerce the monks of S. Albans by excommunicating the abbot and the leading members of the Chapter.[2]

There had by now been no less than five assessments of clerical incomes made since 1217, each entailing a considerable amount of work. Nevertheless it was decided in 1291 to make yet another estimate for the purpose of levying the new tax which had been granted to Edward I upon his taking the cross in Gascony in 1287. It was perhaps a discreet move to make Pontissara, the chief complainant against the previous valuation, one of the assessors for the new taxation. With the assistance of Oliver Sutton, Bishop of Lincoln, the new valuation was made; and once again it was met by a chorus of protest,[3] and had to be revised in 1293.[4]

[1] W. E. Lunt, *Valuation of Norwich*, p. 106. In 1254 the incomes of the clergy were reckoned at £101,600; in 1276 at £213,980.

[2] Rose Graham in *E.H.R.* 1908, p. 439; W. E. Lunt, *Financial Relations*, pp. 320–30; *Valuation of Norwich*, p. 155.

[3] W. E. Lunt, *Financial Relations*, pp. 349–50; cf. Luard, *An. Mon.* iv, pp. 331, 333, 509.

[4] W. E. Lunt, *Valuation of Norwich*, p. 155.

This assessment of 1291 is the most accessible of all as it was published by the Record Commission in 1802.[1] The figure for each parish was based upon evidence supplied by the clergy of the neighbouring churches, given under oath; but how far such figures correspond with the actual values of the livings it is hard to say. Mr Lunt declares that the valuations of 1291 are far below the figures of gross income and probably represent only the actual values or the amounts at which the churches could be 'farmed'.[2] They are, however, considerably higher than the 'Norwich' calculations; and though in many cases they fall below the known value of the livings, in others they are distinctly higher. For example, in the twenty-seven parishes in the Camps deanery the total value, according to the Archdeacon of Ely's book, was £309. 6*s.* 8*d.*, whereas in the *Taxatio* they were valued at £408. 6*s.* 8*d.*[3] Again, in a group of thirty-one parishes in the diocese of York, the figures given in Archbishop Giffard's Register amount to £307. 16*s.* 8*d.*, whereas in the *Taxatio* they are given as no less than £554.[4] These figures would suggest that the clergy were justified in their complaint that the taxation was unreasonably heavy. On the other hand, as Mr Lunt points out, for sixty-one vicarages in the diocese of Lincoln the assessments of 1291 amount to £545. 1*s.* 4*d.*, whereas quite early in the century, when Hugh of Welles was bishop, these same vicarages were rated at a total figure of £571. 6*s.* 8*d.*[5] Again, for forty-seven churches in the diocese of Winchester, the patronage of which belonged to Bishop Pontissara, the total revenue, according to his Register, is £1472. 13*s.* 4*d.*, whereas in the *Taxatio* they are assessed at only £1021.[6]

It is impossible, therefore, to regard the figures in the *Taxatio* as a wholly satisfactory index of what the livings were worth at the close of the thirteenth century. Undoubtedly some are reckoned too high, and many too low. But, bearing in mind the limitations and faults of the valuation, what do we find?

[1] *Taxatio Ecclesiastica Angliae et Walliae auctoritate P. Nicholai IV, c.* A.D. *1291* (London, 1802).

[2] W. E. Lunt, *Valuation of Norwich*, pp. 147, 151.

[3] Feltoe and Minns, *Vetus Liber Archidiaconi Eliensis*, pp. 47–73 and *Taxatio Nicholai*, ad loc.

[4] *Regist. W. Giffard*, pp. 21–90 and *Taxatio Nicholai*, ad loc.

[5] W. E. Lunt, *Valuation of Norwich*, pp. 581–3.

[6] *Regist. J. Pontissara*, pp. 794–7 and *Taxatio Nicholai*, ad loc.

We find, first of all, the greatest possible variation in the value of benefices. The richest living in the country appears to have been Holy Island (Lindisfarne) assessed at £230. 15*s.* 0*d.*, with Bamburgh on the mainland closely following with £230. 9*s.* 4*d.*[1] Next comes the valuable living of Bakewell in Derbyshire with £194 and two Yorkshire parishes, Snaith and Adlingfleet, each valued at £153. 6*s.* 8*d.* Simonburn in Northumberland near the Roman Wall was stated to be worth £136. 4*s.* 2*d.* There were two other rich livings in Northumberland, Norham and Rothbury, and two in Kent, Minster and Teynham, each of which was valued at £133. 6*s.* 8*d.* At the other extreme we find the churches of Buckland Monachorum and Tamerton in Devon each assessed at 3*s.* 4*d.*

These are the extremes of wealth and poverty. So far as the ordinary parishes were concerned, the average gross income appears to have been about £10 a year. For example in the deanery of Chelmsford, which was then part of the diocese of London, the average for twenty-five parishes is £11. 13*s.* 1*d.*, while for the deaneries of Barstaple and Lexden, in the same diocese, it is £9. 13*s.* 5*d.* and £9. 4*s.* 5*d.* respectively. In the deanery of Middlesex, which contained some of the richer London churches, the average is £15. 13*s.* 5*d.*[2] On the whole the parishes in the north of England were worth more than those in the south. Not only were most of the richer livings in the north, but the average for the northern deaneries is generally higher than in the south. For example, the parishes in the deanery of Craven in Yorkshire give an average of £14. 16*s.* 9*d.*, those in the deanery of Durham £18. 1*s.* 5*d.*, and those in the deanery of Derby £20. 6*s.* 4*d.* In the Holt deanery in Norfolk the average is £15, but in that of Newport Pagnell in the diocese of Lincoln the figure is £10. 9*s.* 0*d.*, and in the Dorchester deanery (Sarum) only £7. Going farther west we find that the parishes in the deaneries of Kenn and Shirwell in the diocese of Exeter work out at an average of only £7. 13*s.* 4*d.* and £5. 4*s.* 2*d.* respectively.

[1] In 1254 Bamburgh was valued at £146. 13*s.* 4*d.* In 1312, however, the gross income was estimated to be £383. 11*s.* 9*d.* and the average over 15 years was £297: W. E. Lunt, *Valuation of Norwich*, p. 567.

[2] According to the Norwich valuation the average for the Chelmsford deanery was £13. 7*s.* 5*d.*: for Barstaple £7. 1*s.* 2*d.*: for Lexden just under £7, and for Middlesex £11. 19*s.* 0*d.*: W. E. Lunt, *Valuation of Norwich*, pp. 337–41, 345–7, 358–60.

If the parishes as a whole were worth less than £10 a year the clergy were not overpaid. There may have been other sources of income, for it is not certain whether the figures in the *Taxatio* include oblations and perquisites as well as glebe and tithe; but, at the same time, there were various outgoings of one kind and another. There were synodals and procurations, pensions and portions, poor relief and the upkeep of the church, wages and stipends of cleaners and curates, besides the expense and difficulty sometimes of collecting tithes. For example at Sturminster Newton the living was worth £13. 6*s*. 8*d*. but the expenses were 66*s*. 8*d*. for a chaplain, 7*s*. 4¼*d*. procurations, 2*s*. rent, 3*s*. 4½*d*. synodals and cathedraticum, making a total of nearly £4.[1] Skipsea in Holderness was valued at £23. 6*s*. 8*d*., but the outgoings amounted to £13. 7*s*. 4*d*. besides 43 quarters of oats payable to the Provost of Beverley.[2] In any ordinary parish the expenses must often have been in the neighbourhood of £5 a year, leaving only about £5 for the rector himself, or little more than the average wage of a working man.

Apart, therefore, from the scandals of pluralism, the average rector was in fact a 'pore persoun', finding it difficult enough to make ends meet on an income which would be worth only about £3 or £4 a week in modern currency. Perhaps, then, it was right that the Church should be strict about the paying of tithes and oblations and that it should support its own clergy against those who would defraud them of their dues. 'The labourer is worthy of his hire', and if the hire had always fallen to the labourer we should have no right to complain. But, unfortunately, in too many cases the hire went elsewhere, while the labourer himself received only a very small proportion of it. It was this that made the financial administration of the Church in the thirteenth century so unjust. Far too much money from the parishes found its way into monastic treasuries or into the already full purses of wealthy pluralists and foreigners who did nothing in return. But where a parish was conducted, as it was meant to be, by a resident rector who ministered in person to his flock there can be no doubt that the system of parochial finance was neither unreasonable nor unjust.

1 *Taxatio Nicholai*, p. 178, and Dugdale-Caley, *Monasticon*, i, p. 34.

2 *Taxatio Nicholai*, p. 304, and Bond, *Chron. Melsa*, ii, p. 235.

CHAPTER XI

PRIEST AND PEOPLE

In the confined atmosphere of manorial or village life priest and people were inevitably thrown a good deal together. The collecting of the more perishable tithes, such as milk, eggs and butter, must have kept the parson busy, picking up a little here and a little there to stock his own larder. This whole question of tithe was a continuous strain upon the clergy as well as a potential source of friction between priest and people, especially in times of drought or disaster when stocks were low and everyone had to go short. We shall not, therefore, be surprised to find the clergy sometimes over-anxious to maintain their rights, for constant vigilance was needed to prevent tithe-payers from concealing produce upon which the tenth was payable, or from foisting on the parson the poorest corn or the weakest lambs or yesterday's milk.

In ancient times the laity had been entitled to claim, for the relief of the poor, one quarter of what was paid in tithe; and, by the thirteenth century, some proportion was still regarded as allocated to poor-relief. The importance of this will be realised only when we contrast the prospects of the sick and poor of our own generation with what prevailed seven hundred years ago. It is the claim of our modern politicians that no one in this country need starve. Whether this is as true in practice as it appears in theory may be questioned, but the fact remains that there is nowadays provision for the sick and the poor far beyond the wildest dreams or hopes of our forefathers. Old age and widows' pensions, unemployment money, health insurance and public assistance are at any rate an attempt to ensure that no one shall be entirely without the bare necessities of life—shelter, food and clothes. But in the Middle Ages none of these amenities existed. If a man died or was killed, his widow and children had somehow to fend for themselves. If the bread-winner in a family was sick or unable to work, then his wife must somehow manage to carry on. All 'indigent faint souls past corporal toil' must find relatives to support them. The struggle for existence was a desperately hard one in which the State did nothing for those who fell.

Their only hope then lay with the Church. In theory the

public had its rights, but in practice they were often hard to claim. Under the system of 'appropriations' at least two-thirds of the income of many parishes went into the treasury of some religious house which might be many miles away; and it was little consolation to a woman whose husband was dying of the plague to know that she could receive a pittance if she left him to tramp thirty or forty miles.[1] Meanwhile the vicars whom the monasteries employed to do the work were paid so small a stipend that it was impossible for them to bear the burden of poor-relief out of their very modest incomes of some three or four pounds a year.[2]

The effect of appropriations upon the system of poor-relief was very serious, and undoubtedly a great many folk in desperate need were robbed of the only source of relief which they could claim. Nor were the rectors of those parishes which were not appropriated always conscientious in this duty of providing for the poor. Many of these men were pluralists and absentees who were content that their parishes should be served by parochial chaplains at a salary which scarcely sufficed to keep body and soul together while they themselves lived far away and rarely or never appeared in their parishes.

It was to one such, Peter Blaunc, Rector of Wrotham and Lyminge in Kent, that Archbishop Pecham wrote in 1284. 'As I was recently making a journey through these parishes of yours', he writes, 'I found the cure of souls in them totally neglected, so far as your duties are concerned; while the poorer parishioners, through lack of a good dispenser, are afflicted with hunger and deprived of all material and spiritual consolation.' He orders his proctor to spend a hundred shillings immediately in each parish on the relief of the poor.[3]

[1] In 1261 Alexander IV ordered that where churches were more than four or five miles from the monasteries to which they belonged an eighth or a tenth part of the income was to be set aside for poor parishioners: Bliss, *Cal. Papal. Letters*, i, p. 375. This shows that in many parishes even less than this fraction was being spent on the poor. Bishop Geynsburgh of Worcester, *c.* 1306, granted a licence to the Rector of Lighthorne to be non-resident for three years on condition that he spent £1 a year on the relief of the poor (*Regist. W. Geynsburgh*, p. 128). According to the *Taxatio Nicholai*, p. 219, this living was worth £17. 6*s.* 8*d.* a year.

[2] On this see Coulton, *Five Centuries*, iii, pp. 203 ff., 650–4.

[3] Pecham, *Reg. Epist.* ii, p. 715. Three years later he issued a circular letter to all the clergy of the diocese ordering them to make better provision for the poor in their parishes: *ibid.* iii, pp. 949–50.

One of the few ways in which priest and people could co-operate was in the care of the parish church. Some portion of the receipts from tithe was earmarked for the fabric of the church, but the clergy were not expected to support the whole burden of this, for, from early times, it had been an accepted principle that whereas the chancel was the responsibility of the rector the upkeep of the nave was to be provided for by the parishioners. This agreement seems to have been almost universally observed, for though there are a few instances in which the laity were concerned in the upkeep of the chancel these were generally the result either of some temporary arrangement or of some dispute.[1]

It seems also to be unknown for the rector to have been responsible for the nave, though occasionally the laity tried to shift the burden on to his shoulders. For example, in 1280 the parishioners of Crich, near Matlock, asked the Archbishop of Canterbury to lay the burden of repairing the nave of their church upon the abbey to which it was appropriated since they owned so much land in the parish; but Pecham was unable to do more than to get a division made.[2]

But if it was agreed that the clergy and laity should each be responsible for a definite portion of the fabric of the church, there was no such agreement as to the responsibility of providing the furniture, books, ornaments and vestments. It would seem that in early years these were regarded as the concern of the rector, but it is clear that a determined effort was made to shift the burden from the shoulders of the clergy on to those of the laity.

In the earlier part of the thirteenth century the provision of books, ornaments and vestments was clearly the concern of the clergy, and the only problem was to decide, in the case of appropriated churches, how the burden should be shared between the monastery and the vicar, and in what proportion. Thus at Shabbington (Bucks) in the time of Hugh of Welles (1209–35) the vicar and the monks who held the church shared between

[1] For example, at S. Perran-in-Zabulo in Cornwall, where the laity took over the responsibility since the work was being so negligently performed by the rector (Hartridge, *Vicarages*, p. 138). At Sidbury the vicar and the people were quarrelling as to who was responsible (*Regist. W. Stapeldon*, p. 369), but at S. Mary Church the parishioners appear to have been responsible for the chancel for some time (*ibid.* p. 337).

[2] Cox, *Churches of Derbyshire*, iv, p. 47.

them the burden of providing books and ornaments in addition to repairs to the chancel.[1] In the time of Welles' successor, Grosseteste, there still seems to have been no attempt to shirk this responsibility, for the Vicar of Haxey (Lincs) was ordered to repair the books, ornaments and vestments of the church, the Vicar of Cuddesdon was to supply sufficient books, ornaments and lights, and the Vicar of S. Peter's-in-the-East (Oxford) was to provide lamps, incense, straw, bell-ropes and wafers.[2]

In the diocese of Lincoln, then, it appears to have been an accepted thing in the earlier part of the century that the ornaments and furnishings of a church were the responsibility of the clergy, not of the laity. Meanwhile in the diocese of York Archbishop Gray was making a determined attempt to relieve his clergy from as much of this burden as he could. In his injunctions issued in 1250 he makes the laity responsible for providing the ornaments, vestments, lights, books, bells and ropes. The only responsibility borne by the rector is to repair the chancel and the benches in it.[3] Such was Archbishop Gray's intention, but it is clear that it was not observed, for several instances from the same diocese can be cited in which the responsibility for providing books and ornaments remained with the clergy, not with the people.[4]

Towards the end of the century it is clear that the clergy were gradually succeeding in laying more and more of the onus on the shoulders of the laity. For example at Totternhoe (Beds) in 1293 it is expressly stated that the laity are to provide banners, a cross and candles and the Missal,[5] and at Whalley in 1296 the people were responsible for supplying altar linen.[6] Then early in the following century, at the Council of Merton held in 1305, Archbishop Winchelsey decreed that all the following

[1] *Rot. H. de Welles*, ii, pp. 49–50. At Basingstoke and Old Basing repairs to the church were paid for not only out of tithe but out of the oblations of the people, one-third of the sum thus collected being set aside for this purpose: A. W. Goodman, *Chartulary of Winchester*, p. 174.

[2] *Rot. R. Grosseteste*, pp. 146–7, 451, 454–5.

[3] *Regist. W. Gray*, pp. 218–19.

[4] E.g. at Ruddington (Notts) in *Regist. J. Romeyn*, i, p. 314, and cf. p. 290; at Mattersey (Notts) in *Regist. W. Wickwayn*, pp. 71–2, and at Nafferton (Yorks) in Bond, *Chron. Melsa*, ii, pp. 230–1.

[5] Luard, *An. Mon.* iii, p. 377.

[6] Hulton, *Coucher Book of Whalley Abbey*, i, pp. 306–7.

should be provided by the parishioners: the Missal, chalice and vestments; processional crosses, incense and thurible; lights and bells; candlesticks and the necessary liturgical books.[1] This was now the official ruling of the Church, but even so it was not observed, for in the ordination of a vicarage at Hoo (Kent) in 1327 it is stated that the vicar shall be responsible for finding books up to the value of 2*s.* a year together with bread and wine, processional candles and other things necessary for worship,[2] while the Vicar of Malling in the same county had to provide practically everything needed in the church—ornaments, vestments, books, candles and candlesticks, bread and wine, rochets and surplices, towels, phials and basins, and rushes for the floor.[3] At Hailsham (Sussex) the vicar was to provide the rushes in summer, while the Convent of Bayham sent straw for the winter, besides providing the necessary books and ornaments. Since the vicar was held responsible for the provision of lights, bread and wine, and incense, as well as for all repairs and washing, the burden on the parishioners here must have been light.[4] Indeed, the evidence from the early part of the fourteenth century shows that Winchelsey's decree of 1305 was largely disregarded. To take one instance, in 1349, the year of the Black Death, a vicarage was ordained at Heckington (Lincs) under the terms of which the vicar was to supply incense, wax, bread and wine, books, ornaments and vestments.[5] From this it is clear that no uniform system could be established for the country. In many parishes parson and people had come to some working agreement, the readjustment of which would only cause endless dispute and litigation.[6]

[1] Wilkins, *Concilia*, ii, p. 280. Winchelsey's list is much like that of Archbishop Gray of York.

[2] *Regist. H. Hethe*, pp. 176–8.

[3] *Ibid.* pp. 395–6 (1339).

[4] *Regist. R. Winchelsey*, pp. 103–8.

[5] Dugdale-Caley, *Monasticon*, i, p. 636. Cf. p. 187, and see *Regist. H. Hethe*, p. 50 (Westerham, Kent, 1328), *Regist. R. Baldock, etc.* pp. 90–1 (Ealing, 1308), and *Regist. J. Drokensford*, p. 12 (Thurloxton, Somerset, 1318).

[6] There are traces of this division of burdens in our Prayer Book of 1662. The alms at the Offertory are ordered to be collected, as is generally known, in 'a decent bason to be provided by the parish'. It is also directed that 'The bread and wine for the Communion shall be provided by the Curate and the Churchwardens at the charges of the Parish'. In the First Prayer Book of Edward VI (1549) the elements were to be provided at the cost of the incumbent, who received the offerings for this

A word must now be said about the way in which the laity fulfilled their responsibilities. The returns of the visitation of the Totnes archdeaconry in 1342 show that the laity were no more conscientious about repairs and renewals than the clergy. At Moreton Hampstead the visitors noted several defects for which the laity were responsible; at Ideford the parishioners, although few and poor, were ordered to repair and replace certain things in the church under penalty of fivepence; at Lamerton and Beaworthy the naves of the churches were in need of restoration.[1]

This neglect on the part of the parishioners may have been due partly to lack of organisation. The churchwarden, who has played such an important and honourable part in English Church history, was only just beginning to make his appearance in the thirteenth century. From the middle of the fourteenth century onwards we have records of churchwardens' accounts from several parishes, but there is very little evidence from the period with which we are concerned. As early as 1260 the accounts of Shrewsbury Church speak of 'Guardians of the light of the altar of the Holy Cross' while the register records various gifts to the church of land which was managed by the wardens.[2] Again, in the visitations in Kent in 1292–4, wardens are mentioned at Bilsington and Billswick,[3] while early in the fourteenth century a new officer appears under the title of *yconomus* whose function must have been the upkeep of the house of God.[4]

How this officer was originally appointed we do not know, but it is clear that he must have had some means of raising money for the various tasks which he had to perform. Only a few churches were endowed with land or tenements which brought in a regular income, but most of them possessed sheep

purpose. In the Canons of 1604 the elements are definitely chargeable to the parish, as are also the surplices for the clergy, the parochial register, the great Bible and the Book of Common Prayer, the Communion-table with its appurtenances (including the Ten Commandments painted upon the East wall), a pulpit and a strong box (*Canons* 20, 58, 70, 80, 82–4).

[1] Coulton, *A Visitation of the Archdeaconry of Totnes in 1342*, in E.H.R. 1911, pp. 111, 113, 120, 123.

[2] W. A. Leighton, *Shrewsbury Abbey Parish Church Estate*, in Shropshire Arch. Soc. (1878), i, pp. 19–30.

[3] Woodruff, *Some Early Visitation Rolls*, in *Arch. Cantiana*, xxxii, pp. 154, 161. Unfortunately the editor prints these returns in English, so that it is impossible to say what word is here translated as 'warden'.

[4] *Regist. R. Baldock, etc.* p. 135 (West Tilbury, 1311).

and cattle which were let out to local farmers at a small annual rent. These rents were the churchwardens' main source of income, but they were able to supplement it by doing a certain amount of trading in wool, milk and beef, in letting out appliances for cooking, baking and brewing, and even in providing feasts and entertainments from which some profit might be derived.[1] In emergencies the parishioners appear to have imposed a tax upon themselves, but since this was a voluntary measure it must not be confused with the compulsory Church Rates which became so unpopular in later centuries.[2] At the same time, once the parishioners had agreed upon a general rate for church repairs everyone was expected to pay his quota. Thus at Wembdon, near Bridgwater, in 1325 certain parishioners who failed to pay their contribution toward the rebuilding of their church were reported to the Bishop of Bath and Wells,[3] while in 1330 two men of Snodland, Kent, who had failed to pay a similar rate were forced by the Bishop of Rochester to do so.[4]

By the division of responsibility between clergy and laity the Church was attempting to erect a system which would ensure that the parish churches were kept in repair and adequately provided with the necessities of public worship. By means of constant visitation tours the more conscientious of the bishops were doing their best to keep a vigilant eye on the fabric and ornaments of the parish churches,[5] and several synodal statutes contain lists of what each church must possess.[6] It is true that it is hard to find a single inventory of church property which conforms with the minimum standard demanded by these statutes, but there were undoubtedly many parish churches which were on the whole well stocked with books, vestments and ornaments. The Deanery of Bourn in Cambridgeshire was probably typical of any country deanery, and we find here that

[1] J. C. Cox, *Churchwardens' Accounts*, p. 2; Hobhouse, *Churchwardens' Accounts of Croscombe, etc.* pp. xiii–xiv.

[2] F. W. Cornish, *A History of the English Church in the Nineteenth Century*, i, pp. 158–72.

[3] Hobhouse, *Churchwardens' Accounts*, p. xvi.

[4] *Regist. H. Hethe*, p. 248. One man was ordered to pay 7*s*. and the other 40*d*.

[5] See below, pp. 191–4.

[6] E.g. Richard le Poore in 1220 (Wilkins, *Concilia*, i, p. 580); William of Blois in 1229 (*ibid.* p. 623); W. Cantilupe in 1240 (*ibid.* p. 666); Walter Gray in 1250 (*Regist. W. Gray*, p. 218); P. Quivil in 1287 (Wilkins, *Concilia*, ii, p. 139); and cf. Grosseteste, *Epistolae*, pp. 156, 161.

of the twenty-six churches in it every one had a good set of liturgical books, most of them possessed three complete sets of vestments, and many of them had banners and altar-frontals.[1] The twenty churches in the London diocese visited by Ralph de Baldock, Dean of S. Paul's, in 1297, were all well supplied with the necessities of divine worship. Most of them had two chalices, and there was a great variety of pyxes of wood, glass, ivory, brass, copper, enamel and silver. Vestments, frontals, altar-linen and bridal canopies abounded, and even ivory combs for the use of the priests and fans of peacock's feathers to be gently waved by some little boy to keep flies from disturbing the celebrant. Two of the churches were provided with organs.[2]

On the other hand there is no doubt that many churches were in a bad way. Leaky roofs and broken windows were in many cases causing damp and mildew. Books were often torn and dirty; vestments faded and ragged, ornaments chipped and broken. In some churches there was no surplice or rochet for those who assisted at the altar, in others no pyx for reserving the Sacrament, no thurible for burning incense, no candlesticks for the altar, and even, in some instances, no chalice or no Missal. *Debilis*, *insufficiens*, *fractus*, *deficiens*—'worn out', 'inadequate', 'broken', 'missing'—are words which recur far too often in these visitation returns from typical English parishes during the thirteenth and early fourteenth centuries. Moreover some of the churches were themselves in so terrible a state of dilapidation that it was impossible to use them at all in wet weather while others were desecrated by being used for purely secular purposes.[3]

[1] Feltoe and Minns, *Vetus Liber Archidiaconi Eliensis*, pp. 122–41.

[2] Sparrow Simpson, *Visitations of Churches belonging to S. Paul's, 1297 and 1458*, Camden Society, New Series, vol. lv. It is rather surprising that there were not more organs, for we know that they were common in churches during the twelfth century: F. W. Galpin, *Old English Instruments of Music*, p. 219. An organ is mentioned at Branscombe, Devon, in *Regist. W. Stapeldon*, p. 194.

[3] For evidence of this see the following: (i) Visitations carried out by the Dean of S. Paul's in 1249–52 (*Camden Misc.* ix) and again in 1297 (*Camden Soc.* 1895); (ii) Visitations by the Dean of Salisbury in 1220 (Jones, *Reg. S. Osmundi*, i); (iii) Visitations of Snaith and Selby (*Regist. W. Giffard*, pp. 322–6); (iv) A thirteenth-century account of visitations in the Archdeaconry of Ely (*Vetus Liber Archidiaconi Eliensis*, ed. Feltoe and Minns); (v) Visitation of some parishes in Kent in 1292–4 (*Arch. Cantiana*, vols. xxxii and xxxiii); (vi) Visitation of Sonning churches in

That the churches should have been used as places of entertainment may seem strange in these days. Yet there is reason to suppose that the wide naves were sometimes used for dancing, some of which may have led to horseplay and wild behaviour. Games of various kinds were also played in the churches to such an extent that the Bishop of Exeter in 1306 had to rebuke the clergy of his diocese for indulging in such merry-making which went even to the point of mocking the divine service.[1] Grosseteste referred in 1236 to games being played in the churches as well as in the churchyards;[2] and, nearly a century later, Bishop Baldock of London drew attention to the 'games, dances, wrestlings and other sports meetings' which were being held at Barking both in the parish church and in the church of the nunnery.[3] Grosseteste again refers to what he calls the 'disgusting habit' (*execrabilis consuetudo*) of holding the ceremony known as the 'Feast of Fools', a kind of New Year revel in which the inferior clergy indulged.[4] Churchyards were commonly the scene of buffoonery which sometimes interfered with the prayers of the more devout, for William of Blois, Bishop of Winchester, had to order people not to play during the hours of divine service.[5] Banquets and scot-ales were also often held in the churches, when trestle-tables were erected in the nave and a considerable amount of food and liquor was consumed.[6]

The performance of plays in churches was common throughout this century. We must distinguish here between religious plays, which have been part of the life of the Church from early days, and purely secular (or, more accurately, pagan) entertainments which, like the games and banquets, sometimes found their way into sacred places. The religious plays, which were acted by the clergy, were a development of the dramatisation to which

1300 (*Charters of Salisbury*, pp. 369–70); (vii) Visitation of Devon churches in 1301 (*Regist. W. Stapeldon, passim*); (viii) Visitation of Totnes Archdeaconry in 1342 (*E.H.R.* 1911).

[1] Powys, *The English Parish Church*, p. 72.

[2] Grosseteste, *Epistolae*, pp. 74–5.

[3] *Regist. R. Baldock, etc.* pp. 73: 'lasciviae, choreae, luctae et aliae conventiculae voluptuosae.' Cf. pp. 145–6.

[4] Grosseteste, *Epistolae*, p. 161. On the 'Feast of Fools' see E. K. Chambers, *Medieval Stage*, i, pp. 279–335.

[5] Wilkins, *Concilia*, i, p. 625.

[6] Almost all synodal statutes refer to the custom of holding scot-ales. See, for example, Wilkins, *Concilia*, i, pp. 530–1, 574, 635–40, 672, and Grosseteste, *Epistolae*, pp. 73 and 162.

Christian worship has always lent itself. The 'Easter Sepulchre', for example, was a fairly common liturgical drama in English parish churches in the thirteenth century.[1] By the middle of the century the development of these plays was complete, but from that time onwards they were gradually taken more and more out of the hands of the clergy to be performed by laymen in secular buildings, and in English instead of in Latin.[2] Until this 'secularisation' took place religious plays had been common in churchyards and actually within the churches.[3] Probably many which were planned to take place in the open-air were moved into the church at the last minute, unless the weather in the Middle Ages was more reliable than it is now.

The liturgical and religious dramas had a respectable Christian origin and were to some extent didactic and devotional. It was not so with the other kind of play which was sometimes held in church. Grosseteste speaks of the clergy taking part in such customs as the *Introductio Maii* or *Autumni*, which were nothing but spring or harvest customs descended from pagan fertility festivals.[4] Walter Cantilupe refers to *ludi de rege et regina*,[5] which appear to have been something in the nature of masques, such as the *larvae et theatrales ludi* mentioned by Innocent III and included in the decretals of Gregory IX in 1234.[6] All such performances were liable to find their way into the churches, and it is no wonder that the more conscientious of the bishops did their best to keep them out.

There is reason, also, to believe that the house of prayer was sometimes turned into a house of merchandise by the holding of fairs and markets actually within the walls of the church. These were most commonly held in the churchyards, though this in itself was an act of irreverence, especially since medieval methods of buying and selling sometimes led to quarrels and bloodshed.[7] There is evidence that some of the bigger churches

[1] J. D. Chambers, *Divine Worship in England*, App. p. xxiv.

[2] E. K. Chambers, *Medieval Stage*, ii, pp. 69, 87, 88.

[3] *Ancren Riwle*, ed. Gasquet, p. 240.

[4] Grosseteste, *Epistolae*, p. 317 and cf. E. K. Chambers, *Medieval Stage*, i, p. 91. See also the disgraceful story of the parish priest of Inverkeithing who revived the profane rites of Priapus: *Lanercost Chron.* (tr. Maxwell), pp. 29–30.

[5] Wilkins, *Concilia*, i, p. 666.

[6] E. K. Chambers, *Medieval Stage*, i, pp. 91 and 279.

[7] As at Kirkburton in 1303: *Regist. T. Corbridge*, i, p. 86.

and cathedrals were sometimes turned into markets, the booths of the merchants standing in a double row down the length of the nave;[1] and it is probable that chapmen peddled their wares in smaller parish churches, and slept in them at night.[2] In some churches it was customary for a watchman to sleep there every night in order to guard the treasures. Thus at Southwell the sacrist was ordered to sleep always in the church,[3] and at Colyton in Devon the vicar had been in the habit of providing a deacon to sleep in the church at night.[4] At S. Mary Church, in the same county, the poor condition of the church was due to the fact that the vicar was using it as a brewery and as a store-house for his corn.[5]

Knowing something of the parochial clergy and their shortcomings we shall not be surprised to learn that some of them neglected their high calling to engage in worldly pursuits. In spite of their poverty and loneliness it was not the 'pore persouns' of the country parishes who were most to blame, but the richer men, with time and money to spare, who made little or no attempt to fulfil their responsibilities, and to whom the possession of a benefice was little more than a financial asset.

In the year 1284 John Pecham wrote sadly of the clergy who 'forsake the things of the spirit for those of the flesh',[6] while half a century earlier Grosseteste had waged war in his vigorous way on those who, by their worldliness, 'blasphemed the name of Christ, brought the Holy Scriptures into contempt and made themselves the despicable shame of the learned and the scorn and laughing-stock of the people'.[7] Those whom these two great men were attacking were clergy only in name; in every other way they were laymen, and expected to live as such.

For one thing, they expected to take part in the sporting activities of their friends and neighbours, as the country clergy have done at many times in their history. Many of them kept hawks and hounds, to the great distress of William Langland, who thought that nothing was too bad for the sporting parson.

[1] A. R. Powys, *The English Parish Church*, pp. 66–8.
[2] Cutts, *Parish Priests*, p. 317.
[3] Leach, *Memorials of Southwell*, p. 210.
[4] *Regist. W. Stapeldon*, p. 111. [5] *Ibid.* p. 337.
[6] Pecham, *Reg. Epist.* ii, pp. 694–7.
[7] See his letter to a clergyman in 1233: *Epistolae*, pp. 48–50.

Indeed he was not sure that he ought not to be exterminated altogether.

> Haukyng other hontyng · yf eny of hem hit vsie
> Shal lese ther-fore hus lyue-lode · and hus life parauenture.[1]

Humbler forms of sport, such as dice and gambling, were indulged in by clergy of all ranks, and drew down episcopal wrath[2] besides the censure of moralists like Robert Manning, who complained of clerks playing games like chess on Sunday mornings.[3]

With sporting activities we should expect to find unclerical attire, and, indeed, the clergy were often reprimanded for wearing clothes unsuited to their profession. The Durham Statutes of 1220 forbade the clergy to wear cloaks with sleeves or pointed shoes or to deck themselves with rich trappings and other extravagances, and most reforming Councils endorsed or augmented these regulations.[4] Bishop Quivil said that clerical garments must be all of one colour,[5] and not like those of a chaplain employed by the nuns of S. Mary's, Winchester, who wore a parti-coloured habit.[6] Lyndwood, the canonist, declared that the clothes of the clergy should not be either red or green, nor too smart (*fulgidus*) nor too shabby (*sordidus*); and they must not wear green or red stockings.[7] Pecham forbade the wearing of lay or military attire by the clergy, and wrote to the Bishop of S. Asaph ordering him to make all his clergy dress in a becoming manner.[8] In addition the clergy were expected to have their hair cut correctly as a sign of their profession. This meant not only shaving the top of the head but also the nape and over the ears so as to make of the remaining hair a circlet or *corona*.[9] In a word, the priest was expected to look like one, and was not to go about disguised as a layman.

[1] *Piers Plowman*, C, iv, 469–70; cf. Wilkins, *Concilia*, ii, p. 142 and Owst, *Literature and Pulpit*, pp. 278 n., 279.

[2] Wilkins, *Concilia*, i, p. 574; Grosseteste, *Epistolae*, p. 159.

[3] *Handlyng Synne*, p. 38.

[4] Wilkins, *Concilia*, i, pp. 574, 590 (Oxford, 1222), 652 (Otto, 1237), 669 (Cantilupe, 1240); ii, pp. 4 (Ottobon), 59 (Pecham, 1281), *et alii*.

[5] *Ibid.* ii, p. 141.

[6] *Regist. J. Sandale*, p. 90.

[7] Lyndwood, *Provinciale*, p. 117.

[8] Wilkins, *Concilia*, ii, p. 59 and Pecham, *Reg. Epist.* ii, p. 737.

[9] Wilkins, *Concilia*, i, p. 574; cf. Rock, *Church of our Fathers*, i, pp. 144–6. Dr Owst quotes from Bromyard; 'They are ashamed of the tonsure, therefore they cultivate a fashionable head of hair and have a small tonsure, so as not to be recognised as priests': *Literature and Pulpit*, p. 262.

The wearing of unclerical attire was perhaps not in itself a serious thing: the unfortunate thing was that it was sometimes associated with unclerical behaviour. A *Song on the Corruptions of the Time*, written in the reign of Henry III, spoke of a rural dean 'changing the tune of his tongue with yesterday's garments and migrating with humble speech to low taverns'.[1] Whether or not a priest was responsible for the bibulous song beginning:

'Tis my intention, gentle sir, to perish in a tavern[2]

there were certainly some among the clergy who would have endorsed the sentiments which it expresses.

Drunkenness is, in these days, a thing so degrading and unnecessary that we should rightly be shocked to know of any clergy who were guilty of it. But censures which would be justified to-day can hardly be applied to those who lacked so many of the advantages which we enjoy. Many of the medieval clergy lived in isolated villages and hamlets cut off from all chance of sober relaxation and with none of the solaces of home life or of books. Is it any wonder, then, that they sought companionship and recreation in the taverns?

Finally, there were those who, either from inclination or from the desire to augment their slender incomes, engaged in secular occupations unbecoming to the cloth. Some of them did a little buying and selling, some acted as moneylenders,[3] some (such as the Rector of Bingham in Nottinghamshire) kept public-houses.[4] Some made use of their abilities and education by obtaining posts such as bailiffs and seneschals,[5] while others engaged in the work of the courts, acting as proctors, advocates and assessors.[6] In 1293 Bishop Pontissara wrote to the Rector of Sanderstead citing him to answer various charges, among which was one that he had acted as advocate and judge in a secular court.[7] Many years earlier Grosseteste had refused to admit one of the Passelew family to the living of S. Peter's, Northampton, on the grounds that he was a forest judge.[8]

[1] Wright, *Political Songs*, p. 33.

[2] 'Meum est propositum in taberna mori'; see Wright, *Poems attributed to Walter Mapes*, p. xlv.

[3] Grosseteste, *Epistolae*, p. 158; Wilkins, *Concilia*, i, pp. 627–8.

[4] *Regist. J. Romeyn*, i, pp. 256–7.

[5] Wilkins, *Concilia*, i, p. 586.

[6] *Ibid.* ii, pp. 4, 146.

[7] *Regist. J. Pontissara*, pp. 586–7.

[8] Grosseteste, *Epistolae*, pp. 349–50, and cf. pp. 353–4. On Grosseteste's attitude see Stevenson, *Robert Grosseteste*, pp. 117–19, 171–7.

Occasionally we hear of clergy not only dressing in military array but even going to war, for in 1312 the papal penitentiary had to arrange for the unfrocking of a priest who, having served as a soldier, had 'joined in various acts of homicide'.[1]

That there were clergy who, both in life and in work, preferred the standards of the world to those of the priesthood goes without saying. The proportion of the worldly-minded among the clergy cannot, however, be computed with any accuracy. Episcopal Registers and the decrees of synods and councils are bound to show up abuses, and it may be that only those abuses which were fairly common came up for censure. But, bearing in mind the loneliness and the restrictions in which most of the clergy laboured, and also their poverty and lack of education, it is perhaps no wonder that some of them compromised their high calling by accepting the standards and customs of the world. Yet, in spite of it all, the priest remained a priest, conscious of his position, of his orders and of his authority. And if the Church took a good deal from the people we must remember that it also gave a good deal in return. It gave first, the regular worship of the Church on Sundays and weekdays. It gave also the opportunities of Christian baptism, matrimony and burial, together with a little teaching and some spiritual direction mainly administered in the confessional. Further, it offered to the sick and the dying spiritual comfort and perhaps, in some places, medical help as well. In addition to all this it had the opportunity of exercising in each parish a civilising and elevating influence to counteract the coarseness and tediousness of life.

This was what the Church had to offer, but it is quite certain that in some parishes these opportunities were never presented to the people. Apart from the occasional visit of a bishop or an archdeacon the parish priest was left very much to himself, and we shall not find it hard to believe that many of them grew very slack. When certain parishes in Kent were visited in 1292 it was revealed that at S. Mary-in-the-Marsh the rector was an absentee and the chaplain who had been left in charge could nowhere be found.[2] At the adjoining parish of Eastbridge there

[1] *Regist. A. Orleton*, p. 166. The clergy as a rule were forbidden to bear arms (cf. Grosseteste, *Epistolae*, p. 159; Wilkins, *Concilia*, ii, p. 3), but some were allowed to bear arms in self-defence (Wilkins, *Concilia*, i, p. 670).

[2] Woodruff, *Some Early Visitation Rolls*, in *Arch. Cantiana*, xxxii, p. 149.

was neither rector nor chaplain and the parishioners made an application for a priest to be sent to them.[1] A few years later at Orcop in Herefordshire it was discovered that there was no vicar or chaplain, and that several people had died without receiving the sacraments of the Church.[2] These are just a few examples of gross negligence which could easily be multiplied.[3] In other parishes strange things took place. At Letton in Herefordshire the rector was absent from his parish for ten years through age and sickness, and the chaplains appear to have celebrated Mass during that time without any wine.[4] At Fairfield in Kent the priest in charge had a young woman to assist him at the altar.[5] In a good many parishes there can have been no proper Mass owing to the absence of a chalice.[6] In others there was either no Missal at all, or the wretched condition of the liturgical books meant that there could be no reading of the Epistle and Gospel during certain months of the year.[7]

These are the black spots. There were other parishes, no doubt, where things went well, though we must not be misled by Chaucer's admirable description of the 'pore persoun' and give to a work of fiction the same authority which we must give to records. Nor must we be led into the other extreme by pictures of the pluralists and absentees like Bogo de Clare, Nicholas Lovetot and John Mansel, or of obvious failures like the Rector of Bingham (Notts).[8] It is the average that we want to strike; and it is this that is so difficult since it is always the extremists and they alone who get into the news.

[1] *Arch. Cantiana*, xxxii, p. 149.

[2] *Regist. A. Orleton*, p. 62.

[3] Cf. for example, *Regist. J. Pecham*, p. 154, *Regist. J. Pontissara*, p. 66, and the evidence from Kent quoted in chapter XVI.

[4] *Regist. A. Orleton*, p. 223.

[5] *Arch. Cantiana*, xxxii, pp. 161–2.

[6] There was no chalice at Hill Deverill (1220), All Saints in the Jewry, Cambridge (1275), Chesterton, Landbeach, and Rampton (1275), Snave (1292), Hurst, Sandhurst and Heytesbury (1300), Clyst Honiton (1301). There were only broken chalices at Thorpe (1249), Old Romney and Staple (1292).

[7] There were no books at all at S. Martin's, Old Romney, in 1292. Missals were incomplete at Westley (1249 and 1297), Hope All Saints, and Stanford (1292), Wickham (1297), Hurst (1300). The books at Salcombe Regis (1301) were in a bad way through being left in a damp place.

[8] *Regist. J. Romeyn*, i, pp. 256–7.

If, however, we could visit a number of thirteenth-century English parsonage houses we should find in most of them simple men without much education and perhaps with even less imagination or vision. Their standards of efficiency and conduct were perhaps not very high; but, without stopping to think too deeply of why they were there or what was the real object of their work, they carried on according to the traditions which they had inherited and were generally accepted by the people. Men of genius like Grosseteste might groan at their shortcomings—and, indeed, constant vigilance was necessary to prevent them from sinking into carelessness and apathy—but for the most part they gave the people what they needed and kept alive the rich heritage which later generations of churchmen have enjoyed.

CHAPTER XII

PREFERMENT

With one or two notable exceptions the clergy of England in the thirteenth century were poor men. The average living was worth only about £10 a year, and there were many outgoings. A certain amount was to be spent on the relief of the poor; the upkeep of the church and the provision and maintenance of books, ornaments and vestments would make further inroads, while the support of one or more assistant clergy would absorb a good deal of what remained. It is unlikely, therefore, that the average living was worth more than about £6 a year net.

Even rectors, then, were mostly poor men. The vicars appointed by the monasteries received even less. Bishops as a whole were anxious to see that the minimum stipend for a vicar was five marks a year (£3. 6*s.* 8*d.*), but they did not always succeed in enforcing this. Assistant clergy were supposed to receive about fifty or sixty shillings a year, but some of them certainly had to manage on less than that. Quite apart from the grossly underpaid, the average parochial chaplain probably had to keep body and soul together on what would represent about thirty shillings a week in modern currency. No wonder the archdeacons of the diocese of Lincoln in 1230 included among their enquiries the question: 'Are there any clergy who have not enough to live on?'[1]

With the offer of such very small wages it may be wondered why so many men sought ordination rather than some more lucrative occupation. Most of those who were ordained remained all their lives as assistant clergy with no hope of preferment and never expecting to have more than about £3 a year. Moreover, at their ordination they cut themselves off for ever from all legitimate pleasures of family life. And yet some thirteen hundred boys in England found their way each year into the ranks of the clergy. What, we may well ask, were the attractions?

In the first place we must allow for a sense of vocation. The 'pore persoun' of Chaucer was undoubtedly a man with a high

[1] Wilkins, *Concilia*, i, pp. 627–8.

sense both of his calling and of his responsibility; and it is reasonable to suppose that a good number of men were led by such a spirit into the Christian ministry. Such men are concerned more with their work than with their wages, being content to live on a very small income while in the service of the Son of Man who 'had not where to lay his head'. Among the forty thousand secular clergy in this country in the thirteenth century there must have been many who had no other desire than to serve God and their fellow men.

But not all clergy, as our records show, were moved by any such lofty sense of vocation; and, for such, other motives must be sought. Perhaps the strongest of these was the sense of security. Even the humblest clergy were members of a great organisation with a right to appeal beyond their employers to the higher powers who would be morally bound to see that justice was done. Moreover such security, tenuous though it might sometimes be, was, and still is, to many men worth more than a fluctuating wage which may at some times be ample and at others a mere pittance. The medieval peasant was at the mercy of the weather and the landlord, either of which might ruin him in a single night. The parish chaplain was to some extent at the mercy of his rector, but his position was one which was recognised by all and had the full weight of ecclesiastical law behind it.

Moreover, he could claim the privilege known as 'benefit of clergy', the right to be tried by the ecclesiastical courts, a privilege which might stand him in good stead if he should ever fall into the hands of the law. Benefit of clergy applied to all crimes above the level of misdemeanours, with the one exception of high treason. For all smaller offences the clerk, like any other man, must stand his trial in the ordinary courts;[1] but murder and manslaughter, theft, rape, pillage, assault and highway robbery were among the many crimes which were

[1] See the cases at Norwich: e.g. Robert the parson, who is said to have a measure of ale false and not sealed; John de Fransham, a chaplain, accused of buying corn outside the city and having it conveyed to his house by night in order to avoid payment of toll; Robert the chaplain, who is fined 3*s*. for unlawfully entering the house of Claricia Attegrene; and a certain chaplain who beat the serjeants of the Bailiffs of Norwich and broke their wands: *Leet Jurisdiction in the City of Norwich*, ed. W. Hudson, Selden Society, v (1892), pp. 14, 35, 40, 45.

'clergyable'.[1] Any man who could prove himself a clerk was entitled to be tried for such offences in the ecclesiastical courts. In order to establish his claim it was enough to show his tonsure, and there are instances on record of a man bribing or persuading his gaoler to confer the tonsure on him in order that when he came up for trial he could claim benefit of clergy.[2] In later years the test of clerkship was whether a man could read or not, and the privilege was much abused as literacy spread. If a man established his claim, the secular judges were obliged to hand him over to the ecclesiastical authorities, and he would normally be kept in the bishop's prison until his trial came on. If he escaped, the bishop was liable to a fine of £100.[3]

That the privilege of trial in the ecclesiastical courts was a real advantage to the accused is proved by the evidence of laxity which prevailed there. These tribunals had, it is true, power to sentence a man to imprisonment for life, or to corporal punishment 'short of death', but in point of fact a clerk could often reckon on going unpunished, for the procedure in these courts had become little more than a formality.[4]

This leniency may have served to encourage lawlessness among the clergy and there is certainly some evidence that clerks were from time to time concerned in acts of violence. For instance, in 1220 Hugh Hoppeoverhumbr' accused Thomas of Dean of coming with armed men and shooting Hugh's cousin, William, in the leg as he was walking in the park at Cuckfield so that he died of his wounds. Thomas pleaded benefit of clergy as an acolyte and was handed over to the Bishop of Chichester.[5]

[1] Leona C. Gabel, *Benefit of Clergy in England in the later Middle Ages*, in *Smith College Studies in History*, Oct. 1928–July 1929, pp. 58–9; Pollock and Maitland, *History of English Law*, i, p. 429.

[2] Gabel, *Benefit of Clergy*, p. 64. In a Lincolnshire trial in 1202 a man called Sefrid who had been arrested for pillaging ships shaved the crown of his head in order to claim benefit of clergy, but his pledges gave him away: *Select Pleas of the Crown*, ed. F. W. Maitland, Selden Society, i, p. 19.

[3] Gabel, *Benefit of Clergy*, p. 111. The Bishop of Bath and Wells was amerced for the escape of four thieves from his custody, but no amount is stated: *Somersetshire Pleas*, ed. C. E. H. Chadwyck Healey, p. 323.

[4] Pollock and Maitland, *History of English Law*, i, p. 426: 'little better than a farce'; Gabel, *Benefit of Clergy*, p. 113: 'largely an empty form favourable to the accused.'

[5] *Select Pleas of the Crown*, ed. F. W. Maitland, Selden Society, i, pp. 120–1.

On 6 November 1311 William of Wellington, parish chaplain of Yelvertoft in Northamptonshire, sent his clerk to buy a penny candle. The candlemaker refused to send the candle unless he had the money, whereupon William took a stick and beat the candlemaker to death 'so that his brains flowed forth'.[1] In addition to cases of homicide the judicial records of the thirteenth century give evidence of clerks found guilty of assault,[2] rape,[3] burglary,[4] and even of such offences as receiving hidden treasure[5] and not returning books which they had borrowed.[6]

Considering the general state of the country in the thirteenth century the clergy were probably a good deal better behaved than we might have expected, and there is no real evidence that the clemency of the ecclesiastical courts encouraged clerical lawlessness. Even though the verdict might turn out favourable to the accused, there was a chance of a considerable period of imprisonment pending the bishop's convenience, and we have every reason to suppose that conditions in the prisons were often extremely uncomfortable.[7] Nevertheless the privilege of benefit of clergy was a real advantage to the cleric over the layman and may well have been one of the attractions which drew men to seek ordination.

[1] *Select Cases from the Coroners' Rolls*, ed. C. Gross, Selden Society, ix, p. 69. Cf. *ibid.* p. 91; *Rolls of Justices in Eyre for Yorks., 1218–19*, ed. D. M. Stenton, Selden Society, lvi, pp. 318, 335; *Rolls of Justices in Eyre for Gloucestershire, Warwickshire and Staffordshire, 1221–2*, ed. D. M. Stenton, Selden Society, lix, p. 367; *Somersetshire Pleas*, ed. C. E. H. Chadwyck Healey, pp. 21, 22, 265–6.

[2] *Select Pleas of the Crown*, pp. 24–5, where two men, one of whom was a clerk, assaulted a man while ploughing and cut off his thumb; *Rolls of Justices in Eyre for Yorks.* p. 303, where a rector is accused of maiming a man.

[3] *Rolls of Justices in Eyre for Yorks.* pp. 360–1; *Rolls of Justices in Eyre for Gloucestershire, etc.* p. 376.

[4] *Select Pleas of the Crown*, pp. 102–3 (burglary and abduction); *Rolls of Justices in Eyre for Gloucestershire, etc.* p. 363; *Somersetshire Pleas*, pp. 18, 244.

[5] In 1218–19 a canon of York was suspected of receiving hidden treasure and was committed to the custody of the Archbishop: *Rolls of Justices in Eyre for Yorks.* p. 419.

[6] In 1271–2 the Rector of Donington (Lincs) was summoned to answer for a Breviary which he had borrowed from the Chamberlain of the Exchequer and had not returned: *Select Cases in the Exchequer of Pleas*, ed. H. Jenkinson and B. E. R. Formoy, p. 63.

[7] Bishop Sandale reckoned that it cost only a farthing a day to keep a clerk in his prison, whereas the recognised rate for the support of the Friars Minor was fourpence a day: *Regist. J. Sandale*, pp. xiv–xv.

Another attraction was the fact that the priesthood offered a certain status and prestige. For example, when the priest took the Sacrament to the sick he was to be preceded by lights and a cross and with bells ringing.[1] The reverence was, of course, intended for the Sacrament rather than for the priest, but many a man derives some pleasure from finding himself the object of the attentions of others. So it was all along. The man might break all his vows; he might drink and gamble and swear; he might be dirty, stupid and ignorant; but still he remained a priest, entitled to a respect and even a reverence which as a layman he would long ago have forfeited.

Furthermore, the man who had been ordained believed that he had set his foot firmly upon the narrow way that leadeth to life. Every child was familiar with the great 'doom' painted upon the wall of the church, with its grotesque portrayal of heaven and hell. Almost everyone was haunted all through life by the thought of possible damnation and endless torment. To become a priest did not necessarily ensure salvation, but it put a man on the side of the angels and gave him something to offer at the Judgment Seat of Christ.

And, in addition to all these, the Church gave one of the few opportunities for a man of real ability to rise to the top. Although the medieval Church was in so many ways bound to the chariot-wheels of Feudalism, there were some ways in which it was strikingly liberal and progressive. In an age when class distinctions were infinitely more rigid than they are to-day the Church opened its doors to men of all ranks of society, for preferment was by no means limited to men of the upper and middle classes as it has so often been in more recent years. It is true that the richer livings and wealthy prebends and dignities generally fell to the members of the ruling families or to protégés of the Pope or the King; but so far as real preferment was concerned no man of outstanding ability need despair.

This is shown by a study of the antecedents of the men who were appointed to bishoprics during the thirteenth century, among whom we shall find representatives of all classes and of every degree of ability and aptitude. Four were men in whose veins flowed royal blood; many were drawn from the great baronial families whose names stood high in the land; many came from the smaller landed gentry; a few belonged to the

[1] Council of Westminster (1200) in Wilkins, *Concilia*, i, p. 505; and cf. R. Grosseteste, *Epistolae*, p. 155.

best artisan class, such as Thomas of Corbridge whose grandfather was master-carpenter at York Minster during the building of the transepts;[1] and some were sons of quite humble parents. For example, when John Pecham, himself of lowly birth at Patcham in Sussex,[2] became Archbishop of Canterbury in 1279 he found, among his suffragans, Roger de Molend, a cousin of the King, at Coventry and Lichfield; at London, John de Chishul, who had been chancellor of the exchequer, had had the custody of the great seal, and had served as treasurer; at Worcester, Godfrey Giffard, a member of one of the great land-owning families; and, at Chichester, Stephen de Berkstead, a man of humble origin and of no social pretensions whatever. In the same year the province of York was governed by another Giffard as Archbishop; a courtier, Robert de Chause, had just died at Carlisle, while the great bishopric of Durham was held by the son of poor crofters of Lindisfarne, Robert called 'de Insula'. Thus at a time when the great families exercised far more power than they do now the Church offered a means of promotion to men of every class from royalty to peasantry. With all the growth of democratic ideals it is doubtful whether there has ever been such equality of opportunity in more modern times.

If, then, the bench of bishops in the thirteenth century showed great diversity of class and breeding, the same is true of the training and experience of its occupants. Some were men who had been brought up under the shadow of a great cathedral or abbey; others were men whose interests had lain entirely in the field of military and political affairs and whose acquaintance with the Church which they were destined to lead was only very slight. Again, some were members of families whose roots stretched far and deep into the English countryside, while there were others who knew little or nothing of this country and were even unfamiliar with its language.[3] Or again, there were scholars of international reputation like Pecham and Grosseteste, and there were men like Hubert Walter whose ignorance aroused the scorn of Giraldus Cambrensis,[4] and Boniface of

[1] *Regist. T. Corbridge*, ii, p. xi.

[2] J. Pecham, *Tract. Tres de Paupertate*, ed. Kingsford, Little and Tocco, p. v.

[3] For example, Aymer of Lusignan spoke no English at all (see Hunt's article in *D.N.B.*), and of Peter de Aquablanca Matthew Paris wrote 'Anglicum idioma ignoravit': *Chron. Maj.* v, p. 422.

[4] G. Cambrensis, *Opera*, ii, pp. 344–5.

Savoy of whom Matthew Paris wrote that he 'was noted more for his birth than for his brains'.[1]

The reason for this great diversity among the bishops lay partly in the method of their appointment. By the beginning of the thirteenth century the power of electing a bishop had come to be vested in the cathedral Chapter of the see.[2] In the dioceses of London, Chichester, Hereford, Lincoln, Exeter, Salisbury and York this Chapter was composed of the canons or prebendaries of the cathedral; in the dioceses of Canterbury, Winchester, Ely, Norwich, Rochester, Worcester, Durham and Carlisle the electoral body was formed by the monks, since the cathedrals of these sees were also monastic churches. In the diocese of Bath and Wells and in that of Coventry and Lichfield the election had to be carried out by two separate bodies of which one was composed of 'seculars' and one of 'regulars'.[3] The choice, then, lay with the cathedral Chapters; but there were various interested parties whose powers might have considerable influence on the course of the election.[4] First of all there was the King. A bishop was a big landowner with extensive feudal rights and wide powers over both clergy and laity, and it was therefore very much to the King's interest to see that those who were elected were acceptable to him.[5] But though the powers of the King (especially after the year 1214) were circumscribed, his influence could sometimes make itself felt. In 1250, for example, Henry III browbeat the reluctant monks

[1] 'Plus genere quam scientia choruscus, plus armis martialibus quam spiritualibus formidatus': *Chron. Maj.* iv, p. 425; cf. Pegge's *Life of Grosseteste*, pp. 119–20.

[2] For an account of how the law of election came to be regularised see Gibbs and Lang, *Bishops and Reform*, pp. 55–68.

[3] Bath and Coventry were monastic, Wells and Lichfield secular.

[4] As the Dominican, Hugh de S. Cher, said, in one of his sermons: 'Some [bishops] are not chosen by the Lord, but by themselves, for they violently intrude and force themselves into a prelacy.... Others are chosen by the devil, like those who are elected out of jealousy, that another may be turned out...others are chosen by the flesh, because they are nephews or relations...others are chosen by the world...'; quoted in R. F. Bennett, *The Early Dominicans*, pp. 140–1.

[5] Needless to say, this dual control led to endless disputes. So important was this that when King John granted to the Church freedom of election in 1214 he expressly reserved to himself the right to veto the election if he could show some just cause for so doing, e.g. if the man elected were likely to prove disastrous to the Commonweal: Stubbs, *Charters*, pp. 283–4.

of Winchester into electing his half-brother, Aymer, whom the more spirited Chapter of Durham had turned down in the previous year on account of his youth and ignorance.[1] In the same way the Pope, though he had little direct power over the choice of English bishops, was occasionally able to make his influence felt, especially when, after some dispute, the question of nomination was referred to Rome and the Pope exercised his powers of 'providing' to the vacant see. When, therefore, a vacancy occurred there were likely to be several parties interested in the election, and many factors would enter in, political, personal and even financial; and the Church of the thirteenth century, though nominally free to choose its diocesans, was in fact to some extent under the influence of powers which had ends to serve other than those of the well-being of the Church.

Since in ten out of seventeen sees the choice of bishop lay with a monastic Chapter it was likely that a certain number of those elected should have been monks. Several times during the thirteenth century the electors simply chose the outstanding man among themselves, a man whose qualities and abilities were known to them all.[2] Occasionally they went outside their own circle, for in 1229 the monks of Ely invited Hugh of Northwold, Abbot of Bury S. Edmunds, to be their bishop, and in 1278 the canons of Carlisle elected Ralph de Irton, a canon of Guisborough. On one occasion a head was sought from the members of a different order when the Benedictine Chapter of Ely in 1220 chose the Cistercian Abbot of Fountains to be their bishop. Altogether, among the English bishops of this century, there were fourteen who had previously been members of one or other of the monastic orders. Nine were Benedictines,[3] two

[1] See the account of this in Matthew Paris, *Chron. Maj.* v, pp. 179–85.

[2] In 1216 the monks of Worcester elected their own prior, Silvester of Evesham; in 1257 the Ely Chapter elected their subprior, Hugh Balsham, founder of Peterhouse at Cambridge; in 1261 the Durham monks elected one of their number, Robert Stichel, and again, in 1274, Robert de Insula; in 1266 the monks of Norwich chose their own prior, Roger de Skerning; in 1278 the Chapter of Rochester elected one of their own men, John Bradfield, and lived to regret it; and in 1292 the Augustinians of Carlisle elected John Halton, a canon of the house. Note also that in 1298 the Ely monks elected their prior, John Salmon, but the election was disputed and Salmon was translated to Norwich.

[3] In addition to those mentioned above Ralph Wareham, Prior of Norwich, was elected Bishop of Chichester in 1218, the only example of a monk being chosen by a secular Chapter.

were Augustinians, two Cistercians (including Hugh, Abbot of Beaulieu, who was forced upon the canons of Carlisle much against their will) and one Carthusian, Boniface of Savoy, who had entered that order as a boy but had probably been unable to sustain its very severe discipline for long. Besides those who were monks there were three men who had been friars—Robert Kilwardby, a Dominican, and two Franciscans, John Pecham and Godfrey Giffard.[1]

Most of these were men who had shown ability and leadership in their respective orders, who had been trained as administrators and who had had some experience in the handling of human problems as they arose in the limited atmosphere of a monastic house. Another type of thirteenth-century bishop was the distinguished student who had made his mark in the schools. The moment we begin to study the personnel of the episcopal bench we are struck by the large number of scholars who were promoted to high office. It is a remarkable, and in many ways a most encouraging, fact that, in spite of the influence of King and Pope, six out of the eight men who held the primacy during the thirteenth century were scholars of great merit. Stephen Langton had already acquired an international reputation for his lectures at Paris long before he was called upon to bear office as Archbishop.[2] His successor, Richard Grant, was a writer of some distinction,[3] and the saintly Edmund of Abingdon, who followed him in 1234, had already made his mark as a scholar and teacher.[4] In the latter years of the century Canterbury was governed by men of very considerable academic distinction. The first was the Dominican friar, Robert Kilwardby, who had lectured at Oxford and edited the works of S. Augustine;[5] the second was the Franciscan, John Pecham, who had acquired so high a reputation for his lectures at Rome that even the cardinals and bishops who attended would rise and bare their heads at his entrance;[6] and the third was Robert Winchelsey, whose sermons and lectures in S. Paul's Cathedral and elsewhere

[1] Although Giffard formally entered the Franciscan Order in 1277 it is unlikely that he ever took his membership very seriously, see J. W. W. Bund, *Regist. G. Giffard*, pp. xxxv and 94.

[2] Powicke, *Stephen Langton*, chapters ii and iii.

[3] Tanner, *Bibliotheca*, p. 759.

[4] B. Ward, *S. Edmund, Archbishop of Canterbury*, pp. 33–4, 39–42.

[5] See Tout's article in *D.N.B.*

[6] See Kingsford's article in *D.N.B.*

attracted enormous crowds,[1] and the list of whose writings fills more than two whole pages of Tanner's *Bibliotheca*.

Like the Canterbury monks, many of the secular Chapters looked to the Universities when the time came for them to choose a leader. That learned and extremely able man, Richard le Poore, who had been a pupil of Stephen Langton at Paris, was elected Bishop of Chichester in 1214 and translated to Salisbury in 1217, where he spent eleven years before his final removal to Durham.[2] Chichester was also distinguished in later years by the presence of S. Richard de la Wych, who had made a name for himself as a scholar at Oxford and Orleans.[3] The Salisbury Chapter replaced le Poore in 1228 with another learned man, Robert de Bingham.[4] At Lincoln the outstanding figure of the century was Robert Grosseteste, who had been Chancellor of Oxford and was perhaps the most brilliant scholar of his generation in Europe. At Hereford we find the learned legist, John le Breton, and the scholarly Ralph Maidstone.[5] York was well served by able men, among whom Sewal de Bovill and Thomas Corbridge stand out as men of academic distinction.

In order to complete our list of distinguished scholars who rose to episcopal rank we should notice Nicholas of Farnham, who had been Professor of Medicine at Bologna before becoming Bishop of Durham,[6] John of Pontissara who, before his election to Winchester in 1282, had been Chancellor of Oxford and Professor of Civil Law at Modena,[7] Alexander Stavensby, who had been Professor of Theology at Toulouse before his appointment to the see of Coventry and Lichfield in 1224,[8] and one of his successors in that diocese, Roger de Weseham, who had followed Grosseteste as lecturer to the Franciscans at Oxford.[9]

[1] Stephen of Birchington in Wharton's *Anglia Sacra*, i, p. 11.

[2] He is described by Matthew Paris as 'eximiae sanctitatis et profundae scientiae': *Chron. Maj.* iii, p. 391.

[3] See Mrs Tout's article in *D.N.B.*

[4] M. Paris, *Chron. Maj.* iv, p. 586: 'literaturae scientia ad plenum eruditus'; cf. W. H. R. Jones, *Reg. S. Osmundi*, ii, p. 16: 'Summe literatus et magister a longo tempore in theologia.'

[5] For Ralph Maidstone see Little, *Grey Friars in Oxford*, p. 182.

[6] M. Paris, *Chron. Maj.* iv, p. 86.

[7] Introduction to *Regist. J. Pontissara*, p. vi.

[8] *N. Triveti Annales*, ed. T. Hog, p. 224, and cf. Rashdall, *Medieval Universities* (new ed.), ii, p. 163 n.

[9] Eccleston, *de Adventu Fratrum Minorum*, p. 61, and cf. Little, *Grey Friars in Oxford*, pp. 30 and 31. There had been one lecturer between

All these were men of distinction whose names were familiar to students of all lands; and, on the whole, they made good, conscientious bishops. Many of them had passed through the discipline of poverty, they knew how to work hard without much return, and they had learnt to labour not for their own advancement but for that of truth. Had there been more of such men among those who held high office in the Church of England greater progress might have been made along the path of reform. The weakness of the episcopate during this century was that so many of its members were men who, though they had achieved distinction in other fields of human activity, were neither fitted nor anxious to sustain the responsibilities which were thrust upon them. Just as in our own days ex-Cabinet ministers often become directors of city companies about whose internal affairs they know very little, so in the thirteenth century men were appointed rulers of dioceses without any real interest in the work which they were supposed to direct and inspire.

Among the letters written to Ralph Neville, Chancellor of England and Bishop of Chichester, is one from the precentor of the cathedral, who writes imploring him to come down to Chichester for Easter to celebrate the paschal services. He knows how busy he is about the business of the Court but asks him to give up at least three days to the affairs of the Church, since there are so many matters upon which he needs his advice.[1] Neville was typical of a large class of bishops who were really, by training and inclination, civil servants and statesmen rather than ecclesiastics. Some were judges, some diplomatists, some financial advisers to the Crown, and many of them continued their judicial and administrative work after they had been rewarded with a bishopric. Men like Grosseteste and Pecham,[2] who were really concerned for the well-being of the Church, complained bitterly of those who travelled about as justices itinerant and who neglected their dioceses in order to serve

Grosseteste and Weseham who had become a bishop in Scotland. There is a *Memoir of Roger de Weseham* by Samuel Pegge, 1761.

[1] *Letters to Ralph Neville*, ed. W. H. Blaauw, in *Sussex Arch. Coll.* iii (1850), pp. 75–6.

[2] In 1236 Grosseteste wrote to Hugh of Pateshull, afterwards Bishop of Coventry and Lichfield, pointing out how shamefully he neglects his responsibilities and admonishing him to give up either his worldly business or his pastoral charge: R. Grosseteste, *Epistolae*, pp. 97–100.

their King. But of what avail were such complaints with men who were far more interested in diplomacy than in the endless routine of diocesan administration, who preferred the company of courtiers to that of country clergy, and who found the King's Bench far more comfortable than a cathedral stall?[1]

But though these men may have been faced with an almost impossible task, namely that of leading the Church while they were at the same time servants of the State, yet they were at least men of ability and probity, who had served their apprenticeship in the school of public life and had advanced through their own merits. There remains to consider a group of men who had little or nothing to recommend them and who owed their preferment to the fact that they had won the ear of the King. Among these were several of his own relatives, most of whom proved themselves thoroughly incompetent bishops. The first was Geoffrey, an illegitimate son of Henry II, who, because of his royal descent—albeit left-handed—became Bishop of Lincoln at the tender age of fourteen. He drew the revenues of the see for seven or eight years in spite of the fact that he was only in minor orders and spent most of his time abroad. In 1181 he was offered the archbishopric of York, which he had the honesty at first to decline on the grounds that he was more interested in dogs and hawks than in books and priests. However it served the King's purpose to have him there, and he held the office until 1212. During these years he quarrelled violently with all who stood in his way, devoted himself almost entirely to sport and warfare, and allowed the diocese to sink into a shocking state of neglect.[2]

[1] Among the prelates who also held high office in the state were Hubert Walter, who had been Justiciar of England; Nicholas of Ely, Walter de Merton, and Ralph Neville, who held office as Chancellors; John de Chishul, Walter Langton and John Kirkby, who had been Treasurers; William Raleigh, Simon Walton, William of York, Godfrey Lucy, John Gray, Eustace Fauconberge and John le Breton, who were judges. Silvester de Everdon, Henry de Wingham, and William Kilkenny are described as Keepers of the Seal; Thomas Blunville was an Exchequer clerk and Constable of the Tower of London. For biographical notes and references see articles in *D.N.B.* and Gibbs and Lang, *Bishops and Reform*, pp. 185–92.

[2] See *Vita Galfridi*, by Giraldus Cambrensis in *Opera*, vol. ii; Dixon, *Fasti Eboracenses*, pp. 252–78; and Miss Norgate's article in *D.N.B.* Modern estimates of Geoffrey's incompetence are unanimous and yet the saintly Hugh of Lincoln, when appointed chairman of a commission to

Another such was Aymer de Lusignan, a half-brother of Henry III, who, at an early age, was forced upon the reluctant monks of Winchester in 1250. He also was a man of violence, who used his office simply as a means for providing himself with the funds which he needed for his personal and family affairs. Although he held the see for ten years he was never ordained more than acolyte until within six months of his death. A more illustrious favourite was the Queen's uncle, Boniface of Savoy, whom Henry III nominated as Archbishop of Canterbury on the death of S. Edmund in 1240, a nomination which the monks of Christ Church dare not reject. Estimates of Boniface's character and achievements have been varied. Creighton, basing his judgment mainly on the opinions of monastic writers like Matthew Paris, summed up his article on the Archbishop with the words: 'Boniface did nothing that was important either for church or state in England.'[1] But in more recent years critics have been more sympathetic, if not to the Archbishop's character at least to his work. Miss Gibbs even goes so far as to say that 'for the general history of the period which followed the death of Grosseteste it is a circumstance of real importance that the English episcopate had at its head this forceful, ruthlessly businesslike foreigner, half distrusted by King and clergy and barons, himself principally interested in pressing to their logical conclusions his own rights as metropolitan and the privileges and exemptions of his order'.[2] Politically, no doubt, Boniface played an important part in the affairs of Church and State, and, on the whole, he appears to have been anxious to do his duty and prepared to listen to the advice of better men. But however much we may concede to the customs of the time, we are still left with the picture of a man of God of such violent habits that he could strike a fellow-priest with such force as to fell him to the ground, and of a Primate who was not ashamed, out of the twenty-nine years during which he held office, to spend fourteen

enquire into his misdeeds, said: 'I would as soon be suspended myself as suspend him': Dixon, *Fasti Eboracenses*, p. 271. S. Hugh may have felt that he owed something to Geoffrey, for he had done a good deal for Lincoln and had redeemed the ornaments of the Church which had been pawned to Aaron the Jew: *ibid.* p. 254.

[1] See his article on Boniface in the *D.N.B.*

[2] Gibbs and Lang, *Bishops and Reform*, pp. 22–3.

of them out of England in the pursuit of the military and political fortunes of his own family.

John, Henry III and Edward I were all anxious to secure the appointment of their favourites to lucrative positions in the Church, and they had considerable success. In 1205 Peter des Roches, who was 'by turns warrior, military engineer, builder, financial agent, statesman and diplomatist',[1] became Bishop of Winchester through the influence of King John; Walter Gray, William of Cornhill and Simon of Apulia all owed their preferment to royal influence, while in 1240 Henry III persuaded the canons of Hereford to elect Peter de Aquablanca, who has been described as 'the most unpopular prelate of his day'.[2] A fat and ugly Savoyard,[3] he had no sooner been appointed than he devoted himself to the dual task of filling the cathedral stalls with his own kinsfolk and of procuring his own translation to a more lucrative see.[4] He made no effort to administer his diocese in person, preferring to live abroad, where he devoted himself to political intrigues for the prosecution of which he diverted considerable sums of money destined for the welfare of the Church in this country. The dislike and opprobrium which he aroused is summed up in Matthew Paris' impolite words: 'his memory', he writes, 'exhales a foul and sulphureous stench'.[5]

And there were others little better. There was that 'slippery customer' Robert Burnell who amassed an enormous fortune with which he married off young relatives who were thought to be his daughters to English noblemen;[6] there was Hugh of Beaulieu who played havoc with the affairs of Carlisle;[7] and

[1] See article by W. E. Rhodes in *D.N.B.*

[2] *The Will of Peter de Aquablanca*, ed. C. E. Woodruff, in *Camden Misc.* xiv (1926), p. v.

[3] M. Paris, *Chron. Maj.* v, pp. 622, 647, where reference is made to the fact that he suffered from a polypus in the nose.

[4] Henry III tried to get him elected to Durham in 1241, to Lincoln in 1254 and to Bordeaux in 1256, but without success.

[5] M. Paris, *Chron. Maj.* v, p. 510.

[6] The *Dunstable Annals* describe him thus: 'He was pleasant in conversation with people but was considered mighty slippery (*supra modum lubricus*). By means of his vast treasure he married off his relatives—I won't say daughters (*ne dicam filias*)—to English noblemen. He acquired much property and many manors which he left to his nephews—or sons (*seu filiis*)': Luard, *An. Mon.* iii, p. 373.

[7] Gibbs and Lang, *Bishops and Reform*, p. 8; cf. *Chron. de Lanercost*, p. 30.

there was Anthony Bek, arrogant, wealthy, ostentatious, who played with his hawks while being interviewed by the Pope and quarrelled with everyone who stood in his way.[1] All these owed their preferment to royal influence; but none of them brought much prosperity or happiness to his diocese, or to his clergy.

[1] See Raine, *Hist. Dunelm. Script. Tres*, p. 64 and Creighton's article in *D.N.B.*

CHAPTER XIII

THE BISHOP AT HOME

When a man became a bishop he became at the same time a landlord on a very considerable scale; and, however much he might wish to regard his appointment as a sinecure, he was bound to accept the responsibilities which the ownership of land entailed. The administration of his estates might be largely left in the hands of stewards and bailiffs—just as spiritual work might be delegated to archdeacons and officials—but if the bishop were to ensure that there was no reduction of his income and no infringement of his rights he would be obliged to devote some attention to local affairs.

By far the greater part of a bishop's income was derived from 'temporals', from the ownership of a number of manors either in his own diocese or elsewhere. The bishopric of Winchester carried with it the possession of fifty manors with an income estimated at £3000 a year;[1] the archbishopric of Canterbury included thirty-four manors of which ten were in the diocese of Chichester and four in that of Winchester;[2] London and Exeter had twenty-four each,[3] Hereford and York twenty-three.[4] Robert Burnell, when Bishop of Bath and Wells, was the owner of eighty-two manors scattered over nineteen counties, but many of these were his own personal property and no part of the bishopric.[5] According to the assessments made in 1291 the richest see was Winchester, valued at £2977. 15*s.* 7½*d.*; followed by Durham, Canterbury and Ely, all over £2000. The poorest was Rochester, with a paltry £183. 10*s.* 7*d.*[6]

[1] *Regist. J. Pontissara*, pp. 421–2, 433–4; and cf. *Taxatio Nicholai*, p. 215. In John de Sandale's time there were forty-nine manors, four boroughs and a fair, bringing in a net income of about £5250: *Regist. J. Sandale*, pp. 627–8.

[2] *Taxatio Nicholai*, pp. 6, 139, 140, 206.

[3] *Accounts of Executors of R. Gravesend and T. Button*, Camden Society, 1874, pp. xi and xiii. Cf. *Taxatio Nicholai*, pp. 151, 139, 207.

[4] *Regist. T. Cantilupe*, p. xl; Webb, *Roll of Household Expenses of R. de Swinfield*, ii, p. xxvii; Dixon, *Fasti Eboracenses*, p. 325.

[5] See Tout's article in *D.N.B.*

[6] See the figures in *Taxatio Nicholai* and compare the list in *Regist. H. Hethe*, p. 51. In addition to manors bishops often held a monopoly of fairs and markets; e.g. Simon of Ghent, when Bishop of Salisbury,

The administration of so much property, and the maintenance of the complicated system of manorial rights and responsibilities which went with it, entailed a vast amount of work. Some of the bishops were men who had been brought up on large estates and who therefore understood some of the intricacies and pitfalls of estate management. Others who had come from humbler circumstances, or who were more at home in a lecture-room than in a manorial court, must have found it a heavy burden.

An intimate picture of the relations between a landowner and his steward is revealed by the correspondence addressed to Ralph Neville, who was Bishop of Chichester from 1224 to 1244, by Simon de Senliz.[1] By keeping his ears open for local gossip among other agents Simon was able, on more than one occasion, to do his master a good turn. He knows for certain, from what others have told him, that when the Archbishop of Canterbury comes to Preston he will provide for himself out of his own means; he therefore advises the bishop to write to the Primate and make him an offer of hospitality since he knows that it will not be accepted.[2] On another occasion he writes to say that he has heard rumours that a local landowner, Sir John de Rochford, is ready to mortgage for eight years a carucate of land at Westmill, and Simon suggests that the bishop should make him an offer before anyone else hears of it.[3] He describes with much satisfaction the new windmill at Watersfield of which he says 'it is ready and well fitted up, *and it grinds*'.[4] He gives much advice as to where the best sheep can be bought, urges the bishop to buy twelve mares to draw the marl-carts since horses are 'as dear as gold in Sussex', describes the harvest and the cutting down of trees, and twice asks his master to buy more foxhounds.[5] He also fills his letters from time to time

took a toll of fairs and markets at Yetminster, Sherborne, Ramsbury, Godalming and Chiddingfold: *Regist. S. Gandavo*, i, p. xiv, and cf. Savage, *Great Register of Lichfield*, pp. 102, 141–2, 173.

[1] Published by W. H. Blaauw in *Sussex Arch. Coll.* vol. iii (1850).

[2] *Ibid.* p. 51. [3] *Ibid.* p. 69. [4] *Ibid.* p. 64.

[5] *Ibid.* pp. 52, 54, 63, 65, 46–7. There were many problems arising out of the stock on the various manors. For details of how episcopal manors were stocked see *ibid.* p. 53, and cf. *Regist. R. Swinfield*, p. 87; Dixon, *Fasti Eboracenses*, p. 325; *Accounts of Executors of Gravesend and Button*, Camden Society. The stock on the manors of Sandale, Bishop of Winchester, included 184 horses, 487 head of cattle, 4330 wethers, 162 rams, 4862 ewes and 2693 pigs: *Regist. J. Sandale*, p. 631.

with local scandal, as that he has heard that the Vicar of Mundham has two wives and that he claims to have obtained a special dispensation from the Pope for this doubtful privilege. He adds that no one in the neighbourhood believes this fantastic claim.[1]

The possession of so much land inevitably led to many disputes which were intensified by the medieval passion for litigation. As landlords bishops were constantly brought into collision with their neighbours, both rich and poor. The chief trouble with their poorer neighbours was over the question of game, for the bishops, like all landed gentry who are also magistrates, were very severe on poachers. In 1284 John of Pontissara, Bishop of Winchester, excommunicated certain persons who had been catching rabbits on his estate at Esher, and Thomas Cantilupe even had to take action against some of his clergy for a similar offence.[2]

With their richer neighbours there were perpetual disputes and quarrels, some of them inherited from predecessors, which dragged on for many years and were a constant drain on the resources of the bishopric. Hereford was not one of the richest sees; yet one of its bishops, Thomas Cantilupe, found it necessary to keep five advocates in his service in the King's Bench as well as proctors and attorneys in other courts.[3] Several bishops maintained in their households a *pugil* or champion, for duels were still a part of the method whereby disputes were sometimes settled.[4]

The profit which accrued from the ownership of manors formed by far the greater part of the bishop's income. In addition, each diocesan collected certain small sums which were paid by the parishes,[5] and a few sees benefited from the appropriation of one or more parish churches.[6] Occasionally, when a bishop was hard pressed by his creditors he was allowed to

[1] *Sussex Arch. Coll.* iii, p. 47.

[2] *Regist. J. Pontissara*, p. 451, and *Regist. T. Cantilupe*, pp. 69, 76–8. Cf. also *Regist. R. Winchelsey*, pp. 356–7; *Regist. S. Gandavo*, i, p. 8.

[3] *Regist. T. Cantilupe*, pp. lxix–lxxi, 22; cf. *Regist. J. Pontissara*, pp. lxiv and 735–9.

[4] *Regist. G. Giffard*, pp. xxxi-ii; Luard, *An. Mon.* iv, pp. 467–8. Thomas Cantilupe also kept a champion, Thomas de Bruges, who received a salary of half a mark a year: *Regist. T. Cantilupe*, p. 104; cf. *Roll of R. de Swinfield*, i, pp. 125–6. Thomas de Bruges seems to have been afterwards employed by Bogo de Clare: *Archaeologia*, lxx, pp. 14–15.

[5] See above, pp. 120–3.

[6] See above, pp. 41–2.

employ some temporary financial expedient such as the sequestration of vacant livings[1] or the right to retain the various benefices and prebends which he had held previous to his elevation to the episcopate.[2]

Adding together all the sources, temporal and spiritual,[3] the bishops' incomes must have been very large. It would certainly be no exaggeration to say that the average episcopal stipend represented about £80,000 a year in modern currency, while some of them were even larger. Yet with all this income almost all of the bishops were constantly harassed by debt. The episcopal Registers show the efforts which the bishops had to make to meet their creditors. They borrowed money widely and wildly, from Italian merchants, from the Pope, from the monasteries, from Church dignitaries, even from their own clergy. It was not beneath their dignity to approach anyone who had a little ready cash. And still their debts mounted up.

Winchester was the richest see in England, with an income in modern terms of some £200,000 a year;[4] yet throughout the thirteenth century the bishops who drew this enormous income were constantly and hopelessly in debt. Godfrey Lucy, who was bishop in 1200, had borrowed £3000 from the Chapter; William Raleigh had to borrow a vast sum in order to pay the fees engendered by a long dispute over his election in 1238, and the diocese was impoverished for many years as a result. Aymer of Lusignan let the affairs of the see go from bad to worse; and his successor, John Gervais, inherited a debt of 1300 marks to the Pope, while he himself ran up debts of 8000 marks to various merchants.[5]

At Canterbury, Boniface of Savoy inherited a debt of 22,000 marks (£14,666), but being an able financier and a merciless

[1] M. Paris, *Chron. Maj.* iv, pp. 506–9; Bliss, *Cal. Papal Letters*, i, pp. 71, 238, 267, 292, 380.

[2] E.g. Lawrence of S. Martin, Bishop of Rochester in 1251: Bliss, *Cal. Papal Letters*, i, p. 267. Also Simon Walton, Bishop of Norwich in 1258: M. Paris, *Chron. Maj.* v, pp. 648–9.

[3] The 'spirituals' amounted to far less than the 'temporals', but even so were a great asset. In 1301–2 the spiritualities of the bishopric of Worcester amounted to £109. 11*s*. 11*d*.: Worcester, *Regist. Sede Vacante*, pp. 39–40.

[4] See above, p. 169.

[5] See articles on Lucy, des Roches and Raleigh in *D.N.B.*, and Bliss, *Cal. Papal Letters*, i, pp. 380, 409 and 424. John of Pontissara managed to restore some sort of financial order towards the end of the century: *Regist. J. Pontissara*, pp. xix, liii.

collector of fines and dues he was able to pay this off.[1] He was helped by the fact that he got permission from the Pope in 1247 to collect from the proceeds of vacant livings a sum of 12,000 marks towards the payment of his debts.[2] This, however, did not satisfy him; for in 1251 we find the Pope, Innocent IV, writing to the Deans of Wells, Chichester and Hereford desiring them to curb the predatory activities of the Primate.[3] Robert Kilwardby, Boniface's successor, allowed debts to accumulate again and left an unfortunate legacy to the diocese by carrying off into his retirement at Rome some of the money belonging to the see, together with many of the books and ornaments of the Church and the official Registers.[4] John Pecham thus inherited debts which he was powerless to clear. As a Franciscan he had no private estate and was obliged to turn to the Italian merchants, to the King, to the Pope and even to the citizens of Canterbury in order to find money to pay the vast sums consequent upon his elevation to the primacy in 1279.[5] In the following year he tried to borrow 1000 marks from the Prior and Convent of Ely.[6] By 1295 Archbishop Winchelsey owed the merchants of Pistoia £3000.[7]

Other dioceses fared equally disastrously. Walter Bronescombe found heavy debts at Exeter owing to the action of a group of unscrupulous men who had surrounded the death-bed of his predecessor, Richard Blund, and had issued forged letters in his name disposing of his property and conferring benefices on whom they would.[8] Richard Gravesend of London left debts of £1200.[9] At York, Walter Giffard was continuously in debt. He wrote in 1267 to the Cardinal of S. Prassede to say that he could not pay the money which he owed at Rome and to remind the Cardinal that the late Pope had agreed to let him pay off his debts at the rate of 1000 marks a year.[10] John le Romeyn,

[1] Stephen of Birchington in Wharton, *Anglia Sacra*, i, p. 11; cf. *D.N.B.* and Gibbs and Lang, *Bishops and Reform*, pp. 22–3.

[2] Bliss, *Cal. Papal Letters*, i, p. 238.

[3] *Ibid.* pp. 273–4.

[4] See Tout's article in *D.N.B.*

[5] Pecham, *Reg. Epist.* i, pp. 17, 21–2, 34–5, 49–50.

[6] *Ibid.* pp. 105–7. Cf. an essay by D. Sutcliffe on *The Financial Condition of the See of Canterbury, 1279–92*, in *Speculum*, x (1935), pp. 54–67.

[7] *Regist. R. Winchelsey*, p. 56; cf. *Regist. J. Pontissara*, pp. 505–6.

[8] *Regist. W. Bronescombe and P. Quivil*, p. x.

[9] *Accounts of Executors of Gravesend and Button*, Camden Society, p. xix.

[10] *Regist. W. Giffard*, pp. 106, 110, 117.

in the first six months of his reign at York, had to borrow £2173.[1]

This terrible record of insolvency on the part of those who should have set a good example to men who were trying to keep their heads above water on an income of three or four pounds a year seems very shocking to us. Yet there were some extenuating circumstances over which the bishops had little control. When Walter Giffard wrote to the legate Ottobon in 1267 he explained that the reasons for his insolvency were the difficulty of collecting tithes and the necessity of attending so many parliaments.[2] There were also heavy losses due to bad harvests and murrain among the stock on the manors.[3] Moreover, each bishop on his accession had to pay heavy fees to the King and to the Pope. Pontissara had to pay £2000 to the King for the possession of the see of Winchester and a further £2850 for the crops of the previous year;[4] Pecham had to find 2000 marks for corn and hay growing on the manors;[5] Walter Gray had to produce £10,000 in fees to the Pope before he could get his election to the archbishopric of York ratified,[6] and John Salmon of Norwich had to borrow 13,000 florins to pay his expenses.[7]

But apart from fees and misfortunes the fact remains that many of the bishops' embarrassments were due to their extravagance. John Pecham, in spite of all his debts and in spite of the fact that he was a Franciscan, vowed to the service of Lady Poverty, paid £173. 4*s.* 1*d.* for a mitre in 1288;[8] Godfrey

[1] *Regist. J. Romeyn*, ii, pp. xiii–xiv; Dixon, *Fasti Eboracenses*, p. 330.

[2] *Regist. W. Giffard*, pp. 156–7. He adds that his financial embarrassment has caused him many sleepless nights and that he has had to resort to 'incommoda usurarum'.

[3] For the diocese of Canterbury see the article by Miss Sutcliffe in *Speculum*, x (1935), pp. 54–67.

[4] *Regist. J. Pontissara*, pp. 716, 398–9.

[5] *Regist. J. Pecham* (C. & Y. Soc.), p. 15.

[6] Dixon, *Fasti Eboracenses*, p. 283.

[7] Bliss, *Cal. Papal Letters*, i, p. 582. Even in modern times appointment to high office in the Church is an expensive thing. When Randall Davidson became Archbishop of Canterbury in 1903 his expenses amounted to nearly £10,000, so that he wrote sadly to Lord Knollys, the King's private secretary: 'It is a very grave thing for a man who is not rich to succeed to this sort of office': G. K. A. Bell, *Randall Davidson*, i, p. 395.

[8] Pecham, *Reg. Epist.* iii, p. 957. This must have been exceptional, for Bishop Orleton acquired a mitre which Swinfield had bought for £40

Giffard, who had also been a Franciscan, kept a retinue of one hundred and forty horsemen with whom he once descended upon the unhappy monks of Worcester and demanded hospitality;[1] and Walter Gray entertained the Kings of England and Scotland to a banquet at York at Christmas 1252 which cost him over £2500.[2] It is only on very rare occasions that we find any attempt at economy, as, for example, when William Raleigh, having crippled the diocese of Winchester by his extravagance, was forced to retire to Tours, where he lived for eleven months with a much reduced household.[3]

It was, in fact, in the maintenance of his household that a bishop's main expense lay. There were, first of all, the legal officers, the officials, penitentiaries, apparitors, proctors, advocates, attorneys and sequestrators, each with his clerk or secretary. Then there were the ecclesiastical attendants, the chaplains and clerks of the chapel.[4] Next came a host of men engaged in the management of the bishop's estates, accountants and auditors, stewards and bailiffs, foresters, fowlers, park-keepers and huntsmen. Finally there were the actual members of the household, the squires, valets, servants and pages.[5] Some bishops had, in addition, a personal bodyguard of soldiers.[6] Many of the above were about their master's business in various parts of the diocese or in London, but the majority of them formed the bishop's *familia* or household and followed him in his endless wanderings from manor to manor.

For medieval bishops, like other great landowners of those times, were compelled to live as nomads. They may often have

(*Regist. A. Orleton*, pp. 41–2) and Bishop Drokensford paid £23. 6*s*. 8*d*. for two mitres in 1321 (*Regist. J. Drokensford*, p. 198).

[1] Luard, *An. Mon.* iv, pp. 503–4. Anthony Bek also had a retinue of 140 knights and his display and extravagance were proverbial.

[2] Dixon, *Fasti Eboracenses*, p. 288.

[3] M. Paris, *Chron. Maj.* v, pp. 178–9.

[4] Grosseteste, for example, always had a few friars in his entourage: *Epistolae*, p. 69; Pegge, *Robert Grosseteste*, p. 37.

[5] For mention of bishops' private barbers see Pecham, *Reg. Epist.* iii, p. 1079; *Regist. J. Sandale*, p. 71.

[6] In an inventory of the goods belonging to the Bishop of Winchester at Wolvesey we find 27 steel helmets, 80 shields and 23 crossbows: *Regist. J. Pontissara*, pp. 495–6; cf. *Accounts of Executors of Gravesend and Button*, Camden Society, p. 136. In 1326 Bishop Hethe of Rochester received a royal mandate to arm his retainers for the defence of the realm: *Regist. H. Hethe*, p. 303.

meditated upon the text: 'Here we have no continuing city', as they trundled from one manor to another preceded by the luggage waggons and surrounded by their squires, valets and pages. Transport and distribution were so bad in those days that no manor could support the episcopal household for more than a few weeks, at the end of which it was necessary to pack up and move on to another of the many manors which the bishop owned, where a store of food and fuel would be awaiting them. In addition to these perpetual peregrinations necessitated by the difficulties of catering, a bishop would also be obliged to travel sometimes to London at the command of the King or the Archbishop, sometimes to Rome, sometimes to some other part of the continent 'on his majesty's service'.

A remarkable picture of the day-to-day life of a thirteenth-century prelate is afforded by the fragment of the roll of Bishop Swinfield's household expenses in the years 1289 and 1290.[1] During the 296 days covered by the roll we find that the bishop moved his household no less than eighty-one times. The longest periods of settled life were fifty-seven days at his manor of Bosbury in the autumn and early winter, twenty-nine nights at his manor of Prestbury in the New Year, and thirty-four nights at the manor of Whitbourne in the summer. On the other hand between 10 April and 5 June, a period of fifty-one days, he slept at thirty-eight different places. This was due to the fact that he was then on one of his visitation tours of a part of his diocese.

The organisation necessary for these frequent removals must have been very considerable, for the household consisted of about forty men. These were strictly graded in four classes. First came the five or six squires (*armigeri*), most of whom had definite tasks allotted to them in connection with the management of the estates and the organisation of the household. Their wages varied between one mark (13*s.* 4*d.*) and one pound a year. Next to the squires came the valets (*valetti*), of whom there were about a dozen. They included the clerk of the chapel, two carters who were responsible for transporting the baggage, farriers, a porter, a messenger, a huntsman, a butler and a larderer. Their wages varied between five shillings and eight shillings and eightpence a year. Below the valets came thirteen servants (*garciones*) earning three or four shillings a year, who

[1] *A Roll of the Household Expenses of Richard de Swinfield during part of the years 1289–90*, ed. by John Webb, Camden Society, 2 vols. 1854–5.

Plate IV. Effigy of Godfrey Giffard, Bishop of Worcester.

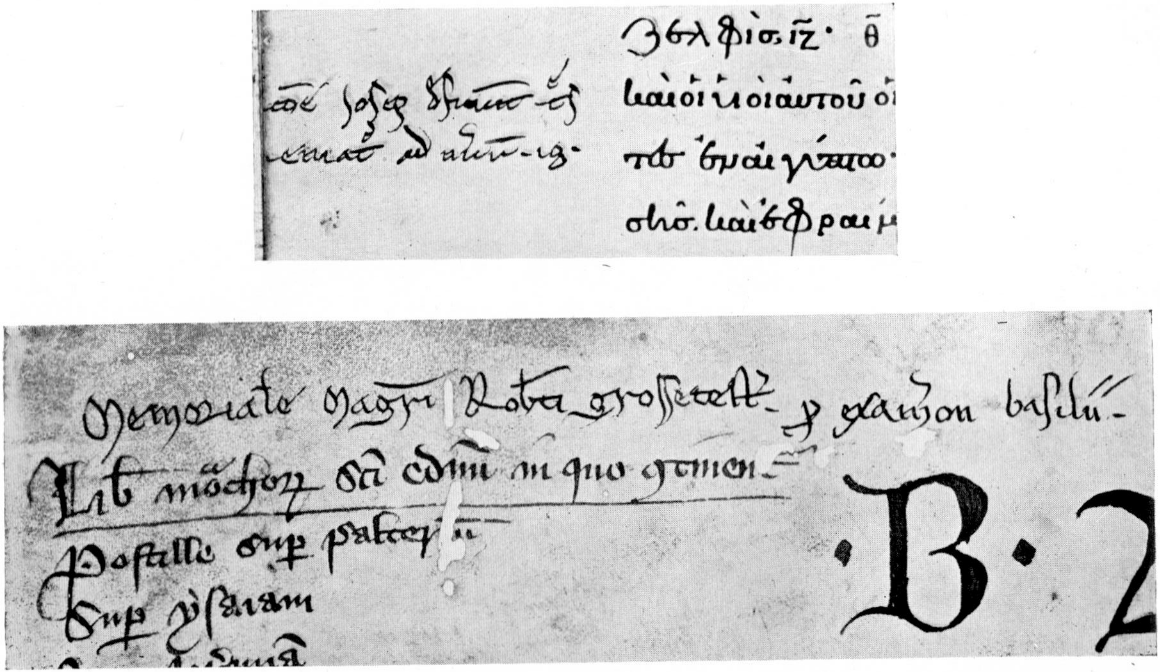

Plate V. Specimens of Grosseteste's Handwriting from MSS at Cambridge.

formed the household and kitchen staff together with some outdoor workers such as a thresher and an under-groom. Last on the list came the pages (*pagii*), some of whom were perhaps hired only for short periods.[1]

John de Kemeseye, the bishop's accountant, kept a most careful record of how the money was spent, together with the exact amount of food consumed each day. Large quantities of cloth were bought, as the bishop was responsible for the clothing of his household as well as for their food and drink. In winter he himself wore keyneth or strong cloth, together with a surcoat trimmed with doeskin, hoods of miniver and a mantle. His head was protected by a fur cap, and for relaxation by his own fireside he spent two shillings on a pair of slippers.[2] Apart from food and clothes the household expenses included replacements of crockery owing to an accident to the kitchen waggon which fell into the ditch near Lechlade, new towels for the guests, a glass window at Bosbury manor, brass kettles and cauldrons.[3] The washing bills for the ten months amounted to £2. 3*s*. $2\frac{3}{4}$*d*.[4] Outdoor expenses included repairs to carts, dog-chains, mending saddles and harness, collecting tithes, extra wages for beaters and for a man who planted shrubs in the garden and for another who sanded the drive.[5]

The bishop's retinue generally consisted of between thirty and forty horses—draught horses, sumpters, nags and palfreys. He also kept a pack of hounds which were freely used in hunting.[6] At the greater festivals the bishop was accustomed to entertain his friends, and we find the number of horses in the stables at these times rising to fifty-five at Christmas, and as many as seventy at Easter.[7]

[1] *Swinfield's Roll*, ii, pp. xxx–xxxi.

[2] *Ibid*. i, pp. 111–14, and cf. ii, pp. xxxvi–vii. Bishop Thomas Button of Exeter spent £3. 6*s*. 8*d*. on his best robe, and among his garments was found a feathered cap: *Accounts of Executors of Gravesend and Button*, Camden Society, pp. 127–9.

[3] *Swinfield's Roll*, i, pp. 137, 191 and 166.

[4] *Ibid*. ii, p. xxxix.

[5] *Ibid*. i, pp. 139–40, 134, 131–3, 172–5, 16, 135–6.

[6] *Ibid*. ii, p. lvi. Most bishops kept hounds in the thirteenth century. Even the austere Archbishop Wickwayn of York kept sporting dogs (*perdriarii*): *Regist. W. Wickwayn*, p. 266. Walter Suffield left a pack of hounds to the King in his will: Blomefield, *History of Norfolk*, iii, p. 488. Cf. *Sussex Arch. Coll*. iii, pp. 46–7.

[7] *Swinfield's Roll*, ii, pp. cxix and clxvii.

His guests can have had no cause to complain of the fare which was provided. Medieval refectory tables were made to stand a considerable strain, but they must have groaned under the vast quantities of food which were sometimes heaped upon them. The actual amount consumed on Easter Day was 1½ carcases of salt beef, 1¾ carcases of fresh beef, 5 pigs, 4½ calves, 22 kids, 3 fat deer, 12 capons, 88 pigeons and 1400 eggs, besides bread and cheese, beer without stint and 66 gallons of Bosbury wine.[1] 'So much for the first release from Lenten diet', comments the editor of the roll. Even supposing that there were eighty people present to share in this repast the amounts to us seem more than ample.[2] Days of abstinence were marked rather by a change of diet than by any reduction of quantity, for on Friday, 28 October, the larderer provided two whole salmon, one conger, over 300 eels, 900 herrings and seven hake in order to satisfy the appetites of some forty or fifty people.[3]

The household had three meals a day, the fare at each being much the same and consisting largely of meat, bread, and beer or wine.[4] The wine was either white wine made locally from

[1] *Swinfield's Roll*, ii, p. clxvii. The roll says eleven sextaries. According to Rogers a sextary contained six gallons: *Hist. of Agric. and Prices*, i, p. 172.

[2] If we assume that a carcase of beef yielded about 150 lb. of meat, a pig or a calf 20 lb., and a kid only 5 lb., the flesh meat consumed on Easter Day by eighty people must have amounted to about 800 lb., or 10 lb. each. In addition, there were the pigeons and eggs. During the fortnight, 13 to 26 November inclusive, the bishop and his household were at Bosbury with apparently no visitors. Three days in each week were days of abstinence, and some of the household were fasting on Mondays as well. This makes about seven meat days in the fortnight. On these seven days they consumed 6 carcases of beef, 5½ pigs, 21 deer, 53 geese, 60 fowls, 49 partridges and some duck and pigeons. This works out at about 6 lb. of meat for each person each day in addition to the poultry. On the days of abstinence they consumed nearly 2000 herrings, 6 salmon, 19 congers, 225 eels, 200 lamperns, 4 hake, 1 cod, 1 stockfish and a quantity of freshwater fish. This would allow about ten of the smaller fish for each man each day. They also had about 2500 eggs. In the household rolls of Eleanor, Countess of Leicester, the bills at the fishmonger include whale, grampus, porpoise and sea-calf: T. H. Turner, *Manners and Household Expenses*, p. xli.

[3] *Swinfield's Roll*, i, p. 13.

[4] In a description of a meal at Beverley in the twelfth century we are told that it consisted of four courses: a kind of broth made of beef and vegetables, fresh meat, game or poultry, and something in the nature of mincemeat. See A. F. Leach, *Early Yorkshire Schools*, i, pp. xl and 80–1.

the vineyards at Ledbury or red wine from abroad. The latter was bought in large quantities, over £10 being spent in December and nearly £14 in July, though these amounts look paltry compared with the £73 paid by Archbishop Walter Giffard in 1268.[1] The meat was obviously served up highly flavoured, for considerable sums of money were spent on spices such as aniseed, cinnamon, carraways, coriander, cummin, ginger, liquorice, pepper and saffron.[2] There was little fruit or vegetables in the dietary although these were beginning to be eaten in England, and no gardener was employed in the establishment.[3] This is surprising, for Hereford was in the heart of the fruit-growing country and we know that apples, pears, cherries and plums were cultivated and much sought after.[4]

Such was the standard of living enjoyed by a bishop in the thirteenth century. But the price which he paid for it was a heavy one, for it meant that he had no permanent home, no place where he could collect his treasures or enjoy his library. Life was very full, for a bishop had to combine with his pastoral duties the responsibilities of a landowner and feudal lord, judge and magistrate, King's Counsellor and Member of Parliament. He was never free from work or from the routine of administration, besides 'the care of all the churches' which weighed heavily upon such as took their work seriously. It is no wonder if little time was left for scholarly activities, nor was the interminable procession from manor to manor conducive to quiet study. Yet many of the bishops were scholars, men who had been brought from the schools to rule over the dioceses; and a man who has once acquired scholarly habits and affections is not likely to give them up, whatever the pressure of other business. We know, for example, that Grosseteste, between 1239 and 1244, when he was in the midst of his work as bishop of the largest diocese in England, made his famous translations from Greek into Latin of the *Testament of the Twelve Patriarchs*

[1] *Regist. W. Giffard*, p. 107. English beer was mostly brewed by women who also kept the beer shops; cf. Turner, *Manners and Household Expenses*, p. xxxix. The bishop, however, had his own brewery.

[2] *Swinfield's Roll*, ii, p. li.

[3] Peas and beans, fennel and onions are all mentioned in the roll of the Countess of Leicester: Turner, *Manners and Household Expenses*, p. xlvii; cf. *Household accounts of Bogo de Clare*, in *Archaeologia*, lxx, p. 26.

[4] Matthew Paris describes the failure of the fruit crop—apples, pears, figs, acorns, cherries and plums—in 1257: *Chron. Maj.* v, p. 660.

and of parts of the *Mystical Theology* of Dionysius the Areopagite, besides writing a book on farming.[1] The following year, while he was waiting at Lyons for the opening of the Council, he had sent to him the *Morals* of S. Gregory and Rabanus *On the Nature of Things*, and was working on his commentary on the *Nicomachean Ethics* of Aristotle.[2] In 1249 he wrote one of his scientific treatises.[3] But Grosseteste was a man of phenomenal energy, far surpassing that of most of his contemporaries. His mind and his knowledge were alike encyclopaedic, for his published works include treatises on theology, logic, ethics, politics, economics, natural science, husbandry, mathematics, ecclesiastical law and astronomy.[4] Indeed his knowledge of the last of these led to his being accused, like his equally brilliant pupil Roger Bacon, of being in league with the powers of darkness. He was reputed to have invented a 'brazen head' which spoke of its own accord on Saturdays, and to have travelled to Rome in a single night on the back of an 'infernal horse'.[5]

Apart from Grosseteste the most voluminous writers among the episcopate were the four Archbishops of Canterbury—Stephen Langton,[6] Robert Kilwardby,[7] John Pecham[8] and Robert Winchelsey.[9] Each of these men wrote many books, but none of them attempted to wander over so many fields of human knowledge as did Grosseteste. How much of their work was actually composed after their elevation to the primacy it is impossible to say, but it is probable that most of it was written

[1] Stevenson, *R. Grosseteste*, pp. 223–8, 230; cf. Wharton, *Anglia Sacra*, ii, p. 347. Copies of the translation of the *Twelve Patriarchs* were soon in circulation, for we find one mentioned in a book list at Glastonbury in 1247 *J. of Glastonbury*, *Chronica*, ed. Hearne, ii, pp. 423–44) and John de Cauz, Abbot of Peterborough 1249–62, possessed a copy (Dugdale-Caley, *Monasticon*, i, p. 356). There was a copy at Christ Church, Canterbury, in 1258: James, *Ancient Libraries of Canterbury and Dover*, p. 118.

[2] Stevenson, *R. Grosseteste*, p. 247.

[3] *De Impressione Aeris*; see Little, *Studies in Eng. Franc. Hist.* pp. 197, 208.

[4] Pegge, *Life of Robert Grosseteste*, pp. 16–17, 304. But see also S. H. Thomson, *The Writings of R. Grosseteste*.

[5] Pegge, *Life of Robert Grosseteste*, pp. 306–8; cf. Gower, *Confessio Amantis*, iv, ll. 234–43.

[6] Powicke, *Stephen Langton*, chaps. ii and iii, and pp. 168–204.

[7] Tanner, *Bibliotheca*, pp. 455–7.

[8] Pecham, *Tract. Tres de Paupertate*, ed. A. G. Little, pp. 1–12. Pecham also wrote a certain amount of poetry.

[9] Tanner, *Bibliotheca*, pp. 778–80.

while they enjoyed the greater leisure of the Universities. Sewal de Bovill's little tract addressed to his priests must have been written after his appointment as Archbishop of York in 1256,[1] and Roger de Weseham wrote *Instituta* for the edification of his clergy, to instruct them in dogma and to suggest topics for their sermons.

If it is hard to know what opportunities the bishops had for writing, it is even harder to know what reading they did. That Grosseteste employed his time profitably while at Lyons we know, and we can take it for granted that other bishops who were of scholarly habits and dispositions would seize such opportunities as were offered for quiet reading. Some light is thrown on the subject by a study of the libraries which they possessed. The collecting of books does not necessarily mean that they are read; and just as merchant princes of the nineteenth century bought their libraries by the yard with no intention of ever reading the books, so no doubt there was many a collector of books in the thirteenth century who liked to have

> at his beddes heed
> Twenty bookes, clothed in blak and reed

without caring very much about their contents.

The lists of books possessed by the bishops are not without considerable interest. When an inventory was taken at Wolvesey Castle in 1287 it disclosed 'seventeen quires of books on various subjects'.[2] Apparently these did not include a Bible, for the bishop had to borrow one from the Prior and Convent of Winchester.[3] Some of the bishops certainly possessed Bibles of their own, for S. Edmund lost one on a Channel crossing,[4] Wickwayn bought one from Master Roger de Holt,[5] and Walter de Merton left one in his will.[6] Godfrey Giffard left his nephew 'a little Bible',[7] and Walter Suffield disposed of 'a little Bible',

[1] Tanner, *Bibliotheca*, p. 664.

[2] *Regist. J. Pontissara*, pp. 495–6: 'xvii peciae librorum de diversis scientiis'. (A *pecia* was an unbound quire. For further particulars see Little and Pelster, *Oxford Theology and Theologians*, pp. 56–64.)

[3] *Regist. J. Pontissara*, p. 712. Anthony Bek, Bishop of Durham, borrowed a Bible from the Convent in 1300 and refused to return it; see *Catalogi Veteres Librorum Ecc. Dunelm.*, Surtees Society, pp. 121–2.

[4] B. Ward, *S. Edmund*, p. 35.

[5] *Regist. W. Wickwayn*, p. 319.

[6] Hobhouse, *Sketch of the Life of W. de Merton*, p. 49.

[7] Thomas, *Survey of Worcester*, App. pp. 77–81.

a copy of the Decretals and other books.[1] Copies of the Decretals, the official law-book of the Church, were certainly in the possession of Richard of Chichester, Richard Gravesend of London, Walter Bronescombe and Ralph de Walpole, who had two copies.[2] The notorious Peter de Aquablanca possessed a 'plain Bible' (*Biblia simplex*), a Bible with gloss, and some books of sermons. The sermons he gave to his nephew John, Dean of Hereford, together with the 'plain Bible'. The larger Bible he directed to be sold in order to provide clothes for the poor.[3]

Walter Bronescombe's library consisted of an Antiphonary and Psalter (for use in the chapel), one part of the Pentateuch with commentary, and a volume containing five works: the *Pantheon* of Godfrey de Viterbo, the Decretals with apparatus, a book about animals, a work by Avicenna, the Moslem physician, and a tract on military science by Vegetius.[4] The saintly and learned Richard of Chichester was well supplied for theological study. He had, besides a Bible, a Psalter with gloss, copies of the four Gospels, Commentaries on Hosea, Isaiah, Job, Acts, the Epistles, the Apocalypse and the Minor Prophets, and annotations on the Psalms. He had also a copy of the *Sentences* of Peter Lombard, the *Summa* of William of Auxerre, Anselm's *Cur Deus Homo?* and a book on Vices.[5]

But by far the most extensive episcopal library of which we have any record was that possessed by Richard Gravesend, Bishop of London 1280–1303. Among his papers is preserved a catalogue of his books with the values attached to them by his executors. There are eighty volumes altogether, valued at a total of £116. 14*s.* 6*d.*[6] These include three Bibles, various books of commentaries and three Concordances, one of which is priced at £4. The Fathers are represented by Jerome,

[1] Blomefield, *History of Norfolk*, iii, p. 489.

[2] *Sussex Arch. Coll.* i, pp. 179–83; *Philobiblon Society Miscellanies*, ii; *Regist. J. Pecham* (C. and Y. Soc.), pp. 205–7; Wharton, *Anglia Sacra*, i, pp. 639–40.

[3] Woodruff, *The Will of Peter de Aquablanca*, in *Camden Misc.* xiv, p. 4.

[4] *Regist. J. Pecham* (C. and Y. Soc.), pp. 205–7. There was a copy of Vegetius' *de Re Militari* in the Library of Christ Church, Canterbury: M. R. James, *Ancient Libraries of Canterbury and Dover*, p. 47.

[5] *Sussex Arch. Coll.* i, pp. 169–83.

[6] Milman, *A Catalogue of the Books of R. de Gravesend*, in *Philobiblon Society Miscellanies*, ii (1855–6) and *Accounts of the Executors of Gravesend and Button*, Camden Society (1874), pp. 50–2.

Eusebius, Gregory the Great and Augustine, and medieval writers by S. Bernard, Peter of Ravenna, Alexander of Hales, Bede and others. There are several volumes of sermons by various writers; but, as we should expect, none of these is priced very high. Among the bishop's law-books are five copies of the Decretals (all of considerable value), and a magnificent *Corpus Iuris Civilis* in five volumes valued at £20. There are in addition a few historical works, including a *Historia Scholastica*, a Life of S. Hugh of Lincoln, and a *Legenda Sanctorum*.

This was a noble library according to the standards of the time, but few of the bishops would ever have been able to find time to enjoy it. Life was hard, and only very few of them lived to taste the pleasures of retirement. Two Archbishops of Canterbury of this century died abroad—S. Edmund, who had fled to Pontigny in 1240, and Robert Kilwardby, who, on becoming a Cardinal in 1278, resigned the primacy and went to live at Rome. Four bishops resigned their sees to enter a religious order—Maugerus of Worcester, who died an exile at Pontigny in 1212; William de S. Mère Eglise who, on resigning the bishopric of London in 1221, became an Augustinian canon at S. Osyth's in Essex; Walter Mauclerk, who left Carlisle in 1248 to become a Dominican at Oxford;[1] and Ralph Maidstone, who resigned from Hereford to live as a Franciscan first at Oxford and then at Gloucester.[2] Nicholas of Farnham retired in comparative comfort from the bishopric of Durham in 1249 and had three manors assigned to him.[3] Grosseteste is said to have offered to resign after his remarkable interview with the Pope in 1250; but if so, his offer was not accepted.[4] Roger de Weseham, on becoming afflicted with paralysis in 1256, retired from the see of Coventry and Lichfield to the manor of Brewood on a pension of 300 marks.[5]

[1] Luard, *An. Mon.* iii, p. 170. According to Matthew Paris he resigned because he was troubled in conscience over his ability to hold office, being of illegitimate birth: *Chron. Maj.* iv, p. 564.

[2] He was a saintly man who is said to have worked with his own hands to carry stones and water for the building of the Franciscan church at Oxford: *Analecta Franciscana*, iv, pp. 330–1. His resignation may have been due to a fall from a rock: Luard, *An. Mon.* iii, pp. 148, 156; cf. Brewer, *Mon. Franc.* i, p. 58; Bliss, *Cal. Papal Letters*, i, p. 348.

[3] M. Paris, *Chron. Maj.* v, pp. 53–4.

[4] *Chron. de Lanercost*, p. 43.

[5] Pegge, *Memoirs of Roger de Weseham*, p. 43.

The rest died in harness, many of them at a ripe old age. In modern times clergy are notoriously long-lived, the reason given by actuaries being that they are regular in their habits and temperate in food and drink. Grosseteste once told a Dominican that the three things necessary to temporal salvation were food, sleep and good humour,[1] and he once ordered a melancholy friar, as a penance, to drink a cup of the best wine.[2] His own table, however, was none too well furnished, and guests used to complain that they did not get enough to eat.[3] Stephen of Birchington describes Archbishop Winchelsey as 'at table affable, benignant and jovial' though he ate very little and would often send the best dishes to the houses of the sick.[4] Others certainly fared well, as the accounts of Swinfield and others show; but in a hard and active life it seems to have done them no harm. If hard work and hard exercise in the fresh air are the secret of longevity, then it is no wonder that the bishops lived long, for they certainly had plenty of both.

[1] 'Cibus, somnus et jocus': Eccleston, *de Adventu Fratrum Minorum*, p. 115. Cf. Roger Bacon's advice on how to keep young: Little, *Studies in Eng. Franc. Hist.* pp. 201–2.

[2] Eccleston, *ibid.*

[3] *Chron. de Lanercost*, p. 44.

[4] Wharton, *Anglia Sacra*, i, p. 13.

CHAPTER XIV

ON THE MOVE

A bishop is primarily a *Pastor Pastorum.* However much he may fancy himself as a politician, or as a writer, or as a champion of deserving causes, his first business is to be a father-in-God to the clergy over whom he presides. The parish priest enjoys a freedom from control greater than that of most men, but this liberty carries with it, in many cases, a corresponding isolation. Even in these modern days, when facilities of transport are so enormously increased, a country parson may live for weeks without speaking to a fellow priest or to anyone his equal in education and culture. In the Middle Ages such isolation was far more common and much more serious. With no means of transport swifter than horses, with no post, no newspapers and very few books, the country clergyman was left almost entirely on his own to struggle against secularism, indolence and the darker sins and vices to which, as a celibate, he was prone. In such circumstances it needed a lofty sense of vocation and an unswerving loyalty to duty and honour to carry him through.

Much depended in this struggle on the degree of sympathy and encouragement which he received from his diocesan. If he had reason to suppose that the bishop was interested in his welfare and was willing to come and visit him in his own parish he would be far more likely to feel that the struggle was of some avail than if he knew himself to be neglected and forgotten. Every bishop, therefore, who took his responsibilities seriously knew that the success or failure of the Church's work in the country parishes would be largely governed by his efforts to visit his clergy. The best of them therefore spared no pains in travelling about their dioceses, from parish to parish, finding out how the work was progressing and correcting abuses.

The difficulties were considerable. Many dioceses were inconveniently large,[1] and contained tracts of country which were so remote that a visitation of them would hardly justify the

[1] The diocese of Lincoln covered eight counties and extended from the Humber to the Thames. It is now divided into five dioceses—Lincoln, Leicester, Peterborough, S. Albans and Oxford. The diocese of Coventry and Lichfield extended from Blackburn in the North to Leamington in the South. It has now been divided into eight.

expense of time and trouble in getting there. The Copeland Deanery, for example, in the diocese of York,[1] consisted of a strip of coastline from Workington to Cartmel containing twenty-seven parishes. It was largely cut off from the rest of the diocese (which stretched as far south as Nottingham) not only by distance but also by the barrier of the Lakeland hills. It was no wonder that the Archbishop of York, with so large a diocese to administer, found it impossible to reach such outlying places.[2]

No bishop, however energetic, could hope to visit every parish in a diocese the size of York or Lincoln or Lichfield; but many of them made determined efforts to know their clergy and to satisfy themselves that a reasonable standard of efficiency and morality was being maintained. John le Romeyn, who was Archbishop of York from 1286 to 1296, was a most energetic diocesan who in the first seven months of his reign visited eighteen priories, one abbey, twelve rural deaneries, the city of York and the jurisdictions of Otley, Ripon and Beverley besides holding two ordinations and attending Convocation.[3] Thomas Corbridge, who succeeded to York in the year 1300, never once left the diocese during the four and a half years that he was there, but devoted his whole time to visiting his clergy. As Professor Hamilton Thompson rightly says: 'There are few examples of consistent diligence in the episcopal office more conspicuous than that which is disclosed to us by the itinerary of Corbridge.'[4] Richard Gravesend of Lincoln aimed at a triennial round of his whole vast diocese of some eight hundred parishes.[5] Godfrey Giffard of Worcester, having been laid up through age and sickness in the winter of 1300, rose up the following summer and carried out a visitation tour lasting thirty-three days, in which he visited eighteen places and travelled

[1] Copeland Forest is the district between Ennerdale and Wastwater.

[2] Even in the nineteenth century there were parts of the York diocese which were completely neglected. In 1835 William Boyd was appointed by University College, Oxford, to the living of Arncliffe in Littondale. On presenting himself before the Archbishop of York for institution the archbishop said: 'Arncliffe? Arncliffe? I have no such living in my diocese, sir.' 'He rang for his registrar, who, on referring to his books, found that it was in his diocese': *Littondale Past and Present*, pp. 3–4.

[3] *Regist. J. Romeyn*, i, pp. v–vi.

[4] *Regist. T. Corbridge*, ii, p. xx.

[5] *Rot. R. Gravesend*, Intro. p. xvii.

over two hundred miles. Several of the Archbishops of Canterbury attempted to visit the whole of the Southern Province besides their own diocese.[1]

On the other hand there were, of course, a good many bishops who were so much occupied with other matters that they could devote little time to their dioceses and left their sheep 'encombred in the myre'. We know that Ralph Neville, who was Chancellor of England, scarcely ever visited in his diocese of Chichester,[2] and many others who held high offices of state were equally negligent. Yet the effects of such neglect must have been disastrous. Indeed we know a little of what a diocese without a bishop was like from the very stern letter which Archbishop Pecham wrote in 1282 to Roger de Molend, Bishop of Coventry and Lichfield. The archbishop had recently been visiting in this diocese and had found many evils in need of correction. Churches had been appropriated without proper provision being made for the spiritual welfare of the parishes, confirmations had been sadly neglected, and the sins of simony and incest were rife among the clergy, not without the connivance of the bishop.[3] What was true of this diocese was doubtless true of others where the bishops were negligent or absentees.

A most vivid picture of what a visitation tour involved is provided by the Household Roll of Richard Swinfield. The hawthorns were putting out their freshest green and the willow-warblers had just returned to fill the woods with their plaintive little cadences when the bishop left his manor of Colwall on Low Sunday, 9 April 1290, with a retinue of thirty riders and rode a few miles north to Cradley, where another of his manors stood. Here, among other things, he interviewed his woodward and paid him sixpence to look after his falcons during the nesting season and to see that the young birds did not escape. On

[1] Tout's article on Kilwardby in *D.N.B.*; and cf. Kilwardby's Itinerary in the diocese of Ely in 1277 in *Vetus Liber Archidiaconi Eliensis*, pp. 19–20; Pecham, *Reg. Epist.* i, p. lxviii; cf. M. Paris, *Chron. Maj.* v, pp. 119–25 and *Regist. W. Bronescombe*, pp. 41 f.

[2] *Letters to R. Neville*, in *Sussex Arch. Coll.* iii, pp. 75–6.

[3] *Reg. Epist.* ii, pp. 479–80. He says: 'magnum defectum invenimus in confirmatione parvulorum' for in every place children are to be found 'in infinita multitudine confirmandi'. He wrote at the same time to the Dean and Chapter of Lichfield complaining that the bishop had winked at many of the evils which were disgracing the diocese (pp. 480–1).

Tuesday he rode nearly ten miles to Bromyard, where he and his household were entertained by Roger de Savernak, one of the three men who held the living.[1] Adam the Marshal fell sick while they were here and had to be left behind the following morning when the party rode another ten miles or so to Tenbury. On Thursday the bishop visited the church of Burford, close to Tenbury, and spent the night there before turning eastwards on the Friday to Lindridge, where he consulted with the interested parties as to the consolidation of the rectory and vicarage. On Saturday he visited at Rock, and on Sunday pushed on to Kinlet, where he spent two nights at his own expense. The bakers had reached the town three days previously and the bishop received various gifts—flour and fuel, hay and oats for the horses, and capons, kids and venison for his own table. The rest of the food was bought at Kidderminster, to which Robert the carter was sent with a guide through Wyre Forest at the cost of one penny. Meanwhile the bishop also sent all the way back to Hereford for some horse-shoes and nails. While at Kinlet Swinfield spent a day in composing a letter to the Pope in which he pleaded for the canonisation of his predecessor, Thomas Cantilupe.

On Tuesday, 18 April, the party was off again, turning westwards to Dudlick, where they stayed at the manor which belonged to the Abbot of Shrewsbury. The bishop apparently was doubtful whether it would be fit for his occupation, as he made arrangements beforehand for it to be thoroughly cleaned. On Wednesday he visited the church at Chetton and was entertained by the rector, on Thursday he was at Morville, and on Friday he made a regular visitation of the parish church of Wenlock. He slept at the priory as the guest of the prior and was off again next morning for Oxenbold, and on Sunday reached the parish of Munslow. The rector here was apparently an absentee but he had deputed his neighbour, the Rector of Stanton Lacy, to offer the bishop three quarters of oats. The bishop went on to Stanton Lacy on the Monday, and on Tuesday passed through Ludlow, where he gave the Austin Friars four shillings for a pittance, and reached Bitterley in the afternoon. On Wednesday he was away to Bromfield; on Thursday he slept in the manor-house at Stoke Say, which still stands much as it stood that night; and on Friday evening

[1] According to the *Taxatio Nicholai* Roger's portion was £8, the other portionists receiving £20 and £16. 13*s*. 4*d*. The vicar's stipend was less than £4: *Taxatio Nicholai*, p. 160.

they dined on cod and salmon at Wistanstow. On Saturday they were the guests of the Prior of Wenlock in the manor-house at Eaton and on Sunday they reached Church Stretton. Again they were off next morning over the hills to Pontesbury,

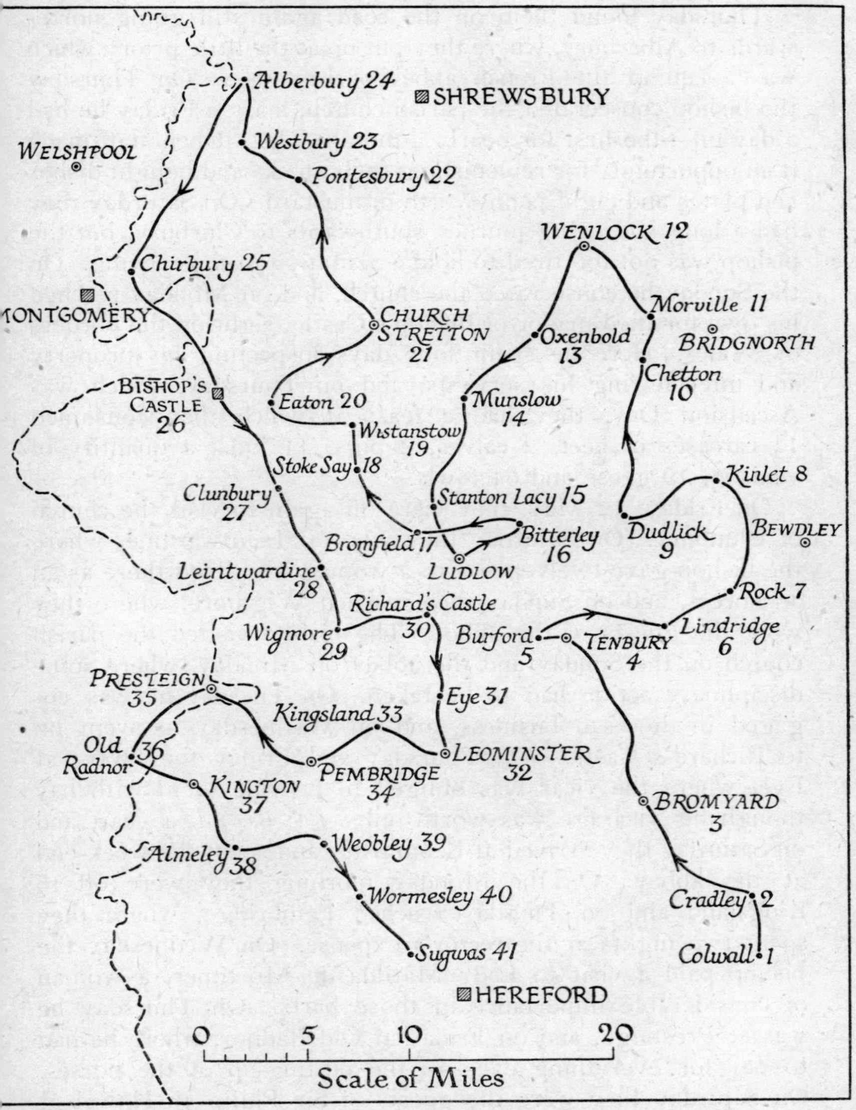

Itinerary of Richard Swinfield, Bishop of Hereford, in 1290

a journey for which they had to have a guide; and on Tuesday they reached Westbury, to which the cooks had been sent on in advance. Here they spent two days, the first at their own expense, the second as the guests of Sir William de Hodnet. On Wednesday they bought some charcoal.

Thursday found them on the road again still going northwards to Alberbury, where they put up at the little priory which was a cell of the French abbey of Limousin. On Thursday the bishop consecrated the parish church, and on Friday he had a day off—the first for nearly a month. The kitchen staff made it an opportunity for replenishing their stocks and bought dishes and plates and eight pennyworth of mustard. On Saturday they had a long and tiring journey southwards to Chirbury, but the bishop was not too tired to hold a visitation in the evening. On the Sunday he consecrated the church, and on Monday reached his own fortified manor of Bishop's Castle, right on the borders of Wales. Here he spent four days inspecting his property and interviewing his servants, and on Thursday, which was Ascension Day, they had a feast at which they consumed $1\frac{1}{2}$ carcases of beef, 2 calves, 2 pigs, 11 kids, a quantity of venison, 19 geese and 64 fowls.

On Friday, 12 May, they were off again to visit the church of Clunbury. On Saturday they were at Leintwardine, where the bishop gave twelvepence to a woman who lived there as an anchoress, and on Sunday they reached Wigmore, where they were the guests of the abbot. The bishop visited the parish church on the Sunday and the abbey on Monday, where some disciplinary action had to be taken. On Tuesday he was engaged in diocesan business, and on Wednesday he went on to Richard's Castle. On Thursday and Friday they were at Eye, where the vicar was obliged to provide them with hay though his vicarage was worth only £4. 6*s*. 8*d*. a year, and on Saturday they arrived at Leominster and spent the week-end at the abbey. On the Monday morning they were off to Kingsland and on Tuesday reached Pembridge, where they spent two nights at the rector's expense. On Wednesday the bishop paid a visit to Lady Matilda de Mortimer, a woman of considerable importance in those parts. On Thursday he was at Presteign, and on Friday at Old Radnor, where he had to pay for everything even to the putting-up of the horses. On Saturday they were the guests of Sir Philip ap Howel at

Kington, where the bishop held an institution; on Sunday they moved on to Almeley. On Monday they were at Weobley; and on Tuesday they reached Wormesley Priory, having visited Dilwyn church on the way. The following day, Wednesday, 31 May, the bishop reached his own manor of Sugwas, a few miles west of Hereford, where he allowed himself five days of what we will hope was comparative peace.

Matthew Paris once described Grosseteste as 'the Bishop of Lincoln to whom quiet is a thing unknown'.[1] Much the same might have been said of any of his contemporaries who carried out their duties as conscientiously as Richard Swinfield. We think of our days as being days of constant movement; but who of us can compete with the restless energy of the medieval bishop, perpetually on the move in all weathers and under all conditions, carrying out the work to which he believed God had called him?

The method whereby each bishop carried out his visitations no doubt varied from one diocese to another; but there seems to have been a certain plan which was generally followed. The visitation began with the bishop sending out either to the archdeacon, or to the rural dean, or possibly to each individual incumbent, a set of most searching questions, designed to discover the actual state of each parish.[2] Which clergy are absentees or pluralists? Are any married or living with concubines (*concubinarii*)? Have any obtained their livings by simony or inherited them from their fathers? Are any of illegitimate birth or insufficiently ordained? What of the finances of the parish? If a vicarage has been ordained, what is it worth? Is it considered sufficient? Do any churches need to be dedicated or reconciled? Are any being farmed out? Are the clergy regular in visiting the sick and in saying the offices? Is the wine used for the Eucharist in fresh condition? Do any of the clergy try to get money illegally for administering the sacraments? Are any mis-spending money which has been given for special purposes? Have the churches proper fonts, and are churchyards

[1] M. Paris, *Chron. Maj.* iv, p. 497. Cf. Adam Marsh's letter to Grosseteste imploring him not to work so hard: *Mon. Franc.* i, p. 143.

[2] Some of these questionnaires have been preserved: see *Regist. W. Giffard*, pp. 266–8; Luard, *An. Mon.* i, pp. 296–8; *Regist. W. Wickwayn*, pp. 116–19; Wilkins, *Concilia*, i, pp. 627–8.

adequately enclosed? Are any of the clergy or laity suspected of witchcraft (*sortilegia*)? Are churches or graveyards being used for markets or games? Are the rural deans and archdeacons carrying out their duties faithfully?

The questions were searching, and many a man's honesty must have been strained in the answering of them. But deceit or subterfuge would be of little avail, for every man knew that the questionnaire was but the prelude to a personal visit of the diocesan, who came not only to admonish and exhort but also to punish and to condemn.

The arrival of the bishop was, for the parson, more of a visitation than a visit—a 'visitation' being, according to the dictionary, 'a heavy affliction, blow or trial'. The bishop came to inspect the property of the church, the efficiency of the clergy and the morals of the whole parish, both clergy and laity alike.[1] He or his officials walked round the churchyard, climbed on to the roof to examine the lead, scrutinised the mass books, had all the vestments turned out, counted up the purificators, and listened to all the scandal and gossip of the parish. Here, for example, is Archbishop Giffard visiting the parish of Snaith in 1275. First his clerk, Nicholas de Wells, makes a careful inventory of all Church property and records the fact that there were twenty books mostly in good condition, three chalices of which one was broken, five sets of vestments, seven copes, eight surplices and about sixteen banners. He then proceeds to examine the clergy. The first witness to be called was Geoffrey, the parochial chaplain or curate of Carleton, a little village about a mile away. He said that the services at Snaith were regularly celebrated each day according to the York 'use'. He also gave evidence that sixteen years ago Thomas, the parish priest, had

[1] In the diocese of York it seems to have been customary for the archbishop to summon not only the clergy but three or four laymen from each parish: *Regist. J. Romeyn*, i, p. 50; *Regist. T. Corbridge*, ii, pp. 27–8. In the visitations carried out by the Dean and Chapter in the diocese of Exeter in 1301 the laymen seem to have been summoned without the clergy: *Regist. W. Stapeldon*, ed. Hingeston-Randolph, pp. 107–11, etc. and cf. Coulton, *Social Life in Britain*, pp. 260 ff. Archbishop Pecham also summoned laymen to his visitations: *Reg. Epist.* ii, pp. 512–14. Four laymen together with the clergy was quite common: Worcester, *Regist. Sede Vacante*, pp. 61–2; *Regist. R. Baldock, etc.*, p. 45. Simon of Ghent sometimes summoned only the laity, as at the churches of Salisbury in 1303: *Regist. S. Gandavo*, i, pp. 134–5.

had a son and daughter, but had not sinned since. Thomas, on being next called, admitted the truth of this accusation. The next witness was one of the parochial chaplains, Alexander, who confessed that Mass was sometimes not said on weekdays. He went on to give evidence against a certain Brother Thomas Gundale, perhaps a monk of Selby, whom he believed to have been keeping company with a woman of Snaith; but, on being pressed, he had to admit that he had this only at secondhand. He also told of another Selby monk, one Alexander, who had had issue by a certain woman seven years since. Robert of Tickhill, another of the chaplains, was then called and was found to agree with what the previous witness had said, adding that the woman with whom Brother Alexander had consorted was a married woman. Finally the two parish clerks were examined —Adam, who announced that the said Brother Thomas Gundale held the church of Snaith in farm for sixty marks; and John, who was clearly a simple soul who knew nothing of the above and was under the impression that all was going well and peacefully in the parish.[1]

At a similar enquiry made at the church of S. German's, Selby, Walter, the parish chaplain, gave evidence against various people in the town. He also said that the font had been moved from the church into the abbey, but by whose authority he did not know. On being asked whether any of the clergy had attended a synod, he replied that none of them had gone, since one of the monks had always represented them all. He further gave evidence that neither the church nor the altar was dedicated, and that it had no graveyard, since the dead were all buried in the cemetery of the great monastery. As to himself, he had been ordained in Ireland, but his orders had been ratified by Archbishop Gray. Thomas, one of the chaplains, who next gave evidence, remarked that he knew a man who was going about slandering the Archbishop and saying that he was a married man. When pressed for further information, Thomas had to admit that he did not know the man's name. He also told of gross immorality of which he believed the Abbot of Selby to be guilty, information which was apparently corroborated by the following witnesses.[2]

[1] *Regist. W. Giffard*, pp. 322–4. Note that there is no incumbent mentioned. Apparently he was an absentee who had farmed out the living to one of the monks.

[2] *Ibid.* pp. 324 ff.

To all this gossip and tittle-tattle the bishop would have to listen, trying to sort out the true from the false and the serious from the frivolous and malicious. Finally he would gather up his papers and retire to his lodgings to rest and to sleep before going on next morning to another parish where the whole weary process would be gone through again.

But the visitation was not only an occasion for inspecting and examining the parish and its clergy. It was also an opportunity for the bishop to address his clergy and people. The *Annals of Dunstable* tell us that in 1237 'Robert, Bishop of Lincoln, carried out a general visitation of the monasteries, archdeaconries and deaneries of his diocese. In each he held a general chapter, preached a sermon and issued decrees. He also suspended many rectors of churches.'[1] It would be interesting to know more about these sermons of Grosseteste's, but no trace of them has been found. All that we know is that he used sometimes to preach in English, especially in later years.[2] On the other hand the scribe of Godfrey Giffard's Register is most careful to give the text of each sermon which his master preached, whether to the members of a religious house, to parish clergy or to the laity.[3] It is interesting to see what method he pursued. He preached far more from the Old Testament than from the New,[4] one of his favourite texts being: 'Take away the dross from the silver and there cometh forth a vessel for the finer',[5] on which he preached six times—to the monks of Pershore, Llanthony, Tewkesbury, Winchcombe and Alcester and in the church of S. Mark at Bristol.[6] Another interesting choice was *Ecclesiasticus*, vii, 6: 'Hast thou a wife after thy mind? forsake her not: but give not thyself over to a light woman.' Strange to say the bishop preached on this text to four different

[1] Luard, *An. Mon.* iii, p. 147.

[2] M. Paris, *Chron. Maj.* v, pp. 256–7; Stevenson, *R. Grosseteste*, pp. 32 and 297. Stevenson points out that Wharton mentions some English sermons (*Anglia Sacra*, ii, p. 344 ff.) but they may have been translations from the Latin (p. 32, n. 4).

[3] There is nothing to suggest that any of Giffard's sermons were in English except the fact that some of them were certainly preached to laymen; e.g. in the churchyard of S. James, Bristol, on Good Friday, 1284: *Regist. G. Giffard*, p. 230.

[4] Of the eighty-five sermons mentioned, sixty-one texts are from the Old Testament and only twenty-four from the New.

[5] *Proverbs*, xxv, 4.

[6] *Regist. G. Giffard*, pp. 164, 233–6, 244.

nunneries—the Cistercians of Whiston and Cokehill and the Benedictines of Wroxall and of S. Mary Magdalene, Bristol.[1] A good, straightforward sermon could, no doubt, be preached on *James*, i, 21: 'Wherefore lay apart all filthiness and superfluity of naughtiness, and receive with meekness the engrafted word which is able to save your souls.' This was used three times, on each occasion at an Ordination Service where, perhaps, the Apostle's advice was particularly desirable.[2]

In addition to the sermon the bishop might use the occasion as an opportunity for administering the rite of Confirmation.[3] We hear surprisingly little of Confirmation in the records of the thirteenth century, and what evidence we have suggests that the bishops took little interest in it. In theory the regulations were quite plain: children were to be confirmed at a very tender age, perhaps before they were a year old, and parents who neglected their duties in this respect were to be punished either by exclusion from church or by fasting on bread and water every Friday until the matter had been put right.[4] Archbishop Pecham added to this the rule that no unconfirmed person was to partake of the Body and Blood of Christ unless he was *in extremis*, or unless his Confirmation had been 'reasonably postponed'.[5]

Such were the regulations; but it is clear that they cannot have been enforced. Many bishops visited their dioceses only on rare occasions, and even those who were most sedulous in their visitations seem to have been reluctant to administer this

[1] *Regist. G. Giffard*, pp. 234, 244, 246.

[2] *Ibid.* pp. 164, 204, 374.

[3] Grosseteste, when preaching before the Pope and Cardinals, said that he had visited each archdeaconry and deanery, calling the clergy together and summoning people to bring their children to be confirmed. The Confirmations had taken two days. Cf. Kennett, *Parochial Antiquities* (1818), i, pp. 343–4. When a Confirmation did take place it was usual for large numbers to be confirmed. In 1336 Bishop Grandisson in quite a small parish confirmed 'pueros quasi innumerabiles': *Regist. J. Grandisson*, ii, p. 820. In 1330 Bishop Hethe was accused of omitting to confirm children, but he was acquitted by the Archbishop of Canterbury: *Regist. H. Hethe*, pp. 424–8.

[4] The *Statutes* of Richard le Poore, 1220, in Wilkins, *Concilia*, i, p. 576, give the age of seven as a maximum. Cf. *Statutes* of Peter Quivil, 1287, where the age is lowered from seven to three: *Concilia*, ii, p. 132. But in the *Statutes* of Worcester and Chichester, 1240 and 1246, the interval between Baptism and Confirmation is reduced to one year: *Concilia*, i, pp. 667, 686.

[5] *Ibid.* ii, p. 53.

sacrament. Perhaps they felt it somehow beneath their dignity, for when that energetic man Richard Swinfield experienced some pricks of conscience about the number of children and adults in his diocese who were unconfirmed, he engaged the services of an Irish prelate, the Bishop of Annadown, to remedy this abuse.[1] In the same way John le Romeyn, Archbishop of York, employed an assistant, the Bishop of Whithorn in Scotland, to confirm people in his diocese, and wrote in 1287 to the Dean of Ryedale to warn all parish priests to announce in their churches that all those who had children to be confirmed must present them to the bishop when he passed through that deanery.[2] When Archbishop Pecham wrote to Roger de Molend, Bishop of Coventry and Lichfield, complaining of many abuses in his diocese, he included among them neglect of the sacrament of Confirmation. Instead, however, of ordering him to make an effort to remedy this, he tells him to provide himself with an assistant bishop to see that the work was done.[3] If we add to this the fact that Godfrey Giffard of Worcester appointed one of his neighbours, the Bishop of Llandaff, to carry out his Confirmations for him in the winter of 1300[4] we have exhausted all the evidence for Confirmation which the thirteenth-century Registers afford. The only conclusion to which we can come is that, in spite of stringent regulations, this sacrament was in fact only very imperfectly administered,[5] even though a few bishops like Thomas Cantilupe might take the precaution of wearing a stole every time they rode through their dioceses so that people might stop them and present their children for Confirmation.[6]

[1] *Regist. R. Swinfield*, p. 499. Dr Capes, in the Introduction to this Register, points out that this is the only reference to Confirmation in twenty-five years of active diocesan work (p. iv).

[2] *Regist. J. Romeyn*, i, p. 166. [3] Pecham, *Reg. Epist.* ii, pp. 479–80.

[4] This was due to Giffard being ill, not to any reluctance on his part to take Confirmations; *Regist. G. Giffard*, p. 517.

[5] It is only in quite recent years that an attempt has been made to invest the Confirmation Service with dignity and reverence. Dr Carpenter has collected evidence of the scenes of confusion and even violence which prevailed even down to the middle of the nineteenth century; *Church and People, 1789–1889*, pp. 252–3; cf. Canon Ollard in *Confirmation*, i, pp. 213–17.

[6] *Acta Sanctorum*, October, i, p. 561. At the Council of Oxford in 1222 it was stated that parents must not wait too long for the coming of the bishop but must take their children to him, when he is known to be in the neighbourhood, as quickly as possible: Wilkins, *Concilia*, i, p. 594, and cf. Lyndwood's notes in *Provinciale*, pp. 34–5.

CHAPTER XV

DIOCESAN AFFAIRS

The regular visitation of the parishes was the principal way in which a diocesan kept in touch with his clergy and attempted to ensure the maintenance of as high a standard as possible of efficiency and morality. In addition, the clergy were expected from time to time to wait upon the bishop that they might take counsel together in solemn synod.[1]

The diocesan synods were normally held each year in the autumn, but in some dioceses there seems to have been a second session in the spring.[2] Their importance as a deliberative assembly of the clergy to discuss their problems, and as an opportunity for the bishop to give spiritual and practical help to his priests, would have been very great had the clergy attended in large numbers; but there is not much evidence that this was so. To leave a parish, say, on the banks of the Thames in Oxfordshire; to make the journey of some one hundred and thirty miles to Lincoln; to find and to afford lodgings in the town for several nights; and then to make the long journey home again, must have been more than many clergy were prepared to do. We know that the clergy of S. German's at Selby, which is only fourteen miles from York, had made no attempt to attend the synods held by Archbishop Giffard, being satisfied that they should be represented by one of the monks from the abbey.[3]

But synods there undoubtedly were; and from them were issued decrees designed to remedy the most glaring of the abuses of the times. Copies of such decrees from every diocese in England, with the exception of Rochester, Hereford and Carlisle, have been preserved, and provide one of the most valuable sources of evidence for the actual state of the Church during the thirteenth century. They are designed to legislate

[1] In the twelfth century synods had been largely concerned with judicial matters and were therefore attended by both laity and clergy. By the thirteenth century they had become far more concerned with ecclesiastical legislation and were therefore generally confined to the clergy. See C. R. Cheney, *English Synodalia of the Thirteenth Century*, p. 33.

[2] *Ibid.* p. 17; cf. *Regist. W. Gray*, p. xxi and Gibbs and Lang, *Bishops and Reform*, p. 147.

[3] *Regist. W. Giffard*, p. 324.

for every aspect of Church life and for almost every problem which might arise.[1]

In a diocese of average size in the thirteenth century there would probably be between two and three thousand secular clergy.[2] No bishop, however diligent and determined, could hope to know all of these personally in the way in which a modern diocesan can know his men. Yet large numbers of them must have passed through his hands at the time of their ordination or of their institution or licensing.

It would be interesting to know to what sort of ordination examination these men were subjected before their acceptance by the bishop. That some attempt was made to test their qualifications is revealed by Walter Giffard's Register, where express mention is made of an examination held at Blyth in September 1273, immediately before the Michaelmas Ordination. It appears also from this record that there were two separate standards, equivalent to what we should call a 'pass' and an 'honours' degree, since the men from the Hospital of S. Leonard at York are described as 'lightly examined'.[3] Nor was the examination a test only of intelligence, for careful enquiry was made into each man's parentage, as to whether he were legitimate or not,[4] and there is even evidence of some physical test being imposed, for in 1289 a certain Master John of Ditenshale, whose 'ring finger of the left hand had been shortened when a child by the unskilfulness of a surgeon who operated on it for a chilblain', applied to the Pope for dispensation to be ordained 'this defect notwithstanding'.[5] Yet though

[1] The synodal decrees will be discussed in chapter XVII below.

[2] See above, pp. 52–5.

[3] 'Leniter examinati': *Regist. W. Giffard*, pp. 187–8. Cf. also *Regist. W. Wickwayn*, p. 22, where a commission is appointed to examine ordination candidates. Pecham's and Winchelsey's ordination lists sometimes mention examinations, but not always. See also Rashdall, *Medieval Universities* (new ed.), iii, pp. 451–2.

[4] For those who were illegitimate a special dispensation 'de defectu natalium' was required. This does not refer, as Gasquet says, to those who were not free men (*Parish Life in Medieval England*, p. 72) but to those who were born out of wedlock or who were the sons of clerks; cf. Lyndwood, *Provinciale*, p. 26.

[5] Bliss, *Cal. Papal Letters*, i, p. 505. Cf. *Regist. A. Orleton*, p. 247, where the bishop allows Robert, Rector of Fownhope, to accept preferment though suffering from a defect in the pupil of one eye (1322). These

the more conscientious bishops made some effort to enquire into the qualifications of their ordination candidates, others must have 'laid their hands suddenly' upon a good many men of whose antecedents and attainments little was known.[1]

Apart from the ordination seasons men were constantly passing through the hands of the bishops as they came to them for institution or collation. At such times the more conscientious bishops took the trouble to enquire into the character and fitness of each nominee, but only the most fearless and determined of them made any sustained effort to challenge vested interests and the power and influence of the great families. The most conspicuous example of such fearlessness was Grosseteste, who was no respecter of persons. He began his episcopal career by flatly refusing to institute to a large and important parish a young man who had appeared before him 'untonsured, in a red suit more like that of a layman or a knight, bejewelled and almost illiterate'.[2] A few years later he had to write to the Dean of York, John le Romeyn, who afterwards became Archbishop, to explain why he could not possibly institute his nephew to a living. 'He who, in a stormy sea strewn with rocks,' he says, 'entrusts the care of a ship full of men to an imbecile, or to a child, or to a paralytic, or to one totally ignorant of the art of navigation, or to one who declines to put his hand to the helm; what else does he but condemn both ship and men to disaster and make himself responsible for their deaths?'[3]

incidents remind us of the Franciscan, Brother Thomas of Ireland, whose humility was such that he cut off one of his thumbs in order to disqualify himself for ever from ordination to the priesthood: Barth. of Pisa, *Liber de Conformitate*, in *Analecta Franciscana*, iv, p. 290.

[1] Even as recently as the nineteenth century the examination of ordination candidates was often a very perfunctory affair. Cf. Overton, *English Church in the Nineteenth Century*, pp. 7–8: 'We hear strange tales of one bishop examining his candidates for ordination in a tent on a cricket field, he himself being one of the players; of another sending a message, by his butler, to the candidate to write an essay; of another performing the difficult process of examining a man while shaving, and, not unnaturally, stopping the examination when the examinee had construed two words.'

[2] R. Grosseteste, *Epistolae*, p. 51.

[3] *Ibid.* pp. 203–4. The passage is repeated almost word for word in *Fasc. Rerum Expetendarum*, ii, p. 252. Cf. a similar passage on p. 152 of the *Epistolae*, where Grosseteste explains to the legate Otto his scruples about instituting the son of Earl Ferrers to a living since he is too young and not in holy orders. For Grosseteste's action on other occasions see *Epistolae*, pp. 63, 68–9 and *Rot. R. Grosseteste*, pp. 232, 233.

Hugh of Welles, Grosseteste's predecessor at Lincoln, had been almost equally severe. He would only institute a certain Robert Malebise, presented by his father to the church of Enderby, on condition that he satisfied his examiners 'in writing and singing'. If he failed, then his father was to appoint someone else.[1] Walter de Toriton was appointed to the living of Kiddington, subject to further examination 'in music and psalmody' as he had not yet made sufficient progress in these arts.[2] Master Stephen de Eketon was instituted perpetual vicar of Shillington on condition that he could prove himself to have been born in lawful wedlock and that he was not the son of the rector of that church.[3]

Such were the efforts made by fearless and conscientious diocesans to keep up a high standard among their clergy. Yet vested interests were sometimes too strong.[4] Much of the patronage was in the hands of powerful laymen; and even when they appointed quite unsuitable candidates—children of ten years old,[5] men who had never been ordained, the 'totally illiterate' and so on—not many of the bishops had the courage to stand up to them.

What is more surprising is the large number of cases in which the bishops themselves collated to livings men whom we should think quite unsuitable. It might be difficult for a bishop to challenge a powerful layman and refuse to institute a young man whom he knew to have the support of some prominent and influential family behind him; but it seems strange that when the right of presentation to a living had fallen into the hands

[1] *Rot. H. de Welles*, i, pp. 19–20.

[2] *Ibid.* i, pp. 22–3.

[3] *Ibid.* i, p. 170. Other bishops who made careful enquiries were Walter Giffard and John Pontissara; cf. *Regist. W. Giffard*, p. 76, and *Regist. J. Pontissara*, pp. 568, 576.

[4] In 1282 Pecham wrote to Cardinal Gaetano in Rome to say that he could not confer a benefice upon Bartolomeo da Ferentino since he could speak neither English nor Latin; and yet a month later we find him writing to the Bishop of Sabinum promising to confer the next vacant living upon a certain Simon da Croce: *Reg. Epist.* i, pp. 350–1, 369–70. In the same way Thomas Cantilupe had to submit to a royal command not to molest a man who was a portionist at Burford (Salop), since he was in the service of the King and therefore immune from the normal regulations as to ordination and residence: *Regist. T. Cantilupe*, p. 169.

[5] E.g. at Cromhall (Glos) in 1294 Roger de Kyngeston was appointed rector at the age of ten: *Regist. G. Giffard*, p. 442. The living was valued at £7 according to the *Taxatio Nicholai*, p. 220.

of the bishop himself he should have given the benefice to a man who was clearly unable to perform the most important functions of his office.

John Pecham was a determined reformer of Church abuses, and yet between 1281 and 1294 he collated to livings in his gift four deacons, ten subdeacons and one acolyte.[1] Godfrey Giffard was another energetic and conscientious bishop, yet he collated an acolyte to Kidderminster in 1281 and another to Peopleton in 1290.[2] William Wickwayn, who deprived the Rector of Rampton for not being a priest, himself collated a subdeacon to Langton and a deacon to Thwing.[3] Richard Swinfield was a man who took his episcopal responsibilities very seriously, yet, of the seventy-six men whom he collated to livings between 1283 and 1317, five were deacons, eight subdeacons and four only acolytes.[4]

The large flock over which a bishop had oversight provided many problems, especially to those diocesans who had a keen sense of responsibility and a firm desire to see that order and discipline were observed. There was, first of all, the perpetual problem of how to deal with aged clergy who are too old to do their work but who yet insist upon remaining in their cures. The most usual solution was to appoint an assistant or coadjutor,[5] but occasionally a bishop went one stage further, as

[1] *Regist. J. Pecham* (C. and Y. Soc.), pp. 44–98. One of the subdeacons was his nephew Walter Pecham (p. 83). In another list of Institutions and Collations from 1279–84 we find Pecham collating four deacons and six subdeacons (pp. 102–39). It is only fair to state that some of these were afterwards ordained to higher orders; e.g. John Bidike, collated rector of Keston in 1286 as a deacon, was ordained priest in Lent, 1287 (Pecham, *Reg. Epist.* iii, p. 1043); John of Shorne, collated to Monks' Risborough in 1289 as a subdeacon, was ordained deacon in December and priest the following Whitsuntide (p. 1052). On the other hand William de Trumpington, having been ordained acolyte in June 1286 and subdeacon in September, was then collated rector of Halstead (Kent). His name does not appear in any subsequent ordination list (pp. 1039–40).

[2] *Regist. G. Giffard*, pp. 128 and 370.

[3] *Regist. W. Wickwayn*, pp. 66–7, 108 and 113.

[4] *Regist. R. Swinfield*, pp. 522–44. John Halton of Carlisle collated a subdeacon to the rectory of Ousby in 1295: *Regist. J. Halton*, i, p. 44. John de Sandale collated a number of acolytes: *Regist. J. Sandale*, pp. 120, 137, 141, 157.

[5] The Vicar of Melton was to have a proper chaplain, since he was aged and feeble and not yet ordained: *Rot. H. de Welles*, i, p. 120. The Rector

when Archbishop Winchelsey gave the custody of the church of Snave in Kent to the Rector of Sturry, who was to make provision for the spiritual needs of the parish, the charges on the church, and the support of the rector who was old and feeble.[1] Sometimes a man was allowed to resign and to take some portion of the stipend as a pension.[2] In 1237 Richard le Poore, Bishop of Durham, obtained permission from the Pope to put all the old, weak and blind clergy together in a home which he proposed to endow.[3]

Another problem was that of clergy who allowed their parsonages and the chancels of their churches to fall into disrepair. Winchelsey, in 1296, ordered the Dean of Sittingbourne to sequestrate the fruits in the rectory barns at Tong until certain repairs to the church and rectory had been paid for.[4] Pecham wrote to the Chancellor of York, who was also Rector of Maidstone, informing him that he had sequestrated the church on the ground of neglect of the fabric and ornaments. He warned the chancellor that even if he appealed to Rome about it his appeal would be fought.[5] At Crambe in the North Riding of Yorkshire Archbishop Corbridge put the church and its chapels under an interdict until repairs were carried out, and also took the precaution of writing at the same time to the rectors of the neighbouring parishes forbidding them to admit parishioners of Crambe to the sacraments.[6] Archbishop Wickwayn wrote to the notorious Bogo de Clare, who was then one of the canons of York, complaining of the shocking state of the minster where the vestments were in need of repair, the thuribles were broken, the candles and incense exhausted, the bells badly hung and without ropes, and the books falling to pieces.[7]

of Bainton is to provide himself with a competent assistant on account of his age: *Regist. W. Wickwayn*, p. 105. John Legat is appointed guardian of the Vicar of Ledbury who 'compos mentis propriae non existit': *Regist. R. Swinfield*, p. 116. Cf. also *Regist. T. Corbridge*, i, p. 146; *Regist. G. Giffard*, pp. 25, 96, 152, 192, etc.; *Regist. J. Pontissara*, p. 81; *Regist. J. Romeyn*, i, p. 71; *Regist. R. Winchelsey*, pp. 320, 371.

[1] *Regist. R. Winchelsey*, p. 143.

[2] *Regist. R. Swinfield*, pp. 276–7, 331.

[3] Bliss, *Cal. Papal Letters*, i, p. 162.

[4] *Regist. R. Winchelsey*, pp. 142–3.

[5] Pecham, *Reg. Epist.* i, pp. 95–6 and cf. iii, pp. 948–50. Cf. *Regist. J. Pecham*, p. 154, and *Reg. Epist.* i, pp. 360–1.

[6] *Regist. T. Corbridge*, i, pp. 136–7.

[7] *Regist. W. Wickwayn*, pp. 286–7.

Occasionally the bishops had to deal with disputes either between parson and people or between one parson and another. At Easton in Hampshire the Bishop of Winchester had to excommunicate certain men who had quarrelled with the rector and locked him up in his own church for four days without food.[1] Reference has already been made to Ferriby in Yorkshire, where there was a dispute between two rival clergy which lasted over many years and became so embittered that at one time the church was fortified by one party and besieged by the rival faction. The Archbishop was not powerful enough to bring about a peaceful settlement, which eventually had to be done by the stronger arm of the King.[2] At Hampton a similar dispute led to the church being burnt down.[3]

Less violent disputes were constantly breaking out in other parishes; and, on the whole, the bishops seem to have handled them with wisdom and with due regard for the needs of the people. For example, in 1276 Thomas Cantilupe was called upon to intervene in a dispute between Thomas of Wichenford and John de Ebulo who were rivals for the church of Wichenford. Thomas seems to have had the weaker case, but he was a local man who would reside in the parish and understand and be understood by the people, whereas John was a favoured papal chaplain, an Italian who already held a number of livings in France and was unlikely to take much interest in a remote Worcestershire village.[4] Cantilupe was determined, therefore, that Thomas should be the rector, whatever the legal claims of the Pope's favourite might be. And in course of time Thomas was instituted, though he had to pay the foreigner 23 marks a year out of his stipend.[5]

[1] *Regist. J. Pontissara*, p. 352.

[2] *Regist. W. Wickwayn*, pp. 97–105, 262–5.

[3] Probably Highampton in Devon: Pecham, *Reg. Epist.* iii, pp. 789–92. Cf. *Regist. J. Pecham*, p. 162; *Regist. W. Giffard*, p. 216; *Regist. R. Winchelsey*, pp. 103–8. Such disputes led to a clause in the Constitutions of Cardinal Otto in 1237: 'Against those who thrust themselves into livings and are prepared to use force of arms to prevent their being dislodged': Wilkins, *Concilia*, i, p. 651 and cf. ii, pp. 5–6.

[4] Bliss, *Cal. Papal Letters*, i, pp. 388, 417.

[5] *Regist. T. Cantilupe*, pp. 99–100. Thomas is described as 'ratione linguae praecipue habilis...ad instructionem parochianorum ecclesiae memoratae', whereas John 'ad regendum ecclesiam eandem vix vel nunquam descendere poterit majoribus occupatus'.

Bishops in all ages have been expected to support 'good causes' both with their alms and with their influence; the only difference, as time goes by, being in the nature of the causes. Among those who, in the Middle Ages, looked to the bishops for help were the promoters of Crusades, of church building, and of the construction of roads and bridges. The Crusades absorbed a good deal of the thought and money of church people in the thirteenth century, though, as the years went by, the Crusading spirit grew weaker and even the appeals issued by the Council of Lyons in 1274, and by individual bishops, aroused little response. In 1275 Godfrey Giffard, in an attempt to follow up the recommendations of the Council, summoned the priests and people of every parish in Worcester to gather in the cathedral to hear him preach to them on the spiritual benefits of taking the cross; but it was of little avail.[1] Meanwhile his brother Walter at York had ordered boxes to be put in the churches to collect alms for the Crusades.[2] But though lists of 'crucesignati' were made out, it is doubtful whether many of those whose names appeared therein ever set sail.[3]

A more popular object for the alms of the faithful was the building of churches and cathedrals, and many of the bishops supported this by granting indulgences to those who were willing to contribute. Archbishop Gray of York was a warm supporter of church building and encouraged his people to give towards the additions and alterations which were being carried out at York, Southwell, Ripon and Beverley and even as far afield as Worcester.[4] He also supported in like manner the Austin Friars of Tickhill and hospitals at Creake in Norfolk, Lechlade in Gloucestershire, and Roncevaux in the south of France.[5] In later years Hugh of Welles at Lincoln had ordered collections to be made in the churches of his diocese for the building of Salisbury Cathedral,[6] as well as for Daventry Priory, Sulby Abbey and some parish churches such as All Saints', Northampton, and S. Mary's, Ketton, in Rutland.[7]

[1] *Regist. G. Giffard*, p. 73.

[2] *Regist. W. Giffard*, p. 277.

[3] *Ibid.* pp. 279 ff. Throughout the century we find bishops releasing people from Crusading vows; e.g. *Regist. W. Gray*, p. 14.

[4] *Regist. W. Gray*, pp. 1, 10, 17, 55–6, 64–5.

[5] *Ibid.* pp. 1, 9, 16, 44.

[6] This was in 1224: *Rot. H. de Welles*, ii, p. 207.

[7] *Ibid.* ii, pp. 228, 243, 253–4.

Episcopal support for the building of roads and bridges may seem less natural until we remember that, up to the time when the State took over the responsibility for such public services, the provision of these amenities was one of the claims upon the alms of the faithful.[1] The traveller, like the poor and the sick, was an object of compassion, and therefore merited the gifts and ministrations of devout folk. That is why Hugh of Welles granted indulgences to those who would contribute towards the building of bridges at Brampton, Rockingham and Aynho,[2] and Walter Gray did the same for those who helped in the construction of a road between Beverley and Bentley.[3]

Not only was a bishop then, as now, expected to throw the weight of his influence into every 'good cause', but many also looked to him for financial support. Nor did they look in vain. Swinfield made himself entirely responsible for the support of two poor scholars—'the boys at Oxford' as they are called in his accounts[4]—and among his expenses we find several entries which show where his sympathies lay. Besides numerous gifts to religious houses, especially the friars, we find him sending three shillings to a poor scholar at Ledbury, two shillings to another at Colwall, seventy-eight shillings spent in cloth for the poor, and a charming gift of fourpence to a boy for leading about a blind man.[5] Walter Giffard's accounts contain similar charitable gifts: 'to a lame clerk at Iveden, two shillings' and 'to a poor man at Wickham, 12*d.*';[6] while in 1276 he was paying two shillings a week to three schoolmasters at Beverley and gave them 30*s.* 7*d.* to buy themselves three gowns.[7] The two brothers Hugh and Jocelyn of Welles founded a hospital at Wells which Hugh endowed in his will;[8] Walter de Merton founded a hospital at Basingstoke in memory of his mother;[9] and Walter

[1] Jusserand, *English Wayfaring Life*, p. 30. S. Richard of Chichester directed in his will that the residue of his property should be divided between poor religious houses, hospitals, roads and bridges, widows and orphans: *Sussex Arch. Coll.* i, p. 191.

[2] *Rot. H. de Welles*, ii, pp. 188, 195, 220.

[3] *Regist. W. Gray*, p. 39; cf. pp. 20, 42, 60–1; *Regist. J. Romeyn*, i, pp. 1–15.

[4] Webb, *Household Roll of R. de Swinfield*, i, pp. 116 ff.

[5] *Ibid.* i, pp. 143, 150–2, 153–5, 188.

[6] *Regist. W. Giffard*, p. 116.

[7] *Ibid.* p. 272.

[8] Wharton, *Anglia Sacra*, i, pp. 563–4, and cf. the Will of Hugh of Welles in G. Cambrensis, *Opera*, vii, pp. 223–7.

[9] Hobhouse, *Sketch of the Life of W. de Merton*, pp. 3, 48.

Suffield spent much of his money in establishing an asylum for aged priests and poor scholars at Norwich.[1] Many other bishops were generous in their alms-giving. Gilbert of S. Lifard, Bishop of Chichester, was described as 'the father of orphans, consoler of widows, a pious and humble visitor at rough bedsides and hovels, and a bountiful helper of the needy',[2] while it was recorded of Oliver Sutton, Bishop of Lincoln, that he spent all the money which he received in fines on the relief of the poor.[3] Richard Gravesend of London left enough money in his will to provide 36,288 poor persons with one penny each on the day of his funeral.[4] As we should expect, such generosity was liable to abuse, and it is therefore no surprise to find Archbishop Wickwayn writing to his clergy to warn them against certain impostors who were going about claiming to be his relatives and saying that they had his approval in asking for financial help.[5]

Occasionally a bishop had to come to the rescue of one of his clergy who had fallen into financial straits. In 1270 Walter Giffard found one of his clergy in very low water and had to send the poor fellow two shillings to buy a shirt,[6] and John le Romeyn had to issue a mandate to the official of the Archdeacon of York ordering him to admonish the clergy to assist a certain poor priest in order to save him from the disgrace of having to go begging.[7] Archbishop Winchelsey once told his official, William de Staundon, that he must induce the executors of the late Bishop of Coventry and Lichfield to make some provision for a certain destitute priest whom the bishop had rashly ordained without a title.[8]

[1] Blomefield, *History of Norfolk*, iii, p. 488. There was also a hospital for poor priests in the parish of S. Margaret, Canterbury: *Register of S. Augustine's, Canterbury*, ii, pp. 557–9.

[2] *Flores Historiarum*, ed. Luard, iii, p. 129.

[3] See Kingsford's article in *D.N.B.*

[4] *Accounts of Executors of Gravesend and Button*, Camden Society, p. xvii. Thomas Button of Exeter left money to provide 10,212 poor persons with a penny each. The same was to be given to each of 235 prisoners; but twelve of them who were clerks received 12*d.* each: *ibid.* p. xvi. Bishop Drokensford of Bath and Wells arranged for the feeding of 200 poor people each day at the rate of a silver farthing each. At Michaelmas they were to have 4*s.* each for clothes. Poor priests were to have special consideration: *Regist. J. Drokensford*, p. 161.

[5] *Regist. W. Wickwayn*, p. 220.

[6] Dixon, *Fasti Eboracenses*, p. 313.

[7] *Regist. J. Romeyn*, i, p. 65.

[8] *Regist. R. Winchelsey*, p. 97.

Another class of person whom the bishops seem to have been always ready to befriend were anchorites and recluses, both male and female. Many of the bishops' wills contain gifts to such persons, and in 1270 Walter Giffard gave '6*s*. 8*d*. to a recluse at Doncaster, 12*d*. to two recluses at Blyth, and 3*s*. to a recluse at Elland'.[1] Swinfield regularly gave small sums to hermits, and we find in his account rolls such entries as: 'to a recluse at Kensington, 6*d*.' and 'to a recluse at Leintwardine, 12*d*.'[2] We are not surprised, however, to learn that anchorites and hermits needed some supervision if they were to be prevented from becoming a burden upon the community. Once a woman called Alice de Falketon applied to Archbishop Giffard for leave to build a house and live as an anchoress in the churchyard of S. Nicholas, Hedon; but before granting his permission the Archbishop wisely ordered the Archdeacon of the East Riding to enquire whether she had enough to live on, and whether her proposal was likely to be to the good of the parish as a whole.[3]

But what would surprise us most about the Church of the thirteenth century would be the power of the bishops over the laity. What should we think, for example, of a Bishop of Worcester ordering some men who had molested the clergy of Little Comberton to go barefooted in procession, in their shirts and breeches only, and to be publicly beaten by the rural deans of Worcester, Gloucester, Bristol, Pershore and Warwick, through the market-places of those towns?[4] Or what should we say of an Archbishop of Canterbury who ordered a wealthy layman, Sir Osbert Giffard, to be flogged three times round the church of the nunnery at Wilton, three times round the market-place at Salisbury and three times round Shaftesbury Church?[5]

The powers of a medieval prelate over the laity were almost as great as those which he exercised over his clergy. Excom-

[1] Dixon, *Fasti Eboracenses*, pp. 312–13. One of the recluses at Blyth fell ill some time afterwards and Wickwayn ordered the Vicar of Blyth to look after her affairs: *Regist. W. Wickwayn*, p. 74.

[2] Webb, *Household Roll of R. de Swinfield*, i, pp. 150, 153.

[3] *Regist. W. Giffard*, p. 108, and cf. p. 185. Note that in the Constitutions of the Council of Durham in 1220 it is enacted that no one is to live as a hermit alone: Wilkins, *Concilia*, i, p. 583. For details as to the life of these anchoresses see the *Ancren Riwle*.

[4] *Regist. G. Giffard*, p. 190.

[5] Pecham, *Reg. Epist.* iii, pp. 916–17.

munications flew about the diocese like sparks from a Catherine wheel; eminent men were publicly flogged and humiliated; knights were cited to appear before their diocesan like schoolboys before their headmaster, and fines and punishments of every sort were inflicted.[1] Corbridge obtained a bond for £10 from Loretta Lady Swanland for good behaviour, and ordered Henry Leve to pay his wife five shillings a year and treat her well.[2] Godfrey Giffard ordered Sir William le Poer either to take his wife back or to make her a maintenance allowance.[3] Archbishop Gray extracted a promise from Hugh of Berwick that he would treat his wife well under penalty of ten marks,[4] and Winchelsey cited Walter de la Mare who had deserted his wife four years previously and was refusing to support her.

Occasionally a bishop had to deal with some unusual problem or dispute, and one very curious incident has found its way into the Register of Godfrey Giffard. The story is as follows. A certain Ella de Sor married a man called Richard Beyngham and in course of time pretended to be pregnant. Two friends, Richard Richmon and Ida de Partunhal, knowing that she was only pretending, went to Banbury where they bought a boy baby for twelvepence, a loaf of bread and a dish of bacon. The boy was baptised by the parish priest as Ella's own child. But a few years later Richard Beyngham, the supposed father of the child, died; and, suspicions having been aroused in the village, enquiries into the parentage of the boy were instituted with a view to deciding who was his legal guardian. In the course of these enquiries Richard Richmon and his friend Ida took fright and confessed what they had done. We are not told what the end of the story was, except that the Bishop of Lincoln excommunicated all the parties concerned for having the infant baptised twice.[5]

The judicial powers of a bishop were thus considerable, embracing the laity as well as the clergy. Each bishop was, in fact, surrounded by a number of officials whose duty it was to find out what was amiss in the diocese, to bring it to the notice of the bishop, and to see that punishment followed. The chief

[1] Cf. *Regist. G. Giffard*, pp. 110, 215; *Regist. W. Giffard*, p. 104; *Regist. W. Wickwayn*, p. 37; *Regist. H. Hethe*, pp. 201, 224, 248, 458.

[2] *Regist. T. Corbridge*, i, pp. 196, 201.

[3] *Regist. G. Giffard*, p. 394. *Regist. W. Gray*, p. 269.

[5] *Regist. G. Giffard*, pp. 538 and 507.

of these officers was the archdeacon, the 'bishop's eye', who had considerable powers and generally a bad name. Other men engaged in the judicial work of the diocese were the bishop's official (now called Chancellor), penitentiaries, vicars-general, sequestrators and apparitors, all of whom were concerned with matters of discipline and the carrying out of the bishop's injunctions. These all worked through the rural deans and even below them, for in the Statutes of Durham in 1220 it is decreed that there shall be in each deanery two or three 'inquisitors' to keep the bishop informed of any misdemeanours or irregularities.[1]

Behind all this system of enquiry lay the bishop's court, which had wide powers over life and property. Clergy who misbehaved or who proved themselves contumacious could be suspended from their livings, or deprived of them altogether, or their goods might be sequestrated until such time as they were prepared to submit to the bishop's authority.[2] If none of these punishments proved effective a man might be sent away on pilgrimage or find himself lodged in gaol; for, by the statutes of the Council of Lambeth in 1261, every bishop was required to provide himself with one or two prisons in his diocese.[3]

There was thus in every diocese a complex machinery for the punishment of evil-doers and for the maintenance of discipline and efficiency. Had it functioned as it was meant to do, the incompetent or nefarious parson would have had little chance of escaping from its clutches. The smallest sign of clerical misbehaviour should have been quickly detected by those whose responsibility it was to pass on information to the authority which had power to enforce the appropriate penalties. Theoretically, at any rate, the parson had far less chance of defying authority in the thirteenth century than he has to-day. And yet, in spite of all this machinery, and in spite of the determined efforts made by courageous reformers among the bishops, conditions in the parishes remained very unsatisfactory, as every intelligent man fully realised.

[1] Wilkins, *Concilia*, i, p. 578.

[2] See e.g. *Regist. T. Corbridge*, i, p. 95; *Regist. W. Wickwayn*, pp. 93, 126; *Regist. J. Pecham* (C. and Y. Soc.), pp. 139–64.

[3] Wilkins, *Concilia*, i, p. 755; cf. *Regist. J. Pontissara*, pp. 461–2; Pecham, *Reg. Epist.* iii, p. 914.

CHAPTER XVI

THE DEMAND FOR REFORM

After the death of Archbishop Pecham in 1292 the see of Canterbury was vacant for nearly two years. During this time the administration of the diocese was in the hands of the Prior and Chapter of Christ Church, Canterbury, who appointed one of their number, Richard de Cliffe, to visit certain parts of the diocese and to report on conditions in the parishes. How many parishes were visited during the interregnum we do not know, but a few records of these visitations have survived through the centuries and are now among the archives of Canterbury Cathedral.[1] As he journeyed from village to village Richard de Cliffe found much in need of correction, all of which he entered in his rolls. Let us, therefore, follow him on his travels and see in what condition he found these parishes, most of which lie in or near Romney Marsh.

We start, then, from the coast town of New Romney, where Richard de Cliffe found several clerks attached to the church all of whom were married. He also reported the absence of a censer among the ornaments of the church. A mile to the north-west lay the village of Hope All Saints. Here the rector appears to have been a minor, for he was still at school and therefore absent from the parish; while William the Chaplain, who ran the parish, had a woman living in the house with him. The dilapidated condition of the Missal in this church must have interfered with the proper conduct of the services.

At the parish church of Old Romney the chaplain lived with a woman whom he called his sister, but the visitor was a little suspicious of this. At the church of S. Martin's the chaplain had to be suspended owing to the sorry state of the church. The chrismatorium and pyx were without locks, the chalice was broken and there were no books at all. The services in this church must, therefore, have ceased altogether.

[1] *Some Early Visitation Rolls at Canterbury*, by C. E. Woodruff, in *Archaeologia Cantiana*, xxxii and xxxiii. Richard de Cliffe may have been disputing at Oxford about 1300: see Little and Pelster, *Oxford Theology and Theologians*, pp. 258–9. He died in 1329, leaving a number of legal works to the library of the convent: M. R. James, *Ancient Libraries of Canterbury and Dover*, p. 140.

The next parish of Brookland revealed nothing more serious than the need of repairs to the roof and the gutters, and little is known of Brenzett except that the tithes were farmed out to a layman called Thomas Quickenham; but at Fairfield things were in a bad way. The rector had let the proceeds of the church to farm and is described as doing no good in the parish. This expression, which Cliffe uses of several incumbents, probably meant that the man spent nothing on the poor or on the upkeep of the church. The Rector of Fairfield certainly took little interest in his church, for the ornaments and vestments were dirty and worn, six of the necessary service-books were missing, and the oil had not been changed for over a year. He was almost certainly an absentee, for the chaplains and clerks were left to their own devices. One had a young woman to serve him at the altar, another had married a widow and was consequently forbidden to assist at the altar in future, a third was described as 'too poor to live decently'.

At Snave the rector was a deacon and a married man. He was made to promise not to minister anywhere near the altar in future, the responsibility being transferred to a competent clerk. How far the services could be performed is doubtful, as there appears to have been no chalice.

The Rector of Ivychurch was Master Hugh de Penebroke, D.C.L., who had been ordained subdeacon and instituted to this parish in 1288.[1] He was never there as he was one of the King's clerks, and, like the Rector of Fairfield, he is described as having done no good in the parish. There was no vicar, and the clerk, being a married man, was forbidden to go near the altar. Whether or not there was any chaplain to say Mass is not recorded.

We come next to the parish of S. Mary-in-the-Marsh, where the rector was found to be an absentee and a pluralist, and the chaplain could not be found at all. At Blackmanstone all seems to have been well except that there was no daily Mass. Orgarswick also presented no difficulty; but, at Dymchurch, Elias the clerk was found to be keeping a woman in his house and both were ordered to be flogged three times round the church.

The church of Eastbridge appears to have been totally neglected, the tithes being farmed by the Vicar of West Hythe,

[1] *Regist. J. Pecham* (C. and Y. Soc.), pp. 81–2. Penebroke was ordained deacon in March 1289 and priest in the following June: Pecham, *Reg. Epist.* iii, pp. 1050, 1051.

who was suspended and deprived of his vicarage for this breach of ecclesiastical law. A certain Amfridus was Rector of Eastbridge in 1289,[1] but he never resided here, and, since there was no chaplain, the parishioners, not without justification, asked to be provided with a priest.

The Rector of Newchurch was also an absentee and 'did no good in the parish'. He allowed the outbuildings of the rectory to fall into complete ruin in spite of the fact that the living was a good one, worth sixty marks a year. The vicar whom he had appointed was supposed to get ten marks a year, but he had not had a fair deal, since the hay-tithe, to which he was entitled, had been largely annexed by the rector, while the draining of the marsh and subsequent ploughing of new land deprived him of most of what remained of his income, since all corn-tithes went to the rector. As a result the vicar pleaded that he was too poor to afford any assistance. This parish, then, had suffered considerably since the arrival of the present rector, for his predecessor had lived and worked in the parish with the assistance of two chaplains, a deacon and other clerks. Now there was only the vicar struggling against poverty and over-work.

At Burmarsh the rector, though he spent a good deal of time away from the parish, was described as a good man who did what he could for the parish. The clerk was married and the chancel roof needed attention. At West Hythe, a chapelry in the parish of Lympne, the vicar in charge had lived many years with a woman who had borne him 'ever so many children' (*quam plures proles*), and when she finally died in his house he took another. The Rectory of Lympne was held by the Archdeacon of Canterbury who was seldom there, the work being carried out by chaplains and a clerk who had married a widow. At Westenhanger the rector was at school and 'did no good in the parish', the chaplain had living with him a woman who was pregnant, and his clerk was married.

In these records, then, we have a picture of one small corner of England at the end of the thirteenth century. It is not very reassuring. Of these nineteen parishes or chapelries only one could be regarded as wholly satisfactory; six of the rectors were absent, and four were described as 'doing no good in the parish'.

[1] Pecham, *Reg. Epist.* iii, p. 1052.

Most of the inferior clergy were unfaithful to the vow of chastity, and in a good many of the churches there were defects either of the structure or of the books and ornaments.

Yet we have no grounds for thinking that these records are false. There was, it is true, some rivalry between the regular and the secular clergy, and it is possible that Robert de Cliffe may have had sharp eyes to see what was wrong; but on the whole the document strikes us as a sober record of conditions as they were found to be in this quiet corner of Kent. Moreover the evidence which has been given in previous chapters shows that this district was not likely to be greatly different from other parts of England. The few visitation records which have come down to us, such as Sonning and Snaith, tell very much the same tale of slackness and neglect. Indeed, this particular district should have had as high a standard as any. The diocese had had at least two energetic and conscientious archbishops, Kilwardby and Pecham, both of whom had really cared about the conditions which obtained in the parishes, and some of the villages in this district were no more than fifteen miles from Canterbury itself. If this was the state of affairs in a small and well-conducted diocese, what must they have been like in a vast diocese like Lichfield or Norwich, or in one which had long been ruled by men who spent most of their lives at Court?

Fortunately there were a good many men who realised how bad things had got and who were clamouring for reform. At the beginning of the century Giraldus Cambrensis, Archdeacon of S. David's, was busy criticising everything and everybody except himself, for whom he had a very high regard. His attacks on the monks are choice material for those who are anxious to show up the worst sides of the monastic system; but his criticisms of the parish clergy and of the bishops were no less severe. Giraldus had been disappointed in the ambition of his life, which was to be elected Bishop of S. David's. The iron had to some extent entered into his soul, and, not having become a bishop himself, he tended to regard with some contempt those who had usurped what he felt should have been his seat. He refers in the *Gemma Ecclesiastica* to 'the wretched bishops of these days' who sell justice, traffic in pardons and visit not once in seven years; and, as if in answer to the question of the ultimate destiny of archdeacons, which was of perennial interest to the medieval mind, he says: 'I do not say that bishops cannot be saved, but I do say that it is in our days harder for them than for other men.'[1] As for the parish clergy the chief evils which he finds among them are simony, ignorance and the vice of making money out of the sacraments.

We must not, however, take Giraldus too seriously. He was a professional critic with a nose sensitive enough to smell out any scandal, and a pen ready dipped in gall to record it for posterity. Moreover his evidence was largely based upon what he had seen in Wales, and we know from no less an authority than the Council of Oxford in 1222 that the Welsh churches were notoriously derelict.[2]

A much more important witness was Robert Grosseteste, who, after fifteen years' pastoral experience as Bishop of Lincoln, could write to the clergy of his diocese of 'so many evils, so serious, so hateful, so foul, so scandalous, so criminal, so wicked, so profane' which, he says, are due to the neglect of the clergy and to the bad example which they set.[3] In the same year, 1250, he drew the Pope's attention to the terribly low standard of the clergy, whom he described as 'utterly sensual, given over to fornication, adultery and incest, sunk in every kind of gluttony, and (to pass over quickly) polluted with every sort of depravity and crime and abomination and as having "gone a-whoring with their own inventions"'.[4] These are hard words, but Grosseteste knew what he was talking about. He had had ample opportunity of seeing the clergy in their homes and in their parishes, and his love of fair play would have prevented him from exposing them to the Pope had he not had abundant evidence for his accusations.

Grosseteste's Franciscan friend, Adam Marsh, was driven almost to despair by the wickedness of the times. His letters abound in such outbursts as 'these most evil and perilous times, as detestable as they are damnable, alack and alas!'[5] or 'these days of astounding wickedness',[6] or 'these most damned

[1] G. Cambrensis, *Opera*, ii, pp. 294–304.

[2] Wilkins, *Concilia*, i, p. 587.

[3] Grosseteste, *Epistolae*, pp. 439–40.

[4] Brown, *Fasc. Rerum Expetendarum*, ii, p. 252.

[5] 'Diebus pessimis periculosissimi temporis...tanto detestabilius quanto damnabilius, heu! heu! heu!' Letters of Adam Marsh in *Monumenta Franciscana*, i, p. 88.

[6] 'His diebus stupendae perversitatis': *ibid.* pp. 198–9.

days'.[1] No doubt Adam Marsh had in mind the general state of the Church throughout the world, but he cannot have been unaware of the conditions which prevailed in the parishes and among those who held high office in the Church.

If Marsh spoke in general terms, and Grosseteste attacked mainly the moral standards of the clergy, the Cardinal Legate, Ottobon, was able to define some at least of the things which disgraced the Church and impaired its efficiency. In the Constitutions which he drew up in 1268 he declared that the three main evils from which the Church was suffering were pluralism, non-residence and men refusing to proceed to holy orders.[2] These were certainly serious enough, but the records of the Visitation of Kent show that there were other things equally grave which Ottobon perhaps thought were less serious.

About the same time Roger Bacon was writing his *Compendium Studii*, in which he groans over the lamentable state of the Church. Like his master, Grosseteste, he realised that the *causa, fons et origo* of all this was the papal court with its veniality and materialism. The 'immeasurable corruption' which is everywhere to be found appears above all, he says, in the Roman Curia, which is dreadfully corrupt. Everywhere, he declares, there is pride, avarice, envy, luxury and gluttony. The regulars have without exception fallen from their first state. The clergy are given over to pride and luxury and greed. Wherever clergy meet together there are quarrels and disturbances. Indeed the Christians have proved themselves worse than the heathen.[3]

Another Franciscan, John Pecham, who, as Archbishop of Canterbury, had more chance of observation than had intellectuals such as Roger Bacon and Adam Marsh, put his finger upon seven main evils which he thought must be the seven phials of the Apocalypse. Writing in 1284 to the Bishop of Tusculum he complained of the following evils in the Church—ignorance of the clergy; clergy who care only for their own well-being; appeals to Rome; litigation; daily limitation of the powers of prelates; neglect of God's law and contempt of the Gospel; and

[1] 'His diebus damnatissimis': *Mon. Franc.* i, p. 116. Cf. 'his diebus pessimis' (pp. 96, 144, 241); 'his sceleratissimis diebus' (pp. 138, 147).

[2] Wilkins, *Concilia*, ii, p. 12.

[3] R. Bacon, *Opera Ined.* pp. 398–402.

worldliness of priests.[1] As we shall see in a few moments, this was by far the most profound of all contemporary judgements.

The above quotations will serve to show that the keenest intelligences of the age were fully alive to the blemishes which marked the Body of Christ and impaired its effectiveness in the world. That there should have been so much dissatisfaction is itself an indication of strength and hope. Uneasiness about the present state of affairs is always the first step towards reform. It is when men are complacent that all hope of progress is lost.

Looking back through the mist of seven centuries, and trying to fit our scraps of evidence together, like pieces of a jig-saw puzzle, to form a whole picture, we are driven to the conclusion that though the thirteenth century was one of great and solid achievement there was yet something radically wrong with a Church system which could tolerate conditions such as those which Richard de Cliffe found in Kent in the course of his visitations in the early 'nineties. When we try to put into words what we feel to have been the real weakness of the Church we find that it divides itself into three statements.

The first sounds paradoxical enough, for it is this: the great weakness of the Church was the fact that it was far too strong. On the continent the Western Church was fighting a continuous battle against heresy and individualism, and the Eastern Church against Islam. But in England the Church knew no rival. It had a complete monopoly of spiritual allegiance and was brought up against no heresy upon which it could sharpen its wits, and against no interference or persecution which would have found out its weak spots. The sin of disunity, disastrous though it is at the present day, has at least the advantage of making each religious community conscious that it has its rivals. But in the thirteenth century there was none of this. The Church knew no competition, and, as a result, could adopt a 'take-it-or-leave-it' policy. At its best it exercised a noble and devoted 'pastoral' ministry: it had little incentive and indeed little opportunity to be 'piscatorial'. The apostles were sent out not as shepherds but as fishers of men, but the Church of the thirteenth century would have claimed that there was no more

[1] Pecham, *Reg. Epist.* ii, pp. 694–7; cf. the more general statements as to the desolate state of the Church in his letters to the Dominicans in 1288 (*ibid.* iii, pp. 958–9) and to the Franciscans in 1289 (pp. 964–6).

fishing to do. As a result it lost the need and the art of making the Gospel winsome, and could adopt the attitude so sternly rebuked by Henry Ward Beecher, who had to point out to a young preacher that it was the duty of an angler to attract fish to his hook, not to cast his line into the water with the cry: 'Bite that or be damned!'

The very power of the Church and its position in society encouraged a totally wrong attitude to the ministry. Unless a man is driven into the priesthood by a strong sense of vocation, and unless his ministry is going to bring out all that is best in him, he will be of little service to the Kingdom of God. It is obvious that many men were ordained in the thirteenth century for quite the wrong reasons. Some went for security, some for prestige, some as an easy way of making a living. The result was that if a man saw a chance of 'bettering himself' by accepting a richer living, or by collecting a number of benefices, he took it readily. This is brought out by Grosseteste's letter to his sister in the year 1232 when he resigned all his preferment except the prebend of Lincoln. He feels sure that his sister, being a nun vowed to poverty, will understand this action which he knows will be regarded with astonishment and contempt by most people.[1]

This totally wrong attitude towards the ministry poisoned the relationship between priest and priest, and between priest and people. Instead of co-operation between the clergy for the good of the Church, we find endless litigation and quarrelling over rights and privileges and precedence. If the clergy had thought more of the souls of the people and less of their tithes and dues things would have been better.

This first point, then, covers three of the 'seven evils' described by John Pecham: clergy who care for their own well-being; litigation; and neglect of God's law and contempt for the Gospel. The second great weakness of the Church was that there were far too many clergy. A parish of two or three hundred souls cannot possibly provide full-time employment for more than two men; yet the average parish, as we have seen, contained four or five clergy. The question which seems to have influenced the bishops most in the selection of ordinands was not: 'Do you think in your heart that you be truly called

[1] Grosseteste, *Epistolae*, pp. 43–4.

according to the will of our Lord Jesus Christ...to the Order and Ministry of Priesthood?' but: 'What guarantee can you give that, once you are ordained, you will be able to support yourself?' Since a great many men seem to have been able to give the requisite assurance, the number of ordained men became very great, with the inevitable result that standards of knowledge and morals were low. If the Church could have taken a strong line, and, for a whole generation, accepted only those who were fully qualified for the work which they were to do and for the position which they were to hold, things would have been far better; and what the clergy would have lost in numbers and power they would have gained in prestige and in the respect in which they would have been held.

This second point includes two more of Pecham's 'seven evils'—the ignorance and worldliness of the clergy. The third great weakness of the Church was its lack of effective discipline. Compared with the chaotic individualism of the reformed churches to-day the medieval Church appears highly organised and efficient. It had a whole system of justice applied through the bishop's courts and officials. It had its councils and synods pouring out statutes and decrees. It had a system of visitation by bishop, archdeacon and rural dean. It even had inquisitors to go round the parishes and report on anything which they found amiss.[1] It had, in fact, the framework of a well-organised and effective discipline. Yet somehow it failed to carry out even the most vital of its own decrees. Sections 13 and 14 of the Statutes of the Lateran Council of 1179 declared that pluralism was henceforward illegal. Provincial and Diocesan Councils in this country willingly endorsed this decree. Yet pluralism continued unchecked throughout this century, largely because the popes continued to sell dispensations to such as could afford them.[2] Farming of livings was also repeatedly condemned by the synods.[3] Yet rectors continued to farm their livings, if and when it suited them, in defiance of all authority.

[1] Wilkins, *Concilia*, i, p. 578.

[2] The Lateran Council of 1215 admitted that the decree of 1179 had borne little fruit, but instead of making a more determined attempt to enforce it the Council gave way to the well-to-do by allowing dispensations for 'sublimes et litteratae personae': Mansi, *Sac. Concil. Collectio*, xxii, coll. 1015–18.

[3] See R. Grosseteste, *Epistolae*, p. 158; Wilkins, *Concilia*, i, pp. 580, 588, 651; ii, 10, 58; Pecham, *Reg. Epist.* iii, pp. 949–50.

The whole system of discipline, then, admirable though it might appear on paper, was defenceless against vested interests and the power of the purse. Popular satirists were never tired of criticising the veniality of ecclesiastical courts and especially of Rome, making puns about a mark gaining more respect than S. Mark, and lucre more than Luke.[1] Grosseteste had no hesitation in declaring that the *causa, fons et origo* of the evil state of the Church was the corruption of the Curia, and even the less fiery Pecham included among the 'seven phials full of the wrath of God' the system of appeals to Rome which shipwrecked every reforming effort of the local prelates.

[1] Wright, *Political Songs*, pp. 11, 16, 31.

CHAPTER XVII

HOW THIS DEMAND WAS MET

Bad though conditions were in many ways, the Church of the thirteenth century was fully alive to the need for reform and anxious that progress should be made. Those who held positions of authority were anxious to get rid of as many of the abuses as they could, and perhaps even to make the Church more the servant of the people and less its master. This is not to say that they were prepared to see the clergy lose any of their rights or their powers, but rather that they desired so to reform the Church that it would be able to rule more by respect and affection and less by threats and punishments. The ideal was to see that each parish was faithfully served, and to do this the first evil to be attacked was pluralism.

Pluralism was an old vice which was known to the Council of Chalcedon as early as A.D. 451. It was attacked by the Lateran Council of 1179 and by that of 1215. So far as this country was concerned, the law, throughout the thirteenth century, was clear—a beneficed clerk who accepted another living vacated *de jure* the one which he already held.[1] Pluralism was forbidden by the London decrees of 1215–22, by the Council of Oxford in 1222 and by Grosseteste in 1238.[2] Richard le Poore not only said that any clerk holding one benefice and accepting another was to lose the first, but added that if he protested against this he should lose both.[3] Both Otto and Ottobon declared that if a man already holding one living were instituted to another that institution should be invalid.[4] Many bishops would only institute men on condition that they did not accept another benefice, and in visiting their dioceses made careful enquiries as to who were pluralists.[5] Pecham was indefatigable in his efforts to root out this disease. Almost immediately after

[1] A. H. Thompson, *Pluralism in the Medieval Church*, in *Associated Architectural Societies' Reports*, 1916–17, p. 42.

[2] *E.H.R.* 1915, p. 298; Wilkins, *Concilia*, i, p. 591; R. Grosseteste, *Epistolae*, p. 159.

[3] Wilkins, *Concilia*, i, p. 600.

[4] *Ibid.* i, p. 652; ii, p. 12.

[5] *Rot. R. Grosseteste*, pp. 94, 140–1; Wilkins, *Concilia*, i, pp. 627–8; Luard, *An. Mon.* ii, 113–15; *Regist. W. Giffard*, pp. 266–8; *Regist. G. Giffard*, p. 516.

his consecration he issued a decree declaring that all benefices held by a pluralist, except the latest to which he had been instituted, were legally vacant; adding, like Richard le Poore half a century earlier, that if anyone protested against this he should lose all that he held.[1] So anxious was he to put an end to this evil that he wrote in this same year to the Grey Friars ordering them to refuse absolution to pluralists.[2]

Yet in spite of these efforts of reforming bishops pluralism survived. The richer incumbents obtained papal dispensations and royal clerks sheltered under the protection of the King.[3] The circle was in every sense a vicious one. Dispensations cost money; but pluralism was profitable, and an outlay of many pounds could be repaid out of the income of a number of benefices. The only person who could break the circle was the Pope, but no Pope of the thirteenth century could afford to lose this financial asset, no matter how disastrous it was for the Church as a whole. We have to wait until the year 1317 for a really bold move at Rome in the bull *Execrabilis*, which has been called 'the last word of the medieval papacy on the subject'.[4]

Closely allied to the evil of pluralism was that of non-residence, as Ottobon observed. Clearly no man can be in two places at once, and the more livings a man held the less time he could spend in each.

The Church was alive to this evil, and various attempts were made to force incumbents to reside;[5] but once again the flow of dispensations from Rome rendered the efforts of reformers of none effect. Various bishops, in instituting men to livings, made it a condition that they should reside there and serve the church *in propria persona*;[6] but the episcopal registers also reveal the fact that a good many men were consistently absent from

[1] Wilkins, *Concilia*, ii, pp. 34, 60. See also *Archbishop Peckham and Pluralities* by W. T. Waugh, in *E.H.R.* 1913, pp. 625–35.

[2] Pecham, *Reg. Epist.* i, p. 68.

[3] Bliss, *Cal. Papal Letters*, i, p. 168.

[4] W. T. Waugh in *E.H.R.* 1913, p. 628. For the effect of this bull see *Regist. R. Baldock, etc.* pp. 184–5; *Regist. A. Orleton*, pp. 59–60; *Regist. J. Sandale*, pp. 94–100: all of which give information as to the number of pluralists in the dioceses of London, Hereford, and Winchester.

[5] See Wilkins, *Concilia*, i, pp. 652, 673, 733; *E.H.R.* 1915, p. 298; R. Grosseteste, *Epistolae*, p. 160; *Vetus Liber Archidiaconi Eliensis*, p. 11; *Regist. J. Pontissara*, p. 212.

[6] E.g. *Rot. H. de Welles*, i, pp. 7, 9, 16, 21, 39, 43, etc.; ii, pp. 40, 48, 58, 61, etc.; *Rot. R. Grosseteste*, p. 187.

their cures.[1] The more disciplinarian of the bishops did their utmost to persuade men to reside, but with only scant success. None was more eager than Pecham, who sequestrated a number of livings of men who were absentees, and ordered the Bishops of Norwich and Chichester to do the same.[2] But Pecham, like every one else who tried to bring order out of confusion, was powerless against the man who could afford to defy authority.

This is brought out in the record of the correspondence between Pecham and Peter Blaunc, Rector of Wrotham and Lyminge, who, as a protégé of Archbishop Boniface and an executor of his will, obtained leave of absence to study at the University of Paris for five years.[3] But in 1281 he was found to be neglecting his parishes so much that Pecham wrote remonstrating with him for this, and at the same time sequestrated the fruits of the two benefices in order to provide for the poor and for the upkeep of the churches.[4] Early in the following year the sequestration was relaxed to the extent of allowing Peter's proctor enough money for tilling the land and feeding the stock, and shortly afterwards the sequestration was removed altogether.[5] The rector, meanwhile, remained in Paris where, instead of pursuing his studies as agreed, he had become chaplain to the Queen of France.[6] In 1284 his licence for non-residence expired, but there is no record of his having returned to his parishes, in which he took throughout not the slightest interest; and fifteen years later we find Pecham's successor, Winchelsey, in correspondence with the Bishop of Amiens about the prospects of inducing Peter to return.[7]

Thomas Cantilupe of Hereford was another bishop who tried to induce his clergy to reside, but he achieved very little by his efforts. Men with powers as great as those of James de Aquablanca, Archdeacon of Shropshire, could defy their bishops with

[1] *Regist. J. Pontissara*, pp. 586–7; *Regist. W. Wickwayn*, pp. 116–19; *Regist. J. Romeyn*, i, p. 375.

[2] *Regist. J. Pecham* (C. and Y. Soc.), p. 163; Pecham, *Reg. Epist.* i, pp. 193–4 and ii, pp. 531–2.

[3] Pecham, *Reg. Epist.* i, p. 8. He was permitted to 'farm' his rectories during this time: *Regist. J. Pecham* (C. & Y. Soc.), p. 23.

[4] Pecham, *Reg. Epist.* ii, pp. 715–16; *Regist. J. Pecham*, p. 146. Cf. above, p. 139.

[5] *Regist. J. Pecham*, pp. 150–1, 153.

[6] Pecham, *Reg. Epist.* iii, p. 828.

[7] *Regist. R. Winchelsey*, pp. 305, 320; cf. *Cal. Close Rolls, 1279–88*, p. 503.

impunity,[1] while Bishop Quivil of Exeter gave way to them by allowing non-residence for such as had instituted vicars in their parishes.[2] So, once again, the efforts of those who wished to reform the Church were wrecked by vested interests and the 'almighty dollar'.[3]

The third great evil of which Ottobon was conscious was that of clergy who had not received the ordination which their work demanded. As we have already seen,[4] a fairly large proportion of those who were inducted into livings were not fully ordained, many of them being only in minor orders. The evil of this is obvious. If a man *couldn't* act as a parish priest it was easy enough for him to say that he *wouldn't*; and if he could draw his income without having to do any work, there was, for some men at least, every temptation to go on doing this for as long as possible.

The first step in fighting this evil was to examine the orders of those who were already beneficed. This was ordered by Poore in 1220, by the Archdeacons of the Lincoln diocese in 1230 and by Archbishop Giffard in 1275.[5] Many men had been (or claimed to have been) ordained in other dioceses or by wandering bishops. The letters of all such were to be closely examined, and if there was any doubt they were to be suspended until further enquiry had been made.[6] So far as vicars were concerned efforts were made—though without any marked success—to ensure that all were ordained priest either before institution or at the next ensuing ordinations,[7] but even this apparently simple regulation was not always observed, and Walter Giffard actually had to deprive Simon Cave, Vicar of Carnaby, of his vicarage on an order from the legate Otto.[8]

If it was difficult to see that vicars were properly ordained it was infinitely more difficult to do the same with rectors. Often enough children were appointed who had to wait long years

[1] *Regist. T. Cantilupe*, pp. 125, 137, 141–2.
[2] Wilkins, *Concilia*, ii, p. 143.
[3] Once again it was papal dispensations which nullified the work of the bishops. See, for example, Bliss, *Cal. of Papal Letters*, i, pp. 129, 174 and *Regist. W. Gray*, pp. 103, 136, 260.
[4] See above, pp. 34–7.
[5] Wilkins, *Concilia*, i, pp. 572, 627–8; *Regist. W. Giffard*, pp. 266–8.
[6] S. Edmund's Statutes in Wilkins, *Concilia*, i, p. 635.
[7] Wilkins, *Concilia*, i, pp. 587, 692, 705; ii, 5–6, 143.
[8] *Regist. W. Giffard*, p. 209.

before they could even qualify for holy orders, while many young men were instituted to 'family livings' without any intention of ever assuming the responsibilities of priesthood.

Grosseteste was the first to launch an attack on the scandal of men holding positions for which they were in no sense qualified. In his Constitutions of 1238 he declared that all beneficed clergy must receive such orders as their work demanded.[1] He did not actually specify that all rectors and vicars must be priests, though his words could hardly be given any other interpretation. That they were taken to mean this is suggested by a story told by Matthew Paris, who declares that in 1252 certain beneficed clergy in the diocese of Lincoln, having been told that they were to proceed to priests' orders 'willy-nilly', appealed to Rome and clubbed together to obtain licence to attend the Schools for a time in order to postpone the evil day when they must be priested.[2]

Pecham, within a few months of his consecration, declared that all rectors and those who had a cure of souls were to be ordained priest within a year.[3] Most bishops, however, were content with a much lower standard. The Council of Oxford in 1222, presided over by Stephen Langton, only went so far as to say that all rectors not in holy orders were to attend at the next Embertide to be ordained 'at least subdeacon'. The rider that if necessary they were to be *compelled* to come shows that the bishops realised how much opposition even this elementary step was likely to arouse.[4] Hugh of Welles at Lincoln would often institute a man only on condition that he was ordained subdeacon. On a few occasions he expected men to proceed to major orders, but he clearly accepted the subdiaconate as the only minimum standard which there was any hope of enforcing.[5] Thomas Cantilupe, on instructions from Pecham, sequestrated the income of Church Stretton until such time as Walter the rector attained the age of eighteen and was ordained subdeacon.[6]

[1] R. Grosseteste, *Epistolae*, p. 160.

[2] M. Paris, *Chron. Maj.* v, p. 279.

[3] Wilkins, *Concilia*, ii, p. 33.

[4] Wilkins, *Concilia*, i, p. 596. Bishop Kirkham in 1255 merely repeated the decree of 1222; *ibid.* p. 705.

[5] *Rot. H. de Welles*, i, pp. 9–10, 137; ii, pp. 1, 5, 8, 10, 13, etc. For those to be ordained deacon see ii, pp. 27, 57, and for those who were to proceed to the priesthood, i, p. 156; ii, pp. 64, 81, 282, 294.

[6] *Regist. T. Cantilupe*, p. 119, and cf. Pecham, *Reg. Epist.* ii, p. 534.

In 1274 the Council of Lyons passed a decree declaring that rectors of parishes must proceed to the priesthood; and, acting on this, many of the bishops in the later years of the century took action against those who refused to conform. Pontissara at Winchester declared the rectory of Thruxton vacant and appointed a new man, because the rector had not proceeded to the priesthood within three years.[1] Wickwayn at York, besides ordering all those insufficiently ordained to attend the next ordinations, refused to accept some of the men presented by the laity on the grounds that, being in minor orders, they were not as yet eligible for institution.[2] His successor, le Romeyn, ordered all beneficed clergy to come to Tadcaster in 1286 to be ordained priest.[3] Meanwhile Pecham at Canterbury was busy sequestrating the churches of forty-five men who defied his commands to attend the ordination,[4] while the Register of Thomas Cantilupe of Hereford gives a list of no less than ninety-five recusants.[5]

Ottobon was probably right in thinking that the main evils of the Church were concerned with the clergy. If men took their responsibilities so lightly that they could live far from their parishes and remain all their lives in minor orders, then there was little hope of reform. But Ottobon himself, and all those of his contemporaries who had the well-being of the Church at heart, were conscious of many matters which called for reform in the day-to-day life of the parish churches.

That services were often carelessly performed is obvious from the evidence which has already been given. Since a good deal of it was due as much to ignorance as to carelessness, many statutes attempted to give some instruction to the clergy and to improve their minds as well as their manners.[6] Any parish priest who purchased a copy of the statutes of Richard le Poore, for example,

[1] *Regist. J. Pontissara*, p. 43. Pontissara also cited the Rectors of Laverstoke and Sanderstead for not being properly ordained (pp. 348, 586–7).

[2] *Regist. W. Wickwayn*, pp. 18, 95.

[3] *Regist. J. Romeyn*, i, p. 15. Cf. *Regist. W. Bronescombe*, pp. 212–13.

[4] *Regist. J. Pecham* (C. and Y. Soc.), pp. 158–60, and cf. his injunctions to the Dean of Risborough in *Reg. Epist.* ii, p. 510.

[5] *Regist. T. Cantilupe*, pp. 302–3.

[6] Wilkins, *Concilia*, i, pp. 573, 650, 731–2; *E.H.R.* 1915, pp. 288–9; R. Grosseteste, *Epistolae*, p. 155.

would find in them a careful statement of the faith which he was expected to teach, while those who invested in the decrees of Alexander Stavensby would find in them what is really a specimen sermon on the Seven Deadly Sins.[1]

But besides instruction on the theoretical side, careful directions as to the right performance of the offices were necessary. Both the necessity of Baptism and the correct method of its administration were constantly stressed. Efforts were made to ensure that every child was christened and that each service was conducted with reverence and dignity.

A great many injunctions are concerned, also, with the right celebration of the Mass. The first thing was to see that the correct words were used. When copies of the Missal were made, mistakes often crept in. Mass-books must therefore be corrected and all errors rectified.[2] Great importance was also attached to the necessity of the words being spoken in such a way that the worshippers could hear them. The Council of London in 1200 ordered all celebrants to utter the words of the Mass plainly and not either gabbled or long drawn-out.[3] William of Blois, Bishop of Worcester, ordered them to be said 'with the utmost clarity and in full'.[4] In order to make the service as dignified as possible, the altar was to have two lights burning upon it, the servers were to be vested in surplices and the clergy were to beware of using sour wine.[5] Bishop Kirkham of Durham gave minute directions in the event of a drop of the consecrated wine being spilled,[6] and care was to be taken to see that the Reserved Sacrament was treated with reverence and renewed once a week.[7]

Some account has already been given of the marriage customs of the thirteenth century.[8] They were hardly of a nature to satisfy the demands of the Church, for the actual marriage service was obviously regarded as little more than an after-

[1] Wilkins, *Concilia*, i, p. 642.

[2] *Ibid.* i, pp. 501, 579, 626; R. Grosseteste, *Epistolae*, p. 162; *Vet. Lib. Arch. Eliensis*, p. 11.

[3] Wilkins, *Concilia*, i, p. 505, and cf. pp. 540 and 579.

[4] 'Maxime distincte, plene et integre': *ibid.* p. 623.

[5] *Regist. J. Pontissara*, p. 208; *Vet. Lib. Arch. Eliensis*, p. 14; Wilkins, *Concilia*, i, pp. 624, 704; R. Grosseteste, *Epistolae*, p. 161.

[6] Wilkins, *Concilia*, i, p. 707.

[7] *Ibid.* i, pp. 501, 657, 667; ii, p. 52; *Regist. J. Pontissara*, p. 208.

[8] See above, pp. 85–6.

thought. In the eyes of the law the purely secular troth-plight was the important thing, and the Church was faced with the fact that couples frequently enjoyed the privileges of matrimony long before seeking the blessing of the priest. The drive of marriage reform was therefore towards making the religious ceremony a necessity for a valid marriage. As early as 1200 Hubert Walter declared that no marriage was to be celebrated except 'in the face of the Church',[1] and later reformers tried to put an end to clandestine weddings, some of which were solemnised in taverns in an atmosphere heavily laden with the smell of food and liquor.[2]

Even more difficult was the problem created by child betrothals which, quite literally, came to grief. Was such a betrothal to be regarded as a valid marriage, or could it be annulled? To this question the Church in the thirteenth century was trying to find a satisfactory answer. Much turned on the form of words used in the declaration of assent when the troth-plight was made. If the words used were *verba de futuro* ('I will take thee, etc.') then the contract was regarded as dissoluble unless the marriage was consummated by cohabitation. In this event even a declaration *de futuro* must be regarded as binding and the marriage could not be annulled. The same applied when the words used were *verba de praesenti* ('I take thee, etc.'). After such a declaration a valid and indissoluble union had been made which could not be annulled.[3] In all this the Church, realising that it was powerless to destroy the ancient customs of the people or to invalidate even clandestine marriages, was anxious to bring some sort of order into the methods whereby marriages were contracted, as well as to put some check on those who could afford the legal processes whereby inconvenient unions might be declared null.

Against the loose-living, which was so common then as now, the Church fought a hard battle, in which the cause of purity was often compromised by the bad example of the clergy them-

[1] Wilkins, *Concilia*, i, p. 507.

[2] *Ibid.* i, pp. 581–2, 641, 707, 733; ii, p. 8; and cf. *Regist. J. Pontissara*, p. 210 and R. Grosseteste, *Epistolae*, pp. 75, 162. Richard le Poore declares that marriages must be 'non cum risu, non joco, non in tabernis, potationibusve, seu commessationibus'. Cf. also A. L. Smith, *Church and State*, p. 63.

[3] A. L. Smith, *Church and State*, pp. 66–86; G. C. Homans, *English Villagers of the Thirteenth Century*, pp. 167–8.

selves. Where immorality was detected the Church could impose very severe penalties, by far the heavier burden falling on the woman. In the Register of Bishop Geynsburgh of Worcester, we read of the punishment of a subdeacon and a woman who had lived together for some years and begotten five children. The man was to fast each Friday for a twelvemonth on bread and water and was to stand by the font on seven successive Sundays reciting psalms, while thirteen poor people attended to pray for him. The woman was condemned to nine strokes with the birch in public on nine Sundays and nine market-days.[1] In the same way the Knight of La Tour-Landry, writing for the edification of his daughters, obviously approves of the customary methods of punishing harlots. 'In sum places', he writes, 'thaire throtes be cutte, in sum places thei be brent, in sum places bothe man and woman putte all quik in erthe.'[2] Nor should they imagine that punishment for immorality was confined to this life, as Robert Manning shows in the affecting tale of the adulterous wife whose skeleton split in two.[3] So great was the Church's passion for chastity that occasionally some moralist would go so far as to declare that even the lawful intercourse of man and wife was sinful, and attempt to frighten young women by the most dismal pictures of the sorrows of married life.[4]

The sin of making money out of the sacraments was one which the reformers constantly and strongly opposed. The Lincoln enquiries of 1230 include a question as to whether any of the clergy have demanded money for the performance of the sacraments or have imposed upon penitents penances which would prove lucrative to themselves.[5] Grosseteste, Balsham, Walter Cantilupe, Kirkham, the Bishops of Norwich and the legates Otto and Ottobon are all agreed in denouncing the sale of sacraments,[6] while the Durham Statutes mention both 'Sacraments and sacramentals' to include the blessing of nuptials, the making of wills and the burial of the dead.[7]

[1] *Regist. W. Geynsburgh*, pp. 64–5.

[2] *The Knight de la Tour-Landry* (E.E.T.S.), p. 162.

[3] *Handlyng Synne*, pp. 63–6.

[4] See *Hali Meidenhad*, ed. F. J. Furnivall, in E.E.T.S. No. 18 (revised ed. 1922).

[5] Wilkins, *Concilia*, i, pp. 627–8.

[6] R. Grosseteste, *Epistolae*, pp. 76, 160; *Vet. Lib. Arch. Eliensis*, p. 13; Wilkins, *Concilia*, i, pp. 650, 671, 707, 733; ii, pp. 2–3.

[7] Wilkins, *Concilia*, i, p. 575, and cf. p. 636.

Laziness about saying the daily offices was another evil which the constitutions assailed. Parish priests were to say the offices reverently and in full,[1] by day and by night,[2] and at times convenient for the people.[3] If the clergy do not rise at midnight to say their Mattins, says the bishop of Salisbury in 1256, they must rise at dawn. Absence of a congregation must not be made an excuse for idleness.[4]

In order that the services may be properly performed many of the synods drew up lists of what each church must possess in the way of ornaments. Some of the bishops, like Grosseteste, were content to state that churches should be adequately furnished with books, holy vessels and vestments and that these should be safely guarded at night.[5] On the other hand, several, like Bishop Quivil of Exeter, gave most careful lists of everything which a church should possess.[6] In addition to providing catalogues of the necessary movables many bishops were anxious to see that high standards were maintained in quality and cleanliness. The London statutes declared that chalices must be of silver and not of pewter or tin,[7] while others pleaded that ornaments, books and vestments should be kept clean and in good repair.[8] S. Edmund of Canterbury ordered that any defects among church property which are discovered on the death of a rector are to be made good out of his estate.[9] The sale of church ornaments was strictly forbidden.[10]

Attempts were also made to see that churches were adequately staffed, the larger parishes being expected to provide two or three priests,[11] and even the smaller ones to have a deacon and subdeacon, or, at the very least, a clerk.[12] Annual chaplains are

[1] R. Grosseteste, *Epistolae*, p. 156; *Vet. Lib. Arch. Eliensis*, p. 11; Pecham, *Reg. Epist.* iii, p. 949.

[2] Wilkins, *Concilia*, i, p. 586.

[3] R. Grosseteste, *Epistolae*, p. 317.

[4] Wilkins, *Concilia*, i, p. 717.

[5] R. Grosseteste, *Epistolae*, p. 161.

[6] Wilkins, *Concilia*, ii, p. 139. Cf. also i, pp. 580, 587, 623, 658, 714; ii, pp. 49, 278–80; *Regist. W. Gray*, p. 218.

[7] *E.H.R.* 1915, p. 300.

[8] Wilkins, *Concilia*, i, p. 732; *Vet. Lib. Arch. Eliensis*, p. 12.

[9] Wilkins, *Concilia*, i, p. 638.

[10] *Ibid.* i, pp. 580, 590; *Regist. W. Giffard*, pp. 266–8; Pecham, *Reg. Epist.* iii, pp. 949–50.

[11] Wilkins, *Concilia*, i, pp. 588, 627.

[12] R. Grosseteste, *Epistolae*, p. 161; Wilkins, *Concilia*, i, p. 707; *Regist J. Pontissara*, p. 210.

not to be turned out by their rectors unless just cause be shown; and, since it is unlawful 'to muzzle the ox that treadeth out the corn', they must be paid a living wage.[1] In return, all parish chaplains were expected, among other things, to attend Mattins, Vespers and the Canonical Hours.[2] All strange and wandering clergy were to be treated with caution.[3]

Taken all together, the various synodal statutes represent an ideal which covered the life of the Church in most of its aspects. But far more important than the life of the Church were the personal lives of the clergy. The most careful legislation about the conduct of services and the performance of pastoral duties could be of little use unless the men to whom these things were entrusted were themselves animated by a keen sense of vocation and responsibility. In the undisturbed isolation in which so many of the clergy found themselves there was often little incentive to a disciplined life, and much of the good seed sown in diocesan and provincial synods fell on the stony ground of sullen indifference. It was one thing for a papal legate or a diocesan bishop to demand that every parish should have complete sets of vestments, silver chalices, banners, frontals, bells, books and candles: it was quite another thing to see that this was enforced, or to goad the reluctant clergy into any effort to provide them. Bishops on their visitation tours might order the clergy to say their daily offices; but, once the bishop and his retinue had ridden away, who was to see that his injunctions were carried out? Ultimately the standard of Church life depends upon the conscientiousness of the clergy, and so long as the bishops continued to ordain so many, and often such unsuitable, men, conditions in the parishes must remain unsatisfactory, and no amount of legislation would ever make it otherwise.

It is surprising, therefore, to find so little effort made by those who had the reform of the Church at heart to ensure a higher standard of devotion, education and discipline among the parochial clergy. Apart from Grosseteste, who tells his clergy that they must attend to their *daily* prayers and Bible-reading,[4] there is very little in the whole series of statutes which concerns the inner life of the priest. And yet, as Chaucer's parson realised,

[1] Wilkins, *Concilia*, i, p. 601. [2] *Ibid.* i, p. 668.
[3] *Ibid.* i, p. 750; Luard, *An. Mon.* i, p. 417.
[4] R. Grosseteste, *Epistolae*, p. 156.

unless a good example were set by the priest there was small hope of a high standard among the laity. The bishops may have realised that there was little point in urging Bible-reading among a class of whom only a very few possessed or had access to any copy of the Scriptures, but some exhortation to the clergy to betake themselves to prayer and meditation might well have been included.

Most of the reforming bishops were genuinely concerned about the low standards of education among the clergy, and many of them were anxious to ensure that parish priests should know at least the rudiments of the Christian faith. The first question to which the archdeacons of the diocese of Lincoln were to apply themselves was whether any of the clergy were 'monstrously ignorant' (*enormiter illitterati*),[1] while various statutes demanded that every parish priest should know the Ten Commandments, the Creed, the Seven Sacraments and the Seven Deadly Sins.[2] Richard le Poore told his archdeacons that they were to instruct the clergy in the outlines of the faith,[3] and Quivil of Exeter expected each man to provide himself with a *summula* under penalty of a fine of one mark for those who neglected to do so.[4] But here again it was easier to state aspirations than to enforce any kind of discipline.

There were three different classes with whom the bishops had to deal. First of all there were those men already instituted to livings. The Bishops of Exeter and Winchester were prepared to suspend any who proved themselves grossly ignorant,[5] and we find other bishops threatening to deprive men whose intellectual standards did not satisfy them.[6] Secondly, there were those who had been presented to livings by lay patrons and who applied to the bishops for institution. Many of these were turned down, or at least their applications deferred, until they could show some progress in knowledge. Many were turned down unconditionally on the grounds of ignorance.[7]

Thirdly, there were the ordination candidates. The Oxford statutes stated that no one was to be ordained unless he had

[1] Wilkins, *Concilia*, i, p. 627. [2] *Ibid.* i, p. 704, and cf. pp. 731–2.
[3] *Ibid.* i, p. 573. [4] *Ibid.* ii, p. 144.
[5] *Ibid.* ii, p. 144; *Regist. J. Pontissara*, p. 216.
[6] *Rot. R. Grosseteste*, pp. 36, 41; *Regist. S. Gandavo*, ii, p. 586.
[7] E.g. *Rot. R. Grosseteste*, pp. 232–3, 499–500; R. Grosseteste, *Epistolae*, pp. 63–4, 68, 203–4.

been examined.[1] William of Blois expected the examination to last three days,[2] while other decrees show that enquiries were made into birth and conduct besides mere knowledge.[3] But, in spite of all these regulations and of the spirited action of some of the bishops, the fact remains that a good many ordination candidates got through on very slender qualifications, and the Church suffered accordingly.

If many of the clergy were ignorant and ill-educated, many also were in danger of forgetting their high calling and of being 'conformed to this world'. This applies both to the richer men who, as we have seen, often took their pastoral duties very lightly, and also to the more humble parish priests.

Action had to be taken to prevent the richer and better-educated men, the *sublimes et litteratae personae*, from deserting their parishes and seeking more lucrative employment in the commercial or juridical or administrative world. Richard le Poore forbade the clergy to engage in 'worldly business', Quivil attacked those who engaged in business or acted as proctors for laymen, and Ottobon referred to the 'horrible vice' of secular jurisdiction.[4] Many others, including Grosseteste, bitterly condemned those of the clergy who acted as bailiffs or sheriffs, barristers or itinerant justices.[5] But so long as large numbers of bishops were regularly employed in secular administration—to the great neglect of their dioceses—it was unreasonable to expect the inferior clergy to renounce occupations which they found both stimulating and profitable.

Akin to the problem of secular employment was that of secular attire. Many of the diocesan statutes refer to this, and try to enforce the wearing of sober and seemly garments; but such is the vanity of man that in 1268 Ottobon had to admit that the various regulations about clerical dress had been widely neglected.[6] The same applied to that badge of the clerical

[1] Wilkins, *Concilia*, i, p. 595, and cf. p. 651.

[2] *Ibid.* i, p. 627.

[3] *Ibid.* i, p. 689; *E.H.R.* 1915, pp. 295–6.

[4] Wilkins, *Concilia*, i, p. 574; ii, pp. 4, 146. Cf. *Regist. J. Pontissara*, p. 211.

[5] R. Grosseteste, *Epistolae*, p. 158, and cf. Stevenson, *R. Grosseteste*, pp. 117, 176. See also Wilkins, *Concilia*, i, pp. 586, 659, 674, 732; *E.H.R.* 1915, p. 298, and *Regist. J. Pontissara*, pp. 586–7.

[6] Wilkins, *Concilia*, i, pp. 502, 574, 652, 670, 706, 716, 733; *E.H.R.* 1915, pp. 296–7; cf. R. Grosseteste, *Epistolae*, p. 51 and Pecham, *Reg. Epist.* ii, p. 737.

profession, the tonsure, which many men had allowed to disappear under fancy coiffures and ringlets.[1]

Secular occupations and secular attire attracted only such as had the talents or the wealth to indulge in them. The poorer parish priests also had their temptations to worldliness, but on a different level altogether. The loneliness and tedium in which some of them lived drove them to find some relaxation in the pleasures of sport or in the less certain pleasures of strong drink. One bishop after another condemned the habit of holding 'scot-ales', or public drinkings,[2] many of which were actually promoted by the clergy, while some were even introduced into the more sober atmosphere of Diocesan Synods and Chapter Meetings.[3] Grosseteste knew the effect of strong drink on a man, 'taking away the use of his reason, distorting in him the image of God and giving rise to countless evils',[4] and many of the bishops did their best to keep the clergy out of the public houses.[5] Alexander Stavensby sternly forbade his clergy to enter a tavern or attend a scot-ale. Those who disobeyed were to be fined six-and-eightpence—a very serious matter to a man earning less than sixty shillings a year.[6] The anonymous *Synodal Constitutions* declare that if clergy attend feasts they must be temperate and, after supper, make an early and sober departure. If they hear wicked things said or sung they must try to stop them or at least show their disapproval.[7] Quivil says that he has heard of clergy spending whole nights in drinking and asks them how they supposed that they would be fit to celebrate the following morning after such carousals.[8]

If it was unseemly for the clergy to follow after strong drink and to be seen of their parishioners making an unsteady progress towards their homes in the grey light of morning, it was equally improper that they should take part in the rough games in which our forefathers indulged. Plays of all kinds were also condemned, together with attendance at performances by jongleurs and mimers.[9] Many of the reformers also stated

[1] Wilkins, *Concilia*, i, pp. 574, 590, 755; ii, pp. 2–3; R. Grosseteste, *Epistolae*, p. 159.

[2] Wilkins, *Concilia*, i, pp. 530–1, 574, 635, 662, 672, 719; R. Grosseteste, *Epistolae*, p. 162; *Vet. Lib. Arch. Eliensis*, p. 12.

[3] R. Grosseteste, *Epistolae*, p. 73.

[4] *Ibid.*

[5] *Ibid.* p. 157; Wilkins, *Concilia*, i, p. 574; *E.H.R.* 1915, pp. 296–7; *Regist. J. Pontissara*, p. 211.

[6] Wilkins, *Concilia*, i, p. 642.

[7] *Ibid.* i, p. 658.

[8] *Ibid.* ii, p. 144.

[9] *Ibid.* i, pp. 574, 706, 733; R. Grosseteste, *Epistolae*, pp. 74, 159, 317.

their disapproval of sports and entertainments in churchyards which finished up with dancing and women singing bawdy songs.[1]

This brings us to the problem of the relationships between the clergy and women, which caused the reformers considerable uneasiness. The evidence quoted in a previous chapter[2] and the findings of Richard de Cliffe's visitations in Kent show that this problem was one of urgency for the bishops. We have enough evidence to know that the law of celibacy was by no means generally observed in this country; and, though the higher clergy had for the most part accepted it by the thirteenth century, conditions among the lower ranks of the clergy—the annual priests, parish chaplains and clerks—were chaotic. All that the reformers could hope for was to show that they had the question in mind, for there was no power in the world strong enough to separate husbands and wives or to enforce strict self-control on men with so little training in discipline.

The first thing was to find out how things stood, and the inquisitions which generally preceded visitation tours naturally sought to find out which of the clergy were married, or had concubines, or were suspected of loose-living.[3] Having collected the evidence, the next thing was to inflict some sort of penalty on all defaulters. Concubinage was regularly condemned by the synodal statutes as incompatible with clerical vows;[4] and Giles de Bridport ordered all clergy to get rid of their concubines within a month,[5] while other statutes forbade any clerk to leave money to his *focaria* in his will.[6] Many of the episcopal Registers show how attempts were made to carry out these decrees. Incumbents were often deprived of their livings through disobedience to the decrees of their bishops,[7]

[1] 'Nec mulieres choreas, luxuriosa carmina canendo, lascive ducere praesumant': *E.H.R.* 1915, p. 298; Wilkins, *Concilia*, i, pp. 662, 666, 734; *Regist. J. Pontissara*, p. 210.

[2] See above, pp. 63–7.

[3] See Luard, *An. Mon.* ii, pp. 113–15; Wilkins, *Concilia*, i, pp. 627–8; *Regist. W. Giffard*, pp. 266–8.

[4] Wilkins, *Concilia*, i, pp. 607, 658, 732; ii, pp. 5, 142–3; *E.H.R.* 1915, p. 296; R. Grosseteste, *Epistolae*, pp. 162, 317; *Regist. J. Pontissara*, p. 211.

[5] Wilkins, *Concilia*, i, p. 717.

[6] *Ibid.* p. 596; *Regist. J. Pontissara*, p. 211.

[7] *Rot. H. de Welles*, ii, p. 55; *Rot. R. Grosseteste*, p. 28; *Rot. R. Gravesend*, pp. 192–3; *Regist. W. Giffard*, p. 26; *Regist. W. Bronescombe*, p. 123.

and others were instituted only on condition that they put their wives and concubines away.[1] The Bishop of Winchester would not allow a 'prestes mare' to enter a church,[2] and S. Edmund told all who had been wives of clergy that they should either get married or enter a nunnery.[3]

In addition to those clergy who had women living in their houses, their wives in all but name, there was a certain amount of promiscuity and loose-living which the reformers were most anxious to stamp out. The difficulties were very great. A married clerk whose wife could be seen going in and out of the parsonage every day, and whose children mingled with those of the laity in the parish, could easily be detected and brought to book; but for evidence of occasional incontinence the bishop would have to rely upon village gossip which might often be misinformed, adulterated or spiteful. Incontinence, declared Alexander Stavensby, was the result of intemperance and overeating, and he took the bold step of declaring that he proposed to punish rectors for the sins of their assistant clergy.[4] Walter Cantilupe of Worcester said that incontinent clergy should be fined and removed from office at the end of a year,[5] while Archbishop Wickwayn refused to allow offenders to officiate in their parishes or indeed anywhere in the province of York.[6] Hamo of Hethe, Bishop of Rochester, punished an incontinent clerk by ordering him to say the Psalter weekly from October to Christmas,[7] but Pecham sent the Rector of Ham on pilgrimage for three years—to Compostella, Rome and Cologne—as a punishment for repeated misconduct.[8]

Each bishop, then, had his own way of dealing with these offenders, but it is extremely doubtful whether they were able to do much good. With such large dioceses and such vast numbers of clergy it was impossible to keep track of them all, and for every case which came in for punishment there were doubtless a good many others which passed unnoticed or for which the evidence was too slight.

[1] *Rot. H. de Welles*, i, p. 79; *Rot. R. Grosseteste*, p. 41; *Regist. W. Bronescombe*, p. 193.

[2] *Regist. J. Pontissara*, p. 211.

[3] Wilkins, *Concilia*, i, p. 635.

[4] *Ibid.* p. 641.

[5] *Ibid.* p. 676; cf. *Rot. R. Grosseteste*, pp. 231, 490; *Rot. H. de Welles*, ii, pp. 23, 72; *Rot. R. Gravesend*, p. 168.

[6] *Regist. W. Wickwayn*, pp. 93, 126.

[7] *Regist. H. Hethe*, p. 250.

[8] Pecham, *Reg. Epist.* ii, pp. 585–6.

The third great evil from which the Church suffered was the lack of any effective discipline. Every would-be reformer found himself thwarted on every side by appeals to Rome which, if they did not result in reversing his decisions, at least had the effect of holding up proceedings, perhaps for years. It was no wonder, therefore, that Pecham included among his 'seven phials' the two evils of 'appeals to Rome' and the 'daily limitation of the powers of prelates'.[1] Nor was it surprising that Grosseteste should have attacked the Curia as the seat of all that was wrong with the Church.

Reform, however, was very much in the air in the thirteenth century. The Lateran Council of 1179, presided over by Alexander III, had made a great effort to bring to an end some of the evils which hindered the work of the Church, and it was followed, thirty-six years later, by the great Council under the presidency of Innocent III which denounced, among other things, pluralism and the immorality and worldliness of the clergy.[2] The decrees of these two great ecumenical Councils formed the basis of Church reforms and were frequently quoted in the various provincial and diocesan statutes of this country. In 1274, the Council of Lyons provided further material for later synods to discuss.

In this country there was a steady flow of diocesan statutes issued by the synods which were held at least once a year in most dioceses.[3] In addition to these there were the decrees issued by the papal legates Otto and Ottobon in 1237 and 1268. A study of the statutes shows that they have much in common, and that most of the reformers borrowed freely from previous Councils. By far the most important set of statutes was that drawn up by Richard le Poore, successively Bishop of Chichester, Salisbury and Durham. Poore, who is described by Matthew Paris as 'a man of great holiness and profound knowledge',[4] was responsible for the abandonment of Old Sarum and the building of the new cathedral, that perfect example of Early

[1] See above, p. 215.

[2] For the *decreta* of these Councils see Mansi, *Sac. Concil. Collectio*, xxii, coll. 212–13, and coll. 981–1068.

[3] See the lists in Gibbs and Lang, *The Bishops and Reform*, pp. 183–4, and C. R. Cheney, *English Synodalia*, p. 36. There is still considerable doubt about the provenance and dates of some of the synodal statutes, and scholars will look forward to the new *Concilia* which has been promised.

[4] M. Paris, *Chron. Maj.* iii, p. 391.

English architecture. His statutes were drawn up in 1220, while he was still at Salisbury, and were reissued by him after his translation to Durham in 1228. He had been present at the Lateran Council of 1215 in his capacity as Bishop of Chichester and the influence of the Council upon his statutes is clearly discernible, though he also borrowed from the Council of London (1200) and from the statutes of Odo de Sully, Bishop of Paris.[1] Other English prelates who attended the Fourth Lateran were the two Archbishops, Stephen Langton and Walter Gray, the Bishops of Rochester, Exeter, Norwich, Lincoln, and of Coventry and Lichfield, and two monks, Silvester of Evesham, who afterwards became Bishop of Worcester, and Hugh, Abbot of Beaulieu, who was subsequently Bishop of Carlisle. Not all of these, so far as we know, issued decrees, or indeed showed much inclination to follow up the work of the Council;[2] but that there was a very considerable output of provincial and diocesan constitutions the pages of Wilkins' *Concilia* will show.

Apart from the comprehensive statutes of Richard le Poore and the work of Stephen Langton, the most important contributions to reform were the efforts of William of Blois, Bishop of Worcester, and his successor Walter Cantilupe; Hugh of Welles and Grosseteste at Lincoln; Alexander Stavensby at Coventry and Lichfield; Peter Quivil at Exeter, Simon of Ghent at Salisbury, and Pecham as Archbishop of Canterbury.

William of Blois, who became Bishop of Worcester in 1218, issued an important set of constitutions and devoted much of his energy to reform of both secular and regular clergy in his diocese.[3] He was fortunate in his successor, Walter Cantilupe, whom Luard described as, apart from Grosseteste, 'decidedly the greatest bishop of his time'.[4] Hugh of Welles set himself, above all else, to improve the lot of the poorer clergy in the diocese of Lincoln, and his name will always be had in honour

[1] C. R. Cheney, *English Synodalia*, p. 55.

[2] Langton presided over the Council of Oxford in 1222 which reissued many of the decrees of the Lateran (see Powicke, *S. Langton*, pp. 151–2); Gray issued his statutes in 1250; the Bishop of Exeter possibly issued a set of decrees about 1220. So far as the other dioceses are concerned we have to depend upon later bishops for statutes. None have survived for the dioceses of Rochester, Hereford and Carlisle.

[3] Gibbs and Lang, *Bishops and Reform*, pp. 28–9.

[4] *D.N.B.* s.v. Willis Bund calls him 'in some respects the ideal of a thirteenth-century prelate'; *Regist. G. Giffard*, p. xix.

by those who admire a man who will champion the cause of the weak. His brilliant and indomitable successor, Grosseteste, who stands head and shoulders above any other English churchman of his century, was as tireless in reform as he was outspoken in criticism of those who stood in the way of it. Alexander Stavensby was both a mystic and a theologian, but he worked hard to improve conditions in his own vast and unwieldy diocese; Quivil in 1287 issued, for his diocese in the far west, a set of constitutions which rank next in importance to those of le Poore; Simon of Ghent hunted down pluralists and other defaulters in the diocese of Salisbury and tried to raise the standard of education among his clergy. Pecham, who counted among his friends Bonaventura and Thomas Aquinas, and who only very reluctantly accepted the burden of the primacy,[1] was tireless in pursuing a policy of reform not only in his own diocese but throughout the whole of the Southern Province.

There was, therefore, no lack of zeal or of energy among those whose ambition it was to bring new life and greater discipline into the Church. Yet when we compare the conditions in the parishes at the close of the thirteenth century with those which obtained in earlier years we can only feel disappointed that so little progress was made. Many of the evils which disgraced the Church during the unhappy years of King John were still present a century later, and, indeed, for many years to come.

Yet it was not for lack of reformers. On the whole the bishops of the thirteenth century were a competent and conscientious set of men, most of whom cared for the welfare of the Church and desired to see abuses in it swept away. But circumstances were against them. For one thing, many of the dioceses were far too big. No bishop, however earnest, could hope to keep in any sort of intimate touch with more than a handful of the parishes in his diocese, while most of them he could visit only on the rarest occasions, if at all. The most conscientious of the bishops did try to visit regularly in the parishes, but many others were so much occupied with political or judicial affairs that they could find time for only occasional journeys to their manors and cathedral cities and never got about among the parochial clergy at all. The fact that in 1268 the legate had to encourage bishops and archbishops to be in their dioceses on

[1] See Luard, *An. Mon.* iv, pp. 279–80.

feast days and in Advent and Lent shows what conditions were.[1] Nor were the archdeacons, the 'bishops' eyes', much help, since so many of them were rich men or scholars with but little interest in parish life.

Many, therefore, of the clergy in country districts were left very much alone. If they were keen and conscientious they would get little encouragement or praise from their superiors, while if they were weak or idle there was very little chance of their being brought to account. Few bishops could afford the time, even if they had the inclination, to go through the whole business of making a man submit to discipline, with the result that many a country parson cheerfully defied authority in the knowledge that the chances of his being seriously challenged were small.

The lesser clergy and those in the more remote districts were, therefore, in most dioceses, free from any very troublesome interference with their liberty. For a time they might groan under the fiery zeal of some reforming prelate, but there was always the hope and the prospect of his being succeeded by a man who would spend most of his time at Court and leave them in peace with their scot-ales and their *focariae*. On the other hand the richer men, the *sublimes*, could afford to defy authority because of the enormous powers of the families to which they belonged. Moreover, even if, in some dispute with their bishop, their cause should fail, they could afford to take the whole thing to Rome, where, at least, a final judgement could be deferred almost indefinitely.

Circumstances were, therefore, very much against the reformers, and obstacles of all kinds lay in their paths and sometimes proved insuperable. Yet we must not think that all the energy generated by the passionate outbursts of men like Adam Marsh and Grosseteste and Pecham was of no avail. Although the diocesan decrees achieved only very slight success in the way of reform, we can detect some real progress during the century.

Perhaps the most important was the improvement which took place in the lot of the inferior clergy—the vicars and the unbeneficed. The rapid growth of the system of appropriation of parochial endowments by the religious houses caused a crisis in the position of the parish priest. Hitherto a man once instituted to a cure of souls could be assured of a livelihood *quamdiu*

[1] Wilkins, *Concilia*, ii, p. 10.

se bene gesserit. But with the rapid snapping up of livings by the monasteries a very large number of rectories disappeared altogether, and only saints or sinners could be content with the miserable wages which were offered. Meanwhile, as more and more clergy were thrown on to the market, wages got lower and lower. Hugh of Welles and some of his contemporaries during the earlier part of the thirteenth century set themselves to arrest this process through the establishment of vicarages with a settled stipend, and by trying to insure that even the humblest of the 'anniversary priests' were paid a living wage. Poor though they were, the inferior clergy of England were better off in 1300 than they had been in 1200, and a great deal better off than they would have been if some check on the system of appropriations had not been imposed.

Another real reform of the thirteenth century was the growth of preaching. The weekly sermon can be a burden to both preacher and congregation, but it is a link between them which nothing else can supply. The fact that a man has got to proclaim some message to his people week by week encourages him in his reading, his prayers, his self-discipline, his visiting (to find out what people are thinking), and his sense of responsibility. Until the advent of the friars there is no doubt that a kind of spiritual lethargy had settled on a good many parishes. The daily or weekly offices were performed, but in a desultory way which made little attempt to meet the needs of the people. The revival of preaching, under the influence of the mendicants, created a new relationship between priest and people which was wholly good.

Hand in hand with this went a distinct improvement in the scholastic standards of the clergy. The thirteenth century was a time of great intellectual activity and even the country clergy could not remain altogether untouched by its influence. As the Universities grew, supplemented by the friars' schools, the lectures of chancellors and theologians at the cathedrals, and by the work of the grammar and parochial schools, so new opportunities were put before the clergy, opportunities which some, at any rate, were willing to take. Many of the bishops of this century were notable scholars, brought to the bench from the schools; and such men were ready both to encourage and to help their clergy to equip themselves more thoroughly for the teaching side of their ministry.

In these ways, and perhaps in others, some definite progress was made during this century. The revelations of Richard de Cliffe in the Romney Marshes in 1292 may seem strange to us, accustomed as we are to such different conditions and standards; but the thirteenth century, like everything else, must be judged not by what it was but by what it was trying to be, and against the scandals which undoubtedly existed must be weighed both the despair of those who saw the evils of the time and the enthusiasm and energy of the reformers.

PART TWO

CHAPTER XVIII

ENGLISH MONASTERIES IN THE THIRTEENTH CENTURY

By the beginning of the thirteenth century monasticism had already had some seven centuries of life in Europe, during the course of which it had undergone some changes from the ideals upon which it had originally been founded. The community which S. Benedict brought into being at Monte Cassino about the year 500, and to which he gave the Rule which is the basis of all later monastic legislation, was a self-contained unit, almost completely isolated from the outside world, living a simple life of prayer, study and labour, a 'family' over which the abbot watched with fatherly care. The type of religious house which the Rule envisages is, according to Dom David Knowles, 'a community ruled by an abbot elected by the monks for life, supported by the produce of its fields and gardens and having within the wall of its enclosure all that is necessary to convert the produce into food and to make and repair clothing and other articles of common use. It has no function in the life of the Church save to provide an ordered way of life based on the teaching of the gospel, according to which its inmates may serve God and sanctify their souls apart from the life of the world. No work done within it, whether manual, intellectual or charitable, is directed to an end outside its walls. It is the home of a spiritual family whose life and work begins and ends in the family circle.'[1]

Such was the ideal which animated S. Benedict when he founded what was intended to be a model for all houses of Black Monks; but even a cursory comparison of the conditions at Monte Cassino with the average Benedictine house of the thirteenth century will show many remarkable changes. We have only to read, first, the Rule of S. Benedict and then Jocelin of

[1] D. Knowles, *The Monastic Order in England*, p. 4.

Brakelond's frank and intimate account of life at Bury S. Edmunds to see what a revolution had taken place. The old simplicity has gone; and the picture of a group of men supporting themselves by the labours of their hands, cut off from the sights and sounds of the world, conforming to the standards of living appropriate to peasants, has changed to one of a flourishing community, owning vast estates and employing large numbers of men, involved in all the anxieties and excitements of the business world, and enjoying a standard of living which was shared only by their richer neighbours. How far these changes were inevitable, and how far they interfered with the devotional life of the community, it is hard to say. We can only point to the fact that when big reforms were introduced they took the shape of an attempted return to the poverty and simplicity of the early days. But by the thirteenth century the days of such reforms were over. The initiative in advocating the simple life had passed from the monks to the friars, and the reforming activities of the monks were directed more towards the establishment of uniform conditions in the various houses, and the checking of obvious abuses, than to any large-scale attempt to change the whole life of the monks by putting the clock back and undoing the work of centuries. In fact the members of the older monastic orders, even including the Cistercians, whose bold effort to reintroduce the simplicity of primitive Benedictinism was barely a century old, seem during the thirteenth century to have been content with the general conditions in which their lives were cast. And when we have discovered what those conditions were we can easily understand why this was so.

So far as this country was concerned the earliest monasticism was of two kinds, Benedictine and Celtic. Each had its own distinctive features but both perished almost completely by the time of the Danish invasions. The revival of monasticism in England was due above all else to the labours and genius of Dunstan about the middle of the tenth century.[1] With the coming of the Normans about a century later monastic life received fresh encouragement and a great many new houses were set up under the inspiration of Lanfranc and Anselm, both

[1] For a full and admirable account of this see D. Knowles, *Monastic Order*, chaps. iii and iv.

of whom were Black Monks.[1] During the twelfth century the foundation of new houses went on apace so that by the year 1200 there were fifty-seven independent Benedictine houses in England and Wales. By this time, however, the enthusiasm for the establishment of new convents had begun to wane, for, from the year 1200 onwards to the Dissolution, only two additions were made—Snelshall in Buckinghamshire founded about 1219 and Upholland in Lancashire just a hundred years later.[2]

Most of the Benedictine houses had a number of 'cells', scattered all over the country and sometimes even overseas. S. Albans, for example, had no less than eleven such dependencies, of which two were in Northumberland; Durham had nine; Evesham had a cell at Odensee in Denmark. Altogether the English Benedictine houses had eighty-three cells, each a *monasteriolum* in itself with its own prior, officers and servants, and yet each under the direct control of the mother house. Very few new cells were founded after the year 1200, the most important being the two colleges which were established at Oxford for Black Monks, Gloucester College in 1283–4 and Durham College in 1289.

In addition to the independent houses and their cells in England there was also a large number of alien houses, dependencies of Norman or other monasteries. Many of these also had cells of their own.

Taken all together there were in England during the thirteenth century rather more than two hundred houses of Black Monks. These varied enormously in size and importance from the largest houses, such as S. Albans and Canterbury, down to the smallest cells where only two or three monks were to be found. Each, however, was bound by the same rule, and each was organised according to the same plan.

Various events combined, during the early centuries, to make great changes in the life of the Benedictines, and it was inevitable that some decay should set in once the primitive rural

[1] The most important new foundations after the Conquest were Battle (1067), Whitby (before 1077), Rochester (1077), S. Mary's, York (c. 1078), Durham (1083), Bardney (1087), Chester (1093), Colchester (1095), Norwich (1096), Tewkesbury (1102).

[2] In all dates of foundations I have followed Dom David Knowles in *The Religious Houses of Medieval England*.

simplicity had given way to a more sophisticated urban life. There were, therefore, from time to time, revivals among the Black Monks, not with the purpose of starting anything new but of returning to a stricter interpretation of the Benedictine Rule.

The first great monastic revival was that of Cluny, founded in 910. The most distinctive feature of the Cluniac system was that each house, instead of being a self-contained and independent community, was under the authority of Cluny itself. In the ordinary Benedictine house the abbot ruled supreme and was answerable only to the bishop, who had powers of visitation. The Cluniac houses, on the other hand, were exempt from episcopal supervision but were all dependent upon Cluny itself.

The Cluniac system, inaugurated only a generation before the time of S. Dunstan, had a considerable influence upon the course of the monastic revival in this country.[1] There was, however, no actual Cluniac foundation in England until shortly after the Conquest, when William de Warenne founded the monastery of Lewes. By the year 1200 the order had made some progress, but even then there were only eleven independent houses. Most of these had families of cells, and there were a few priories which owed allegiance to foreign Cluniac houses.

The second great monastic revival was that associated with the names of Stephen Harding of Cîteaux and Bernard of Clairvaux early in the twelfth century. Once again the purpose of the revival was a return to the hardship and simplicity of the early days. The accounts of the early Cistercian settlements in this country and of the privations which their members endured are among the high lights of monastic history. Realising that Benedictine monasticism belonged rather to the country than to the towns, the Cistercians chose out the wildest spots of the Yorkshire dales or of the Welsh valleys to plant their monasteries.

The Cistercian order was very popular in this country. The earliest foundation was at Waverley in 1128, but by 1200 there were no less than sixty-two houses in this country, and, by 1300, twelve more had been added to this number. Like the Cluniacs, the Cistercians were free from episcopal control, but each house was visited by the house from which it was originally founded. Abbots were also expected to attend an annual Chapter General at Cîteaux.

[1] D. Knowles, *Monastic Order*, p. 145.

On a far smaller scale, and on totally different lines, was the Carthusian order, which began in England with the foundation at Witham in Somerset in 1178–9 but added only one other house, Hinton, before the year 1300. The Carthusian system was an attempt to combine the solitary, hermit life with the idea of a community. Each individual monk had his own plot of land and cell in which he worked and prayed, cooked his dinner, ate and slept. His only contact with his fellow-monks was in church or chapter; there was little common life except the sense of living together within one enclosing wall. In many ways the Carthusian experiment was a return not to primitive Benedictinism but to the methods adopted by Pachomius in the desert nearly two centuries before S. Benedict.

Similar in many ways to the Benedictine houses were the bodies of canons living together according to a rule and presided over by an abbot or prior. Groups of priests living a regular life in community had existed from very early times, though there was no life in England which could be strictly called 'canonical' until the time of Edward the Confessor. The early history of the Canons Regular is confused by the difficulty of deciding when a body of priests ceased to be 'secular' and became fully 'regular'.[1] It is, however, generally agreed that the earliest houses of regular canons were those of the Augustinians, and that the first of these to be established in this country was at Colchester in 1106.[2] The expansion during the twelfth century was very rapid, for, by the year 1200, there were 150 Augustinian houses with fifteen dependent cells. The foundation of new houses continued throughout the thirteenth century and by the year 1300 there were over 200 abbeys, priories and cells. All of these were subject to episcopal control.

Similar to the Augustinians were the White Canons or Premonstratensians who owed their origin to S. Norbert at Prémontré, near Laon, in 1120. In organisation they resembled the Cistercians rather than the Benedictines, since they were inspected not by the bishop but by a visitor appointed by the mother house. This order never made much progress in England.

[1] See W. H. Frere, *The Early History of Canons Regular*, in *Fasciculus J. W. Clark dicatus*.

[2] A. H. Thompson, *English Monasteries*, p. 21; but cf. D. Knowles, *Monastic Order*, p. 141, where it is suggested that Barnwell, S. Gregory at Canterbury and Huntingdon may have been houses of 'regular' canons rather earlier than this.

By 1200 there were only twenty-eight independent houses in this country, and only three were added from that time onwards.[1]

Of greater interest to us was the purely English order of S. Gilbert of Sempringham which also began during the twelfth century. The Gilbertine houses were at first small nunneries to which a group of men was attached as canons. This order therefore had the unusual feature of a number of 'double' houses of men and women, each with their own cloister and living accommodation but meeting together in church. In 1200 there were sixteen Gilbertine foundations in this country and eight were added during the century. The order never spread outside England.

Benedictines, Cluniacs, Cistercians, Augustinians and Premonstratensians all had houses for women as well as for men. Compared with the fifty-seven independent Benedictine monasteries in the year 1200 there were no less than seventy-five nunneries and a few more were added during the first half of the thirteenth century. But the ardour for building nunneries dried up about 1250, the last foundation being Easebourne some time before 1248. There were only two Cluniac nunneries in England, Arthington and de la Pré; but there were twenty-seven Cistercian houses in 1200 and thirty-one in 1300. The Augustinians increased considerably during the thirteenth century, beginning with eight houses and finishing with seventeen. There was only one house of Premonstratensian canonesses—Orford in Lincolnshire.

The twelfth century had been a particularly successful and busy time for the monasteries, for it had seen the foundation of some hundreds of houses for monks, canons, and nuns. During the thirteenth century, however, there was not very much new building. It was not only that something like 'saturation point' had been reached. Men who gave large sums to found religious houses wanted to be quite sure that what they were endowing was really meritorious and that the prayers of the men whom they were supporting would really be of some avail. But could they be certain of this? So long as the monasteries were the only form of the 'regular' life, rich benefactors were satisfied that the support of such life was the best way of investing their

[1] There were, in addition, three dependencies.

money. But the thirteenth century saw the rise of a new type of regular life—the mendicant friars—and men began to wonder, when they saw the holiness and hardship of their lives, whether these men were not now more worthy of their endowments than either monks or canons. Thus the foundation of new monasteries practically ceased just about the time when the Dominicans and Franciscans invaded this country, for the zeal of benefactors was now turned into a new direction. Nothing could be nearer to the evangelical perfection than the ideal of the mendicants; and patrons hastened to welcome them and to shower gifts upon them. The first Dominicans arrived in this country in 1221 and the Franciscans in 1224, and by the close of the century each had over fifty houses in England and Wales. Meanwhile other smaller groups of friars had made their way to these shores—Carmelites, Austin Friars, Friars of the Sack and of the Order of Martyrs, Crutched Friars, Pied Friars and Friars of S. Mary. By the year 1300 there were no less than 169 friaries in this country. Cambridge contained the houses of no less than seven different orders of friars.[1]

The thirteenth century was not at all an easy time for the monasteries. Outwardly they gave every appearance of wealth and security—building was going on apace, their lands and estates were growing, their abbots were men of power and influence in the land. Yet behind all this show of prosperity and power lay much anxiety and, in many houses, a burden of debt which threatened to overthrow them.

The apparent wealth of the monasteries was itself one of their greatest trials. At a time when both Pope and King were desperately anxious to raise money the religious houses seemed

[1] This brief survey of the religious houses in England would not be complete without some mention of the Hospitals. It is a debatable point whether these should be included among the religious houses or not. Gasquet includes them in his tables in *English Monastic Life*, but Knowles omits them from the lists in *Religious Houses of Medieval England*. Some of the Hospitals were of ancient origin, but the great period for the foundation of Hospitals lies in the latter part of the Middle Ages. The thirteenth century saw over 250 new foundations in all parts of the country, thus bringing the total from 155 in 1200 to 415 in 1300. The figures are based on the tables in R. M. Clay, *Medieval Hospitals of England*. By the time of the Dissolution there were about 728 Hospitals in this country.

to offer one of the most hopeful fields for plunder.[1] From time to time very heavy burdens of taxation were laid upon the monks, while individual houses were sometimes called upon to provide money for the needs of the King.[2] Meanwhile the wealth of the religious houses provided a constant temptation to marauders of all kinds.

The disturbances at the close of the reign of King John brought great hardship to some of the abbeys. Rochester Cathedral was rifled by the King in 1215,[3] Crowland was sacked the following year when priests were dragged from the altars while saying Mass,[4] S. Albans was attacked and despoiled twice in 1217, once by Fawkes de Breauté and once by French soldiers.[5] In the North, various houses suffered grievously from Scottish raids. In 1216 Holm Cultram near Solway Firth was pillaged by King Alexander of Scotland, whose soldiers carried off much booty, even stripping the coverlet off a monk who was dying in the infirmary.[6] The Nunneries of Lambley and Holystone both suffered severely from Scottish invasions,[7] and in 1296 and the following year Hexham Priory was raided and largely destroyed, the school being set on fire with all the boys in it.[8] Furness Abbey was devastated by the Scots early in the fourteenth century.[9]

Other monasteries suffered greatly from fires, some of which were due to carelessness and some to the malevolence of men.[10]

[1] According to the *Waverley Annals* King John demanded 33,300 marks from the Cistercians; Luard, *An. Mon.* ii, p. 265. Matthew Paris complains of the enormous burden of taxation which was laid upon the monasteries; *Chron. Maj.* ii, pp. 530–1.

[2] See, for example, Bond, *Chron. Melsa*, i, p. 329; *Chron. of Louth Park* (Lincolnshire Record Society), p. 11; *V.C.H.*, *Somerset*, ii, p. 73; M. Paris, *Chron. Maj.* v, p. 362; Stapleton, *Chron. Petroburg.* p. xi; Dugdale-Caley, *Monasticon*, i, pp. 356–7; *V.C.H.*, *Sussex*, ii, p. 73.

[3] Wharton, *Anglia Sacra*, i, p. 351.

[4] *V.C.H.*, *Lincs.* ii, p. 108.

[5] M. Paris, *Chron. Maj.* iii, pp. 12, 16. See also *V.C.H.*, *Bucks.* i, pp. 347–8 for plundering of Luffield in 1244, and J. Wilson, *Worcester Liber Albus*, pp. 124–6 for losses at Worcester at the close of the century.

[6] Dugdale-Caley, *Monasticon*, v, p. 593; Grainger and Collingwood, *Register of Holm Cultram*, pp. 128–9; Gilbanks, *Records of… Holm Cultram*, p. 113.

[7] E. Power, *Medieval English Nunneries*, pp. 426–7.

[8] Raine, *Priory of Hexham*, i, pp. lxxx–ii.

[9] *V.C.H.*, *Lancs.* ii, p. 117.

[10] E.g. at Guisborough in 1289 (Brown, *Guisborough Chartulary*, ii, pp. 353–4), though here the disaster was turned to good account by the

Floods also caused havoc from time to time,[1] and the serious murrain among sheep which broke out in 1276 and lasted for many years was a great disaster for the Cistercians who, as sheep-farmers on a large scale, suffered heavily.[2]

All these were misfortunes over which the monks themselves had little or no control. It was not their fault that the burden of taxation was so heavy, or that raiders destroyed their crops and their churches, or that floods or disease swept away their flocks. This was the kind of disaster which everyone in the Middle Ages had to be prepared to face, and the monasteries fared no worse than their neighbours. There were, however, other causes of distress which came not from any 'act of God' but from the incompetence and sinfulness of man.

Considering the very large number of religious houses it is inevitable that we should find some bad abbots and priors among the many hundreds who held office during the thirteenth century. The pathetic incompetence of Abbot Hugh of Bury has been revealed in Jocelin's intimate narrative of events at S. Edmunds.[3] Hugh was obviously totally unaware of the very unsatisfactory state of the abbey's finances and was not apparently unduly worried by the spectacle of Jews wandering about the cloister and the church demanding the money which was owing to them. The energy of Abbot Samson disclosed some of the shortcomings of his predecessor, and built up again the ravages which mismanagement had caused. Selby had a very bad abbot towards the close of the century who made no attempt to keep

canons' obtaining permission to appropriate three parish churches in order to repair the damage. Similarly the Worcester monks, after a fire in 1202 which largely destroyed their church, secured the canonisation of S. Wulfstan and paid for the rebuilding of their church out of the offerings of pilgrims at his shrine: *V.C.H.*, *Worcs.* ii, p. 98. For other accounts of fires see Luard, *An. Mon.* i, p. 66 (Pershore); Dugdale-Caley, *Monasticon*, v, p. 687 (Hayles); vi, p. 444 (Stoneleigh); *Gesta Abbatum Mon. S. Alb.* i, p. 273 (Hatfield Peverel); J. W. Clark, *Lib. Memorandorum*, pp. 220–1 (Barnwell); S. W. Williams, *The Cist. Abbey of Strata Florida*, pp. 153–4.

[1] H. Brakspear, *Waverley Abbey*, pp. 6–7; *V.C.H.*, *Surrey*, ii, p. 70; Craster and Thornton, *Chron. of S. Mary's, York*, p. 7; *Chron. Oxenedes*, pp. 247–8.

[2] *V.C.H.*, *Gloucester*. ii, p. 95. There were further outbreaks in 1302 (*Regist. T. Corbridge*, i, p. 177) and 1349 (Wilson and Gordon, *Compotus Rolls of Worcester*, p. xii).

[3] Jocelin of Brakelond, *Chronicle*, tr. L. C. Jane, pp. 4–5, 10–11, 60.

the Rule, was quarrelsome and sometimes violent, allowed the property of the house to decay or be dispersed, was extravagant and immoral, and even descended to witchcraft in order to find the body of his brother who was drowned in the Ouse.[1]

The Cluniacs of Wenlock suffered a good deal from the incompetence and dishonesty of their prior in 1279,[2] and the Augustinian houses of Bolton, Cirencester, Felley and Thurgarton all passed through a period of mismanagement, though all recovered through the wise intervention of their bishops.[3] The most notorious instance of a thoroughly bad abbot occurred at Evesham during the earlier part of the century.[4] The culprit here was a man called Roger Norreys who had escaped from Christ Church, Canterbury, after causing trouble there, and had been imposed by royal influence upon the monks of Evesham in 1191. Things soon began to go wrong, for Norreys was a man totally unsuited to the delicate and responsible task of ruling over a company of men and directing the affairs of a wealthy corporation. When eventually the legate visited in 1213 he found the abbey in a sorry state. The monks were starving and complained that they got nothing but bad bread and water. The divine office was neglected because the monks had no suitable clothes in which to attend. Masses could not be said since the Rule would not allow a man to celebrate without his breeches and many of the monks had none. When the abbot's chaplain was due to celebrate, Norreys had to lend him his own breeches, to be returned immediately after the service. While the monks were reduced to beggary and suffered from cold and hunger the abbot himself was living delicately in his lodgings, wearing secular clothes and entertaining young women. Hospitality had been abandoned, the poor went unprovided for, the goods of the abbey were dissipated and the buildings fell into

[1] *Regist. W. Wickwayn*, pp. 22–4, recording a visitation of Selby Abbey in 1280.

[2] Duckett, *Visitations of Cluniacs*, pp. 28–30. The visitor was so disgusted with the monks here that he wrote: 'it is almost impossible to elicit the truth from English monks'.

[3] *Regist. W. Giffard*, pp. 302–4, 316–18; *Regist. G. Giffard*, pp. 86–7; *Regist. J. Romeyn*, i, pp. 242–3.

[4] The whole story has been told from two rather different points of view by Dr Coulton in *Five Centuries*, ii, pp. 347–78, and by Dom David Knowles in *Monastic Order*, pp. 331–45. Both of these accounts should be read in order to reach a just estimate of Roger Norreys and his misdemeanours.

such a state of dilapidation that during wet weather services could be held only in those portions of the church which had vaulted roofs since in other parts of the building the rain was coming in.[1] Such were the conditions revealed in 1213. Norreys was deposed; but, instead of being punished, he was transferred to the cell of Penwortham as Prior. Evesham eventually recovered under the firm rule of Abbot Ralph, and his successors—Thomas de Marlberge, Richard le Gras and Henry.[2]

Norreys was deposed by the representative of the Pope, acting on the evidence of the monks themselves and at their instigation. In this instance the abbey as a whole benefited by the determination of its members to rid themselves of a wholly objectionable and inefficient head. In other houses there were disputes among the members which brought nothing but harm. Many of them would have been avoided if the monks had been prepared to sacrifice their personal interests to the general well-being of the community. But this they were most reluctant to do. Like most people of their age they seem to have enjoyed quarrelling, and had little of the sense of shame which we should feel if a group of men dedicated to what was commonly supposed to be the highest form of Christian life was torn by intense strife and discord. For example, the really serious quarrel at Durham in 1300, which caused a schism in the community and led to violence and bloodshed, was described by the chronicler not in terms of sorrow or shame but as a 'gorgeous row' (*pulcherrima disputatio*).[3] If that was the common attitude of the monks towards the strife which occasionally disturbed the peace of the monasteries it is no wonder that there are various instances of such 'gorgeous rows' in the records of monastic life. There was a sharp dispute at Bury in 1213 over the election of a successor to the great Samson, a dispute which grew so serious that the Pope had to appoint a commission of enquiry.[4] In 1249 Grosseteste had to intervene at Peterborough where the monks were at odds with their abbot, whom they accused

[1] Macray, *Chron. Abb. de Evesham*, pp. 237–46.

[2] The period covered by these abbots has been termed 'the golden age of the abbey'; Tindal, *History and Antiquities of Evesham* (1794), p. 32. This shows that the ravages of a man like Norreys could be repaired if wise leaders were appointed.

[3] *Gesta Dunelm.*, ed. R. K. Richardson, in *Camden Misc.* xiii, p. 22.

[4] Arnold, *Memorials of S. Edmund's Abbey*, ii, pp. x, xii–xiii.

of enriching his relatives at the convent's expense;[1] and a few years later there was a schism among the monks of Winchester,[2] and later still at S. Mary's, York.[3] At Dover in 1290 the monks rebelled against their prior, whom they kept a prisoner for seven weeks in his own monastery.[4] Bishops who visited Augustinian houses often found evidence of strife and had to remove canons to other houses for the sake of peace and quiet.[5]

Nor were these quarrels confined to angry words. In 1248 the Prior of Thetford was murdered by one of his monks,[6] the same thing happening to the Abbot of Jervaulx in 1279.[7] There were quarrels at Christ Church, Canterbury, in 1248 which led to bloodshed and to the death of one of the monks.[8] At Wootton in 1281 there was a fight between the prior and one of the brethren, and at Llanthony a canon was chained and flung into prison for biting the prior's finger.[9] In 1308 there was an affray at Royston, when the prior was wounded and the subprior dragged from bed and despoiled of all his clothes.[10] A monk of Rievaulx in 1279, when under examination for leprosy, drew a knife and stabbed the examiner in the hand. He immediately fled, but was captured, brought back to the abbey, and so severely beaten that he died.[11]

Life, therefore, in a monastery was not always as quiet and uneventful as some writers would have us suppose. The monks were, after all, men of like passions with ourselves, and yet they were trying to live what must have been an extraordinarily difficult life, cut off from so many of the contacts which help men to a right judgement in all things. In many ways they

[1] M. Paris, *Chron. Maj.* v, p. 84.

[2] *Ibid.* iii, p. 590.

[3] *Regist. T. Corbridge*, i, pp. 87–8.

[4] Haines, *Dover Priory*, pp. 220–34.

[5] Felley, 1276 (*Regist. W. Giffard*, pp. 316–18); Drax, Newburgh and Shelford, 1280 (*Regist. W. Wickwayn*, pp. 55–6, 134–6, 144–5); Chirbury, 1286, and Wigmore, 1287 (*Regist. R. Swinfield*, pp. 102–3, 132–3); Blackmore, 1310 (*Regist. R. Baldock, etc.* pp. 120–2). Cf. Salter, *Augustinian Chapters*, pp. 8, 9, 25, 46.

[6] M. Paris, *Chron. Maj.* v, pp. 31–3.

[7] *V.C.H., Yorks.* iii, p. 141.

[8] M. Paris, *Chron. Maj.* v, p. 33.

[9] *Regist. G. Giffard*, pp. 129–32, 182.

[10] *Regist. R. Baldock, etc.* pp. 69–73. Monks, of course, always slept in their clothes.

[11] *V.C.H., Yorks.* iii, pp. 150–1. For other instances of violence see *Regist. W. Wickwayn*, pp. 134–6; Raine, *Priory of Hexham*, i, App. pp. xxx–xxxii; *V.C.H., Notts.* ii, p. 92; Duckett, *Visitations of Cluniacs*, pp. 18–19.

were like a ship's company, crowded together in a small space for long periods at a time, with no privacy and with little choice of companions. In such circumstances it was no wonder if petty jealousies sometimes became unduly magnified, or if tempers, strained by the rubbing of shoulders day and night with the same group of men, occasionally became uncontrollable.

But the real cause of the decay of the monasteries in the thirteenth century was not taxation or misfortune, nor yet mismanagement, extravagance or strife. The older monasteries fell into bad ways because they ceased to attract the best type of man. When monasticism first began it appealed to the highest in men. Those who joined S. Benedict at Monte Cassino, or S. Columba at Iona, were men of high ideals with a burning desire to work out their salvation along the path of prayer, discipline and mortification. As the abbeys grew and prospered the demands which they made upon men became less, while the attractions which they offered grew greater. Inevitably the type of man deteriorated, and what was meant to be a religious community became more and more a residential country club.

Each monastic revival, therefore, took the form of a return to primitive strictness, the greatest of all revivals—the Cistercian—being a deliberate attempt to reproduce the conditions under which S. Benedict and his companions had lived. In the early days of the Cistercian movement the demands which it made on postulants were very high; but no attempt was made to throw off the burden of accumulating wealth; and, by the beginning of the thirteenth century, the Cistercians differed little from the Benedictines either in what they offered or in what they demanded. Throughout this century Black Monks and White Monks, and Canons of all Orders, appeared as men of the world, conservative, reactionary and living in comparative wealth and security. They were not, as has sometimes been suggested, vicious or immoral; but nor were they particularly virtuous or ascetic. They were, therefore, unlikely to attract young men of vision and ideals.

In fact, by the beginning of the thirteenth century the great days of monasticism were over. It survived in this country for another three hundred years and was able to do some useful work for society in various ways; but it had ceased to offer any challenge to the world and its complacency. Meanwhile new movements were stirring, demanding the best that a man could offer, appealing to his zeal, his courage, his industry. One of these was the growth of the Universities, the other the appearance and rapid expansion of the various orders of Friars. The Universities appealed to the scholar, and, by demanding a high standard, attracted only those with a thirst for knowledge and those who had made some offering of themselves at the shrine of Athene. Even greater was the challenge of the mendicant orders which, like Garibaldi in 1849, offered 'neither pay nor quarters nor provisions; [but] hunger, thirst, forced marches, battles and death'. Was it any wonder that the keenest minds and the more earnest souls of the thirteenth century wanted to throw in their lot either with the young Universities or with the even younger friars rather than with an institution which must have appeared to them reactionary and decaying?

CHAPTER XIX

OCCUPANTS OF THE RELIGIOUS HOUSES

By no means everybody living in a monastery was a monk. In point of fact not more than a third of the monastic population were professed monks or canons, the other two-thirds being made up of servants and lodgers. The typical religious house of the thirteenth century was, therefore, not a brotherhood of men, 'living as a self-contained unit almost completely isolated from the world', but rather a thriving community of monks and laymen, from which the monks spread their influence far and wide over the countryside and in whose employment large numbers of men found their livelihood.

About one-third of the monastic population were 'regulars', the numbers in the various houses differing considerably. The average number of monks in the large Benedictine houses was about fifty. Some, such as Pershore, Boxgrove and Coventry, had only half this number or less; some, such as Bury, the two Canterbury houses, Durham, Glastonbury, Peterborough, Norwich and Winchester, had over sixty members. S. Albans was probably the largest abbey, with a community of nearly a hundred monks. The Benedictine cells were very much smaller. Dover contained a dozen monks; Finchale, a cell of Durham, had nine; Wetherhal and S. Bees, cells of S. Mary's, York, had seven or eight; Dunster, a cell of Bath Abbey, had five; and Saintoft, another cell of York, had for a time only one member. We may take it, then, that the average number of monks in the dependent cells was about five or six.

As far as the Cluniac houses are concerned we know fairly accurately how many monks they contained during the thirteenth century from the visitation returns which have been preserved. In the eleven independent houses which were visited there were found to be 322 monks, and in the twenty-one cells about 180. This gives an average for each Cluniac house of thirty men, and for each cell of about nine.

The Cistercian abbeys had been very large in the twelfth century. Rievaulx under Ailred is said to have contained no less than 140 choir monks and 600 lay brothers,[1] and Fountains

[1] F. M. Powicke, *Ailred of Rievaulx and his Biographer*, p. 97.

sent out 150 monks in eight years to colonise new foundations.[1] But during the thirteenth century the numbers had fallen considerably. Waverley had 70, Louth Park 66, and Meaux between 50 and 60. Bordesley early in the fourteenth century had 34, Cleeve appears to have had about 28; Beaulieu was founded in 1204 for 30 monks and Hayles in 1246 for only 20. Rewley, which was established at Oxford for Cistercian scholars, never had more than sixteen members before 1300. The average complement for a Cistercian abbey during the thirteenth century was not more than about forty or fifty choir monks.

The Augustinian houses were considerably smaller. Waltham in 1273 had forty-eight canons, but this was unusually large. Barnwell had thirty; Cirencester, Hexham, Nostell, S. Osyth's, Thornholm and Worspring each had between twenty and thirty. But the majority of houses had a good deal less than this, while some, such as Bushmead, Newstead-by-Stamford, Blythburgh, Tandridge and Wroxton had only four or five members. The only figures which we possess for Premonstratensian houses are Beauchief with thirteen canons, and Eggleston with twelve. In the year 1200 there were said to be 600 canons in the various Gilbertine houses.

The numbers in the friaries are fairly well known owing to a royal custom of making a grant of a day's food (4*d.*) to each friar in the houses with which the King was brought into contact. From the sums which appear under this heading in the royal accounts, and from other sources, we can determine the number of friars in most of the houses; and we find that the Dominican and Franciscan houses contained about thirty-five or forty friars, making them nearly equal in size to the average Cistercian or Benedictine houses. The Carmelite and Austin houses were a little smaller, and the friaries of the lesser orders very small indeed.

Working on these figures, we can arrive at some estimate of the total number of 'regulars' in the country. The Benedictines must have numbered about 3800 men distributed over 200 different houses; there were also about 525 Cluniacs and 3250 Cistercians. The Augustinian canons must have numbered about 2850; the Premonstratensians nearly 500 and the Gilbertines about the same. This would make a total of monks and canons of about 11,500 men. In addition to this there were nearly

[1] D. Knowles, *Monastic Order*, p. 223.

2000 Dominicans, at least as many Franciscans, and about 1000 friars of other orders. The total, therefore, of 'religious' in this country in the thirteenth century was about 16,500. In addition to this we ought to add about 7000 nuns and perhaps 1500 men and women living under vows in the various hospitals.[1]

The monastic movement was, in its original form, intended largely for laymen. The priest-monk is mentioned in the Rule of S. Benedict, but obviously as an exception to the general rule, and he is not to expect any special privileges on account of his orders.[2] As time passed, however, the proportion of ordained men among the monks gradually rose until it became the normal thing for monks to proceed to holy orders.[3] This very important change came slowly. At S. Gall, in 895, out of 101 monks 42 were priests, 24 deacons, 15 subdeacons and 20 laymen.[4] Lanfranc's Constitutions of about the year 1070 speak of 'clerks and laymen' among the monks, as if a monastery normally contained some of each.[5] How, then, did things stand during the thirteenth century? There can be little doubt that by this time it was considered the normal thing for a monk to be ordained, and the Ordination lists are full of the names of regulars who proceeded to both major and minor orders. A study of these lists, however, shows that many of those who were ordained remained in minor orders at any rate for many years if not for life. During the eighteen years from 1282 to 1299 the Archbishops of Canterbury ordained 265 men who belonged to the monastic orders. As far as we can tell, of these 265 men 77 were ordained priest in due course, 82 proceeded as far as the diaconate, 76 remained as subdeacons, and 30 as acolytes. Of course some may have been ordained to higher orders in later years, and a few may have received ordination from some other bishop; but many must have remained in minor orders all their lives. In 1284, for example, Pecham ordained one acolyte and two subdeacons from S. Augustine's, Canter-

[1] For full details of the numbers in the religious houses see Appendix, pp. 402–11.

[2] *Reg. S. Ben.* cap. lx. In cap. lxii S. Benedict says that if the abbot at any time requires a priest among the community he is to choose one of the monks and send him to the bishop for ordination.

[3] D. Knowles, *Monastic Order*, p. 19.

[4] C. Butler, *Benedictine Monachism*, pp. 293–6.

[5] Lanfranc, *Consuetudines*, in Migne, *Patr. Lat.* vol. cl, col. 501.

bury, and in 1285 he ordained to the subdiaconate two canons of Leeds, and, to the diaconate, five monks of Christ Church. During the next fifteen years none of these names occurs again in any Ordination list of the diocese of Canterbury.[1] These statistics make us feel that Grosseteste was probably right when, in a letter to the legate about the behaviour of the monks of Christ Church, Canterbury, he stated that only certain of them were in holy orders.[2] If the ordination lists are reliable, then it must appear that a good many of the regulars did not proceed to the order of priesthood. A little further light is thrown on the question by a statute passed by the Benedictine Chapter of 1253 which states that no outside administration is to be given to a young monk until he has been priested.[3] This was no doubt intended to encourage men to be ordained, but there probably remained a good many who had no ambition to hold office and who were content to remain in minor orders.

S. Benedict was particularly anxious that there should be no class-distinction among the Black Monks.[4] Within the cloister all were to be equal, recognition being given only to such as had been appointed to high office by their fellows. This principle seems to have been maintained, for the *Reformatiuncula* of Abbot Nicholas Thorn of S. Augustine's, Canterbury, of about the year 1275, say that no distinctions must be made, even between bond and free.[5] As a result, the monasteries were perhaps the most 'democratic' institutions of the period. Whereas among the secular clergy class-distinctions counted for a good deal owing to the power of the wealthy families, in the monasteries they were practically ignored.[6] When the monks of Bury S. Edmunds disputed among themselves as to the sort of abbot whom they wanted, the question of class is scarcely mentioned, and the man eventually appointed, Samson, was clearly of

[1] The particulars are taken from the Ordination Lists in *Regist. J. Pecham* and *Regist. R. Winchelsey* published by the Canterbury and York Society.

[2] R. Grosseteste, *Epistolae*, p. 326.

[3] Pantin, *Chapters of English Black Monks*, i, p. 50, and cf. p. 74 (1277–9).

[4] *Reg. S. Ben.* cap. ii.

[5] E. M. Thompson, *Customary of S. Augustine's, Canterbury, and S. Peter's, Westminster*, i, p. 37.

[6] This would not apply to the nunneries, which were 'essentially aristocratic institutions, the refuge of the gently born': Power, *Medieval English Nunneries*, pp. 4, 13.

humble birth since we know that when he was a young student he had no money to pay for his education.[1] Robert de Insula, the son of poor crofters on Lindisfarne, rose to be, first, prior of Finchale and finally prince-bishop of Durham. Humble birth was therefore no bar to advancement in the Benedictine Order.

The same cannot be said of the Augustinians, among whom class-distinctions were carefully observed. The decrees of the General Chapter of Leicester in 1276 record certain quarrels about precedence and declare that special seats are to be allotted to those who have been rich in the world, or are of noble birth, or have given large sums to the house.[2] Similarly, at Barnwell, the distribution of food and clothes was to be made not on any equalitarian basis but according to what each man had been accustomed to in the world.[3]

When the Bury monks were discussing the perfect pastor reference was constantly made to the question of scholarship. Some wanted a learned abbot, others thought that they would be better off with a foolish or stupid pastor who, by his ignorance, would be driven to seek their help and advice. On the whole, the monks were fairly well educated and were certainly expected to be literate, since reading and meditation formed an important part of the daily routine of the cloister. In the early days most of the monks had grown up in the monastery from childhood and had been educated by the masters appointed for this purpose. Those, however, who came later in life were often illiterate or, at best, of only very elementary education. Innocent III tried to prevent the monks of Malmesbury from accepting illiterate men,[4] while at Gloucester no postulants were to be admitted unless 'learned in letters and in singing'.[5] Similar standards were demanded from nuns, who were expected to be able to read and sing,[6] and from canons.[7] A postulant at Dunstable in 1288 was actually turned away on the grounds that he was not

[1] Jocelin of Brakelond, *Chronicle*, pp. 16–20, 71.

[2] Salter, *Augustinian Chapters*, p. 9.

[3] J. W. Clark, *Barnwell Observances*, pp. 3–7, and cf. p. 121. Wickwayn's Injunctions for Kirkham say that ranks are to be observed; but this may refer to seniority, as at Westminster: *Regist. W. Wickwayn*, pp. 88–90; Pearce, *Monks of Westminster*, p. 24.

[4] Brewer, *Regist. Malmesburiense*, i, p. 376.

[5] Hart, *Hist. et Cart. Gloucest.* i, p. lxxxiv.

[6] Power, *Medieval English Nunneries*, p. 245.

[7] Clark, *Barnwell Observances*, p. 121.

sufficiently educated.[1] All Cistercian abbots were expected to be learned men.[2]

In addition to the monks there was, in most houses, a number of novices awaiting their profession. From the very earliest times it had been the custom for parents to offer their sons to some religious house at an early age.[3] Such children were brought up in the monastery and eventually professed, whether they wished it or not. Such a system of 'oblation' was perhaps the most unsatisfactory element in S. Benedict's ideal, and as such it was gradually abandoned. By the beginning of the thirteenth century the children of the cloister had practically disappeared altogether. The change came during the twelfth century, and, when it came, was very rapid. Lanfranc's Constitutions of *c.* 1070 are full of references to the boys[4] who, in his day, played an important part in the monastic system. A century later there was hardly a boy to be found. Moreover, the Cistercian and Carthusian revivals both forbade the system of 'oblation' of children altogether.[5] Boys hardly appear at all in monastic records of the thirteenth century, though a few were sometimes accepted as pages in the abbot's household and some might be receiving their education in the cloister.[6] Both boys and girls were accepted as boarders in nunneries when their parents wanted to be rid of them for a time,[7] though Pecham strongly disapproved of boys lodging with the nuns at Wherwell.[8] But the old system of 'oblation' had gone by the year 1200, and successive legislation saw to it that none were admitted under the age of eighteen or nineteen.[9] The principle

[1] Luard, *An. Mon.* iii, p. 342.

[2] Canivez, *Stat. Ord. Cist.* ii, pp. 246–7.

[3] *Reg. S. Ben.* cap. lix, and Knowles, *Monastic Order*, p. 418. According to Dr Coulton the commonest age in Benedictine cloisters was seven: *Five Centuries*, i, p. 223.

[4] *Consuetudines*, in Migne, *Patr. Lat.* vol. cl, coll. 446, 506.

[5] Coulton, *Five Centuries*, i, p. 229; Fowler, *Cistercian Statutes*, p. 73; D. Knowles, *Monastic Order*, p. 634. Canivez, *Stat. Ord. Cist.* i, pp. 264 and 275, shows that this regulation was not always strictly observed.

[6] Snape, *English Monastic Finances*, p. 9.

[7] Power, *Medieval English Nunneries*, pp. 568–81. In nunneries oblate girls were taken at a very early age: *ibid.* pp. 25–6.

[8] Pecham, *Reg. Epist.* ii, p. 653.

[9] Pantin, *Chapters of English Black Monks*, i, pp. 10, 234; M. Paris, *Chron. Maj.* iii, p. 499; vi, p. 236 (where the age of 15 is given, perhaps

lying behind this change is important. In early days the child was offered, generally with a sum of money,[1] on the assumption that he would take kindly to the life of the cloister when he grew up. But there must have been many misfits, bringing sorrow and anxiety to those in authority as well as to the men who had to suffer from the misguided zeal of their parents. It was, therefore, wise that the system should be abandoned and that entry into the cloister should depend upon a man's personal conviction based upon a full realisation of what his subsequent vows would entail.

Throughout the thirteenth century, therefore, the normal recruit to the monasteries was already grown up, or at least an adolescent who had reached years of discretion. Even so, care was to be taken to test his vocation, so far as such a thing is ever possible. Winchelsey found some monks at Christ Church, Canterbury, and again at Gloucester, who had little sense of vocation, and ordered that none were to be admitted in future except such as had a real call.[2] At some Augustinian houses the bishop, as visitor, claimed the right to say who should be admitted and who refused.[3]

Once accepted, the postulant entered his novitiate, which normally lasted a year, and which was a time of trial and instruction.[4] The number of such novices was very small, since

erroneously for 18); Wilkins, *Concilia*, i, p. 592. As early as 1168 the Pope had forbidden S. Augustine's, Canterbury, to take boys under the age of 15, whereas before they had been taken 'as soon as weaned': Hardwick, *Hist. Mon. S. Aug.* p. 427, cf. Hart and Lyons, *Cart. Rameseia*, ii, pp. 204–7.

[1] *Reg. S. Ben.* cap. lix.

[2] *Regist. R. Winchelsey*, pp. 826–7; Hart, *Hist. et Cart. Gloucest.* i, p. lxxxiv. The examination of postulants at Ely was to be conducted by three or four of the brothers: Statutes of R. de Walpole in *Ely Chapter Ordinances*, in *Camd. Misc.* xvii, pp. 14–15.

[3] See, for example, *Regist. W. Giffard*, pp. 204–6 for S. Oswald's, Gloucester, and *Regist. T. Corbridge*, i, p. 282 for Newstead. Cf. also *Regist. R. Swinfield*, pp. 132–3 for Wigmore. Postulants sometimes brought considerable wealth with them: cf. Alan de Hyde at Dunstable in 1240 in Luard, *An. Mon.* iii, p. 154 and William of Tourney at Louth Park in 1239 in *Chron. of Louth Park*, p. xxxvii. See also what is said of Fraternities and *ad succurrendum* on pp. 300–1 below.

[4] According to the Rule of S. Benedict the novice would hear the Rule read three times during his novitiate. He must distribute all his goods to the poor or hand them over to the monastery. His own clothes were to be kept in case he wanted to leave: *Reg. S. Ben.* cap. lviii. The Cistercians also had a year's novitiate: Canivez, *Stat. Ord. Cist.* i, p. 487. So did the Augustinians: Clark, *Barnwell Observances*, p. 133.

in a community of forty or fifty men there could scarcely be more than one or two vacancies a year. There also appears to have been some reluctance to undertake the responsibilities of full profession and some men tried to prolong the novitiate beyond the appointed time.[1] Normally, however, at the year's end the novice would make his vows and so take his place in the community.

So far we have been concerned only with monks, either professed or on their way to profession. These formed only a small part of the monastic population. Our next concern is with the lay-brothers or *conversi* who stood half-way between the monks and their servants. The word *conversus*, as used in medieval literature, must be treated with caution since it is patient of more than one meaning. Among the Cistercians and Augustinians it means a man living according to a rule, but one not so strict as that of the monks or canons. Such lay-brethren were engaged largely in manual work, they had their own living-quarters, their own chapter and their own part of the church. Among the Benedictines a *conversus* may mean a lay-brother in this sense, or it may refer to a man who joins a monastery as an adult (as opposed to the *nutriti* who had grown up in the cloister), or it may mean a monk not in holy orders.[2]

The Cistercian *conversi* formed a most important part of the monastic economy. In early days they often largely outnumbered the monks. Walter Daniel mentions 600 at Rievaulx compared with 140 monks,[3] and there were 120 of them at Waverley with 70 monks in 1187,[4] and at Louth Park in 1226–46 150 *conversi* and 66 monks.[5] The thirteenth century, however, saw a gradual reduction in the number of lay-brothers. As Mr Snape says: 'The *conversi* seem to have been turbulent and

[1] Wilkins, *Concilia*, ii, pp. 15–16; M. Paris, *Chron. Maj.* iii, p. 500; *V.C.H.*, *Sussex*, ii, p. 57 (Boxgrove, 1205). In the Augustinian houses profession was not to be deferred more than three months: Salter, *Augustinian Chapters*, p. 29. Any Cistercian novice who contracted leprosy or epilepsy was to be sent away, but the monastery was bound to provide for him: Fowler, *Cistercian Statutes*, p. 82.

[2] The subject is discussed in Knowles, *Monastic Order*, pp. 419–20, 719–20.

[3] F. M. Powicke, *Ailred of Rievaulx and his Biographer*, p. 97.

[4] Luard, *An. Mon.* ii, p. 244 and cf. H. Brakspear, *Waverley Abbey*, p. 9.

[5] *Chron. of Louth Park*, p. 15.

unruly, a difficult class to deal with, and, when placed in control of monastic property—a practice very generally adopted in the granges and manors in demesne—liable to fall into the sin of owning private property, or becoming "proprietaries", as it was technically called.'[1] But private property was not the only trouble. The Cistercian Statutes made it a rule that all lay-brothers should be illiterate. They were to learn a few prayers and formulae by heart, but even the rudiments of education were denied to them.[2] In these circumstances was it any wonder that the *conversi* sometimes became unruly and violent? There was misbehaviour among the lay-brothers at Strata Florida in 1196; at Margam in 1206 they threw the cellarer from his horse and locked the abbot in his bedroom; at Neath in 1269 they stole the abbot's horses.[3] Thus these men, whom the monks were so anxious to keep in their place, got more and more out of hand, and, by degrees, the system was allowed to die out.[4] Paid servants proved more manageable than semi-monks.

The Augustinian *conversi* occupied a position much like that of the Cistercians, though at some houses they seem to have been allowed to receive some instruction.[5] They were, however, kept strictly subservient to the canons, to whom they must show respect, rising to their feet when one of the canons passes, and so on.[6] They seem to have been employed a good deal on the land and in the outlying granges, but it is unlikely that there were ever very many of them in any of the Augustinian houses.[7]

Lay-brothers of this type certainly existed among the Black Monks during the thirteenth century. The revised Statutes of 1253 refer several times to 'monks and *conversi*' as if they

[1] Snape, *English Monastic Finances*, p. 9.

[2] Fowler, *Cistercian Statutes*, p. 97.

[3] Canivez, *Stat. Ord. Cist.* i, pp. 199, 324; iii, p. 72: cf. Bond, *Chron. Melsa*, i, p. 432. In 1277 three *conversi* of Strata Marcella were imprisoned in Montgomery Castle, but we are not told the cause; see *Cal. Close Rolls, 1272–9*, p. 404.

[4] For example at Meaux there were 90 in 1249, 7 in 1349 and by 1396 none at all: Bond, *Chron. Melsa*, ii, p. 65; iii, pp. xliii, 229. Bordesley had only 7 *conversi* in 1332 (*V.C.H., Worcs.* ii, p. 153).

[5] E.g. at Thurgarton: *Regist. W. Wickwayn*, pp. 145–7.

[6] Clark, *Barnwell Observances*, p. 227; *Regist. W. Giffard*, pp. 204–6.

[7] The Gilbertines had lay-brothers and lay-sisters. The latter were completely subordinate to the nuns, whom they attended practically as servants (R. Graham, *S. Gilbert and the Gilbertines*, pp. 64, 69).

normally existed side by side in Benedictine houses,[1] though they appear to have been in practice little more than servants.[2] Some of them were put in charge of outlying estates, for one of the abbots of Evesham, about the year 1300, had to recall the *conversi* who were living on the manors in order that they might perform their vows in the monastery 'with prayer and fasting'.[3]

With the gradual disappearance of manual labour from the daily life of the cloistered monk it was inevitable that others should be found to perform it. The system of keeping large numbers of lay-brothers was not altogether satisfactory, and there consequently appeared, in every monastery, paid servants. They were certainly very numerous. Bury, for example, in 1286 had a population of 80 monks and 122 servants;[4] Norwich, with a total of 62 monks, had 146 servants;[5] Ramsey had about 50 monks and nearly 100 servants.[6] Some of the Augustinian houses were even better off. The fourteen canons of Bolton Priory employed over 30 servants,[7] while at Nostell there were 77 servants to look after 26 canons.[8] That the numbers sometimes got far too high is shown by the anxiety of visiting bishops to keep them within reasonable limits.[9]

[1] M. Paris, *Chron. Maj.* vi, p. 239.

[2] The Statutes of 1279 mention *conversi* and servants working together in the kitchen: Pantin, *Chapters of English Black Monks*, i, p. 116.

[3] Macray, *Chron. Abb. de Evesham*, pp. 284–5. The lay-brothers in this instance seem to have been giving some trouble, as the Cistercians found.

[4] Dugdale-Caley, *Monasticon*, iii, pp. 158–9.

[5] Saunders, *Introduction to Norwich Rolls*, p. 163.

[6] Hart and Lyons, *Cart. Rameseia*, iii, pp. 236–41 and Dugdale-Caley, *Monasticon*, ii, p. 549. Compare the following figures: Glastonbury, 50–60 monks and 80 servants (Domerham, *Hist. de Rebus Glaston.* ii, pp. 385–6); Abingdon, about 50 monks and 85 servants (Stevenson, *Chron. Monast. de Abingdon*, ii, pp. 237–43); Worcester, over 40 servants (Hale, *Reg. Prioratus Wigorn.* p. 119); Boxgrove, 10 monks, 28 servants (Haines, *Dover Priory*, p. 331 n.).

[7] Whitaker, *History of Craven*, pp. 341–2.

[8] Burton, *Monasticon Eborac.* pp. 301–2.

[9] See Hart and Lyons, *Cart. Rameseia*, ii, pp. 204–7; *Regist. R. Winchelsey*, pp. 852–6; *Regist. J. Romeyn*, i, pp. 199–202; Brown, *Guisborough Chartulary*, ii, pp. 360–2; Raine, *Hexham Priory*, i, App. pp. xvii–xxii; *Regist. W. Wickwayn*, pp. 144–5; Webb, *Household Roll of R. de Swinfield*, ii, pp. cxcix–ccii. The Cistercians tried to keep the number of servants within reasonable proportions. According to the Statutes of 1237 only those abbeys with less than 8 *conversi* might have servants (Canivez, *Stat. Ord. Cist.*

By the thirteenth century, then, a large staff of servants had become an essential part of each monastic house; so much so that when Evesham fell on evil days, through the mismanagement of Roger Norreys, the monks even went without food themselves in order that the servants might be fed, 'since without them', says the Chronicler, 'we cannot live'.[1]

The servants were of every possible kind. At Abingdon we find a chaplain, porter, butler, larderer, cook, doorkeeper and scullion; servants in the infirmary,[2] refectory, brewery, bakehouse and garden; a man to look after the fires, a woodsplitter, a carpenter, a man to attend to the gutters, a tailor, a laundryman, farm hands of all kinds, stablemen, woodmen, a cupbearer, and various servants attendant upon the cellarer, the sacrist and the almoner.[3] The cellarer of Norwich employed no less than thirty-two men, including a collector of rents, a curer of herrings, a sauceman, two boatmen and a master-keeper of the pigs.[4] The 'indispensable' servants of Evesham included those who wash the monks, those who prepare their baths and those who sit with them when dying.[5] The Bury monks also had bath-attendants besides writers, a wax-keeper, a keeper of cressets or lamps, a vestry-chaplain and a plumber and his mate (*serviens suus*).[6] Winchester had a beer-drawer,[7] and Worcester had five sailors on the Severn and four weir-keepers each with his boy.[8] Nor were women-servants unknown, for we find washer-women mentioned among the domestic staffs at Abingdon, Ely and Norwich,[9] while Worcester employed a woman to make candle-wicks,[10] and Mottisfont seems to have had a

ii, p. 169); none were to be admitted unless they take the threefold vow, thereby making them almost equal to lay-brothers (Fowler, *Cistercian Statutes*, p. 86), and none were to serve in the kitchen or at the abbot's table (*ibid.* pp. 57–8).

[1] Macray, *Chron. Abb. de Evesham*, p. 240: 'sine quibus esse non possumus.'

[2] Servants in the infirmary are mentioned as early as the *Concordia Regularis* of S. Dunstan: Dugdale-Caley, *Monasticon*, i, p. xliii.

[3] Stevenson, *Chron. Monast. de Abingdon*, ii, pp. 237–43.

[4] Saunders, *Introduction to Norwich Rolls*, p. 99.

[5] Dugdale-Caley, *Monasticon*, ii, pp. 27–31.

[6] *Ibid.* iii, pp. 158–9, 162.

[7] *Regist. J. Pontissara*, pp. 655–7.

[8] Hale, *Reg. Prioratus Wigorn.* p. 120a.

[9] Stevenson, *Chron. Monast. de Abingdon*, ii, pp. 237–43; Chapman, *Sacrist Rolls of Ely*, ii, p. 5; Saunders, *Introduction to Norwich Rolls*, pp. 99, 119.

[10] Hale, *Reg. Prioratus Wigorn.* p. 120a.

whole staff of women whom Archbishop Pecham tried to expel in 1284, excepting only those over sixty years of age.[1] At some houses, such as Kirkham and Lesnes, the servants brought their wives and relatives to live in the monastery, thereby creating yet more problems.[2]

If the monks formed roughly one-third of the monastic population and the servants about half, the remaining fraction was made up of lodgers of various kinds.

The most difficult type of lodger was the ex-abbot or prior who, having retired from office, lived on in the house in a room or rooms of his own and with his own household, a constant burden to the community and often a great anxiety to his successor. A good many houses were saddled in this way with some retired prelate. Among the Benedictines we find Robert, Abbot of Glastonbury, retiring in 1234 with a pension of £60 a year; while his successor, Michael of Ambresbury, followed him into retirement eighteen years later on a pension of £160 a year, the manor of Mere, and an ample allowance of food each day from the monastic kitchens.[3] Adam, Abbot of Eynsham and author of the *Life of S. Hugh*, having been deposed in 1228 for perjury and waste of the monastery's goods, lived on in the house and had his own manor of Little Rollright to support him.[4] Ex-priors of the cells belonging to S. Albans were allowed to retire on a money pension to be fixed according to the amount of useful work which they had done.[5]

Resignation was very common among Augustinian heads of houses. At Barnwell, during the thirteenth century, three priors retired. The first, Henry de Eya, resigned in 1254 but lived on in the house for sixteen years, during which he continued to entertain the brethren hospitably. Jolan de Thorley retired on a very good pension in 1264 and lived for over sixteen years. In 1297 Simon of Aschele resigned but died shortly afterwards.[6]

[1] Pecham, *Reg. Epist.* ii, pp. 645–9. Women servants were not allowed by the Statutes: see M. Paris, *Chron. Maj.* vi, p. 244.

[2] *Regist. W. Wickwayn*, pp. 88–90; *Regist. R. Winchelsey*, pp. 842–4.

[3] Domerham, *Hist. de Rebus Glaston.* ii, pp. 520–1; Dugdale-Caley, *Monasticon*, i, p. 6.

[4] Salter, *Eynsham Cartulary*, p. xx. Another ex-abbot of Eynsham had his rations cut down by Pecham in 1284: Pecham, *Reg. Epist.* iii, pp. 843–5.

[5] *Gesta Abbatum Mon. S. Albani*, i, pp. 451–2.

[6] Clark, *Liber Memorandorum*, pp. 70, 72, 73–4.

Adam de Newland, Prior of Guisborough, who retired in 1281, was granted a good chamber of his own near the infirmary, precedence over all others if he enters the cloister, a canon companion and a secular servant to look after him, the usual allowances from the kitchen and ten marks a year pocket-money.[1] The ex-abbot of Wigmore who resigned in 1318 was to have provision for himself, a fellow-canon, a servant and a boy, and was to have for his own use either the 'black room' or the 'painted chamber' and 100*s.* a year for clothes.[2] Where such accommodation was available it would obviously suit the pensioner to remain in the monastery, where he could enjoy the company of his friends; but occasionally arrangements were made for an ex-abbot or prior to live on one of the manors, an arrangement which must have appeared more satisfactory to the man who succeeded him. In 1275 Richard of Bachampton resigned the priory of Bolton and went to live at Ryther near Selby on a pension of £20 a year from the canons;[3] and a few years later we find an ex-abbot of S. Augustine's, Bristol, living on his own manor.[4]

In most cases ample provision was made for the abbot who wished to retire. He could generally count on having a set of rooms, adequate domestic help, good food and a settled income for private expenses. These privileges were, however, sometimes abused. We hear, for example, of an ex-prior of Luffield who had 'turned his liberty into an occasion for damnable sloth' and who was punished by being made to live in future as a cloistered monk, while the door leading from his room to the orchard (and which seems to have been the cause of the trouble) was to be sealed up.[5] Similarly, John of Worcester, ex-prior of Little Malvern, lost all his privileges and was forced to live with the community.[6] The ex-prior of Porchester was given the usual allowances in 1282; but two years later he was

[1] Brown, *Guisborough Chart.* ii, pp. 362–4. For similar allowances see *Regist. J. Romeyn*, i, pp. 317–19 for John de Laxton, ex-prior of Newstead; *ibid.* pp. 56–7 for John of Lund, ex-prior of Bolton; *Regist. W. Wickwayn*, pp. 145–7 for the ex-prior of Thurgarton.

[2] *Regist. A. Orleton*, pp. 99–102. According to the Augustinian Chapters, when the head of a house resigned the bishop was to fix his allowance. He was not to have too much lest he become a burden to the house and encourage others to resign: Salter, *Augustinian Chapters*, p. 7.

[3] A. H. Thompson, *Bolton Priory*, p. 65.

[4] *Regist. G. Giffard*, p. 233.

[5] Pecham, *Reg. Epist.* iii, pp. 854–5.

[6] *Regist. R. Winchelsey*, pp. 864–6.

reduced to the rank of an ordinary canon because he had made a suspicious-looking door and had obtained goods from the community by fraud.[1]

Apart from those who, having served the house for many years, continued to reside there after their retirement from active work, there was always a certain number of people living in a monastery who had acquired the right to do so either by purchase or by some other arrangement with the convent. Reference has already been made to the vicar who held a 'corrody', and who served the parish church while living in the monastery either with the monks or with the servants.[2] Corrodies were often sold to wealthy laymen who, in exchange for some acres of land or a bag of money, could demand board and lodging for themselves and their families in their old age. A corrody was, therefore, a form of annuity, and, as such, was of great value to men and women who had few ways of providing for their declining years. On the other hand the monasteries regarded it as a convenient way of raising a little ready money, though the sale of a corrody often meant that a house was burdened for many years.

In the year 1250 Selborne Priory sold to Roger de Cherlecote and Isabella his wife a corrody of 18 canons' loaves, 28 servants' loaves, 15 gallons of convent beer and 14 of second quality, and 12 dishes weekly, the price paid being about 40 acres of land and a mill.[3] Dunstable in 1234 sold, for a carucate of land, a corrody to cover a man and his wife, two sons, a daughter and the wife's maid.[4] Merton sold a corrody to a man for 20*s.*, and the man lived for twenty-nine years to the great distress of the canons.[5] Sometimes the terms of the corrody included other things beside board and residence. At Darley, for instance, in 1252, a corrody was sold to Ralph de Wistanton for himself and his wife which was to include also some provision for their two sons, who were to become free servants of the house if they chose to do so;[6] and at Bayham a corrody was to include the support of a crippled son, a clerk, teaching the two younger sons some trade, pin-money for the daughters, the paying off of the

[1] Pecham, *Reg. Epist.* i, pp. 292–3, ii, pp. 666–9. Cf. the ex-prior of Newburgh who held too many 'confabulations' in his chamber: *Regist. W. Giffard*, pp. 328–30.

[2] See above, pp. 46–7.

[3] Macray, *Charters and Documents of Selborne*, p. 35.

[4] Luard, *An. Mon.* iii, p. 139, and cf. pp. 287, 395.

[5] Heales, *Records of Merton*, p. 170.

[6] *V.C.H., Derbyshire*, ii, p. 49.

man's debts, a pension to the family lawyer and leave for him to visit the abbey for relaxation.[1] Corrodies were sometimes sold to Jews;[2] and, just as women could by this method take up residence in a monastery, so men sometimes boarded in nunneries.[3]

Other corrodies were for board without residence. Eynsham Abbey, for instance, in 1250, sold a corrody to Isabella de Cuillardeville under which the monks agreed to send food and firewood regularly to her house.[4] About 1310 Roger de Redenhall and his wife acquired a corrody at Waverley and built a house for themselves close to the abbey gate.[5] Malmesbury sold a corrody to a man which gave him certain rights of pasture and permission to roam through the abbey woods with a tool called a 'hackare' (? hacker or bill-hook) as well as receiving food and clothes.[6] A corrody at Dunstable included the support of two boys, one of whom was at school.[7] Corrodies were also sometimes given to monastic servants.[8]

The corrody system was very popular throughout the thirteenth century, for it offered advantages to both buyer and seller. Many a man was glad to be relieved of the burden of managing his estates in his old age and welcomed an opportunity of settling quietly with his wife and servants in the pleasant surroundings of a religious house, where the necessities of life would be regularly provided and where he would be certain of a high degree of security. On the other hand many a hard-pressed abbot, desperate for a little ready money, turned eagerly to this method of raising it, knowing that if the holder of the corrody survived for a long time the abbot himself would probably not live to feel the burden. Corrodies were therefore sold fairly freely. Crowland in 1328 had ten 'corrodars' living on the premises;[9] Selby in 1322 had fifteen, each with servants.[10]

The burden which the corrodies placed upon the convent was

[1] *V.C.H., Sussex*, ii, pp. 86–7.

[2] Fowler, *Dunstable Charters*, p. 103.

[3] Power, *Medieval English Nunneries*, pp. 414–15.

[4] Salter, *Eynsham Cartulary*, i, pp. 186–7. For similar grants see Wigram, *Cart. of S. Frideswide's*, i, p. 286; ii, p. 320.

[5] Brakspear, *Waverley Abbey*, p. 17.

[6] Brewer, *Regist. Malmesburiense*, ii, pp. 326–7.

[7] Fowler, *Dunstable Charters*, p. 228 and cf. pp. 149–50.

[8] Salter, *Eynsham Cartulary*, i, pp. 231–2; Heales, *Records of Merton*, p. 82.

[9] Dugdale-Caley, *Monasticon*, ii, p. 121.

[10] *V.C.H., Yorks.* iii, p. 97.

considerable. In 1324–5 the canons of Bolton were spending over £22 on their lodgers,[1] and in 1279 a corrodar at Thetford was costing more to keep than the whole community of twenty-three monks put together.[2] Abbot Roger of S. Albans in his old age burdened the house considerably by a rash sale of corrodies,[3] and it was no wonder that bishops tried to keep the traffic within bounds and to check this unsatisfactory method of 'quick returns'.[4]

The visitor to a thirteenth-century monastery would thus find a considerable variety among its occupants. As he passed through the great gate into the courtyard he would probably see groups of lay people, both men and women, walking about or sitting under the shelter of the great west wall of the church, watching their children playing in the sun until a bell summoned them to return to their rooms, where their servants had prepared the tables for their dinner and laid on them the steaming dishes and the great pots of ale brought up from the monks' kitchen. Meanwhile the visitor would see a constant stream of servants and officials moving about on their lawful occasions, looking after the interests of the monks and attending to their needs. In the kitchen an army of cooks would be preparing meals for this large family; cleaners would be hard at work in the church, in the refectory, in the dormitory and elsewhere; in the stables, grooms and stable-boys would be looking after the horses; in the gardens men and lads would be hard at work. Meanwhile, what of the monks? Unless it was actually the hour of divine service these would be scattered about the monastery. Some would be in church attending to the books and ornaments and vestments; others would be in the library or cloister, reading, copying or writing books; others would be interviewing their own particular households, supervising the work and managing their financial affairs; others perhaps would be out visiting friends or hunting. Everywhere there would be signs of life and activity, though it might not be quite the sort of life or activity which men like S. Benedict, S. Augustine or S. Bernard intended.

[1] Burton, *Monasticon Ebor.* pp. 121–33.

[2] Duckett, *Visitations of Cluniacs*, pp. 34–5.

[3] *Gesta Abbatum Mon. S. Alb.* i, p. 484.

[4] See Hart, *Hist. et Cart. Gloucest.* i, pp. lxxxiv–xcii; *Regist. J. Romeyn*, i, pp. 199–202; *Regist. W. Giffard*, pp. 204–6; *Regist. W. Wickwayn*, pp. 130–1, 134–6.

CHAPTER XX

ADMINISTRATION

The responsibilities of a monastic chapter—as landowners, administrators and employers of labour—were very great; and, as time went by, they became increasingly intricate and laborious. Ownership of land carried with it many duties when the land was tilled by paid or forced labour, while the manorial system, under which so much land was held, laid upon the owner many responsibilities of a judicial and administrative kind. By the thirteenth century the estates of some of the monasteries were very extensive. It is estimated, for example, that the Cistercian Abbey of Meaux in East Yorkshire owned no less than 19,600 acres,[1] and the chartularies of any of the larger abbeys will show that this is not likely to be any exaggeration. The Chartulary of Fountains Abbey gives details of land in 151 different places,[2] while even a comparatively small house, such as the Augustinian Priory of Bridlington, held estates in over a hundred parishes scattered far and wide.[3] Worcester owned 25 manors,[4] Peterborough 29,[5] Gloucester 30,[6] and Bury S. Edmunds no less than 170.[7] The Cluniac Priory of Lewes in Sussex held land in as many as 223 different parishes lying as far apart as Norfolk and Dorset,[8] and the Crowland estates were spread over five counties.[9]

The management of these vast and often scattered estates entailed a great deal of work, demanded considerable business acumen, and absorbed a very large part of the monks' daily life. The burden, in fact, became so heavy that some form of decentralisation was essential. If the Chapter as a whole were to be consulted about every detail of the management of these estates a great deal of time would be wasted, men would be taken away unnecessarily from other duties, and there would be endless discussion and delay. In these circumstances it was

[1] Bond, *Chron. Melsa*, iii, p. lxiii.
[2] Lancaster, *Chartulary of Fountains Abbey*, passim.
[3] Burton, *Monast. Ebor*. pp. 213–46.
[4] Hale, *Reg. Prior. Wigorn*. pp. ii–iii.
[5] Dugdale-Caley, *Monasticon*, i, pp. 396–7.
[6] Hart, *Hist. et Cart. Gloucest*. iii, p. 2.
[7] Dugdale-Caley, *Monasticon*, iii, p. 165.
[8] *Ibid*. v, pp. 8–9.
[9] Page, *Estates of Crowland Abbey*, p. 9.

obviously better that the administration of the monastic property should be divided among those of the monks who were best qualified to deal with it, each of whom would thereby become responsible for his own share of the burden and could be made to render an account from time to time. From the twelfth century onwards this process of devolution went on apace, monastic bodies becoming more and more divided into different departments each with its own income and duties.

The first and most important division was between the abbot and the convent. The seeds of this lay in the Rule of S. Benedict where the abbot is set somewhat aloof from his fellow-cloisterers, not that he lived apart from them but because of his authority and responsibilities. There was, moreover, one very important moment at which the abbot was separated from his monks, and that was at meal times. So important was the duty of hospitality to all and sundry who looked for a welcome at the monastery that S. Benedict ordained that the abbot should have his own kitchen and his own table where he would dine either alone, or with his guests, or with such of the brethren as he might choose to invite to join him.[1]

This decision opened the door in later years to a gradual separation of abbot and convent.[2] With the growth of abbatial estates the abbot was taken more and more away from the monastery on endless journeys to his manors, interviewing bailiffs, holding his court, threshing out all the multitudinous problems of land tenancy and the customs attached to it, settling disputes over rent and service, hunting down defaulters and bringing them to justice. Besides all this, his position as a great feudal lord brought him into the arena of public affairs and necessitated periodic journeys to Court.

A medieval abbot therefore lived very much like a medieval bishop—constantly on the move from manor to manor. The Abbot of Westminster was lord of fourteen manors, and, as Dr Pearce has shown, was constantly on tour, watching over his interests and supervising his employees.[3] Samson of Bury

[1] *Reg. S. Ben.* capp. liii, lvi.

[2] Dom David Knowles has shown how this separation grew during the twelfth century: *Monastic Order*, p. 276. At Bury it was apparently not completed until 1281: *Chron. Oxenedes*, p. 235.

[3] Pearce, *Walter de Wenlok*, pp. 69–75.

S. Edmunds was away from home so much that the monks complained that they hardly ever saw him,[1] and the Abbot of S. Benet of Holme seems to have made himself responsible not only for the administration of his own manors but for those of the convent as well.[2] We do sometimes come across evidence of a prelate who was content to leave these affairs in the hands of stewards,[3] but the normal thing, as Dom Butler has pointed out, was for an abbot to be absent from his monastery for a large part of every year.[4]

Participation in political, judicial and diplomatic affairs kept some abbots away from their convents for long periods. They were regularly summoned to meetings of Parliament, some acted as judges,[5] and several were sent by the King as envoys on diplomatic journeys.[6] Others kept away from the monasteries more from choice than from necessity. Jocelin tells us that Samson was 'happier and in better spirits anywhere than at home', an observation which can scarcely be regarded as complimentary to his fellow-monks.[7] But if so conscientious and responsible a person as Samson was depressed by the society of his monks and recovered his spirits only when separated from them, it is no wonder that lesser men took such opportunities as offered themselves to escape from the cloister. Perhaps this accounts for the fact that when Walter de Wenlok, Abbot of Westminster, had to go on a visit to the Pope he actually took a house in Orvieto and remained there for some time, no doubt preferring the pleasures of Italian society to the irritations and tedium of life at Westminster Abbey.[8] Archbishop Pecham had to tell the Prior of Christ Church, Canterbury, that he was to

[1] Jocelin of Brakelond, *Chronicle*, p. 55.

[2] West, *S. Benet of Holme*, Norfolk Record Society, iii, p. 209.

[3] Page, *Estates of Crowland*, p. 29.

[4] Butler, *Benedictine Monachism*, pp. 195–7.

[5] E.g. Samson of Bury (Jocelin of Brakelond, *Chron.* p. 53), the Abbot of Ramsey in 1238 (Hart and Lyons, *Cart. Rames.* iii, p. 181), the Abbot of Crowland (Grosseteste, *Epistolae*, p. 262). In 1273 Edward I ordered the Abbot of Chertsey to go to Kingston to see that a tournament which the King had forbidden did not take place: *V.C.H., Surrey*, ii, p. 59.

[6] The Abbot of Beaulieu was regularly employed in this way (Fowler, *History of Beaulieu Abbey*, pp. 115–30); the Abbot of Robertsbridge was away in 1212, 1222 and 1225 (*V.C.H., Sussex*, ii, p. 72); and in 1290 the Abbot of Welbeck was sent to Norway (A. H. Thompson, *Welbeck Abbey*, p. 70).

[7] Jocelin of Brakelond, *Chron.* p. 55.

[8] Pearce, *Walter de Wenlok*, pp. 14–22; cf. *V.C.H., London*, i, p. 441.

spend more time in the cloister, as he was in the habit of absenting himself for long periods,[1] while it is said of William de Trumpington, Abbot of S. Albans, that 'despising the society of his fellow-monks he betook himself to worldlings and lived with them'.[2] Others spent a good deal of time at the papal court, Richard of Croxley, Abbot of Westminster, serving there as a papal chaplain.[3] In 1262 the Abbot of S. Mary's, York, having had some difference of opinion with his monks, kept away from them for over a year,[4] and in 1284 the Prior of Lewes went overseas and never returned.[5]

Many communities, therefore, saw very little of the 'father abbot', and even when he was at home he lived almost entirely apart from his fellow-monks. Reference has already been made to the passage in the Rule of S. Benedict which empowered the abbot to have his own kitchen and his own table; and the step from this to the abbot living in almost complete seclusion was not very large. By the thirteenth century most heads of houses had their own lodgings in the monastery with their own households, and even their own chapel and chaplain, so that in point of fact they may rarely have mingled with the monks even when they were at home, in the intervals between their constant journeys.

In the seclusion of their own quarters many abbots kept great state. The abbot's lodgings had become a separate establishment, conducted like any other large household of the period, with a very large number of retainers. At Westminster the abbot employed forty-three men, including musicians and actors, in his household,[6] while the Abbot of S. Augustine's, Canterbury, had no less than sixty-five.[7] The Prior of Norwich's household contained nine squires, six clerks, and about thirty-five other men.[8] At Ely in 1307 the prior's household was con-

[1] Pecham, *Reg. Epist.* ii, pp. 397–403.

[2] *Gesta Abbatum Mon. S. Alb.* i, p. 254.

[3] M. Paris, *Chron. Maj.* v, p. 303; cf. William of Taunton, Prior of Winchester (*ibid.* iii, p. 568) and the Abbot of S. Augustine's, Canterbury, in Dugdale-Caley, *Monasticon*, i, p. 122 and *W. Thorn's Chronicle*, tr. Davis, p. 258.

[4] Craster and Thornton, *Chronicle of S. Mary's, York*, p. 7.

[5] Dugdale-Caley, *Monasticon*, v, p. 5.

[6] Pearce, *Walter de Wenlok*, pp. 99–104.

[7] Thompson, *Customary of Canterbury and Westminster*, i, p. 64.

[8] Saunders, *Introduction to Norwich Rolls*, pp. 86–7.

sidered to be too great a burden upon the community, partly because of the lavishness with which he entertained.[1]

The standard of living in the abbot's household was often very high. In 1214, and again in 1216, the Chapter General of the Cistercians tried to put some check upon Hugh, second Abbot of Beaulieu, who was living in a manner hardly suited to an order which claimed to be founded upon simplicity of life.[2] Samson of Bury began with twenty-six horses, which was obviously considered a very small stable;[3] the Abbot of Ramsey took thirty-nine on his journey to London early in the fourteenth century.[4] The weekly consumption of food in the abbot's household at Bury S. Edmunds was said to be $6\frac{3}{4}$ carcases of beef, $15\frac{1}{2}$ pigs, 31 geese and 155 fowls;[5] but this must have been in the more prosperous times, for there was a period when the Abbot of Bury was so poor that he had to break up his establishment and live in so modest a fashion that he was unable to attend the installation of the Abbot of S. Benet of Holme.[6] Indeed, in spite of the appearance of great prosperity, many of the abbots and priors were hard put to it to make ends meet. The accounts of Walter de Wenlok, Abbot of Westminster, were carefully studied by Dr Pearce, who says that 'it is beyond question that this lord of broad acres was often but ill supplied with ready cash'.[7] Sometimes through mismanagement or extravagance, but more often through the vicissitudes of bad harvests, or civil disturbances, or the perpetual burden of

[1] Evans, *Ely Chapter Ordinances*, in *Camden Misc.* xvii, p. 32. Cf. *Regist. J. Halton*, i, pp. 119–22 for Carlisle.

[2] Canivez, *Stat. Ord. Cist.* i, pp. 445, 460. Hugh was said to dine with 3 counts and 40 knights and to have a large number of servants. He afterwards became Bishop of Carlisle, where he was very unpopular (see *Chron. de Lanercost*, p. 30).

[3] Jocelin of Brakelond, *Chron.* pp. 40–1. On being criticised for keeping so few horses Samson replied: 'A child must first crawl, and afterwards he may stand upright and walk.'

[4] Dugdale-Caley, *Monasticon*, ii, pp. 583–6.

[5] *Ibid.* iii, pp. 161–2. Many abbots had large quantities of plate. Walter de Wenlok was handed fifty-five pieces when he became Abbot of Westminster (Pearce, *Walter de Wenlok*, p. 23) and when Walter, Abbot of Peterborough, died, his executors found in his rooms a great quantity of plate including gold cups, silver bowls, silver plates, silver spoons, two gold necklaces and thirty gold rings (Sparke, *Hist. Anglic. Script. Varii*, pt. ii, p. 122).

[6] Arnold, *Memorials of S. Edmund's Abbey*, iii, p. 37.

[7] Pearce, *Walter de Wenlok*, p. 114 and cf. the whole of chap. vii.

taxation, abbots got into financial difficulties from which it was not easy to escape.

This, again, helped the process of separation between the abbot and the convent. On the death of an abbot the King took over and administered the affairs of the barony until a new appointment was made. In early days, when the abbot and convent were one, this meant that the entire finances of the community fell under royal control. But by the separation of the estates of the abbot from those of the convent the monks were able, during a vacancy, to prevent their own financial affairs from falling into the hands of the King.[1]

The multiplication of duties which took an abbot away from his monastery, and his confinement to his own lodgings even when at home, made a very wide gulf between the head and the rest of the body, and sometimes threw the two into some degree of opposition. If abbots recovered their spirits when they were away from their monks, no doubt the monks also felt happier when they saw their father-in-God riding away down the road and knew that he would not be back for some months. The separation of abbot and convent had destroyed that intimate touch between the shepherd and his flock which the Benedictine Rule intended; the abbot had become an august personage whose occasional visits to the monastery were associated in the minds of the monks with inspection, anxiety and discipline.

Yet many attempts were made during the thirteenth century, both by the monks themselves and by their Visitors, to bridge the gulf which they saw to be growing between the head and the members of so many religious houses. The Chapters of the Black Monks, set up in response to a decree of the Fourth Lateran Council, repeatedly urged abbots to mix more with their convents,[2] while at a good many houses bishops encouraged such co-operation when they sent in their visitation injunctions.[3]

[1] Snape, *English Monastic Finances*, pp. 27–8. Cf. Jocelin of Brakelond, *Chron*. pp. 127–8, which shows how much the monks of Bury were concerned that their affairs should not be 'mingled and confounded' with those of the abbot.

[2] Pantin, *Chapters of English Black Monks*, i, pp. 8–9, 35–6, 65–6, 232.

[3] *Regist. W. Wickwayn*, pp. 147–8, for Blyth; *Regist. G. Giffard*, pp. 100–2, for S. Augustine's, Bristol; *Regist. T. Cantilupe*, pp. 147–9, for Chirbury; *Regist. W. Giffard*, pp. 204–6, for S. Oswald's, Gloucester; Pecham, *Reg. Epist.* iii, pp. 782–4, for Haverfordwest; *Regist. R. Winchelsey*, pp. 842–4, for Lesnes; *Regist. R. Baldock, etc.* p. 26, for Holy Trinity, London.

But the process of separation had often gone too far; and, however much an abbot might wish to mix with his convent, the exigencies of his work and of his responsibilities made it impossible.

Meanwhile, there were, of course, some monasteries in which there was a certain amount of friction between abbot and convent, friction which generally arose either over questions of jurisdiction or of the division of property. The latter was the cause of a dispute which lasted for some years at Westminster Abbey. In 1225 the abbot, Richard de Berking, had drawn up an agreement with the convent whereby he assigned to them seven manors, three farms, a pension of £6 from Oakham Church, and promised to supply a dish of flesh-meat for the misericord every day from Epiphany to September, and to entertain all the monastic servants on the greater feasts.[1] In spite of this agreement disputes over property broke out again in 1249 and continued for some years.[2] A similar agreement was drawn up between the prior and convent of the alien Priory of Tutbury, a cell to S. Pierre-sur-Dives, in 1230. Under this settlement the prior undertook to provide, for the monks' kitchen, 26 marks (£17. 6*s.* 8*d.*), 30 good live hogs (or 10 live oxen), 6 sextaries of wine, 45 cheeses, 3 lb. of pepper, 3 lb. of mustard, 1 sextary of salt, 5 bushels of white beans in Advent and a quarter at Easter, and a quarter of flour. On the day of the Assumption he was to provide the 'great feast'.[3]

On the question of jurisdiction there was a good deal of controversy. According to the Rule of S. Benedict the abbot was in all things supreme. He and he alone was responsible for every decision. He might listen to the advice of his Chapter, but he was under no obligation to act upon it. Against his decisions there was no appeal.[4] Yet by the thirteenth century determined attempts were being made to limit the autocratic powers of the abbots and to place the religious houses upon a much more democratic basis. The Benedictines themselves, in their General Chapters, introduced decrees forbidding abbots to alienate the goods of their monasteries, or to appoint men to benefices, or

[1] Pearce, *Walter de Wenlok*, pp. 134–7.
[2] M. Paris, *Chron. Maj.* v, pp. 83, 230–1, 303.
[3] Dugdale-Caley, *Monasticon*, iii, p. 389.
[4] *Reg. S. Ben.* capp. ii and iii; cf. Butler, *Benedictine Monachism*, p. 187.

to receive new members, without the consent of their Chapters.[1] At Selby in 1233 Archbishop Gray demanded that the abbot should seek and act upon the advice of a small committee of four senior monks,[2] and Pecham did much the same, fifty years later, at Christ Church, Canterbury, and at Bardney in Lincolnshire.[3] The same process was applied to the Augustinians. At Barnwell, Felley and Newstead the consent of the whole chapter was to be sought;[4] at Bridlington, Hexham and Mottisfont the advice of the senior and wiser members;[5] at Llanthony and Wigmore the prior was to consult a small inner circle of the canons.[6] By this means the old autocratic powers of the abbot or prior were very considerably limited. It was one of many significant changes which were taking place in monastic life during the thirteenth century.

The gulf which appeared between abbot and convent was largely caused by the accumulation of wealth. As time went by, the estates of the monasteries became so enormous that the abbot found himself almost fully occupied in the administration of his lands and in the various responsibilities which this entailed. A similar process of division of estates and duties was taking place at the same time among the monks themselves. When this process began is not certainly known; but by the thirteenth century it was fully developed.[7] Each monastery was divided into what were practically separate departments, each

[1] Pantin, *Chapters of English Black Monks*, i, pp. 233, 249, and M. Paris, *Chron. Maj.* v, p. 240.

[2] *V.C.H., Yorks.* iii, pp. 96–7.

[3] Pecham, *Reg. Epist.* i, pp. 341–8, ii, pp. 397–403, iii, pp. 823–6.

[4] Clark, *Barnwell Observances*, p. 49; *Regist. W. Giffard*, pp. 313–14; *Regist. W. Wickwayn*, pp. 143–4.

[5] *Regist. W. Wickwayn*, pp. 87–8; Raine, *Hexham Priory*, i, App. p. xvii; Pecham, *Reg. Epist.* ii, pp. 645–9.

[6] *Regist. G. Giffard*, pp. 87–9; *Regist. R. Swinfield*, pp. 363–4. Mr R. A. L. Smith has recently shown how the Exchequer at Christ Church, Canterbury, composed of the *seniores et saniores*, came to handle not only the financial affairs of the house, but also many questions concerning the daily life of the monks. See *The 'Regimen Scaccarii' in English Monasteries*, in *Trans. R. Hist. Soc.* 1942, pp. 87–90.

[7] Dom David Knowles has shown that it was well established on the Continent by the beginning of the eleventh century: *Monastic Order*, p. 433. At S. Augustine's, Canterbury, the division into several departments was made by Abbot Hugh de Trottiscleve, 1124–51: Dugdale-Caley, *Monasticon*, i, pp. 121–2.

with its own income and its own special responsibilities. The officer in charge of each department was known as an 'obedientiary'. To him certain sources of income were assigned; he had his own household and servants; and the burden of his office was such as to occupy a very large part of his time.

In an average monastery there were about fifteen obedientiaries, though in the larger houses there might be up to twenty. Abingdon had fifteen, Evesham seventeen, Glastonbury thirteen, Bury S. Edmunds twenty.[1] At the Augustinian Priory of Barnwell there were seventeen obedientiaries among only thirty canons.[2] It is obvious, therefore, that any monk of average intelligence and ability could count on receiving some form of office in due course, and that he would spend a good many years of his monastic life in the administration of his department.

It has been pointed out that the obedientiaries were grouped according as their duties centred round the Prior, the Church and the House.[3] Most monasteries in addition to the abbot or prior had a sub-prior, and many had a third prior as well. The obedientiaries connected with the church were the Sacristan and Sub-sacristan who looked after the church, the Precentor and Succentor who were responsible for the singing and for the Choir-School where such existed; and the keepers of various shrines. Those connected with the House were the Cellarer, who was in charge of all the catering and often had the assistance of a Sub-cellarer; the Bursar or Treasurer, who became increasingly important as the financial affairs grew more complex; the Refectorer, the Kitchener, the Infirmarer, the Chamberlain, in charge of clothes and bedding, the Almoner, the Guest-master, the Master of the Works, who looked after the fabric; the Gardener, the Forester, the Librarian, the Novice-Master, the Pittancer to supervise the monks' pittances; and occasionally a number of smaller offices such as the Keeper of the Herb Garden (Winchester), the Chamberlain of the Infirmary (Abingdon), and the Master of the Book-press (Bury).[4]

[1] Knowles, *Monastic Order*, p. 713.

[2] Clark, *Barnwell Observances*, p. xxxiii. For nunneries, see Power, *Medieval English Nunneries*, pp. 131–4.

[3] Snape, *English Monastic Finances*, p. 29, quoting from Kitchin, *Compotus Rolls of the Obedientiaries of S. Swithun's, Winchester*.

[4] See Snape, *English Monastic Finances*, p. 32; Knowles, *Monastic Order*, p. 713; and, for Winchester, *Reg. J. Pontissara*, pp. 655–7.

Each of these obedientiaries had his own income derived from manors, estates, rents, appropriated churches, and various offerings and dues. The Consuetudinary for Abingdon, drawn up about 1180, sets forth in great detail the incomes of the various officers. The Chamberlain, for example, received annually some £67 together with various gifts in kind. To begin with, he owned the manors of Welford and Chieveley with all manorial rights pertaining to them. These two manors were valued at £37 and £16 respectively. He also received *52s. 3d.* for the monks' clothes and sandals, and ointment for greasing the sandals three times a year; 40*s.* from the tithes of Tadmarton; 6*s.* from a meadow at Stockgrave to provide bath-mats for the brethren; rents in various places to a total of £7. 13*s.* 4*d.*; and such perquisites as oats for two horses when he goes on a journey, food for his servants, churchset[1] and gifts of hens.[2] The Almoner received various tithes and rents, and £5 from the abbot, being 10*s.* from each of his manors. By this means the abbot delegated to the monks' almoner his responsibilities for giving alms—a wise move when we consider how often the abbot was away from home.[3] The Precentor received two-thirds of the tithes of 30 virgates of land in Dumbleton and a few small sums in rents, all of which were 'for making books and looking after the organ'. On the days when he washed the covers of the books in the choir he was to receive from the Cellarer a loaf of bread, an allowance of beer and one ordinary ration (*generale*) from the kitchen. These were clearly meant for the man who was hired for the occasion.[4] The Kitchener received rents from nine manors together with 27,000 eggs, 1224 fowls and 54 bushels of vegetables. He also had the right to collect 100 herrings from every ship coming up the Thames.[5]

At Durham the incomes of the various departments were very large. The Cellarer, for example, had an annual income of over £800, and the Guest-master of £272, while the Bursar handled nearly £4000 a year, a turn-over in present-day currency of something approaching a quarter of a million pounds.[6] There were at that time about eighty or ninety monks.

[1] See above, p. 132.

[2] Stevenson, *Chron. Monast. de Abingdon*, ii, pp. 299–306.

[3] *Ibid.* ii, pp. 327–8.

[4] *Ibid.* ii, p. 328.

[5] *Ibid.* ii, pp. 322–3, 329.

[6] Fowler, *Durham Account Rolls*, i, pp. 6, 113; ii, p. 492. In 1293 the Bursar's receipts were £3741, in 1295 £3975 and in 1297 £3626.

At Norwich the Sacrist had an annual income of £167 derived from various appropriated churches (£80), offerings at numerous shrines in the Cathedral (£60–70), and a few rents. He spent, during the year, about £50 on wax for candles, a small amount on books, and no less than £40 on his own table.[1] This last entry is significant, for it shows that some at any rate of the obedientiaries had their own households and even took their meals apart from their fellow-monks. This is borne out by entries in the Account Rolls at Ely, which show that the Sacrist used to retire periodically to a grange or farm-house at Turbutsey where he used to entertain parties of his fellow-monks and townsmen of Ely with mutton, veal, chicken, bread, beer and wine.[2] The Sacrist of Ely had an income of between £250 and £300 a year derived from four appropriated churches and a pension, receipts from land, and offerings at various shrines, crosses and altars in the Cathedral.[3]

Each obedientiary, then, was the head of a department. He had his own sources of income, out of which certain responsibilities must be met. What was left over he spent as he thought fit. The Guest-master at Durham, for example, received tithes and rents to the value of £272. 2*s.* 2*d.* a year. Out of this he paid £6. 16*s.* 4*d.* to the vicar of an appropriated church, £2. 6*s.* 8*d.* to a chaplain in charge of another parish, £6. 13*s.* 4*d.* to the Prior, 6*s.* 8*d.* to the Sacrist, 10*s.* to the Marshal, 22*s.* to the Infirmarer, 6*s.* to his washerwoman and three guineas in servants' wages. This left him about £250 for running the Guest-house. But not all of this was spent on the guests, as he managed to provide extra pittances for his fellow-monks, presented them with a number of gifts, and bought his own clothes.[4] The Precentor of Norwich had an income of about £25, which was meant to provide books for the church; but actually most of it went in buying clothes and spices for the monks, only £2. 9*s.* 4*d.* being spent on books.[5] The Almoner at Norwich received annually about £110, but the gifts to the poor, though they were sometimes as much as 83 per cent of this, in other years fell to only 20 per cent. Since most of this

[1] Saunders, *Introduction to Norwich Rolls*, pp. 102–8.

[2] Chapman, *Sacrist Rolls of Ely*, i, p. 3, and cf. ii, p. 8. This party cost him nearly £14 or the combined annual income of four vicars (ii, p. 5).

[3] *Ibid.* i, p. 111.

[4] Fowler, *Durham Account Rolls*, i, pp. 113–17.

[5] Saunders, *Introduction to Norwich Rolls*, pp. 134–5.

went towards the upkeep of the Grammar School there must have been very little left for the poor of what was one of the largest cities in the country.[1]

There can be little doubt, therefore, that the Obedientiary System suited the monks very well. The novice at Barnwell, before his profession, was asked whether he felt able 'to endure with a good heart nocturnal vigils, the dull life of the cloister, continual services in choir, prolonged silence, the strictness of the Order and of this particular house, and the different characters of the brethren'.[2] Yet at this house we know that more than half the canons were obedientiaries, who would see very little of the 'dull life of the cloister' since so much of their time would be taken up with the performance of their manifold duties in charge of their own departments. The average obedientiary was a very busy man who was obliged to spend a good deal of time away from the monastery and, when at home, had many details of administration and finance which demanded his attention. He had his duties either as an assistant to the prior, or in connection with the church, or in feeding or clothing the monks, or in caring for the guests, or in supervising the gardens or some other part of the estate. Then he had his household to manage, servants to engage, bills to pay, entertainments to organise. If he acted as cellarer or chamberlain he would have to spend much time visiting fairs and markets in search of good food or good cloth. Above all, he was constantly 'outriding', visiting his manors and his estates, interviewing his tenants and his bailiffs and trying to fulfil all the complicated and exacting responsibilities of a man of property. As Dom David Knowles says: 'Save in monasteries such as Winchester, Canterbury and S. Albans, where strong intellectual or artistic interests existed, business of this kind was the career which absorbed all the talent of the house.'[3]

The provisioning of a household of several hundred men was indeed a formidable matter in days when transport was difficult and dangerous. We have already seen that the larger households solved the problem by a continuous progress from one manor to another. The monks' inability to do this made it necessary for them to find some method which would ensure the regular

[1] Saunders, *Introduction to Norwich Rolls*, pp. 121–7.
[2] Clark, *Barnwell Observances*, p. 133.
[3] Knowles, *Monastic Order*, p. 438.

delivery of foodstuffs at the monastery. There were two ways in which they utilised their estates for this purpose. One was to put their own servants and officials to cultivate the lands and to arrange for regular supplies to be sent up for the monastic kitchen. The other method was to let the lands at a fixed rental and to spend the money in the markets nearer home.

Throughout the thirteenth century both of these methods were in practice, for each could be made profitable.[1] The period was one of great progress in agricultural methods; more and more land was being brought under cultivation by draining fens and marshes, cutting down forests and clearing rough ground; and several monastic houses, under the leadership of capable and far-seeing abbots, were greatly improving their estates and increasing their production. Henry of Eastry, for example, who was Prior of Canterbury from 1285 to 1331, has been described as 'one of the most remarkable farmers in medieval history'.[2] Under his influence not only was much land reclaimed but the stock on the manors was improved and increased. This 'high' or 'demesne' farming was typical of the thirteenth century and many of the religious houses profited by it. Meanwhile, in order to remove some of the administrative difficulties, the monks were busy consolidating small parcels of ground to form larger units.[3] Where, for example, a parish church had been appropriated to a religious house it would be convenient to acquire land in the neighbourhood in order that the produce of the fields might be added to the tithes of the parishioners. From these manors and granges, under the direct control of the monks and their officials, large quantities of food were regularly supplied for the maintenance of the monastic household. It was customary to draw up a schedule of what each unit should provide, some estates being responsible for a week's supply, some for a fortnight, some for a month.[4]

These estates which were held in demesne were normally administered by bailiffs who were responsible to the member of the convent to whom the land was allotted. Some of the abbeys also appointed a seneschal or steward to be in charge

[1] N. Neilson in *Cambridge Economic History*, i, p. 466.

[2] R. A. L. Smith, *High Farming on the Canterbury Estates*, in *Canterbury Cathedral Chronicle*, May 1940, p. 13.

[3] T. A. M. Bishop, *Monastic Granges in Yorkshire*, in *E.H.R.* 1936, pp. 193–213.

[4] R. A. L. Smith in *Canterbury Cathedral Chronicle*, May 1940, p. 11.

of all the manors and so to relieve the obedientiaries of some of their work.[1] In other houses the administration of the manors was placed in the hands of one of the monks, sometimes known as the 'outside cellarer', who must have spent most of his time out of the cloister. Occasionally we find the entirely unjustifiable practice of allowing a monk or canon to live permanently on one of the manors. When, for example, the Premonstratensian house, originally established at Otham, moved to Bayham in Sussex they left one of the canons behind to look after their estates at the old home.[2] This separation of one religious from the rest of the community was entirely opposed to the principles of claustral life, and, when practised, must often have led to disastrous results. Jocelin tells us of one such case. Four of the manors belonging to Bury S. Edmunds—Barton, Pakenham, Rougham and Bradfield—had been entrusted to the care of one of the monks, Geoffrey Ruffus, who was a good man of business. 'When the abbot heard ill reports of his morals, for a long while he concealed the matter, perchance because Geoffrey was clearly useful to the whole community. At last, when the truth was known, he suddenly caused his chests to be taken and placed in the vestry, and all the stock of the manors to be strictly guarded, and placed the said Geoffrey in the cloister. There was found a great store of gold and silver to the value of two hundred marks, and all of this the abbot decreed should be devoted to the building of the front of the shrine of S. Edmund. And when Michaelmas came it was decided in the Chapter that two brothers, and not one alone, should succeed to the custody of the manors.'[3]

During the thirteenth century demesne farming was certainly the most popular and the most profitable method of administering the monastic estates. Many of the monks were enthusiastic farmers, interested in the problems of agriculture and stock-breeding,[4] and their estates benefited by their knowledge and

[1] E.g. at Crowland (Page, *Estates of Crowland Abbey*, pp. 30–1) and Norwich (Saunders, *Introduction to Norwich Rolls*, p. 35).

[2] *V.C.H.*, *Sussex*, ii, p. 86.

[3] No doubt two would be better than one; but the fact remains that monks ought not to have been taken away from the community in order to administer the manors. See Jocelin of Brakelond, *Chron.* pp. 190–1.

[4] Several monastic library catalogues of the thirteenth century contain books on agriculture; e.g. the Peterborough catalogue includes the entry: 'Liber qui vocatur Housbondrie, Gallice'; Gunton, *History of the Church of Peterburgh* (1686), p. 224.

wisdom. On the other hand some of the religious houses found it less trouble to let their lands to lay tenants who paid a fixed rental and made what they could out of the bargain. This method relieved the monastic owners of much of their responsibility and provided them with a fixed income in cash which could be used to advantage in the local markets and fairs. As time went on this method of letting their estates became more and more popular and 'we see a withdrawal of the monasteries from an active share in the management of the sources of their income'.[1]

The great wealth of the monasteries, and the wide powers which it gave them over the lives and liberties of their tenants, carried great responsibilities and many duties. In addition to manorial administration many of the larger abbeys had very considerable powers over the towns or villages in which they were situated. At Bury S. Edmunds this 'banlieu', or exempt area, included twelve hides; at Ely it comprised the whole of the island on which the town was built;[2] at Ramsey it extended in all directions to a distance of a mile and a half from the high altar of the church.[3] Within this area the abbot and convent had complete control of the administration of justice together with various commercial and financial privileges which were highly profitable.

Our most complete information concerning these powers comes from the great abbey of Bury S. Edmunds.[4] Here the rights and privileges were shared by the sacrist and the cellarer. The sacrist not only had control of the administration of justice but also acted as archdeacon of the banlieu, thereby claiming both judicial and ecclesiastical powers over the people. The cellarer's rights lay mainly in control of the market, in the ownership of certain lands and tenements, in the collection of various taxes, and in the enjoyment of a number of monopolies, some of which caused great indignation among the burgesses.

[1] Snape, *English Monastic Finances*, p. 94; cf. R. A. L. Smith in *Canterbury Cathedral Chronicle*, May 1940, p. 15, speaking of the period after the death of Eastry in 1331.

[2] M. D. Lobel, *The Ecclesiastical Banleuca in England*, in *Oxford Essays in Medieval History presented to H. E. Salter*, pp. 123–4.

[3] W. O. Ault, *Court Rolls of the Abbey of Ramsey and the Honor of Clare*, p. xxxiii.

[4] See M. D. Lobel, *The Borough of Bury S. Edmunds* (1935).

Meanwhile, farther afield, beyond the banlieu, lay the manors with their regular courts over which some of the obedientiaries were obliged to preside. On the manors belonging to Durham the halmote court was held three times a year, the bench being occupied by the steward, the bursar and the terrar, and sometimes by the prior himself.[1] Other courts, such as those of the Abbey of S. Benet of Holme in Norfolk, were held every three weeks.[2] At Ramsey the courts were held at indefinite periods.[3] Although the main business of these courts was the enforcement of labour services we find among the convictions such offences as cutting timber without permission, bad ploughing, failure to manure the land, growing the wrong crops, coming late to the court, poaching and playing football (*ad pilam*).

The exercise of such wide judicial powers and the financial privileges which they entailed naturally led to a certain amount of friction between the monks and the laity. With the progress of municipal self-consciousness this was naturally most likely to arise in the places where the burden of monastic control seemed to be hostile to the growth of civic liberty. The very extensive privileges of the cellarer of Bury, who not only bought and sold in the market on terms which gave him a great advantage over all others but also controlled the supply of certain raw materials and levied taxes on the people of the town, caused considerable indignation in the borough; and Jocelin tells us how 'the old women appeared with their distaffs, threatening and cursing the cellarer and his men'.[4] This shaking of distaffs by the old women was one of the first signs of the determination of the burgesses to shake off the bands with which they were tied by the abbey. In 1264 the grandsons of these old women formed themselves into a gild, the *gilda iuvenum*, to try to set up their own alderman and bailiffs and so obtain some measure of freedom from monastic control.[5] Quarrels occurred between these young progressives and the monastic servants, and for a time both the sacrist and the cellarer were shut out of the town. Eventually the older and wiser men of the borough intervened

[1] Longstaffe and Booth, *Halmota Prioratus Dunelmensis*, Surtees Society, pp. xxviii–xxxi.

[2] West, *S. Benet of Holme*, Norfolk Record Society, iii, p. 230.

[3] Ault, *Court Rolls of Ramsey*, pp. xxxiv–v.

[4] Jocelin of Brakelond, *Chron.* p. 156.

[5] M. D. Lobel, *The Borough of Bury S. Edmunds*, pp. 126–7.

and the young men's gild was dissolved. Nearly thirty years later further riots took place, but the abbey was still too strong, and a long dispute ended in a sweeping victory for the monks. Resentment, however, remained; and in 1327 the anger of the townsfolk broke out again in the most serious riots of all.[1]

Most of the other big abbeys were faced with the same dangers. Townsfolk were getting restive, chafing under the constant restrictions and petty exactions of the religious houses, and from time to time resentment flared up and assaults were made either upon the monastery itself or upon its servants. At S. Albans in 1276 there was a sharp dispute between the burgesses and the abbot, who refused to let them set up their own mills.[2] At Gloucester the quarrel between abbey and town was mainly concerned with the monks' exemption from toll.[3] At Norwich a quarrel began in 1256 over the payment of land-gable, relations growing steadily worse until 1272 when serious riots took place and much of the monastery was burnt down by the mob. For this outrage the townsfolk were fined three thousand marks towards the rebuilding of the priory.[4] At York, Westminster and Colchester there was a good deal of friction,[5] and at Dunstable the people of the town complained of the action of the prior in refusing to allow the butchers to set up wooden sheds.[6]

Besides this constant friction between abbey and town there was also a certain amount of tension between the religious and the local clergy. It was, as has been already explained, comparatively rare for monks to act as parish priests,[7] and, as a rule, their paths seldom crossed. At the same time certain parochial functions were lucrative, and some of the religious houses were not averse to trying to appropriate these functions with the customary fees attached. The Cistercian Abbey of Meaux, for example, claimed the right to prove the wills and baptise the children of all their tenants, a right which, if sub-

[1] See the whole account in M. D. Lobel, *The Borough of Bury S. Edmunds*, pp. 118–42; Arnold, *Memorials of S. Edmund's Abbey*, ii, pp. xxxix–xlvii.

[2] *Gesta Abbatum Mon. S. Albani*, i, pp. 410–13, 421.

[3] Hart, *Hist. et Cart. Gloucest.* iii, pp. xxii–xxiii.

[4] Dugdale-Caley, *Monasticon*, iv, pp. 3–5.

[5] Craster and Thornton, *Chron. of S. Mary's, York*, p. 6; *V.C.H., London*, i, p. 439; *V.C.H., Essex*, ii, p. 95.

[6] Luard, *An. Mon.* iii, p. 281.

[7] See above, pp. 48–51.

Plate VI. Lay-brothers' Refectory at Fountains Abbey.

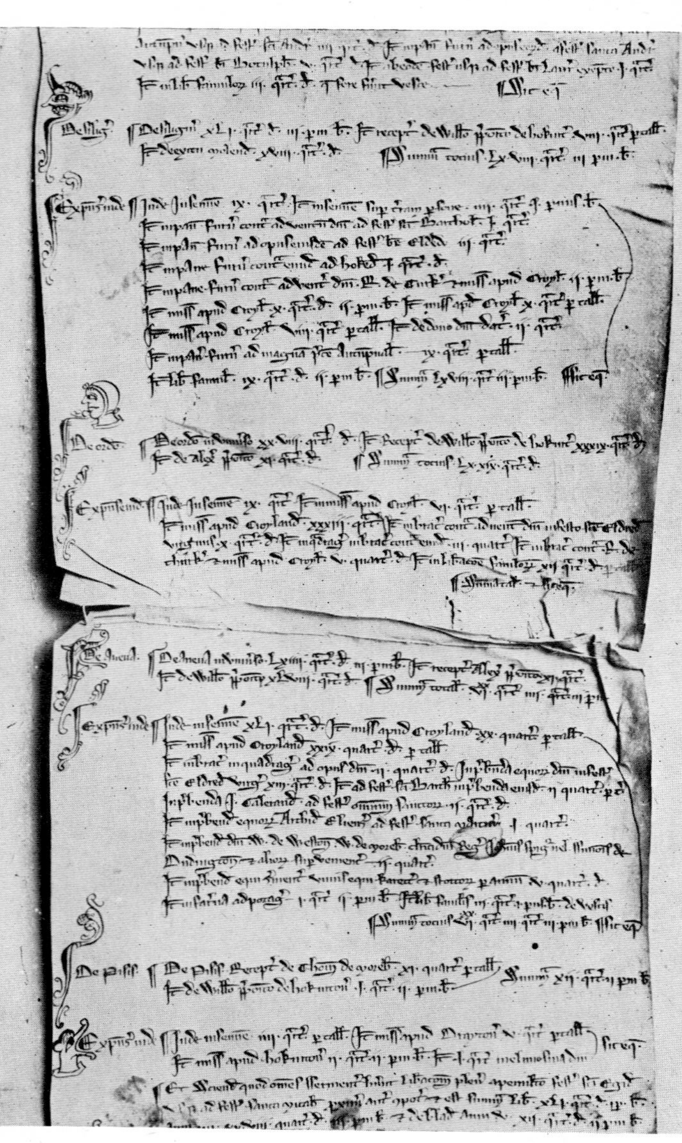

Plate VII. Crowland Abbey Account Roll, 1258.

stantiated, would have deprived the local clergy of much of their income.[1] Similarly, when Archbishop Giffard visited the parish church of S. German's at Selby he found that the font had been removed bodily from the church into the monastery, and that there was no cemetery, since all the dead were buried in the graveyard of the abbey.[2] Many of the rich ended their days in a monastery, either as corrodars or actually in the monastic habit; and they too would contribute nothing towards the parochial clergy when the end came. Friction between religious houses and the clergy arose also from conflicting claims over land,[3] and from the immunity from the payment of tithe which most monasteries enjoyed. As more and more land was bought by the monks, or given to them, so the parish clergy lost more and more of the main source of their incomes, and in such circumstances it was no wonder if a certain amount of bad blood was stirred up.

During the thirteenth century, then, the monks as a whole were beginning to hear the rumblings of popular resentment against their wealth, their privileges and their powers. Perhaps as a result of this there was some closing of their ranks against the possibility of open rebellion. We see this in an increasing number of agreements drawn up between various houses, not always of the same order, with the idea of providing some form of accommodation should the abbey fall on evil days or be brought to desolation. Such agreements had existed from early times[4] and were allowed for among the Cistercians, whose *Carta Caritatis* states that if an abbey is known to be in distress other houses must go to its assistance.[5] The same aspiration formed part of the decrees of the English Black Monks,[6] and agreements between Benedictine houses became common. S. Augustine's, Canterbury, formed treaties of mutual assistance with Bury in 1200 and with Winchester in 1254; Westminster Abbey did the same with Bury, Worcester and Malmesbury; S. Benet of

[1] Bond, *Chron. Melsa*, ii, pp. 121–2. The Cistercian Statutes include a clause forbidding their abbots and monks to baptise: Fowler, *Cistercian Statutes*, p. 24.

[2] *Regist. W. Giffard*, p. 325.

[3] See M. Paris, *Chron. Maj.* vi, pp. 87–9; Stapleton, *Chron. Petroburg.* pp. 35–8; Goodman, *Chartulary of Winchester*, p. 171.

[4] Knowles, *Monastic Order*, pp. 472–5.

[5] *Carta Caritatis*, cap. ix, in Fowler, *Cistercian Statutes*, p. 15.

[6] Pantin, *Chapters of English Black Monks*, i, pp. 19, 86.

Holme was in alliance with Bury; and Evesham with Whitby, York, Odensee and Alcester.[1] Under these agreements the houses were joined in a mutual confederation, monks from any of these houses could claim hospitality at any time at any other house allied with their own, and each Chapter agreed to say Requiem Masses for the souls of members of the other house.

More interesting are the alliances which were drawn up between houses of different orders. While it was comparatively easy (though contrary to the vow of *stabilitas* which confined every Black Monk to the house in which he was professed) for a monk of Westminster to be absorbed into the community of S. Augustine's, Canterbury, it was a very different matter for a Benedictine or Cistercian to be adopted by a house of Augustinian canons. Yet agreements between houses of different orders were sometimes made. In 1248 the Benedictines of Coventry fell into such distress that there was some danger of the house being broken up. This indeed would have occurred had not the Augustinians of Darley in Derbyshire taken pity upon them and accepted a considerable number of the Coventry monks into their cloister. This led to a close friendship between the two houses which lasted for some years, and which was cemented by an interchange of presents, the Darley canons supplying Coventry with needles and soap while the monks provided the canons with saddles and bridles.[2] Similarly the Cistercians of Bordesley were accustomed to make the Benedictines of Worcester an annual present of fifty pairs of slippers.[3] In the year 1208 an agreement was signed between the Cistercians of Furness and the Augustinians of Conishead; but the motive which lay behind this was not so much mutual aid as the desire of the stronger house to limit the influence of the weaker, for the monks of Furness imposed upon the canons of Conishead a rule that the number in their house should not exceed thirteen and that they should pay fifty shillings a quarter to the monks.[4] A good many similar treaties were drawn up between monasteries and hospitals whereby their conflicting claims were defined.

[1] *W. Thorn's Chronicle* (tr. Davis), pp. 136, 230–1; *V.C.H., London*, i, p. 438; Arnold, *Memorials of S. Edmund's Abbey*, iii, p. 2; Knowles, *Monastic Order*, p. 475.

[2] *V.C.H., Warwicks.* ii, p. 55.

[3] Wilson, *Worcester Liber Albus*, p. 9.

[4] *V.C.H., Lancs.* ii, p. 141.

Such agreements were made between S. Augustine's, Canterbury, and the hospital at Ospringe, between Chester and the hospital of S. John in the same city, and between the monks of Malmesbury and a hospital near by.[1] The arrival of the friars also led inevitably to friction with the older established houses.[2]

Quite apart from mutual agreements between different religious houses there was a certain amount of movement on the part of individuals between the different orders. Each new order tended to attract men who were already in the cloister and who desired either a greater asceticism or to associate themselves with the newest form of religious life. When the Carthusians established their first houses in England—Witham in 1178 and Hinton Charterhouse about 1225—it was inevitable that they should attract some members of other orders. Thus, in 1241, some of the monks of Christ Church, Canterbury, disgusted with the thought of having Boniface of Savoy as their Archbishop, left the monastery and were received by the Carthusians.[3] In 1287 Nicholas Thorn, having been for some years Abbot of S. Augustine's, Canterbury, left it to join the Carthusians.[4] In 1218 Walter, Prior of the Augustinian house at Merton, yearning for a stricter form of life, departed to join one of the Charterhouses. The Waverley Chronicler, in recording this event, tells us that Walter was led to take this step through 'despising the riches and pomp of the world and longing for the quiet of solitude'[5]—a very surprising statement when we remember that he was already a member of a religious order!

[1] Turner and Salter, *Register of S. Augustine's*, ii, pp. 509–10; Tait, *Chartulary of Chester*, ii, p. 299; Brewer, *Regist. Malmesburiense*, ii, p. 77.

[2] E.g. *Gesta Abbatum Mon. S. Albani*, i, pp. 385–7; Clark, *Liber Memorandorum*, pp. 209–19; Arnold, *Memorials of S. Edmund's Abbey*, ii, pp. 263–85; and see below pp. 373–6.

[3] M. Paris, *Chron. Maj.* iv, p. 105. This passage in the *Chronica* was afterwards erased, perhaps because Paris considered that it suggested that the Carthusians were better than the Benedictines.

[4] *W. Thorn's Chronicle* (tr. Davis), pp. 324–5.

[5] 'Divitias et pompam seculi spernens et solitudinis quietem diligens': Luard, *An. Mon.* ii, p. 290. The Carthusians, however, did not have it all their own way, for a decree of the Cistercians that no Carthusian was to be received by them without permission shows that there was some movement in the opposite direction: Canivez, *Stat. Ord. Cist.* i, pp. 368–9 (1210).

We hear from time to time of Benedictines going over to the Cistercians and that for various reasons. The cell at Wetherhal which belonged to the abbey of S. Mary's at York lay close to the White Monks of Holm Cultram. Wetherhal was a very small community, and it is not therefore altogether surprising to read of monks leaving the cell and being received into the Cistercian house.[1] In 1275 the Prior of S. Augustine's, Canterbury, left to join the Cistercians at Beaulieu in Hampshire, and in 1248 an Augustinian canon of Dunstable, terrified at the prospect of a visitation of the house by Robert Grosseteste, broke out, fled half-way across England, and threw himself into the arms of the Cistercians at Merevale in Warwickshire.[2] The White Monks of Sawtry in Huntingdonshire were reprimanded in 1303 for admitting apostate Dominican friars.[3]

The mendicant orders, after their arrival in this country round about the year 1220, naturally attracted a certain number of men. In 1233 two canons of Dunstable escaped from the cloister by breaking a window, and joined the Franciscans.[4] The following year the Abbot of Osney gave up his office to join the Grey Friars,[5] and in 1241 the Abbot of Walden became a Dominican.[6]

These are just a few instances which have found their way into the chronicles. There were no doubt others which are not recorded. But on the whole the movement between the various orders was probably very slight. Monastic life was not unpleasant, and, by its system of obedientiaries, held good prospects for those who showed ability and were prepared to wait until a vacancy occurred. To run away from a house in which you had struck your roots was to cut yourself off from all hope of future appointment, while the attractions of other orders were not always very powerful. In the early days of any new movement—such as the Cistercians and, later, the mendicants—we should expect to find some more ardent souls longing for the sacrifices which their stricter rules demanded; but, as

[1] Craster and Thornton, *Chron. of S. Mary's, York*, pp. 7, 29.

[2] Luard, *An. Mon.* iii, p. 178.

[3] *V.C.H., Hunts*, i, p. 391.

[4] Luard, *An. Mon.* iii, p. 133.

[5] *Ibid.* iv, p. 82.

[6] M. Paris, *Chron. Maj.* iv, p. 164. Dom Bede Jarrett says that 'an abbot of Romsey [? Ramsey] and several Benedictine priors' entered the ranks of the Dominicans, but there seems no evidence for this; see *The English Dominicans*, p. 22.

the new orders lost their original zeal, and the fires of an eager self-denial began to burn low, there was very little to tempt a man away from the cloister which he had made his home. Here, after all, lay his interests; here lay his hope of preferment. These were solid advantages to weigh against the doubtful prospects of life in a new house or in a new order.

CHAPTER XXI

FINANCIAL AFFAIRS

All the evidence which we possess—and which is considerable—goes to prove that almost every English religious house in the thirteenth century was deeply in debt. The causes of this embarrassment are many and not all of them were under the control of the monks; but the fact remains that with enormous resources, and with an income which in some houses represented a modern equivalent of at least £1000 a year for each monk, financial stability was but seldom achieved. As Mr Snape says: 'The financial difficulties of the religious houses were frequent and serious throughout the thirteenth century. They seem, if anything, to have grown more serious as the century progressed.'[1] In this chapter an attempt will be made to show what the resources of the monasteries were; what were the causes of the heavy debts which they contracted; and what efforts were made to get out of the toils of the money-lenders.

The sources of monastic income may be conveniently divided into four headings: 'temporalities', or income from land; 'spiritualities', or income from ownership of parish churches; trade and industry; and 'takings' of various kinds from well-wishers and others.

The landed estates of the monasteries were, of course, very large.[2] Some of their land lay close to the monastery—the home farms worked by the monastic servants and supplying the day-to-day needs of the monks. Other estates lay farther afield, such as the sheep-runs which Dunstable Priory owned in the Peak District. With the land went all kinds of rights and privileges which carried financial advantages with them. Many monasteries owned mills with the right to grind all the corn grown on the manor; often there were fishing rights, rights of felling timber, rights of cutting peat or reeds. Other land included such things as salt pans,[3] and Spalding Abbey claimed the right to wreckage of the sea for three leagues of the Lincoln-

[1] Snape, *English Monastic Finances*, p. 119.

[2] See above, pp. 272–3.

[3] Fowler, *Chartulary of Newminster*, p. xix; Prescott, *Wetherhal Priory Register*, p. xxv; Brown, *Guisborough Chartulary*, ii, p. 115.

shire coast.[1] Markets were another fruitful source of income, and many monasteries could also levy toll on traffic passing over or near to their estates. Abingdon, for example, took a toll of a hundred herrings from every ship passing up the Thames,[2] and at Blyth in Nottinghamshire the monks, after a dispute with the local inhabitants over the question of tolls, were allowed to take ½*d.* on every cartload of timber or bread passing through the town, and 2*d.* on every load of any other material; 1*d.* on every horseload of salmon and ½*d.* on every load of any other commodity; ¼*d.* for every pack of merchandise, ½*d.* for every horse or cow for sale, ¼*d.* for every pig or sheep, and 4*d.* on every sack of wool.[3] In 1296 the canons of Dunstable stopped a cart going through the town, taking fish to the Earl of Cornwall, and demanded toll.[4]

The second main source of monastic income came from the churches appropriated to the religious houses. This system, whereby at least two-thirds of the value of a living passed into the coffers of the monks while the remaining portion was used to pay a vicar or chaplain to minister to the people, has already been described,[5] and it will not therefore be necessary now to do more than draw attention to its being a source of great profit to the religious houses. In addition to wholly appropriated parishes the monks also drew pensions from a good many other churches. Many of these were small, but at the same time they carried no responsibilities with them and were therefore pure gain. Thus at S. Albans the kitchener owned three churches, the sacrist three churches and one pension, the refectorer five churches and two pensions, the chamberlain four churches, the infirmarer one, and the almoner a number of portions.[6] At Norwich no less than twenty-two churches within the city, and sixty-five outside, contributed in one way or another to the finances of the priory.[7] In a privilege drawn up by Eugenius III about the year 1150 for the abbey of S. Benet of Holme in Norfolk at least twenty-three churches are mentioned, even though this was in the early days of appropriations.[8] The Cluniac house of S. Andrew's at Northampton, which contained

1 *V.C.H., Lincs.* ii, p. 120.
2 Stevenson, *Chron. Monast. de Abingdon*, ii, p. 309.
3 *V.C.H., Notts.* ii, p. 85.
4 Luard, *An. Mon.* iii, p. 407.
5 See above, pp. 38–41.
6 Dugdale-Caley, *Monasticon*, ii, p. 241.
7 Saunders, *Introduction to Norwich Rolls*, p. 61.
8 Dugdale-Caley, *Monasticon*, iii, pp. 89–90.

about thirty brethren, was well supplied with appropriated churches, for a document drawn up by Hugh of Welles (and, incidentally, witnessed by Robert Grosseteste) mentions no less than twenty-four.[1] The Premonstratensians of Welbeck owned eleven parish churches.[2]

The third source of monastic income was from trade and industry. Jocelin of Brakelond has given us a remarkable picture of the cellarer of Bury S. Edmunds taking advantage of the privilege (whereby those who bought corn from him were free of toll) to sell at a higher price than the ordinary merchants.[3] Such privileges were common and were jealously regarded by the monks. As the editor of the Bury records says: 'Naturally the monks regarded the town as existing merely for the glory and by the favour of S. Edmund, and for the good of his monastery'; the conventual view was that 'the town belonged to the convent and to the altar, and specially for the purpose of finding lights for the church'. But no less naturally, the view of the burgesses of Bury was different.[4] Trade in corn was probably common, since the vast estates of the monasteries produced far more than the monks themselves would need.[5] At other houses other kinds of trade were being carried on. For example when Archbishop Walter Giffard visited the Augustinian priory of Newburgh in 1275 he found the cellarer breeding horses and doing a certain amount of horse-dealing. This, said the Archbishop, must stop.[6] Similarly at Carlisle in 1300 Adam the prior was found to be doing a brisk trade in wine.[7] The Cistercians of Newminster carried on a considerable industry in basket-making,[8] and both Rievaulx and Louth Park owned iron-mines which brought them in a good deal of money.[9]

But by far the most profitable of the trading interests of the monks was in wool. Dom David Knowles has given us an

[1] Dugdale-Caley, *Monasticon*, v, p. 19.

[2] A. H. Thompson, *Premon. Abbey of Welbeck*, p. 35.

[3] Jocelin of Brakelond, *Chron.* pp. 162–4.

[4] Arnold, *Memorials of S. Edmund's Abbey*, ii, p. xxxviii.

[5] R. A. L. Smith, *High Farming on the Canterbury Estates*, in *Canterbury Cathedral Chronicle*, May 1940, p. 12.

[6] *Regist. W. Giffard*, pp. 328–30.

[7] *Regist. J. Halton*, i, pp. 119–22.

[8] Fowler, *Chartulary of Newminster*, p. xix.

[9] Atkinson, *Chart. of Rievaulx*, pp. 57–60; Lincolnshire Record Society, *Chron. of Louth Park*, p. xxx.

account of the almost accidental way in which the Cistercians, seeking out the wildest parts of the country for their habitations, found a new and extremely profitable source of income in the breeding of sheep. 'Among the village communities of England previous to the thirteenth century', he writes, 'there was little facility or incentive for sheep-farming on any scale.[1] In the great plain counties, and the inhabited valleys of the west and south-west, good enclosed pasture was reserved for horses and cattle, and waste land was either forest or heath; in the wolds and moorlands of the north the population was too scanty and conditions too unsettled for any exploitation of the grassland. But it was precisely in these desolate open spaces that the White Monks first settled; wool was necessary for their habits and cowls, and it so happened that their sheep were set to graze upon the rolling pastures of Lincolnshire and Yorkshire, which ever since that time have proved among the best in the world for the rearing of noble sheep and the production of the finest fleeces. Sheep farming on a large scale, which had been utterly outside the purview of the small village cultivator, fettered as he was by divided strips, fold-service and labour-dues, was eminently practicable under the grange system of the Cistercian abbeys in the valleys of Lincolnshire, Yorkshire and, later, North Wales, and before the reign of John the annual yield of wool of their fleeces had become one of the assets of the country.'[2]

To the Cistercians certainly belongs pride of place in the wool industry of this country in the thirteenth century, but other orders were equally energetic in those parts of the country where there was good grassland. Bolton Priory in Wharfedale had every opportunity for successful sheep-farming on the moors of Craven. In the year 1301 the canons owned over 2000 sheep and a considerable portion of their income came from the sale of wool.[3] Similarly the Dunstable canons kept a number of

[1] This statement should be supplemented and corrected by reference to Eileen Power's *Medieval English Wool Trade*, where it is shown that 'thousands of peasant farmers all over England were keeping sheep' (p. 29).

[2] Knowles, *Monastic Order*, p. 352. In 1301 Kirkstall had 4000 sheep on their manors (Dugdale-Caley, *Monasticon*, v, p. 528) and in 1270–80 Meaux had 11,000 (Bond, *Chron. Melsa*, ii, pp. 156–7). Vaudey in 1291 made over £200 from wool (Dugdale-Caley, *Monasticon*, v, p. 489).

[3] Whitaker, *History of Craven*, pp. 327–8, and Burton, *Monasticon Eboracense*, pp. 121–33. See also Snape, *English Monastic Finances*, p. 93 for a discussion of the financial aspects.

sheep on some land which they owned in the Peak District as well as on the Chilterns nearer home. How large their flocks were is not recorded, but in 1243 the annals record the death of 800 of their sheep in Derbyshire.[1] The Black Monks showed less aptitude for sheep-farming on a big scale, but a few houses certainly kept large flocks. Durham pastured a good many sheep on the northern moors,[2] and when Michael of Ambresbury, Abbot of Glastonbury, retired in 1252 he left the manors well stocked with over 6700 sheep.[3] Again, the South Downs in Sussex lent themselves so admirably to sheep-farming that we are not surprised to find that the Cluniac priory of Lewes had discovered how profitable the production of wool could be, or that when it was visited in 1279 it was found to be in possession of 6000 sheep.[4] The Gilbertines of Malton in Yorkshire also did well out of the flocks which they pastured on the wolds, since during fourteen years from 1244 to 1257 they made over £5224.[5]

The wool trade, therefore, in many parts of the country was a most profitable concern. Tracts of country which had been chosen as the most bleak and barren that could be found had been turned by this 'accident' into a source of great wealth, and the religious houses were quick to see their good fortune and to seize the opportunities which were given to them. First, the wool gave them warm clothes with which to face the rigours of the northern climate; then, as supplies increased, they found a ready sale in the neighbourhood; and finally the monks opened up negotiations with Flemish and Italian merchants. Indeed the people of Louth in Lincolnshire complained very bitterly in the thirteenth century that since the monks paid no tolls or market-dues they could undersell their neighbours in the Flemish wool trade and thereby gain an unfair advantage.[6]

The fourth source of monastic income was from 'takings' of one sort or another, some of them voluntary offerings and some rights to which the monks were entitled. Many of these were associated with manorial customs such as the heriot or

[1] Luard, *An. Mon.* iii, p. 163; cf. also pp. 160, 195, 305–6.

[2] Fowler, *Durham Account Rolls*, ii, p. 487, where the Bursar's accounts for 1278 include 9*s.* for dipping and shearing sheep.

[3] Domerham, *Historia de rebus gestis Glastoniensibus*, ed. T. Hearne (1727), ii, pp. 522–3.

[4] Duckett, *Visitations of Cluniacs*, pp. 35–6.

[5] Graham, *Ecclesiastical Studies*, p. 264.

[6] Lincolnshire Record Society, *Chron. of Louth Park*, pp. xxxi–xxxii.

payment due when a man died. Others arose through the appropriation of churches, the monks often claiming some portion of the offerings of the people. In the town parishes these may have amounted to a good deal, but in country districts, where there was less ready money, they can never have been very large, and some portion of them was almost always reserved for the vicar.[1] On the other hand the offerings of pilgrims and worshippers at the abbey churches were often very considerable. The shrine of S. Thomas at Canterbury was an attraction to pilgrims from all over the world and provided the monks of Christ Church with a substantial income. The receipts of the treasurers in 1220, the year of the translation of the martyr's bones from the crypt to the new shrine, were £2707, and a high figure was maintained for many years.[2] Canterbury was exceptional and not every abbey had a 'holy blisful martir' whom the faithful would long to visit and at whose shrine they would be willing to cast their crowns and guineas. But the sacrist of Norwich reckoned on an annual income of some £60 or £70 from collections in the cathedral priory,[3] and even at Ely, in its solitary, fenland glory, well over £22 a year was taken out of the boxes by the high altar and the cross by the font.[4]

Apart from the offerings of the faithful the monks often added to their incomes by various 'pickings'. At Reading and Bury, for example, they had the right of coining;[5] at Peterborough the abbot collected a certain amount each year from the property of felons and fugitives,[6] while the Malmesbury monks made a small income of thirty shillings a year from organising feasts or scot-ales, in spite of the fact that these were constantly banned by episcopal constitutions.[7]

[1] See above, p. 127.

[2] Sheppard, *Literae Cantuarienses*, ii, p. xlvi. See also C. E. Woodruff, *The Financial Aspect of the Cult of S. Thomas of Canterbury*, in *Archaeologia Cantiana*, 1932, pp. 13–32.

[3] Saunders, *Introduction to Norwich Rolls*, p. 102.

[4] Chapman, *Sacrist Rolls of Ely*, ii, pp. 12–13.

[5] Dugdale-Caley, *Monasticon*, iv, pp. 33–4; M. D. Lobel, *The Borough of Bury S. Edmunds*, p. 53.

[6] £41 in 1285: Stapleton, *Chron. Petroburg*. pp. 119–24.

[7] These scot-ales were held three times a year—on the Sunday before Michaelmas Day, the fourth Sunday in Advent and the fourth Sunday in Lent: Brewer, *Regist. Malmesburiense*, ii, p. 85. For episcopal denunciations of scot-ales see Wilkins, *Concilia*, i, pp. 530, 574, 635, 672; R. Grosseteste, *Epistolae*, p. 162.

Yet another source of income, irregular but sometimes very valuable, was provided by the gifts of newcomers to the community or of those who desired to be received by the monks into their 'fraternity'. According to the Rule of S. Benedict postulants were either to distribute all their property to the poor, or, by a solemn deed of gift, they might make it over to the monastery. The choice seems to have lain entirely with the man himself.[1] No doubt many rich men who sought admission brought large sums with them, and monastic finances must often have benefited considerably by these windfalls. We know, for example, that when William of Tourney, Dean of Lincoln, having been deposed by Grosseteste, sought shelter with the Cistercians of Louth Park in 1239 he brought a very considerable fortune with him.[2] About the same time a rich landowner of Holderness, Sir John Fryboys, having helped the monks of Meaux for some years, entered the house as a novice, no doubt bringing a good deal of wealth with him.[3] This custom of old men taking the habit in their declining years, or even on their death-bed, was often a great financial asset to the monks. Not only was it a common belief that a monk stood a better chance of salvation than anyone else, but, in days when medical service was extremely primitive, by far the best hospitals were the infirmaries of the monks, and many a layman knew that he would get more comfort and better treatment there than in his own home. But in order to enter the monastic infirmary a man must take the habit. Hence arose the custom known as *ad succurrendum*.[4] In some ways it was an obvious abuse. It introduced into the cloister men with no vocation to the monastic life, and it was very often made to depend upon the ability of the postulant to pay heavily for the privilege. It was no wonder, then, that the early Cistercians, in their desire to break away from the cash-nexus which bound the older monasteries, legislated against it.[5]

[1] *Reg. S. Ben.* cap. lviii.

[2] Lincolnshire Record Society, *Chron. of Louth Park*, p. xxxvii.

[3] Bond, *Chron. Melsa*, ii, pp. 28–9.

[4] This explains the problem left unresolved on p. 123 of S. W. Williams' *Cistercian Abbey of Strata Florida*, where he mentions the large number of distinguished people who died at the abbey, and appears to be under the impression that the public were admitted if not to the infirmary at least to some other part of the precincts.

[5] Knowles, *Monastic Order*, p. 477; cf. Coulton, *Five Centuries*, i, pp. 93–4; iii, pp. 19–20.

A further link between the monks and the laity—and incidentally a further source of income to the former—was the system of Fraternities. These had grown up in fairly early times as a means whereby lay men and women could be brought into spiritual fellowship with the religious houses, demand burial in the monastic cemetery, and thereafter count upon the prayers of the monks. In the twelfth century, when the monasteries stood high in public estimation and were receiving extensive gifts from the laity, this system of fraternities was popular. In the thirteenth century, when the passion for endowing monastic houses was dying down, the enrolment of *confratres* became less common, though it continued down to the Dissolution.[1] That the privilege was often granted to benefactors is natural enough, though it opened the door to what appeared on the surface to be no more than a business transaction. For example, when we read that about the year 1200 Serlo de Plesley gave four bovates and sixteen acres of land, and pasture for 100 sheep, 10 cows and a bull to the Augustinian canons of Felley in Nottinghamshire in exchange for membership in the fraternity and permission to be buried with the canons, it is difficult not to see in this a perfectly simple example of a religious house selling a privilege to a man who could afford to buy it.[2] Similarly in 1285 William de Roos, lord of Ingmanthorpe, gave to the canons of Healaugh Park two bovates of land in North Deighton, in exchange for which he and his wife, Eustachia, and their sons and daughters were received into the fraternity of the house.[3] Poor men with nothing to contribute to the monasteries may have been given this privilege, but there is no evidence of this from the thirteenth century.

Another privilege which the religious houses exchanged for gifts of land or money was the right to nominate to membership of the community. This was important both to the regulars themselves and to their benefactors. The tendency in the religious houses during the thirteenth century was to keep the numbers down, since every additional member was an extra financial burden to the house.[4] On the other hand the monasteries pro-

[1] Knowles, *Monastic Order*, pp. 475–6.

[2] *V.C.H.*, *Notts.* ii, p. 110.

[3] Purvis, *Chart. of Healaugh Park*, pp. 77–8.

[4] This does not apply to the nunneries, which tended to grow very large and were frequently ordered to reduce their numbers: Power, *Medieval English Nunneries*, p. 213.

vided the laity with an exceedingly convenient asylum for poor relations and younger sons who had not much opportunity of standing up to the struggle for existence. It was therefore not unnatural that laymen should want to buy such right of presentation to a religious house, or that the regulars should be willing to grant it only at a price. The chronicles and chartularies of the monasteries contain a number of such agreements. For example, at Merton, towards the end of the twelfth century, the Prior and Convent sold to Luke de Hardres the right of presentation to a canonry in the house.[1] In 1261 the Augustinians of Selborne were engaged in a sharp dispute with Ralph de Camays, Kt., about the advowson of West Tisted Church. The Prior and Convent eventually won their case, but the price which they had to pay for it was to grant to Ralph the right to present 'one fit clerk' to be a canon of the house.[2] In 1281, in return for various benefactions by Master Simon de Eylondia, the Prior and Convent of S. Botolph's at Colchester bound themselves to maintain an extra canon, presumably to be nominated by the said Master Simon.[3]

With so many sources of income there would seem to be no excuse for the financial chaos in which so many of the religious houses of this country were sunk. Almost everywhere we turn among monastic chronicles and records we are brought up against a picture of insolvency and of almost desperate remedies to get out of the toils of the moneylenders. In some houses incompetence and extravagance were responsible for debts which assumed such gigantic proportions that the community had to be dispersed among other houses until some sort of order could be brought to their financial affairs.

There could surely be no better picture of financial disorder and anxiety than the opening pages of the Chronicle of Jocelin of Brakelond. 'In those days', he writes, 'Abbot Hugh grew old, and his eyes were dim. He was a good and kindly man, a godfearing and pious monk, but in temporal matters he was unskilful and improvident. . . . The townships and all the hundreds of the abbot were given to farm; the woods were destroyed, and

[1] Heales, *Records of Merton*, pp. 31–2. The price in this case is not mentioned.

[2] Macray, *Charters and Documents of Selborne*, p. 54.

[3] *V.C.H.*, *Essex*, ii, p. 149.

the houses on the manors were on the verge of ruin. From day to day all things grew worse. The abbot's sole resource and means of relief was in borrowing money, so that it might at least be possible to maintain the dignity of his house. For eight years before his death, there was never an Easter or Michaelmas which did not see at least one or two hundred pounds added to the debt.' Jocelin then goes on to explain how each obedientiary was contracting debts of his own, how 'golden vessels and other ornaments of the church' were being pawned, and how everyone turned for help to the Jews who roamed about the monastery and even invaded the sanctuary during High Mass in their endeavours to wring something out of the unhappy monks.[1]

Jocelin's account is the most intimate and picturesque which we possess, but the more prosaic records tell the same story. Matthew Paris tells us that the monks of Christ Church, Canterbury, in spite of the great financial asset of the 'holy blisful martir', were over £2500 in debt in 1255, while at Rochester the debts were 'inestimable'.[2] Gloucester and Peterborough each had a debt of £2000 about the middle of the century,[3] while S. Mary's Abbey at York in 1300 owed no less than ten thousand marks (£6666) to the Earl of Lincoln.[4] Even the small priory of Dover, a cell to Canterbury, ran up a debt of nearly £800.[5] Pecham on visiting Reading Abbey in 1281 found what he called an 'intolerable burden of debt',[6] and at Winchester in 1286 the prior was so heavily involved in debt that he could not meet the demands of his monks.[7] Eynsham and both the Canterbury houses were, like Bury S. Edmunds, in the toils of Jewish moneylenders,[8] while the monks of Bath were reduced to borrowing from the local clergy.[9] At Ramsey in 1300 the abbot had got into such financial difficulties that the monks

[1] Jocelin of Brakelond, *Chron.* pp. 1–6 and 15.

[2] M. Paris, *Chron. Maj.* v, pp. 502–3.

[3] Dugdale-Caley, *Monasticon*, i, p. 533; Stapleton, *Chron. Petroburg.* p. 20.

[4] Craster and Thornton, *Chron. of S. Mary's, York*, p. 31.

[5] Haines, *Dover Priory*, p. 235.

[6] Pecham, *Reg. Epist.* i, pp. 223–6 and cf. Dugdale-Caley, *Monasticon*, iv, pp. 30, 32; *Regist. R. Swinfield*, p. 165.

[7] Goodman, *Chart. of Winchester*, pp. 53–4.

[8] Salter, *Eynsham Cartulary*, i, p. 235; *W. Thorn's Chronicle* (tr. Davis), pp. 249–50; R. A. L. Smith, *Central Financial System of Christ Church, Canterbury*, in *E.H.R.* 1940, p. 356.

[9] Hunt, *Two Chartularies of Bath*, pp. 84–5, 87.

refused to accept any responsibility for his debts and, knowing his love of music, threatened to cut off the singing in the choir until the abbot got himself out of 'Queer Street'.[1]

The Cistercians, in spite of their flourishing trade in wool, were no better off than the Benedictines. Bruerne in 1284 owed over 2000 marks; Meaux in 1270 had debts of £3678; Kirkstall in 1284 was in debt to the tune of £5248, while Fountains was in such a bad way at this time that the Archbishop of York had to report to the Abbot of Clairvaux to inform him that the monks of Fountains were 'temporally ruined', 'in a desperate condition', 'a cause of scandal and derision to the whole kingdom', 'in dire need and lamentable poverty'.[2]

The Cluniac houses visited in 1262 and 1275 were almost all in debt, Lewes to the extent of 4000 marks and Pontefract of 3200.[3] Bermondsey became deeply involved in debt through the foolishness of Abbot John, who allowed himself to get into the toils of Adam de Stratton, a notorious moneylender.[4] The Augustinians fared no better. In 1267 the canons of Bolton had borrowed £324 from their neighbours, and by 1300 their debts were £445.[5] Dunstable owed 400 marks in 1262, Newburgh was over £700 in debt in 1275, Nostell by 1328 had contracted debts to a sum of more than £1000, and in 1231 some of the canons of S. Oswald's at Gloucester were sent into exile because they had pledged their house to the Jews.[6]

The results of this appalling insolvency were sometimes disastrous. The time came when even the patience of the moneylenders could last no longer and monks and canons were reduced to the position of beggars, depending upon what charitable neighbours would give them. In 1275 the monks of Faversham

[1] Macray, *Chron. Abb. Rameseiensis*, p. 393. See also, for other Benedictine houses, Evans, *Ely Chapters*, in *Camd. Misc.* xvii, p. viii; M. Paris, *Chron. Maj.* iv, p. 586; Wilson and Gordon, *Early Compotus Rolls of Worcester*, pp. 15–23.

[2] For Bruerne: *V.C.H.*, *Oxon.* ii, p. 80; for Meaux: Bond, *Chron. Melsa*, ii, pp. 156–7; for Kirkstall: Dugdale-Caley, *Monasticon*, v, p. 528; for Fountains: Walbran, *Memorials of Fountains*, i, pp. 180–2.

[3] Duckett, *Visitations of Cluniacs*, pp. 33, 35–6.

[4] R. Graham, *La Charité-sur-Loire and Bermondsey*, in *Eng. Eccl. Studies*, pp. 102–5.

[5] *Regist. W. Giffard*, pp. 145–6; Whitaker, *History of Craven*, p. 327.

[6] For Dunstable: Luard, *An. Mon.* iii, p. 221; for Newburgh: *Regist. W. Giffard*, pp. 328–9; for Nostell: Dugdale-Caley, *Monasticon*, vi, p. 90; for S. Oswald's: Luard, *An. Mon.* i, p. 78.

were found to be practically starving, since they had been so long in debt that no one would give them credit and their stocks were exhausted.[1] In 1228 the canons of Grimsby received permission to go begging for alms,[2] and there was a time when the canons of S. Augustine's at Bristol were reduced to the same straits.[3] In 1301 one of the canons of S. Oswald's at Gloucester complained that he and his companions were getting ill through lack of food,[4] and at Rochester in 1200 the monks were reduced to melting down the silver shrine of S. Paulinus in order to supply themselves with a little ready cash.[5] At the small Cluniac house of S. James' at Exeter the visitors in 1279 could not be received by the canons, who had sunk into such poverty that only the prior and one aged colleague remained.[6] In 1253 the nuns of S. Mary's at Chester were found to be going out daily asking for alms,[7] and in 1284 Pecham found that the nuns of Romsey were starving.[8]

The causes of all this poverty and debt were many, and not all of them were within the control of the monks themselves. Taxation and forced loans, civil disturbances and Scottish raids, floods and fires, bad harvests and murrain; all these made great inroads on the resources of the monasteries.[9] The very serious outbreak of disease among sheep, which began in 1276 and lasted for many years, was partly responsible for the collapse of some of the big Cistercian houses and of all those which depended upon the wool trade. On top of all this there was the continuous burden of providing hospitality, which fell most heavily upon those houses which stood on or near the main thoroughfares.

On the other hand much of the financial distress from which the religious houses suffered was due to the extravagance and incompetence of the monks themselves. Most monasteries were busy with building operations during the thirteenth century,

[1] *V.C.H., Kent*, ii, p. 138. [2] *V.C.H., Lincs.* ii, p. 161.

[3] *V.C.H., Gloucs.* ii, p. 77. During the disastrous abbacy of Roger Norreys at Evesham the monks were obliged to go out begging in the neighbourhood; see Macray, *Chron. Abb. de Evesham*, pp. 238–40.

[4] *V.C.H., Gloucs.* ii, p. 96.

[5] Dugdale-Caley, *Monasticon*, i, p. 156.

[6] Duckett, *Visitations of Cluniacs*, pp. 25–6.

[7] Power, *Medieval English Nunneries*, p. 172.

[8] Pecham, *Reg. Epist.* ii, pp. 651, 659–60.

[9] See above, pp. 248–50.

seeing nothing incongruous in spending vast sums on erecting new and sumptuous buildings at a time when the state of their finances demanded the most rigid economy. Meanwhile the monks' standard of living remained high, in spite of those statutes which tried to check luxury and extravagance.[1] But perhaps the most potent cause of poverty was to be found in lack of business ability. Many abbots like poor old Hugh of Bury were totally incompetent to administer the complicated finances of a large abbey with an income of some hundreds of thousands of pounds in modern currency. Abbot Hugh, as Jocelin tells us, was in complete ignorance of the condition of affairs in his own monastery and allowed himself to be hopelessly deceived as to the state of its finances.[2] Nothing but his death, and the force and wisdom of his successor Samson, saved the house from disaster.

Abbot Hugh must have been typical of many heads of houses who ought never to have accepted administrative responsibility. Over and over again we come across mismanagement and recklessness plunging a house into debt from which it tries to get free by shortsighted policies which promise a quick return but do nothing to remove the real cause of the disaster.[3] Typical of these expedients was the sale of corrodies. Faced with mounting debts, and with the indignity of having to argue with dunning Jews who forced their way into the sanctuary of the church during divine service, many an abbot was thankful to be able to lay his hands suddenly on a little ready money, even though it meant placing a burden on his successors which they might be totally unable to support. In the same way much land was sold during these years, often at a low price, simply in order to settle some account which had become too pressing to be comfortable. By these desperate remedies no real solution of the problem was achieved, and unless some really able ruler could be found to set their house in order the monks fell into poverty and their buildings into decay and dilapidation.[4]

[1] M. Paris, *Chron. Maj.* vi, p. 238. See below, Chapter xxiii.

[2] Jocelin of Brakelond, *Chron.* pp. 4–5.

[3] For example, the Cistercians of Pipewell were desperately in need of money in 1280, some of which they raised by chopping down their woods and cutting off the tops of growing trees to sell as firewood. *V.C.H., Northants.* ii, p. 118.

[4] At Felley in 1276 the rain was coming into the church and the infirmary: *Regist. W. Giffard*, pp. 316–18; at S. Clears in 1279 the visitors

Such, indeed, were the conditions in a good many houses, but there were convents in which financial stability was sought along the road of discipline, retrenchment and efficiency. To our way of thinking, the normal way to get out of debt is to consider what economies may be effected, but this method does not seem to have occurred so readily to the monks, who generally regarded retrenchment as the very last resort when all other methods had failed.

Jocelin of Brakelond shows us how, under the firm rule of Samson, the financial troubles of Bury S. Edmunds were largely removed. Master Denis the cellarer halved a debt of £60 by rigid economies, and Samson himself helped to restore order by enjoining both obedientiaries and monks to take their meals in the refectory instead of in their own rooms.[1] At S. Albans, at about the same time, the monks agreed to give up wine for fifteen years in order to save money for the building of the dormitory.[2] A century later, at Reading, Abbot Whaplode, with a view to introducing economies, formed a committee of eight monks with whose help he managed to cut down days of feasting to ten in the year, and, while maintaining the ordinary allowances of bread and beer for the convent, cut out all the tasty and expensive extra dishes which had become part of the daily fare of the monastery.[3]

Similar economies were also from time to time forced upon the religious houses by visiting bishops. In 1277 Thomas Cantilupe ordered the canons of Chirbury to cut down their expenses in food and clothing in order to carry out some necessary repairs to their church and to the outer wall of the monastery;[4] John of Pontissara demanded economies in food at Winchester in 1286, and Archbishop Winchelsey did the same at Dover Priory in 1299.[5] At Glastonbury, Ely and Winchcombe efforts were made to check the extravagance of the

wrote that 'as far as constructions or buildings go in the aforesaid house they may be considered nil for everything has been made away with': Duckett, *Visitations of Cluniacs*, p. 26. Cf. also Oliver, *Monasticon Dioc. Exoniensis*, p. 204 (Hartland), and Macray, *Chron. Abb. de Evesham*, p. 240.

[1] Jocelin of Brakelond, *Chron.* pp. 8 and 140.

[2] *Gesta Abbatum Mon. S. Albani*, i, p. 220.

[3] Coates, *History and Antiquities of Reading* (1802), pp. 285–7.

[4] *Regist. T. Cantilupe*, pp. 147–8.

[5] Goodman, *Chartulary of Winchester*, pp. 53–5; Haines, *Dover Priory*, pp. 252–6.

abbot or prior,[1] while at Gloucester and Thurgarton some reduction of hospitality was suggested.[2]

Apart from economies there were two other ways whereby financial order and stability might be achieved. One was to institute a regular audit of the monastic accounts; the other was to appoint one or two members of the community to act as treasurers for the whole house. At Winchester it appears that there was a regular audit of accounts soon after the middle of the twelfth century;[3] and there is not much doubt that, when the Council of Oxford in 1222 ordered all obedientiaries and heads of houses to present half-yearly or quarterly accounts to a committee of the monks, it was only trying to make general what was already being done in a number of houses.[4] The introduction of the obedientiary system had led to considerable confusion and loss. Jocelin tells us that no less than thirty-three of his fellow-monks at Bury were found to have their own seals, and were quietly contracting debts without the knowledge of the Chapter or of the abbot himself.[5] As a result of episcopal visitations a strenuous effort was made to see that accounts were regularly rendered. The terms varied from once a year at Reading to once a week at Evesham.[6] Meanwhile the monks and canons were themselves anxious to see that a proper system of accountancy was introduced into every house. The Benedictine Chapters ordered all abbots to give an annual report on the state of their houses and also to present their accounts either once or three times a year.[7] The Cistercians insisted

[1] Pecham, *Reg. Epist.* i, pp. 259–65; Evans, *Ely Chapters*, in *Camd. Misc.* xvii, p. 25; *Regist. A. Orleton*, p. 69.

[2] Dugdale-Caley, *Monasticon*, i, p. 533; *Regist. T. Corbridge*, i, pp. 272–3.

[3] R. A. L. Smith, *The 'Regimen Scaccarii' in English Monasteries*, in *Trans. R. Hist. Soc.* 1942, p. 74.

[4] Wilkins, *Concilia*, i, p. 590.

[5] Jocelin of Brakelond, *Chron.* p. 60, and cf. p. 2.

[6] *Regist. R. Swinfield*, pp. 165–9; Dugdale-Caley, *Monasticon*, ii, pp. 27–31. Cf. also *Regist. W. Wickwayn*, pp. 147–8 (Blyth, 1280); *Regist. R. Winchelsey*, pp. 852–6 (Boxgrove, 1300); Raine, *Hist. Dunelm. Scriptores Tres*, p. 72 (Durham, 1283); Thompson, *Cust. of S. Augustine's, Canterbury, and S. Peter's, Westminster*, i, pp. 34–5 (S. Augustine's, 1273–83); Raine, *Priory of Finchale*, Preface, p. xxii; *Regist. J. Romeyn*, i, pp. 199–202 (Bridlington, 1287); *Regist. G. Giffard*, pp. 100–2 (S. Augustine's, Bristol); Pecham, *Reg. Epist.* ii, pp. 645–9 (Mottisfont, 1284).

[7] Pantin, *Chapters of English Black Monks*, i, pp. 36, 84–5, 238; M. Paris, *Chron. Maj.* iii, p. 501.

upon their cellarers giving an annual financial statement,[1] and the Augustinians expected all their obedientiaries to keep the convent informed of their dealings either once or twice a year.[2] William Hotot, Abbot of Peterborough, about the year 1246 ordered the treasurers whom he appointed to give an annual account of their stewardship,[3] while Samson at Bury audited his accounts every week.[4]

The other method of introducing greater efficiency into the monastic accountancy was to appoint one or two of the monks to act as bursars or treasurers for the whole house. Christ Church, Canterbury, seems to have been one of the pioneers in this movement. As early as 1169 there is evidence of a treasurer at this house,[5] and in 1202 Archbishop Hubert Walter, who must have known something of the system at Canterbury, ordered the monks of Ramsey to nominate three of their members as 'receivers' to handle the entire income of the abbey.[6] The idea was then taken up by the Augustinians who, in 1220, decreed that every house should in future have two receivers who should be responsible for all money coming in.[7] In 1233 Archbishop Gray imposed a similar arrangement at Selby, and it was introduced into Peterborough about 1246.[8] Seeing, as he said, how well this system was working in other houses,[9] Pecham made it one of his favourite methods of trying to save the monasteries from financial chaos. At Glastonbury, for example, in 1281 he ordered that all money, including that of the abbot, should go into one account, to be paid out by the treasurers. Any obedientiary who raised any objection was to be deprived of his office for three years. Any surplus at the year's end was to be devoted towards paying off the debts which the abbey had contracted.[10] In the same year he

[1] Fowler, *Cistercian Statutes*, p. 67.

[2] Salter, *Augustinian Chapters*, pp. 22–3 (1220).

[3] Sparke, *Hist. Anglic. Scriptores Varii*, p. 126.

[4] Jocelin of Brakelond, *Chron*. p. 66.

[5] R. A. L. Smith, *The 'Regimen Scaccarii' in English Monasteries*, in *Trans. R. Hist. Soc.* 1942, p. 74; cf. also his article on the finances of Christ Church, Canterbury, in *E.H.R.* 1940, pp. 353–4.

[6] Hart and Lyons, *Cart. Mon. de Rameseia*, ii, pp. 204–7, and cf. Dugdale-Caley, *Monasticon*, ii, p. 580.

[7] Salter, *Augustinian Chapters*, pp. 22–3.

[8] *V.C.H., Yorks.* iii, pp. 96–7; Sparke, *Hist. Anglic. Scriptores Varii*, p. 126.

[9] Pecham, *Reg. Epist.* ii, p. 622.

[10] *Ibid.* i, pp. 259–65.

introduced a similar reform at Reading, which was followed up by the Bishop of Salisbury in 1284 and by Pecham again in 1285 when he appointed twelve of the monks to see that the accounts were not faked, and gave orders that any obedientiary who got into debt was to be put in prison.[1] In at least eleven other houses similar reforms were introduced.[2] There was, of course, nothing new in Pecham's methods; what was new in his policy was his invariable insistence upon the combination of treasurers and auditing committees.[3]

Anxious though the reformers might be to introduce a uniform system of accountancy it is clear that their efforts were only partially successful. We can well understand that obedientiaries who had had almost unlimited freedom in the management of their financial affairs resented any interference and clung tenaciously to their seals and their separate incomes. At some houses it was found to be impossible to touch the revenues which were definitely allocated to separate departments.[4] At the same time, the twofold method of establishing a central bursary and of arranging for a regular scrutiny of accounts helped to save the monasteries from financial disaster.

In all these instances the monks themselves were considered competent to manage their affairs so long as these were put on right lines. In many houses, however, there was no one to be found with sufficient ability to handle their financial affairs, and it therefore became necessary to apply for assistance outside. This was especially true of the nuns, whose finances were constantly falling into a state of chaos. The poor things had so little training in money matters that they were often quite incapable of handling the considerable incomes which their houses enjoyed. It therefore became advisable to put the whole finances of the nunneries into the more capable hands either of a local monk or canon or of some neighbouring parish priest. The nunnery at Swine in Holderness was regularly managed by one of the Premonstratensian canons of Croxton, Catesby by a regular from Canons Ashby, Grimsby by a canon of Wellow, and Handale and Basedale by a monk of Whitby.[5] Pecham put

[1] Pecham, *Reg. Epist.* i, pp. 223–6; *Regist. R. Swinfield*, pp. 165–9.
[2] Snape, *English Monastic Finances*, p. 40.
[3] R. A. L. Smith in *Trans. R. Hist. Soc.* 1942, p. 78.
[4] *Ibid.* pp. 81–3; *E.H.R.* 1940, pp. 358–9.
[5] *Regist. J. Romeyn*, i, pp. 203–4; Power, *Medieval English Nunneries*, p. 231 n.; *V.C.H., Lincs.* ii, p. 179; *Regist. W. Giffard*, p. 54.

the finances of Davington, Usk and the Holy Sepulchre, Canterbury, and Romeyn those of Arthington, Wilberfoss, Moxby and Sinningthwaite, in the hands of some local clergyman.[1]

Several monasteries were driven to a similar expedient. Rochester in 1255 put its affairs into the hands of John of Gaddesdon who, according to Matthew Paris, was so severe in the economies which he demanded that the monks complained that they could scarcely subsist on the very short commons which he allowed them.[2] Bindon Abbey summoned the assistance of Henry de Montfort in 1275,[3] and both Bruerne and Grimsby sought secular help early in the following century.[4] But by far the commonest action for a convent which had fallen upon evil days was to surrender to the King, who generally appointed one of his clerks to examine the affairs of the monastery and to see what could be done to establish financial stability. Reading and Luffield among the Benedictines; Aberconway, Flaxley, Fountains and Waverley among the Cistercians; and Healaugh Park, Newstead and Thornholm among the Augustinians were all driven to this expedient during the thirteenth century, followed a few years later by Bardney, Bittlesden, Grimsby and Bicknacre.[5]

If none of these methods availed then there was no other course than for a house to be dispersed until its finances could be put on a solid basis. Coventry, as we have seen, was in danger of dispersion in 1248 but was rescued by the generosity of the Augustinians of Darley;[6] on the other hand the convent of S. Mary's, York, was actually broken up for a time between the years 1253 and 1255.[7] Earlier in the century, during the troubles of the Interdict, both Waverley and Meaux were scattered;[8] and, later in the century, other Cistercian houses suffered the same calamity. The monks of Woburn were dispersed for

[1] Pecham, *Reg. Epist.* i, pp. 72–3, ii, pp. 708–9, iii, p. 806; *Regist. J. Romeyn*, i, pp. 234, 157, 86.

[2] M. Paris, *Chron. Maj.* v, p. 503. [3] *V.C.H., Dorset*, ii, p. 83.

[4] *V.C.H., Oxon.* ii, p. 80; *V.C.H., Lincs.* ii, p. 161.

[5] Dugdale-Caley, *Monasticon*, iv, p. 30; *V.C.H., Bucks.* i, p. 348; Ellis, *Reg. et Chron. Aberconway*, in *Camd. Misc.* i, p. 10; *V.C.H., Gloucs.* ii, p. 95; Walbran, *Memorials of Fountains*, i, p. 182; *V.C.H., Surrey*, ii, p. 83; Purvis, *Chart. of Healaugh Park*, p. 227; *V.C.H., Notts.* ii, p. 113; *V.C.H., Lincs.* ii, p. 167; *ibid.* pp. 98, 161; *V.C.H., Essex*, ii, p. 144.

[6] See above, p. 290.

[7] M. Paris, *Chron. Maj.* v, pp. 362–3, 503.

[8] Luard, *An. Mon.* ii, p. 255; Bond, *Chron. Melsa*, i, pp. 353–4.

a time in 1234, and Flaxley in 1281.[1] By this time the murrain among sheep was hitting the Cistercians very hard and in the 'eighties and 'nineties Kirkstall, Fountains, Rievaulx, Bruerne and Pipewell all applied to the Chapter General for dispersion.[2] After the disasters of the Scottish raids in 1297 the canons of Hexham had to be sent to Bridlington since their own priory had suffered so terribly from the invasion.[3]

Such were the vicissitudes through which many of the monastic houses were passing during the thirteenth century. As we read these records of insolvency, and of the desperate remedies which were sometimes adopted by the monks to get out of the clutches of their creditors, we cannot fail to be struck by the extraordinary vitality of the religious houses and by their powers of recuperation. Reading some of the records which have survived, especially those of the smaller houses crippled with debt and dilapidations, and sometimes reduced to a mere handful of men, we should expect to find at least some trace of complete collapse and annihilation. And yet it is true to say that not a single religious house in this country perished until long after the close of the thirteenth century. Even houses which had been dispersed somehow managed to coalesce after a few years and to pick up again the threads which they had had so hurriedly to throw down.

The roots of this vitality lay partly in the fact that, although a monastery might fall on evil days, it had, behind it, vast resources. Most religious houses were, by the thirteenth century, heavily endowed; and though by extravagance or by incompetence they might become deeply in debt, they still had their property behind them; and if they had to surrender some of this to raise a little ready money, they could always throw themselves on the charity of their bishop, and, by pleading poverty, acquire the appropriation of some parish church to replace what they had, by their own carelessness, lost. Nor must we be misled by the colossal debts which the monks contracted. Most of them were no doubt of their own making, but some were taken over from benefactors who, tired of resisting

[1] Luard, *An. Mon.* iii, p. 140; Canivez, *Stat. Ord. Cist.* iii, p. 215.

[2] Canivez, *Stat. Ord. Cist.* iii, pp. 212, 258, 266, 286.

[3] Raine, *Hexham Priory*, i, p. lxxxvi, and cf. *Regist. T. Corbridge*, i, pp. 170–1, for S. Oswald's, Gloucester, in 1302. The Gilbertine house at Chicksands was dispersed for a time in 1257: Luard, *An. Mon.* iii, p. 205.

the demands of their creditors, were glad to hand over the whole burden to some religious house together with a gift of some acres to sugar the pill. In a sense it is true to say that, in the Middle Ages, everyone lived on credit, just as industry is nowadays run on a capitalist basis. Landowners, both ecclesiastical and lay, were burdened with enormous debts which they had neither the power nor the intention of clearing and which they handed on, as they themselves had received them, to their heirs or successors.

All these things helped to carry the monasteries through evil times and to save them from disaster. But the greatest thing of all was the fact that, under God, periods of mismanagement and incompetence in a community were often terminated by the appearance of some really strong man who was able to bring order out of chaos and to save his house from disaster. We see this at Bury, where the ability and courage of Samson were able to restore the ravages of poor old Hugh's dotage. The same thing happened at Evesham, where the disasters caused by Roger Norreys were repaired by the wisdom of Abbot Ralph and his successor Thomas de Marlberge. No doubt if our records were more complete many such examples of the cycle of decay and reform could be quoted. So long as the monastic system could continue to produce men of administrative and financial ability there would be no danger of houses becoming submerged beyond hope of recovery.

CHAPTER XXII

DAILY LIFE OF THE MONASTERIES

The accumulation of large estates profoundly influenced the daily life of the monks. So long as religious communities remained small groups of men wedded to the simple life and living on the proceeds of their own labours in the fields immediately surrounding the cloister it was possible for them to regulate their lives according to a definite time-table or *horarium*. But by the thirteenth century this primitive type of religious life had disappeared. The monks were now landowners on a large scale and employers of labour, and were invested with all the powers and responsibilities of manorial tenure. With so many duties to perform, and with so much business to transact, it had become impossible for many of the monks to adhere to any regular time-table or to devote to the activities of the cloister the time which these normally required.

S. Benedict had quite clearly in his mind the sort of programme to which he expected his monks to adhere. Part of the day was to be devoted to the worship of God, part to reading and meditation, and part to manual work. The hours devoted to each of these would vary considerably according to the length of daylight. The difficulties of determining at what hour any particular event actually took place are very great. In days when the only method of measuring time was by water-clocks, sundials or candles, and when the hour was reckoned not as the twenty-fourth part of a whole day but as a fraction of the time when the sun was above the horizon, it was clearly impossible to keep to any programme which would remain constant. Efforts therefore to fix the exact hours, according to modern reckoning, at which events in the daily life of the monks took place are doomed to failure,[1] and every statement concerning time must be regarded as only approximate.

[1] This is illustrated by the attempts made to draw up an *horarium* by Dom Cuthbert Butler and Dom David Knowles. Both have studied the monastic regulations with great diligence but their conclusions differ widely—e.g. Butler makes the monks retire to bed at 5.0 p.m. in winter whereas Knowles puts the time as 6.30 p.m. There are actually only a few points at which they are in entire agreement. See C. Butler, *Benedictine Monachism*, pp. 278–83; D. Knowles, *Monastic Order*, pp. 448–53, 714–15. For an attempt to draw up a programme for the Cistercians see J. T. Micklethwaite in *Yorks. Arch. Journal*, 1900, pp. 260–5.

Visitors to monastic ruins, or to some surviving portion of a medieval religious house such as Hexham Priory, are often struck by the presence of the night staircase. This immediately suggests to their minds the thought of men rising from their warm beds in the middle of the night and descending into a cold and draughty church to sing their night office. It is indeed true that monks rose every morning between 1.30 and 2.30 a.m. and that their first office began at 2.0 or 3.0 o'clock in the morning. The reason for this very early start is to be found in two phrases in the Rule of S. Benedict, one of which says that the monks' day must end before sundown, the other that the brethren shall rise 'at the eighth hour', which was roughly 2.0 a.m.[1] The result of this was that while the monks' day was in fact no longer than ours it was always five hours ahead of our modern manner of living. We tend nowadays in winter time to rise at dawn and sit for some five hours by artificial light at the end of the day. The unfortunate monk was obliged to *begin* his day with five hours of darkness, retiring to bed at about 6.0 o'clock when darkness fell. In summer time he rose at 1.30 a.m. and went to bed at 8.0 in the evening, but he also had a siesta of two hours in the early afternoon.

Under this arrangement the monk could count upon eight hours of sleep both in summer and winter. Of the sixteen waking hours the regulations allowed for four to be devoted to the saying of the offices, one to meals, about four to reading, and the remaining seven to work of various kinds.[2]

S. Benedict called his experiment at Monte Cassino 'a School of the Lord's Service', and it is clear from his legislation that he intended the recitation of the divine office to take first place in the daily life of his monks.[3] The liturgical injunctions of the Rule are however designed to work hand in hand with the other activities of the monks, a balance being held between physical, intellectual and spiritual pursuits. When this equilibrium was upset by the changing conditions of monastic life and the disappearance of manual labour there was a tendency

[1] *Reg. S. Ben.* cap. xli and viii. Cf. Butler, *Benedictine Monachism*, pp. 277–8.

[2] These figures are only approximate, as the time-table varied considerably from summer to winter. In the Cluniac houses the divine office occupied a good deal more time than in the Benedictine and Cistercian monasteries.

[3] *Reg. S. Ben.* cap. xliii, where he says that nothing must come before the *Opus Dei*.

to lengthen the periods of worship, in order, as Dom Cuthbert Butler says, 'to give them [the monks] something to do and to keep them occupied'.[1] By the thirteenth century the burden of these much enlarged offices was felt to be too irksome. The monks were busy men; and, in order to get through their day's work some of them were getting into habits of arriving late or of going out before the service was over, while some even stayed away altogether.[2] In order to meet the demands of the times, and also to bring some order out of the confusion which had arisen, the Benedictine Chapter General of 1277 made a deliberate attempt to cut out some of the accretions which had arisen and to return to the standards of the Rule.[3] This experiment was no doubt made in the hope of restoring a regular and general attendance of the whole community when the offices were said. But the evidence of later years shows that these aspirations bore but little fruit. When Pecham visited the priory of Christ Church, Canterbury, in 1281 he found many of the convent absenting themselves from the services, especially in the early morning, and ordained that those who were absent from Mattins, Mass or the Canonical Hours were to lose their pittances on that day. A few years later Winchelsey found that little improvement had been made, and in 1298 had to order all the monks to come punctually when the bell was sounded and to stay for the whole of the worship.[4] At Glastonbury, Reading, Worcester and elsewhere similar instructions were given.[5]

The Cluniacs had a far heavier programme of daily worship than either the Black or White Monks, and it is encouraging to know that when Bermondsey and Wenlock were visited in 1262 it was found that the services were being properly carried out. On the other hand, in some of the smaller houses such as S. Clears, Monks Horton and S. James', Exeter, they were either 'totally neglected' or performed in a hurried and slovenly manner.[6]

[1] C. Butler, *Benedictine Monachism*, p. 296.

[2] On this see Knowles, *Monastic Order*, pp. 451–2. The obedientiaries, he says, attended the services only 'partially and occasionally'.

[3] Pantin, *Chapters of English Black Monks*, i, pp. 22–3, 60, 67–71.

[4] Pecham, *Reg. Epist.* i, pp. 341–8; *Regist. R. Winchelsey*, pp. 91–3, 814. Cf. *W. Thorn's Chronicle* (tr. Davis), p. 280.

[5] Pecham, *Reg. Epist.* i, pp. 259, 223–6; *Regist. R. Winchelsey*, p. 873. See also M. Paris, *Chron. Maj.* iii, p. 502; vi, p. 235; Pantin, *Chapters of English Black Monks*, i, p. 256 (1287).

[6] Duckett, *Visitations of Cluniacs*, pp. 13–15, 20–2, 25–7, 36–7.

Among the canons regular the same tendency to neglect the offices is noticeable. In 1223 the General Chapter held at Newburgh legislated against this habit, and there is evidence of negligence and haste from various Augustinian houses during the century.[1]

Despite attempts to accommodate busy men by shortening the offices it appears that there were some in every Chapter who had become very casual about their attendance. There is evidence of this even in so orthodox a document as the Decrees of Lanfranc. In the section devoted to the abbot, careful instructions are given to allow the abbot to sleep quietly in the morning if he wishes to do so. No one is to make a sound while the abbot lies abed, and, if he sleeps long, the schoolmaster must get the boys up in silence and make them sit quietly until the abbot awakes.[2] If this was the sort of example set by the abbot, can we wonder if humbler members of the monastery became careless about their attendance in the early morning?[3] And how could regulations against sleeping during the services be enforced if the monks knew that their father-in-God was peacefully sleeping upstairs while they were trying to keep awake in a cold, dark church?

In S. Benedict's monastery Mass was said only on Sundays and upon the greater festivals. As time went by, and the number of priests in each community grew, it was inevitable that there should be more frequent celebrations, and by the thirteenth century at least one Mass was said each day. The modern custom of requiring every priest to celebrate a daily Mass had not been generally enforced by this time, and there is a good deal to show that some of the regulars who were in priest's orders said Mass only on rare occasions. In 1202 the Chapter General of the Cistercians noted that the Abbots of Aberconway, Caerleon and Valle Crucis celebrate very seldom (*rarissime*) and absent themselves from the altar.[4] The General Chapter of the Black

[1] E.g. Newburgh, Bridlington and Bolton (*Regist. W. Wickwayn*, pp. 55–6, 87–8, 131–3); S. Augustine's (Bristol), and Llanthony (*Regist. G. Giffard*, pp. 100–2, 87–9); Coxford (Pecham, *Reg. Epist.* i, pp. 162–5); Breamore (*V.C.H., Hants.* ii, p. 170); Leeds (*Regist. R. Winchelsey*, pp. 844–6); Leighs (*Regist. R. Baldock, etc.* pp. 112–15).

[2] Lanfranc, *Decreta*, in Migne, *Patr. Lat.* vol. cl, col. 483.

[3] See, for example, Pecham, *Reg. Epist.* iii, p. 823; Raine, *Hexham Priory*, i, App. pp. xvii–xxii; *Regist. W. Giffard*, pp. 145–6.

[4] Canivez, *Stat. Ord. Cist.* i, p. 281.

Monks in England in 1256 also took notice of this tendency to neglect one of the primary duties of a priest and ordered all priest monks not to abstain from celebrating for more than four days at a time.[1] In 1268 this was endorsed by the papal legate, Ottobon.[2]

Similar conditions prevailed among the Austin canons. At the Chapter held at Nostell in 1253 it was ordained that any priest in good health who for eight consecutive days does not say Mass is to be cut off from the rest of the community. But this decree does not seem to have achieved much success, for thirty-five years later the Chapter put on record the fact that some priest canons were refusing to celebrate for fifteen days or even a month at a time, and declared that any who absent themselves from the altar for more than eight days are to fast on bread and water.[3] At Wigmore in 1318 Bishop Orleton demanded that canons in priest's orders should say Mass every day.[4]

This evidence of reluctance to offer the Sacrifice of the Mass sounds strange in our ears. Yet during the thirteenth century we find numerous attempts being made by the monks themselves to avoid the responsibility of officiating at the altar. Most monks were at this time in priest's orders, and it would seem therefore that there should be no shortage of celebrants. Nevertheless our records leave us in no doubt that in many religious houses secular chaplains were employed to relieve the monks of the duty of saying Mass. We find, for example, in the account books of the Sacrist of Ely a sum of 10*s*. which was paid each year to a secular chaplain, while one of the Bishops of Ely, William Kilkenny, left 200 marks in his will to endow two chaplains in the priory to pray for his soul.[5] At Evesham, Abbot Henry, about the year 1260, appointed and paid a chaplain to say a daily Mass for the monks;[6] the monks of Chester supported two chaplains to celebrate in the abbey for the soul of one of

[1] Pantin, *Chapters of English Black Monks*, i, pp. 70–1.

[2] Wilkins, *Concilia*, ii, pp. 18–19. At Ely priest monks were to celebrate at least once in three days: Evans, *Ely Chapters*, in *Camd. Misc.* xvii, p. 7. Cf. also *W. Thorn's Chronicle* (tr. Davis), p. 281, for neglect at S. Augustine's, Canterbury.

[3] Salter, *Augustinian Chapters*, pp. 33, 44–5.

[4] *Regist. A. Orleton*, pp. 99–102.

[5] Chapman, *Sacrist Rolls of Ely*, i, p. 4; Wharton, *Anglia Sacra*, i, p. 636.

[6] Macray, *Chron. Abb. de Evesham*, p. 281.

their benefactors, Sir William Burnell;[1] and at Ramsey in 1285 the abbot, William of Gomescestre, left money to endow a secular priest.[2] At Durham, clerks were paid to sing the Psalter on All Souls' Day—obviously with the intention of relieving the monks of this onerous task.[3] The same applied to the Augustinian houses. Barnwell, for example, supported two chaplains, students of the University of Cambridge, as well as three stipendiary priests in the almonry.[4]

It is beyond any doubt that S. Benedict intended his monks to do their own manual work. 'The brothers must occupy themselves in manual work' he writes; and again: 'true monks are they when they live by the labours of their hands'.[5] This does not necessarily mean that the monks did all the heavy work of the fields, but it does assume that manual work was a definite and inescapable part of the monks' daily life.[6] Gradually, however, this manual work was allowed to disappear from the monks' time-table. Under the monastic revival in this country in the tenth century very little heavy agricultural work was done by the monks, and by the year 1200 it had become 'a thing of the legendary past'.[7] The Cistercians in the twelfth century made some effort to revive manual labour among the choir-monks, but this experiment very soon died out. Canons were always exempt from working with their hands, except for small, light tasks about the house.

Against this background it is interesting to notice the few references to manual work in the records of the thirteenth century. In 1215 the water which supplied the lavatory of the

[1] Tait, *Chartulary of Chester*, i, pp. 224–5.

[2] Hart and Lyons, *Cart. Mon. de Rameseia*, ii, pp. 233–5.

[3] Fowler, *Durham Account Rolls*, ii, p. 484.

[4] Clark, *Liber Memorandorum*, pp. 94, 96–7. See also Fowler, *Dunstable Charters*, p. 166; Purvis, *Chart. of Healaugh Park*, p. 90.

[5] *Reg. S. Ben.* cap. xxxv, xli, xlvi, xlviii: 'Occupari debent fratres in labore manuum'; 'Vere monachi sunt si labore manuum suarum vivunt.'

[6] Knowles, *Monastic Order*, pp. 6–7; cf. C. Butler, *Benedictine Monachism*, pp. 285–6.

[7] Knowles, *Monastic Order*, p. 687. But it is interesting to note that in 1279 the Black Monks asked at their General Chapter how they could be expected to do manual work if they attended all the services and the lectures in theology: Pantin, *Chapters of English Black Monks*, i, p. 74. Is this evidence of a desire to re-introduce manual labour into the monks' daily life?

Cistercians at Waverley dried up; and one of the monks, Simon by name, undertook to make a new conduit in order that there might be running water in which the brethren could wash their hands. That a choir-monk should attempt so arduous a task fills the chronicler with admiration and surprise.[1] In 1250 Archbishop Gray of York visited the Augustinian canons of S. Oswald's, Gloucester. He found that some of them had been helping in the fields, leading hay and engaging in other rural pursuits (*opera rusticana*), and ordered them to desist at once.[2] In 1279 the Cluniac visitors came to the small cell of S. Clears where, to their obvious surprise and dismay, they found the prior 'taking upon himself all sorts of manual labour'.[3]

Except for one or two strange individuals who shocked or grieved their fellows by digging drains or making hay, the regulars as a whole had given up manual work altogether. But this naturally left a good deal of time on their hands which it was the duty of the authorities to fill. Thus it came about that in 1277–9 the Chapter General of the Black Monks ordered all abbots to give their monks plenty to do 'in the place of manual work'.[4] Many monks were already fully occupied with the administration of their departments. For the rest intellectual work was suggested such as reading, copying, illuminating or correcting manuscripts.

Sacred study had been from the first an important element in the life of the cloister. S. Benedict had laid down instructions as to the hours which his monks were to devote to their reading and had decreed that books suitable for the *divina lectio* should be given out at the beginning of Lent.[5] Archbishop Lanfranc had enlarged upon this in his constitutions drawn up about the year 1070. According to his statutes all the books were to be brought together into the chapter house on the Monday after the first Sunday in Lent, there to be laid out upon a carpet. Each brother would then bring to the Chapter the book which he had borrowed twelve months previously; and, when he heard

[1] Luard, *An. Mon.* ii, pp. 284–5. The Chronicler describes how Brother Simon applied himself to the problem of providing a new water supply and how he bravely girded himself and 'with much toil and sweat' dug the new channels through which the water was to run.

[2] *Regist. W. Giffard*, pp. 204–6.

[3] Duckett, *Visitations of Cluniacs*, p. 26.

[4] 'Loco operis manualis': Pantin, *Chapters of English Black Monks*, i, p. 74.

[5] *Reg. S. Ben.* cap. xlviii.

his name read out, he was to step forward, hand in the volume which he had read, and receive a new one in its place. If he had been idle and had neglected to read the book he must confess his fault.[1] When we consider that the monk had had a whole year in which to read a single volume we may be surprised that this last sentence was considered necessary; but it is wise to remember that manuscript books are not read as easily as printed works, that the reader was meant to meditate at length upon what he read, and that medieval volumes often contained several separate works.

The Carthusians received two books each, which they carried away to their cells, and of which they were instructed to take the utmost care. The Augustinians and Premonstratensians were also intended to do a good deal of reading, since the customs provided not only for a regular distribution of books but also for a collection to be 'kept at hand for daily use...in some common place to which all the brethren can have easy access for inspection and selection of anything which seems to them suitable'.[2] The same arrangement of a number of open presses from which the brethren could help themselves obtained among the Benedictines of Christ Church, Canterbury.[3] At Reading a separate collection of books was kept in the dormitory to be read in the refectory, or in church, or privately at night.[4]

From the very earliest times the monasteries had been collectors of books[5] and by the year 1200 most of the houses had

[1] Lanfranc, *Decreta*, in Migne, *Patr. Lat.* vol. cl, coll. 453–4. J. W. Clark points out that Lanfranc must have had the Cluniac Customs in mind when he drew up this regulation: J. W. Clark, *The Care of Books*, p. 68. Lanfranc himself gave a number of books to the library at Christ Church, Canterbury: M. R. James, *Ancient Libraries of Canterbury and Dover*, pp. 52–3, 88.

[2] J. W. Clark, *Barnwell Observances*, p. 15, and cf. *The Care of Books*, pp. 70–2.

[3] M. R. James, *Ancient Libraries of Canterbury and Dover*, pp. xl–xli.

[4] S. Barfield, *Lord Fingall's Cartulary of Reading Abbey*, in *E.H.R.* 1888, pp. 113–25; J. R. Liddell, *Some Notes on the Library of Reading Abbey*, in *Bodleian Quarterly Record*, 1935, pp. 47–54.

[5] A good deal of work on monastic libraries has been done in recent years; see especially: E. A. Savage, *Old English Libraries*; N. R. Ker, *Medieval Libraries of Great Britain*; G. Becker, *Catalogi Bibliothecarum Antiqui*; J. W. Clark, *The Care of Books*; F. S. Merryweather, *Bibliomania in the Middle Ages*; E. Edwards, *Memoirs of Libraries*; and M. R. James, *The List of Libraries prefixed to the Catalogue of John Boston*, in *Collectanea Franciscana*, vol. ii.

considerable collections.[1] During the next hundred years notable additions were made to these libraries both by the monks themselves and by gifts from outsiders. Chronicles of monastic history from time to time mention benefactors who enriched the libraries of the house, and many ancient catalogues of the libraries give the names of donors. We have, unfortunately, no catalogue of the library at S. Albans, which must have been among the very finest in the country, for this house was renowned for its learning and support of the arts. All that we know is that Abbot Roger, who died in 1290, gave to the library a number of law books, a copy of Seneca which he had written himself and various other books and pamphlets.[2] Many monastic libraries were indebted to their abbots for gifts of books. Thomas de Marlberge of Evesham was a notable benefactor who enriched the monks' library with books on theology and grammar, civil and canon law, medicine and history, besides volumes of Cicero, Lucan and Juvenal.[3] At Glastonbury Abbot Henry towards the close of the twelfth century had made notable additions to the library,[4] which by the year 1247 was very extensive.[5] Another abbot, John of Taunton, bequeathed some forty volumes, including some modern theology, in 1290.[6] Many of the abbots of Peterborough were collectors of books, a number of which seem to have found their way into the convent library. Some of the volumes, however, appear to have been passed on from one abbot to another. A copy of Grosseteste's *Templum Domini*, for example, which appears among the books of Walter of S. Edmund

[1] There is a catalogue of an unidentified monastery of the twelfth century in Becker, *Catalogi Bibliothecarum Antiqui*, pp. 216–17; of Burton-on-Trent *c.* 1175 in *Zentralblatt für Bibliothekswesen*, ix, pp. 201–3; of Bury S. Edmunds *c.* 1200 in James, *On the Abbey of S. Edmund at Bury*, pp. 23–32; of Durham, cent. xii, in *Cat. Vet. Librorum Ecc. Dunelm.* pp. 1–10 and in *Durham Cathedral MSS.*, ed. R. A. B. Mynors, pp. 10–11; of Rochester in 1202 in *Arch. Cantiana*, iii, pp. 47–64; of Whitby, cent. xii, in Becker, *Cat. Bibl. Ant.* pp. 226–7, and of Welbeck, cent. xii, in James, *Cat. of MSS. at S. John's Coll., Cambridge*, pp. 10–13. See also J. S. Beddie, *Libraries in the Twelfth Century*, in *Haskins Anniversary Essays*.

[2] *Gesta Abbatum Mon. S. Albani*, i, p. 483.

[3] Macray, *Chron. Abb. de Evesham*, pp. 267–8.

[4] Hearne, *History and Antiquities of Glastonbury* (1722), pp. 141–3.

[5] *Numerus Librorum Glaston. Ecclesiae anno 1247*, in John of Glastonbury, *Chronica*, ed. Hearne, ii, pp. 423–44.

[6] *Ibid.* i, pp. 251–2. The modern theology included works by Robert Kilwardby and Thomas Aquinas.

who died in 1245, during Grosseteste's own lifetime, appears to have been inherited by two subsequent abbots, William Hotot and John de Cauz.[1] The Cistercian house at Newenham which was founded in 1247 owed the beginnings of its library to its first abbot, John Godard, who gave the monks what was probably his own library of twelve volumes on theology and grammar.[2]

S. Augustine's at Canterbury was another house which owed much to generous abbots. To the very extensive collection which had been built up perhaps since the days of S. Augustine himself most of the thirteenth-century abbots made bequests, from the gift of a Bible and book of canon law made by Robert de Bello in 1252 to the splendid collection of 114 volumes bequeathed by Thomas Fyndon in 1309.[3] At the cathedral priory of Christ Church there was another magnificent library which included among its benefactors such great names as Lanfranc, Anselm and Thomas Becket.[4] Most of the thirteenth-century priors added to the collection, the most valuable bequest being that of John de Sidingbourne (1222–32), who appears to have left some thirty-five volumes to the house including works by Stephen Langton and Alexander Neckham.[5]

Apart from the larger bequests made by abbots and priors many monastic libraries were growing steadily by small gifts from the monks themselves or from outsiders. The catalogue made by Prior Eastry at Christ Church (Canterbury) sometime before 1331 gives the names of those who presented books to the library. So far as these names can be identified no less than sixty-six belong to the thirteenth century. Similarly at Ramsey, which had a most interesting library, many of the books came in small bequests from members of the house, local clergy, and others.[6] The library of the Grey Friars at Exeter was founded in 1266 by Roger de Thoris, Archdeacon of Exeter, who gave his books to the friars on condition that they might also be consulted by the Dominicans.[7] The Franciscan library at Oxford

[1] Dugdale-Caley, *Monasticon*, i, pp. 355–6.

[2] J. Davidson, *History of Newenham Abbey*, p. 14.

[3] M. R. James, *Ancient Libraries of Canterbury and Dover*, pp. lxxii–lxxiii, and, for Robert de Bello, pp. 197, 398.

[4] *Ibid.* pp. xxix, xxxi, xli–xlii.

[5] *Ibid.* pp. 109–11.

[6] Macray, *Chron. Abbatiae Rameseiensis*, pp. 356–67.

[7] Little and Easterling, *Franciscans and Dominicans of Exeter*, p. 59; Oliver, *Mon. Dioc. Exon.* p. 332.

probably received its first considerable collection of books from Adam Marsh, who inherited the library of his uncle, Bishop of Durham, in 1226. In 1253 Grosseteste left to this library all his books, a few of which have been identified in recent years.[1]

There was, thus, much expansion of monastic libraries during the thirteenth century and some very fine collections were formed, among the most extensive being those of the two Canterbury houses, Bury S. Edmunds, Durham, Peterborough and Glastonbury. In each of these libraries the books ran into many hundreds, while in many other houses there were smaller but yet adequate collections to provide the monks with material for their reading for many years according to the pace which was then usual. Catalogues dating from the thirteenth or early fourteenth century have survived for the Benedictine houses of Reading, Coventry, Leominster, Deeping, and Durham College at Oxford;[2] for the Cistercian houses of Rievaulx and Flaxley,[3] for the Cluniacs of Bermondsey, the Augustinians of Anglesey, Waltham and one of the northern houses, possibly Bridlington;[4] and for the Premonstratensians of S. Radegund's near Dover.[5]

Although by the thirteenth century the system of offering boys to the monasteries at an early age had been abandoned many of

[1] Little, *Grey Friars in Oxford*, pp. 57–60. The Franciscans were such keen collectors of books that in 1357 Richard Fitzralph, Archbishop of Armagh, said that 'in the faculties of Arts, Theology, Canon Law, and, as many assert, Medicine and Civil Law, scarcely a useful book is to be found in the market, but all are bought up by the friars' (*ibid.* pp. 60–1). Richard de Bury in the *Philobiblon* also bore witness to the friars' passion for book-collecting.

[2] For Reading see S. Barfield, *Lord Fingall's Cartulary of Reading Abbey*, in *E.H.R.* 1888, pp. 113–25, and J. R. Liddell, *Some Notes on the Library of Reading Abbey*, in *Bodleian Quarterly Record*, 1935, pp. 47–54; for Coventry, Dugdale-Caley, *Monasticon*, iii, p. 186; for Leominster, S. Barfield, in *E.H.R.* 1888, pp. 123–5; for Deeping, Dugdale-Caley, *Monasticon*, iv, p. 167; and for Durham College, H. E. D. Blakiston, *Some Durham Coll. Rolls* in Oxford Hist. Soc., *Collectanea*, iii, pp. 36–8.

[3] For Rievaulx see M. R. James, *Cat. of MSS. at Jesus College, Cambridge*, pp. 45–56; and, for Flaxley, *Zentralblatt für Bibliothekswesen*, ix, pp. 205–7.

[4] For Anglesey (Cambs) see E. Hailstone, *History and Antiquities of Bottisham and the Priory of Anglesey*, Camb. Antiq. Soc. 1873, p. 247; for Waltham, M. R. James, *MSS. from Essex Monastic Libraries*, in *Essex Arch. Soc. Transactions*, 1937, pp. 41–5; and for (?) Bridlington, *Zentralblatt*, ix, pp. 203–5.

[5] For S. Radegund's see A. H. Sweet, *The Library of S. Radegund's Abbey*, in *E.H.R.* 1938, pp. 88–93.

the religious houses had been places of education and we should therefore expect to find in their libraries the standard books on grammar, together with the mathematical, musical and scientific works which formed the basis of the *Quadrivium*. When we turn to the catalogues we find it as we expect. At Bury, Glastonbury, Durham, Reading, Ramsey, Peterborough, Rochester and the two Canterbury houses books necessary for the arts course are common. In later years these books came into their own again when an attempt was made to raise the intellectual standards of the monks.[1]

More important were the theological works, of which there were vast quantities. Most catalogues of monastic libraries begin with the Bible, several copies of which were often to be found. The monks of Christ Church (Canterbury) had, early in the fourteenth century, no less than thirty-five copies, besides many separate books of the Scriptures and a wealth of commentaries. 'It is a calumny without a shadow of foundation to declare that the monks were careless of Scripture reading' says a Victorian writer who was a severe critic of monasticism as a whole.[2] Miss Deanesly has shown more recently that although the monks were well supplied with Bibles not all of them could read them.[3] But the fact remains that, in so far as the regulars studied at all, they had abundant opportunity for reading the Vulgate. At Christ Church (Canterbury) there were also copies of *Genesis* and of *Acts* in Anglo-Saxon and three French Psalters,[4] while the monks of S. Augustine's and of Ramsey had French Bibles.[5] Greek and Hebrew were very little studied in the religious houses, the chief exception being at Ramsey, where Robert de Dodford and Gregory of Huntingdon, about the middle of the thirteenth century, devoted themselves to the study of these languages and provided themselves with a Hebrew Bible, some Hebrew commentaries, a Hebrew Grammar and Phrase-book, a Greek Grammar and two Greek Psalters. All of these passed in due course into the monastic library.[6]

[1] See below, pp. 328–33.

[2] Merryweather, *Bibliomania in the Middle Ages*, pp. 24–5.

[3] M. Deanesly, *The Lollard Bible*, pp. 168–74.

[4] M. R. James, *Ancient Libraries of Canterbury and Dover*, pp. 51, 111, 129.

[5] *Ibid*. p. 198; Macray, *Chron. Abbatiae Rameseiensis*, p. 356.

[6] Macray, *Chron. Abbatiae Rameseiensis*, p. 365. See also a copy of the Greek and Hebrew alphabets at Christ Church, Canterbury: M. R. James, *Ancient Libraries*, p. 40.

Patristics were always very well represented in the monks' libraries. In most catalogues this class occupies a large proportion of the whole collection. Augustine was the most widely read, but most libraries had copies of Ambrose, Jerome, Origen, Basil, Gregory the Great and Cyprian. Copies of Irenaeus, on the other hand, were extremely rare, the only known volume having been at Christ Church, Canterbury. Among the more recent standard authors we find all the great names represented —Anselm, Bernard, Bede, Alcuin, William of Auxerre, Ivo of Chartres, Peter Lombard and many others. The libraries also took pains to keep up to date, for, as the thirteenth century progressed, we find books by Stephen Langton, Adam Marsh, Alexander of Hales, Richard Fishacre, Alexander Neckham and of course Robert Grosseteste. By the end of the century most of the large libraries had good collections of the works of Bonaventura and Thomas Aquinas.

Copies of the Rule of S. Benedict, often with running commentaries and occasionally in a French translation, were known in most of the libraries of the Black Monks; and some houses had copies of the Rule of S. Basil and S. Pachomius,[1] while the Peterborough library numbered among its volumes a copy of the Testament of S. Francis and the Rule of the Grey Friars.[2]

History was represented by the standard *Historia Scholastica* of Peter Comestor and by various chronicles and local histories. There were also large collections of the Lives of various saints from the Apostles to Thomas of Canterbury. Most libraries also contained the necessary law books, which were no doubt constantly consulted in the interminable litigation in which so many of the monastic houses were involved; some of the larger libraries had copies of the decrees of the Lateran Councils and of the constitutions issued by English prelates and the two legates Otto and Ottobon.[3] Scientific works were collected in fairly large numbers, partly for practical purposes, partly for use in teaching. Medical books in great variety were very much in evidence, many of them in the vernacular, and they were no doubt used by those who served in the infirmary or who worked

[1] M. R. James, *Ancient Libraries*, p. 132; Dugdale-Caley, *Monasticon*, i, p. 358.

[2] S. Gunton, *History of the Church of Peterburgh*, pp. 173–224.

[3] See, for example, M. R. James, *Ancient Libraries*, pp. 50, 70, 74, 79, 134.

outside the cloisters as general practitioners.[1] Among the medical books should be included Herbals and various other botanical and biological works.

Almost all the monastic libraries, except those of the Cistercians,[2] contained large collections of the classics. Virgil, Horace, Ovid, Juvenal, Cicero, Pliny, Seneca, Plautus, Terence are all found in fairly large quantities, together with a great many of the minor classical authors. Plato, Aristotle and even Homer were known in Latin translations.[3] Service books were, of course, kept in vast quantities. Ramsey Abbey had over a hundred Psalters and seventy Breviaries, and most of the larger houses must have had almost as many.

Finally, most book lists contain a certain number of volumes which seem a little out of place in the cloister. Glastonbury, for example, had a book on matrimony, Peterborough had two books on chess and some French romances, and Christ Church, Canterbury, possessed a spiritualistic work entitled: *Disputatio inter spiritum puellae post mortem et amatorem suum.*

The monks, therefore, had every opportunity for reading, if they were anxious to do so. A considerable part of each day could be devoted to intellectual pursuits by those who kept themselves free from administrative work, and at almost any time of the day members of the community would be found in the cloister engaged upon reading or writing. In early days the monks sat together in the cloister; but as time went by the custom arose of dividing a part of the cloister into small alcoves or 'carrells' in which the student would not only enjoy a greater privacy, but would also be to some extent protected from the cold winds which swept these corridors and so numbed the fingers as to make writing impossible. The appearance of these carrells seems to have been a thirteenth-century innovation

[1] Jocelin relates how one of the Bury monks, Walter by name, contributed to the building of a stone aumbry a large sum of money which he had made 'from the practice of medicine': *Chron.* p. 152.

[2] None of the catalogues of Cistercian libraries in the thirteenth century shows any sign of the classics, but a copy of Cicero which once belonged to Byland has been traced: N. R. Ker, *Medieval Libraries of Great Britain*, p. 15. Beddie's remark that 'by the thirteenth century...the Cistercian libraries were not to be distinguished from those of their neighbours, from the point of view of contents' (*Haskins Anniversary Essays*, p. 22) would therefore not apply to this country.

[3] There was a copy of Homer at Whitby: Becker, *Catalogi Bibliothecarum Antiqui*, pp. 226–7.

and to have originated with the Augustinian canons.[1] By the end of the century they had become a regular feature of most cloisters and were later rebuilt of stone, as in the splendid example which has been preserved at Gloucester. The building of these carrells had a profound influence on monastic life, for it was a move away from the old conception of a completely common life, in which no member of the community had any place which he could call his own, towards the idea of a monk having a little 'den' which was exclusively his own and in which he could keep his personal property. It was no wonder that the decrees of General Chapters and of visiting bishops were full of references to these carrells, the appropriation and locking of which had often made them hiding-places for illicit property.[2]

In spite, however, of the facilities for study, the impression derived from the perusal of any monastic chronicle is not of a community of learned men. Jocelin's Chronicle of Bury is full of details about administration both internal and external, and there is much about property and finance; but there is little to suggest that many of the monks were students, or that they cared very much for scholarship. The same is true of other chronicles, such as those of S. Augustine's (Canterbury), Peterborough, S. Mary's (York), Meaux and Dunstable.[3]

At the same time there was a distinct movement during the thirteenth century to improve the intellectual standards of the monasteries. This was done in two ways: partly by the establishment of theological lectures in the cloister, and partly by sending the more promising members to the Universities, where they could receive the best education then available. The first indication of any policy of encouraging and organising study among the Black Monks comes from the Chapter General of 1247, where it was agreed that in each house there should be a lecturer to give instruction in theology or canon law every day.[4]

[1] J. W. Clark, *The Care of Books*, pp. 90–9. Clark is not quite accurate in saying (p. 98) that the first mention of carrells is at Westminster between 1258 and 1283. They are mentioned in the Augustinian Chapters as early as 1232: Salter, *Chapters of Augustinians*, p. 26.

[2] See below, pp. 340–2.

[3] According to Rashdall, by the thirteenth century 'the days were over in which the Benedictine monasteries had been the repositories of the learning of the age.... The Benedictine monks of this period were above all things men of the world': *Medieval Universities* (new ed.), iii, pp. 184, 190.

[4] Pantin, *Chapters of English Black Monks*, i, pp. 27–8. This decree may have been based on a similar piece of legislation passed two years previously by the Cistercian Chapter General at Cîteaux. According to

How far this decree was observed is hard to say: but it is interesting to hear of a Franciscan being invited to lecture to the Benedictines of Christ Church, Canterbury, in 1275,[1] while in 1303 the Worcester monks had a lecturer in divinity of their own and in 1308 were invited to send one of their members to S. Augustine's, Canterbury, to give instruction in theology there.[2]

Of the second method—that of sending young monks to the Universities—we know a good deal. The first move seems to have come from the Cistercians. About the year 1272 Edmund of Cornwall founded a house for six White Monks at Oxford. Nothing is known of its history during the next eight years, but in 1280 it was enlarged to form a college and in the following year an abbot was appointed.[3] Meanwhile the Black Monks at their General Chapter in 1277 had decided to found a Benedictine School at Oxford and had imposed a special levy of 2*d.* in the mark on the income of each house to raise the necessary funds.[4] The response was not very encouraging,[5] and the scheme seems to have been in abeyance for eleven years. During this time, however, in 1283, Sir John Giffard of Brimpsfield bought a house in Oxford and presented it to the Benedictines of the province of Canterbury in order to allow thirteen monks to study there. The Order invited S. Peter's, Gloucester, to take charge of this, and in 1284 the house came into being under a prior called Henry of Heliun.[6] Four years later the General Chapter of the Benedictines again discussed the question of a

this there was to be in each province at least one abbey with a school of theology to which abbots may send promising monks: Canivez, *Stat. Ord. Cist.* ii, pp. 289–90.

[1] Cotton, *The Grey Friars of Canterbury*, pp. 34–6.

[2] Wilson, *Worcester Liber Albus*, pp. 54–5, 76–7, 106–8. In 1290 the Pope gave a licence to the Prior and brethren of S. Gilbert of Sempringham to have within their house 'a discreet and learned doctor of theology to teach those of their brethren who desire to study that science': Bliss, *Cal. Papal Letters*, i, p. 516.

[3] *V.C.H., Oxon.* ii, pp. 81–2. The first monks were sent from Thame and the house came to be known as Rewley. In 1282 the Cistercians at Oxford were told to obey their abbot and to imitate the life of the students at Paris: Canivez, *Stat. Ord. Cist.* iii, p. 217.

[4] Pantin, *Chapters of English Black Monks*, i, p. 75.

[5] Some houses flatly refused to pay and many others ignored the demand: V. H. Galbraith, *New Documents about Gloucester College*, in *Snappe's Formulary*, Oxford Hist. Soc. 1924, p. 343.

[6] Galbraith, *New Documents*, p. 341, and cf. Dugdale-Caley, *Monasticon*, i, pp. 533–4. In 1291 Giffard increased his benefaction by presenting four more houses.

college at Oxford, and in the following year, 1289, the Prior of Durham founded at Oxford an independent college for monks of his own house.[1] So far, then, the hesitation and delay of the Chapter General had been somewhat compensated by the initiative and generosity of some individuals. Gloucester cell was well established and had opened its doors to monks from any house who wished to attend the schools. The Bursar of Worcester, for example, paid 20*s.* to 'the monks at Oxford' in 1291, 36*s.* 6*d.* in the following year, and in 1294–5, £2. 8*s.* 2*d.*, since there was now more than one scholar monk.[2]

In 1298 the General Chapter was at last persuaded to take some action; the old Gloucester cell was abolished; and an entirely new foundation was created under the control first of Eynsham and subsequently of Malmesbury, where Sir John Giffard was now residing. This was neither a college, nor a monastic cell, nor an independent priory, but a collection of separate rooms (*camerae*) each of which belonged to one of the Benedictine monasteries and all of which were bound together by some measure of corporate life.[3] By the end of the century, therefore, there were three houses for scholar monks at Oxford: the Cistercian house at Rewley for White Monks, and Durham and Gloucester Colleges for Benedictines. The Gilbertines acquired a house at Cambridge in 1290 and in the following year established a small convent at the old chapel of S. Edmund-the-King near Peterhouse; and in 1292 they founded a small college at Stamford which, however, did not survive for long.[4] We know also of Augustinian canons who were sent to Oxford, though they had no college of their own and it is uncertain where they were housed.[5] All of these monks were supported by their own communities.[6]

[1] Raine, *Hist. Dunelm. Scriptores Tres*, pp. 72–3.

[2] Wilson and Gordon, *Early Compotus Rolls of Worcester*, pp. 8–32. In 1295 a royal mandate ordered the monks of Gloucester dwelling at Oxford to receive brethren from other houses: Galbraith, *New Documents*, p. 345.

[3] See the whole discussion, with plans, in Galbraith, *New Documents*, pp. 341–2. Although the house still bore the name of 'Gloucester College' it had now separated completely from S. Peter's Abbey at Gloucester: *ibid.* p. 348.

[4] R. Graham, *S. Gilbert and the Gilbertines*, pp. 44–5; Knowles, *Religious Houses of Medieval England*, pp. 99–100.

[5] Thornton-on-Humber was ordered to send one in twenty of its canons to the University: *V.C.H., Lincs.* ii, p. 164.

[6] The Cistercians appear to have had an allowance of 60*s.* each per annum, but some, at any rate, of the Benedictines had as much as £10: *V.C.H., Oxon.* ii, pp. 81–2; Dugdale-Caley, *Monasticon*, i, pp. 533–4.

Evidence of how these monks fared at the Universities is scanty. The first Benedictine to take a doctorate was William de Broc, a monk of Gloucester, who incepted in 1298 at Oxford. The occasion was marked by the entire convent and a number of visiting monks going to the University city to be present at the ceremony.[1] Three years later another Gloucester monk, Lawrence de Honsom, incepted in theology under William de Broc, who was now styled Prior of Gloucester.[2] About the same time three monks of Worcester—John of Dumbleton, Ranulph de Calthorp and Richard de Bromwich—were all studying at Oxford and in due course graduated.[3] Meanwhile the Cistercians at Rewley were beginning to make their influence felt, for early in the fourteenth century Richard de Straddel, Abbot of Dore, took his D.D. at Oxford,[4] a certain Master Robert, a Cistercian of Margam, was a regent master,[5] and there is some trace of a Thomas de Kirkeby who disputed about the year 1300.[6] It is clear, then, that these monastic centres at Oxford were being used and that the monks were acquitting themselves well.

Yet the purpose of sending monks to the Universities was not to bring the older religious houses into contact with the world of ideas. As Rashdall said: 'The aim of these monastic colleges was probably very simple and practical.... What the monastic houses wanted was not to produce great theologians or to contribute to the advancement of learning, but simply to have a few instructed theologians capable of preaching an occasional sermon to their brethren and of imparting an elementary theological education to the novices.'[7] The truth of this statement could only be attested by a study of the monasteries in the fourteenth century, since the results of the educational experiments made in the latter part of the thirteenth century would only begin to show themselves some years later. Rashdall, as a historian, is unreasonably critical of the monasteries, whose

[1] Hart, *Hist. et Cart. Gloucest.* i, pp. 34–5. [2] *Ibid.* p. 35.

[3] Little and Pelster, *Oxford Theology and Theologians, c. 1282–1302*, Oxford Historical Society, 1934, pp. 236–42. Worcester seems to have had a reputation for scholarship, as in 1289 the monks were given permission to preach in neighbouring churches since they were 'learned in theology': Bliss, *Cal. Papal Letters*, i, p. 510.

[4] *Annales Dorenses*, in *Mon. Germ. Hist.* (*Scriptores*), xvii, p. 530.

[5] Little and Pelster, *Oxford Theology and Theologians, c. 1282–1302*, p. 225. [6] *Ibid.* p. 268.

[7] Rashdall, *Medieval Universities* (new ed.), iii, p. 190.

reputation, he says, 'as houses of learning had decayed with the decay of the positive or contemplative theology which had once flourished within their walls'. It is only rather grudgingly that he admits, on another page, that 'to the monasteries belongs the credit of producing the great medieval historians'.[1]

The output of the Benedictine monks as historians and chroniclers during the twelfth and thirteenth centuries was remarkable, and much of our knowledge of those ages is due to their labours. Nor is it true to suggest that they were interested only in their own monasteries, since many of the chroniclers deal largely with events of public interest and are often disappointingly reticent about the domestic affairs of the houses from which they originated.[2] It is, however, those which reveal something of the daily life in the monasteries which are most valuable. We have only to mention Jocelin of Brakelond at Bury, Adam de Domerham at Glastonbury, Coldingham and Graystanes at Durham, Elias Trickingham at Peterborough, and Matthew Paris at S. Albans,[3] to see how much we owe to these local historians, whose work has stood up well to the test of time and to the fierce light of scientific research and criticism. The Benedictine houses were, in fact, full of very creditable historians even though their contribution to scholastic philosophy may have been weak.[4]

The Cistercians produced no writer of any great distinction during the thirteenth century, either as historian or theologian;[5] and the only regular canon who achieved real fame was Alex-

[1] Rashdall, *Medieval Universities* (new ed.), iii, pp. 184 and 190.

[2] E.g. the Chronicles of Matthew Paris and Thomas Wykes tell us very little about S. Albans or Osney. On the S. Albans School of historians see C. Jenkins, *The Monastic Chronicler and the Early School at S. Albans*.

[3] I refer here to Matthew Paris' *Vitae Abbatum*, which was incorporated many years later by Thomas Walsingham in his *Gesta Abbatum Mon. S. Albani*.

[4] Other historians, of whom particulars will be found in Bale, *Illustrium Maioris Britanniae Scriptorum Summarium* (Basle, 1548) and in Tanner's *Bibliotheca*, were: Roger of Wendover (S. Albans), Hugo Candidus (Peterborough), Richard of Ely (Ely), Thomas Sprott (S. Augustine's, Canterbury), Gregory of Winchester (Gloucester) and Ralph Niger (Bury). The most distinguished Benedictine theologian of the thirteenth century was Adam of Barking, a monk of Sherborne: J. C. Russell, *Dictionary of Writers of Thirteenth Century England*, p. 1 and *D.N.B.* s.v. Adam.

[5] The most distinguished was a theologian, James of Chichester: Bale, *op. cit.* pp. 322–3; cf. *D.N.B.*

ander Neckham,[1] whose philosophical works, which covered a fairly wide field, found their way into most libraries after his death in 1217.[2]

Although it is true that by the thirteenth century the Universities and the friars were attracting the ablest minds, the monasteries still had a good deal to offer to a man of intelligence and ability. The 'dull life of the cloister' of which the Barnwell novice was to be warned can hardly have existed in a busy house such as most monasteries had become by this time. According to the Rules long hours were to be spent in church and in the performance of household duties and of work in the fields and gardens, but ways and means of escaping from these responsibilities had been found, at any rate for the older men and for those of an intelligence above the normal. The monasteries, in fact, offered a field in which men of studious and literary tastes, as well as those who cared about estate management and manorial administration, could find a congenial atmosphere;[3] and although, to a novice studying the Rule of S. Benedict, or the *Carta Caritatis*, or the Observances of a house like Barnwell, the prospect of life in the cloister might appear rather bleak and forbidding, most honest monks who looked back over the years spent in the cloister would be bound to admit that there had been much that was pleasant, and that the limitations of a disciplined, celibate life had been fully compensated by the security and well-being which they had enjoyed.

[1] See *D.N.B.* s.v.

[2] I have noted fourteen in the Christ Church, Canterbury, library catalogue of Prior Eastry. Cf. also catalogues of Peterborough, Ramsey and Reading.

[3] Quite a number of monks were poets. Russell, in his *Dictionary of Writers of Thirteenth Century England*, includes the following: Adam of Barking, Adam of Dore, Henry de Burgo, John de Cella (Abbot of S. Albans), John of S. Omer, Nicholas (a monk of Rievaulx), Simon of Walsingham, Walter (Abbot of Margam), William (Precentor of Combe) and Simon (a monk of Waverley). Most of these wrote in Latin, but Simon of Walsingham wrote in Anglo-Norman.

CHAPTER XXIII

THE MONKS' STANDARD OF LIVING

Critics of the monasteries have sometimes forgotten that the ideal which S. Benedict set before his followers was not that of a life of extreme austerity, but of a simple, disciplined, communal life spent in the service of God. In the Prologue to the Rule he declares that he has deliberately avoided anything 'harsh or rigorous', and in the final chapter he refers to what he has written as 'this least of Rules...written for beginners'.[1] Compared with the asceticism of the desert monks the Rule of S. Benedict is undoubtedly lenient. It was designed not to win grace for its adherents by self-immolation, but rather to cut out all luxury and to reduce the standard of living to that of simple peasants.[2]

It is obvious, however, that with the passage of time and the growth of the order some modification of the original Rule was necessary. The monks of the thirteenth century were as far removed from the days of S. Benedict as we are from the thirteenth century, and any standard of living is bound to alter a good deal during a period of seven hundred years. Also, regulations as to food and clothes which were suitable to the warm climate of Central Italy could hardly be applicable to monasteries in the Yorkshire dales or in Scotland. Unfortunately, however, the Rule made no allowance for differences of temperature, and the monks of northern climates were thrown into the unfortunate dilemma of either disobeying the Rule or going cold and hungry. We must not think too harshly of them if they generally chose the former alternative.

Dom David Knowles has explained how modifications in the diet of the English Black Monks had gradually been introduced before the beginning of the thirteenth century. The chief of these innovations were a larger number of meals, especially in winter; the introduction of flesh-meat under certain conditions; and the multiplication of extra dishes or pittances.[3] The efforts of

[1] *Reg. S. Ben.* Prol. et cap. lxxiii.

[2] Poverty is only once mentioned in the Rule: C. Butler, *Benedictine Monachism*, p. 159.

[3] D. Knowles, *Monastic Order*, pp. 456–65.

reformers during the thirteenth century were directed not to the abolition of these innovations but only to their control.

By far the most important departure from the dietary regulations of the original Rule was the introduction of flesh-meat. S. Benedict clearly intended his monks to be vegetarians; butcher's meat was to be given only to those who were sick or weakly.[1] By the thirteenth century this must have appeared a great privation. The quantities of meat which were a regular part of the daily fare of the rich have already been mentioned in the description of the household of Bishop Swinfield.[2] To such standards many of the monks would have been accustomed in their youth—especially so now that the system of children being placed in religious houses at a very tender age had been discontinued and most postulants had had some experience of the world. Nothing but a very high degree of self-discipline would have made the standards of S. Benedict acceptable to the monks of the thirteenth century; and we have every reason to believe that on the whole such standards did not obtain in the average monastery.

There is no doubt, therefore, that the eating of meat had become common and, indeed, accepted in many religious houses. But in order to clothe this practice with the appearance of regularity and loyalty to the Rule various subterfuges had been found. The first of these was for a certain number of the community to feed each day at the abbot's table, where meat was allowed for the benefit of any guests who might be present. That abbots were accustomed to eat meat is clear from the chance remark of Jocelin of Brakelond, who tells us that after the fall of Jerusalem in 1187 Samson gave up eating flesh-meat.[3] Another device was for some of the community to dine each day in the infirmary, where meat was allowed by the Rule. The decrees of visiting bishops are full of references to this habit and of attempts to restrict the use of the infirmary to those who were definitely sick or aged. Thirdly, in many religious houses a room known as the misericord had been built,

[1] *Reg. S. Ben.* cap. xxxvi, xxxix. Benedict's prohibition covers only the flesh of quadrupeds, and there was some argument as to whether game and fish could be eaten by the monks or not; cf. Pantin, *Chapters of English Black Monks*, i, p. 116. [2] See above, p. 178.

[3] Jocelin of Brakelond, *Chron.* p. 63. Cistercian abbots were repeatedly told to abstain from flesh-meat: Canivez, *Stat. Ord. Cist.* ii, p. 85; iii, p. 80.

in which some of the monks were accustomed to dine each day and where the dietary rules were not considered binding.

Moreover, in addition to the more or less recognised methods of overcoming the rules as to the consumption of meat, there was always a certain amount of irregularity. At Rochester, for example, the cellarer was accustomed to have his own table in a room under the hall, where, no doubt, the ordinary rules were not considered relevant.[1] In many houses, also, various obedientiaries had their own rooms in which they ate with their friends and households. At Boxgrove meat had certainly been introduced into the refectory itself,[2] while the canons of Bolton Priory did themselves well on venison, beef, mutton, pork and poultry, as their account-books show.[3]

For a time it seems as if there was a good deal of confusion over this question of eating meat. The old rule of total abstinence except for the sick and aged had become a dead letter. By the exercise of a little ingenuity a good many of the brethren were getting meat several days a week, and it was hopeless for reformers to imagine that they could persuade the monks to return to the strict vegetarian standards of the past. The efforts of disciplinarians were therefore directed not to the abolition of meat-eating but to its control. Since the dietary regulations were taken to apply only to meals served in the refectory and not to those served in the infirmary or the misericord, it was advisable that some effort should be made to see that the brethren took at least some of their meals in the refectory where the rules could be enforced. Visiting prelates sometimes found the refectory more or less deserted while the community fed in other parts of the house on a diet which they regarded as outside the scope of the ordinary regulations. One of the first reforms was, therefore, to see that the refectory contained each day at least some proportion of the community. For example, in the careful directions drawn up for Malmesbury Abbey in 1293 it was ordained that, apart from the sick and those invited to the abbot's table, half the number of the brethren should feed in the refectory and half in the misericord, and that there

[1] *Regist. R. Winchelsey*, pp. 838–42.
[2] *Ibid.* pp. 852–6.
[3] Whitaker, *History of Craven*, pp. 325–41. At Evesham, Abbot Henry, 1256–63, actually devoted certain rents to the purchase of meat for the monks—'ad recreationem singulorum in esu carnium': Macray, *Chron. Abb. de Evesham*, p. 281.

should be a minimum of thirteen in the refectory. Since there were probably between fifty and sixty monks at Malmesbury the thirteen in the frater represent only about a quarter of the community. If a rota were made out this would mean that each individual would dine in the refectory on only seven days in each month.[1] Similar arrangements were made elsewhere. When Archbishop Romeyn visited Blyth in 1287 he found the whole community taking their meals regularly in the misericord while the refectory was totally deserted. He ordered two-thirds of the brethren to eat in the frater each day.[2] At many houses it was necessary to put an end to the habit of brethren who were neither sick nor aged taking their meals regularly in the infirmary.

Other reforms were directed towards prohibiting the consumption of meat during certain seasons. The Benedictines in their Chapter General of 1273 ordered that no meat should be eaten during Advent and Lent,[3] while the Augustinians added Wednesdays and Fridays as well as the recognised seasons of abstinence.[4] At Healaugh Park no meat was to be served on Mondays and Wednesdays to the 'strong and healthy'.[5] In addition to these regulations attempts were made to restrict the eating of meat to the older members, or to certain parts of the house. At Winchester in 1276 it was ordained that no young monk should eat meat,[6] and at the two Canterbury houses the consumption of meat was to be restricted to the abbot's or prior's chamber, the misericord, the infirmary and the guest-house.[7] From these measures it will be seen that, whereas some check on the unrestricted introduction of meat into the monks' daily fare could be imposed, it was clearly considered impossible to enforce the strict standards of the Rule. As a result, it is unlikely that in many monasteries any member of the community went without meat on more than two days each week.

1 Brewer, *Regist. Malmesburiense*, ii, pp. 383–5.

2 *Regist. J. Romeyn*, i, pp. 269–70.

3 Pantin, *Chapters of English Black Monks*, i, pp. 37, 249; cf. Wilkins, *Concilia*, ii, pp. 16–17.

4 Salter, *Augustinian Chapters*, pp. 7, 24, 29, 33, 45.

5 *Regist. W. Wickwayn*, pp. 130–1; cf. Bridlington: *Regist. J. Romeyn*, i, pp. 199–202; Haverfordwest: Pecham, *Reg. Epist.* iii, pp. 782–4.

6 *Regist. J. Pontissara*, pp. 640–4.

7 Thompson, *Customary of Canterbury and Westminster*, i, p. 40; *Regist. R. Winchelsey*, pp. 91–3.

With the addition of meat to the monastic diet had also come the multiplication of extra dishes or 'pittances', many of them given to celebrate the anniversary of some former abbot or benefactor. These pittances took various forms. At Evesham, on the anniversary of a former prior, William de Walcote, the monks were to have a dish of salmon or of the best fish available, together with an allowance of the choicest wine.[1] At Malmesbury a pittance included wine *clarus et purissimus*.[2] At Bruton a pittance was endowed consisting of one simnel cake, one gallon of wine and three dishes of flesh or fish for each canon in the house.[3] As the amount of money available for these 'treats' grew, a 'pittancer' was often added to the number of the obedientiaries with the sole responsibility of arranging that these various relaxations were faithfully carried out.[4]

With the introduction of meat and of numerous pittances the daily fare of the average monastery was certainly very good. There were, of course, exceptions. Some houses fell on evil days, and, for a time, their members had to tighten their belts and were even sometimes reduced to begging in the streets. But for the most part the monks looked after themselves well, as account-rolls and other evidence show. One or two examples must suffice. At Durham the cellarer's accounts reveal the purchase of large quantities of beef, veal and pork; also sugar, olive oil, 760 lb. of almonds and various spices. In 1278 the bursar spent nearly £80 on wine, and in 1299 his purchases included saffron, sugar, almonds, 155 lb. of rice and 50 lb. of ginger.[5] At Norwich a community of about two hundred people (sixty of whom were monks) consumed no less than 9000 eggs a week, an average of over six each *per diem*.[6] At Newstead no canon was to be offered less than three eggs or three herrings at a time by the Archbishop's orders,[7] while at Winchcombe the cook was instructed to provide four fried eggs for each monk in the refectory at supper-time.[8] In a single year the canons

[1] Dugdale-Caley, *Monasticon*, ii, p. 35.

[2] Brewer, *Regist. Malmesburiense*, ii, p. 380.

[3] Somerset Record Society, *Chartularies of Bruton and Montacute*, p. 23.

[4] E.g. at Meaux: Bond, *Chron. Melsa*, i, p. 360; ii, p. 64.

[5] Fowler, *Durham Account Rolls*, i, pp. 3–6; ii, 487–8, 495.

[6] Saunders, *Introduction to Norwich Rolls*, pp. 96–7. See also the eel-tarts and black and white sugar mentioned on p. 80.

[7] *Regist. W. Giffard*, pp. 211–15.

[8] Dugdale-Caley, *Monasticon*, ii, p. 306.

of Bolton, in addition to the quantities of meat already mentioned, bought large quantities of almonds, rice, figs and raisins, and 1764 gallons of wine, besides the regular supplies of beer.[1]

The quantities of drink which were consumed were certainly, to use Dom Knowles' phrase, 'on a heroic scale'.[2] The monks of Abingdon were apparently allotted twenty-four pints of beer a day for each man;[3] and, if this were considered a reasonable allowance, one cannot help wondering what the Council of Oxford considered 'inordinate drinking' among the monks.[4] A great many efforts were made to stop private and excessive drinking (*privatae potationes, secretae potationes et gulosae ingurgitationes, inordinatae potationes*, etc.), especially in the evening after Compline.[5] Public and private feasts were also held from time to time, when enormous quantities of food and drink were consumed. Giraldus Cambrensis' account of the feast at Christ Church, Canterbury, when sixteen courses followed each other,[6] may be compared with a banquet at the sister house of S. Augustine's in 1309 when 30 oxen, 200 sheep, 1000 duck, 963 fowls, 200 sucking-pigs and a quantity of mallard, partridge and larks were consumed.[7] Private parties such as those which the sacristan of Bury used to hold in some buildings in the churchyard, or which the canons of Llanthony held 'in the house by the weir', were eventually prohibited,[8] but feasting undoubtedly went on.

If a certain amount of luxury and extravagance had entered the kitchen it had also found its way into the chamberlain's office. It was obvious that the quantities of clothes fixed by S. Benedict could not reasonably be supposed to apply to the climate of England;[9] but there was no reason why the primitive

1 Whitaker, *History of Craven*, pp. 342–3.

2 Knowles, *Monastic Order*, p. 717.

3 Stevenson, *Chron. Monast. de Abingdon*, i, pp. 346–7.

4 Wilkins, *Concilia*, i, p. 593.

5 Pantin, *Chapters of English Black Monks*, i, p. 257; Pecham, *Reg. Epist.* i, pp. 259–65; Dugdale-Caley, *Monasticon*, iv, pp. 624–5; Canivez, *Stat. Ord. Cist.* i, p. 472; iii, p. 127; *Regist. W. Giffard*, pp. 211–15; Salter, *Augustinian Chapters*, pp. 5–6, 32.

6 *The Autobiography of G. Cambrensis*, tr. H. E. Butler, pp. 70–2.

7 Dugdale-Caley, *Monasticon*, i, pp. 144–5.

8 Jocelin of Brakelond, *Chron.* p. 48; *Regist. G. Giffard*, pp. 87–9. The canons of S. Osyth's were holding parties in the town in 1304: *V.C.H., Essex*, ii, p. 158. Cf. also Evans, *Chapters of Ely*, in *Camd. Misc.* xvii, p. 35.

9 The question was raised by the Black Monks themselves: Pantin, *Chapters of English Black Monks*, i, p. 118.

standards of roughness and simplicity should be abandoned. S. Benedict intended his monks to dress as peasants, and would have been horrified at the silks and furs which he would have found at Abingdon, Christ Church (Canterbury), Durham, Ely, and no doubt at other houses also.[1] Compared with the standards of later centuries[2] the requirements of the thirteenth century were reasonable enough. At Gloucester, for example, each monk was to receive one tunic, short and thick; a leather coat and slippers; shirts and breeches; short, thick stockings; a new cowl and habit once a year; day-shoes once in eighteen months, and night-boots once in five years.[3] The difficulty, however, was to prevent monks and canons from abandoning the uniform of the order altogether and arraying themselves in the bright and fancy garments which they purchased for themselves or which their relations sometimes sent them. Against this abuse reforming Chapters and visiting prelates waged a continuous war.[4]

Such reformers were also constantly on the look out for a certain abuse which had grown up in some houses. With the improvement of the monks' clothing it was often possible for them to make their clothes last longer than was anticipated, and, when the day for the issue of a new outfit came, to receive a sum of money instead of a new set of clothes.[5] This was regarded as a serious abuse because it was contrary to one of the fundamental principles of monasticism, namely, that no member of the community should hold any private property. S. Benedict had been most insistent upon this point: private property was to be totally eradicated, and no monk must regard

[1] At Abingdon the monks wore lambskin and cats' fur: Stevenson, *Chron. Monast. de Abingdon*, ii, p. 300. At Christ Church, Canterbury, Archbishop Winchelsey found silk girdles and furs in 1296: *Regist. R. Winchelsey*, pp. 91–3. The Durham monks bought lambskin, squirrel, miniver and other furs: Fowler, *Durham Account Rolls*, ii, p. 495. Silk girdles and jewelry were among the things forbidden at Ely in 1300: Evans, *Chapters of Ely*, in *Camd. Misc.* xvii, p. 10.

[2] See the extraordinary 'clothes-list' for an Ely novice quoted by Snape, *English Monastic Finances*, p. 160.

[3] Hart, *Hist. et Cart. Gloucest.* i, p. lxxxix.

[4] See, for example, *Regist. R. Winchelsey*, pp. 91–3; Pantin, *Chapters of English Black Monks*, i, pp. 11, 236; Wilkins, *Concilia*, i, p. 590; M. Paris, *Chron. Maj.* vi, pp. 239–40; Fowler, *Cistercian Statutes*, p. 94; *Regist. W. Wickwayn*, pp. 88–90; Heales, *Tanridge Priory*, pp. 16–19.

[5] On this see Coulton, *Five Centuries*, iii, pp. 375–7.

even his body or his will as his own. Even the beds were to be inspected from time to time to see that nothing was hidden in the straw.[1] As time passed, however, the urge for a few personal possessions became very strong, and it was evident that very stringent measures would be needed to control it in days when the general discipline of the religious houses was on the decline. Pecham, the Franciscan, was obviously shocked at the growing habit of monks collecting a little private property, which he saw to be totally contrary to the spirit and intentions of the Rule.[2] The General Chapters also made some attempt to get rid of it.[3] But it certainly continued throughout the thirteenth century and was encouraged by the growing habit of regulars having lockers by their beds and of carrells being erected in the cloisters. Not only had carrells been built in Augustinian cloisters as early as 1232, but the canons had begun locking them up.[4] Over and over again, therefore, we find visiting bishops demanding that carrells shall be opened and searched at regular intervals, three or four times a year, in order that any hidden property might be brought to light.[5]

We have no certain knowledge of what these lockers contained in the way of private property. No doubt some of the monks were in the habit of receiving gifts from their relations and friends, and these would find their way into some locked chest or carrell. In some monasteries also the members received a certain amount of pocket-money, most of which would be spent on small personal possessions. At S. Augustine's, Canterbury (so William Thorn tells us), each member of the community received a sum of money once a year at Candlemas. The abbot received £4, the prior 30*s*., the sub-prior and precentor 15*s*. each, the twenty-six senior monks 13*s*. each, the eighteen intermediaries 11*s*. 2*d*. each, and the rest 7*s*. 6*d*.

[1] *Reg. S. Ben.* capp. xxxiii and lv. When Grosseteste visited Ramsey Abbey in 1251 he inspected the beds, an action which Matthew Paris regarded as 'inhuman': M. Paris, *Chron. Maj.* v, 226–7.

[2] At Christ Church, Canterbury, he spoke of *proprietas* as something 'plurimum absurdum' and as 'abusum dampnatae proprietatis': Pecham, *Reg. Epist.* i, p. 342, ii, pp. 400, 539–40.

[3] Pantin, *Chapters of English Black Monks*, i, pp. 9, 10; Wilkins, *Concilia*, i, p. 593; ii, p. 16; M. Paris, *Chron. Maj.* iii, pp. 500–1; vi, p. 241; Canivez, *Stat. Ord. Cist.* ii, p. 202.

[4] Salter, *Augustinian Chapters*, p. 26.

[5] E.g. at Blyth, S. Augustine's (Canterbury), Ely, Worcester, Bury, Bolton, Bridlington, Kirkham, Newstead, Shelford, Drax and Worksop.

apiece.[1] The monks of Ely also received *graciae* administered by the Sub-prior and Third Prior.[2] The Westminster monks received tips (*exennia*) on certain occasions, such as when a priest-monk said his first Mass or when one was promoted to a higher table in the refectory; but these gifts may have been in kind.[3] Samson at Bury allowed the monks to have up to 2*s*. each to spend on charity or on poor relations.[4] Pecham had to make a rule that no monk at Christ Church, Canterbury, should receive more than 6*s*. 8*d*. in cash without the consent of the Chapter.[5]

The 'tedium of the cloister' was interrupted from time to time by periods of recreation and by a certain amount of entertainment which was no doubt much enjoyed. The men of the Middle Ages believed very strongly in the tonic effects of a periodic letting of blood or *minutio*. In earlier days this was regarded as in the nature of a cure for certain bodily disorders and was resorted to only when the patient was in need of treatment; but it gradually came to be accepted as a regular break in the routine of the cloister, and was looked forward to with pleasure by the monks. The pleasure lay not in the operation itself but in the fact that it was regarded as a general holiday when the restrictions of daily life were relaxed, extra food was supplied, and tongues wagged more freely than usual. Jocelin describes it as the season when 'cloistered monks were wont to reveal the secrets of their hearts'.[6] So pleasant had this become that in the regulations of the Benedictine Chapter in 1293 the *minutio* was clearly regarded not as a surgical operation, nor as a necessity of good health, but as a privilege which could be taken away as a punishment for some misdemeanour.[7] At Worcester we find mention of *potionandi*, those 'about to be dosed', suggesting that in this house a milder and less painful form of tonic had been adopted.[8]

Besides the *minutio* most of the monks were given opportunities for holidays and recreation. The monks of Durham had an

[1] *W. Thorn's Chronicle* (tr. Davis), p. 283.
[2] Evans, *Chapters of Ely*, in *Camd. Misc.* xvii, p. 34.
[3] Pearce, *The Monks of Westminster*, pp. 22–4.
[4] Jocelin of Brakelond, *Chron.* p. 61.
[5] Pecham, *Reg. Epist.* ii, pp. 397–403.
[6] Jocelin of Brakelond, *Chron.* p. 21.
[7] Pantin, *Chapters of English Black Monks*, i, p. 262.
[8] Hale, *Regist. Prioratus Wigorn.* p. 129b.

estate at Beaurepaire (now Bearpark), three miles out of the town, where some of the community would generally be found enjoying a short holiday.[1] The monks of Westminster Abbey had an estate at Hendon,[2] those of S. Albans had a house in London and another at Great Yarmouth,[3] and when the riots occurred at Bury S. Edmunds in 1326 it was discovered that half of the monks were away from home on holiday.[4] The canons of Hexham were given leave to go away for 'the inside of a week' each year to have a short respite on one of the manors,[5] and the Prior of Barnwell was told to take some of the younger canons with him each time he visited the manors in order that they might get some recreation and a change of air.[6]

Even while at home opportunities for recreation were provided. Jocelin tells us that Samson 'made many parks, which he filled with beasts, and had a huntsman and dogs. And whenever any important guest arrived, he used to sit with his monks in some retired grove and watch the coursing for a while; but I never saw him interested in hunting.'[7] This last sentence would not apply to some of his fellow-abbots. Bishop Swinfield found the Prior of Leominster to be a keen sportsman who delighted in the chase so much that he had to be reproved for deserting the religious life and devoting himself to sport 'with dogs, birds and shady characters'.[8] The Abbot of Gloucester, however, was allowed to keep eight sporting dogs and four greyhounds with two fewterers to look after them;[9] the Abbots of Chester and Peterborough had sporting rights in the vicinity of their houses;[10] and the monks of Whitby roamed the moors with bows and arrows in search of game and amusement.[11] The

[1] Raine, *Hist. Dunelm. Script. Tres*, pp. 46, 49, 52.

[2] Pearce, *Walter de Wenlok*, p. 98.

[3] *Gesta Abbatum Mon. S. Albani*, i, pp. 289–90.

[4] Arnold, *Memorials of S. Edmund's Abbey*, iii, p. 39.

[5] Raine, *Hexham Priory*, i, App. pp. xxxv–xl.

[6] Clark, *Observances at Barnwell*, p. 49.

[7] Jocelin of Brakelond, *Chron.* p. 44.

[8] 'Cum canibus, avibus et personis inhonestis': *Regist. R. Swinfield*, pp. 149–50.

[9] Hart, *Hist. et Cart. Gloucest.* i, pp. lxxxiv–xcii; and cf. Hart and Lyons, *Cart. Mon. de Rameseia*, i, pp. 228–30.

[10] Tait, *Chart. of Chester*, i, p. 88; Stapleton, *Chron. Petroburg.* p. 135.

[11] *V.C.H., Yorks.* iii, pp. 102–3. Any dog which got into the cloister was to be soundly beaten (*rigide castigetur*). For mention of bows and arrows cf. *Regist. R. Winchelsey*, pp. 844–6 (Leeds Priory, 1299).

Austin canons were equally addicted to sport. The canons of Bicknacre in Essex had the right to hunt hare, fox and cat,[1] the Prior of Dunstable used to go ferreting on the downs near Eaton Bray,[2] the canons of Lanercost had their own deer-leap and kept a pack of eight hounds,[3] and the Prior of Coxford in Norfolk was given permission by so strict a disciplinarian as Pecham to ride to hounds, though he was not to go coursing (*canes sequi peditanter*).[4] At other places, such as Reading and Christ Church, Canterbury, Pecham forbade the monks to go hunting or hawking;[5] all Cistercians were ordered not to keep sporting dogs or birds;[6] and attempts were made to prohibit expeditions on to the Yorkshire moors by canons of Bridlington and Bolton.[7]

During bad weather there were indoor games. Reference has already been made to the presence, in the library at Peterborough, of some books on chess. Chess had been introduced into Europe during the eleventh century and found its way into some of the religious houses as a quiet and thoughtful form of amusement. Pecham found the canons of Coxford playing it when he visited there in 1281,[8] and it was certainly played at Gloucester and Hexham.[9] In 1289 the Chapter General of the Cistercians had to pass a decree saying that any White Monks caught playing chess were to be punished.[10] At Newstead, Archbishop Romeyn found the canons playing dice.[11] Account-books also reveal the presence of minstrels and buffoons to bring a little life and laughter into the cloister. The Norwich rolls contain several references to the employment of strolling players, especially on Trinity Sunday.[12] Walter de Wenlok, Abbot of Westminster,

[1] *V.C.H., Essex*, ii, p. 144.

[2] Luard, *An. Mon.* iii, p. 374.

[3] *V.C.H., Cumberland*, ii, p. 155.

[4] Pecham, *Reg. Epist.* i, pp. 162–5.

[5] *Ibid.* i, pp. 223–6, 341–8.

[6] Canivez, *Stat. Ord. Cist.* iii, p. 229 (1283).

[7] *Regist. W. Wickwayn*, pp. 87–8, 131–3. Cf. also pp. 148–50 (Cartmel), 55–6 (Newburgh); Raine, *Hexham Priory*, i, App. pp. xvii–xxii; *V.C.H., Gloucs.* ii, p. 77 (Bristol, S. Augustine's).

[8] Pecham, *Reg. Epist.* i, p. 165. It had been introduced here by a certain Robert de Hunstanton. Pecham speaks of 'ludum scaccorum et consimilia scurrilia solatia'.

[9] Hart, *Hist. et Cart. Gloucest.* i, p. lxxxviii; Raine, *Hexham Priory*, i, App. p. xxiii.

[10] Canivez, *Stat. Ord. Cist.* iii, p. 243.

[11] *Regist. J. Romeyn*, i, pp. 317–19.

[12] Saunders, *Introduction to Norwich Rolls*, pp. 182–3.

employed a lute-player, three actors and a boy, and a dancer from Chertsey.[1] The Durham monks engaged a minstrel from Newcastle whom they paid 2*s.* for his services,[2] and at Worcester payments to the jester of Sir Philip Burnels and to a band of minstrels figure among the monastic accounts.[3] Minstrels and buffoons were also employed at Bolton and Bridlington.[4]

In its early days Western monasticism had been associated with the country rather than with the towns; but, as time went on, a change took place in this relationship. As the monasteries grew in wealth and influence, and as they came to employ more and more secular servants and officials, it was inevitable that fairly flourishing communities should spring up outside the abbey gates. The effect of this was sometimes disastrous. The essence of monachism was withdrawal from the world, a complete and permanent separation from intercourse with people still living in the world and with the sights and sounds of daily life. Although S. Benedict made some allowance for monks who were travelling from one place to another, he clearly intended his brethren to spend the whole of their time in the cloister and to mingle only with their fellow-monks. But with the decline in discipline of later centuries, and with the temptations of a vigorous city life at the very gates of the monastery, it was inevitable that the old ideal of complete claustration should fall into decay. It was partly in order to remove the temptation to mingle with seculars that the Cistercians, in their first zeal, chose out the wildest and loneliest spots in which to build their monasteries.

The evidence from the thirteenth century is that in many houses of monks and canons there was a good deal of going in and out and of social contact between the regulars and the laity. Over and over again, as we read the accounts of visitations by bishops and others, we find some decree forbidding the brethren to go out so frequently. Chaucer's monk, who held it absurd to compare a monk out of his cloister to a fish out of water, was typical of a good many men of the previous century. Dr Pearce, for example, gives details of a number of the brethren from

[1] Pearce, *Walter de Wenlok*, pp. 75–6, 130.
[2] Fowler, *Durham Account Rolls*, ii, p. 486.
[3] Wilson and Gordon, *Early Compotus Rolls of Worcester*, pp. 8–14, 15–23.
[4] Whitaker, *History of Craven*, pp. 342–3; *Regist. J. Romeyn*, i, pp. 199–202.

Westminster Abbey who travelled about a great deal. One of them, William de Chalk, went to Rome, Scotland, Northampton, twice to Carlisle and once to an unknown destination. Another, Robert de Beby, was for a time at the court of the Bishop of Winchester, after which he spent thirty-one days on a journey from Westminster to Gloucester. During the next month he visited Windsor, Oxford, Worcester, Pershore and Hartlebury.[1] Thomas Cantilupe found some of the canons of Wormesley away from home in 1277, having taken posts in the households of laymen, and Swinfield discovered the same thing at Wigmore ten years later.[2] As early as 1219 the Cistercians had to pass a decree that English abbots who had sent monks or *conversi* into the service of bishops and seculars were to recall them at once,[3] and in 1237 the Augustinians in Chapter at Northampton passed a similar resolution.[4]

The granges and cells also helped to undermine the old idea of *stabilitas* which meant so much to S. Benedict.[5] The granges were outlying farms which monastic obedientiaries visited from time to time and at which they sometimes stayed for considerable periods. Many of the granges became almost small monasteries, with chapels, guest-houses and small refectories and dormitories.[6] The dangers of such places becoming an excuse for an escape from the discipline of the cloister are obvious. But if the granges were regarded by the monks themselves as an opportunity for a change of scene, the cells were often used by the abbots as a convenient place to which refractory or difficult members of the community could be banished. Earl's Colne in Essex, for example, was turned into little less than a prison for the more troublesome monks of Abingdon,[7] and

[1] Pearce, *The Monks of Westminster*, pp. 66–72.

[2] *Regist. T. Cantilupe*, pp. 144–5; *Regist. R. Swinfield*, p. 132.

[3] Canivez, *Stat. Ord. Cist.* i, p. 509.

[4] Salter, *Augustinian Chapters*, p. 7. In this case, however, permission might be obtained from the bishop.

[5] '*Stabilitas* was to S. Benedict what Poverty was to S. Francis': C. Butler, *Benedictine Monachism*, p. 128. *Stabilitas* meant, primarily, that every monk must remain in the house in which he was originally professed, and could not therefore move, or be moved, to any other. It implied also the monk's isolation from the world and permanent confinement to the cloister.

[6] R. Graham, *S. Gilbert and the Gilbertines*, p. 65; cf. Fowler, *Cistercian Statutes*, pp. 22, 72; Canivez, *Stat. Ord. Cist.* i, p. 307.

[7] *Regist. R. Baldock, etc.* pp. 77–9.

several abbots of S. Albans found the cell at Tynemouth in Northumberland a most admirable place of exile for men who were difficult to manage in the cloister.[1] At S. Mary's, York, on the other hand, Abbot John de Gilling, a weak and unpopular man, had banished all his best monks to the cells, since he feared their powers and influence over their fellows.[2] At any given moment, therefore, it may be safely assumed that some members of each monastic community were away from home, either by choice or by compulsion.

Meanwhile the close connection between many religious houses and the towns in which they were situated meant that there was much wandering in and out of the abbey gate. When Winchelsey forbade the canons of S. Osyth's to leave the cloister some scribe wrote in the margin: *Ista est onerosa.* The ideal of claustration had certainly become 'onerous' to a good many of those who had chosen this way of life; and, unless and until authority intervened, they got rid of the burden by taking the law into their own hands.[3] The early monks had fled from the Cities of Destruction to the solitude of the desert; the monks of the later ages were trying to find their way back again.

Monasticism was born of fear and disgust. In the fourth century many ardent souls considered it impossible to live in the world without becoming contaminated by worldly standards. Monastic life was the direct result of that belief. In this it differed wholly from the ideal of the mendicant orders, which

[1] William Pyggun, after stealing the convent seal and forging a false charter, was banished to Tynemouth: *Gesta Abbatum Mon. S. Albani*, i, pp. 221–4; cf. pp. 251, 257–8; ii, p. 50. 'More than one of those so banished' says Dom David Knowles, 'appealed, not without some reason, to the monastic vow of stability which he had taken': *Monastic Order*, p. 302.

[2] Craster and Thornton, *Chronicle of S. Mary's, York*, pp. 55–6.

[3] To give all the references for this would occupy too much space; but injunctions forbidding regulars to wander about the towns or the countryside will be found in the visitation records of Blyth, Boxgrove, Dover, Glastonbury, Gloucester, Rochester, Winchester, Worcester, Christ Church and S. Augustine's (Canterbury), Bolton, Bridlington, Cartmel, Chirbury, S. Oswald's (Gloucester), Hexham, Shelford, Southwark, Tandridge, Worksop, Healaugh Park, Mottisfont, Newstead, S. Osyth's and Thurgarton. Cf. also for the Cistercians, *V.C.H., Lincs.* ii, pp. 143–4. Also Pantin, *Chapters of English Black Monks*, i, p. 11; M. Paris, *Chron. Maj.* vi, 243–4.

was to live out the full Gospel standards of perfection in the midst of the sin and depravity of the world. Neither experiment was successful for very long: the monks found their way back to the world, and the friars succumbed to the temptations whereby they were continuously surrounded.

The return of the monks to the world, which so often lay immediately outside the gate of their abbey, sometimes had disastrous results. A man like Roger Norreys at Evesham had obviously no intention of conforming to the Rule, and he certainly became a very immoral man.[1] The Priors of Leominster and Farleigh were also found to be guilty of incontinence,[2] and at Felley and Worksop many of the community were unfaithful to their vows of chastity.[3] Immorality seems also to have been very bad in the nunneries, though the standards fell most rapidly during the fourteenth and fifteenth centuries.[4] Not only were monks going into the towns on unlawful occasions, but there was also a good deal of entertaining of women in the cloister. Some monastic churches were open to the public and were frequented by women of all ages. The temptation to invite the more attractive of them to round off their devotions with a little party in the cellarer's office may sometimes have been irresistible. Visitation decrees reveal various attempts to keep women out of the cloister;[5] but they were not always obeyed. At the same time it must not be forgotten that entertaining young women in a religious house is not immoral, though it may be a breach of monastic discipline. That there was a certain amount of licence both within the monasteries and outside, can be proved; but it was certainly on a much smaller scale than has sometimes been suggested by modern critics. Bishops who visited the monasteries would make it one of their first duties to discover the moral state of the house, and yet one can search the decrees drawn up after such visitations and find scarcely any mention of actual vice, though suspicious circumstances

[1] Macray, *Chron. Abb. de Evesham*, pp. 245–6.

[2] *Regist. R. Swinfield*, pp. 149–50; Duckett, *Visitations of Cluniacs*, p. 27.

[3] *Regist. W. Giffard*, pp. 313–14; *Regist. W. Wickwayn*, pp. 141–3.

[4] Power, *Medieval English Nunneries*, cap. xi, and especially pp. 471–2 and 597–601.

[5] Cf. *Regist. J. Pontissara*, pp. 640–4; *Regist. J. Romeyn*, i, pp. 199–202; *Regist. W. Wickwayn*, pp. 130–1, 148–50; *Regist. T. Cantilupe*, pp. 144–5, 147–9; *Regist. W. Giffard*, pp. 204–6; *Regist. R. Baldock, etc.* pp. 112–15, 174–6; Pecham, *Reg. Epist.* i, pp. 162–5, ii, pp. 645–9.

were sometimes noticeable.[1] Again, it is significant that the General Chapters of the Benedictines and of the Augustinians, which met regularly during the thirteenth century and discussed many problems of monastic discipline, seem never to have considered the question of sexual relationships. The only legitimate conclusion to be drawn from these facts is that at this period the standard of morals in the religious houses was a great deal higher than has sometimes been thought.

On the whole, then, the standard of living in the monasteries was high. Grosseteste's three essentials of well-being—'food, sleep and laughter'[2]—were all provided in full measure. The plain fare envisaged by S. Benedict had been considerably modified by the addition of flesh-meat and of numerous pittances; the rough and sombre clothing of the early days had been embellished by warmer and softer garments; manual labour had been replaced by reading or administration, and the tedium of the cloister was constantly interrupted by entertainments, holidays and expeditions into the towns or into the woods where game abounded. Under such conditions the monasteries had a good deal to offer, as is shown by the surprisingly small number of absconders. A few monks ran away from time to time, but mostly either to join some other monastery or to make off with some of the property of the house. S. Benedict made provision for absconders, but there is little evidence of his legislation having to be invoked in the thirteenth century. The perils and hardships to which a vagabond monk would be exposed were a serious consideration to weigh against the undoubted comforts and security of the cloister.

[1] It is worth noting here that even the rare cases of incontinence which are mentioned may not have been very serious. Pecham informed the monks of Christ Church, Canterbury, that he regarded secret kissing as equivalent to incontinence: 'Incontinentiae vero nomine intelligimus sollicitationem ad peccandum et tactus impudicos, nec oscula clandestina a specie impudicitiae credimus aliena': *Reg. Epist.* i, p. 345.

[2] Brewer, *Monumenta Franciscana*, i, p. 64.

CHAPTER XXIV

THE MONASTIC CONTRIBUTION TO SOCIETY

The basis of monasticism is separation from the world. The early monks had fled from the world because they despaired of finding, in the rough-and-tumble of daily life, that 'strait and narrow way' which would bring them to salvation. To live in the world was to make some compromise with the standards of worldly men, and thereby to hinder one in the pursuit of heaven's bliss. The only hope lay in a complete separation from ordinary life, cut off from the sights and sounds of Vanity Fair, sheltered from the temptations of the world, alone with God and with a small company of Christian aspirants who were all seeking to tread the same path. The cloister was designed to be an asylum for such as were willing to turn their backs for ever upon the 'pomps and vanities of this wicked world' and to work out their own salvation along the way of prayer, discipline and mortification.

Based upon such an ideal, monasticism could offer very little to society outside the cloister. It was not really interested in the world beyond its own walls; and even though it provided a good deal of hospitality and poor-relief it did so primarily in order to save its own soul by the exercise of charity.[1] The monastic contribution to society in early days was therefore only indirect. The world was evil: the monastic life was good; and just as Abraham pleaded with God for the cities of the plain—'peradventure there be fifty righteous within the city: wilt thou consume and not spare the place for the fifty righteous that are therein?'—so the monk might plead for the world not on its own merits but upon the merits of the minority who had renounced the world and adopted the regular life. For the world itself monasticism had no gospel; the most which it could do was to offer men a retreat from the world and a way of life for those who aspired to perfection.

But by the thirteenth century conditions had changed a good deal. The old idea of the monks' complete separation from the

[1] See Knowles, *Monastic Order*, p. 4: 'No work done within [the monastery], whether manual, intellectual or charitable, is directed to an end outside its walls.'

world was breaking down and with it came the collapse of the popular idea that the monastic life was the 'religious' life *par excellence*. Not only were people beginning to realise that there was much in the life of the regulars which was not conspicuously other-worldly, but they had discovered also that there was much 'true religion and undefiled' in the lives of quite ordinary citizens who laid no claim to a monopoly of sanctity. By the beginning of the century men like Walter Map and Giraldus Cambrensis were sharply criticising the monks; but we see the complete change in public opinion most clearly in the pages of Chaucer, and especially in the *Prologue* to the *Canterbury Tales*. Probably neither the monk nor the 'pore persoun' was typical of his profession; the significant thing is that Chaucer went out of his way to show up the regulars as utterly worldly and self-indulgent, while he made his parish priest a paragon of simplicity and devotion to duty.

With this change in public opinion, amounting almost to loss of confidence in the monasteries as the nearest approach to evangelic perfection, we should expect to find some signs of disintegration in the monastic system. As long as men believed that the prayers of the monks were helping to save the world, and as long as they were satisfied that the regulars were vicariously relieving them of their obligations to personal discipline and renunciation, so long would they support the monasteries by their gifts, and men of high ideals would be anxious to attach themselves to some community. But once men lost faith in the virtue of the regular life, financial support would tend to diminish and the stream of postulants to dry up.

The religious houses survived this crisis for two reasons. One was that they had, during previous centuries, built up such vast resources that, given wise handling, they could support themselves without relying upon the gifts of the faithful; the other was that the monasteries offered a kind of existence which was undeniably attractive. The standard of living in most houses was high and, in many, a good deal higher than that of the world outside; there was much in the life of the monk or canon that was interesting and varied; and there were good prospects, since most members of a community could count on becoming heads of departments in due course. There were, of course, disadvantages, though many of them had been considerably mitigated. The restrictions of the cloister could certainly be oppressive; but through regular trips to outlying manors, the possibility of sending the more disagreeable members of the community to distant cells, and the various opportunities for getting out of the cloister and into the world for a time, these restrictions became much less onerous. Again, the discipline of the regular life, though it remained in theory as strict as it had ever been, was considerably relaxed through a whole series of dispensations and evasions. Or again, the ban of celibacy which to our modern way of thinking would be one of the chief obstacles to the religious life, seemed much less formidable in days when this privation was accepted, at least in theory, by almost all professional men, and lay no more heavily upon the regulars than upon the secular clergy, the schoolmasters, the lawyers and most of the doctors.

The prospect of life in a monastery in the thirteenth century was, in fact, by no means unattractive. For those who sought sanctification there was great opportunity for every kind of religious exercise—worship, prayer, meditation and mortification. No one can doubt that in each monastery there were some who devoted themselves to such pursuits. Such men do not leave very much behind them except a sweet memory in the minds of those who have lived with them; consequently the monastic chronicles tell us little about the holy and humble men of heart. But as we read the rather tedious records of the earthly fortunes of the religious houses we occasionally catch sight of some saintly figure whom we know to have lived close to things infinite and eternal.[1]

Again, for those whose interests were literary, the monasteries, with their well-stocked libraries, offered a pleasant, sequestered existence with abundant opportunity for studying the great literature of the past, both sacred and secular. It is true that on the whole the flow of scholarly works from the older monasteries is disappointingly small. This is due to the fact that by the thirteenth century the more active and ambitious students were sharpening their wits in the invigorating atmosphere of the schools. But not all men of scholarly interests are either

[1] Judging by the devotional books which he collected, Walter of S. Edmund, Abbot of Peterborough, who died in 1245, was one such: Dugdale-Caley, *Monasticon*, i, p. 355. Another was Stephen de Easton, Abbot of the Cistercian house of Salley in Yorkshire, who wrote a number of devotional books: J. C. Russell, *Dictionary of Writers of Thirteenth Century England*, p. 156.

ambitious or particularly industrious; and for such as desired an opportunity for becoming acquainted with the masterpieces of literature, without the necessity of having to make either a reputation or a living out of this employment, the monasteries certainly offered a pleasant field.

Again, for such as had administrative gifts, but were not blessed with any property upon which to exert them, the monasteries, with their vast estates, offered much scope. Buying and selling of land, managing their estates and their tenants, organising their own households and accounts—all these were occupations into which men of the world could throw themselves wholeheartedly, as well as into the endless pastime of litigation which the medieval mind seems to have found so irresistible.

The chief contribution of the monasteries to society in the thirteenth century was, therefore, the provision of a kind of life which was admirably suited to various types of men and women. Consequently, even with the growth of the Universities and the coming of the friars the older religious houses were able to keep up their numbers, and not a single house came to an end during this period.

But the monasteries did a good deal for society apart from merely offering a pleasant form of life to those who wished to join them. Over and over again when a Chapter applied to their bishop for an increase in their financial resources through the appropriation of a church they pleaded the burden of having to provide hospitality for large numbers of people. No doubt these pleas were sometimes exaggerated, or made an excuse for acquiring a little extra money; but there was certainly much movement about the country during the thirteenth century, and such houses as stood near to the great thoroughfares would undoubtedly be called upon to find lodging for a good many guests.

The Barnwell Observances lay down careful rules for the reception of visitors. The hostiller was to be a man of good class in order that he may set the monastic life in a good light, 'for friends are multiplied by agreeable words'. He was to see that a high standard of comfort was maintained in the guest-house by providing clean cloths and towels, silver spoons, mattresses, blankets, sheets, pillows and quilts pleasing to the eye; a fire that does not smoke, writing materials, rushes on the floor, locks on the doors with keys left in the locks and good bolts on the inside.[1] Such preparations, and the slightly ulterior motive suggested by the words in inverted commas, implied an expectation of wealthy guests. The sturdy beggar would hardly have felt comfortable in such surroundings, nor would the canons have felt very comfortable about their silver spoons. In spite of S. Benedict's hope that in the exercise of hospitality special consideration should be shown to the poor,[2] the evidence from the thirteenth century strongly suggests that the monks were far more interested in their richer visitors who, in course of time, might become benefactors to the house. Members of other religious houses who sought hospitality, and relatives and friends of the monks themselves, were also to receive special consideration.[3] At the Cistercian Abbey of Cleeve there seem to have been four separate guest-houses, one for the rich, one for the poor, one for travelling Cistercians and one for religious of other orders.[4]

The burden of entertaining great men and their retainers was sometimes very heavy. King John frequently imposed himself upon some unfortunate house, which often suffered considerably as a result. He visited Waverley in 1208,[5] was three times at Bath, where his sojourn laid heavy financial burdens upon the monks,[6] while his visit to Bury S. Edmunds, when the only present which he left behind was a silk cloth which his servants had borrowed from the Sacristan and never paid for, has been described by Jocelin of Brakelond.[7] Both Ramsey and Glastonbury were burdened with royal guests from time to time,[8] while a visit of Edward II to Peterborough in 1310 is said to have cost the abbot £1543. 13*s*. 4*d*.[9]

Women visitors presented a problem of another kind. Many reformers and disciplinarians would have liked to exclude them

[1] J. W. Clark, *Barnwell Observances*, p. 193.

[2] *Reg. S. Ben.* cap. liii.

[3] See Salter, *Augustinian Chapters*, p. 4; Evans, *Chapters of Ely*, in *Camd. Misc.* xvii, p. 40.

[4] Walcott, *S. Mary's Abbey, Cleeve*, p. 121.

[5] Brakspear, *Waverley Abbey*, p. 66.

[6] Hunt, *Two Chartularies of Bath*, pp. lii–liii.

[7] Jocelin of Brakelond, *Chron.* pp. 181–2.

[8] Macray, *Chron. Abb. Rameseiensis*, pp. 342–5; Adam de Domerham, *Hist. de Rebus gestis Glaston.* ii, p. 587.

[9] Dugdale-Caley, *Monasticon*, i, p. 539.

altogether but dare not risk offending rich and powerful ladies with whom it was expedient to keep on good terms. When Archbishop Winchelsey gave his orders for the monks of Christ Church, Canterbury, in 1298 he told them that no women were to be admitted except noble ladies and sisters of the monks.[1] This was in accordance with a regulation passed by the Black Monks in their Chapter in 1249[2] and was the usual practice in most religious houses at this time.[3] The Cistercians were the most strict. According to their rules, when a new abbey had been built women were to be allowed to visit it for nine days but must not be allowed to pass the night in it.[4] However, in 1205 the Chapter General deputed the Abbot of Savigny to enquire into the case of the Abbey of Quarr in the Isle of Wight where a certain countess and other women are said to have been entertained for six nights contrary to the regulations.[5] Sometimes the hospitality extended to noble ladies had rather embarrassing consequences, as at the Cluniac house of Lenton. The guest-house at this priory had a high reputation; Henry III stayed here in 1230; and here, in 1263, the wife of Nicholas de Cauntlow gave birth to a son, William, who was baptised in the Priory Church on Palm Sunday.[6]

In spite of the fact that the monasteries often pleaded that the claims of hospitality were more than their meagre resources could sustain, there is no doubt that the company of laymen was often very much enjoyed. Even with all the opportunities for getting out of the cloister there must have been periods when time passed slowly and the same circle of familiar faces grew irritating. At such times the arrival of a traveller, with news of the outside world and perhaps a fund of jokes and good stories, would be a welcome diversion. Visiting bishops were constantly waging war against the unnecessary entertainment of strangers,[7]

[1] *Regist. R. Winchelsey*, p. 816. He did the same at Lesnes: *ibid.* pp. 842–4.

[2] Pantin, *Chapters of English Black Monks*, i, p. 42.

[3] Cf. *Regist. J. Romeyn*, i, pp. 199–202 for Bridlington, where no woman was to enter the choir and none was to stay the night except great ladies whom the canons could not well refuse.

[4] Fowler, *Cistercian Statutes*, p. 21.

[5] Canivez, *Stat. Ord. Cist.* i, p. 319.

[6] *V.C.H., Notts.* ii, p. 95.

[7] E.g. Bridlington (*Regist. J. Romeyn*, i, pp. 199–202); Marton (*ibid.* p. 160); Holy Trinity, London (*Regist. R. Baldock, etc.* pp. 26–31); Hexham (Raine, *Hexham Priory*, i, App. pp. xvii–xxii); Worksop (*Regist. W. Wickwayn*, pp. 141–3); Llanthony (*Regist. G. Giffard*, pp. 87–9).

and efforts were made to ensure that no visitors should take their meals in the infirmary, except those who came for specified purposes, such as a lawyer or a doctor.[1]

Besides providing accommodation for those who were travelling about the country, whether kings, nobles, bishops,[2] monks or laymen, the religious houses also rendered a notable service to the community by providing lodgings for those who were tired of the world and desired to spend their declining years in the peace and security of a monastery. Reference has already been made to these corrodies,[3] most of which were bought at a price, though a few were given to people who had served the house well over a number of years. That these corrodies were regarded as valuable by society as a whole is shown by the large prices which were paid for them by those who could afford to invest in this form of annuity. Occasionally we come across evidence of corrodies being demanded by the King, who was anxious to provide for some member of his household. At S. Albans, for example, Edward I charged the monastery with a corrody for life for a member of the household of his brother Edmund, who complained that he had been received by the abbey with insufficient respect;[4] and at Ramsey, in 1303, he forced the monks to give a corrody to his aged surgeon, regardless of their complaint that they were already looking after two of the King's old servants.[5]

To the rich, the monasteries were thus very useful as providers of accommodation either for a short visit or for life. To the poor they were expected to supply regular gifts of food, drink and clothes. Both the Rule of S. Benedict and the *Concordia Regularis*[6] laid down careful instructions about the administra-

[1] *Regist. W. Wickwayn*, pp. 143–4; Raine, *Hexham Priory*, i, App. p. xxiii.

[2] Houses which were subject to visitation were of course regularly visited by their bishops who could demand procuration. Bishops also used the monastic guest-houses on their journeys, just like any other wealthy travellers. The Bishop of Winchester stayed at Waverley as a guest in 1274 (Luard, *An. Mon.* ii, pp. 383–4), a Norwegian bishop was for a time at Bury (Jocelin of Brakelond, *Chron.* p. 23), and Swinfield on his journeys in 1289–90 stayed at Reading, Newent, Flaxley, Tintern, Dore, Wenlock, Alberbury, and Clifford (Webb, *Household Roll of R. de Swinfield*, vol. ii, *passim*).

[3] See above, pp. 269–71.

[4] *Gesta Abbatum Mon. S. Albani*, i, p. 469.

[5] Macray, *Chron. Abb. Rameseiensis*, p. 381.

[6] For the *Concordia Regularis* see Dugdale-Caley, *Monasticon*, i, p. xliii.

tion of alms to the poor, but there is a good deal of evidence that these were not strictly carried out at a number of English monasteries during the thirteenth century. All the food that remained after a meal was to be given to the poor, but it is clear that a good deal of it found its way to other destinations. This might not always be the fault of the monks. In the more isolated districts the number of poor people who could actually attend each day at the appointed hour might be small. At the same time Visitation decrees are full of commands that the broken meats shall go to the poor and not either to relatives and friends of the monks, or to the dogs.[1] In the same way money which was left to the monks for the sole purpose of providing alms for the poor was sometimes diverted into other channels, to the advantage of the monks and the defrauding of those who depended upon charity for their daily bread.[2] It was in order to check these irregularities that the General Chapters of the Black Monks passed resolutions that those who defrauded the poor of the broken meats which were their due should be punished, and that doors were to be locked during meal-times to prevent the illicit conveyance of food to friends and relations of the monks instead of to the genuine poor.[3]

Though it is true that there was some reluctance to distribute to the poor all that remained from the monks' tables, and that through contact with the outside world the monks had formed friendships and attachments with people in the district whom they were anxious to help as much as they could, yet there is evidence of a good deal of genuine poor-relief administered by the religious houses during the thirteenth century. Not all of

[1] See, for example, *Regist. R. Winchelsey*, pp. 817, 852–6 (Christ Church, Canterbury, and Boxgrove); Pecham, *Reg. Epist.* i, pp. 259–65 (Glastonbury); ii, pp. 622–5 (Rochester); pp. 782–4 (Haverfordwest); Hart, *Hist. et Cart. Gloucest.* i, pp. lxxxiv–xcii (Gloucester); *Regist. R. Swinfield*, pp. 131–2 (Leominster); *Regist. J. Pontissara*, pp. 782–4 (Winchester); Raine, *Hexham Priory*, i, App. pp. xxxv–xl (Hexham); *Regist. R. Baldock, etc.* pp. 26–31 (Holy Trinity, London, where it appears that the canons were sending food outside. For each offence they were to be punished by receiving three strokes of the birch and by fasting on bread and water for one day).

[2] Haines, *Dover Priory*, pp. 252–6 (Dover); *Regist. W. Wickwayn*, pp. 87–8 and *Regist. J. Romeyn*, i, pp. 199–202 (Bridlington); Pecham, *Reg. Epist.* ii, pp. 645–9 (Mottisfont); *Regist. R. Baldock, etc.* pp. 60–2 (S. Osyth's).

[3] Pantin, *Chapters of English Black Monks*, i, pp. 37, 257.

it was distributed at the abbey gate, for the Constitutions of Lanfranc had given instructions that the almoner should visit the houses of the sick, accompanied by two of his household. On arrival at a house all the women folk were to be turned out before the almoner entered. If the patient were a woman the almoner must not go in but must send one of his attendants.[1] When we read, then, of a distribution of loaves or of boots, it was probably carried out in this way, either by the almoner himself or by the members of his household. At Durham we find considerable sums spent on bread for the poor, besides the purchase of boots and shoes for the same purpose.[2] At Norwich the almoner disposed of cloth, shoes, ale, meat, fish, eggs, bread and peat.[3] At Ramsey thirteen poor men were supported, each receiving daily 1½ loaves, half a gallon of beer, a dish of pottage and half a monk's ration of whatever was cooked in the kitchen. On fast-days each was to have three herrings for dinner and one for supper. They also received some cloth and either a pair of boots or 4*d.*[4]

Many religious houses maintained a certain number of poor men actually within their walls. At Barnwell, for example, five poor men lived in the almonry together with some young clerks who were supported by the canons.[5] The canons of Dunstable in 1272 took into their infirmary a blind clerk who remained there 'for a very long time' (*diutissime*),[6] and seculars seem to have been looked after in the infirmaries of a number of Cistercian abbeys, including Waverley, Pipewell, Meaux and Newminster.[7] At Fountains, towards the end of the twelfth century, during a time of plague, the poor flocked to the abbey and tents had to be erected to accommodate them, both nurses and priests being provided by the monks to care for the sick.[8]

[1] *Decreta* of Lanfranc in Migne, *Patr. Lat.* vol. cl, col. 491.

[2] Fowler, *Durham Account Rolls,* ii, pp. 484, 485, 487, 492, 497. The usual price for a pair of boots for the poor was 3*d.*, though the bursar spent 1*s.* 10*d.* for each pair of boots for the monks. Some shoes for widows cost 5*d.* a pair.

[3] Saunders, *Introduction to Norwich Rolls,* pp. 170–1.

[4] Hart and Lyons, *Cart. Mon. de Rameseia,* ii, pp. 233–5. Christ Church Priory in Hampshire was renowned for its almsgiving: *V.C.H., Hants.* ii, pp. 154–5.

[5] Clark, *Barnwell Observances,* pp. liv and 175.

[6] Luard, *An. Mon.* iii, p. 255.

[7] Fowler, *Chartulary of Newminster,* p. xv.

[8] *V.C.H., Yorks.* iii, p. 135.

Bermondsey, which was found to be dispensing alms in a perfectly satisfactory way in 1262 when inspected by the Cluniac visitors,[1] had a hospital built in 1213 for converts from the Jewish faith and for poor boys.[2] Gilbertine houses also had hostels attached for the care of the poor and the sick, lepers and orphans.[3] Feasts in the monasteries to which the poor were invited were also common, in addition to the regular distribution of gifts on Maundy Thursday. Poor were fed in the hall at Norwich;[4] at Winchcombe 100 poor people were to be fed on the morrow of All Saints;[5] at Butley in Suffolk the poor were fed seven times a year,[6] and at Newminster, on S. Katharine's Day, 100 poor persons were to receive two oatcakes and two herrings each.[7] At Evesham thirty poor were fed once a year in the parlour on the anniversary of Prior Thomas.[8] Several individual abbots and priors were noted for the generosity of their almsgiving. Hugh of Durham, for example, was so popular that when he was returning home the poor would flock to meet him and conduct him to the priory with singing.[9]

Monastic account-books prove beyond any doubt that a certain amount of almsgiving was carried out by the religious houses. The accounts of Bolton Priory for the year 1324–5 show that, out of a total expenditure of £647. 10*s*. 2¼*d*., £2. 5*s*. 4*d*. went in alms, though this would not include broken meats distributed at the door.[10] At Norwich Dr Saunders reckons that 11 per cent of the income of the house was actually devoted to the relief of the poor.[11]

Economically the monasteries also had some contribution to make to the life of this country during the thirteenth century. The monks were landowners on a very large scale; and, on the whole, they seem to have administered their estates reasonably

1 Duckett, *Visitations of Cluniacs*, pp. 13–14.
2 Luard, *An. Mon.* iii, p. 452.
3 R. Graham, *S. Gilbert and the Gilbertines*, pp. 24–5, 42.
4 Saunders, *Introduction to Norwich Rolls*, pp. 170–1.
5 *V.C.H.*, *Gloucs.* ii, p. 67.
6 Dugdale-Caley, *Monasticon*, vi, p. 379.
7 Fowler, *Chartulary of Newminster*, p. 108.
8 Dugdale-Caley, *Monasticon*, ii, pp. 27–31.
9 Raine, *Hist. Dunelm. Script. Tres*, p. 47.
10 Burton, *Monasticon Eboracense*, pp. 121–33.
11 Saunders, *Introduction to Norwich Rolls*, pp. 170–1.

well according to the recognised standards of their day. There were, no doubt, instances of injustice and exploitation; but those who have studied the question closely have been driven to the conclusion that the monastic landlords were certainly no worse than any others, and, on the whole, were better. Miss Page, after a most careful and exhaustive study of the Crowland Abbey administration, sums up in these words: 'A general review of Crowland administration is on the whole a tribute to the ecclesiastical landlord.... There are many examples of a general kindliness of administration. During "the hard years" at Drayton, about the year 1322, several concessions were made by the Abbot to alleviate distress.'[1] Again, the editors of the records of the Durham Halmote are driven to the conclusion that the Prior 'always appears to have dealt with his tenants, either in person or through his officers, with much consideration; and in the imposition of fines we find them invariably tempering justice with mercy';[2] while Dr Coulton, after many years of close research into monastic history, has stated what he calls his 'final conviction' about monastic landlords in these words: 'I judge the monk to have been, on the whole, a slightly better landlord than the layman. His conservatism inclined him to the harder side, since his whole economic position was fundamentally capitalistic; but his religion and his traditions of social amenity, which even at the worst kept him on a higher moral plane than the average lay lord, weighed rather more heavily in the milder scale.'[3] If these judgements are true, then the monasteries, as landlords, must be allowed to have made a considerable contribution to society.

Intellectually and artistically the output of the religious houses in the thirteenth century was less than we might have expected. This was no doubt largely due to preoccupation with other affairs. The management of estates kept a large part of the community fully occupied; only the minority gave themselves up to literary work and much of this was desultory and dilettantist. Apart from the historians and chroniclers, to whom reference has already been made,[4] there was little first-class theological or philosophic work among the older religious houses. The initiative here had passed to the friars and to seculars. Nor can

[1] F. M. Page, *The Estates of Crowland Abbey*, pp. 49–50.

[2] Longstaffe and Booth, *Halmota Prioratus Dunelmensis*, p. ix.

[3] Coulton, *Medieval Village*, p. 142.

[4] See above, pp. 332–3.

we picture the average cloister or *scriptorium* of the thirteenth century as the home of busy monks copying out and illuminating books. Most of the copying was by now in the hands of secular clerks who were employed by the monks for this purpose.[1] A few abbeys kept up a tradition of good artistic work,[2] but monastic account-books show that even the money allocated to the provision of books was often diverted into other channels. The Precentor of Norwich, for example, had an income of about £25 a year, but most of this was spent on clothes and spices and very little went towards the provision of new books.[3]

At a few monasteries there was some first-class artistic work, notably at S. Albans. Here under Abbot John (1195–1214) some paintings executed by one of the monks were placed in the church,[4] but it was during the next generation that the great work was done by Walter of Colchester and his brothers and nephew. Walter seems to have come to S. Albans about the year 1200 and shortly afterwards did some fine work, which was continued in later years by his nephew Richard.[5] He was also, for a time, employed by the monks of Canterbury, who invited him to make the new shrine for the bones of S. Thomas in readiness for the translation which took place in 1220. At Bury S. Edmunds, Samson was a patron of the arts, and, according to Jocelin, took some trouble to decide what paintings should be placed in the choir.[6] Hugh, the sacrist at this time, made the screen and rood, and about a century later another monk, John Wodecroft, painted the choir.[7] At S. Benet of Holme another Samson, elected abbot in 1229, was himself a painter,[8]

[1] See J. W. Clark, *Barnwell Observances*, p. 63; Floyer and Hamilton, *Cat. of MSS. in the Chapter Library of Worcester Cathedral*, pp. xiv–xv.

[2] Dom Knowles mentions Winchester, Canterbury and S. Albans: *Monastic Order*, p. 438. To these might be added Reading, which produced some good scribes who presented King John in 1208 with thirteen volumes; see J. R. Liddell, *Some Notes on the Library of Reading Abbey*, in *Bodleian Quarterly Record*, 1935, p. 49.

[3] Saunders, *Introduction to Norwich Rolls*, pp. 134–5; but see also the essay by H. C. Beeching and M. R. James, *Library of the Cathedral Church of Norwich*, in *Norfolk Archaeology*, xix (1917), pp. 67–116.

[4] *Gesta Abbatum Mon. S. Albani*, i, pp. 232–3.

[5] *Ibid.* i, p. 279, and, for a list of Walter's paintings etc., M. Paris, *Chron. Maj.* vi, pp. 202–3. For further details see Swartwout, *The Monastic Craftsman*, pp. 43–4.

[6] Jocelin of Brakelond, *Chron.* p. 14.

[7] M. R. James, *The Abbey of S. Edmund at Bury*, pp. 130–1.

[8] *V.C.H., Norfolk*, ii, p. 332.

and Abbot John de Brookhampton of Evesham is said to have beautified the church and other parts of the monastery with frescoes, though these may not have been executed with his own hands.[1]

On the whole, then, the monks must be regarded as patrons of art and learning rather than as workers themselves in these fields. The same might be said of their contribution to the educational facilities of the time.[2] In earlier days most religious houses had contained a number of boys who had entered the cloister at an early age and were being educated there by the community. This method of recruitment had, as we have already seen, come to an end before the thirteenth century, but in a good many places schools were actually owned and run by the monks though they did not teach in them themselves. Jocelin tells us that Samson, having bought some houses in Bury S. Edmunds, turned them into schools which he endowed in order that the boys of the town might have free education, whereas formerly each scholar had paid 1*d*. or 2*d*. a year.[3] At Dover in 1284 a school was established by the priory, which was bound to keep a master and provide the school buildings.[4] The almoner of Norwich largely supported the Grammar School, in which thirteen boys received their education,[5] and at Hoxne, a cell to Norwich, the monks kept a school for the children of the parish and supported and boarded two of the scholars.[6] Hexham had a school which was destroyed by the Scots in 1296, Thornton in Lincolnshire kept a school for fourteen boys, and S. Frideswide's had two schools in Oxford.[7] Other religious houses supported scholars at other schools and at the Universities. When Archbishop Winchelsey ordered the almoner of Rochester to keep a number of poor scholars he was only telling him to do what several other houses had been doing for some time.[8] The accounts at Norwich show that small amounts were paid out

[1] Macray, *Chron. Abb. de Evesham*, pp. 286–7.

[2] The monastic contribution to education has already been mentioned above in chapter viii.

[3] Jocelin of Brakelond, *Chron*. pp. 72, 150.

[4] Haines, *Dover Priory*, pp. 350–1.

[5] Saunders, *Introduction to Norwich Rolls*, pp. 124–7.

[6] *V.C.H.*, *Suffolk*, ii, p. 76.

[7] Raine, *Hexham Priory*, i, pp. lxxix–lxxxii; *V.C.H.*, *Lincs*. ii, p. 164; Wigram, *Cartulary of S. Frideswide's*, i, p. 447.

[8] *Regist. R. Winchelsey*, pp. 838–42.

from time to time for the support of some poor boy, perhaps the son of one of the monastic servants, whom the Chapter wished to help.[1] Again, the bursar's rolls at Worcester mention a sum of 12*s.* 6*d.* paid to the scholars at Oxford;[2] those at Durham refer to 4*s.* paid to 'a certain scholar';[3] while the Eynsham monks were at one time paying £5 a year to a student at Oxford called Alfonso da Siena 'as a gift of pure charity'.[4]

A discussion of the monastic contribution to society would not be complete without some mention of the way in which the great resources of the religious houses, both financial and literary, were sometimes put at the disposal of the public. There is a document in the Whitby Chartulary in which Galfrid, son of Thomas of York, leaves to the abbey a plot of land in Flowergate in consideration of money advanced to him by the monks when he was in dire necessity.[5] Several Chapters engaged from time to time in a certain amount of money-lending, not only for the purpose of serving the community but also as a means of making a little money for themselves. Osney, for example, during the thirteenth century, appears to have carried on a flourishing banking concern in which it gave no interest to those who entrusted their money to its keeping, but made some profits for itself by investing in property in Oxford.[6] The Premonstratensian abbey of Dale in Derbyshire also did a good deal of money-lending,[7] and we get scraps of evidence from Carlisle and Selborne of fairly large sums being lent in the neighbourhood.[8]

Books were also fairly frequently lent outside the monasteries. Bishops, whose nomadic life gave them little opportunity for collecting large libraries of their own, were often glad to turn to the monasteries for the loan of some volume which they were needing. Bishop Pontissara borrowed from the Prior and Convent of S. Swithin at Winchester a Bible in two volumes, well glossed, for the safe return of which he formally bound

1 Saunders, *Introduction to Norwich Rolls*, pp. 119–20, 184–5.
2 Wilson and Gordon, *Early Compotus Rolls of Worcester*, pp. 8–14.
3 Fowler, *Durham Account Rolls*, ii, p. 497.
4 Salter, *Eynsham Cartulary*, i, p. 249.
5 Atkinson, *The Whitby Chartulary*, i, p. 20.
6 *V.C.H.*, *Oxon*. ii, p. 91.
7 Trueman and Marston, *History of Ilkeston, etc*. p. 325.
8 *Regist. J. Halton*, i, pp. 119–22; Macray, *Charters of Selborne*, p. xii.

himself.[1] Whether the monks ever got their Bible back again is not known; but, at about the same time, the Chapter of Durham were obliged to go to law with their bishop, Anthony Bek, who had failed to return a number of books which he had borrowed from their library. The books which the bishop had taken away included some books of canon law, a Tripartite History, a Bible, a *Historia Anglorum*, a Missal and a Life of S. Cuthbert 'in which are written the secrets of the house' and which was valued at £200.[2] The Bishop of Norwich borrowed a copy of Suetonius, Josephus and some volumes of Augustine and Jerome,[3] and several houses such as Anglesey, Bermondsey and Albury near Guildford were willing to lend books to local clergy and laity, and sometimes had to be told to take greater care that the volumes were returned.[4] Most monastic libraries were also willing to lend to one another, mainly for the purpose of making new copies.[5]

Thus, by the thirteenth century the religious houses had a considerable contribution to make to society, different though it may have been from what the founders of Western monasticism had intended. The essence of monasticism is solitude, as the very name implies. The man who cuts himself off from the world and declines to consider anything except the salvation of his own soul, obviously cannot make much direct impression upon the society which he has for ever renounced. The early religious houses, separated as they were from the life of the world and interested only in their own affairs, could have little to offer to those outside. But as the old isolation gradually gave place to a system under which the monk mingled a good deal with his fellow-men, both within the cloister and outside it, the monasteries found that they could give more and more to the world. It is very easy to criticise the religious houses of the later Middle Ages and to complain that they had betrayed

[1] *Regist. J. Pontissara*, p. 712.

[2] *Catalogi Veteres Librorum Eccl. Dunelmensis* (Surtees Society), pp. 121–2.

[3] H. C. Beeching and M. R. James, *Norwich Library*, in *Norfolk Archaeology*, 1917, p. 68.

[4] Hailstone, *History of Bottisham*, p. 247; Denholm-Young, *Edward of Windsor and Bermondsey Priory*, in *E.H.R.* 1933, p. 438; *Regist. J. Pontissara*, pp. 119–21.

[5] Merryweather, *Bibliomania in the Middle Ages*, pp. 11–13; Edwards, *Memoirs of Libraries*, p. 71.

the principles on which the whole monastic system had been founded, but at the same time it is well to remember that this very departure from the original ideals enabled the monasteries to play more and more part in the life of the community and to make a contribution to that life which society appreciated and valued.

CHAPTER XXV

THE GLORY OF THE FRIARS

The glory of the friars belongs wholly to the thirteenth century. The first decade witnessed the foundation of the two great mendicant orders, the Franciscans and the Dominicans: by the end of the century decay had already set in, a decay which came rapidly and went deep. Up to the year 1250 the friars represented by far the purest and most virile aspect of the Church's work in this country: by the time of Langland, Chaucer and Wycliff they had become an object of contempt in the eyes of thoughtful people. The mendicant ideal, as it evolved in the minds of Francis and Dominic, was a great and heroic experiment; but it was an experiment which failed. The history of the friars in this country, during the first century of their existence, shows both the triumph of their early ventures of faith, and the first symptoms of decay.

The two great orders of S. Francis and S. Dominic were not, as has been suggested, the last stage in the evolution of the monastic ideal;[1] rather they were a protest against the whole conception of the monastic life which sought to separate men and women from the world. In principle the monastery was a self-contained community with no responsibilities towards the world which lay beyond its precinct wall; the friars, on the other hand, lived almost entirely among their fellow-men, using their friaries as lodging-houses in an endless pilgrimage through the world. So revolutionary was this new experiment that efforts were made on more than one occasion to persuade S. Francis to give it up and to affiliate his brotherhood to one of the existing monastic orders. Francis resisted such proposals with indignation. 'Brothers, brothers,' he cried, 'the Lord hath called me by the way of humility, and He has shown me the way of simplicity, and I do not want you to mention to me any other rule, neither that of S. Augustine, nor of S. Benedict, nor of S. Bernard. And the Lord told me that He wished me to be a new fool (*novellus pazzus*) in the world and that He did not want to lead us by any other way than by that wisdom; for by your learning and your wisdom God will confound

[1] See H. B. Workman, *The Evolution of the Monastic Ideal.*

you.'[1] S. Francis had seen the failure of the monastic ideal and was determined to break right away from it.

The same might be said of S. Dominic, though the motives behind his experiment were very different from those which inspired S. Francis. Dominic saw that neither the secular clergy nor the regulars were capable of wrestling with the growing force of heresy. The parochial clergy were far too ignorant and the regulars far too exclusive and remote. The only power which could meet this challenge would have to be something which was neither secular nor monastic. It must be 'regular', for there must be discipline and training; yet at the same time it must be free to go among men, proclaiming at every opportunity the truth of the Christian faith.[2]

Francis and Dominic were, therefore, united in their determination not to allow their plans and ideals to be fettered by too close an attachment to the old monastic system. Apart from this they had very little in common. Dominic started his career as an Augustinian canon and priest: Francis as a layman. Dominic worked out a policy for the salvation of the Church from the assaults of heresy: Francis had no policy except to follow literally the commands of Christ. Dominic was concerned above all things with truth, and planned an order of preachers well taught and well trained, who would put study before all things, even worship itself:[3] Francis was highly suspicious of learning

[1] *Verba S. Francisci*, cap. v, in *Documenta Antiqua Franciscana*, ed. Lemmens, i, p. 104.

[2] This and the following chapter will be concerned mainly with the Franciscan and Dominican orders, since so much more is known of them than of the others. The Carmelites first came to England in 1241–2 and settled at Cambridge in 1249, Oxford and London in 1253 and York in 1255, but little is known of their life and work. The same may be said of the Austin friars, who made their first appearance in this country about 1250. Both these orders were influenced a good deal by the Dominicans. The Friars of the Sack founded twelve houses in England during the thirteenth century, but none of these had a very long existence as the order was wound up early in the fourteenth century. The smaller orders also founded a few houses. See Little, *The Mendicant Orders*, in *Camb. Med. Hist.* vi, pp. 757–61; and, for dates of foundations, D. Knowles, *Religious Houses of Medieval England*, pp. 113–22.

[3] Dr Little writes: 'With the Dominicans learning was regarded as a religious occupation, a kind of divine service, which asserted its right side by side with the divine services properly so called.' He mentions also decrees forbidding the friars to spend too much of their time in church (*The Educational Organisation of the Mendicant Friars in England*,

and refused to let his friars have even the books necessary for their daily worship. To Dominic poverty was but a means to an end, an asset to the friar as a preacher and evangelist: to Francis poverty was an end in itself, an integral part of the imitation of Christ.

The two orders, therefore, were founded upon quite different conceptions. The ideal Dominican was a specialist, a highly-trained preacher and teacher who lived a life of simplicity and poverty in order that he might be the more free to pursue the object of his life, the proclamation of the truth and the victory over heresy. The ideal Franciscan had no pretensions to learning or skill of any kind; he lived only to follow Christ in abject poverty and humility, content to be treated as an outcast and a beggar, finding his perfect joy in cold and hunger and nakedness.

Such were the origins and ideals of the two orders. But as the years passed each had a considerable influence on the other. Impelled by the rivalry of the Franciscans the Dominicans were driven to accept poverty as a necessity of their lives, while the Franciscans developed into the most learned community in Europe. Indeed, so far did this process of assimilation advance, that the old distinction between the two orders vanished almost completely, so that Chaucer, in introducing a friar into the company which set out on pilgrimage from the Tabard in Southwark, does not bother to tell us of which order he was a member. The fortunes and history of the friars in England had a good deal to do with this process of assimilation.

The Dominicans or Preaching Friars arrived in this country in 1221, followed three years later by the first company of Friars Minor. There had already been some connection between the two orders and the Church in England. Nicholas Trivet mentions the fact that Alexander Stavensby (afterwards Bishop of Coventry and Lichfield) was a great admirer of S. Dominic, and there is some reason to suppose that Dominic was actually one of his pupils when he was a lecturer at Toulouse.[1] There

in *Trans. R. Hist. Soc.* New Series, viii (1894), pp. 59–60). S. Francis would have been deeply shocked by this; see Celano, *Vita Secunda*, §§ 194–5, and *Opuscula S. Francisci*, ed. Lemmens, p. 10.

[1] *N. Triveti Annales*, ed. T. Hog, pp. 224–5. Cf. R. F. Bennett, *The Early Dominicans*, pp. 24, 52, where he writes of 'a strong tradition' that the first seven friars attended Stavensby's lectures.

was certainly one Englishman, Lawrence, among Dominic's first companions, and it is probable that the leader of the expedition to this country in 1221, Gilbert de Fresnay, was of English birth.[1]

The Franciscans also counted several Englishmen among the first disciples. In the lower church of S. Francis at Assisi lies the body of Brother William, who was a friend of the saint;[2] Jacques de Vitry tells us of a clerk of his, Colin the Englishman, who joined the Franciscan order about the year 1220;[3] Eccleston mentions two brothers, natives of this country, one of whom opposed S. Francis when he proceeded to pull down the new buildings at the Portiuncula,[4] and we know that at least three of the nine friars who came here in 1224 were of English birth—Richard of Ingworth, Richard of Devon and William of Ashby.[5] There were also some distinguished Englishmen who joined the order at Paris, among whom were Alexander of Hales and Haymo of Faversham.[6]

There was, therefore, some connection between this country and the two great mendicant orders before any friar set foot on these shores. Hither in 1221 came a party of thirteen Dominicans. They were welcomed by Peter des Roches, Bishop of Winchester, who took them to Canterbury and presented them to Stephen Langton. When the Archbishop heard that they were preachers he invited one of them to take his place as preacher at a neighbouring church, and was so much impressed with the performance that he immediately took them under his protection. They did not, however, remain long in Canterbury, but pushed on to London and from thence to Oxford, which they reached on 15 August, and which they had obviously made their goal.[7] This was entirely in keeping with the policy of S. Dominic, who particularly wished his followers to capture the strongholds of learning.[8]

Three years later a party of nine Franciscans, four of whom were clerks and five laymen, landed at Dover and followed the

[1] Jarrett, *The English Dominicans*, p. 1.

[2] See the article *Brother William of England, Companion of S. Francis*, by A. G. Little in *Collectanea Franciscana*, i, pp. 1–8.

[3] Golubovich, *Biblioteca Bio-bibliografica*, i, p. 8.

[4] Eccleston, *de Adventu*, ed. Little, pp. 39–40.

[5] *Ibid.* pp. 4–6.

[6] *Ibid.* pp. 34–5 and cf. articles in *D.N.B.*

[7] *N. Triveti Annales*, p. 209.

[8] R. F. Bennett, *The Early Dominicans*, pp. 24–6.

same route to Canterbury, London and Oxford.[1] Their progress differed, however, from that of their predecessors; for whereas the Dominicans kept together with a view to settling as a community at Oxford, the Franciscans left a few of their members in each town—five in Canterbury and two in London—to establish friaries there. Moreover, the purpose of the two orders in turning towards the University town was different. The Dominicans went there in order to study and preach, the Franciscans in the hope of attracting capable and active young men into the order.[2]

From these early settlements both orders spread rapidly, their success being due to the immediate popularity which the friars achieved. Many of the bishops welcomed them with open arms, as if they saw in these vagrant evangelists the first signs of that revival of Church life which was so sorely needed.[3] Reference has already been made to Peter des Roches and Stephen Langton welcoming the first Dominicans. Grosseteste was eager to help the members of both orders, taking both Dominicans and Franciscans into his household and becoming in due course the first lecturer to the Grey Friars at Oxford.[4] Richard le Poore introduced the Friars Minor to Salisbury soon after 1225;[5] Stavensby gave considerable help to the Dominicans at Chester and to the Franciscans at Lichfield,[6] while in later years many bishops gave support to the mendicants[7] and at least two resigned their sees in order to join the friars—Ralph Maidstone, who gave up the bishopric of Hereford in 1239 to become a Franciscan, and Walter Mauclerk, who left Carlisle in 1248 to join the Black Friars.[8] Richard Swinfield's accounts

[1] Eccleston, *de Adventu*, pp. 3–11.

[2] Dr Little writes: 'The Franciscans at this period regarded a University town not as a place of study but as a place where young men of impressionable age congregated—a place where there was hope of a "good catch" of souls': *The Friars and the Faculty of Theology at Cambridge*, in *Mélanges Mandonnet*, ii, p. 396.

[3] Eccleston, *de Adventu*, p. 75.

[4] B. Formoy, *The Dominican Order in England*, p. 56; Little, *Grey Friars in Oxford*, p. 30.

[5] A. R. Martin, *Franciscan Architecture in England*, p. 241.

[6] Grosseteste, *Epistolae*, p. 120; Martin, *Franciscan Architecture*, pp. 163–4.

[7] See Goldthorp, *Franciscans and Dominicans in Yorkshire*, in *Yorks. Arch. Journal*, 1936, p. 272; Little and Easterling, *Franciscans and Dominicans of Exeter*, pp. 19, 21; Martin, *Franciscan Architecture*, p. 207.

[8] Luard, *An. Mon.* iii, p. 170; Little, *Grey Friars in Oxford*, p. 182.

mention frequent gifts to the friars in the towns which he visited;[1] Walter Giffard, Wickwayn and Romeyn all gave financial help to the friars in the diocese of York;[2] and Godfrey Giffard, himself a Franciscan, assisted the Grey Friars of Worcester.[3] Almost all episcopal wills which have been preserved contain legacies to the friars.[4] Kilwardby, the Dominican Archbishop of Canterbury, and his successor Pecham, the Franciscan, were both warm supporters of the mendicants. The only recorded instance of hostility on the part of the bishops was at Chester, where Alexander Stavensby put some obstacles in the way of the Franciscans in 1236. The cause of this, however, was not antipathy to the Friars Minor, whom he warmly supported at Lichfield, but concern for the welfare of the Dominicans, who were already established in the town.[5]

Royalty was equally generous in its attitude towards the friars and there was scarcely a house in the country which did not owe something to the liberality of the King. Many convents received gifts of money or building materials or clothes; while Henry III instituted annual grants from the Exchequer for the Grey Friars of Oxford, Cambridge and Berwick.[6] There was even, at one time, a proposal that the friars should be permanently supported out of state funds in order to put an end to begging, but the Franciscans refused to surrender the principle of mendicity which had meant so much to them in the early days.[7] In a few places the King actually gave the buildings to the friars. At Cambridge, for example, he handed over to the Franciscans in 1238 a house which had belonged to Benjamin the Jew,[8] and at York in 1228 he gave the Dominicans their

[1] Webb, *Household Roll of R. de Swinfield*, i, pp. 147–50; ii, p. clxvii.

[2] Dixon, *Fasti Eboracenses*, pp. 313–14, 323–4; *Regist. W. Wickwayn*, pp. 311, 317; *Regist. J. Romeyn*, i, p. 67.

[3] *Regist. G. Giffard*, p. 231.

[4] Richard of Chichester left money and books to eight houses of friars (*Sussex Arch. Coll.* i, pp. 171–5), Walter de Merton and Walter Suffield gave to various houses (Hobhouse, *Life of W. de Merton*, pp. 45–6; Blomefield, *Norfolk*, iii, p. 488), and Peter de Aquablanca left a small sum to the Franciscans of Hereford (*Camd. Misc.* xiv, p. 2).

[5] Eccleston, *de Adventu*, p. 100; Martin, *Franciscan Architecture*, p. 226; Grosseteste, *Epistolae*, pp. 120–1.

[6] Oxford received 50 marks, Cambridge 25 marks and Berwick 20 marks; Little, *Studies in Eng. Franc. Hist.* p. 24. The Dominicans of Oxford also had 50 marks a year: *V.C.H., Oxon.* ii, p. 111.

[7] Little, *Studies in Eng. Franc. Hist.* pp. 87–9.

[8] Eccleston, *de Adventu*, pp. 167–8.

first site.[1] Edward I regularly gave money to the friars in the towns through which he passed, his customary gift being fourpence for each friar in the house at the time, the price of a day's food.[2]

In return for these marks of royal favour the friars were expected to help the King in various ways, both spiritual and political. Henry III, who was genuinely fond of the friars and had a great admiration for them, frequently chose mendicants as his confessors,[3] and even provided rooms at Court for the convenience of the Grey Friars.[4] He also used many of them 'on his majesty's service', finding them intelligent, knowing and, of course, inexpensive. Agnellus of Pisa, the first Provincial Minister of the Franciscans in England, died in 1233 from dysentery brought on by the cold and fatigue which he had undergone in his efforts to make peace between the King and the Earl of Pembroke.[5] Adam Marsh was twice sent abroad by the King on diplomatic missions,[6] and several Dominicans were employed in his service.[7] Royalty also found the friaries convenient guest-houses for themselves or for their retainers on their constant journeys. Edward I stayed with the Black Friars of Pontefract and Yarm, and in 1327 Edward III and the Queen Mother settled at the Franciscan house in York for six weeks, during the course of which the Queen gave a feast in the friars' dormitory at which there were at least sixty ladies present.[8]

With the townsfolk the friars seem to have been almost universally popular in the early days. Owing to their rules against the possession of property it was a common thing for their land and buildings to be legally held by the citizens, who gave the friars the use of them. Often the land was actually bought out of public money. In the Preface to the first volume

[1] Goldthorp, *Friars in Yorkshire*, in *Yorks. Arch. Journal*, 1936, pp. 6, 365.

[2] This shows that by the end of the century the friars' standard of living was fairly high. Fourpence a day is over £6 a year, whereas the statutory allowance for parish priests and vicars was £3. 6*s*. 8*d*. or less. See above, pp. 45–6, 55.

[3] B. Formoy, *The Dominican Order in England*, p. 85; Little, *Grey Friars in Oxford*, p. 137.

[4] Eccleston, *de Adventu*, p. 177.

[5] *Ibid.* p. 95.

[6] Little, *Grey Friars in Oxford*, p. 137, and cf. p. 7.

[7] Formoy, *The Dominican Order in England*, p. 79; cf. Bennett, *Early Dominicans*, p. 134.

[8] Goldthorp in *Yorks. Arch. Journal*, 1936, pp. 399, 417 and 275–6.

of the *Monumenta Franciscana* Brewer described the close relationship which existed between the friars and the towns, and pointed out how the merchants welcomed the friars partly because of their contacts with foreign countries and markets.[1] Unlike the Cistercians, who had fled to the loneliest valleys of the Pennines or the Welsh mountains, the friars deliberately settled in the larger centres of population, since it was here that the largest congregations could be attracted to their sermons. Most of the early houses were built inside the walls of the towns, the wall itself often serving as part of their boundary.[2] At Cambridge the Franciscans were provided at first by the townsfolk with an old synagogue near the prison;[3] at Oxford they inhabited for a time a house which Richard le Muliner gave to the citizens for their use;[4] at London the burgesses not only provided them with land but also paid for the erection of their convent;[5] at Ipswich they were established through the generosity of the Dean of Coddenham and the citizens of the town;[6] and at Shrewsbury one of the townsfolk, Richard Pride, built them their church.[7]

The relations between the friars and the inhabitants of the towns seem to have been cordial on the whole. The citizens were quick to appreciate the courage and enthusiasm of the first friars who came to live among them and to serve them, and their support lasted so long as their confidence in the friars remained unshaken. There was some danger of a rift in 1256, when the friars of London, both Franciscan and Dominican, lost a good deal of popular support through their courageous advocacy of the cause of the Jews; but the flow of donations and bequests which began again shortly afterwards shows that friendly relations were not permanently disturbed.[8]

With the older monastic orders relations were not so happy. At the very first the monks seem to have treated the friars with some generosity, but as soon as they realised that these wandering preachers would become their most formidable rivals

[1] *Monumenta Franciscana*, i, p. xiv.

[2] Martin, *Franciscan Architecture*, p. 8.

[3] Eccleston, *de Adventu*, p. 28. [4] *Ibid*. pp. 27–8.

[5] C. L. Kingsford, *Grey Friars of London*, pp. 31, 35.

[6] Eccleston, *de Adventu*, pp. 169–70. [7] *Ibid*. pp. 28–9.

[8] Little, *Studies in Eng. Franc. Hist*. pp. 48–9; M. Paris, *Chron. Maj*. v, p. 546; Kingsford, *Grey Friars of London*, p. 17; *V.C.H., London*, i, pp. 498–9.

they adopted a very different attitude. The first Franciscans owed to the kindliness of the monks of Fécamp their expenses in crossing over to England in 1224, and their first two nights in this country were spent as guests of the Benedictines of Christ Church, Canterbury.[1] Such hospitality, however, was not always forthcoming; for, a few weeks later, when two of them were on their way from London to Oxford, they were turned away by the monks of a grange belonging to the Abbey of Abingdon at which they had sought shelter, and were accommodated in a hay-loft only through the kindness of a young monk with more understanding and charity than his seniors.[2]

At Reading and Bristol the monks seem to have given some help to the friars,[3] but in most places they recognised that the friars would do them no good, and put up a spirited resistance to them. There were several reasons for this opposition. In the first place the monks realised that the old monopoly which they had so long enjoyed was now seriously threatened, and there is little doubt that the drying up of the flow of gifts to the monasteries, which had been so conspicuous during the twelfth century, was largely due to its being diverted to the friars who had captured the imagination of the public. Again, the privations under which the early mendicants lived were bound to make a striking contrast with the easy-going ways of the monks, and so to make the older communities more unpopular than they were already. Once again, the monks realised that the friars might take the side of the laity in the tension which always existed between town and cloister, and might encourage them in their struggle for liberty from the burden of monastic privilege and restraint.[4]

Once the monasteries realised who these friars were, the

[1] Eccleston, *de Adventu*, pp. 7–8.

[2] The story is from Bartholomew of Pisa, *Liber de Conformitate*, in *Analecta Franciscana*, iv, p. 329 and is printed in Eccleston, *de Adventu*, pp. 136–40. The narrative goes on to say that, during the night, the young monk had a dream in which his companions were all condemned, at the judgment-seat of Christ, to be hanged from an elm tree in their own cloister. In the morning the monks were found dead in their beds, and the young monk, who alone survived, immediately joined the Franciscans.

[3] Eccleston, *de Adventu*, pp. 171–2; Weare, *A Collectanea relating to the Bristol Friars Minors*, p. 17. At Bedford in 1310 the site of the Grey Friars was enlarged by various gifts, including one from the canonesses of Harrold: Martin, *Franciscan Architecture*, p. 154.

[4] Little, *Studies in Eng. Franc. Hist.* p. 98.

generosity which was occasionally shown in the early days turned to a stiff resistance. The most detailed account of such resistance comes from Bury S. Edmunds. The monks here were exceedingly powerful, yet their position was beginning to be threatened by the growing self-consciousness of the townsfolk.[1] The Franciscans made their first attempt to settle here in 1233;[2] but it was not until 1257 that they finally secured a footing, fortified with a privilege from Alexander IV. They arrived under cover of darkness, carrying a portable altar with them, and established themselves in a farmhouse at the north end of the town. On discovering this, the monks were extremely indignant, and, regardless of the bull which protected the friars, they drove them out. The friars immediately appealed to the Pope, who ordered the monks to provide them with accommodation in the town and directed the Archbishop of Canterbury and the Dean of Lincoln to see that this was done. But once again the monks proved too powerful and drove away both the friars and the delegates whom the dignitaries had sent on their behalf. This time the friars turned to the secular arm and lodged an appeal with the King. With his help they managed to get possession of a site, where they maintained a precarious footing for five and a half years. But on the death of Alexander IV in 1261 the monks found a new champion in his successor, Urban IV, who ordered the friars to leave the town and pull down their buildings. Finally a reconciliation was reached, the friars agreeing to leave the town and the monks giving them land at Babwell, a few miles away, where they remained until the Dissolution.[3]

At Scarborough both Franciscans and Dominicans fell foul of the Cistercians, to whom the local parish church was appropriated. In 1240 an attempt by the Franciscans to settle in the town led the monks to appeal to Rome. Grosseteste was appointed by the Pope to hear the dispute, but, after two days of discussion, the friars suddenly withdrew their claim on the grounds that it was against their rule to seek privileges from the Pope. So deep and so favourable an impression did this make on the monks that they would have cancelled their opposition

[1] See above, pp. 286–8. [2] Luard, *An. Mon.* iii, p. 134.

[3] See the full account: *Processus contra Fratres Minores, qualiter expulsi erant de villa S. Edmundi*, in Arnold's *Memorials of S. Edmund's Abbey*, ii, pp. 263–85.

had not the Abbot of Cîteaux insisted upon the expulsion of the friars. Thirty years later the friars tried again, but the opportunity of a peaceful settlement had been lost. The friars themselves had lost something of the humility of the early days, and the monks had by now realised the power and influence of their rivals. This second attempt, therefore, led to a bitter dispute which lasted fifteen years, though it resulted finally in the establishment of a friary.[1]

These quarrels at Bury and Scarborough were typical of what happened in a good many places when the friars came into opposition with the monks. The Benedictines of Coventry put some obstacles in the way of the Franciscans in 1234 but appear to have withdrawn their opposition later.[2] At Winchester Eccleston speaks of 'great difficulties' which the friars had to face—an almost certain reference to monastic interference.[3] At Oxford the Dominicans came into conflict with the Augustinians of S. Frideswide's over the building of an oratory,[4] and at Dunstable they quarrelled with the canons, who complained that they had set up an altar in secret and to the great injury of the Prior.[5] The regulars as a whole, therefore, were suspicious of the friars, whose coming they viewed with much distaste. Writing, some years later, of the year 1224 John, Abbot of Peterborough, uttered the following lament: 'In that year, O misery! O more than misery! O cruel scourge! The Friars Minor came to England.'[6]

Apart from the opposition of the older religious houses the friars seem to have been generally respected and popular, and the orders spread rapidly. In the first twenty years of their existence in this country the Black Friars established nineteen houses, mostly in the larger towns such as Oxford, London, Norwich, York, Bristol, Northampton, Winchester, Canterbury, Cambridge, Lincoln and Stamford. From 1242 to 1260 they added a further seventeen friaries, and by the end of the

[1] Little, *Studies in Eng. Franc. Hist.* pp. 93–5, and cf. the authorities there quoted. For the Dominicans' effort at Scarborough see Goldthorp in *Yorks. Arch. Journal*, 1936, pp. 406–7.

[2] Martin, *Franciscan Architecture*, p. 63.

[3] Eccleston, *de Adventu*, p. 100.

[4] *V.C.H., Oxon.* ii, p. 107.

[5] M. Paris, *Chron. Maj.* v, p. 742.

[6] 'Eodem anno O dolor! O plus quam dolor! O pestis truculenta! Fratres Minores venerunt in Angliam': Little, *Studies in Eng. Franc. Hist.* p. 99, quoting Sparke, *Hist. Anglic. Script. Varii*, pt. iii, p. 102.

century had fifty-one. The Franciscans began at Canterbury in 1224 and spread quickly to London, Oxford, Northampton, Norwich and so on, so that after twenty years they had no less than thirty-nine houses.[1] By the year 1300 they had fifty-five. Since each house of Grey or Black Friars had an average of about forty members it is clear that the mendicant ideal was making a strong appeal to the people of this country.[2]

The type of recruit varied considerably, especially in the early days. S. Francis had numbered among his immediate disciples men of all ranks; but, as the order grew more scholastic it tended to appeal more directly to educated men and to cater for them. The same is true of the Dominicans. Among them in early days, men of peasant status would have been found; but, since the illiterate were given no share in the government of the order, it was only natural that it should come to appeal almost entirely to men of education. Evidence of the personnel in English friaries in the thirteenth century is meagre, but, such as it is, it suggests that the recruits were mostly drawn from the merchants and tradespeople of the towns and from the Universities. Eccleston records that when the Grey Friars settled in Oxford they were joined by 'many men of noble birth and many eminent bachelors',[3] while between 1227 and 1232 a number of masters entered the order.[4] The two bishops who became friars have already been mentioned, and to them should be added John, Abbot of Osney, who joined the Franciscans in 1234, and the Abbot of Walden, who became a Dominican about the same time.[5] The number of parochial clergy who gave up their livings in order to join the mendicants does not seem to have been very large, but there were certainly a few, such as Peter de Eport, Rector of Stoke Prior, who joined the Minorites at Worcester in 1226,[6] and Adam, Rector of Askham, who attached himself to the Dominicans at York in 1268.[7]

[1] According to Eccleston there were, in 1256, forty-nine Franciscan houses containing 1242 friars: *de Adventu*, p. 14.

[2] See Appendix for further details as to numbers. In the year 1300 there were over 5000 friars in this country.

[3] 'Multi probi bachelarii et multi nobiles': Eccleston, *de Adventu*, p. 27.

[4] Little, *The Franciscan School at Oxford*, in *Archivum Franc. Hist.* 1926, p. 805.

[5] Luard, *An. Mon.* iv, p. 82 and M. Paris, *Chron. Maj.* iv, p. 164.

[6] Luard, *An. Mon.* iv, p. 410.

[7] Goldthorp in *Yorks. Arch. Journal*, 1936, p. 371.

Adam Marsh had not only been rector of the rich parish of Wearmouth but was also a man of considerable wealth when, in Matthew Paris' words, he gave up 'all worldly greatness and a large income' in order to enter the Franciscan house at Worcester.[1]

For a rich man to cast in his lot with the friars in the early days was indeed an act of renunciation and faith, for, as Dr Little has said, 'certainly at first the friars in England revelled in poverty with a zest which may well have cheered the heart of S. Francis in his last sad years'.[2] On their first arrival they often had to put up with quarters which were cramped, unhealthy and sometimes offensive. At Canterbury the Friars Minor lived for a while in a cellar under a school, from which they emerged in the evening, when the boys had gone home, and sat for a while round what was left of the fire, on which they warmed up the dregs of beer from the boys' cups.[3] In London they made their first home in a house in Cornhill, where they built cells, stopping up the chinks with grass, before moving to an unsavoury part of the town near the shambles known as Stynkynglane.[4] At Exeter the district in which they settled was so objectionable that the Earl of Hereford, having lodged there for a night, described the place as detestable and the stench unbearable.[5] At Reading, Lincoln, Worcester, Boston and Oxford the houses were damp and liable to flooding.[6]

When the friars began to build houses of their own, efforts were made to see that a high standard of simplicity was observed and that the buildings were suitable for knights of Lady Poverty. The early churches of the Grey Friars were mostly very small—at Cambridge the roof was put on by a single carpenter in one day and consisted of fifteen split tree trunks[7]—and were almost invariably made of wood and plaster, in accordance with the wishes of S. Francis himself.[8] All the early Provincial Ministers

[1] M. Paris, *Chron. Maj.* v, pp. 619–20. See also an Essay on Adam Marsh by Father Cuthbert in *The Romanticism of S. Francis.*

[2] Little, *Studies in Eng. Franc. Hist.* p. 5.

[3] Eccleston, *de Adventu*, p. 8.

[4] *Ibid.* p. 11; Kingsford, *Grey Friars of London*, p. 16.

[5] Little and Easterling, *Franciscans and Dominicans of Exeter*, p. 15.

[6] Little, *Studies in Eng. Franc. Hist.* p. 11.

[7] Eccleston, *de Adventu*, p. 28.

[8] Martin, *Franciscan Architecture*, p. 13. For the intentions of S. Francis see *Intentio Regulae*, §§ 14–15; Sabatier, *Speculum Perfectionis* (1898), pp. 26–9, and cf. pp. 17–18, 94–101.

of the Franciscan order in this country were determined to maintain a high standard of poverty and simplicity. Agnellus of Pisa saw to it that the early settlements were poor and squalid enough, for he had the infirmary at Oxford built so low that a man could scarce stand upright in it, and he replaced the stone walls of the dormitory at London with mud.[1] Albert of Pisa, his successor, appears to have been very strict about building, for he destroyed a stone cloister at Southampton in the teeth of considerable opposition from the citizens who had built it, and when prevented from pulling down a chapel at Reading which had been provided by the King he remarked that, since he was not allowed to demolish it, he hoped that it would be struck by lightning.[2] The third Minister, Haymo of Faversham, was distinguished for his sturdy support of a high standard of poverty, for he appeared at the Provincial Chapter in rags and insisted upon sitting on the ground.[3] William of Nottingham, his successor, in his effort to adhere strictly to the rule, had the carved bosses in the cloister at London knocked off, and, when one of the brothers complained that there was no outer wall, William replied that he did not join the Franciscans in order to build walls.[4] At Shrewsbury he pulled down the stone walls of the dormitory and rebuilt them with mud.[5]

Everything, therefore, was done to see that the wishes of S. Francis were observed in the matter of building. The early homes of the friars were poor enough, often mere huts 'of clay and wattles made', quite in keeping with the hovels of Rivo Torto and the brushwood booths of the Portiuncula. Equally severe were the standards of clothing and of food. S. Francis has told us that, in the early days, he and his first disciples were 'satisfied with one habit, patched within and without, if they so wished, and the cord and breeches'.[6] By 1223 the official dress had been modified and the friar was now allowed two tunics and, if need be, shoes.[7] In England the Franciscans certainly maintained a very strict standard in dress. There is abundant evidence that the Grey Friars as a rule went barefoot even in the depths of winter. Royal gifts of clothing to the friars often

[1] Eccleston, *de Adventu*, p. 55.
[2] *Ibid.* pp. 99–100.
[3] *Ibid.* p. 108.
[4] *Ibid.* p. 57.
[5] *Ibid.* pp. 28–9.
[6] *Testamentum S. Francisci*, in *Opuscula S. Francisci*, ed. Lemmens, p. 79; and cf. Celano's account of the early days in his *Vita Prima*, § 39.
[7] *Regula Secunda*, cap. ii, in *Opuscula*, p. 65.

include shoes for the Dominicans but not for the Franciscans,[1] contemporary pictures and descriptions show us the friars going with bare feet,[2] and the *Lanercost Chronicle* tells a story of how the heart of an unfriendly knight was touched by the sight of two Franciscans travelling near Oxford in winter, leaving upon the snow the marks of blood from their feet cut by the ice.[3] So rough were their clothes that they were often indistinguishable from peasants, while they gloried in the privations and hardships which made them sometimes huddle together like pigs to get a little warmth.[4] Three things, said Albert of Pisa, distinguished the order in this country: that the friars went barefoot, that they wore shabby clothes, and that they refused to accept money.[5] Such distinction would have brought joy to S. Francis.

The strictness of the English Franciscans had some influence upon the Preaching Friars. S. Dominic had not made poverty one of the foundation-stones of his order, but he was forced to adopt it by the example which the followers of S. Francis were setting.[6] By the Constitutions of 1228 the Black Friars were allowed to wear shoes, three tunics and an overcoat;[7] but the extreme poverty of the rival order in this country may have made them reluctant to claim even the comforts to which they were entitled. The chief temptation to which the English Dominicans seem to have been prone was to build large and expensive schools, for at the General Chapter of 1250 several English priors were punished for building schools too large,[8] while between 1237 and 1250 the Black Friars of Canterbury had received nearly £500 from the King, besides gifts of timber.[9]

Schools were, in fact, the chief interest of the Preaching Friars.

[1] E.g. Lib. 17, Henry III, m. 2, quoted in Eccleston, *de Adventu*, p. 165, and cf. Little, *Studies in Eng. Franc. Hist*. pp. 56–60.

[2] Eccleston, *de Adventu*, p. 43, and cf. the drawings from Matthew Paris reproduced in *Collectanea Franciscana*, i; also the description in M. Paris, *Chron. Maj.* iv, p. 279: 'ipsi Minores nudi pedes et viliter tunicati cincti funiculis.' The Franciscans at Winchester appear to have worn shoes: Little, *Grey Friars in Oxford*, p. 4 n.

[3] Stevenson, *Chron. de Lanercost*, pp. 30–1.

[4] Eccleston, *de Adventu*, pp. 15–16.

[5] *Ibid*. p. 102.

[6] R. F. Bennett, *The Early Dominicans*, pp. 42–3.

[7] Denifle, *Die Constitutionen des Prediger-Ordens*, in *Archiv für Litt. und Kirchengeschichte*, i, p. 204.

[8] Reichert, *Acta Cap. Gen. Ordinis Praedicatorum*, i, pp. 54–5.

[9] *V.C.H., Kent*, ii, pp. 177–8.

When Dominic sent a small company to Paris it was to 'study, preach and form a convent'; and wherever his followers went they devoted themselves to study and preaching, even to the comparative neglect of worship in their oratories.[1] Each convent was to have a teacher, and novices were to be examined in knowledge as well as in character.[2] The order existed to save the world from heresy: the instrument was the spoken word: the preparation of the instrument long and close study of the Bible and commentaries, and even of languages such as Arabic and Hebrew.[3] The training of the Dominican was designed to make him an effective preacher, and knowledge which might lead him away from this end was to be eschewed. Even the Arts course at the University was at first condemned (though the academic authorities in time forced the friars to modify their rules in this matter), as were also such subjects as medicine and alchemy. For the adequate training of the preacher a whole system of schools was established, from the theological lectures in each convent to the advanced courses at the University, with the result that the order produced a number of learned men and effective preachers. The names of Robert Bacon, Richard Fishacre, Robert Kilwardby and John of Darlington are all honourable in the history of English philosophy and theology.

Yet the curious fact remains that it was the Franciscans, who began by glorying in their ignorance and simplicity, who produced the greatest scholars in this country in the thirteenth century. S. Francis' attitude towards learning has already been noted. So anxious was he that his followers should proclaim their message, not by rousing oratory or by persuasive sermons, but by the sincerity and humility of their lives, that he at first forbade his friars to possess any book or to devote any time to study. The nine Franciscans who landed at Dover on 10 September 1224 were men after S. Francis' own heart. They came to show men the dignity of poverty and humility, to dress as peasants and to live as tramps, to show that the Gospel could best be preached to the poor by the poor, to hold up before the world a reflection of the days when Christ and His apostles walked among the Galilean hills.

[1] R. F. Bennett, *The Early Dominicans*, pp. 24–6.

[2] 'In moribus et scientia': Little, *The Educational Organisation of the Mendicant Friars*, in *Trans. R. Hist. Soc.* 1894, pp. 50–1.

[3] R. F. Bennett, *The Early Dominicans*, pp. 59–60.

And yet within thirty or forty years of their arrival in this country—*idiotae et subditi omnibus*, as S. Francis would have boasted—the English Franciscans had become one of the most learned communities in the world, sending teachers of international reputation to many of the greatest Universities of Europe.[1] The order which despised learning had quickly changed into a fellowship of scholars. And the man who was mainly responsible for this turn in the fortunes of the order was not a Franciscan at all but a secular priest, Robert Grosseteste.

Two of the original party of Franciscans who came to this island—Richard of Ingworth and Richard of Devon—pressed on to Oxford soon after their arrival, in the hope of attracting young men into the order. They were hospitably received here by the Dominicans, with whom they lived for eight days, before settling in a house of their own where they remained for eight or nine months. They then went on to Northampton.[2] During those months there can be little doubt that they came into contact with Robert Grosseteste, who at this time was Chancellor of Oxford and by far the most distinguished lecturer in the University. Grosseteste had already seen something of the Preaching Friars, but the Franciscans, coming a few years later, seem to have won his warmest approval, an approval which turned to a deep affection and to a devotion which at one time very nearly persuaded him to take the habit himself. It needs no great powers of imagination to see why this should have occurred. Grosseteste was passionately concerned to raise the low standards of the parochial clergy and to find some powerful force which would sweep through the land bringing before people's minds a vision of what the Church might be. In the Grey Friars he believed that he had found the instrument which he had been seeking. Here were men prepared to face every kind of hardship and privation, to live in slums and hovels, men who despised most of what the world holds dear, who had no desire for worldly success and no ambition except to serve God and their fellow-men. Grosseteste obviously felt—as he had not felt when he met the Dominicans—that God had sent the very men whom the world most needed.

There was only one point on which Grosseteste failed to see eye to eye with the Franciscan ideal, and that was on the subject

[1] E.g. Paris, Lyons and Cologne: Brewer, *Monumenta Franciscana*, i, p. lxxxi.

[2] Eccleston, *de Adventu*, p. 11.

of learning. Grosseteste was a scholar, a man whose highest gifts and greatest energies had been dedicated to the pursuit of knowledge; Oxford was his home and his delight. But the University needed 'conversion' just as much as the countryside to save it from becoming a place where men equipped themselves for lucrative posts or idled their time away in trivial and useless discussion. So greatly was Grosseteste impressed by the friars that he resolved to make them not only the saviours of the parochial life of England but also of the Universities.

Thus it came about that Grosseteste, in his desire to develop the intellectual as well as the devotional and evangelistic gifts of the Grey Friars, became their first lecturer. To what extent he was the first to hold office as lector to any Franciscan house or province cannot be determined with certainty. A letter of S. Francis to S. Anthony of Padua (the authenticity of which, however, has been disputed) speaks of his 'expounding the words of theology to the friars' in the province of Romagna,[1] and Jordano tells us that in 1228 John Parenti appointed a lector to the friars in Germany, for he had heard that they were without one.[2] On the other hand the Grey Friars in Paris, although they settled there in 1220, appear to have had no theological school of their own for some years.[3] Certainly up to the year 1228 or thereabouts there is not much sign that the intention of S. Francis to discourage intellectual pursuits was being disregarded. Unlike the Dominicans the early Franciscans were more concerned with preaching and with evangelism than with the academic life.

It now seems to be clear that Grosseteste began his work among the Grey Friars in Oxford in the year 1229. In that year the house of William de Wileford with all its appurtenances was bought by public subscription and given to the mayor and good men of Oxford for the use of the friars.[4] Agnellus of Pisa took this an an opportunity for instituting a school and invited Grosseteste to come as their lecturer.[5] Grosseteste must, therefore, have begun his lecturing to the friars about

[1] For a discussion of this letter and a translation, see my *Sources for the Life of S. Francis*, p. 22.

[2] Boehmer, *Chronica Jordani*, p. 47.

[3] Rashdall, *Medieval Universities of Europe* (new ed.), i, p. 348 n.

[4] Little, *Franciscan Papers, Lists and Documents* (1943), pp. 56–7.

[5] Eccleston, *de Adventu*, p. 60.

the same time as Brother Simon in Germany. But the important thing is that Grosseteste was totally different from all other lectors to the Franciscans in that he was not only the foremost scholar of his day, but a secular.[1] The result was that the Franciscan house at Oxford immediately acquired a position and an importance quite different from that of other friaries elsewhere. Whereas the typical friary was a centre of spiritual activity among the poor and the ignorant, the house at Oxford became, under the influence of Grosseteste, one of the most famous spots in the town, the home of the very best teaching which the University could offer.[2] The decision of Agnellus to invite Grosseteste to become lecturer to the friars at Oxford, and his readiness to accept the proposal, must have had a profound influence on the whole future of the order. The Franciscans became, like the Dominicans, a learned order, establishing schools in many parts of the country, sending scholars to teach abroad, and even providing lecturers at some of the Benedictine houses, such as Christ Church, Canterbury, and Worcester.[3] Apart from Grosseteste himself most of the greatest scholars and thinkers of the thirteenth century were Franciscans—Roger Bacon, John Pecham, Thomas of York, William of Ockham, Duns Scotus and Adam Marsh.[4] Poverty the English Franciscans loved and served faithfully for many years; but once the influence of Grosseteste had begun to bear on them the old fear of learning, which had provoked S. Francis to exclaim that every scholar who joined the order ought to surrender even his knowledge in order that he might offer

[1] Alexander of Hales, a few years later and while still a secular, began lecturing to the Franciscans at Paris: Rashdall, *Medieval Universities of Europe* (new ed.), i, p. 374.

[2] The Franciscan school at Oxford appears to have been open to students who were not members of the order: Little, *Studies in Eng. Franc. Hist.* pp. 168–9.

[3] In 1275 the monks of Christ Church, Canterbury, established a school of theology and invited a Franciscan, William of Everel, to be their lector. He was succeeded by at least two other Franciscans, Ralph of Wodehay and Robert of Fulham: Cotton, *Grey Friars of Canterbury*, pp. 34–6. In 1285 Godfrey Giffard, Bishop of Worcester, asked for a friar to be appointed as lector to the monks of Worcester: *Regist. G. Giffard*, p. 263. Friars also lectured in the Cathedral schools: Little, *Franciscan School at Oxford*, in *Arch. Franc. Hist.* 1926, p. 821.

[4] See D. E. Sharp, *Franciscan Philosophy at Oxford in the Thirteenth Century*, for a discussion of the work of most of these thinkers.

Plate VIII. Choir of the Franciscan Church, Chichester, from the N.E.

Plate IX. Effigy of Layman buried in Franciscan Habit at Conington, Huntingdonshire.

himself naked to Christ,[1] was forgotten. All over Europe this process was taking place; the strict interpretation of S. Francis' wishes was being left to a few scattered and persecuted idealists, the *zelanti*, while the rest of the friars were either beginning to lose their footing on a slope which would eventually bring them to the disasters of the fourteenth century, or were finding a new ideal in the alliance of Poverty and Learning. 'Paris, Paris,' cried Brother Giles, 'thou hast destroyed Assisi'; and in a sense this was true. All that we can say is that if 'Assisi' was to be destroyed it was better that it should be destroyed by Paris or Oxford than by the worthless creature who set out with Chaucer's party on that April morning from Southwark.[2]

The first generation of mendicant friars in this country were certainly worthy of the welcome which was given to them. Largely cut off from the disruptive movements which were affecting the orders in South Europe, they were able to live out an ideal of simplicity and evangelistic service which was an example to the whole world. Indeed, when the saintly John of Parma, Minister General of the Franciscans and an upholder in theory and in practice of the strictest standards of poverty and humility, came to this country in 1248 he declared: 'Would that a province such as this had been set in the midst of the world that it might be an example to all.'[3]

[1] Celano, *Vita Secunda*, § 194.

[2] For an account of the breakdown of the Franciscan ideal see Gratien, *Histoire de la Fondation et de l'Évolution de l'Ordre des Frères Mineurs au XIIIe Siècle* (Paris, 1928), and Vida Scudder, *Franciscan Adventure* (1931). The subject is also discussed in my *Sources for the Life of S. Francis* (1940).

[3] Eccleston, *de Adventu*, p 123.

CHAPTER XXVI

CHANGE AND DECAY

There is abundant evidence that the fire which had inspired the friars in the early days had more or less spent itself by about the year 1250, and that from that date onwards a change came over the orders which led in time to the abuses which were so conspicuous in the following century. Eccleston's Chronicle of the Grey Friars, written about the year 1258, gives us an intimate picture of what the early life of the Franciscans in this country was like, a picture which can be supplemented by scraps of evidence from other contemporary literature and from such fragments as remain of the first mendicant foundations.

The earliest friars were generally accommodated in some temporary shelter until money could be found to provide them with a permanent home. Even these first friaries, built at public expense, were generally very small. Eccleston reveals the fact that for some time the Franciscans in London had no chapel of their own, but used the local parish churches for their worship.[1] It was not until 1239—fifteen years after their arrival—that they were provided with a church for their own use through the munificence of one William Joyner, Mayor of London.[2] The Grey Friars of Oxford appear to have had the same experience, for they arrived in the city in 1224 but, so far as we know, they did not start to build their church until at least 1239, for it was in that year that Ralph Maidstone resigned the bishopric of Hereford to join the Friars Minor, and Bartholomew of Pisa describes how he and the ex-abbot of Osney worked with their hands in the building of the church.[3] At Cambridge, where the Franciscans settled about 1230, the first indication of the building of a church is in 1238, when Henry III gave them a site and ten marks towards the building of their little chapel.[4] This delay in the building of the churches is significant. Among the older monastic orders the building of the church was normally the first concern of the monks when

[1] Eccleston, *de Adventu*, pp. 16–17.

[2] C. L. Kingsford, *Grey Friars of London*, p. 16.

[3] Bartholomew of Pisa, *de Conformitate*, in *Analecta Franciscana*, iv, pp. 330–1.

[4] Eccleston, *de Adventu*, pp. 28, 167–8.

a new house was founded. A monastery without a church would be an absurdity, for the community's primary duty was to meet together to worship God in the regular round of the daily offices. The friars, on the other hand, lived so much more in the world that there was nothing to prevent them from using the parish churches for their worship as well as for their preaching. This, indeed, seems to have been their general practice in the early days. It would, however, be wrong to suppose that the friars were in any sense casual about the daily offices. At Cambridge, for example, they were most conscientious about saying the Hours in full, although there were only three brothers that were clerks; and Eccleston assures us that the offices were regularly said in the friaries and that one could nearly always find one of the brothers at prayer at any hour of the night.[1] They had, moreover, a special reverence for the Eucharist, which was quite in accordance with the intentions of S. Francis.[2]

The domestic buildings of the friars were generally on a small scale since land in the towns was so costly. Sometimes, in order to save space, rooms were built over the cloister or some other part of the buildings. The total area of the friars' land was generally small, often no more than three or four acres, while the Grey Friars of York owned but one acre.[3] Into this confined space were packed not only the conventual buildings but also the friars' gardens, which played an important part in their daily life, for it was here that the friars grew some of their food.

The word 'mendicant' as applied to the orders of friars is in some ways a misnomer. It is true that S. Francis begged for his food on many occasions, and that he taught his disciples to regard almost with reverence the scraps which they received in alms. But the Rule makes it perfectly clear that the friars were a community of workers who only resorted to begging when they had no other means of sustenance.[4] The Rule, however, does not contemplate the possession of land on which to work, for the friars were expected to labour in the fields, receiving, as a reward of their toil, a night's lodging or a little

[1] Eccleston, *de Adventu*, pp. 28, 31. [2] *Ibid*. p. 120.

[3] Martin, *Franciscan Architecture*, p. 9.

[4] *Regula Prima*, cap. vii: 'Et fratres qui sciunt laborare laborent.... Et possint pro labore accipere omnia necessaria praeter pecuniam. Et, cum necesse fuerit, vadant pro eleemosynis....Omnes fratres studeant bonis operibus insudare': see *Opuscula S. Francisci*, ed. Lemmens, pp. 33–4.

food. In England the earliest friars were so devoted to poverty that they hated the idea of owning any land of their own; but under the third Provincial Minister, Haymo of Faversham, they were encouraged to grow a little food and therefore to have gardens attached to the friaries. He declared that 'he would rather that the brethren should have ample areas and cultivate them, in order that they might have food-stuffs at home, than that they should beg them from others'.[1] Haymo may have been influenced in this, as in other things, by Grosseteste, who believed that 'there was a higher degree of poverty than mendicancy, namely to live of one's own labour; hence he said that the Beguines are of the most perfect and holy religion because they live of their own labours and do not burden the world with exactions'.[2]

Under Haymo's encouragement several of the friaries enlarged their sites in order to provide themselves with gardens in which they might grow their food, though there is no evidence of their acquiring large estates. The Grey Friars of Babwell at the time of the Dissolution owned 43 acres, and Llanfaes in Anglesey 30.[3] At these houses, then, some agricultural work must have been carried on; and we know that this was so at Llanfaes, and for a special reason. The friary here was founded in 1237; but by the end of the century the village in which it was placed had moved; and the friars, being left isolated in the country, took to farming as a means of keeping themselves alive.[4] At Babwell the rather large estate may well have been due to the fact that the monks of Bury S. Edmunds successfully prevented the friars from settling in the town where alms would have been more plentiful. The Grey Friars of Dunwich appear to have done a certain amount of fishing, for we have a record that in 1305 the King gave them a boat.[5]

The friars, then, lived mostly by alms, supplemented by a certain amount of manual labour on their own plots. Like everyone else at that time they were sometimes in debt, though efforts were made to save them from falling into the chaotic financial conditions in which some of the older religious houses found themselves. On several occasions the King generously intervened with gifts to pay off debts which the friars had con-

[1] Eccleston, *de Adventu*, pp. 55–6. [2] *Ibid*. pp. 123–4.
[3] Little, *Studies in Eng. Franc. Hist*. p. 17.
[4] Martin, *Franciscan Architecture*, p. 173. [5] *Ibid*. p. 79.

tracted,[1] while a few of the custodians, such as Martin de Barton at York, set themselves to prevent the accumulation of debts in any house under their jurisdiction.[2]

The picture which we get of the first thirty years or so of the friars' existence in this country is certainly a very pleasant one. Conditions were rough, but the orders were attracting the best type of man, and there was a vitality and virility in them which the older religious orders seemed to have lost. Unlike the monks, also, they were generally respected by the people, who valued their ministrations and welcomed them into their towns. Intellectually, also, they were far in advance both of the monks and of the general run of the secular clergy, while as popular preachers they quickly made a name and a reputation which preceded them all over the country. People flocked to their sermons, for they knew that they would receive the spiritual food of which they had long been starved. Under the friars' influence, exercised by the quality of their lives no less than by the power of their words, men were brought into a new and far more intimate relationship with God; they began to realise how much God cared for each one of them, and that it was to save ordinary people like themselves that Christ came into the world. The effect of this upon the religious life of the country was profound. Whatever aspect of practical or mystical religion we study, the impact of the friars in the earlier part of the thirteenth century is felt.[3] In the Universities and in the country lanes, in city slum and on the village green, in the castles of the rich and in the hovels of the poor, everywhere the friars made their influence felt, and the country was the richer and the happier for the new hope and strength which were grafted into its spiritual life.

The high standard of the early days was, however, not maintained. As we read the records of the thirteenth century we see, from about the middle of the century, a gradual falling away from the high ideals which had animated the early friars. Popularity seems to have gone to their heads; and we cannot

[1] Eccleston, *de Adventu*, p. 9. [2] *Ibid.* pp. 44–6.

[3] For a most interesting study of the influence of the friars upon religious art, see *Franciscan Influence in English Medieval Wall-painting*, by Professor Tristram, in *Franciscan History and Legend in English Medieval Art*, ed. A. G. Little, pp. 3–11. Tristram writes that under the influence of the friars painting became 'less meditative...more vital and more definitely associated with the needs and habits of the people at large' (p. 5).

but notice a growing laxity and an increasing concern over rights and dues which ill accords with the original teaching of S. Francis and S. Dominic.

S. Francis had insisted over and over again that his friars were to be subservient to the parochial clergy, and were not, under any circumstances, to set up as rivals. If they received permission from the seculars they might preach to the people and hear their confessions: if the clergy withheld their permission the friars must go on to the next place and try again. In no circumstances must they try to force themselves into the parishes or claim any right or privilege to override the wishes of the parish priest.[1] This ideal of humility was one which could scarcely be maintained once the friars had discovered their own skill as preachers and the enormous need of good evangelistic sermons in the parishes. It was also one which could not possibly have appealed to S. Dominic, whose whole intention had been to send his men among the people as preachers of the faith. But it was inevitable that the popularity and power of the friars should in time arouse the jealousy and resentment of the parochial clergy and lead to bitter conflict.

The quarrel between the friars and the parish priests turned on three things: the friars' right to preach, to hear confessions, and to bury the dead in their churches and cemeteries. As preachers the mendicants received much support, not only from popular approval but also from the encouragement given to them by the bishops. Conscious of the slackness and incompetence of so many of the parish clergy, the bishops regarded the friars as an instrument in the hands of God to bring new life and vigour into the parishes; and accordingly they were quick to provide them with licences as preachers. The clergy in the parishes naturally viewed these itinerant preachers in a very different light. It was extremely galling for the incumbent of a parish to find himself in an empty church on a Sunday morning, knowing all the time that his flock were assembled on the village green, enjoying the racy stories and pulpit oratory of some wandering friar.

[1] See, for example, the *Testamentum*, where S. Francis writes: 'Si haberem tantam sapientiam quantam Salomon habuit, et invenirem pauperculos sacerdotes huius saeculi, in parochiis, in quibus morantur, nolo praedicare ultra voluntatem ipsorum': *Opuscula S. Francisci*, ed. Lemmens, p. 78.

The problem of the friars' right to hear confessions was even more difficult. Had the parochial clergy been more competent, the responsibility of giving spiritual help through the confessional should certainly have been reserved for them. A wise priest, capable of giving sound advice and placed in such a position that he could watch over the spiritual health of his parishioners, would obviously be a better confessor than a man who came as a complete stranger and went off afterwards into the unknown. But the problem was not so simple as this. Many of the parish clergy were incapable of acting as spiritual guides to their people, and those of the laity who most needed moral and devotional help would often be the most conscious of the hopelessness of finding, at the hands of their clergy, what their souls and minds required. Again, as far as the villages were concerned, the friar who came to preach what would nowadays be termed a 'mission' sermon often ended with an encouragement to penitence; and it was only natural that he should then and there hear the confessions of the people and give them advice and absolution. On the other hand, in the towns where friaries were established, the objection that the friar could give no *regular* spiritual help did not apply. In order as far as possible to avoid conflict the Dominicans were often ordered, in their preaching, to encourage the laity to confess once a year to their parish priests;[1] but, as time went on, the hearing of confessions became more and more profitable, and the right to do so was jealously claimed by the mendicants.

The struggle between the friars and the secular clergy over preaching was largely one of prestige. Over the hearing of confessions it was one of prestige mingled with some financial considerations. Over the burial of the dead it was wholly financial. A funeral was often a most profitable undertaking. The right to burial in some holy place was one for which people would pay heavily; and offerings at interments seem often to have been on a generous scale. Up to the coming of the friars the parish clergy could generally count on this source of income, since few of the laity acquired the right of sepulture in monastic ground.[2] But with the advent of the friars all this was changed. Friary churches and cemeteries became popular burial grounds,

[1] Goldthorp in *Yorks. Archaeological Journal*, 1936, p. 408.

[2] Only those who assumed the habit *ad succurrendum* or who had acquired some special privilege.

and the unfortunate parish priest had to face the melancholy prospect of losing not only his prestige and influence over the living, but also his right to some portion of the goods of the dead. It was, therefore, over the right of burial that the conflict between the friars and the parish clergy became most bitter.

In the first flush of enthusiasm the friars tried to discourage burials in order to avoid competition with the parochial clergy.[1] Their very restricted space and lack of proper oratories also made the burial of outsiders almost impossible. But as the high standards of the early days began to break down, and as the friars acquired more land and larger churches, it was inevitable that this problem should become very acute. Dr Little speaks of 'a series of unedifying squabbles between friars and rectors of churches for the possession of corpses', and quotes Rishanger's Chronicle, which says that the friars 'hung round the corpses of wealthy men like dogs round carrion, each waiting greedily for his bit'.[2] At Exeter the Dominicans quarrelled most bitterly with the Dean and Chapter over the possession of the body of Sir Henry Ralegh who died in 1301 after having lived with the friars for some time as a *confrater*. At his death the Dean and Chapter demanded that the body should be brought to the cathedral for the first Mass (at which the offerings would be made). Upon the friars refusing to comply, two canons were sent to carry it away by force. This they did; but when they brought it back again for burial the friars 'made fast their gate and wolde not receive it, by meanes whereof the said corps lay so long unburyed that it stanke and the Canons were dryven to bury the same yn S. Peter's churche'. But this was by no means the end of the dispute, which lasted for some years.[3]

Quarrels between the friars and the seculars over the three questions of the friars' right to preach, to hear confessions, and to bury the dead, were disturbing the peace of the Church all over Europe, and were certainly no worse in this country than elsewhere.[4] After various attempts at reconciliation—in one of

[1] Formoy, *The Dominican Order in England*, p. 36.

[2] Little, *Studies in Eng. Franc. Hist.* p. 110.

[3] Little and Easterling, *Franciscans and Dominicans of Exeter*, pp. 40–3. There was a similar quarrel over a corpse at Worcester between the monks and the Franciscans: Luard, *An. Mon.* iv, pp. 499–504.

[4] For the Franciscans see Gratien, *Histoire de la Fondation...de l'Ordre des Frères Mineurs*, pp. 200–5, 252–5, 323–5, 337–59, 475–81. For the Dominicans see Bennett, *The Early Dominicans*, pp. 128–44.

which the Franciscans and Dominicans put aside their own personal quarrel in order to co-operate in seeking a settlement—the Pope made a final effort to achieve an agreement between the friars and the seculars in the bull, *Super Cathedram* (1301), which eventually became part of the canon law. The main provisions of this bull were that it gave the friars the right to preach in their own churches and in public places (except at certain times), but put an end to friars forcing their way into the parish churches. It also insisted upon the friars choosing certain of their members to be licensed as confessors, the number of such to be limited by the size of the population. With regard to burials, the friars might bury whom they liked in their churches, but must give one quarter of all offerings and legacies to the parish priest.[1]

There is little doubt that in this prolonged struggle the friars did very well for themselves. Their early popularity served them in good stead and brought them much support from influential people. But, in the orders, there were already signs of decay. The grand, uncompromising poverty and enthusiasm of the first years was passing away, and, during the second half of the thirteenth century, we see unmistakable signs of degeneracy.

The most obvious symptom of the failure of this early idealism is shown in the extensive building schemes which were taken in hand about this time. Dr Little has collected evidence of enlargement or rebuilding in thirty-four English friaries between the years 1270 and 1320. This was partly due to the increase in numbers, but was far more the result of a desire for larger and better buildings and for more elegant and spacious churches.[2] William of Nottingham had, indeed, advised the Grey Friars to build fairly large buildings, mainly, it appears, to save the friars from the temptation to make them even bigger.[3] Certainly larger churches were necessary, as time went

[1] The bull, *Super Cathedram*, is printed in Sbaralea, *Bullarium Franciscanum*, iv, pp. 498–500; and, for a summary, see Little, *Studies in Eng. Franc. Hist.* pp. 114–16.

[2] There was certainly an increase in numbers during the latter half of the thirteenth century, but this does not mean that the numbers in each house were getting any bigger, for several new friaries were founded between 1250 and 1300.

[3] Eccleston, *de Adventu*, p. 57.

by, to accommodate the great congregations which assembled to hear the friars' sermons, and in order to provide space for the growing number of people who sought burial in a Franciscan church.[1] With this rebuilding there was often removal to pleasanter and more commodious sites, since the cramped positions of the early friaries would not allow of much expansion. The new churches, however, remained small compared with the enormous structures of the monasteries or of the secular canons. The Grey Friars' church in London was 296 feet in length, but most of their churches were well under 200 feet.[2] Nor were the domestic buildings on any scale which would justify Matthew Paris' remark that the friars' houses were as grand as royal palaces.[3]

Side by side with improvement of the buildings went a growth of luxurious habits. The Dominicans seem to have fallen in this matter more quickly than the Franciscans. The acts of the General Chapters of the Preaching Friars contain constant warnings against extravagance in dress, travelling, food and buildings,[4] the Prior of Newcastle-on-Tyne coming in for especial censure at the Chapter General held at London in 1250.[5] Some of the houses of Black Friars even seem to have started the practice of keeping servants. Servants were forbidden in the acts of the General Chapters of 1233 and 1239 but are not mentioned from that time onwards.[6] This, however, does not mean that the hopes of the Chapters had been fulfilled, for we know that at Yarm, in 1302, servants were employed by the friars, since some of them were roughly handled by the townsfolk in an assault upon the friary.[7] In several ways, therefore, there was a steady relaxation of the high standards of the early days, a relaxation which 'by about 1250...was assuming threatening proportions, and repeated steps were taken to check it. But

[1] Martin, *Franciscan Architecture*, pp. 10–12.

[2] *Ibid.* p. 192, and see plans facing p. 22. Winchester Cathedral is 555 feet in length, York and Durham both over 500 feet, and Lincoln 482 feet.

[3] M. Paris, *Chron. Maj.* iv, p. 280. It should be remembered, however, that Matthew Paris was writing of the early days. He did not live to see the later improvements.

[4] Formoy, *The Dominican Order in England*, pp. 31–3; Jarrett, *English Dominicans*, pp. 25–6.

[5] Reichert, *Acta Capitulorum Generalium Ord. Praedicatorum*, i, p. 55.

[6] Bennett, *The Early Dominicans*, p. 149.

[7] Formoy, *The Dominican Order in England*, p. 43.

the labour of thirty years produced little or no result, and the legislators themselves became affected before the end of the century.'[1]

The Friars Minor gave way more slowly. Even in the very early days, however, Agnellus of Pisa had had to reprove the friars of London for extravagance; while a few years later Stephen de Belase, Warden of Lynn and Custos of Hereford, is said to have wept when he saw the relaxations in the order.[2]

But perhaps the most serious breakdown of the original idealism may be discerned in the friars' attitude towards begging. Reference has already been made to the intentions of S. Francis. The friars were to work for their living, but in case of necessity should resort to the alms of the charitable. S. Dominic began by accepting money, but gave it up in 1219 in favour of mendicancy, provisions for one day only to be sought. In the days when the friars were mostly on the move, such a system was practicable. It failed when the friars began to settle down and build themselves houses. The story of the gradual desertion of the ideal of mendicancy is a long one which need not be told in this place.[3] By the end of the thirteenth century the quest for alms had been organised in such a way as to achieve the greatest results with the least trouble. In the early days the duty of collecting alms had been assigned to certain friars in each house called 'procurators'. These developed into the 'limitors' of later ages, men to whom the rights of begging were farmed out at a fixed rent. Chaucer's friar—to whatever order he belonged—was one such.

> He was the beste beggere in his hous,
> For thogh a widwe hadde noght a schoo
> So plesaunt was his *In principio*
> Yet wolde he have a ferthing er he wente.
> His purchas was wel bettre than his rente.

This professional begging, whereby the friar paid a fixed 'rente' for the privilege and expected to make something out of it, was obviously a travesty of what the founders of the

[1] Bennett, *The Early Dominicans*, pp. 154–5.

[2] Eccleston, *de Adventu*, pp. 9, 111.

[3] For the Dominicans see Bennett, *The Early Dominicans*, ch. ix; and for the Franciscans, Gratien, *Histoire de la Fondation...de l'Ordre des Frères Mineurs*, pp. 173–88, and Little, *Studies in Eng. Franc. Hist.* pp. 55–91.

mendicant orders had intended. It led moreover to disputes between various houses over the territory which each regarded as its own preserve. The Black Friars of Dunwich, for example, quarrelled with the neighbouring house at Norwich, about 1260, over the territory which each house was to cover for eleemosynary as well as spiritual purposes;[1] and rather more than a hundred years later the Franciscans of Cambridge and Ware were at variance over a similar problem.[2] The friars certainly became 'sturdy beggars', whose importunity was often a source of embarrassment to the general public. The income necessary to support a community of forty to fifty men, even on the moderate standards which prevailed among the friars, was, of course, considerable; and a good deal of ingenuity was needed to raise it. Bonaventura, in fact, declared that the people were as much afraid to meet a friar as a highway robber, for he was certain to take some money off them.[3]

Towards the end of the thirteenth century, therefore, the friars had drifted a good way from the idealism which had inspired the early settlements and from the intentions of their founders. The friaries were being converted into the very thing which S. Francis had feared—a new crop of monastic houses. It is true that they never reached that pitch of extravagance and easy-going aloofness which characterised the homes of the monks and canons, but by the time of Chaucer there was obviously little to choose between a friar and a monk, each being equally unpopular in the eyes of the people. If the monasteries represented a reactionary spirit and seemed to have outlived their day, the friaries were no less a burden on the community owing to the worldliness which had invaded them. The real failure of the friars belongs to the fourteenth century, but before the thirteenth century had run its course the symptoms of decay had appeared.

It is natural, therefore, to ask how it was that the dual experiment inaugurated by Francis and Dominic deteriorated so quickly. Each movement started off with great enthusiasm, and the Franciscans at any rate could claim that they owed their origin to a man of outstanding religious genius, a man whom Ernest Renan described as 'the one perfect Christian'.[4] Yet

[1] *V.C.H.*, *Suffolk*, ii, pp. 121–2.

[2] Wadding, *Annales Minorum*, ix, p. 438.

[3] Bonaventura, *Opera Omnia*, ed. Quaracchi, viii, p. 468, quoted in Little, *Studies in Eng. Franc. Hist.* p. 31.

[4] 'Le seul parfait chrétien': *Nouvelles Études d'Histoire Religieuse*, p. 334.

by the end of the first century of their existence the orders had departed a long way from the intentions of their founders, and had lost much of the popular support and respect which they had won in the early days.

The failure of the Franciscans was probably the more lamentable on the principle of *Corruptio optimi pessima.* S. Francis' primary ambition was to obey in his own life the most uncompromising commands of Christ, even though the cost might be starvation and death. When others joined him he expected them to do what he was doing. But as the brotherhood grew into an order it was inevitable that some organisation should be introduced, and that, with the organisation, should come some limitation of the original idealism of the saint.

When the Grey Friars came to England in 1224 they certainly had high ideals. Their poverty and patient endurance of hardship were obvious to all, and their evangelistic fervour was a most stimulating influence on the religious life of the country. But within a few years (or perhaps even a few months) of their arrival the fortunes of the order in England took a new turn, and one which was to have a profound influence on the future and to contribute indirectly to their failure. Strange to say the influence behind the innovation was that of Robert Grosseteste, who helped to turn a community of evangelists and mendicants into an order of scholars. His work undoubtedly had a profound effect on the fortunes of the order. It raised it to a position of pre-eminence in the academic world, but it was in sharp contrast to the intentions of S. Francis and would certainly have been deplored by him. The results of this new move were many. In the first place it destroyed the ideal of absolute poverty. Some degree of simplicity is undoubtedly compatible with scholarship, but the uncompromising penury which would allow a man no books or writing-materials, and which would keep him constantly on the move, is clearly hostile to any serious study. If the Grey Friars were to be scholars they must settle down; and if they were to settle down they must give up the ideal of complete poverty. Another effect of the change was that, as the years passed, the leaders of the movement were chosen mainly from the convents in the university towns. Of the first twenty who held office as Provincial Minister in England, all except three were connected with Oxford or Cambridge, and twelve had served as lector, the highest scholastic post to which the friars could attain. Officially, therefore, the

Franciscan order in this country was a learned order, and only those who had some hopes of academic achievement stood much chance of promotion. Is it any wonder if some of the others became dispirited, or lost some of the fervour which had animated the friars in the early days? So long as the main objective of the order was evangelism by the method of living a life as nearly as possible in conformity with the standards of the Gospels, then everyone had a contribution to make; but once the order set itself to turn out good scholars there was bound to be a distinction made between the learned and the ignorant.

Looking at the question solely from the point of view of S. Francis and his immediate friends, Grosseteste certainly did the order a bad turn when he became its tutor and encouraged it in its academic life and work. From the point of view, also, of the life of the Church as a whole, Grosseteste must be regarded as having 'backed the wrong horse'. If he wanted to lend the great weight of his position at Oxford, and his encyclopaedic knowledge, to the support of a learned order, he should have attached himself to the Dominicans rather than to the Franciscans.

The Dominican order failed in this country for two reasons. In the first place the Preaching Friars existed to combat heresy, but this country seems to have been one of the few places in Europe where heresy did not exist. In a way, then, the *raison d'être* of the Dominicans was taken from them the moment that they landed at Dover in 1221. In the second place, the rivalry of the Franciscans was too much for them. Both the striking poverty of the early Minorites and the academic distinction which the order achieved were undoubtedly considerably in advance of the attainments of the Dominicans.

In many ways the ideals of the Franciscans and Dominicans were well suited to save the Church at a moment when some form of regeneration was essential. Had it been possible for the two orders to have worked together, the effect upon the Church might well have been stupendous. As it was, the good which each could have done was largely spoilt through constant rivalry and jealousy among the friars. If the Franciscans had concentrated on the people in the towns and left the Universities to the Dominicans, and if both orders had set themselves to co-operate with the parochial clergy, the Church might have been roused from spiritual lethargy and so have saved itself from the disastrous turmoil of the sixteenth century.

Co-operation, however, was not a very prominent characteristic of Church life in the thirteenth century. Churchmen of all ranks, from the two Archbishops to the humblest parish priests, were so much concerned with their rights and privileges that any idea of subordinating these to the welfare of the Church as a whole does not seem to have occurred to them. And the friars picked up the same habits. Members of various orders crowded together in the same towns, where they were constantly rubbing shoulders and quarrelling over precedence and prestige, when, with a little planning and control from above, they could have been distributed over the country. At Chester the Franciscans found their rivals already established in 1236; but, when the bishop of the diocese, Alexander Stavensby, suggested that they might go elsewhere, they immediately sought the protection and support of Grosseteste, Bishop of Lincoln.[1] Similarly, at Exeter the Dominicans opposed the removal of the Franciscans to a new site in 1285 and managed to get the bishop, Peter Quivil, on to their side.[2] At Oxford the friars quarrelled over their methods of recruitment, and at least one lecturer to the Grey Friars had to be removed from the convent, and another suspended from office, for causing offence to the Dominicans by the things which they said about them.[3] Matthew Paris was, of course, quick to notice the dissension between the two rival orders. 'The Preachers', he said, 'asserted that theirs was the earlier order and that therefore they were the more worthy; and they were more seemly in their dress and had merited their name and office by their preaching...but the Minors replied that as they had chosen in God's service a life of more rigour and humility, and one of greater worth because of more holiness, brethren might pass freely over from the Preachers to themselves as from a lower to a higher and more ascetic order.'[4] A little later we find the two provincial ministers, both destined to become Archbishop of Canterbury, Kilwardby and Pecham, quarrelling over the question of poverty and the merits of their respective orders.

All this argument and rivalry naturally weakened the friars' position in the world. What men wanted was the Gospel, not

[1] Martin, *Franciscan Architecture*, p. 226; R. Grosseteste, *Epistolae*, pp. 120–1.

[2] Little and Easterling, *Franciscans and Dominicans of Exeter*, pp. 15–16.

[3] Little, *Grey Friars in Oxford*, p. 71.

[4] M. Paris, *Chron. Maj.* iv, p. 279.

vindications of one order against the other. Had there been some degree of co-operation, some division of labour, and some definite attempt to subordinate all personal ambitions to the needs of the Kingdom of God, much good might have been done. And the same applies to the relations between the friars and the secular clergy. The parish priest, cut off as so many of them were from much contact with the outside world, should have felt able to welcome the wandering friar bringing spiritual regeneration to his flock. But the behaviour of the friars became such that both priest and people learnt to dread rather than to welcome their coming.

The glory of the friars, then, was beginning to fade well before the thirteenth century had run its course. And yet, taking the century as a whole, the friars undoubtedly represent the purest and strongest element in the life of the Church. The parish clergy, poorly educated and often with low standards of personal behaviour, were little equipped for the spiritual guidance of their people. The monks, living upon the spiritual capital which earlier generations had built up, had little to offer to the world except a quiet escape from its own problems. Except for a few individuals here and there, there was no branch of Church activity which could be regarded as making much contribution to the moral and spiritual needs of men. Then came the friars. Unlike the monks they were prepared to share in the hardships and sufferings of the poor, to take upon themselves the burden of poverty and insecurity, to go among the people with the message of the Gospel. Dressed as peasants and thankful to regale themselves with the dregs of beer that even schoolboys would not drink, they showed that all Christ's words about renunciation and humility could be taken literally even twelve centuries after they were spoken. On the other hand, compared with the general level of the parish clergy, they were better educated, more progressive, and, above all, inspired with a desire to share with all men 'the eternal gifts of Christ the King'.

For a time, then, the friars captured the imagination, and won the respect, of all who really cared for the well-being of the Church. They brought new life into the parishes, stirring up the minds and the affections of men and women, bringing them face to face with their Redeemer. They aroused even the clergy to a deeper sense of responsibility and encouraged them to give more help to their people. They captured the Universities, forcing them to look higher than mere academic discussions of trivialities and to see the part which the lecture-rooms could play in meeting the spiritual and mental hunger of men. They built up a whole network of schools from which all could benefit. Above all, they provided a system, full of life and vigour and austerity, in which those who were prepared to forsake all for Christ's sake could find their spiritual home.

As we look back through the mist of seven centuries and try to form some mental picture of the Church life of those days, we shall be wise to look not to the homes of the parish clergy, nor to the great houses of the monks, but to something like that cellar under the boys' school at Canterbury, where a little group of Friars Minor were huddled together, cold, hungry and in a strange land, and yet burning with an inner joy—'as poor yet making many rich: as having nothing and yet possessing all things'.

APPENDIX

EVIDENCE OF NUMBERS IN ENGLISH RELIGIOUS HOUSES IN THE THIRTEENTH CENTURY

A good deal of work has been done from time to time on this question. Mr Snape publishes some figures for twenty-eight religious houses on p. 21 of his *English Monastic Finances.* Dr Coulton devotes a number of pages to the same subject in *Five Centuries of Religion*, vol. iii, pp. 697–706. Dom David Knowles gives figures for English Black Monks, mostly before 1200, in *The Monastic Order in England*, pp. 713–14. Dom Ursmer Berlière published two articles on *Le Nombre des Moines dans les anciens Monastères* in *Revue Bénédictine*, vols. xli and xlii.

The following pages contain evidence from a number of English religious houses in and around the thirteenth century. The totals suggested at the end are, of course, only approximate, but will give some idea of the monastic population of England during the period under review.

i. BENEDICTINES

House	Status	Date	Numbers	Reference
ALBANS, S.	Abbey	1195–1214	max. 100	*Dugdale*, ii, p. 189; *Gesta Abbatum*, i, p. 234
BATH	Abbey	cent. xiii	max. 41	*Chartularies of Bath*, p. xx, and cf. pp. li–ii
BEES, S.	Cell to York	1258 1286	7 8	*Chronicle of S. Mary's, York*, pp. 2, 24
BOXGROVE	Priory	1230	19	Snape, *English Monastic Finances*, p. 21
		?	10	Haines, *Dover Priory*, p. 331 n.
BURY S. EDMUNDS	Abbey	1213	70–80	*Memorials of S. Edmund's*, ii, p. 75
		cent. xiii (late)	80	*Dugdale*, iii, p. 117
CANTERBURY, S. AUGUSTINE'S	Abbey	*c.* 1250	65	Turner and Salter, *Register of S. Augustine's*, p. 3
		1287	50+	*W. Thorn's Chronicle*, p. 283
CANTERBURY, CHRIST CHURCH	Cathedral Monastery	1207	*c.* 80	Knowles, *Monastic Order*, p. 714
		1298	? 70	*Regist. R. Winchelsey*, pp. 257–8
CHESTER	Abbey	*c.* 1250	40	*Dugdale*, ii, p. 373
COVENTRY	Abbey	1292	26	Snape, *English Monastic Finances*, p. 21
CROWLAND	Abbey	1328	41	*Dugdale*, ii, p. 121

BENEDICTINES (*cont.*)

House	Status	Date	Numbers	Reference
DOVER	Dependency of Canterbury	cent. xiii	12	Haines, *Dover Priory*, p. 331
DUNSTER	Dependency of Bath	cent. xiv	5	*V.C.H.*, *Somerset*, ii, p. 81
DURHAM	Cathedral Monastery	1240	20	Bliss, *Cal. Papal Letters*, i, p. 192
		1300	80+	*Gesta Dunelmensia*, pp. 8–10
ELY	Cathedral Monastery	1241–54	under 70	*Ely Chapter Ordinances*, p. 1
		1335–53	48	*Ibid.* pp. x–xii
EVESHAM	Abbey	1206	30–40	Knowles, *Monastic Order*, p. 714
		1213–29	70	*Dugdale*, ii, pp. 27–31
EYE	Priory	1297–8	9	*V.C.H.*, *Suffolk*, ii, p. 73
FINCHALE	Dependency of Durham	1317	9	*The Priory of Finchale*, pp. xxiii–iv
GLASTONBURY	Abbey	1192	50	Domerham, *Hist. de Rebus Glast.* ii, pp. 385–6
		up to 1200	statutory no. 72	*Ibid.* p. 417
		1202	stat. no. 60	*Rentalia et Custumaria*, p. xx
HENES	Cell to York	1286	1	*Chronicle of S. Mary's, York*, p. 24
HOXNE	Cell to Norwich	?	7–8	*V.C.H.*, *Suffolk*, ii, p. 76
HYDE	Abbey	cent. xiii	30–40	*Revue Bénédictine*, xlii, pp. 29–31
LEOMINSTER	Dependency of Reading	1287	under 12	*Regist. R. de Swinfield*, pp. 131–2
LINCOLN	Cell to York	1258	3	*Chronicle of S. Mary's, York*, pp. 4, 24
		1286	3	
MALVERN, GT.	Dependency of Westminster	1315	26	*Worcester Liber Albus*, p. 138
NORWICH	Cathedral Monastery	?	max. 62	*Dugdale*, iv, p. 8
OXFORD, DURHAM COLLEGE	Dependency of Durham	*c.* 1290	6–10	*V.C.H.*, *Oxon.* ii, pp. 68–9
OXFORD, GLOUCESTER COLLEGE	Dependency of Gloucester	1283	13	*Dugdale*, i, pp. 533–4
PERSHORE	Abbey	1288	17+	Snape, *English Monastic Finances*, p. 21
PETERBOROUGH	Abbey	1219	80	Snape, *English Monastic Finances*, p. 21
RICHMOND	Cell to York	1258	2	*Chronicle of S. Mary's, York*, pp. 4, 24
		1286	2	

BENEDICTINES (*cont.*)

House	Status	Date	Numbers	Reference
ROCHESTER	Cathedral Monastery	?	stat. no. 60	Wharton, *Anglia Sacra*, i, p. 346
RUMBURGH	Cell to York	1258	4	*Chronicle of S. Mary's, York*, pp. 4, 24
		1286	2	
SAINTOFT	Cell to York	1258	1	*Chronicle of S. Mary's, York*, p. 4
TEWKESBURY	Abbey	cent. xiii	57	*Dugdale*, ii, p. 81
TICKFORD	Alien Priory	1233	8	*V.C.H., Bucks.* i, p. 361
WESTMINSTER	Abbey	1283	*c.* 50	Pearce, *Walter de Wenlok*, p. 11
		1303	49	Pearce, *Monks of Westminster*, p. 11
WETHERHAL	Cell to York	1258	7	*Chronicle of S. Mary's, York*, pp. 4, 24
		1286	7	
WHITBY	Abbey	1175	37	*Dugdale*, i, p. 407
		c. 1175	39	*Cart. Abb. de Whiteby*, i, pp. xxx–i
		1176	38	*V.C.H., Yorks.* iii, p. 102
WINCHESTER	Cathedral Monastery	1261	61	Goodman, *Chart. of Winchester*, p. li
		1325	64	
WORCESTER	Cathedral Monastery	1313	50	*Worcester Liber Albus*, pp. 124–6 and lxvii
		1317	47	
WYMONDHAM	Abbey	1260	36	Snape, *English Monastic Finances*, p. 21
YORK, S. MARY'S	Abbey	1258	34	*Chronicle of S. Mary's, York*, pp. 2–3, 23–4
		1286	49	

ii. CLUNIACS

House	Status	Date	Numbers	Reference
BARNSTAPLE	Priory	1279	6	Duckett, *Visitations*, p. 25
BERMONDSEY	Priory	1262	32	Duckett, *Visitations*, pp. 13–14
		1275	20	*Ibid.* p. 16
		1279	18	*Ibid.* pp. 20–2
BROMHOLM	Cell to Castle Acre	1276	16	Duckett, *Visitations*, p. 19
CARESWELL	Cell to Montacute	1279	4	Duckett, *Visitations*, p. 26
CASTLE ACRE	Priory	1276	32	Duckett, *Visitations*, p. 19
		1279	35	*Ibid.* p. 34
EXETER, S. JAMES	Alien Priory	?	5	*Dugdale*, v, p. 105
		1279	2	Duckett, *Visitations*, pp. 25–6
FARLEIGH	Cell to Lewes	1276	18 2 conversi	Duckett, *Visitations*, pp. 17–18
		1279	18	*Ibid.* p. 27
HOLME, E.	Cell to Montacute	1279	3	*V.C.H., Dorset*, ii, p. 81
		1281	? 4	

CLUNIACS (*cont.*)

House	Status	Date	Numbers	Reference
HORKESLEY	Cell to Thetford	1279	5	Duckett, *Records of Cluni*, ii, p. 143
LENTON	Priory	1262	22 2 conversi	Duckett, *Visitations*, p. 11
		1276	27 4 conversi	*Ibid.* p. 18
		1279	25	*Ibid.* p. 31
LEWES	Priory	1240	100	Bliss, *Cal. Papal Letters*, i, p. 186
MONKS HORTON	Cell to Lewes	1275	12	Duckett, *Visitations*, p. 15
		1279	13	*Ibid.* pp. 36–7
MONTACUTE	Priory	1262	25	Duckett, *Visitations*, p. 12
		1276	20	*Ibid.* p. 17
		1279	28	*Ibid.* pp. 23–4
NORTHAMPTON, S. ANDREW	Priory	1262	34	Duckett, *Visitations*, p. 13
		1275	30	*Ibid.* pp. 16–17
		1279	25	*Ibid.* pp. 22–3
PONTEFRACT	Priory	1262	16	Duckett, *Visitations*, p. 14
		1279	27	*Ibid.* p. 33
PRITTLEWELL	Cell to Lewes	1276 1279 1305	15 14 11	*V.C.H.*, *Essex*, ii, p. 139; cf. Duckett, *Visitations*, pp. 19, 35
STANESGATE	Cell to Lewes	?	4 or 5	*V.C.H.*, *Essex*, ii, p. 142
THETFORD	Priory	1262	22	Duckett, *Visitations*, p. 12
		1276	24	*Ibid.* pp. 18–19
		1279	22	*Ibid.* pp. 34–5
WENLOCK	Priory	1262	34	Duckett, *Visitations*, p. 13
		1276	40 3 conversi	*Ibid.* p. 18
		1279	35	*Ibid.* pp. 28–30

iii. CISTERCIANS

House	Status	Date	Numbers	Reference
BEAULIEU	Abbey	1204	30	Knowles, *Monastic Order*, p. 367
BORDESLEY	Abbey	1332	34 monks 1 novice 7 conversi	*V.C.H.*, *Worcs.* ii, p. 153
CLEEVE	Abbey	cent. xiii (late)	28	Walcott, *Abbey of S. Mary, Cleeve*, p. 108
CROXDEN	Abbey	1198	50	Coulton, *Five Centuries*, iii, p. 698
HAYLES	Abbey	1246	20	*Dugdale*, v, p. 686
LOUTH PARK	Abbey	1226–46	66 monks 150 conversi	*Chronicle of Louth Park*, p. 15

CISTERCIANS (*cont.*)

House	Status	Date	Numbers	Reference
Meaux	Abbey	*c.* 1240	49–50	Bond, *Chron. Melsa*, ii, p. 28
		1249	60 monks, 90 conversi	*Ibid.* ii, p. 65
		1349	42 monks, 7 conversi	*Ibid.* iii, pp. xxxvi–vii
Newenham	Abbey	1246	13 monks, 4 conversi	Davidson, *Hist. of Newenham Abbey*, pp. 11–13
Rewley	Abbey	*c.* 1272	6	*V.C.H., Oxon.* ii, pp. 81–2
		1280	15	
		1294	16	
Waverley	Abbey	1187	70 monks, 120 conversi	H. Brakspear, *Waverley Abbey*, p. 9; cf. Luard, *An. Mon.* ii, p. 244
Whalley	Abbey	1296	24	Whitaker, *Hist. of Whalley*, pp. 65–6

iv. AUGUSTINIANS

House	Status	Date	Numbers	Reference
Barnwell	Priory	1254	30	Clark, *Liber Memorandorum*, p. 71
Blythburgh	Priory	?	3 or 4	*V.C.H., Suffolk*, ii, p. 93
Bolton	Priory	average	15 canons, 2 conversi	Whitaker, *Hist. of Craven*, p. 341
		1275	14	A. H. Thompson, *Bolton Priory*, p. 70
Brinkburn	Priory	cent. xiv	12	Page, *Chart. of Brinkburn*, p. 213
Bushmead	Priory	1283	4	*V.C.H., Beds.* i, p. 385
Calwich	Priory	?	4	Fortescue, *Hist. of Calwich*, pp. 5–6
Chetwode	Priory	?	3 or 4	*V.C.H., Bucks.* i, p. 380
Cirencester	Abbey	1307	23	Worcester, *Regist. Sede Vacante*, pp. 99–100
Conishead	Priory	1208	max. 13	*V.C.H., Lancs.* ii, p. 141
Dunmow	Priory	*c.* 1291	10 or 11	*Dugdale*, vi, p. 146
Hexham	Priory	?	stat. no. 27	Raine, *Hexham Priory*, i, p. cxxxv
		1268	21 or 22	
		1311	24	*Ibid.* i, App. p. xlviii
Mottisfont	Priory	?	stat. no. 11	Tanner, *Notitia Monastica*, p. 165
		1294	11	*V.C.H., Hants.* ii, p. 173
Newstead-by-Stamford	Priory	cent. xiii	7	*V.C.H., Lincs.* ii, p. 176
Nostell	Priory	1312	26	Burton, *Monast. Ebor.* pp. 301–2
Osyth's, S.	Abbey	1304	20	*Regist. R. Baldock, etc.* pp. 60–2
Stonely	Priory	?	*c.* 7	*V.C.H., Hunts.* i, p. 395

AUGUSTINIANS (*cont.*)

House	Status	Date	Numbers	Reference
TANDRIDGE	Priory	?	5	Heales, *Hist. of Tanridge*, p. 3
THORNHOLM	Priory	? cent. xii	20	*V.C.H., Lincs.* ii, p. 166
THORNTON	Abbey	—	fairly large	*V.C.H., Lincs.* ii, p. 164
WALTHAM	Abbey	1273	48	Bliss, *Cal. Papal Letters*, i, p. 446
WORSPRING	Priory	1243	26	*V.C.H., Somerset*, ii, p. 45
WROXTON	Priory	1221	6	Bliss, *Cal. Papal Letters*, i, p. 85

v. PREMONSTRATENSIANS

House	Status	Date	Numbers	Reference
BEAUCHIEF	Abbey	cent. xiii	13	Addy, *Hist. Memorials of Beauchief*, p. 135
EGGLESTON	Abbey	*c.* 1200	12	*V.C.H., Yorks.* iii, p. 250

vi. GILBERTINES

House	Status	Date	Numbers	Reference
CHICKSANDS	—	1257	over 52 nuns	Luard, *An. Mon.* iii, p. 205
MALTON	—	? cent. xiii	*c.* 30 canons 35 conversi	R. Graham, *English Eccl. Studies*, pp. 260–2
(Total)	—	*c.* 1200	960 women 594 men	Graham, *S. Gilbert and the Gilbertines*, p. 40

Note. For statutory numbers see Knowles, *Religious Houses*, pp. 99–100.

vii. ALIEN PRIORIES

House	Owning House	Date	Numbers	Reference
ALBERBURY	Limousin	1295	6	Graham, *English Eccl. Studies*, p. 234
COGGES	Fécamp	?	2	Salter, *Newington Longeville Charters*, p. xvi
CRASWALL	Grandmont	1295	9	Graham, *English Eccl. Studies*, p. 234
GROSMONT	Grandmont	1225 1295	13 9	*Ibid.* pp. 227, 234
NEWINGTON LONGEVILLE	S. Foy de Longueville	?	1 or 2	Salter, *Newington Longeville Charters*, p. xvi
TOTNES	Angers	?	max. 13	Watkin *Hist. of Totnes*, ii, p. 967

viii. DOMINICAN FRIARS

House	Date	Numbers	Reference
ARUNDEL	1297	12	*V.C.H., Sussex*, ii, p. 93
	1299	13	Poland, *Friars in Sussex*, p. 19
	1324	20	*V.C.H., Sussex*, ii, p. 93
BEVERLEY	1299	33	*Yorks. Archaeological Journal*, 1936, p. 389
	1300	32	
	1301	36	
	1304	38	
	1310	42	
CANTERBURY	1289	50	*V.C.H., Kent*, ii, pp 177–8
	1300	*c.* 30	
CHICHESTER	1297	34	*V.C.H., Sussex*, ii, p. 94
	1324	21	
DERBY	1323	26	*V.C.H., Derbyshire*, ii, p. 79
EXETER	1297	36	Little and Easterling, *Friars of Exeter*, p. 52
GLOUCESTER	cent. xiv (early)	30–40	*V.C.H., Gloucs.* ii, p. 111
GUILDFORD	1302	12	*V.C.H., Surrey*, ii, p. 114
	1324	24	
LINCOLN	1300	over 21	*V.C.H., Lincs.* ii, pp. 220–2
LONDON	1243	80	Jarrett, *English Dominicans*, p. 4
	1313	70	*V.C.H., London*, i, p. 499
NORTHAMPTON	end of cent. xiii	35–40	*V.C.H., Northants.* ii, p. 145
OXFORD	1276	60	*V.C.H., Oxon.* ii, p. 111
	1277	70	
	1305	96	
PONTEFRACT	1300	30	*Yorks. Archaeological Journal*, 1936, p. 399
	1301	29	
STAMFORD	1300	40–42	*V.C.H., Lincs.* ii, pp. 226–7
SUDBURY	1299	30	*V.C.H., Suffolk*, ii, p. 123
WARWICK	cent. xiii	30–40	*V.C.H., Warwicks.* ii, pp. 101–2
WINCHESTER	1239	28	*V.C.H., Hants.* ii, p. 189
	c. 1245	31	
	1325	46	
YARM	1299	30	*Yorks. Archaeological Journal*, 1936, p. 417
	1319	33	
YORK	1299	50	*Yorks. Archaeological Journal*, 1936, pp. 371–2
	1300	47	
	1307	60	
	1310	57	

ix. FRANCISCAN FRIARS

House	Date	Numbers	Reference
Babwell (Bury)	1300	*c.* 40	*V.C.H., Suffolk*, ii, pp. 124–5
Beverley	1299	32	*Yorks. Archaeological Journal*, 1936, pp. 292–3
	1300	38	
	1301	34	
	1304	38	
Boston	1300	*c.* 30	*V.C.H., Lincs.* ii, p. 215
Cambridge	1326	70	Little, *Grey Friars in Oxford*, p. 44 n.
Canterbury	1289	60	Cotton, *Grey Friars in Canterbury*, pp. 31–2
	1297	39	
	1299	34	
	1300	30	
	1320	35	
Cardiff	1284	18	Martin, *Franciscan Architecture*, p. 160
Chichester	1253	26	Little, *Studies in Eng. Franc. Hist.* p. 68
Doncaster	1299	30	*Yorks. Archaeological Journal*, 1936, p. 298
Dorchester	1296	32	*V.C.H., Dorset*, ii, p. 93
Dunwich	1277	20	Martin, *Franciscan Architecture*, p. 79
Exeter	1297	34	Little and Easterling, *Friars of Exeter*, p. 22
Gloucester	1277	24	Martin, *Franciscan Architecture*, p. 84
	1284	40	
	1326	40	Little, *Grey Friars in Oxford*, p. 44 n.
Grantham	1300	*c.* 20	*V.C.H., Lincs.* ii, p. 217
Lewes	1299	24	*Sussex Archaeological Coll.* ii, p. 146
London	1243	80	Kingsford, *Grey Friars of London*, p. 62
	1300	79	
Lynn	1326	38	Little, *Grey Friars in Oxford*, p. 44 n.
Newcastle-on-Tyne	1299	68	Little, *Grey Friars in Oxford*, p. 44 n.
Norwich	1326	47	Little, *Grey Friars in Oxford*, p. 44 n.
Oxford	1275–1350	70–80	Little, *Grey Friars in Oxford*, pp. 43–4
Reading	1239	13	Eccleston, *de Adventu*, p. 174
	1326	26	Little, *Grey Friars in Oxford*, p. 44 n.
Stamford	1300	39–46	*V.C.H., Lincs.* ii, pp. 227–9
Winchester	1243	23	Little, *Grey Friars in Oxford*, p. 44 n.
	1315	43	
Worcester	1301	34	Martin, *Franciscan Architecture*, p. 250
York	1299	52	*Yorks. Archaeological Journal*, 1936, p. 275
	1300	43	
	1312	38	
(Total)	1255	1242	Eccleston, *de Adventu*, p. 14

x. OTHER ORDERS OF FRIARS

House	Order	Date	Numbers	Reference
AYLESFORD	Carmelite	1326	20	*V.C.H., Kent*, ii, pp. 201–2
CANTERBURY	Friars of the Sack	1289	3	*V.C.H., Kent*, ii, p. 205
GLOUCESTER	Carmelite	1337	31	*V.C.H., Gloucs.* ii, p. 112
LINCOLN	Austin	1300	*c.* 30	*V.C.H., Lincs.* ii, pp. 219–20
	Carmelite	1300	*c.* 28	*Ibid.* p. 224
	Friars of the Sack	1300	4	*Ibid.* p. 225
OXFORD	Austin	1317	43	*Archivum Franciscanum Hist.* 1926, p. 820
	Carmelite	1317	45	(as above)
	Trinitarian	1286	64	*V.C.H., Oxon.* ii, p. 151
SANDWICH	Carmelite	1326	20	*V.C.H., Kent*, ii, p. 204
STAMFORD	Friars of the Sack	1300	4	*V.C.H., Lincs.* ii, p. 230

xi. NUNS

House	Status	Date	Numbers	Reference
HOLYSTONE	Priory	1291	27	*Dugdale*, iv, p. 197
NUNEATON	Priory of Order of Fontevrault	1234	93	Power, *Medieval English Nunneries*, p. 215 n.
ROMSEY	Abbey	cent. xiii	90–100	Power, *Medieval English Nunneries*, p. 215 n.
SHAFTESBURY	Abbey	1218	100	Power, *Medieval English Nunneries*, p. 215 n.

ESTIMATED TOTAL NUMBER OF REGULARS IN ENGLAND IN THE THIRTEENTH CENTURY

i. *BENEDICTINES*

58 Houses of about 50 in each	2900	
85 Cells of about 5 in each	425	
35 Alien Priories of about 10 in each	350	
27 Alien Cells of about 5 in each	135	
	——	3810

ii. *CLUNIACS*

11 Houses with a total of about	322	
21 Cells of about 9 in each	189	
3 Alien Priories of about 5 in each	15	
	——	526

iii. *CISTERCIANS*

In 1300 there were 74 Houses of about 44 in each	3256	
	——	3256

NOTE. In 1200 there were only 62 Houses, but probably rather more in each.

Various small Houses, say		60
Total Number of Monks		7652

iv. *AUGUSTINIANS*

In 1300, 185 Houses of about 15 canons	2775	
18 Cells of about 5 canons	90	
	——	2865

v. *PREMONSTRATENSIANS*

In 1300, 31 Houses of about 12 canons	372	
18 Cells of about 5 canons	90	
	——	462

vi. *GILBERTINES*

In 1200 there were about 600 canons		600
Total Number of Canons		3927

viii. *DOMINICAN FRIARS*

In 1300, 51 Houses of about 37 Friars	1887

ix. *FRANCISCAN FRIARS*

In 1300, 55 Houses of about 44 Friars	2420

x. *CARMELITES*

In 1300, 26 Houses of about 20 Friars	520

xi. *AUSTIN FRIARS*

In 1300, 17 Houses of about 25 Friars	425

xii. *OTHER FRIARIES*

In 1300, 20 Houses of about 5 Friars	100
Total Number of Friars	5352

Total Number of Monks	7,652
Total Number of Canons	3,927
Total Number of Friars	5,352
	16,931

Add to this about 7000 Nuns, and about 1400 men and women living under rule in the Hospitals.

INDEX

CAMBRIDGE: PRINTED BY W. LEWIS, M.A., AT THE UNIVERSITY PRESS